Models, Strategies, and Methods for Effective Teaching

Models, Strategies, and Methods for Effective Teaching

Hellmut R. Lang
University of Regina, Emeritus

David N. Evans
University of Regina

Boston • New York • San Francisco
Mexico City • Montreal • Toronto • London • Madrid • Munich • Paris
Hong Kong • Singapore • Tokyo • Cape Town • Sydney

Executive Editor and Publisher: *Stephen D. Dragin*
Series Editorial Assistant: *Meaghan Minnick*
Marketing Manager: *Tara Kelly*
Editorial Production Service: *Omegatype Typography, Inc.*
Composition and Manufacturing Buyer: *Andrew Turso*
Electronic Composition: *Omegatype Typography, Inc.*
Photo Researcher: *Omegatype Typography, Inc.*
Cover Administrator: *Joel Gendron*

For related titles and support materials, visit our online catalog at www.ablongman.com.

Between the time website information is gathered and then published, it is not unusual for some sites to have closed. Also, the transcription of URLs can result in typographical errors. The publisher would appreciate notification where these errors occur so that they may be corrected in subsequent editions.

Library of Congress Cataloging-in-Publication Data

Lang, Hellmut R.
  Models, strategies, and methods for effective teaching / Hellmut R. Lang, David N. Evans.—1st ed.
     p. cm.
  Includes bibliographical references and index.
  ISBN 0-205-40841-9
    1. Teachers—Training of—United States. 2. Effective teaching—United States. I. Evans, David N. II. Title.

LB1715.L24 2006
370'.71'1—dc22

2005048918

Printed in the United States of America

5   6   7   8   9   10   VOCR   13   12   11   10

Contents

Preface   ix
Using This Text   xiii

part 1 Aspects of Teaching   1

1 Teacher Preparation: Becoming a Professional Teacher   2

Applying the Research   2
A Teacher Preparation Model   9
The Professional Development Process   18

2 Communication and Interpersonal Skills   41

Introduction to Communication Skills   41
Basic Communication Skills   45
Interpersonal Skills   47

3 Teaching for Diversity   58

Importance of Teaching about and for Diversity   58
Learning Styles   61
Cross-Cultural Teaching   71
Special Needs Learners   84
Children of Poverty   92
Accommodating Gender Differences in the Classroom   94
Diversity Issues and Approaches   99

4 Energizing Learners: The Affective Domain and Motivation   107

Taxonomies of Educational Objectives   107
The Affective Domain   108
Motivation   112
At-Risk Students   116
Teaching Attitudes and Values   121

5 Assessment and Evaluation   132

Introduction   132

Assessment Techniques   135

Preparing Test Items   146

Marking Systems   149

Other Forms of Assessment   152

Accommodating Special Needs Learners   154

Assessment Issues and Trends   155

part **II** Mastering the Fundamentals   163

6 Classroom Management   164

Background for Classroom Management   164

Preventive Approaches   168

Supportive Approaches   173

Corrective Approaches   186

Guidelines for Classroom Management   191

7 Facilitating Learning: Lesson and Unit Planning and Delivery   201

Planning Approaches   201

Planning Variables   207

Instructional Variables   213

Lesson and Unit Planning   218

8 Engaging Learners: Questioning, Discussion, Seatwork, and Homework   245

Questioning   245

Discussion   257

Seatwork and Homework   265

9 Teaching Concepts   277

The Nature of Concepts   277

Concepts and Teaching Approaches   287

10 Teaching Skills   306

The Nature of Skills   306

The Teaching of Skills   315

Demonstrations   327

p a r t **III**   Selecting Instructional Approaches   335

11 Direct Instruction and Individual Study   336

The Nature of Direct Instruction   339

Direct Instruction Teaching Methods   343

The Individual Study Strategy   352

12 The Indirect and Experiential Instruction Strategies   368

The Indirect Instruction Strategy   368

The Experiential Instruction Strategy   379

13 The Collaborative Learning Strategy   394

Group Skills   394

Collaborative Instruction and Learning   401

Cooperative Learning   415

14 Teaching for Thinking and Problem-Based Learning   443

Thinking Skills and Processes   443

Classic Teaching Approaches   448

Current Issues and Teaching Approaches   453

Critical and Creative Thinking   460

Problem-Based Learning   467

Epilogue   474

References   481

Index   495

Preface

Models, Strategies, and Methods for Effective Teaching has been written to respond to the challenges to teacher education presented by national and state legislation and the frustrations expressed by teacher education graduates who found it difficult to transfer what was studied on campus to the reality of modern schools and classrooms. This book was written to help you whether you are a teacher education student or practicing professional.

There is significant research-based information on what makes an effective teacher. For example, Danielson (1996) has identified the essential components that teachers need to master to promote improved student learning. Her framework provides a road map for novice teachers, guidance for professional excellence, and a structure for focusing improvement efforts and communication with the larger community. Teachers can have a clear idea of what they need to know and do to be effective and how to help the public understand what teachers do.

In the United States there are several sources of guidelines for the teacher in the new millennium. These include the Professional Assessments for Beginning Teachers (PRAXIS) series, the Interstate New Teacher Assessment and Support Consortium (INTASC), and the National Board for Professional Teaching Standards (NBPTS), which sets standards for teachers. Universities and colleges also have guidelines to help the novice teacher become a successful educator.

In this text we present a pre-service and in-service model, the Teacher Competence Profile (TCP). The TCP is built on the Intern Professional Profile (IPP) developed by Art McBeath, Hellmut Lang, and others at the University of Regina, Saskatchewan, Canada, in collaboration with school system personnel. It has been used successfully since the 1980s and continues to be used for pre-service and in-service professional development by the University of Regina and school districts. The set of descriptors for each competency (designed by Hellmut Lang and David Friesen) is particularly useful. We have modified and added to the IPP descriptors to provide an up-to-date set of competencies and descriptors. It is these descriptors, based on research, that take the profile a step beyond the Danielson rubric. Although it can be used as an assessment tool, the TCP is a valuable profile and functional source of competencies for teacher professional development.

The research is there. We know what needs to be achieved and how to develop effective knowledge, skills, and practices. More and more teacher training programs reflect a constructivist approach through which the novice teacher can build success through a blend of theory and practice. As McLeskey and Waldron (2004) observe,

> Knowledge for practice is perhaps the most widely accepted perspective on teacher learning. . . . This perspective holds that the more teachers know about subject matter, instructional strategies, effective interventions, and so forth, the more effectively they will teach. . . . [The] new image of teacher learning and related professional development has moved to a more constructivist model of instruction, and away from a transmission model. (pp. 5–6)

Another potentially positive development in the United States is the No Child Left Behind (NCLB) Act of January 8, 2002. This is so even though, as reported by Dobbs (2005) in the *Washington Post,* teachers' unions and some state legislatures have depicted the law as an underfunded federal mandate, overly cumbersome and bureaucratic. The four pillars of NCLB are (1) accountability and testing, (2) flexibility and local control, (3) funding for what works, and (4) expanded parental options. It replaces the federal Elementary and Secondary Education Act (ESEA) of 1965 and is the principal federal law affecting K–12 education in the United States today. President Bush pronounced, "Today begins a new era, a new time for public education in our country. Our schools will have higher expectations—we believe every child can learn. From this day forward, all students will have a better chance to learn, to excel, and to live out their dreams." These are high ideals, and the act has already had profound positive and negative effects on schooling.

Teacher preparation is at a crossroads. On one hand, the potential for excellence has never been better, with so many approaches to teaching possible; on the other hand, teachers and teacher educators are faced with state-imposed requirements and trends that threaten to reduce the act of teaching to transmission of knowledge in order to meet the pressures of standardized test requirements.

There is a danger that national and state standards will be used, not to guide and enhance teacher education and practice, but to force teachers to follow a rigid formula that contravenes their beliefs of what students need and deserve. There is a danger that the NCLB movement will lead to teachers drilling students for success, mainly in language arts and mathematics, to the neglect of other parts of a well-rounded curriculum. School districts may respond to the call for accountability by overusing or misusing standardized tests to meet the required standards.

Thorough, high-quality teacher education is critical. A 2004 education symposium to discuss teacher quality was hosted by the James B. Hunt, Jr., Institute, with governors, state education advisors, and experts in attendance. The conclusion was that college graduates with education degrees are unprepared for the rigors of the classroom, especially in schools with large numbers of poor, minority, and special needs students; and that too many teachers wash out of the profession each year as a result of inadequate preparation. Schools of education, particularly at public universities, have failed to provide the training needed to prepare teachers. This issue has gained urgency because of NCLB, which will require all classroom teachers to have bachelor's degrees, pass state subject and pedagogy tests, and be fully certified in their state by 2006. Therefore, it is critical that colleges and universities prepare students well.

We believe that the means to address the positive and negative concerns is provided through this text. The framework is the Teacher Competence Profile. Chapter by chapter, the essential knowledge and skills for effective teaching are presented. Each chapter contains recent research and good practice with respect to the theme discussed. This is followed by guidelines for the teacher, and, finally, practical approaches are presented. For example, in Chapter 6, on classroom management, the current and classic scholarship on classroom management are presented first; then specific guidelines and suggestions for effective practice are explored; followed by examples, cases, and activities. Novice teachers can use case studies, activities, microteaching, and school classrooms to construct personal meaning and develop teaching skills.

We are aware that "new" is not always better. Over the years, educators, psychologists, philosophers, and others have made major contributions to teaching research. People such as Piaget, Dewey, Vygotsky, Bloom, Maslow, and Kounin have added to the knowledge base of teachers. We have endeavored to build on these contributions.

Finally, we recognize that theory grows out of practice and practice informs theory—the relationship is symbiotic. We suggest ways in which novice teachers can use action research to contribute to teacher education knowledge and practice. For example, teachers can consider the question, "Will more higher-level questions enhance the learning of my students?" Teachers can follow the guidelines in this text as the basis for investigation and arrive at their own research results.

This text, with its professional development TCP model, can guide you to best practice. Congratulations in having chosen one of the world's great professions!

Acknowledgments

The inspiration for *Models, Strategies, and Methods for Effective Teaching* has been years of partnerships with the stakeholders in teacher education in Saskatchewan, Canada. Teacher education programs that collaborated and piloted the model and content were the Faculty of Education, University of Regina; the Saskatchewan Urban Native Teacher Education Program (SUNTEP) Gabriel Dumont Institute; and the Teacher Education Department, First Nations University of Canada (FNUC). Saskatchewan cooperating teachers and administrators have provided valuable feedback. Special thanks go to the many teacher education students for their involvement and ideas. Other important collaborators have been the Regina Public and Separate School Systems, the Saskatchewan Department of Education, and the Saskatchewan School Trustees Association.

The Saskatchewan Urban Native Teacher Education Program (Regina) deserves much credit for this book. It provides teacher education for Métis and Indian students, and offers an outstanding teacher education program that was a major inspiration for this text. Hellmut Lang helped design the program and taught in it for over twenty years.

The dedication, drive, and innovativeness of Art McBeath have had a major impact on the creation of this text. Valuable input has been received from Errol Young, Cyril Kesten, Donna Scarfe, Sandra Blenkinsop, George Richert, Ray Petracek, Larry Lang, David Friesen, and Fred Bessai.

We would like to thank the following reviewers for their comments on this manuscript: Louise D. Baucom, University of North Carolina at Charlotte; Robert H. Fowler, University of Victoria; William Michael Hessmiller, II, CET Editors and Training Associates; Melba Spooner, University of North Carolina at Charlotte; and M. Thomas Worley, Armstrong Atlantic State University.

H. R. L.
D. N. E.

Using This Text

The structure of this text is predicated on the needs of the novice teacher and requirements of the federal government and many states and provinces for teachers to meet certain standards. These standards are presented in Chapter 1. When the practice teacher completes an internship, he or she is often assessed by a set of standards similar to the one that frames this text. We present, as our standards, what we call the *Teacher Competence Profile (TCP)*. As the title implies, the new teacher, aided by an experienced cooperating teacher, can build a personal profile of competence during the internship. Experienced teachers can also use the TCP as a basis for planning their professional development.

Novices need to become aware of the standards and competencies of effective teaching, not only during the internship, but also at the outset of their teacher education program. Based on the literature on effective teaching and "good practice," the TCP specifies descriptors of effective teaching competencies. We recommend that TCP competencies be the basis for analyzing personal capability and, through reflection, for targeting growth areas and specifying how these may be achieved.

As novices use the TCP, they will move through stages. This involves a kind of spiral development (moving from simple to complex) through mastery of single competencies within lessons and then the grouping of competencies, as adapted to the context, involved in successful teaching. The first stage is *awareness*. This is followed by ongoing discussion, reflection, and practice. Let us look at a specific example: Chapter 6 examines the critical area of classroom management. It identifies eleven areas of competence:

Classroom Management
1. Creates a positive classroom climate conducive to student-centered learning
2. Communicates and monitors expectations
3. Establishes and uses effective classroom routines and procedures
4. Handles minor disruptions in a positive way
5. Uses a problem-solving approach to misbehavior
6. Uses consultation when necessary
7. Anticipates problems and plans for successful (preventative) management
8. Uses management skills effectively
9. Involves students in formulating classroom rules and consequences
10. Exhibits understanding of student behavior
11. Practices fairness and is consistent

The list is not exhaustive. We encourage student teachers, when they are ready, to consider other examples and design their own teacher competence criteria.

We examine the first of the above competencies in the table at the top of the next page. The goal for the student teacher is to explore the possibilities listed on the left side of the descriptors in the table. First, theory can be discussed in the college classroom. Ideas in the text can be explored. Practical approaches can be considered in student groups. How can school students be involved in classroom management? What kinds of consequences

Effective	Not effective
Uses a problem-solving approach to misbehavior	
Uses a constructive problem-solving approach to discipline; involves the student and, as appropriate, others; ensures understanding of consequences of actions; sensitive to pupil self-concept and promotes pupil accountability.	Autocratic, teacher-centered punishment oriented; insensitive to pupil self-concept; lack of pupil accountability.

might be applied? How can self-concept be respected? What is accountability? What does the research say? Articles can be critiqued. Specific approaches can then be tried in microteaching and initial school practice. During internship, the intern will have a sound body of knowledge and awareness as a foundation for an effective personal approach to dealing with behavior problems. Approaches can be tried in school practice and the results analyzed.

Not all competencies can be observed directly in the classroom. Some involve knowledge, attitudes, and values that are developed through research, discussion, experience, and reflection. For example, an effective teacher does the following:

- Promotes the worth of all students
- Shows interest and commitment to teaching
- Demonstrates confidence and enthusiasm
- Demonstrates creativity and flexibility
- Exhibits understanding of student behavior
- Observes a professional code of ethics

These competencies are developed over time. They are part of the general education and experience of an effective teacher. They are part of the holistic nature of good teaching, which is addressed in the text. All teacher competencies relate to the need for each teacher to be widely and well informed. This text provides a foundation.

Each chapter approaches theory and practice logically. Chapters open with an overview concept map and the specific competencies that apply. The first section of each chapter treats current research and theory, followed by practical suggestions—what can be done to be effective in the use of competencies (e.g., questioning, assessment, or in a particular approach such as indirect or inductive teaching). Every chapter includes case studies that can be a basis for discussion. Chapters conclude with practical activities.

Chapter 1 and the Epilogue are like bookends holding the other chapters together. The important elements of teacher training, with emphasis on the essential standards and competencies of teaching, are introduced in Chapter 1. Chapters 2–14 provide theoretical and practical approaches to the standards and competencies. In the Epilogue are models for successful internships in which all the competencies can be practiced in a school setting. The text is highly adaptable but is designed to ensure that new teachers are well prepared. The authors have worked closely with novice and mentoring teachers at every stage of teacher preparation, through successful internship experiences and entry into the teaching profession. This text can provide the foundation for a well-prepared and informed teacher.

Education students bring personal understandings of teaching. We encourage students not to accept the descriptors blindly. They need to ask questions and critique the descriptors in discussion with instructors and peers so they can make their own decisions about teaching. On the basis of the "behavior problem" example discussed above, typical questions might include: How did teachers who taught me approach behavior problems? What is unique about the students I teach? What would work for me? When teacher education students do this, they are, as Maxine Greene (1991) states, "constructing their identities as teachers in situations marked by tension between what seems given or unalterable and what may be perceived as possibility" (p. ix). Standards and competencies are presented in the text to provide a basic foundation for practice teachers, but they are alterable and can be deconstructed for meaning and significance. They should lead practice teachers to constructing personal standards of good practice.

The importance of clear guidelines and the need for students to go beyond them is emphasized by Duncan (1998):

> A well-articulated set of guidelines for teacher practice as well as a list of well-documented research is a vital component of a well-rounded teacher education program. This type of wisdom only goes so far, however, and teachers must step beyond this kind of knowledge. To become good teachers they must learn what works best for them, and this is something that can never be learned by a set of procedures or guidelines.

We have provided a "well-articulated set of guidelines" and "well-documented research," but student teachers must, through their own experiences and studies, apply these to their own situations. Britzman (1991) decries teacher education being viewed predominantly as vocational preparation: "The vocational model of teacher education poses the process of becoming a teacher as no more than an adaptation to the expectations and directives of others and the acquisition of predetermined skills—both of which are largely accomplished through imitation, recitation, and assimilation" (p. 29). Although this text, without apology, presents skills that are part of good practice, these need to become part of a student teacher's lived experience of teaching.

Models, Strategies, and Methods for Effective Teaching

part I

Aspects of Teaching

In Part I, several critical elements of becoming a reflective practitioner are discussed that are important to the novice teacher:

- Being an effective communicator
- Knowing that students approach learning in different ways
- Being able to adapt instruction for diverse learners
- Managing and motivating individuals and groups
- Creating a positive, supportive learning environment
- Understanding and practicing formal and informal assessment approaches
- Continually evaluating instructional approaches
- Having sound subject matter knowledge
- Having knowledge and ability to apply research
- Using written reflection to give meaning and perspective to experiences

Think back to your most effective teachers. They were good communicators who knew and understood their students, respected diversity, and used a wide variety of instructional approaches and activities. Their classrooms were interesting and challenging, and assessment was fair because there were different ways you and your classmates could show what you had learned. The teacher is an organizer of growth experiences for students. *Authentic instruction,* through which pre- or inservice teachers construct meaning, is the focus of this text. Your professional development will be enhanced through knowledge of the latest research and ongoing reflection, which will add meaning and perspective to your on- and off-campus teaching experiences.

1 Teacher Preparation

Becoming a Professional Teacher

Applying the Research

It is because of the emerging body of research and scholarship in effective teaching and teacher education and criticisms by decades of teacher education graduates that a different approach to teacher education has been developed and this book has been written. The approach advocated has resulted in relevant, high quality teacher preparation.

Although the emphasis is on preservice teacher education, teacher educators can use this text in a variety of ways. For preservice teachers, the intent is to prepare students for an extended practicum and, ultimately, success as a teacher. The key principle is that not only must teachers know about the principles and practices of effective teaching, they also must acquire performance capability. They must know *how to,* not just *what* and *why.* Teachers need to make decisions about content and instruction and then reflect on the decisions and the results. Capabilities are not learned in a linear way. A teacher does not first know about teaching and later learn how to teach. Constant interplay occurs as each aspect of knowledge and performance is improved and incorporated into a personalized act of teaching.

Recent literature reinforces the concept of clear standards or competencies the teacher needs to understand and practice. Cruickshank, Bainer Jenkins, and Metcalf (1999) believe the effective teacher must have characteristics that include: a motivating personality with enthusiasm, warmth, humor, and credibility; and an orientation to success. Teachers need to be encouraging and supportive to their students. They require a professional demeanor that is businesslike, goal orientated, serious, deliberate, organized; and, being adaptable, flexible, and knowledgeable (p. 331).

Walls, Nardi, Von Minden, and Hoffman (2002), in studying the characteristics of effective and ineffective teachers, found five major themes:

1. *Emotional environment:* being warm, friendly, and caring
2. *Teacher skill:* being organized, prepared, and clear

OBJECTIVES

You will be able to:

1. Describe research-based components of teacher preparation.
2. Describe the use of standards and competency profiles in teacher education.
3. Describe and use a professional decision-making process.
4. Describe the general areas of teacher competence presented in this chapter.
5. Assess your present teaching capability using the Teacher Competence Profile in this chapter.
6. Demonstrate effective use of a professional journal.
7. Describe the view of the teacher as a decision maker.

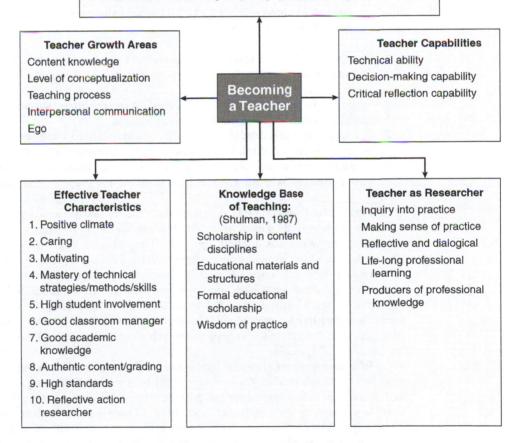

Essentials of a Teacher Education Program
- Meaningful theory with ongoing practical experiences
- Cooperation between college and educational community
- Theory and practice in generic skills
- Reflection and discussion of why skills are effective
- Awareness of how students learn
- Teacher preparation of creative and critical thinkers
- The ability to organize instruction
- Understanding of assessment
- Understanding of motivation theory
- Addressing the challenge of diversity
- Awareness of how schools and community function as social units and organizations
- The need for a constructivist approach
- Solid professional research base
- A shift of focus from the teacher to the learner
- Provision of a wide range of pedagogical repertoires

Teacher Growth Areas

Content knowledge

Level of conceptualization

Teaching process

Interpersonal communication

Ego

Becoming a Teacher

Teacher Capabilities

Technical ability

Decision-making capability

Critical reflection capability

Effective Teacher Characteristics
1. Positive climate
2. Caring
3. Motivating
4. Mastery of technical strategies/methods/skills
5. High student involvement
6. Good classroom manager
7. Good academic knowledge
8. Authentic content/grading
9. High standards
10. Reflective action researcher

Knowledge Base of Teaching:
(Shulman, 1987)

Scholarship in content disciplines

Educational materials and structures

Formal educational scholarship

Wisdom of practice

Teacher as Researcher

Inquiry into practice

Making sense of practice

Reflective and dialogical

Life-long professional learning

Producers of professional knowledge

3. *Teacher motivation:* caring about learning and teaching and being enthusiastic
4. *Student participation:* having activities that involve students in authentic learning, interactive questioning, and discussion
5. *Rules and grades:* having little difficulty with classroom management, caring about student accomplishment, fair rules and grading, requiring and maintaining high standards of conduct, and academic work (pp. 45–46)

Acknowledging Gallagher (1994), Leinhardt and Greeno (1991), and Peterson and Comeaux (1987), Walls et al. (2002) report that expert teachers emphasize process over product, relying "more on procedural knowledge" (emphasizing discovery and understanding). Those who are less apt in their "professional field or task depend more on declarative knowledge" (transmitting information and procedural skills). "Expert teachers would appear (a) to have better developed schemata for classroom teaching with strong links between subject matter and ways to teach it, (b) to be more effective lesson planners and implementers, and yet (c) to be more reflective and flexible in meeting student needs and facilitating student social and academic growth" (p. 46).

Recent literature reinforces the belief that teaching is a professional activity that needs to meet strict standards. Berry (2001) asserts there are no shortcuts to preparing good teachers. He lists four criteria:

1. Strong academic and pedagogical coursework that provides teachers with the subject matter and teaching knowledge needed to help students reach state curriculum teaching standards
2. Intensive field experience in the form of an internship or student teaching under the direct daily supervision of an expert teacher
3. A requirement that candidates meet all state standards for subject matter and teaching knowledge for a standard certificate before becoming a teacher
4. A guarantee that new teachers meet all state teacher quality standards, including passing the assessments given to their traditionally prepared counterparts (p. 35)

Perry and Power (2004) compare the "theory, skills, and knowledge through coursework" provided by most university teacher education programs, and "the field setting where knowledge is applied" (p. 125). They observe that "general propositional knowledge about teaching has always been given a privileged place in teacher education programs—it is 'Truth' with a capital 'T' whereas experiential practical knowledge generated from localized, systematic inquiry accompanied by dialogue and reflection has been regulated to 'truth' with a small 't'" (p. 126). They recommend, for university coursework, "a constructivist view of what preservice teachers need to know and how to learn [that] necessitates emphasis on experiences which actively involve learners in constructing knowledge" (p. 126).

Effective teaching requires certain personal attributes; it also requires continuous professional development. Walls et al. (2002) believe that "knowing how effective and ineffective teachers behave does not provide a prescription for shortening or easing the route to proficiency and excellence in teaching." There must be "balance between formal knowledge of educational practice and the application of concepts of effective teaching." This can be achieved by "giving preservice teachers multiple opportunities to teach in progressively more complex, multidimensional, and realistic environments" (p. 46). The literature suggests a constructivist approach, active learning, and problem-based learning so that education graduates not only "know about" effective teaching and learning but have the capacity "to do," that is, to perform with a high level of skill and competence.

This text supports and addresses the views of the above authorities. It provides a constructivist knowledge base developed from the latest research. Theory and practice are linked through modeling, microteaching, field experience, and reflection. Full collaboration with colleges of education, schools, and the community is emphasized. In an age when many teacher education programs emphasize study *about* education and teaching rather than preparation *for* teaching, this text stresses that teachers need generic skills and knowledge of, and practice in, a range of instructional strategies, methods, and skills. Although attention is given to the act of teaching, the focus is on how teaching influences the learner and how the learner constructs capability. The need to be aware of the diversity of learners and of the rapidly changing technological world is recognized.

Walberg (1990) says, "Over the past decade, there has been an explosion of research activity centering on the question of what constitutes effective teaching." He recommends that we look over the development of various approaches. "Surveying the vast literature on the effects of various instructional methods allows us to consider the advantages and disadvantages of different techniques—including some effective ones that are no longer popular" (p. 470).

A refreshing current approach is one in which teachers become their own researchers. Action research is an approach favored to foster continuous professional development. McLaughlin, Watts, and Beard (2000) recommend that we "use action research to keep a strong focus on answering practical questions about improving instruction" (p. 290).

Maxie (2001) addresses the increasing importance of the "development of standards for teacher preparation; the crafting of a teaching performance assessment for pre-service candidates; and, the building of a flexible teaching credential architecture" (p. 115). In her discussion of a blended teacher education program, she encourages early field experiences and "the introduction of the professional knowledge base and its integration with subject matter preparation" (p. 116). She places the teacher education approach emphasized in this text into a historic context. She describes the 1970s "disconnection between teacher preparation and the practice of teaching" and the initial development of increased field experience and linking university teaching programs and public schools. She points out the recognition in the 1980s of the "shift that recognizes teacher development and field experience as complex processes," the "focus on reflection and inquiry into teaching," and the "practice of teaching through collaborations between universities and schools" (p. 116). These developments led to increasing integration of subject matter and professional pedagogy and partnerships between universities, schools, and teacher organizations in the 1990s and 2000s.

Although current research supports and frames the structure of this text, classic educators are not ignored. Hatton and Smith (1995), drawing on the hierarchy of Van Manen (1977), say that teaching involves a hierarchy of three levels of capabilities: technical, decision-making, and critical reflection (Figure 1.1). These may be seen as a hierarchy of importance, but we think the hierarchy is more a series of stages of development: as student teachers accomplish more at each level, they are inclined to be

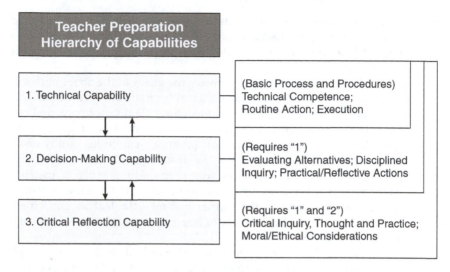

FIGURE 1.1   *Hierarchy of Capabilities and Teacher Preparation*
Source: Adapted from Van Manen, 1977.

capable and interested in the next higher level. This text encourages attention to each level throughout.

- *Technical capabilities.* Technical capabilities are required if effective daily instruction and routine action (e.g., direction giving and questioning) are to occur. Technical capabilities are basic and include the use of fundamental teaching processes, skills, and procedures. The technical skills of teaching, to create meaningful experiences for students, are not just valuable, they are essential to getting things done—the teacher must know "how to," knowing "what and why" is insufficient. In this chapter we introduce what we call the Teacher Competence Profile (TCP). The TCP presents the essential processes, skills, and procedures needed by the novice teacher.

- *Decision-making capabilities.* Decision-making capability involves making choices that result in action after alternatives have been evaluated. It can occur "on the spot" or during either short- or long-term planning. Decision making requires knowledge of, and capability in, the technical aspects. Decision-making capabilities include the ability to select from alternatives and require understanding and mastery of the fundamental competencies. As skills are mastered, the novice teacher becomes more adept at decision making—for example, when best to use an inductive approach to a lesson rather than a deductive approach. Decision-making capabilities are essential in the setting of goals and in planning.

- *Critical reflection capabilities.* Critical reflection, which requires technical and decision-making capabilities, facilitates creative reflective inquiry. Reflective inquiry requires keen observation, reasoned analysis, and weighing of the ethical and moral ramifications of decisions and actions. Reflection can enhance professional development. To be effective, reflection needs to be based on the concrete world of classrooms and the work of teachers therein. A *continuing dialectical relationship* is needed as theory informs practice and practice informs theory. Reflection, based on knowledge, is essential to growth as a teacher. "Why did the experiential approach work in this lesson?" "How can I incorporate experiential learning in other parts of my teaching?"

Good teacher education moves beyond the technical. Although development of teaching capability is not linear, it is logical that emphasis begins with the technical, moves to decision making, and then on to critical reflection. All three, however, should always be present, and all three require conscious attention through articulated theory and practice. Preservice teachers can gradually move beyond emphasis on technical improvement to reflection on "why and what" to teach and the ethical and social consequences of actions; this suggests, among other things, the narrative ways of "knowing," such as the use of journals and supervisory conferences based on microteaching and classroom teaching experiences.

Teacher preparation as presented in this text is ongoing and evolutionary, not static and fractionalized. The text structure emphasizes teacher growth and, eventually, autonomy. Teacher education, the authors believe, needs to be concerned with five growth areas:

1. *Content knowledge:* knowledge of instructional and curriculum content, going beyond the text, extending student knowledge of subject matter, and restructuring knowledge
2. *Level of conceptualization:* ability to identify problem areas or areas for improvement of one's own teaching ability, identifying alternate behaviors, applying theories and ideas, and designing professional development plans
3. *Teaching process:* capability in and appropriate use of a variety of instructional and classroom management skills, methods, and strategies
4. *Interpersonal communication:* ability to communicate with students, school staff, and parents
5. *Ego:* knowledge of oneself and willingness to take responsibility for one's own behavior, being concerned for others, responding positively to feedback, being objective and honest, facilitating growth in others, developing a positive self-concept, and increasing self-esteem

The interaction of growth areas must be considered by the student and faculty as development takes place over the entire period of teacher education. No one area can be ignored; they are interrelated. Over time, more complex levels of understanding and performance develop. This text provides a solid foundation of theory *and* practice, so graduates can face the challenges of the present and future.

Theory and Practice in Teacher Education

How will all this influence you? As a new teacher you will learn theories about teaching, such as the nature of effective questioning, and then, circumstances permitting, practice these in microteaching labs and school classrooms. Much traditional teacher education is founded on the assumption that students use theory to understand practice. Normally, however, *practice must be mastered before theory becomes meaningful.* Theory cannot be separated from practice, so we suggest that your teacher preparation learning experiences follow a spiraled, developmental, personalized approach that integrates theory and practice.

You will begin with several prescriptions and principles discussed on campus and apply these in lab and real classroom contexts to develop into a thoughtful, competent practitioner. Principles and practices that are basic to classroom teaching should be learned well at early levels and practiced at advanced levels. For example, you will learn effective communication skills early in your teacher education experience but practice them throughout your internship.

Whether to study the whole of teaching or parts is a matter of controversy in teacher education literature. Some think that breaking teaching into specific skills destroys the nature of teaching, which, they argue, is not the sum of those particular skills. We believe that learning certain fundamental aspects of the teaching process requires an approach that is systematic and adds parts to the whole. It involves concentration on specific aspects of the teaching act and reduction of the number of variables that must receive simultaneous attention. The Teacher Competence Profile presented in this text identifies the essential knowledge and skills and processes you will need as a novice teacher. Skills and processes are presented, beginning with the basic essentials. At first, one learns specific skills and processes; later, selection depends on reflection, personal need, and decision making.

Emphasis on selected skills or perspectives is preferable to learning many skills but poorly. It is logical for students to begin by learning skills that are fundamental to classroom teaching. These need to be practiced until they are mastered. Initial emphasis needs to be on basic planning, classroom management, questioning, and presentation skills—basic, everyday classroom skills that will free you to be creative and sensitive to student needs.

The presentation in this book includes concepts—principles—linked with practical applications or skills. The skills include, for example, the use of wait time to promote the development of thinking capability. The approach is consistent with constructivist thinking because knowledge becomes personal and arises out of experiences unique to an individual.

As you plan your lessons, restricting emphasis to one rule, principle, or procedure lets you think about, reflect on, and change your understanding of the rule, principle, or procedure and your way of operationalizing it. Instead of being studied in a vacuum, the rule, principle, or procedure is part of the whole lesson. This eases transfer to other lessons and inclusion into your repertoire of teaching competencies so it can be available in the future, consciously "as is" or as modified. To use questioning as an example, when you teach a lesson you might decide to work on the principle that waiting longer after you ask a question before naming a student to respond will lead to more meaningful responses to your questions. So, "wait time" is the skill that is the focus (target) of your lesson. As you reflect on the effectiveness of wait time, it becomes a part of your repertoire and increases your knowledge and awareness.

The approach to the skills and principles in this book encourages you to interpret and apply the principles in new situations. You will find that a more extensive understanding of the principles and concepts will happen as you work with these in real situations. For example, you might want to see if the use of higher-level questions will lead to better answers. You can try the approach, collect data, and so be an action researcher.

The demands on teachers and their practice are real and pressing. Although teachers need specific skills and competencies, they also need to know how to question these and build on skills as they create principles for effective practice. "Most teacher activities seem to have a component of both knowledge and practice, but at least at the beginning, when learning how to teach, it is extremely helpful to focus on those things that can be articulated in a systematized way" (Duncan, 1998).

A Teacher Preparation Model

Imagine the would-be teacher entering a university or college faculty of education. What combination of classes and school practice would best prepare this student? A model, based on extensive research and experience in teacher preparation, is presented in this book. The components of the model are as follows.

1. *Clear criteria, description, and explanation of the essential standards of what is involved in being an effective teacher.* We call these *competencies* and present a Teacher Competence Profile that lays out the essentials of what an effective teacher needs to know and be able to do. These standards exist in various forms. Danielson (1996), in *Enhancing Professional Practice: A Framework for Teaching,* identifies components of a teacher's responsibilities documented through research to promote improved student learning. In this book, we introduce the Teacher Competence Profile first developed by the University of Regina education faculty and cooperating teachers (including the authors) during the 1980s. The TCP, within a series of domains, outlines standards of effective teaching and responsibilities: professional qualities, interaction with learners, classroom management and discipline, planning and organization, teaching competence, and personal qualities. The TCP is described in this chapter.

2. *Meaningful theory on campus with ongoing practical experiences in microteaching.*

3. *Extensive field experience with increasing involvement and responsibility.* A possible approach might be weekly visits to a school in the first and second years of training, with guided practice of a specific competence explored in the class and practiced with peers in microlessons. In the third year the practice teacher teaches during a period of from several weeks to a semester. The intern's skill and competence as a teacher can be assessed at all stages by the TCP.

Profiles or Frameworks for Professional Practice

A profile of what effective teachers are like and do emerges from the professional literature. Student teachers, faculty, and practicing teachers can benefit from a guiding framework of good teaching. Through research, Danielson (1996) identifies components of a teacher's responsibilities to improve student learning (Figure 1.2). The framework specifies what professional teachers should know and be able to do. She identifies four domains: (1) planning and preparation, (2) classroom environment, (3) instruction, and (4) professional responsibilities. Within each domain, distinct aspects or behaviors are specified (pp. 1–4).

The Danielson model and the TCP are remarkably similar, although developed independently. The TCP provides descriptions of instructional strategies, methods, and skills that can be used as professional targets by intending teachers. Under Domain 3, Instruction, Danielson addresses, for example, communication, questioning, and discussion, which are key components of the TCP.

The Danielson Framework

Danielson's framework (and the TCP) can help you set professional targets as a novice teacher, remind experienced teachers of professional expectations, provide potential

FIGURE 1.2 *Danielson's Components of Professional Practice*

DOMAIN 1: Planning and Preparation	DOMAIN 2: The Classroom Environment	DOMAIN 3: Instruction	DOMAIN 4: Professional Responsibilities
Component 1a: Demonstrating knowledge of content and pedagogy Knowledge of content Knowledge of prerequisite relationships Knowledge of content-related pedagogy	*Component 2a: Creating an environment of respect and rapport* Teacher interaction with students Student interaction	*Component 3a: Communicating clearly and accurately* Directions and procedures Oral and written language	*Component 4a: Reflecting on teaching* Accuracy Use in future teaching
Component 1b: Demonstrating knowledge of students Knowledge of characteristics of age group Knowledge of students' varied approaches to learning Knowledge of students' skills and knowledge Knowledge of students' interests and cultural heritage	*Component 2b: Establishing a culture for learning* Importance of the content Student pride in work Expectations for learning and achievement	*Component 3b: Using questioning and discussion techniques* Quality of questions Discussion techniques Student participation	*Component 4b: Maintaining accurate records* Student completion of assignments Student progress in learning Noninstructional records
Component 1c: Selecting instructional goals Value Clarity Suitability for diverse students Balance	*Component 2c: Managing classroom procedures* Management of instructional groups Management of transitions Management of materials and supplies Performance of noninstructional duties Supervision of volunteers/paraprofessionals	*Component 3c: Engaging students in learning* Representation of content Activities and assignments Grouping of students Instructional materials and resources Structure and pacing	*Component 4c: Communicating with families* Information about the instructional program Information about individual students Engagement of families in the instructional program
Component 1d: Demonstrating knowledge of resources Resources for teaching Resources for students	*Component 2d: Managing student behavior* Expectations Monitoring of student behavior Response to student misbehavior	*Component 3d: Providing feedback to students* Quality: accurate, substantive, constructive, and specific Timeliness	*Component 4d: Contributing to the school district* Relationships with colleagues Service to the school Participation in school and district projects
Component 1e: Designing coherent instruction Learning activities Instructional materials and resources Instructional groups Lesson and unit structure	*Component 2e: Organizing physical space* Safety and arrangement of furniture Accessibility to learning and uses of physical resources	*Component 3e: Demonstrating flexibility and responsiveness* Lesson adjustment Response to students Persistence	*Component 4e: Growing and developing professionally* Enhancement of content knowledge and pedagogical skill Service to the profession
Component 1f: Assessing student learning Congruence with instructional goals Use for planning Criteria and standards			*Component 4f: Showing professionalism* Service to students Advocacy Decision making

Source: Adapted from Danielson, 1996 (pp. 3–4).

points of discussion between cooperating teachers and interns or between experienced teachers and novices, and set benchmarks of teaching excellence and continuous professional development.

Danielson believes that her framework provides: *a road map for novices* (a map of the territory; a pathway to excellence); *guidance for professional excellence* (what the effective teacher knows and does in the performance of duties); *a structure for focusing improvement efforts* (for novice teachers working with their mentors; to determine which aspect of teaching requires attention); and *communication with the larger community* (to define clearly what constitutes excellence in teaching, and guidelines for professional development) (pp. 6–7).

Danielson traces the origin of components of professional practice to Madeline Hunter, whom Danielson considers to be one of the first to argue convincingly that teaching is more than an art and is also a science. There was a need to create performance assessment systems as a basis for licensure. Various states have developed performance assessments similar to Danielson's framework. Danielson observes that the earliest systems had a tendency to identify specific teaching behaviors—for instance, writing learning objectives on the board. Later systems were based on a more complex view of teaching and included the efficacy of a teacher's judgment regarding what she calls more sophisticated tasks such as asking meaningful questions (pp. 7–8).

In *Teacher Evaluation: To Enhance Professional Practice,* Danielson and McGreal (2000) discuss an effective approach to teacher evaluation. They note that use of feedback or evaluation forms alone is not enough, and an evaluation system must contain three elements: (1) a coherent definition of the domain of teaching ("What?"), including decisions concerning the standard for acceptable performance ("How good is good enough?"); (2) techniques and procedures for assessing all aspects of teaching ("How?"); and (3) trained evaluators who can make consistent judgments about performance, based on evidence of the teaching as manifested in the procedures (p. 21).

The "what" is described in detail in Danielson's "components of professional practice" in her 1996 book, *Enhancing Professional Practice: A Framework for Teaching.* The "how" is the assessment procedures used when observing an intern, novice, or experienced teacher. The procedures used may involve feedback forms based on good practice.

Danielson and McGreal's (2000) views on the issue of trained evaluators are interesting. First, they believe, evaluators must be able to recognize examples of evaluative criteria in action. Classroom events and instructional artifacts are mere data; data evaluators need to select as evidence different evaluative criteria. The evidence selected should be not only relevant but also representative. Second, evaluators must interpret the evidence for an aspect of teaching against evaluative criteria. There is more than one possible interpretation of an event. Correct interpretation is important. Third, the evaluator must make a judgment about a teacher's performance, linking interpretations to the descriptors of levels of performance; and evaluators must be able to conduct reflective conversations and provide constructive feedback (pp. 23–24).

Danielson and McGreal speak of "making a judgment." The authors of this text (while believing the Danielson approach is sound) argue that the gathering and interpretation of evidence (descriptive data) should be a shared process between a teacher and an observer. In our experience, an intern observed by a peer, an intern observed by a cooperating teacher, or a practicing teacher observed by a peer or administrator can gather valuable data and interpret it, leading to plans for improvement. A meaningful judgment can be made by the teacher who was observed upon examining the data as the observer acts as a nonjudgmental helper. In other words, self-evaluation, we believe, should be part of the process. Then, the teacher can prepare plans for professional development, based on what was learned and facilitated by the observer.

Danielson says the intended use of her framework and rubric is in contrast to how some districts apply it to teacher evaluation. She believes the checklist of skills should be used as a guide, not as a rigid formula. She says that it is better to use the rubrics for feedback and dialogue followed by a holistic judgment. She prefers to limit the use of judgments about whether further training is needed (Finkel, 2003).

Finkel observes that some districts comply closely with the intent of the Danielson model, the belief being that the rubric provides stable targets to work toward and benchmarks for administrators. Critics, however, say the rubric may be misused because it is not tied to student performance in class and on tests. Furthermore, critics claim, it requires excessive, labor-intensive documentation, and it can be used punitively. The rubric could be used for anything from teacher pay to teacher dismissal.

PRAXIS, INTASC, and NBPTS

The use of performance assessment is reflected in the Professional Assessments for Beginning Teachers (PRAXIS) series that is to replace the National Teacher Examination (NTE). On a national level in the United States, there are standards for novice teachers, the Interstate New Teacher Assessment and the Support Consortium (INTASC). These set guidelines in the same way as the National Board for Professional Teaching Standards (NBPTS) sets standards for experienced teachers.

Page, Rudney, and Marxen (2004) discuss "the pattern of development through which students become teachers" (p. 26), linking this pattern of awareness to INTASC. The authors emphasize, "Standards of proficiency must be met but pre-service teachers must be allowed to construct their own knowledge" (p. 27). Standards, such as the Teaching Competence Profile used in this text, are not a final checklist. They are, however, sophisticated, research-based criteria that provide sources of professional competencies and a means of reflection as interns construct meaning through a structured inservice experience. Successful standards are achieved "with the nurturing guidance, feedback, and challenges of knowledgeable others such as university faculty and cooperating teachers" (Page et al., 2004, p. 40).

The Teacher Competence Profile (TCP)

The Intern Professional Profile (IPP) developed by Art McBeath, Hellmut Lang, and others at the University of Regina in cooperation with school system personnel, has been successfully used since the 1980s and, with adaptations in keeping with current research, is used for preservice and inservice professional development by the University of Regina and school districts. The set of descriptors for each aspect and component (originally designed by Hellmut Lang and David Friesen) is particularly useful. It is these descriptors, based on research, that have an approach similar to the Danielson rubric. An example from the IPP is shown in Figure 1.3. Although it can be used as an assessment tool, like the Danielson rubric, it is primarily a guide and a source of targets for teacher professional development.

The Joint Field Experience Committee (2004), of the Faculty of Education, University of Regina, has prepared two Intern Placement Profiles (IPPs), one for the elementary teacher education program (including middle years), and another for the secondary program. Figure 1.3 is a blend and adaptation of the two. We call this model the Teacher

FIGURE 1.3   *Blended Elementary/Secondary Teacher Competence Profile*

These are the essential competencies or standards for becoming an effective teacher. They follow the sequence of chapters in the text. Descriptors of each competency, providing a profile of desired and also undesirable behavior, are at the end of this chapter.

Communication Skills (Chapter 2)
Models appropriate voice and spoken and written language
Makes effective use of interpersonal skills

Diversity Issues (Chapter 3)
Promotes the worth of all students
Responds to the needs of all
Is attentive to learning styles
Is adept at intercultural communication

Attitudes and Values (Chapter 4)
Helps students understand attitudes and values
Creates a positive classroom climate conducive to student-centered learning
Shows an interests in individual students
Encourages and supports students
Motivates students to participate

Assessment and Evaluation (Chapter 5)
Identifies student academic, personal, and social strengths
Assesses change in student development
Involves students in assessment
Evaluates student progress
Keeps thorough, well-organized records
Provides diagnosis and remediation

Classroom Management (Chapter 6)
Creates a positive classroom climate conducive to student-centered learning
Communicates and monitors expectations
Establishes and uses effective classroom routines and procedures
Handles minor disruptions in a positive way
Uses a problem-solving approach to misbehavior
Uses consultation when necessary
Anticipates problems and plans for successful (preventative) management
Uses management skills effectively
Involves students in formulating classroom rules and consequences
Exhibits understanding of student behavior
Practices fairness and is consistent

Lesson, Unit Planning, and Delivery (Chapter 7)
Planning
Integrates skills and knowledge common to all subjects and adapts curriculum to individual needs
Plans varied learner-centered activities
Outlines long-range plans to guide student development

Plans interdisciplinary thematic units
Involves learners in the planning process
Includes classroom management in plans

Instruction
Demonstrates competence in basic instructional skills
Teaches for holistic development (physical, social, emotional, cognitive)
Varies teaching approaches and activities
Ensures the participation and success of all students
Engages students in instructional dialogue
Provides motivating set and closure
Orders and sequences content to meet learner needs
Provides for transfer of learning

Curriculum
Adapts curriculum to student needs
Knows subject matter
Exhibits knowledge of local and state curricula

Questioning, Discussion, Seatwork, and Homework (Chapter 8)
Has effective questioning skills
Conducts effective class discussion
Sets meaningful seatwork and homework

Teaching Concepts (Chapter 9)
Provides effective teaching of concepts and explanations

Skills Teaching (Chapter 10)
Provides effective teaching of skills and demonstrations

Direct Instruction and Individual Study (Chapter 11)
Effective direct instruction/deductive/expository methods
Effective use of the individual study strategy
Employs resource-based teaching/learning with a wide variety of media and resources
Uses instructional technology to enhance student learning

Indirect and Experiential Learning (Chapter 12)
Provides effective use of indirect/inductive/inquiry methods
Uses experiential learning regularly to encourage active learning

Collaborative and Cooperative Learning (Chapter 13)
Develops group skills in the classroom
Uses collaborative and cooperative learning methods regularly

continued

FIGURE 1.3   *Continued*

Thinking Skills and Problem-Based Learning (Chapter 14)
Uses specific instruction in the nature and use of thinking
    skills and processes
Incorporates key thinking operations and core thinking
    skills into teaching
Ensures that students use critical thinking procedures
Ensures that students think creatively
Skilled and effective approach to problem-based learning

Professional Development Practica (Chapter 15)
General internship skills
Shows interest and commitment to teaching
Demonstrates initiative
Manner is dependable and mature
Deals effectively with personal and interpersonal stress
    and conflict

Demonstrates confidence and enthusiasm
Demonstrates creativity and flexibility
Collaborates and cooperates with school staff
Relates effectively to students' caregivers
Gets involved in student-related school activities
Practices a professional code of ethics

Professional Development Process
Practices the Professional Development Process
    (target selection, pre-/postconferences,
    data collection methods, and analysis
    of data)
Implements change (plans for growth) based on
    reflection on experiences
Evaluates planning, instruction, and management
Participates in planned professional development

Competence Profile. Each item describes performance along a continuum ranging from "ideal" to "unsatisfactory." (See descriptors on pp. 29–40.)

The Professional Development Model

The teacher preparation model we recommend is based on the frame of reference of the purposes and tasks of effective teachers. It is recommended that delivery of the program take place in one of two ways. The preferred way (Figure 1.4) involves both microteaching and field classroom application. If this is not possible, cases and activities can be used (Figure 1.5) in place of microteaching.

Principles and practices are studied and practiced, one by one, and integrated cumulatively into an individual's repertoire. Teaching is a complex act in which the components of decision making, implementation of instructional decisions, and evaluation of their efficacy are interrelated. Though skills and strategies are practiced separately, the whole act is maintained regularly when the cycle includes practice in simulated and real classrooms.

Acquiring Competencies and the Delivery Cycle

To become an effective teacher you will need to have command of many competencies; several often come into play simultaneously. Many of these competencies are described in the Teacher Competence Profile. As you focus on a particular competency for mastery, you might call this your "target," a term used in some internship programs. The process of teaching is based on generic skills or principles that must be organized and structured into teaching strategies and applied to content that is individualized to suit a class and individuals.

As you select and use a variety of instructional skills, methods, and strategies, you need subject matter knowledge and need to organize it for learning—the natural order of a discipline and organization for instruction may not be identical. You must respond to individual and cultural differences; be competent in communication, interpersonal, and group skills; manage the class; and use disciplinary techniques as necessary. To acquire these capabilities, you need reflective practice using a systematic, comprehensive, and personalized approach to professional development.

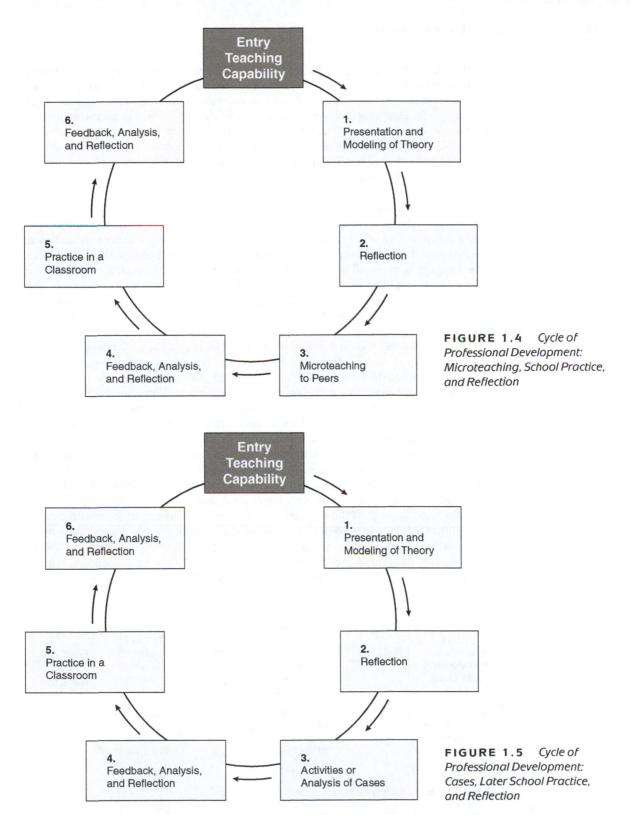

FIGURE 1.4 *Cycle of Professional Development: Microteaching, School Practice, and Reflection*

FIGURE 1.5 *Cycle of Professional Development: Cases, Later School Practice, and Reflection*

DELIVERY CYCLE.   If it is possible in your program, use a cycle (or sequence) of theory presentation and modeling, reflection, microteaching, reflection, classroom practice, and reflection (Figure 1.4). For example, a three-week cycle can be used to cover each topic, with a new cycle beginning each week: theory/modeling the first week, microteaching the second week, and school practice the third week. If microteaching or school lessons are not possible, some form of application experience such as a lab activity or case study can be provided and reflected upon so theory can be personalized and enlivened, and the possibility of transfer to actual teaching increased (Figure 1.5). Another view of the cycle is shown in Figure 1.6.

Ideally, you will be actively involved in meaningful, personalized learning through deliberate use of the cycle. An example of how this works using a professional competency or target is exploration of the competence, "giving directions." First, theory presentation, instructor modeling, and debriefing of effective direction giving takes place. Preservice teachers engage in personal professional reflection about their in-school experiences as students. Next, in a microteaching lab, each student teacher presents a minilesson. The purpose of lab lessons is to practice direction giving. Presenters give their lessons and receive feedback from their group. The group has from six to ten peers and a lab instructor. When all have taught, debriefing on the target of direction giving occurs. Reflections about lab experiences are recorded in personal professional journals. Then, each teacher-learner (who, with a peer partner, will have been placed in a school classroom) will teach a lesson to practice giving directions in a school classroom. As each teaches, she or he will be observed by his or her partner and classroom teacher, who will provide feedback on the use of direction giving. Finally, reflections about school "tries" of the professional target will be recorded. The cycle is repeated with a new target or competence. The target of giving directions becomes a continuing secondary target until it is mastered.

As indicated, to foster comprehension, internalization, and capability in direction giving, teacher-learners keep a record in a personal professional journal of reflections about their growth. In the journal, they can reflect about each on-campus class, lab, and school experience by recording a description of what was experienced, the impact (learning and feelings) because of the experiences, and the resulting intent (commitment) for specific future action to achieve the target. Here the practice teacher is describing his or her lived experience of teaching an approach and comparing the experience to the theory.

Typically, because of program restraints and lack of time and resources, teacher preparation may not follow the entire model. Follow-up studies of teacher education grad-

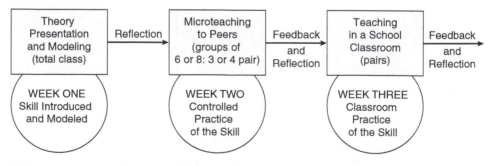

FIGURE 1.6   *Delivery Cycle*

uates reveal that graduates often believe their preparation to be irrelevant to real classrooms. When teacher education students speak with their cooperating teachers, they are often told to ignore what university instructors told them. Often, instructors present theories of instruction and tell their students what they should be doing; then, students are asked to critique readings, have a discussion, or write a paper and a test. Later, students experience a practicum, often with scant or inconsistent supervision by faculty, that is loosely, if at all, integrated with what they have been studying in classes. Students often have little opportunity to practice what they have studied. The result often is that practice teachers copy what their cooperating teachers do and become socialized to what exists. The stress is on what works, not on what should be done. Follow-up studies of graduates show that when the cycle described above is used, methods classes are thought to be relevant and are rated favorably.

Students typically move through five stages (Figure 1.7) as they acquire a professional competency: (1) unaware, (2) aware, (3) awkward, (4) consciously competent, and (5) internalized (Campbell, Cordis, McBeath, and Young, 1987, pp. 16–19). By using the materials in this text, practice teachers will first become aware of a skill and, though awkwardly, try it. They likely will not reach the characterization stage until well into their extended practicum. As they practice new targets, they gain further practice in previous targets, though these are secondary to the practice of each new target.

Team Planning and Delivery

Effective preservice study of the principles and practices of teaching requires the cooperation of several significant actors: you and your peers, microteaching lab instructors (if these are part of the cycle), other instructors who also teach you, administrators (on campus and in the school system), the person responsible for school placements, and the teachers with whom you and your peers are placed. It is critical that all of these key people are familiar with the Teacher Competence Profile.

A team approach to planning and delivery is best. Periodic meetings can be held to discuss content and delivery procedures. Using a team approach ensures that the program will not be static and components will not clash. The program can be kept up to date and fit the needs of students, faculty, the school system, and what is being discovered about effective teaching and teacher education. Constructive, adaptive change should, and can, take place. Teaming also can ensure that all concerned will stress common (rather than contradictory) objectives and the actors will be consistent in the approach chosen. All personnel involved need to know what knowledge and skills are being learned. Change should take place through a consensus process. Some flexibility in choice to meet the needs of students should be possible. Because delivery of topics (targets) follows a schema that affects others, content selection and arrangement and delivery procedures should be altered only after careful examination.

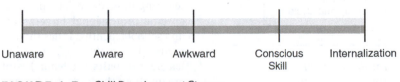

| Unaware | Aware | Awkward | Conscious Skill | Internalization |

FIGURE 1.7   *Skill Development Stages*

The Professional Development Process

The Model

A model called the *professional development process (PDP)* can be used to help you acquire the behaviors and reflection-in-action capability of an effective teacher (Figure 1.8). The PDP can be used as described or may be adapted to a particular situation. Opportunity for continuous professional growth is provided as personal knowledge about teaching is reconstructed as the process is experienced. Stress is on fundamental principles and practices of teaching and the development of a strong personal professional self-concept. The goal is holistic development moving from known to not yet known, from simple to complex, and from parts to the whole. You apply principles as you practice in a context that requires reflection and allows the "art" and humanistic aspects to be enhanced. Emphasis is on the development of ego, a strong personal professional self-concept. Over time, focus shifts from specific competencies to broader processes or frameworks. The shift is not perfectly linear. If needed, the focus can return for a time to a specific competency.

This approach is different from a theory-into-practice model, which can lead to separation of means and ends. It is an integrative approach in which the PDP recognizes the dialectical relationship between theory (which helps develop practice) and practice (which deepens understanding of theory). Theory must be personalized—it is only meaningful if it is based on experience. The process provides experience and requires reflection. Theory can exist within the mind and enhance professional decision making and performance. The process fosters integration of professional knowledge, the content being taught, and application experiences (microteaching or classroom).

As you experience the PDP you participate in the broad act of teaching and, though attention may center on a specific competency or process, understanding of teaching deepens as you gain experience. You develop self-analysis ability and own and are accountable for your professional development.

The capabilities of the technical-rational and reflection-in-action approaches are brought together in the **PDP.** It is concerned with increasing technical, decision-making, and reflective skills. It involves theory, action, and reflection. Without action, reflection goes nowhere. Implementation depends on the ability to apply understandings about teaching and principles of teaching. The process lets you acquire critical, specific professional competencies, proficiency with reflection-in-action, and a reconstructed understanding. Over time, these are brought together and refined. A practice cycle, in a collegial context of research-validated prescriptions and principles, is used because action is a necessary precursor to reflection. The professional development process stresses collegiality, reflection-in-action, performance capability, and reordered understanding of teaching in its cycle. The process is used to practice specific professional targets during microteaching and school teaching. It has three interrelated components: (1) a *conferencing procedure* with (a) teacher-learners in pairs (or teams) conferencing before a lesson about the target to be practiced, (b) collection

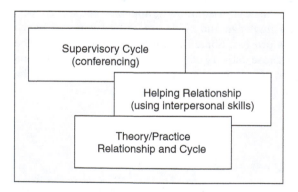

FIGURE 1.8   *The Professional Development Process*

of data about the target during the lesson, and (c) after the lesson, debriefing student learning and the teacher's growth regarding the professional target; (2) use of a *helping* (facilitating, supportive, but nonjudgmental) *relationship frame of reference* during conferencing; and (3) *practice of targets* following the professional development cycle.

As you follow this process, a *helping relationship* mode of conferencing should be used. Communication and interpersonal skills and descriptive, nonjudgmental data collection and feedback should be taught and used. The class (or staff) should be divided into pairs (though teams of three or four could be used) for laboratory or school lessons and pairs alternate as "helper" and "helpee" as they prepare for, deliver, and analyze the lessons they teach. A preconference is held before a lesson. The lesson is taught by one while the others observe and collect data on the chosen professional target in the manner decided in the preconference. In a postconference, the data collected are analyzed by the "teacher," with the help of the data collector(s).

Pre- and postconferences deal with (1) achievement of lesson objectives by students, and (2) achievement of a specific professional target (or competency) by the teacher.

Principal focus is on a specific target, not everything done during a lesson, one target at a time. You cannot focus on all the components of the act of teaching simultaneously. To use an analogy, a beginning golfer cannot concentrate on numerous elements, including the correct grip, stance, body turn and thrust, backswing, stroke, and follow-through simultaneously with the hope that all will be improved simultaneously. So, too, a teacher-learner, while teaching a lesson, cannot be expected to improve simultaneously all the elements of the complex act of teaching.

In each preconference, pairs preview and, as appropriate, you as the "teacher" revise plans for the lesson topic, content, objectives, prerequisite learning, set, development, closure, materials and aids, evaluation, professional target, ways of achieving the target, and how data will be collected. While the lesson is being taught it is observed, and data are recorded about the presentation and how the target was used. Data collection needs to be objective and descriptive, not sketchy and judgmental. It is up to you to analyze the data that mirror what occurred.

The postconference includes debriefing on lesson elements, reviewing the target agreed upon, nonjudgmental presentation of the data collected, analysis of data by you with the help of the observer, decisions by you about the significance of the data, and a decision by you about future action. The task of the "helper" is to present the data collected and to be a nonjudgmental facilitator. Ownership of the data, analysis, and a decision about future action rests with you.

Giving and Receiving Feedback

Good feedback (Figure 1.9) promotes growth by providing information about what the teacher-learner has been doing and the effect on students. When targets are practiced, feedback should be given after each attempt. Feedback should be nonthreatening and non-judgmental, and received as information intended to help. Comments such as "good" or

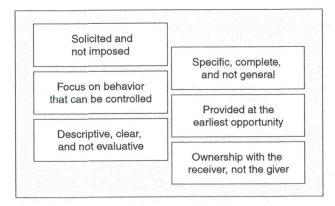

FIGURE 1.9   *Characteristics of Effective Feedback*

"bad" should be avoided by the feedback provider. Effective feedback is solicited, descriptive, and clear; focused on behavior that can be controlled; provided at the earliest opportunity; specific and complete; and ownership is with the receiver (not the giver).

How feedback is given and received makes a big difference to your overall development as a practice teacher. The following guidelines are suggested.

Guidelines for Giving Feedback

1. Allow for receiver readiness. The receiver must indicate readiness to listen and accept feedback.
2. Feedback is descriptive, not interpretative. Feedback is a description of your perceptions and reactions.
3. Feedback should be given as close to the time of the behavior as possible. It should cover recent happenings.
4. Give feedback at appropriate times. Avoid giving feedback when others are present.
5. Feedback should give new, not obvious information.
6. Feedback should be on what can be changed. Feedback is valuable when behavior can be modified.
7. However, feedback does not demand a change. It is up to the receiver to make the change.
8. Do not overload the feedback. To not give too much feedback or bring up too many points at once.
9. Feedback is given to be helpful. Always consider your motivation when you give feedback.
10. Share something. Feedback can lead to an imbalance in the relationship. Sharing feelings and concerns can make the other more comfortable.
11. Be as specific as possible. Avoid generalizations. Quote, give examples and details.

Guidelines for Receiving Feedback

1. Check for understanding through paraphrasing and other forms of communication.
2. Ask for feedback on specific things. This also shows areas of readiness.
3. Share your reactions to the feedback. This lets others know where you stand, so the relationship can grow. It also avoids uncertainty, so the giver feels positive about sharing and giving feedback.

Guidelines for Disclosure

1. You control your own disclosure. No one can make you share information that you do not feel comfortable sharing.
2. Disclosure should be relevant to the situation and the relationship. Usually this is about resources, experiences, talents, capabilities, likes and dislikes in the work you are sharing. If you disclose information to another, and that person misuses it, it is still your responsibility and judgment that is at fault.

Laboratory Microteaching to Practice the Target

Ideally, laboratory settings are available for microteaching. Microteaching allows controls of the nature of the tasks being learned before you are placed in the complex crucible of a classroom. Preparation, as in other professions, should include use of controlled clinical and laboratory experiences before experiences in natural classrooms. Microteaching works! It has substantial effects.

Small groups of six or eight students (three or four pairs) can be used so each student has an opportunity to teach a lesson. The microteaching lab should provide a "safe" environment for the practice of targets. If the first practice was in an actual classroom it would be difficult to concentrate on a target. The teacher-learner would have to attend to many variables and feel obligated to teach each lesson as well as possible. In microteaching, the general success of the lesson can be secondary and attention can be devoted to achieving the target. The overriding purpose is to practice and receive feedback on tries of a skill. Microteaching to peers can free students to do this because the number of variables is reduced. Students "crawl before they walk, walk before they run, and run after they have learned to walk." Being less pressured, the teacher-learner benefits from initial tries before a new skill or method is practiced in a school.

To help provide a "safe" learning opportunity, topics chosen should not be complex, nor require subject matter depth, and be no longer than ten minutes. The topics should be suitable for practice of the target at hand. For example, if questioning technique is the target, the content and teaching method must lend itself to the use of questioning.

While the major purpose of labs is for teacher-learners to make "safe" tries of targets, a continuing secondary consideration is becoming increasingly proficient with past targets, with conferencing, observation, and data collection, and with communication and interpersonal skills. A collegial or "helping relationship" should be established and maintained, and teacher-learners need to learn about themselves and how to be effective observers who can collect meaningful, descriptive data.

A procedure you can adapt to meet the realities of your program follows. If groups of six are used, a time block of two hours is needed so each student can practice the target. Twenty to thirty additional minutes will be needed if groups of eight are used. A lab instructor should act as a facilitator. At the end of the lab, the instructor debriefs learning about the target and the nature of data collection and conferencing. Initially, pairs should conference in front of the whole lab group so they can learn effective conferencing techniques. Later, the instructor can circulate from pair to pair. Then, in personal professional journals, learning and feelings about plans for school practice of the target can be recorded.

Ideally, your lessons should be videotaped at least twice during the term, to allow comparison of "before" and "after" performances. The following is a suggested procedure for microteaching labs.

Steps for Practicing Targets in the Microteaching Lab

1. *Teacher-learners are paired.* Pairs preconference, observe and collect data, and postconference on the lessons each teaches.

2. *Every teacher-learner prepares a lesson plan for each lab.* The plan should outline what the teacher-learner is trying to do to achieve lesson objectives and what will be done to achieve the professional target. Lesson plans are handed in to the lab instructor for written suggestions. These are returned at the next lab.

3. *Each pair of teacher-learners holds a preconference about the lesson to be presented.* One student acts as a "helper" to the "teacher" whose plans for the lesson are being discussed. The helper finds out what the other is intending to do regarding: (a) lesson objectives, content, materials and aids, set, development, closure and evaluation, and (b) how the other intends to go about achieving the professional target, and how data are to be recorded. Behaviors of the helper include listening, seeking information, clarifying, and seeking alternatives and consequences of these. The helper does not say what to do. She or he helps the other examine the plan, surface concerns, facilitates problem solving, and provides empathetic and nonjudgmental support. The "teacher" may revise the plan because of the conference, and should have a better understanding of, and be comfortable with, what is to be done in the lesson.

4. *The lesson is taught and data are collected.* Teacher-learners, in turn, teach their lessons to their lab group. The partner of each student observes from an appropriate vantage point and collects data. Before teaching the lesson, the "teacher" may ask group members to role-play a certain age group and tells them what prerequisite knowledge or skill(s) they will be presumed to possess.

5. *Each pair holds a postconference about the lesson.* Opportunity should be provided for the "helper" to consider the significance of the data and how they can be presented in a way that helps the "teacher" analyze the data and plan. The helper is a facilitator, not a judge. The helper presents the data to the teacher. Data are analyzed and their significance determined. A decision is made by the teacher about the degree of success of the practice of the target. If the target requires further practice, a decision must be made about the aspect(s) requiring attention and when and how to conduct it. If, for example, the target was direction giving, the teacher may decide that more practice is needed and also a plan for "checking up" on students more effectively; and that, in the school lesson, the target should emphasize "checking up" to see if directions were understood. A postconference checklist is provided in Figure 1.10.

6. *Debriefing on target trials, the nature of data collection, and conferencing.* Under the guidance of the lab instructor, about ten minutes should be taken to examine learning about the target and data collection and conferencing. "Teachers" are encouraged to think further about how they will try the target in their school lesson. Lesson plans and the recorded feedback are handed to the lab instructor for comments and suggestions.

7. *Teacher-learners reflect about their professional target attempts.* Before professional targets are attempted in a classroom, "teachers" consider what they have learned and what they will try to do before they try the target again. It is useful for students to keep a journal in which to house lesson plans and feedback, and record reflections about their experiences and plans for the next practice. More microteaching practice may be helpful if time is available.

Though performance of a specific target is emphasized during microteaching lessons, the process is not mechanical. You plan to apply the principles involved in the target during the lesson taught. This is content designed to increase understanding of teaching principles. It occurs through application (or transfer) of the principles to new content. A checklist that can be used is included in Figure 1.10.

The TCP and the Field Experience

Two sets of standards for teacher competencies have been presented in this chapter. One is "Danielson's Components of Professional Practice" (Figure 1.2); the other is the "Blended Elementary/Secondary Internship Placement Profile" (Figure 1.3). Figure 1.3 is the Teacher Competence Profile. It specifies criteria for teaching skills and competencies. Most are treated in the subsequent chapters and, ideally, are practiced by the novice teacher during microteaching and initial field experiences. The profile provides a learning plan and means of assessing progress in the development of teaching skills. A critical

FIGURE 1.10   *Pre- and Postconference Checklists*

Preconference Checklist	Postconference Checklist
____ Topic	____ Debriefing on the lesson regarding plans for achievement of objectives by students
____ Identification of content	
____ Prerequisite learning	____ Review of target and method of data collection as agreed
____ Set	
____ Development	____ Presentation of the data collected
____ Closure	____ Analysis of data by you (as assisted by a helper if available)
____ Materials and aids	
____ Evaluation	____ Decision by the teacher about the significance of the data
____ Identification of target	
____ Actions proposed to achieve target	____ Decision by the teacher re specific action for the future
____ Data collection method	

use of the profile is during the novice teacher's extended practicum (field experience). The TCP on pages 29–40 contains descriptors for each competence. Descriptors occur along a continuum from "effective" to "ineffective."

During the field experience you will have two goals: (1) helping students learn, and (2) personal professional development (Figure 1.11). Teaching is based on lesson and unit plans. To achieve help students learn, the teacher decides what to teach, the objectives to be achieved, and the assessment to be used to discover how well students have met the objectives. Focus is on the learners. The goal of personal professional development is to discover how effective he or she is in delivering the lesson. Objective descriptive information needs to be collected on the teacher's performance. To get this information you decide on a particular professional competence (we call this a *target*) on which you would like feedback data. The focus is on your professional development.

Practicing Professional Decision Making

ASSESSING PRESENT TEACHING CAPABILITY. It is important to use the criteria in the TCP selectively as competence develops. The following competencies work well for the first- or second-year teacher:

- Lesson planning
- Communication skills
- Interpersonal skills
- Set and closure
- Giving directions
- Basic management skills
- Handling minor disruptions
- Questioning skills
- Varying the presentation
- Teaching a skill
- Concept teaching

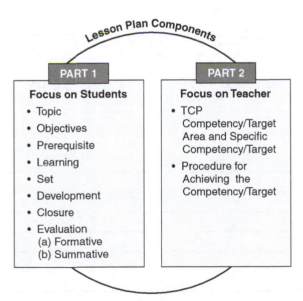

FIGURE 1.11   *Two Goals in Teaching a Lesson*

We suggest: (1) Read the text description of the competency. (2) Give a tentative assessment of your present teaching capability. (3) Read the criteria in the competency profile. (4) Select or design a basic data sheet (samples are appended to this chapter). (5) Microteach a lesson with one of the above competencies as a focus, with your teacher and/or a partner collecting data.

USING THE TEACHER COMPETENCE PROFILE TO PLAN TARGETS AND DESIGN DATA SHEETS.   A listing of competencies as well as descriptors is appended to this chapter. When you plan to achieve a target, read the descriptor for that target. An example of using a competency to plan targets and design a data sheet is shown in Figure 1.12. The data collected should be descriptive. Judgmental statements such as "great voice" or "too quiet" are not helpful. It is better to describe what occurred, for example, "All questions were audible from all parts of the room," or "All words were clearly enunciated and heard by the class," or "Some responses to the class were given while students were talking." Sometimes during the data collection simple "+'s" can be used for positive observations and "–'s" to suggest that an alternative may be desirable. Data sheets can be sophisticated, with additions such as the time or beginning, middle, end of lesson, questions or responses to particular students using a seating plan, and teacher position in the room.

   Before teaching a lesson, you, in a preconference, tell your cooperating (observing) teacher or partner about your two goals (intended student learning and professional tar-

FIGURE 1.12   *Example of a Professional Target of Spoken Language Using the Appropriate TCP Descriptor*

A: Personal and Professional Qualities
   3. Models appropriate voice and spoken and written language

---

Spoken Language

Descriptor: Audible, clear, pleasant, and expressive; enunciation is correct and distinct; absence of distracting mannerisms; excellent language usage modeled; matches pupils' ability levels; ability to relate to pupils through language.

   [*Note:* Based on the above criteria, the teacher makes a simple data sheet and asks the cooperating teacher to collect descriptive information.]

Spoken Communication

Observations:

Audible _____

Clear _____

Pleasant and expressive _____

Correct and distinct enunciation _____

Distracting mannerisms _____

Language usage _____

Matches pupils' abilities _____

get) to be achieved. After the lesson is taught, hold a postconference. Discuss the lesson and professional target—first, "how the lesson went," and then, based on data collected by the cooperating teacher, whether the target was achieved or needs further attention.

Data collected should be given to you in the postconference. You make a judgment based on personal analysis of the data. For example, rather than the cooperating teacher saying, "You were too loud," it is better if you, as the one who taught the lesson, interpret the data and say, for example, "I notice I tend to speak too loudly at the beginning of a lesson to get attention. I'll work on that."

Through the use of this professional development process you can build, over the duration of the field experience, a bank of competencies. The cooperating teacher builds a picture of your growing development based on valid data. The final rating of your performance can be based on descriptive evidence shared with and agreed on by you and your cooperating teacher.

DESIGNING OTHER TYPES OF TARGETS AND DATA SHEETS.   You are encouraged to design your own data sheets. Initially, we recommend you use the data sheets at the ends of the chapters. Each sheet is based on research and can be used as an initial foundation for data collecting. Subsequently, feel free to adapt the sheets in keeping with your objectives and in relation to the development of the lesson plan. We recommend that the target and nature of the data sought be identified in the lesson plan.

There are other sources of targets as well as data sheets and the TCP, A target is an example of good practice. If, for example, you witness the management skills of an experienced teacher, these skills and approaches can be described and used as targets. Or an article that describes the success of a particular questioning or discussion approach can be the source. Many schools and school districts produce booklets of good practice. These, too, can be sources. The point is, targets need to reflect good practice. You can try a particular target to see if it will work for you.

Classroom Teaching to Practice the Target

After you have studied the theory and rationale for a target, have seen it modeled, and have practiced in a microteaching laboratory, you will be ready to practice the target in the more complex, less "safe" setting of a classroom. This is where the school–university partnership comes into play.

One, two, or more persons can be placed with a cooperating (or sponsor or mentor) teacher. The major purpose of the classroom placement is to practice specific targets in a realistic setting. Theory integration with practice is fostered. Feedback can be received from placement partners and cooperating teachers. Bristor, Kinzer, Lapp, and Ridener (2002) build on this theme when they say, "One of the major postulates to come out of the teacher education reform movement was the importance of school–university partnerships" (p. 688). Citing a range of research sources, they discuss the importance of higher education and school co-involvement in teacher education. They advocate many of the themes critical to this text, including awareness of the "rapid development of information technologies on teacher education," the "need to be prepared to teach in culturally diverse settings" and the need to relate theory to practice, instructional practices to learning and development, and to connect content knowledge with methods (p. 689). Bristor et al. stress the importance for teachers "to make the university methodology part of the classroom reality and their own experiences, rather than experiences only existing within the confines of the university" (p. 697).

The value of the university–public school partnership was studied by Dever, Hager, and Klein (2003). The critical importance of the cooperating teacher or mentor and the need for them to have training in the supervision or professional developmental process is described. "Teacher education programs are more likely to be effective if they use mentor teachers who have received supervisory training" (p. 245–246). We recommend that the cooperating teacher and intern share a joint preparation workshop and that the cooperating teacher, intern, and university faculty advisor follow a model such as the TCP. Dever et al. (2002) stress, "For university education programs to be effective, the collaborative effort of university faculty in academic settings and public school teachers in classrooms is required." Such partnerships lead to benefits such as "congruence between academic and field experiences," keeping "university faculty abreast of the realities of teaching," and increased "opportunities for communication between university and public school facilities" (p. 246).

PROCEDURE.   A cooperating teacher is selected to work with each pair (the pair is the same as in the microteaching lab). A cooperating teacher orientation session should be held to explain the purposes of the practicum experience and the roles of student teachers, cooperating teachers, and the faculty instructors. Teachers should be given:

- An information sheet about each person in the pair
- Material that explains the procedures being used and the targets that are to be practiced, with data collection instruments matching the topics that will be studied
- A schedule outlining the weekly cycle for learning about and practicing professional targets

The process should continue to be used as in labs.

A pair can conduct conferencing with input from the cooperating teacher (who listens and comments). Ownership and responsibility for learning continues to rests with the "teacher." Cooperating teachers are not experts who "tell." They are "helpers" who provide opportunity to teach lessons that lend themselves to the practice of the specific targets that are the primary goals of lessons. School lesson content should be relatively simple and not require extensive preparation time.

Suggested Steps for Practicing the Target in a Classroom

1. *Each pair is placed with a classroom teacher.* Before their first visit, students phone their cooperating teachers to introduce themselves and arrange to meet them. The first visit is for orientation to the school and classroom, and for students and teachers to get to know each other and discuss their roles. A teacher training institution contact person is named, and cooperating teachers are given an orientation to the program.

2. *The cooperating teachers assign students a lesson topic.* During the first visit, the topic for the following visit may be agreed on, or students may phone at a predetermined time to have a topic assigned congruent with the schedule of the classroom and suitable for practice of the target.

3. *Preconferencing takes place before each lesson is taught.* Student–teacher pairs preconference with the help of their cooperating teachers. Each "teacher's" partner and cooperating teacher act as "helpers" in the manner described above for microteaching.

4. *Lessons are taught and data are collected.* Partners and the cooperating teachers observe and collect data. Stress is on practice of the target, although secondary targets can be solicited by the teacher-learner and agreed on by the "teacher" and "helper(s)."

5. *Teacher-learners hold postconferences with their partners and cooperating teachers.* Opportunity should have been available for the helpers to consider the significance of the data collected and how the data can be presented so the teacher-learner can analyze them and formulate plans for future tries. Teacher-learners analyze the data and decide their significance. A decision is made about the degree of success of the lesson and target attempt. If the target requires further practice, a decision is made about the specific aspect(s) that require attention and when, and how, further practice is to take place.

6. *Reflection about learning through the classroom practice of the target occurs.* Students should think carefully about what they have experienced and what to do in the future to develop further proficiency in the use of the target. Students should include lesson plans for the lessons they taught, feedback received, and reflections about these in their professional journals.

Reflection: Using a Professional Journal

REFLECTION AND DECISION MAKING. The goal is to help you as a teacher-learner to become a self-analyzing, self-actualizing decision maker. Record reflections about your learning and plans for future target attempts in a *professional journal*. Consider also how a specific target fits into the total teaching act. While targets are initially practiced separately, they do not occur in a vacuum. They should become part of a teacher-learner's decision-making repertoire. Just as the artist who paints in oils must acquire the knowledge and techniques of the medium and knowledge of form, line, balance, and texture, so must the teacher-learner thoughtfully learn the skills and strategies used by effective, creative teachers.

THE PROFESSIONAL JOURNAL. Written reflection about development experiences can be a powerful constructivist experience! You should sit back and think about what has occurred and should occur. Effective journalizing involves the cognitive acts of recalling, analyzing, synthesizing, evaluating, and planning. A record of professional growth emerges as entries are made. You can visualize where you have been, where you now are, and where you hope to go. Periodic "stocktaking" entries prompt review of several weeks' progress and plans for professional growth. Suggestions for keeping a journal follow.

Keeping the Journal

1. *Dividers.* Have a title page and dividers to separate journal sections in your binder. Use the headings: Class Experiences; Microteaching Lab Experiences; Classroom Experiences; Special Investigations; Stocktaking; and Career Choice. Place a Journal Checklist at the front.

2. *Class experiences.* The main focus for the on-campus classes section should be the weekly professional target(s). Use the headings: Description (What was presented, discussed, and modeled? What activities took place?); Impact (What was the impact for you as a developing professional? What did you learn? How do you feel about it?); Intent (What do you intend to do because of what you have learned when you practice the target in the lab? Specifically what? How? When?).

3. *Microteaching lab experiences.* For the microteaching labs section, reflect about how your lesson went regarding the target and what you learned about the target because of the rest of your lab experiences. Under the heading "Description," briefly describe what happened in the lab; under "Impact," note what you learned about, and how you feel about, your target because of your lesson and the other lessons; and under "Intent," tell, specifically, what you will do because of your learning and feelings when you practice the target in your school. Attach your lesson plan and the feedback you received (include the verbal feedback you received).

4. *Classroom experiences.* For the classroom experiences section, under the heading "Description," describe: (a) how you practiced your target; (b) how your partner practiced the target; and (c) how your cooperating teacher uses the target. Under "Impact," describe what you learned and how you feel about your practice of the target; and your partner's practice of the target. And under "Intent," tell, specifically, what you will do when you next practice the target. Attach your lesson plan and all feedback.

5. *School observations.* Record things you saw or heard in class, the lab, or the building that made an impression, or caused you to wonder. Did you read something or interview the principal, a teacher, a student, or somebody else?

6. *Stocktaking.* Do an inventory of your professional growth. Indicate what you knew and could do as a teacher at the start of the term, what you now know and can do, and what you still need to know and be able to do. Take stock again at the end of the term, picking up from were you left off at mid-term.

7. *Career choice.* At the end of the term, comment on your choice to become a teacher. Do you still want to be a teacher? Why? What grade or age level? Future plans? What other alternatives do you have? What is influencing your choice?

Summary

There have been many changes in teacher education over the past two decades. An effective teacher has knowledge of and skill in the use of the basic principles and practices of teaching. You need to discover the latest research, and acquire sound theoretical knowledge and a repertoire of precise teaching skills. A sound teacher education program must be comprehensively planned and must be developmental. The basic essentials of effective teacher education are suggested in this chapter. A teacher must possess certain capabilities and characteristics. Teaching, like any other profession, has its own knowledge base. It is suggested that today's teacher become an ongoing researcher and reflective practitioner and life-long learner and producer, not just consumer, of professional knowledge. A sound approach to teacher education blends modeling theory and microteaching in the college classrooms with practical teaching experience in the schools. A framework for professional development that forms the structure of this text is the Teacher Competence Profile. Other models include the extensively used Danielson (1996) approach. The models provide a plan and a foundation for teacher training. Adapt these to your personal teaching needs as you live your learned experiences.

Descriptors for Competencies in Your Personal Profile

The following descriptors match the competencies listed in the preceding profile. Two statements are made with respect to each competence. The first statement describes an effective use of the competence and the second statement describes an ineffective use of the competence.

TEACHER COMPETENCE PROFILE

Effective Performance	*Ineffective Performance*

COMMUNICATION SKILLS (Chapter 2)

Models appropriate voice and spoken and written language

Generally audible, clear, pleasant, and expressive; controls volume appropriately, enunciation is correct and distinct; correct spelling and grammatical usage; excellent language usage modeled; written handouts are easily understood and match level of students; written work is neat and presentable.

Inaudible or monotone; incorrect enunciation; poor English usage; students have difficulty understanding the teacher; little effort to improve language usage; written work is messy and confusing.

Makes effective use of interpersonal skills

Empathetic (tries to understand others) and helps others understand him/herself; is other- rather than self-centered; models, teaches, and expects the use of interpersonal skills by students.

Poor listener; unempathetic (does not try to understand others), doesn't help others to understand him/herself; is self- rather than other-centered; does not teach or expect use of interpersonal skills by students.

DIVERSITY ISSUES (Chapter 3)

Promotes the worth of all students

Demonstrates a caring professional manner toward all students regardless of developmental level, intellectual capacity, appearance, health, exceptionality, socioeconomic status, gender, religion, race, or cultural background.

Discriminates or stereotypes or acts on personal preferences; tends to treat all students the same way regardless of individual needs; delays responding to individual needs.

Responds to the needs of all

Attends to needs of all students; secures needed resources; encourages and recognizes growth according to individual ability.

Treats all students the same regardless of individual needs; delays responding to individual needs.

Is attentive to learning styles

Aware of the range of learning styles, hemispheric mode, and learning modalities; knows about the range of intelligences; is capable of creating a differentiated classroom; individual approaches to instruction; varied materials to draw on student interest.

Little awareness of the range of teaching styles; has a narrow sense of the meaning of intelligence; whole-class instruction is dominant and instruction is text driven.

Is adept at intercultural communication

Respects and works along with the range of cultural differences in the classroom; is aware of ways of communicating between and within cultures.

Little or no acknowledgment of the range of cultural diversity in the classroom: all or most lessons reflect the view of the dominant culture.

continued

Effective Performance	*Ineffective Performance*

ATTITUDES AND VALUES (Chapter 4)

Helps students understand attitudes and values

Demonstrates love of learning and respect for others; helps students understand their attitudes and values; sets objectives and selects appropriate activities for the development of attitudes and values; helps students overcome negative attitudes and low self-esteem.	Models disinterest in learning and lack of respect for others; concentrates solely on cognitive and psychomotor objectives; oblivious to student attitudes and self-esteem.

Creates a positive classroom climate conducive to student-centered learning

Creates an enjoyable environment conducive to learning; fosters participation by all learners; deals quickly with interpersonal tensions; creates a positive attitude toward and excitement for learning.	Creates negative attitudes toward others and learning; allows interpersonal tensions to build.

Shows interest in individual students

Discovers individual student interests; promotes the development of specific abilities and interests of individual students; makes an effort to know students personally; establishes appropriate relationships to enhance student development.	Does not make an effort to discover individual student interests and abilities; does not establish a cordial relationship with each student.

Encourages and supports students

Encourages individuals and class to try their best and fosters development of a positive self-concept; fosters development of positive attitudes toward others and the school; sets challenging but achievable goals; shows confidence that students can achieve goals.	Does not encourage students to overcome barriers or to achieve potential; does not show confidence in students; is sarcastic or belittles and generally attacks self-concept of individuals; allows or encourages negative attitudes toward self, others, or the school.

Motivates students to participate

Student attention stimulated and maintained; uses a variety of stimulation techniques; accommodates student needs and interests; builds success experiences appropriate for individuals and class; encourages and recognizes effort.	Uninspired approach to instruction; oblivious of student and class needs and interests; does not reinforce achievement by individuals or class; teaches only to the best students or "down the middle."

ASSESSMENT AND EVALUATION (Chapter 5)

Identifies student academic, personal, and social strengths

Uses formal and informal methods to identify students' strengths; shares assessment of strengths with students; incorporates knowledge of student strengths into planning for student assessment.	Tends to dwell on inefficiencies and weaknesses; does not assess student strengths or share them with students.

Assesses change in student development

Uses formal and informal methods to assess change in student development; maintains accurate and comprehensive records of each student's progress.	Does not document student development.

Effective Performance	Ineffective Performance

ASSESSMENT AND EVALUATION (Chapter 5)   *continued*

Involves students in assessment

Students are regularly given opportunities to set criteria for their work and to assess their progress; students are involved in individual conferences with the teacher; assessment is treated as a learning experience.

Students are not given the opportunity to assess their work; no dialogue with students about progress.

Evaluates student progress

Various assessments are interpreted to evaluate student progress; the basis for evaluation is clearly and regularly reported to students and parents; evaluation is used to set goals for future growth.

Student evaluation is not based on regular formal and informal assessment; evaluation is reported as marks, with little or no reference criteria or interpretation.

Keeps thorough, well-organized records

Record keeping thorough, well organized, and accessible (e.g., attendance, marks, student progress, assignment and test schedules, record of professional targets, progress in essential learning).

Little or no evidence of usable record keeping.

Provides diagnosis and remediation

Uses and acts on standardized and teacher-made evaluation techniques for remediation or enrichment; refers to other professionals when appropriate.

Does not diagnose or provide remediation or enrichment.

CLASSROOM MANAGEMENT (Chapter 6)

Creates a positive classroom climate conducive to student-centered learning

Creates an enjoyable environment conducive to learning; fosters participation by all learners; deals quickly with interpersonal tensions; creates a positive attitude toward and excitement for learning.

Creates negative attitudes toward others and learning; allows interpersonal tensions to build.

Communicates and monitors expectations

Consistently provides clear and achievable directions; models and fosters appropriate behavior norms; clear standards; checks for understanding. Monitors behavior expectations; immediate attention to behavior, i.e., feedback and correctives as appropriate; checks up periodically as needed.

Poor direction giving; does not model or promote appropriate behavior; inconsistent or inappropriate standards; does not check for understanding; does not notice (or allows) inappropriate behavior that often escalates; does not reinforce appropriate behavior.

Establishes and uses effective classroom routines and procedures

Maximizes on-task behavior through establishment of appropriate routines and procedures.

Routines and procedures nonexistent or inconsistent; much off-task behavior.

Handles minor disruptions in a positive way

Is aware of and deals unobtrusively and immediately with minor disruptions; watches for recurrence.

Is unaware of, does not respond to, or responds inappropriately or inconsistently to minor disruptions.

continued

Effective Performance	Ineffective Performance

CLASSROOM MANAGEMENT (Chapter 6)   *continued*

Uses a problem-solving approach to misbehavior

Uses a constructive problem-solving approach to discipline; involves the student and, as appropriate, others; ensures understanding of consequences of actions; sensitive to student self-concept and promotes student accountability.

Autocratic, teacher-centered punishment oriented; insensitive to student self-concept; lack of student accountability.

Uses consultation when necessary

Recognizes personal limitations for dealing with unique needs or situations; provides appropriate documentation and involves others as needed (i.e., cooperating teacher; principal, guidance counselor, MD, social services, parents, etc.).

Does not recognize personal limitations in dealing with unique needs or situations; fails to involve appropriate personnel.

Anticipates problems and plans for successful (preventative) management

Anticipates and plans for potential problems, which helps maximize on-task behavior.

Does not anticipate or preplan responses to inappropriate behavior; much off-task behavior occurs.

Uses management skills (Kounin) effectively

Consistently demonstrates awareness of off-task student behavior; plans for and monitors a consistent flow of meaningful activities; makes smooth transitions from one activity to another; is able to deal with minor problems without disrupting classroom routines.

Often unaware of off-task student behavior; does not plan for organized classroom; transitions often disrupt; ineffective use of time.

Involves students in formulating classroom rules and consequences

Promotes student self-discipline; involves students in setting and monitoring classroom rules and consequences; rules and consequences are appropriate to grade and age level.

Sets rules and consequences that are inappropriate; relies on punishment rather than rewards; does not involve students in setting and maintaining classroom rules and procedures.

Exhibits understanding of student behavior

Able to anticipate problems and identify sources of classroom problems; uses cues to control behavior without interrupting entire class; clearly established behavior standards can distinguish between major and minor disruptions and responds appropriately; reprimands are consistent with infractions, reacts quickly and decisively in handling discipline cases.

Is hesitant and indecisive when dealing with discipline cases; generally does not identify problem source; interrupts entire class to reprimand major and minor infractions; behavior standards are not established or are seldom adhered to; reprimands are not consistent with infractions.

Practices fairness and is consistent

Is, and is perceived to be, fair and consistent in enforcing rules and promoting positive behavior; positive behavior is rewarded and rule violation results in suitable consequences.

Is inconsistent in applying consequences or rewarding appropriate behavior; relationship between behavior and consequence is not congruent.

Effective Performance	*Ineffective Performance*

LESSON, UNIT PLANNING AND DELIVERY (Chapter 7)

Integrates skills common to all subjects and adapts curriculum to individual needs

In planning units and lessons, incorporates the skills common to all subjects; adapts curriculum plans to individual needs.	Unaware of common essential skills; does not incorporate skills common to all subjects; does not adapt curriculum plans to individual needs.

Plans varied learner-centered activities

Plans enable students to be actively involved in a broad range of motivating activities congruent with objectives and evaluation; development level and student needs and interests recognized; activities often learner selected; aware of the need to adapt to individual and group needs.	Prescriptive activities chosen and sequenced randomly or inappropriate to developmental level and student needs and interests; often incongruent with objectives and evaluation; activities always teacher selected; unaware of the need to adapt to individual and group needs.

Outlines long-range plans to guide student development

Logically sequenced; variety in presentation and student activities; addresses student readiness; plans adaptable to a variety of student needs; provides for evaluation; plans available prior to teaching.	Generally fails to plan units or drafts or series of lessons, with little coherence, variety, or attention to student needs; plans not available in advance.

Plans interdisciplinary thematic units

Plans units that focus on a specific theme/ problem/issue, which integrate several areas; themes are realistic, relating to student interests and abilities.	Units always subject area specific.

Involves learners in the planning process

Learners are involved in planning units.	Students are never consulted or involved in unit planning.

Includes classroom management in plans

Unit plans contain detailed plans for classroom management.	Unit plans do not incorporate classroom management.

INSTRUCTIONAL VARIABLES (Chapter 7)

Demonstrates competence in basic instructional skills

Provides motivating lesson introduction (set); gives clear explanations; words questions clearly; provides for review and practice; checks for student understanding; provides lesson summary (closure).	Lessons introduced in unmotivating, vague ways; explanations confusing; questioning skills poorly developed; no effective closure.

Teaches for holistic development (physical, social, emotional, cognitive)

Lessons consist of activities that address physical, social, and emotional as well as cognitive needs.	Lessons are primarily cognitive.

continued

Effective Performance	*Ineffective Performance*

INSTRUCTIONAL VARIABLES (Chapter 7)   *continued*

Varies teaching approaches and activities

Consistently uses a variety of teaching strategies and methods appropriate for the content and students; experiments with a variety of ways of teaching.	Uses only one or two teaching strategies and methods; tries new methods only when urged to do so.

Ensures the participation and success of all

Assesses ongoing individual student development; modifies activities for active participation to ensure success of all students.	Little individual assessment; students expected to engage in the same activity regardless of level or ability.

Engages students in instructional dialogue

Engages students in dialogue about their experiences and learning; debriefs the processes of learning with students; teaches specific learning strategies; monitors use of learning strategies.	Learning activities seldom debriefed; learning processes not taught to students; learning strategies not monitored.

Provides motivating set and closure

Always provides a motivating set for lessons and units that facilitates transfer from previous to new learning; always provides closure to lessons and units, which reviews and provides transfer.	Begins lessons and units without a set; lessons end abruptly, without review or transfer.

Orders and sequences content to meet learner needs

Orders and sequences content to meet learner needs; recognizes when text organization is inappropriate; uses advance organizers and in-progress and post-organizers well; fosters student capability to recognize structures and patterns in content.	Rigidly follows the text or curriculum guide without considering learner needs; content is a smorgasbord of information; no use of organizers; students not helped to discover structures in patterns of content.

Provides for transfer of learning

Deliberate provision for transfer (bridging) within the subject, across subjects, and to life; examples are relevant and interesting.	No attempt to bridge previous and new learning, or transfer learning within the subject, to other subjects or life.

CURRICULUM KNOWLEDGE (Chapter 7)

Adapts curriculum to student needs

Selects material appropriate to learner needs and interests; sets curriculum goals taking into account learner differences and interests; can restructure content for various ability and interest levels.	Uses prescribed curriculum without adjusting for learner needs and interests; cannot restructure content for various ability and interest levels; rigid application of curriculum guidelines.

Knows subject matter

Has an excellent grasp of subject area content (concepts, information, skills, theories); can articulate the structure of different subject areas; can see inter-	Treats subject content as a body of disjointed information; unable to construct relationships within individual subject areas; unable to build relationships

Effective Performance	*Ineffective Performance*

CURRICULUM KNOWLEDGE (Chapter 7)   *continued*

relationships among subject areas; rich in breadth and depth; presents information, skills, and methods of the subject accurately and in appropriate sequence; uses teacher and student resources well.	among subject areas; inaccurately, poorly used and sequenced information; superficial skills and methods; inadequate use of sources.

Exhibits knowledge of local and state curriculum

Understands local and state core curriculum requirements; uses local and state curriculum guides effectively.	Not aware of the value of local and state curriculum guides in planning.

QUESTIONING, DISCUSSION, SEATWORK, AND HOMEWORK (Chapter 8)

Has effective questioning skills

Excellent use of questions: choice; steps in; conducting; wait time; cognitive level; prompts, probes, and redirects; and distribution.	Rarely uses questions; unaware of effective steps, effective use of wait time, and cognitive level; up and down rows distribution; repeats questions and answers; accepts chorus responses and call-outs.

Conducts effective class discussion

Conducts effective classroom discussions; helps class focus on topic; fosters participation; varies interaction so all participate; brings closure and summary; conducts guided and open discussions.	Discussions have no apparent structure; little evidence of planning; a few students dominate; no satisfactory summing up and closure.

Sets meaningful seatwork and homework

Seatwork and homework assignments follow a clear school or classroom policy; guidelines clear to students; assignments match student ability and challenge reasonably; students given some choice; prompt, meaningful feedback.	Little consistency or policy to the seatwork and homework assignments; haphazard setting of homework; no clear guidelines; care not taken to match student ability; no choice in assignments; inadequate feedback; assignments returned late.

TEACHING CONCEPTS (Chapter 9)

Provides effective teaching of concepts and explanations

Prior analysis; students learn critical and noncritical attributes and appropriate definitions; effective examples and nonexamples and understanding extended over time; effective selection of the number and sequence; concepts presented in a lesson or unit interrelated; appropriate choice and use of inductive and deductive approaches.	No prior analysis; definitions often "muddied" with noncritical attributes; definitions presented without emphasis on understanding; relationships not identified; poor or inadequate selection of examples and absence of nonexamples; approach always deductive.

continued

Effective Performance	*Ineffective Performance*

SKILLS TEACHING (Chapter 10)

Provides effective teaching of skills and demonstrations

Prior analysis of skills; developmental level of students accommodated and desired skill level determined; demonstrations clear and systematic; effective guided practice and feedback before independent practice; appropriate choice and use of deductive and inductive approaches.	No prior analysis; readiness of students ignored; absence of or ineffective demonstration; absence of guided practice and feedback; approach always deductive.

DIRECT INSTRUCTION AND INDIVIDUAL STUDY (Chapter 11)

Effective direct instruction/deductive/expository methods

When used, fit content and learner needs; effective principles of lecture and assigned question methods demonstrated; stimulates student participation; makes effective use of audiovisual aids, discussion, and question and answer.	Exclusive use of expository approach; instruction highly abstract and not learner centered; students passive; no use of audiovisual aids, discussion, or question and answer.

Effective use of the individual study strategy

Students taught research skills and use of computer technology; homework and seatwork is well planned and monitored; students encouraged to develop individual responsibility and life-long learning skills and interests; students taught to think carefully about their academic tasks.	Limited use of individual study approaches; students rarely do meaningful homework and seatwork; individual research and computer skills rarely taught or required.

Employs resource-based teaching/learning and a wide variety of media and resources

Students involved in individual and group research projects; school resources used beyond classroom including community resources; students taught how to use resources; inquiry-oriented climate promoted; students involved in planning and assessing their learning.	Bound to prescriptive materials; lesson formats are stereotypical; students not taught to process information; lack of variety in resources; direct instruction orientated; students not involved in planning and assessing their learning.

Uses instructional technology to enhance student learning

Uses computers effectively to enhance student learning; effectively uses a range of audiovisual technology and approaches; teaches students to use technology and the Internet with skill and awareness; a variety of nonprint material used.	Computer and Internet illiterate; seldom uses nonprint materials; does not teach students to use available technology and resources.

INDIRECT AND EXPERIENTIAL LEARNING (Chapter 12)

Provides effective use of indirect/inductive/inquiry methods

Use matches content and learner needs; instruction highly learner centered; student discovery fostered; appropriate learning materials available; sensitive to learners' experiential backgrounds; learners presented with problems or issues to be explored and solved.	Instruction exclusively teacher centered and expository or deductive; information-centered instruction almost always used.

Effective Performance	*Ineffective Performance*

INDIRECT AND EXPERIENTIAL LEARNING (Chapter 12) *continued*

Uses experiential learning regularly to encourage active learning

Able to design experiences that facilitate active participation in learning; debriefs student experiences; gets students to discover generalizations from experiences; gets students to apply learnings to new situations.

Students seldom engage in actual experiences to generate active learning; no debriefing of student experiences.

COLLABORATIVE AND COOPERATIVE LEARNING (Chapter 13)

Develops group skills in the classroom

Builds rapport with whole class and a cohesive class group; sets achievable, challenging goals for the class or small groups; uses effective interpersonal and group skills (i.e., participation, consensus seeking, problem solving, conflict resolution, group accountability); models, teaches, and expects use of group skills.

Unaware of the class as a social group and appropriate student and teacher behaviors; does not model, teach, and expect the use of group skills.

Uses collaborative and cooperative learning methods regularly

Uses collaborative and cooperative learning appropriately; teaches social skills; monitors group work and gives regular feedback; able to develop positive interdependence among group members; uses a variety of collaborative and cooperative learning methods; allows students to evaluate group effectiveness and accountability.

Uses groups without teaching social skills; no feedback given to groups; unable to create positive interdependence among group members; group effectiveness not evaluated by students; collaborative and cooperative learning used inappropriately.

THINKING SKILLS AND PROBLEM-BASED LEARNING (Chapter 14)

Uses specific instruction in the nature and use of thinking skills and processes

Specific instruction in the nature and use of thinking skills and processes; emphasis on problem-solving and critical thinking skills; objectives and evaluation reflect emphasis on thinking skills acquisition; asks many "why" and "what if" questions.

Sole focus on facts and information of an area of study; right answer emphasized; no opportunity for problem solving or critical thinking.

Incorporates key thinking operations and core thinking skills into teaching

Key thinking operations such as comparing and classifying are a key part of teaching, as are core thinking skills such as organizing and analyzing.

Teaching tends to focus on basic factual information and accepted at face value without organizing of material into new patterns through comparison, classification, and analysis.

continued

Effective Performance	*Ineffective Performance*

THINKING SKILLS AND PROBLEM-BASED LEARNING (Chapter 14)   *continued*

Ensures that students use critical thinking procedures

Ensures students are familiar with the difference between facts and value claims, and that they check for bias, validity, and relevance in their research.	Students tend to accept all information at face value. Little attempt by the students to check material for bias, validity, and relevance; students unaware of critical thinking procedures.

Ensures that students think creatively

Encourages creative potential of students; welcomes novel and imaginative responses; uses divergent approaches; models creativity and allows open-ended expression; experiential, inductive, and hands-on approaches.	Creativity not apparently welcomed; reliance by teacher on standard information; only "right" answer welcomed; little attempt to encourage and welcome novel, imaginative, and creative ideas.

Skilled and effective approach to problem-based learning

Skilled at setting up student-centered problem-based learning approaches; teacher is facilitator, ensuring students explore problems themselves; carefully selects problems as focus of learning; students develop problem learning skills as they direct their learning; meaningful information provided or suggested.	Few or no student-centered approaches; teacher tends to control and dominate the learning process; problems selected not authentic or challenging; students learn few meaningful skills; information provided uninteresting or inadequate.

EPILOGUE—PROFESSIONAL DEVELOPMENT PRACTICA

Shows interest and commitment to teaching

Active effort to improve teaching and extensive involvement in school programs and professional development opportunities: displays genuine concern for and enjoyment of children.	Lack of commitment to teaching; avoids getting involved in school, extracurricular, and professional development activities.

Demonstrates initiative

Shows active interest and inner self-direction by volunteering constructive suggestions and assuming responsibility.	Shows apathy or reluctance to be involved; waits to be asked and/or directed.

Manner is dependable and mature

Fulfills commitments responsibly; positive, but realistic, outlook; is concerned with self-betterment; acts independently but is sensitive to the needs and feelings of others; accepts and acts on constructive criticism; cooperative and pleasant without being compliant; addresses problems in a professional rather than personal way; shows excellent professional judgment; is tactful.	Unreliable, duties neglected or fulfilled in a haphazard or sloppy way; must be reminded or checked up on; defensive when constructive criticism is offered; moody and uncooperative; problems addressed personally rather than handled professionally; makes inappropriate professional judgments; is not tactful.

Deals effectively with personal and interpersonal stress and conflict

Calm and composed under stress; maintains "professional cool"; seeks and fosters satisfactory solutions to	Easily flustered; displays unprofessional behavior such as sarcasm or blaming rather than seeking

Effective Performance	*Ineffective Performance*

EPILOGUE—PROFESSIONAL DEVELOPMENT PRACTICA   *continued*

disagreements, conflicts, or misunderstandings; handles emergency solutions calmly and expeditiously; seeks assistance when appropriate; able to remain objective.	solutions; never admits that help may be needed; avoids addressing problems; acts in a defensive manner when challenged.

Demonstrates confidence and enthusiasm

Responds positively to new experiences and is willing to risk; is not threatened by unexpected events; is decisive and communicates a positive outlook, enjoyment, and high levels of interest to inspire others in a variety of situations; is dynamic.	Withdraws from challenge; makes inappropriate decisions based on emotion; avoids making decisions; is pessimistic, lacks expression of interest and enjoyment; is uninspiring.

Demonstrates creativity and flexibility

Actively incorporates new ideas and materials or uses traditional ideas and models in different integrative ways; models and encourages imagination; is able to change activities as the situation demands.	Follows commonly prescribed or suggested methods, in own presentations and in responding to others; focuses on specifics; limited imagination exhibited; cannot adapt teaching to changing demands.

Collaborates and cooperates with school staff

Typically listens to constructive criticisms and suggestions of others and is able to contribute criticisms and suggestions of his/her own with sensitivity to the norms of the school and needs of others; is tactful.	Typically submissive; follows directives from colleagues or makes inappropriate or indiscreet comments; antagonizes or irritates others.

Relates effectively to students' caregivers

Communicates effectively with students' caregivers; makes caregivers feel comfortable in the school; listens to concerns of caregivers without making premature judgments; encourages and achieves caregiver participation in the classroom.	Avoids students' caregivers and discounts their concerns.

Gets involved in student-related school activities

Actively contributes to the school co-curricular program; initiates new activities for students.	Avoids co-curricular activities; does not contribute in his/her areas of expertise.

Practices a professional code of ethics

Observes principles of a professional code of ethics; commitment to students, school, profession, and community; resolves conflicts with sensitivity.	Violates precepts of a professional code of ethics; lacks commitment to students, school, profession, and community.

Practices the Professional Development Process: (target selection, pre-/postconferences, data collection, and analysis of data)

Consistently sets appropriate generic and subject-specific professional targets for each lesson and unit without being urged to do so; progresses creatively, as ready, from simple to sophisticated.	Seldom, if ever, sets targets; sets only when urged; inappropriate to content of lesson; seldom varied.

continued

Effective Performance	*Ineffective Performance*

In the preconference, based on preplanning, clearly presents and collaboratively plans for all essential lesson elements and a specific target; in the postconference, participates actively and receptively in analysis of feedback and plans for future.	Uncooperative; avoids conferences; unprepared; does not solicit feedback; unreceptive to feedback.
Appropriately uses available instruments; often designs suitable instruments that result in specific, objective, and observable behavior.	Data collection instrument rarely provided; often inappropriate for target or lesson; onus on cooperating teacher.
Reviews data and initiates identification of key elements and patterns; forms and takes ownership of appropriate generalizations or implications.	Usually doesn't analyze and interpret feedback; if attempted, fails to identify, or accept, data implications; relies on cooperating teacher's analysis and interpretation.

Implements change (plans for growth) based on reflection on experiences

Incorporates feedback for improvement of: future lessons and professional growth through suitable targets; in an attempt to gain understanding about classroom practice and personal professional growth, often reflects on key events, records these and shares thoughts and questions with the cooperating teacher and faculty advisor; as a result, sets new directions and goals.	Rarely uses feedback to improve future lessons or select targets; does not reflect about, or ask questions about, personal professional growth or classroom practice through a journal or dialogue with the cooperating teacher or advisor.

Evaluates planning, instruction, and management

Periodically self-evaluated by reviewing documented process; sets long-term professional goals to direct future progress; uses the Teacher Competence Profile monthly.	Seldom takes time to evaluate progress; avoids effective use of the Teacher Competence Profile.

Participates in planned professional development

Regularly participates in staff development activities; seeks information on professional development opportunities; attends professional meetings.	Avoids planned professional development opportunities; avoids professional meetings.

Source: Adapted and expanded from the IPPs of the Joint Field Experience Committee (2004).

2 Communication and Interpersonal Skills

Introduction to Communication Skills

Effectiveness in teaching depends on a number of factors. Knowledge of subject matter, use of appropriate techniques and media, awareness of principles of applied learning, and skill in classroom management. . . . More important than these, however, are the skills you yourself possess—your life skills. (Gazda, Asbury, Balzer, Childers, Phelps, & Walters, 1999, p. 1)

A teacher needs to be an effective communicator. A teacher communicates with students, colleagues, administration, parents, and the public at large. Effective communication requires many kinds of knowledge and skills. These include knowledge of self, knowledge of subject, knowledge of students' learning approaches, and skill in interpersonal communication. Effective communication outside the school involves knowledge of education as a discipline and being an advocate of its importance.

Kauchak and Eggen (2003), based on research, identify five components of effective communication:

1. *Precise terminology*—eliminating vague and ambiguous words and phrases
2. *Connected discourse*—presentation logically connected and leading to a point
3. *Transition signals*—signals that an idea is ending and another beginning
4. *Emphasis*—signaling that an idea or topic has special significance
5. *Congruent verbal and nonverbal behavior*—conveying the message without spoken words (pp. 135–137)

The above are examples of communication skills within the classroom. "Teachers in a democratic society have to play a role in the formulation of professional practice, educating the public, and educational policy making" (Kincheloe, 2004, p. 52).

The significance of communication is demonstrated in the PRAXIS/Professional Assessments for Beginning Teachers and the INTASC/Interstate New Teacher Assessment and Support Consortium.

OBJECTIVES

You will be able to:

1. List and describe the kinds of classroom interactions presented in this chapter.
2. Plan and deliver a microteaching or school lesson that includes the professional target of verbal and nonverbal messages.
3. State reasons why positive interpersonal relationships are important in the classroom and list behaviors needed for positive interpersonal relationships.
4. Demonstrate awareness of effective verbal and nonverbal communication skills.
5. Demonstrate use of the skills of paraphrasing, perception checking, feelings description, and behavior description.

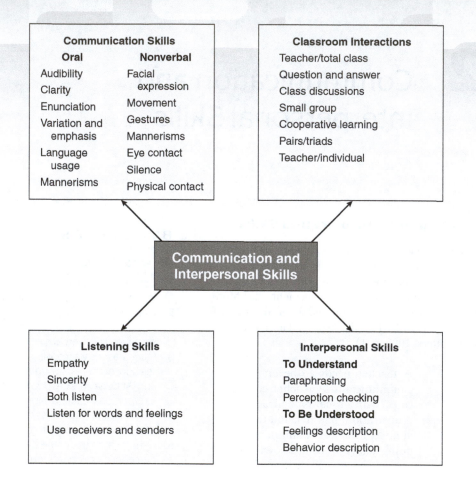

The Teacher Competence Profile

The Teacher Competence Profile (TCP) introduced in Chapter 1 presents the essential skills that need to be mastered by the preservice teacher. The chart at the top of the next page identifies key communication skills treated in this chapter. The descriptors on the left describe effective and on the right describe ineffective use of the competence. Data sheets based on the positive descriptions can easily be designed. Examples of these can be found in the Chapter Appendices.

Beyond the Cognitive

A focus on cognitive approaches, which has such a major place in teaching, is no longer enough in today's classrooms. "Beginning teachers must develop the ability to apply knowledge appropriately in different contexts while handling the dozens of cognitive, psychological, moral and interpersonal demands that simultaneously require attention in a classroom" (Darling-Hammond & Cobb, 1996, p. 45). Norris (2003) adds, "If we recognize that schools are social and emotional places, and we are social and emotional beings, then we must place emphasis on more than our cognitive brain" (p. 314).

TCP COMMUNICATION AND INTERPERSONAL SKILLS

Models appropriate voice and spoken and written language

Generally audible, clear, pleasant, and expressive, controls volume appropriately, enunciation is correct and distinct; correct spelling and grammatical usage; excellent language usage modeled; written handouts are easily understood and match level of students; written work is neat and presentable.

Inaudible or monotone; incorrect enunciation; poor English usage; students have difficulty understanding the teacher; little effort to improve language usage; written work is messy and confusing.

Makes effective use of interpersonal skills

Empathetic (tries to understand others) and helps others understand him/herself; is other- rather than self-centered; models, teaches, and expects the use of interpersonal skills by students.

Poor listener; unempathetic (does not try to understand others), doesn't help others to understand him/herself; is self- rather than other-centered; does not teach or expect use of interpersonal skills by students.

Teachers, say Elksin (2003), need to be aware of social-emotional learning. They note that, according to Mayer and Salovey (1997), this involves perceiving accurately, appraising, and expressing emotion (p. 63). The emotional quotient of schooling, they believe, has five domains: knowing one's emotions; managing one's emotions; recognizing others' emotions; using social skills when with others; and learning social-emotional skills, particularly by at-risk students—which needs to be taught (pp. 64–74).

Instructional objectives include cognitive, psychomotor, and affective outcomes. Teaching, however, is first and foremost a "people business." Every person you will work with has unique needs, feelings, attitudes and values, and a unique history of life experiences. This is why teaching is such a complex, demanding, and often stressful profession.

The Teacher as a Learning Facilitator

The perceived role of a teacher has shifted from that of knowledge disseminator to that of a learning facilitator. To be an effective learning facilitator you must know subject matter, have a good grasp of learning and developmental theory, and have command of a wide repertoire of instructional skills. You will also need well-developed communication, interpersonal, and group skills:

- Awareness of self and personal values and understanding of the values and feelings of others
- Knowledge of your own culture and the culture of others
- Ability to analyze your own feelings
- Understanding the power of being a role model
- A sense of ethics
- Ability to determine the degree of responsibility for others and yourself

You can become a more effective interpersonal communicator by improving your people skills. Further, you can teach these same skills to your students as you cover the curriculum. You can model and teach communication, interpersonal, and group skills and expect that your students use them as well.

Self-Knowledge

"Know thyself!" Self-knowledge is fundamental to good interpersonal relations. How do you see yourself at this moment? How do others see you? The way you see yourself? What are your strengths? Weaknesses? Aspirations? Potential?

We are products, often prisoners, of our experiences. We make judgments from personal perspectives. Before teachers can work effectively with others, they must understand themselves and their value systems. There are two main ways we can learn about ourselves: (1) by luck and (2) through conscious effort. The "Johari awareness model" or "Window" (in Civikly, 1992, pp. 148–150) is an excellent way to develop a realistic perception of what you are like and your potential. When you construct a personal Johari Window you reveal, receive, and think about information about yourself. The window presents four areas (panes) to explore about yourself.

1. The *public area* (your open area) represents information you know about yourself and that most other people (e.g., family, friends, and classmates) know about you. It is behavior and motivation known to yourself and others (e.g., appearance, brothers and sisters).

2. The *blind area* (your blind spot) is information about you that you do not know but that others do. Others can see things about us of which we are unaware (e.g., halitosis, speech mannerisms). You may be blind to either pleasant or unpleasant things.

3. The *hidden area* (your private self) is information about yourself that you know but others do not (e.g., you feel uncomfortable and anxious in a social situation when others seem to exclude you from the conversation). These are things about yourself that you typically keep secret.

4. The *unknown area* (your mystery area) is information about you that neither you nor anyone else knows. This is the area where neither you nor others are aware of certain behaviors or motives (e.g., perhaps you could be a good photographer but neither you nor anyone else realizes you have this potential). It may include untapped talents or unconscious desires, aspirations, or fantasies—things that may later become a strong force in your life. For graphic examples, see www.augsberg.edu/education/edc210/johari.html.

Good communication skills (sending clear messages in a sensitive-to-others way), interpersonal skills (understanding others and being understood by others), and group skills (working with two or more others) are basic to good teaching. You can become a better interpersonal communicator by improving your interpersonal skills. Furthermore, you can model these for your students, and teach them to your students.

Increasing the size of your public window (shown by an enlarged "public" window pane) is a goal you can have to better your interpersonal skills. A person with much self-knowledge has a large public area. Increasing the size of this area means that information must be moved from the other areas. Do this by: revealing more about yourself, reflection, inviting and accepting feedback about yourself, or taking part in, and reflecting about, activities that let you learn more about your behavior and motives. When you help others, you often use yourself, your perceptions and needs, as a point of reference. Be aware of the effects of your behavior and motivations on others and avoid projecting personal values and needs on them.

Basic Communication Skills

New teachers are often surprised by the demands of their first teaching experience. Despite spending hours planning the lesson, they are most struck by the vital importance of communication. Suddenly, each spoken word and gesture has significance. "What do I say? How shall I say it? What can I do with my hands?" This section is designed to help you improve your ability to communicate. From the moment a teacher walks into a classroom, he or she sends all sorts of messages. An effective teacher is warm, friendly, caring, organized, prepared, and clear. This teacher cares about teaching and learning, is enthusiastic, and is skilled at questioning and discussion. These qualities need to be reflected in the teacher's verbal and nonverbal behaviors.

Effective teachers have a range of communication, interpersonal, and group skills. Communication skills include writing, speaking, reading, listening with eyes and ears, and body language. The focus in this chapter is on oral and nonverbal communication skills, which we consider basic communication skills. There is something of an actor in every effective teacher.

Basic Oral Communication Skills

The human voice brings words to life. The words we speak, their meanings, and how they are delivered (firmness, modulation, tone, tempo, rate, pitch, and loudness) shape the messages we send to students. Verbal communication is a refined means for stimulating thoughts, ideas, concepts, and feelings. Speaking, or oral language, is a major medium used by teachers to give messages. Indeed, speaking is what many people think of when the word *communicating* is mentioned. The language you choose and the way you use it should lead to clear understanding and positive feelings. To be effective in the classroom and meet expected standards, we suggest the following.

Oral skills with which you should become proficient include:

- *Audibility.* Speak loudly enough for all to hear, but not so loudly that listeners are irritated.
- *Clarity.* Choose words and sentence structure that are descriptive, concise, and suitable to the listeners' level of understanding; avoid "run-on," fragmented, or incomplete statements and questions.
- *Enunciation.* Speak so each word, and each sentence, is distinct, with consonants and vowels phrased correctly, and with crisp word beginnings and endings.
- *Variation and emphasis.* Vary your speech rate, volume, inflection, tone (timbre and resonance); use silence for emphasis or to allow thinking time; avoid speaking in a monotone.
- *Language usage.* Use grammatically correct language, avoid slang, and avoid sloppy speech (e.g., "gonna," "kinda," and "won't ya").
- *Mannerisms.* Eliminate speech mannerisms that distract or annoy (e.g., frequent use of "OK," "uh-huh," "and-uh," and throat clearing).

Basic Nonverbal Communication Skills

We rarely trust words alone. We use body language continuously, expressing nonverbal messages through body stance or posture, body movement, gestures, facial expression or color, and even tactile contact. Learners "read" the shoulder shrug, frown, lift of an eyebrow, or movement of the hand of the teacher. Amundson (1993) reports that 93 percent of a message is sent nonverbally. You may be unaware of the nonverbals you use, but you can learn how to use nonverbal communication effectively.

The importance of congruence between verbal and nonverbal messages in communicating feelings cannot be overstressed. Students are more in tune with how we say things than with what we say. If students feel that messages are contradictory, they may be anxious and distrust the teacher. To be an effective communicator, try the following approaches.

Nonverbal skills with which you should become proficient include:

- *Facial expression.* Support your words with appropriate facial expressions; avoid being expressionless and dull (if the teacher is enthusiastic, it should show).
- *Movement.* Vary the stimulus by moving around the room or to the chalkboard or other aids while maintaining eye contact; attend to individuals or groups; support speech with body movement.
- *Gestures.* Direct attention, using gestures for emphasis or to aid understanding, in a way that supports rather than distracts.
- *Mannerisms.* Avoid distracting or annoying mannerisms (e.g., scratching, playing with a pencil, wetting your lips, swaying, or cracking your knuckles).
- *Eye contact.* Make all students feel that they are personally being addressed, included, or noticed; look at the person you are addressing; avoid looking excessively at notes, a certain spot in the room, an object, or the chalkboard.
- *Silence.* Use silence to gain attention, for emphasis, to provide time to think, or to deal with a minor disruption.
- *Physical contact.* Use tactile contact to, for example, guide a student's hand movement, gain attention, or show approval. However, use tactile contact only with much discretion and depending on the age level or gender of the student.

Geddes (1995) offers suggestions to improve the nonverbal components of communication:

- To show you like and respect people, face them when you interact.
- Observe the posture of others, because this can provide clues to their feelings—good posture is connected with confidence or enthusiasm.
- Note facial expressions. Some people mask emotions by remaining expressionless, others exaggerate expression to hide their real feelings. If you suspect either of these, gently probe deeper.
- In many cultures, frequent eye contact indicates interest and confidence, whereas avoidance communicates the opposite.
- In general, the less distance there is between people, the more intimate and informal is the relationship. Staying behind your desk gives a cold impression.
- People who are well dressed—not overdressed—tend to earn more respect from others.

An instrument you can use for feedback about your basic communication skills is included as Appendix 2.1. During your early microlessons and first in-school teaching experience, have a partner or the teacher collect data on your communication skills. Another useful—if sometimes daunting—experience is to arrange for your early lessons to be videotaped.

Interpersonal Skills

A teacher's work involves a steady stream of interactions with individuals, small groups, and the class as a whole. As we interact, using words and body language, we constantly send and receive messages that communicate information and feelings.

Communication Clarity and Congruence

Use of verbal and nonverbal communication skills was discussed earlier. These are key in sending clear messages. Messages that are ambiguously worded, indifferent, incoherent, or in which the words used and nonverbal signals conflict obstruct communication. Statements that teachers make must be clear and concise. When you communicate, it is important that you understand others and that they, in turn, understand you. Effective interpersonal communication requires congruence between the message sent and the message received (see Figure 2.1). If the two are not the same, frustration, even anger, may result. Not only must the message sent be sent clearly, an appropriate response is unlikely unless the receiver listens effectively (Tubbs & Moss, 2003).

Communication cannot be taken for granted. You must make an effort to ensure that you state clearly what you wish to convey, that your nonverbal behavior supports your words, and that you check for understanding. Using interpersonal skills effectively will increase the possibility of congruence between message sent and message received.

Using and Teaching Listening Skills

How often have you caught yourself not really paying attention when another person was speaking? Listening problems "stem from focusing on ourselves rather than the messages of others" (Beebe, Beebe, Redmond, Geerinck, & Milestone, 2000, p. 121). To be successful, listening should be an *active* process. In *active listening,* understanding and evaluating the meaning of a message must occur before a listener can respond. The listener must work actively at listening while a speaker is talking. This requires concentrating on what the other person is saying even when you disagree with it (Borich & Tombari, 1995). As a teacher, listen to the words students are using *and* their tone. That is, listen to what a student is *actually* saying as well as what the student is *trying* to say. For good two-way communication to occur: (1) both people must listen; (2) listening must involve listening for feelings as well as words; and (3) listening must be responsive. Use your "receivers," as well as your "senders." Listening involves paraphrasing, checking for meaning, accepting feelings, and searching for further information. The speaker must know you are listening through your body language and how you respond verbally. Model listening skills, teach your students how to use them, and expect them to use

EFFECTIVE COMMUNICATION	INEFFECTIVE COMMUNICATION
Occurs when Message sent equals message received	Occurs when Message sent and message received differ
Result: *CONGRUENCE*	Result: *DISSONANCE*

FIGURE 2.1   *Congruence between Sending and Receiving Messages*

them. Hal Macomber (2003), after reviewing the literature, put together a list of "The Top Ten Listening Skills":

- Stop talking.
- Put all your energy into listening.
- Notice your own filters when listening.
- Don't argue mentally.
- Inhibit your impulse to immediately answer questions.
- Adjust to the situation.
- When in doubt about whether to listen or speak, keep listening.
- Don't assume you have to do anything but listen.
- Work at listening.
- Listen generously with a willingness to be influenced.

Attributes for Effective Interpersonal Relations

People who display good interpersonal skills have positive, but realistic, self-concepts and respect others as persons. They avoid being patronizing, judgmental, negatively critical, ridiculing, or belittling. They share the attributes of empathy and genuineness.

Interpersonal skill is based on *empathy* (trying to understand what a person is saying and feeling, as opposed to sympathy, which means agreeing with, or feeling the same as, the other). Empathy allows the skills involved in understanding others and being understood to function.

Effective teachers are *genuine*. They are sincere in their concern for others and have time for them. They listen, help students probe into problems, offer alternatives, and help students understand the consequences of choice. Good teachers tend to use interpersonal skills when working with students, colleagues, and parents—both skills to help understand others and skills that help them to be understood (Figure 2.2).

Skills to Help You Understand Others

Good interpersonal skills are vital in many professions. So too in the teaching profession. Through this section you will be helped to develop and practice these skills. When people interact, the process begins with an attempt to communicate a meaning or feeling to someone else. The sender has a mental image that is encoded into language, a drawing or diagram, or body language. How you encode depends on your background, frame of reference, values, and the way you interpret things. This may be different than the interpretation of the person who receives the message, who may have another frame of reference or way of communicating. Checking may be needed to discover whether the message was received accurately.

The two major skills for understanding others and helping ensure the message intended is the same as the message received are (1) *paraphrasing* (to understand the information, ideas, and suggestions of others), and (2) *perception checking* (to understand the feelings of others).

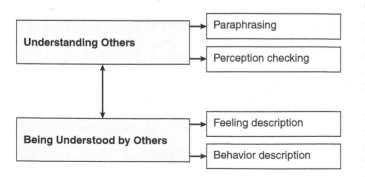

FIGURE 2.2   *Kinds of Interpersonal Skills*

PARAPHRASING.   Paraphrasing is a test to ensure that the message received is the same as the one sent. It involves putting another person's statement into your words or giving an example that shows what you think the other is talking about. The real purpose of paraphrasing is not to clarify what another person meant, but to show what it meant to you. Good paraphrases are often more specific or more concise than the original. They give another person a chance to check whether the message was received accurately. This helps eliminate misunderstanding, frustration, or anger.

Paraphrasing is a like holding up a mirror: it *reflects* what the other person said. When you restate (or mirror) a statement, you may be checking the ideas or information stated or trying to understand the feelings behind the words. Paraphrasing is a powerful way of saying, "You are important. I have time for you. I respect your ideas. I want to understand." It also allows the other person to make sure the right thing was said (or communicated), providing an opportunity for a correction. How often have you meant to say one thing but unknowingly said another. For example, "Did I say Monday? I meant to say Tuesday." Some guidelines for paraphrasing are given below.

Guidelines for Paraphrasing
- No judgments! Don't indicate approval or disapproval.
- Put the statement into your words. Avoid mere repetition or mimicking.
- Be attentive, interested, and open to the sender's ideas or feelings. Concentrate on what the sender is trying to say.
- Listen for the feelings behind the words.
- Preface your paraphrase with leads such as "You think . . . ," "Your position is . . . ," "Do you mean . . . ," "Do you feel that . . . ," "It seems to me that . . . ," "I heard you saying. . . ." Continue the interchange until agreement about meaning is reached.

Consider the following examples of effective paraphrasing:

SUPERVISING TEACHER: For the next lesson I would like you, using lots of color information, to present the various kinds of appeals that advertisers could use to get consumers to buy products.

PARAPHRASE BY STUDENT TEACHER: Do you mean that you want me to teach about the various ways color can be used in advertising?

SUPERVISING TEACHER: No. I'd like you to present the various emotional appeals that advertisers use to influence consumer choice, supporting each category of appeal with real-life examples.

PARAPHRASE BY STUDENT TEACHER: Oh. Using actual examples from the media, you want me to teach the psychological appeals used by advertisers.

SUPERVISING TEACHER: You got it!

PERCEPTION CHECKING.   Perception checking (or feelings checking) is used to make sure you are interpreting another person's feelings accurately. Inaccurate impressions are often drawn from the words or nonverbal behaviors used by others. This may be because we unconsciously interpret the words and body language of others from our own frame of reference—projecting our own feelings, attitudes, or desires. Perception checking can be done *indirectly* (for example, listening more carefully, looking for more cues in the speaker's nonverbal behavior) or *directly* (asking straight out if your interpretation of the speaker's message is correct—describing what you think is the other person's emotional state) (Beebe et al., 2000). In short, we try to find out if we *decoded* the message correctly. Like paraphrasing, perception checking avoids misunderstanding and feelings of frustration or anger.

Good perception checking requires careful listening and observation of nonverbal clues. From this, a tentative inference is drawn; then, the feeling inferred is clearly, unemotionally stated. The other person can then tell whether the interpretation was correct. It is only a check, not a statement of fact. Good perception checking lets the other person know you wish to understand, that you care enough to want to understand how the other feels, and so you do not act on false assumptions. It does not express approval or disapproval of the other person's feelings or motives. Examples of perception checking statements include:

> "I get the impression that I have made you angry, are you? Have I?"
> "Am I right in thinking that you are disappointed with what happened?"
> "I get the impression that you are pleased with the results."
> "It seems that I hurt your feelings. Did I?"
> "You look bewildered. Are you?"
> "You seemed to agree with the way I handled the situation. Do you?"
> "You appeared to be nervous when I asked you to. . . . Were you?"
> "I'm not sure if you were pleased or displeased with the results."

Skills to Help Others Understand You

Not only is it important that you understand others, it is equally important that others understand you. You might ensure understanding by, when appropriate, using the skills of (1) behavior description (helping others understand the behavior you are responding to) and (2) feelings description (helping others understand how you are feeling).

BEHAVIOR DESCRIPTION.   Sometimes you react in a certain way because of what you think you observed. The skill of describing behavior lets others know the behavior you are responding to when you describe it clearly enough so they know what you observed. Behavior description allows the other to agree or disagree. Description should be specific, nonaccusative, and without judging it good or bad, right or wrong.

When you offer a behavior description, focus on the specific and observable, and recognize when you are making an inference. Phrase your description in language that reflects the tentative nature of your interpretation and that you want to check it out. Remind yourself to describe specific action. Behavior descriptions begin with stems such as "I see that . . . ," "The following things occurred: . . . ," "I noticed that . . . ," "I observed. . . ." Consider the following examples of improving perception checking:

> "Nathan, you seem to take the opposite side of whatever I say today." *Not:* "Nathan, you are just trying to show off!" (This would be an accusation of unfavorable motivation.)
> "Mae, you began to speak before Leroy had finished his comment." *Not:* "Mae, you deliberately didn't let Leroy finish!" (This implies that Mae deliberately cut Leroy off. All that one can observe is that she did cut him off.)
> "José, when I was telling the story you were smiling. I'm puzzled." *Not:* "José, why were you leering at me when I was telling the story?" (This implies a negative motive on José's part.)

Judgmental statements build the ego of the giver while inviting the receiver to feel inadequate or attacked and may promote retaliation. Good behavior description reduces the possibility of defenses being raised and increases the possibility of understanding. The message is, "You are important, I want to understand."

Here are two examples of what a student teacher's classroom teacher might say:

> "While you were giving your demonstration, Jeff, Susan, Maria, and Sam were off-task." *Not:* "The class was not paying attention during your demonstration. You should have done something about it." (Nondescriptive, judgmental statement.)
>
> "You asked six questions at the analysis level or higher." *Not:* "That was really good, you really had the kids thinking." (Nondescriptive, judgmental statement.)

FEELINGS DESCRIPTION. Feelings description is a valuable skill. How often have you said, or someone has said to you, "If only I had known. . . . I wish you'd told me." We all have feelings. Communication is aided when people are free to describe their feelings and when this occurs in a sensitive, nonaccusing way. If feelings are not expressed, they may be misinterpreted. Tears, for example, may signify several things (fear, anger, hurt, joy, or hay fever), but the observer may not know which, or may jump to a wrong conclusion.

Many people find it hard to express feelings; and, indeed, expressing feelings involves risk. Perhaps we think we should be tough, "keep a stiff upper lip," contain our emotions, or we fear our feelings will be discounted and we will be put down. However, it is often far better that we express feelings rather than have them eat away at us or that we build resentment toward another. Unexpressed feelings can impede communication and damage a relationship. Sharing one's "inner state" is necessary if two people are to understand each other and improve their relationship. Describing feelings carries a deeper meaning: "I trust you. You are important to me. I need you to understand. By disclosing myself to you, I create the potential for trust, caring, commitment, growth, and self-understanding."

To express your feelings accurately, you have to be aware of them, accept them as yours, and know how to communicate them. Feelings can be expressed through (1) *statements* (words): they can be clearly described ("I feel very nervous"), expressed as a metaphor ("I have butterflies in my stomach"), or stated as a preference ("I feel like running away"); or (2) *nonverbal actions:* examples include sighing, becoming silent, turning away, frowning, smiling, or keeping somebody waiting. Nonverbal actions are particularly susceptible to misinterpretation, and it is often better to express the feeling verbally. The way you express feelings can be misinterpreted. Care must be taken to describe feelings so the other person is not made to feel guilty or coerced. Feelings description should be matter-of-fact and give information. Examine the following four situations.

1. A person blurts out, "Oh, shut up."
   Better: "I feel angry with you when you. . . ."
   Or "I feel hurt by what you said and wish you would stop."
   Or "I know what you are going to tell me, and you are right."
2. A person says, "You shouldn't have done that."
   Better: "I really like your gift to me."
   Or "Your gift makes me feel obligated to you."
   Or "I feel bad because I gave you a far cheaper gift."

3. A person suddenly becomes silent.

    Better: "I feel that you are putting me down."

    Or "What you said reminded me of something sad."

    Or "I'm worried about what I'm going to do in tomorrow's lesson."

4. A person states, "You're always, always late."

    Better: "I'm upset with you because I had to wait so long in the cold."

    Or "I was worried that something had happened to you."

    Or "You won't have time now to pick up the DVD we need and now I must change my plans for the lesson."

Often, the purpose of describing your feelings is to improve a relationship. Someone may need to know how you feel if your feelings are to be taken into account. The expression, "If you loved me, you'd know," rarely matches reality. Ignoring negative feelings is like ignoring the oil warning light in your car when it lights up. Serious damage can result. It is possible your feelings resulted from a false perception of the situation or motives. On the other hand, the other person may not even be aware of the effect of his or her words or actions on you and may not have intended to hurt or annoy. Bringing feelings into the open can lead to problem solving and a strengthened relationship. A data collection instrument you can use to analyze your use of interpersonal skills is shown in Appendix 2.2.

Intercultural Communication

It is unlikely that, year after year, you and your students will share the same culture. You will find many "ways of life" in your classes. What is your comfort zone with other cultures? How can you work with students with different cultural backgrounds? Effective communicators do more than recognize differences; they respect and learn how to work with differences.

Ways of communicating differ *between* cultures and *within* cultures (Gazda et al., 1999, p. 36). An example of the latter is that Northern Cree and Southern North American Cree people tend to differ in the degree of assertiveness deemed acceptable—one leaning toward forwardness, the other toward reticence. Tubbs and Moss (2003) observe that, especially in countries as diverse as the United States and Canada, while citizens share the national culture, they may also share a "co-culture—that is, a culture within a culture" (p. 299). Those in a co-culture may share a common language system, values, and communication patterns. "Among such groups are Asian Americans, African Americans, gays, lesbians, women, and people with disabilities" (p. 299).

A teacher might say to a student, "Look at me when I'm speaking to you!" To that student, from the perspective of his culture, looking directly at an adult may show disrespect. The teacher, however, may interpret the student looking down as a sign of indifference or hostility. Miscommunication can cause intercultural discomfort and anxiety. Communications, both verbal and nonverbal, differ from one culture to another in *what* is said, *how* it is said, *when* it is said, or *why* it is said. If you are unfamiliar with another's culture or if you do not recognize that there is more than one way of doing things, you can easily jump to a wrong conclusion.

As a beginning, effective teachers become aware of their own cultures. Ethnocentrism, even unintended, and stereotyping are complex and formidable barriers to communication with students of different backgrounds.

Cultural differences should be celebrated. The classroom community is a place where "various groups and co-cultures can coexist and flourish" (Tubbs & Moss, 2003, p. 324)—diversity is a *good* thing. Gudykunst and Kim (1997, pp. 381–383) propose principles for building community that apply to a classroom community. As adapted to a teacher these are:

- Be committed to procedures that foster a productive classroom community.
- Think about what you say to and do with students. Focus on process, not outcome.
- Accept your students as they are. Don't try to change them, but value diversity. Do not judge students based only on their diversity.
- Be concerned both about yourself *and* your students. Engage in dialogue as much as possible. Listen. Be open to their ideas.
- Recognize how ethnicity and culture affect the way you think and act. Seek commonalities, balance fear or anxiety with reason.
- When working with students, behave in a way that is morally right, do not use behavior that is merely a means to an end.
- Strive for harmony. Avoid being secretive, deceitful, or violent. Keep your promises.

To help you in your quest to become a good cross-cultural communicator, you may wish to review Chapter 3, "Teaching for Diversity," which deals with becoming a good cross-cultural teacher.

Summary

As a teacher in your role of learning facilitator, you need to communicate effectively with students, staff, and parents. This requires knowledge of self and subject matter and facility with instructional approaches, verbal and nonverbal communication skills, and interpersonal skills. The words you use and accompanying body language need to be congruent. Interpersonal skills to master include listening, paraphrasing, perception checking, behavior description, and feelings description. Diversity is the norm in classrooms, so being able to communicate in different ways is important. In particular, become a good intercultural communicator and learn how to communicate with special needs children.

LINKING PRACTICE TO THEORY

Think about your communications and interpersonal skills. What part do they play in your dialogue with other teachers and in the creation of an effective climate in your own classroom? How do you relate to other teachers? What behaviors to enhance communication are important? Reflect on these and related questions as you shape your skill as a communicator.

CASE 2.1

Communication Skills: Talkers and Listeners

Two education students, who are majoring in psychology, are working in the college library. The table is piled with books and papers. They are in a discussion on social psychology, especially interpersonal communication. Carl, pushing aside the papers and looking at his friend Selina, says, "You know, I've been thinking about which kinds of people are good at different kinds of communication . . . who have good oral and nonverbal skills."

"That's an interesting thought," replies Selina. "Let's see. Good talkers—actors, lawyers, preachers, teachers, maybe politicians, and of course, radio and television announcers. As for those good at nonverbal as well, I should think actors again, dancers, athletes, perhaps good friends."

"That's not bad!" says Carl, smiling. "What about good listeners?"

"Now that's more of a challenge," says Selina. "Doctors? Psychiatrists? School counselors? Lawyers?

Teachers should be. Good friends are good listeners. Why do you ask?"

"I just realized," replies Carl, "teachers need to be all of these. They have to speak well, communicate well with gestures, eye contact, and that rare thing . . . silence. And, they have to listen for words *and* feelings. Teachers need every communication skill in the book."

"Maybe," Selina says, closing up her books, "that's why you decided to be a teacher and not a psychologist."

"Who says I don't need to be a psychologist or a psychiatrist?" Carl replies, also packing up. A tome by Jung is noticeably at the top of the pile.

"Yes, Carl," smiles Selina, nodding knowingly at his books, "you were well named!"

Activities

1. Join a group of five. Groups should be mixed by teaching major or area of specialization. Taking turns, each person speaks to the rest of the group for three to five minutes using the stem phrases provided below. Using the data collection form, listeners collect written data on the oral or nonverbal behavior used by the speaker, one on the first three aspects of oral behavior, the second on the next three, the third on the first three aspects of nonverbal behavior, and the fourth on the last four aspects. At the conclusion of the talk, listeners provide descriptive, nonjudgmental feedback to the speaker on the skills observed. Appendix 2.1 can be used by your peers to collect data.

   ### Stem phrases
   "I think that (name of student's teaching subject specialization) is important because. . . ."
   "I think that study of (specialization name) is fascinating because. . . ."
   "Some students do not like (specialization name) because. . . ."
   "Teaching (specialization name) could be improved by. . . ."

2. Do you know the old "telegraph game"? It involves relaying a message from one person to another. A message is given to the first person, who in turn passes it on to the next, and so forth. The last person repeats what she heard to the whole group. The original and last messages are compared and the message is traced backward to the person who first said it. Debrief. Consider the effect of one-way communication and that feelings or emotions are part of all messages. An example of a message is

   > Methuselah ate what he found on his plate. He wasn't disturbed about granular fat or nutritional value or cancer or calorie count. He ate it all so his friends would not be hurt. And yet, he lived over 900 years.

3. Divide your group into pairs and sit back to back. One of the pair is given a diagram and the other a pencil and note pad. As the first describes the diagram, the other must draw it. Questions of clarification cannot be asked. When the first is finished describing, the pair compares diagrams. Debrief on what occurred (including the feelings involved). An alternative, before debriefing, is for the same pair to repeat the exercise with a different diagram, only this time questions, feedback, paraphrasing, and information seeking are permitted. Then compare the two experiences.

4. Join a triad (group of three). Student A makes a statement (in less than two minutes) about an idea or belief about a teaching-related issue to B.

Note: Activities 3–9 have been adapted from *Internship Seminars for Interns and Cooperating Teachers,* Faculty of Education, University of Regina, Regina, Saskatchewan, 1988–2003.

B then paraphrases A's statement four times, each time trying to get deeper meaning, with A responding with only a "yes," "no," or "partly." If B still has not achieved understanding, A should offer more explanation. C monitors the interchange and, if B has failed, paraphrases A until understanding is achieved. The three then debrief. Roles are rotated until each person has played each of the three roles.

5. Join a triad. One acts as message sender, another as perception checker, and the third as observer. A picture is picked from a magazine by the sender, who, while holding the picture up so the checker can see it, makes a brief statement about the picture. The perception checker states what he or she believes is the sender's emotional state about the picture. If the checker's impression was not correct, the observer makes a perception-checking statement. Roles are rotated until all have had a turn at each role. The trio debrief after each exchange.

6. Pair up. Pairs sit opposite each other with knees touching (or nearly so). Looking into each other's eyes, they concentrate on the feelings of the other. After one minute, they state their impressions of the other's feelings at the beginning, middle, and end of the minute (i.e., "At the beginning, I thought you were feeling . . . ," "In the middle, I thought you were feeling . . . ," "At the end, I thought you were feeling . . ."). The other agrees or describes how he or she was feeling.

7. Join a triad. The exercise involves a pair of participants and an observer. Pairs sit back to back on chairs or on the floor and, in turn, describe an exciting recent event to each other. The observer describes how each person was feeling during the various stages of the story. Participants then can confirm or clarify the observer's perceptions.

8. Five people sit in a circle to complete a task (e.g., without talking, build a house with two playing cards for each person, solve a puzzle, or do a human hand sculpture). Five other people sit around the first circle, each observing a specific person in the inner circle and recording his or her behavior. The exercise runs for five minutes. Behavior of inner-circle individuals is described by the observers, who also must make a statement about the feelings they thought were exhibited and then ask whether their perception was accurate. Then, each person whose behavior was described tells what she or he was feeling. The exercise can then be repeated with the people in the inner and outer circles exchanging places and roles.

9. Groups of five build a free-standing shelter using only newspaper and masking tape. They have five minutes for verbal communication before building the shelter in silence. Debrief.

APPENDIX 2.1 *Communication Skills*

PROFESSIONAL TARGET—BASIC COMMUNICATION SKILLS

Please describe what was said or occurred.

Communication Skill	Descriptive Notes
1. **Oral Communication:**	
Audibility	
Clarity	
Enunciation	
Variation and emphasis	
Language usage	
Mannerisms	
2. **Nonverbal Communication:**	
Facial expression	
Movement	
Gestures	
Mannerisms	
Eye contact	
Pauses (silence)	
Physical contact	

APPENDIX 2.2 *Interpersonal Skills*

DATA COLLECTION—INTERPERSONAL SKILLS

Please record what was said and done and how students reacted.

Name of Skill	Description
Paraphrasing	
Perception checking	
Behavior description	
Feelings description	
Other behaviors used to understand others	
Other behaviors used to help others understand you	

3 Teaching for Diversity

Importance of Teaching about and for Diversity

Let us put our minds together and see what we can do for our children. (Chief Sitting Bull)

Students entering the nation's schools come with such widely diverse backgrounds, capabilities, interests and skills that meeting their needs and finding appropriate learning activities requires a great deal of care and skill. (Emmer, Evertson, & Worsham, 2003, p. xiii)

A teacher is in her classroom. The lesson has been prepared, strategies thought out, and materials are ready. A group of students enters the room. They smile and greet their teacher. She enjoys and respects her students, and when she is planning her lessons, keeps their interests and abilities in mind. She knows that the boys and girls approach learning differently, and that some of her students catch on to ideas quickly, while others need help. She knows, too, that she must vary her approaches to address the different ways her students learn. She has students from different ethnic backgrounds, and she is aware that this must be considered. She is a teacher who tries to accommodate the diversity of her students.

OBJECTIVES

You will be able to:

1. Define and give examples of learning style, hemisphericity, and modality preferences.
2. Use your knowledge of style, hemisphericity, and modality in lesson and unit planning.
3. Define culture and its components, and describe the cultural makeup of people in your region of your country.
4. Define racism and its causes, and be aware of the "hidden curriculum."
5. Describe effective methods of cross-cultural teaching/learning.
6. List ways in which cultural bias may exist in print materials and in teacher behaviors.
7. Describe how to set a classroom climate for cross-cultural teaching.
8. Teach a lesson that has, as a major objective, cross-cultural or antiracist learning.
9. Describe ways of teaching exceptional students.
10. Define mainstreaming, and list its potential advantages and disadvantages.
11. Recognize and be able to use strategies for reducing gender discrimination.

Diversity in today's classrooms is more complex than we may realize. It has several dimensions (see Figure 3.1). Learners vary in learning style, hemisphericity, and learning modality; classrooms represent a variety of cultures and subcultures and students of different social and economic status; learners may be slow, gifted or talented, bilingual, or disabled; and learners represent different genders and sexual preferences. These are the subject of this chapter. Although we are far from knowing everything about the fac-

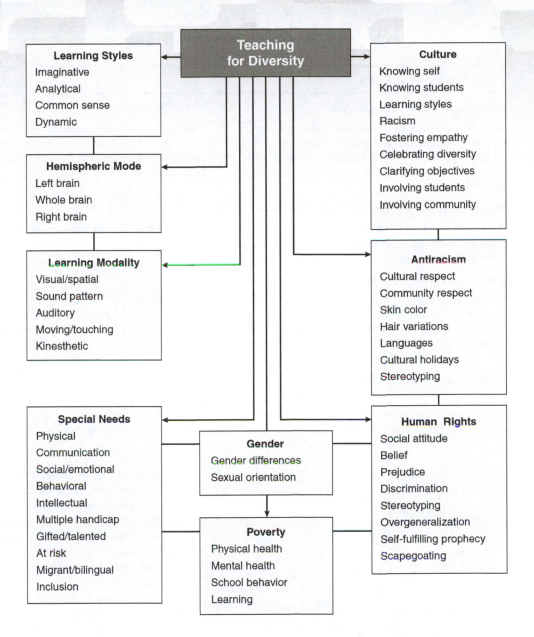

tors that affect learning, we should do our best and keep our minds open to emerging knowledge.

Every classroom includes a mix of learners, and diversity should be an expected, valued characteristic. Classes represent a cross section of the local community, and sometimes the whole country. Not all learners benefit from conventional instruction, some content taught in schools is not appropriate for all learners, and learners respond differently to various instructional approaches. Because individuals are different, no single curriculum or way of teaching works for everyone. To be successful, education needs to adapt teaching to individual differences. Low achievement by at-risk children or children labeled "slow learners" should not be blamed on deficits in the children or their families. The school

TCP DIVERSITY ISSUES

Promotes the worth of all students

Demonstrates a caring, professional manner toward all students, regardless of developmental level, intellectual capacity, appearance, health, exceptionality, socioeconomic status, gender, religion, race, or cultural background.

Discriminates or stereotypes or acts on personal preferences; tends to treat all students the same way regardless of individual needs; delays responding to individual needs.

Responds to the needs of all

Attends to needs of all students; secures needed resources; encourages and recognizes growth according to individual ability.

Treats all students the same regardless of individual needs; delays responding to individual needs.

Is attentive to learning styles

Is aware of the range of learning styles, hemispheric mode, and learning modalities; well informed on the range of intelligences; is capable of creating a differentiated classroom; individual approaches to instruction; varied materials to draw on student interest.

Little awareness of the range of teaching styles; has a narrow sense of the meaning of intelligence; whole-class instruction is dominant and instruction is text driven.

Is adept at intercultural communication

Respects and works along with the range of cultural differences in the classroom; is aware of ways of communicating between and within cultures.

Little or no acknowledgment of the range of cultural diversity in the classroom: all or most lessons reflect the view of the dominant culture.

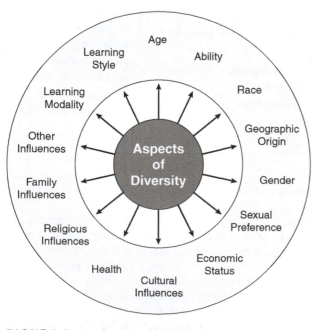

FIGURE 3.1   *Aspects of Diversity*

must not ignore or criticize family or community differences, or it will risk crushing the self-esteem of students. School structure must accommodate the diverse interests and abilities of a heterogeneous student body rather than stress uniformity if it is to avoid complications caused by different behavior patterns and achievement.

All persons deserve to be treated with dignity, recognizing that all are equal in rights and responsibilities regardless of race, disability, gender, age, ancestry, religious belief, place of origin, marital status, sexual orientation, source of income, or family status. Teachers are responsible for recognizing, fostering, and celebrating the diverse composition of society. Fordham University (2004) stresses, "In an ever-increasingly-diverse society, educators must understand how learners in all educational contexts are unique." The knowledge base about diversity is significant and includes differences in: intelligence, emotional intelligence, giftedness, cognitive styles and exceptionalities, cultural diversity, socioeconomic diversity, ethnic and racial diversity, linguistic diversity, gender and role identity, multiculturalism, diversity in classrooms, critical pedagogy, and inclusive education.

Sleeter, Torres, and Laughlin (2004) assert that prospective teachers need not only an awareness of others, they need to know more about themselves through "developing a critical consciousness of their own reality as persons of a specific race, ethnicity, gender, and socioeconomic status, with specific abilities, and stories" (p. 84). The authors add that teacher education students should learn the difference between the experience white preservice teachers bring to teaching compared with those of color. They say that white preservice teachers "bring very little cross-cultural background, knowledge and experience, and little awareness or understanding of discrimination, especially racism" but that preservice students of color, by contrast, "tend to bring greater commitment to multicultural teaching, social justice, and providing children of color with an academically challenging curriculum" (p. 81).

Increasingly, educators are aware of the need to accommodate the differences in learning preferences of students. For example, recognizing that North American schools are multicultural, the Florida Assembly has passed legislation requiring schools to examine differences (Stevenson & Dunn, 2001, p. 483). An issue is, how adaptable should teachers be in dealing with diversity in the classroom? For example, should students have the right to express themselves in African American or other dialect? More and more states legally recognize the language approaches of African American students with court-mandated programs. An in-depth exploration can be found in Lisa Delpit's *Other People's Children: Cultural Conflict in the Classroom* (1995).

New teachers need to know a great deal about the diversity of students and how to accommodate it. Also, they need to know about themselves, their own learning styles and preferences, and how personal background influences teaching.

"Every child has the capacity to succeed in school and in life. Yet far too many children, especially those from poor and minority families, are placed at risk by school practices that are based on a sorting paradigm in which some students receive high-expectations instruction while the rest are relegated to lower-quality education and lower-quality futures. . . . [A]ll children are capable of succeeding in a rich and demanding curriculum with appropriate assistance and support" (CRESPAR, 2002). Diversity needs to be recognized and celebrated.

Learning Styles

Learning Style Is Personal

The first aspect of diversity that we will examine is learning style. Everybody has a learning style. Yours may be very different from that of your best friend, brother, sister, mother, father, or partner. Whenever we observe, interpret, or judge something, we tend to do this from our frame of reference or way of doing things. Our perspective may be different from that of others. We may organize our thoughts in a linear, step-by-step way, or in a nonlinear, leaping, chunking, or holistic way; some of us think with our sensory apparatus, some with our hearts, some with our intuition, and some with our intellect. Some have to "see it to believe it," while others just "feel it in their guts"; some plan very carefully, others "go with the flow"; some prefer to work alone, others in groups; and some are "open" with people and others "closed." Consider the challenges to a teacher in adapting teaching to such variety.

Defining Learning Style

Learning style can be described in several ways. In general, it is about the unique ways that people learn. It can encompass the fairly consistent pattern of how a person perceives, grasps, and processes knowledge. It is a "biologically and developmentally imposed set of personal characteristics that make the same teaching method effective for some and ineffective for others" (Dunn, Beaudry, & Klaves, 1989, p. 50). Gregorc (1979) defines learning style as "distinctive behaviors that serve as indicators of how a person learns from and adapts to his environment. It also gives clues about how a person's mind operates" (p. 234). Learning style describes how a student learns, not how well or how much. It is different from ability. Always trying to match learning style differences is not realistic, but a teacher can have a repertoire of teaching methods from which to choose that, at least at times, fit individual differences.

POPULAR BELIEFS ABOUT STUDENT LEARNING.   Dunn and Dunn (1987) point out that you can increase student academic achievement and decrease discipline problems by modifying instruction to accommodate individual learning styles (p. 55). Based on research, they are critical of basic beliefs about student learning:

Not all students learn best:

- When "properly" seated at a desk or table.
- In a setting that is absolutely quiet.
- In well-lighted areas; reading in low light does not damage eyesight.
- Early in the morning (this is based on the mistaken belief that this is when students are most alert). Actually, most learners prefer late morning or afternoon and are not "morning alert."
- When sitting perfectly still.
- Through whole-group instruction.
- When the temperature is between 68 and 70 degrees Fahrenheit.
- When teaching involves a sequence of clearly stated objectives and detailed, step-by-step, sequential explanations.

Dunn and Dunn (1987) add:

- For most students, being self-motivated does not guarantee they will achieve well.
- Some students learn well when they eat, drink, or chew on objects.
- Whatever the length of a class period, students can learn well when mobility is possible, furniture is suitable, and when they can learn through perceptual strengths rather than just through lecture.
- Students who cannot remember verbal instructions are not necessarily less intelligent than those who can.
- Homework does not always have to reinforce what was presented or be assigned from a text after a lecture.
- Older students do not necessarily find it easier to adapt to a teacher's style than younger students. (pp. 55–59)

WHY LEARNING STYLES ARE OF CONCERN TO EDUCATORS.   With greater awareness of the importance of the learning style movement and its widespread publicity, the realization has grown that the learning of all students (not only the weak) may be enhanced when students are taught in a manner that matches learning style. Dunn and Dunn (1987) say that students do best when instruction and learning context match learning style (p. 55). Other authorities concur, saying that attention to students' learning styles can have a strong effect on achievement (Kolb, 1976, 1984; Gregorc, 1979; McCarthy, 1986; Gardner, 1993; Performance Learning Systems, 2003; Raab, 2004). McCarthy claims that "students vary on two continuums: *perceiving* (sensing/feeling versus thinking) and *processing* (doing versus watching). This suggests, McCarthy says, that students can be located in one of four major learning styles. By using these categories, she believes, teachers can accommodate instruction through building on learners' strengths. Good and Brophy (1995) present McCarthy's learning styles as follows.

> *Imaginative learners.* Imaginative learners perceive cognitively and then process the information reflectively. They listen, share, and try to integrate school experiences with self-experience.
>
> *Analytic learners.* Analytic learners perceive abstractly and process information reflectively. They like both details and ideas, prefer sequential thought, and value ideas more than people.
>
> *Common sense learners.* Common sense learners perceive abstractly and process information actively. They value concrete problem solving and tend to be pragmatic learners. They like "tinkering" and experimenting.
>
> *Dynamic learners.* Dynamic learners perceive concretely and process information actively. They usually integrate experience and apply and value new learning. They like trial-and-error learning and are good at taking risks. (p. 532)

Interestingly, studies suggest that matching learning activities with learning style has no effect on achievement. One can hypothesize that the research was not sophisticated enough to discover that attending to learning style matters. Be that as it may, experienced teachers know that children usually have preferences in the way they learn; and exemplary teachers use a variety of instructional approaches to help students construct personal meaning. Teachers who have, and use, more teaching strategies and methods produce more student learning (Orlich, Harder, Callahan, Kauchak, & Henson, 1994). As well, research suggests that learners who are actively engaged in learning will be more likely to succeed. Recent research stresses that today's teachers need to be better prepared to teach in increasingly multicultural situations. Although many K–12 teachers (and professors) "teach like they have been taught," our current times call for new pedagogy and instructional delivery systems. The key to keeping students actively engaged is discovering their learning style preferences. A range of instructional approaches (as described in Part C of this book) is needed.

Although each person has unique ways of learning, people also share learning similarities. Knowing similarities can help you plan learning experiences in your classroom.

FIELD DEPENDENCE OR INDEPENDENCE. Several writers (Fritz, 1992; Borich & Tombari, 1995; Cruikshank et al., 2003) comment on two dimensions of learning style: field dependence ("seeing the forest") and field independence ("seeing the trees"). *Field-dependent* people focus on "the big picture," viewing content globally. They tend to impose personal structure on the task and have difficulty distinguishing parts of a task from the whole. They tend to be gregarious. They prefer to approach learning in an unstructured way, rather than focusing on details. They are sensitive to criticism, positive or negative.

They like learning material with social content (e.g., literature and social sciences) and tend to be holistic in their approach.

Field-independent people can dissemble parts of a task from a pattern and devise an alternate pattern to comprehend information. They focus on details, are task oriented, like problem solving, and are not constrained by structure. They tend to be curious, self-reliant rather than conforming and obedient, and less prone to want to work with others. They may not care for social content, and they are less affected by praise or criticism. Field-independent learners tend to be highly analytic.

Hemispheric Mode

How does your brain work best? What is your preference for processing information, left or right brain mode? McCarthy's (1987) premises are that: (1) left and right mode processes are different; (2) individuals favor different approaches to learning along the left-to-right continuum; and (3) both kinds of processing are equally valuable. She presents the characteristics of left and right mode learners and how they process content as described below.

LEFT MODE LEARNERS.   Left mode learners are analytic/deductive ("splitters" who prefer logic). They are rational and respond to verbal instructions. Controlled and systematic, they solve problems logically and sequentially by looking at parts. Judgments are made objectively (preferring small steps leading to understanding). They are good planners. They are analytic readers, and behavior is planned and structured. They prefer established and certain information and conventional classrooms. They rely on language, thinking, and remembering. Feelings are controlled. Hierarchical authority structures are preferred. They like multiple-choice tests and respond to the structure of the environment. Being splitters, distinction is important. They like talking and writing, are logical, see cause-and-effect relationships, and draw on previously accumulated and organized information.

RIGHT MODE LEARNERS.   Right mode learners are intuitive/deductive ("chunkers" who see patterns). They are intuitive, like open-ended, random experiences, and want instructions to be demonstrated. Problems are solved through hunches or by discovering patterns. Judgments are often made subjectively, in a fluid and spontaneous way. They enjoy working with elusive, uncertain information. They rely on drawing or manipulating, and they prefer essay tests. Feelings are freely shared, and they are good at metaphoric language and imagery. They like synthesizing, bringing things together, experimenting, and prefer an experiential approach. Their approach is holistic.

"The goal of education should be to help our students develop the flexible use of their whole brain." Schools tend to reward left brain learners more than right brain learners. More emphasis should be on right brain characteristics such as synthesis, intuition, and feelings. The "dichotomy between the two modes of learning has gone on long enough. It is a false dichotomy" (McCarthy, 1987, p. 75).

HEMISPHERIC MODE PREFERENCES OF TEACHERS.   McCarthy (1987) describes the preferences of 1,873 teachers—1,243 females and 570 males—as left brain, whole brain favoring left, whole brain, whole brain favoring right, and right brain (see Table 3.1).

The balance between right mode and left mode preference is heartening, but one wonders why "the educational system is so strongly biased in favor of left-mode struc-

TABLE 3.1 *Hemispheric Mode Preferences of Teachers*

	Total Sample	Females	Males
Left brain	40.0%	35.1%	49.3%
Whole brain favoring left	9.2	8.9	9.3
Whole brain	7.8	7.8	7.9
Whole brain favoring right	9.7	10.5	7.5
Right brain	33.4	37.7	26.0

Source: McCarthy, 1987, pp. 82–83.

tures and teaching methods" (p. 82). Schools stress correct information, conformity, and compartmentalized content and resist whole-brain approaches to learning and instruction. Teachers might find McCarthy and Morris's (1994) *4MAT CourseBook* a useful guide.

Learning Modality Preferences

"Sensory preferences influence the ways in which students learn. . . . Perceptual preferences affect more than 70 percent of school-age youngsters" (Dunn, Beaudry, & Klavas, 1989, p. 52). There are three *modalities:* (1) visual, (2) auditory, and (3) tactile (kinesthetic). Modality preferences (Figure 3.2) are the result of many factors, including experience, culture or race, gender, and handedness. Modality strengths occur singly or in combination, change over time, and become more integrated with age. Your modality strengths influence the way you teach. You can enhance learning by becoming aware of your preferences and their influence on your choice of instructional technique. Use approaches that are of mixed modality.

Students have preferred learning modalities. Some have very strong dominance, while others are comfortable with multiple modalities. A study of kindergarten to grade 6 students by Barbe and Swassing (1979) showed: visual dominance, 33 percent; auditory dominance, 24 percent; kinesthetic dominance, 14 percent; and mixed modalities, 29 percent. The following descriptions of learning modalities are adapted from Barbe and Swassing.

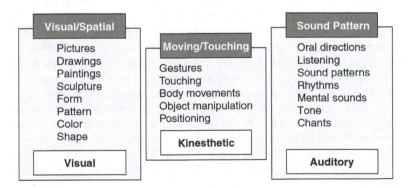

FIGURE 3.2 *Learning Modality*

VISUAL LEARNERS.   Visual learners learn by watching, seeing, or imagining, and they often think in pictures. They like descriptions, and may visualize or imagine what is being presented. They remember faces rather than names and often write things down to remember them. They can be distracted by visual disorder. They often doodle or find something to watch, and they tend to be quiet, neat, orderly, well planned, and organize by writing things down. They normally prefer the visual arts and often focus on details rather than on the work as a whole.

People who prefer the visual style often think in images or pictures. They take in what is heard or read and translate it into images in their brain. When they want to recall what they have learned, they may glance upward and look at the image stored in their minds. It is like recalling what was seen, reviewing pictures, and talking about the pictures. They may say, "I see, I get the picture."

Visual learners usually do well in school, because testing is often written and "visual." Most classroom standards, sitting quietly, writing neatly, and being organized are easily accommodated.

AUDITORY LEARNERS.   Auditory learners learn through listening and verbalizing. They like plays and dialogues but avoid long descriptions. They may, when learning, vocalize silently and even move their lips. They can remember names but may forget faces. They may memorize through auditory repetition and can be distracted by sounds. Solutions may be tried verbally and by talking things through. Sometimes, when talking to others or themselves, they even hum. They may like listening but can hardly wait to talk. Music is more appealing than the visual arts, and they often focus on the whole, thereby missing details.

Auditory learners like to learn by hearing or listening. They tend to filter incoming information through listening and repeating. They can be good at telling stories and solving problems through "talking them through." They may say things such as "I hear," "that sounds right," "that rings a bell." In school these learners learn by listening, easily repeating teacher statements. They like class discussions. They may be talkative and have difficulty writing.

Auditory learners need to be taught how to be visual learners if they are to succeed in school, because tests tend to be centered on a visual approach. Alternately, these students could be allowed to do some assignments orally or by a performance.

TACTUAL (KINESTHETIC) LEARNERS.   Tactual (kinesthetic) learners learn by manipulating and doing. They are action oriented and like to be physically involved. They tend to fidget and need to move often. Memory for things done is better than for what was seen or heard. These learners like to approach problems in a physical way or by manipulating models or objects. They are not particularly good listeners, and they may gesture when speaking. They tend to respond to music by moving and want to touch pictures or sculpture. They prefer situations involving the body and movement.

Tactual learners, so they can process and remember, want to learn through their body or feelings. In class, they may be restless and have trouble paying attention. They may say, "I feel, I'd like to get a better handle on the info." They may have trouble demonstrating or writing what they know. Tactual learners focus on the present, and developing a sense of time may be difficult. They may be good at "acting things out" or building projects.

Theory of Multiple Intelligences

Intelligence is a composite of heredity and experience. We know that intelligence has a variety of attributes. A theory of learning style that now receives much attention is Howard Gardner's (1983, 1991, 1993) theory of *multiple intelligences.* Gardner defines intelligence as an ability or set of abilities that let a person solve a problem or produce a product that is valued by society. Armstrong (1994) notes that Gardner believes every person has distinctive sets of capabilities that work together, not in isolation. Originally, Gardner identified seven forms of intelligence, and in 1997 he added an eighth (Checkly, 1997): (1) linguistic, (2) logical-mathematical, (3) spatial, (4) kinesthetic, (5) musical, (6) interpersonal, (7) intrapersonal, and the (8) naturalist (added to the original seven). People possess all eight intelligences, but in varying degrees of strength and skill. Traditional schooling, Gardner says, to a large extent, tends to develop only the first two.

Gardner's definition of intelligence suggests a broad view of cognitive functioning, which is in sharp contrast to intelligence as defined by the intelligence quotient (IQ). IQ theory (based on linguistic and logical-mathematical intelligences) assumes a person's intellectual potential is a fixed, genetically determined trait that can be measured early in life and will determine an individual's potential. Until Gardner's arrival, this unitary model of intelligence was perceived throughout the world as the norm. Gardner emphasizes the cultural context of multiple intelligences, believing that each culture emphasizes particular intelligences. The theory of multiple intelligences continues to open the minds of educators, psychologists, and parents worldwide about how learning and education can be bettered so all persons may be guided to achieve their potential. The theory continues to get positive reviews from numerous students and educators. Skeptics argue that the theory does not fit the standards-based reform movement, which emphasizes that students' learning needs to be relatively uniform.

Critics observe that experimental studies to back the theory are lacking. However, some scientific evidence in support of the theory is emerging. A number of school systems deliver programs on this theory. A summary of the intelligences and application (Gardner, 1993; Eric Digests, 1996; Guignon, 1998) follows.

The Intelligences

Spatial. The ability to perceive the visual spatial world accurately and perform transformations upon one's perceptions. This intelligence is highly developed in hunters, scouts, guides, interior designers, artists, and inventors.

Bodily-kinetic. Expertise in using one's whole body to express ideas and facility in using one's hands to produce or transform things. Highly developed in actors, athletes, sculptors, craftpersons, mechanics, and surgeons.

Musical. Capacity to perceive, discriminate, transform, and express musical forms. Highly developed in musical performers, aficionados, and critics.

Linguistic. Capacity to use words effectively, orally and in writing. Highly developed in story tellers, orators, politicians, poets, playwrights, editors, and journalists.

Logical-mathematical. Capacity to use numbers effectively and to reason well. Highly developed in mathematicians, tax accountants, statisticians, scientists, computer programmers, and logicians.

Interpersonal. Ability to perceive and make distinctions in the moods, intentions, motivations, and feelings of others. This intelligence can include sensitivity to facial expressions, voice, and gestures, and the ability to respond effectively to such cues—for example, to influence other people.

Intrapersonal. Self-knowledge and the ability to act adaptively based on that knowledge. This intelligence includes having an accurate picture of one's moods and motivations, and the capacity for self-discipline.

Naturalist. Ability to observe and operate hands-on in nature and the environment. Awareness of conservation practices and how to care for plants. Being sensitive to stimuli from the natural word, recognize patterns, or classify organic and inorganic species.

Armstrong (1994, pp. 38–41) provides a concise definition of each intelligence:

Spatial: picture smart
Bodily-kinetic: Body, sports or hand smart
Musical: music smart
Linguistic: word smart
Logical-mathematical: number/logic smart
Interpersonal: people smart
Intrapersonal: self smart
Naturalist: environment smart [added by the authors]

Applying the Theory

- The traditional view of intelligence (mainly linguistic and logical abilities) is too narrow.
- By cultivating a broad range of intelligences, teachers can uncover hidden strengths of students who don't do as well at verbal or mathematical tasks.
- Students who shine in a paper-and-pencil environment may be weak in other areas (e.g., bodily-kinesthetic or interpersonal skills).
- Teachers should nurture students' strengths and challenge them in areas where they are less developed.
- Two or more intelligences can be worked into lessons; four or more may be too many. Over a series of lessons, a balance of all seven should occur.
- Some topics call for a certain intelligence or a certain combination.
- Techniques such as learning centers/projects can draw on the seven intelligences.
- Teachers of various subjects can cooperate in a multidisciplinary approach to assignments or projects. These can tap the strengths of students.
- Students can be grouped heterogeneously by preferred intelligence and learn through sharing responsibilities and interacting with one another.
- Teachers should use multiple assessments instead of relying only on paper-and-pencil tests.
- Students should have encounters with nature through observation, field trips, and natural-world simulations and should engage in sensory stimulation exercise.

Bruce Campbell (1990), a researcher and author about Gardner's multiple intelligences school, conducted an action research project with his third-grade classroom of twenty-seven students "to explore student reactions to a multiple intelligences-based instructional model. Student behavior, attitudes, and abilities to work in non-traditional ways such as with music, movement, visual arts and cooperation were studied" (p. 7).

Seven centers were set up, each involving one of Gardner's seven intelligences, and students circulated from one center to another. The centers were as follows:

Gardner's Identified Intelligence	Center Name
Kinesthetic	Building Center
Visual-spatial	Arts Center
Mathematics-logical	Math Center
Musical	Music Center
Linguistic	Reading Center
Interpersonal	Working Together Center
Intrapersonal	Personal Work Center

Campbell discovered:

1. Students displayed increased independence, responsibility, and self-direction over the course of the year.
2. Students previously identified as having behavioral problems made significant improvement in their behavior.
3. Cooperative skills improved in all students.
4. Ability to work multimodally in student presentations increased throughout the school year, with students using a minimum of three to five intelligence areas in their classroom reports.
5. The more kinesthetic students particularly benefited from the active process of moving from center to center every fifteen to twenty minutes.
6. Leadership skills emerged in most students.
7. Parents frequently reported that behavior improved at home, more positive attitudes about school were exhibited, and attendance was increased.
8. Daily work with music and movement in content areas helped students retain information.
9. The role of the teacher changed during the year, becoming less directive and more facilitative, more diversified, less of a taskmaster and more of a resource person and guide.
10. Students became progressively more skilled at working effectively in the nontraditional classroom format.

Campbell observed, "in planning for such a diversity of activities, I began to grow more creative and multimodal in my own thinking and learning. I learned to write songs and sing. I improved my ability to draw and paint. I began to see growth and development within myself" (1990, p. 7). The message for teachers is that multiple intelligences can be a key part of teaching for diversity.

Learning Style and Cultural Perspective

How we see the world is affected by the way we were raised, the behaviors and value systems of our peers, and the social systems to which we belong and accept. People of differing cultures view the world differently. The cultural perspectives of individuals in classrooms (the students and you) are different—but *all perspectives are "valid."* Cultural background affects learning-style strengths and preferences. It is up to you to respect other cultures and teach children from these cultures in ways that allow them to have positive self-concepts and value their cultures. Learn how culture affects the learning styles of children. Teach them in the way they prefer, but help them acquire alternative ways of learning. Begin by discovering your preferences and the influence on your choice of learning and teaching approach. Culture and diversity is addressed later in this chapter.

Adapting to Different Learning Styles

Many teachers normally do not like to risk or deviate from their preferred learning and teaching style by experimenting with alternative strategies. This may even be true of "good" teachers who are dynamic, warm, caring, enthusiastic, knowledgeable, and hard-working. Teachers can learn to respond to various learning styles if they understand why certain teaching methods are not effective with all students and if they use different methods.

Learning style includes "motivation, on-task persistence versus the need for multiple assignments simultaneously, the kind and amount of structure required, and conformity versus nonconformity" (Dunn et al., 1989, p. 50). Use a variety of teaching methods and grouping patterns. Whenever possible give students optional approaches to tasks. That is, be flexible, be cross-culturally wise, and help students acquire the ability to use different learning styles. The payoff will be higher student motivation, achievement, and satisfaction. Teacher training colleges emphasize giving new teachers the skills for teaching. However, as stressed in this chapter, focus must also be on how learners learn.

Teaching Style

Teachers develop a characteristic style of teaching. Teachers are influenced by the way they were taught and how they personally achieve academic success. Dunn and Dunn (1979) say teachers have observable preferences that relate to:

> *Attitudes:* Toward different instructional programs, teaching methods and resources, and the kinds of children they prefer to work with
> *Instructional planning:* Diagnosing, prescribing, and evaluating; how students are to be grouped; and room design
> *Teaching environment:* Scheduling instruction and options for students regarding resources and mobility
> *Teaching characteristics:* Standards about flexibility, perceptions of what is important and how much is to be taught, and the degree and kind of direction and supervision to be provided
> *Teaching methods and evaluation:* Preferred instructional approaches and modes of assessment (pp. 241–242)

As a teacher you cannot assume your students will enjoy and prefer the learning experiences you do. To be effective, provide variety. Teachers, Marshall (1991) found, assumed the correct formula for instruction involved having: students in rows, a quiet learning environment, teacher-dominant whole-group instruction, text and lecture formats, students learning by looking and listening, little student movement, and emphasis on paper and pencil (p. 225). He asked teachers why they teach they way they do. Common responses were: "It's the way I was taught"; "It's the way I learn"; and "It's the easiest [most expedient] way to cover the material" (p. 225). Marshall suggests that it is easy to understand why teachers teach the way they do. "After all, it was the way they were taught, and *they* had been successful. . . . The way I learn is the way everyone learns. Therefore, if I teach, and the student doesn't learn, the student has the problem" (p. 226). She asserts that teachers must be willing and ready to change approach to suit the learning-style patterns of students. "If students do not learn the way we teach them, then we must teach them the way they learn!" (p. 226).

Cross-Cultural Teaching

Multicultural education needs to extend beyond the borders of North America. Brown and Kysilka (2002) assert that global education does not receive the attention it deserves. They argue that, because of their privileged position, U.S. citizens "tend to be insular and poorly informed about issues elsewhere" (p. 4). Diaz, Massialias, and Xanthopolous (1999) agree, saying global perspectives in the classroom lead to awareness of citizen duties and positive global attitudes. We can add that global multicultural education can lead to better international relations.

What Is Culture?

We are cultural beings. *Culture,* which influences everything we do, is basically the unique lifestyle of a particular group of people or the rules that generate and guide behavior. Culture is acquired; although it is influenced by the past, it is the present and it constantly changes. It is manifested in the language we speak and in our behavior. Common style and patterns of communication ensure that a group of people can live and work together. We all belong to a dominant culture and several subcultures. The influences of our ethnic group, social class, occupation, regional beliefs and customs, religion, geographic location, and outside influences intersect to form our *functioning culture.* Become familiar with the following.

Social stratification: The hierarchical structuring of society with regard to a person's (or group's) political, economic, and social power.

Majority: The dominant group whose members yield the greatest degree of political, economic, and social power. The number of people belonging to the majority may be less than those in the minority.

Minority: A subordinate group whose members yield a lesser degree of social, economic, or political power relative to the majority. (*Note:* Not all minorities are ethnic groups, nor are all ethnic groups minorities.) Ogbu (1999) distinguishes between *voluntary minorities* (e.g., Chinese, Vietnamese, East Indian) and *involuntary minorities* (e.g., African Americans brought here against their will and Native Americans who were conquered).

Ethnic group: A group of people who share a common language, religion, culture, values, behavior patterns, and sense of togetherness. The group has a common history and may have a common destiny.

Ethnicity: The degree to which individuals identify with their particular ethnic group. Ethnicity is voluntary and may change.

COMPONENTS OF CULTURE.   Culture can be seen to have five components: (1) *personality:* attitudes, values, and beliefs; (2) *language:* basic communications, symbolism, and jargons; (3) *social structure:* family, cities, villages, customs, religion, specialization, technology, and education; (4) *occupations:* gathering, service, agriculture, manufacturing, and government; and (5) *environment:* land forms, vegetation, climate, and wildlife.

LIFESTYLES OF A GROUP.   We can categorize the cultural analysis of the lifestyles of a group as (1) communication and language, (2) mental process and learning, (3) beliefs and attitudes, (4) values and norms, (5) sense of self and space, time and time consciousness, (6) relationships, rewards, and recognition, (7) dress and appearance, and (8) food and feeding habits. Another way to analyze a culture is through the process by which a group organizes itself: kinship, education, religion, association, economics, politics, health, recreation, ethnicity, and poverty.

There is substantial evidence that students from certain ethnic groups and also those subjected to the "culture of poverty" (which should not be linked to ethnic heritage) are not achieving in schools. They experience discrimination and their needs are not being met. The most obvious North American examples are African American, Hispanic American, and American Indian and Métis (people of European and American Indian ancestry) students. Dropout rates for American Indian and Métis students are high. The impact on the academic achievement and self-concept of many children is often devastating.

When children from a minority group live in a low-socioeconomic neighborhood and play with other children from their group, their contact with other segments of society is limited. They do not interact with children and adults who have learned the behavior patterns that help one get ahead in the dominant culture. This can lead to lowered self-concept and underachievement in school.

Schools expect the behaviors approved by the majority culture. Lessons taught in school to a child from a minority culture (regardless of socioeconomic status) may not fit well with the attitudes or beliefs of that child. Confusion or conflict should be expected if the child or the child's family disagrees with what you or the school thinks is important. Become sensitive to the cultural mix in your classroom and to students who may be experiencing one or a combination of low socioeconomic and minority statuses. Think about your attitudes and values and how these differ from people in the minority group. Learn the cultural milieu in your state or region. The information you gather may surprise but help you become more sensitive to human rights and differences.

Respecting Human Rights and Differences

If you belong to the majority culture in your country, you probably have certain expectations. You value competition and individual achievement; because of your orientation to time and the future, you value planning and saving; people should be busy, on the move and achieving; nature should be controlled, even through technology, to serve people; and, individual freedom and autonomy are cherished values. In contrast, people from some minority groups may think people should cooperate to help the group achieve; concentrate on the present and the group will provide for the future; or the past, tradition, and ancestors must be valued; be relaxed, meditative, and methodical; people should respect and become one with nature; and loyalty to the group is more important than individual freedom. Your teaching should show that you value, cherish, and celebrate pluralism and the traditions of the cultures represented in your classroom.

You, like most teachers, will not knowingly practice discrimination. However, things you say and do with the best of intentions may be interpreted as discrimination. You can gradually learn to avoid unintended discrimination by becoming knowledgeable and proficient in cross-cultural sensitivity and teaching procedures. You can help yourself respect human rights and differences. A first step is to learn the basic concepts associated with human rights, discrimination, and racism. These, just as relevant today, were addressed by the Alberta Human Rights Commission in 1978.

SOCIAL ATTITUDE.   A social attitude is a "readiness to respond favorably or unfavorably to a person, object, situation, or event. It is a person's mental set; the feelings an individual has towards various problems that determine the way he or she will act. It is a readiness to verbalize or behave."

BELIEF.   A belief is "something that is thought to be true" (p. 5). Compare the following:

"I can't stand Blacks." (social attitude)
"Blacks aren't bright; all they do is play basketball, dance, and use jive talk." (belief)

"I would never let my daughter marry an East Indian." (social attitude)
"East Indians always treat their wives as servants." (belief)

"I'd never associate with the white boys in my classroom." (social attitude)
"White boys have no morals." (belief)

Obviously, beliefs can be incorrect and attitudes may be based on erroneous beliefs. The result is prejudice.

PREJUDICE.   Prejudice is "an attitude or belief formed or held without really considering the facts. It is for or against something or someone" (p. 6). Prejudiced attitudes and beliefs normally are based on faulty or incomplete information. "Prejudging" occurs—attitudes and beliefs are "preconceived." If John Doe and Mary Buck are about to meet Harry Brit, who just stepped off the airplane from England, and John and Mary are inclined to believe that Harry will be a pushy know-it-all, they are being prejudiced. Expecting male artists to be effeminate is another example of prejudice. You may think that "prejudice" is always a negative thing, but assuming that Japanese people will be polite is another form of prejudice—a positive prejudice. Prejudices can be positive or negative. Both have undesirable effects. We all have prejudices and should avoid preconceived notions.

DISCRIMINATION.   Discrimination is "prejudice transmitted into action. It is a definite behavior that is the result of a prejudiced attitude or belief" (p. 6). Whereas prejudice is an attitude or mind state, discrimination is action resulting from such an attitude. When students reject other students because of skin color or because they do not speak standard English, this is discrimination. Discrimination creates categories—the privileged and those not privileged. Categories that are often the basis for discrimination are skin color, race, religion, national origin, social class, gender, sexual orientation, and age (p. 6).

STEREOTYPING.   Stereotyping involves a "fixed set of ideas, often exaggerated and distorted . . . [that] regards all members of a group as being the same" (p. 8). It is a mental picture that does not allow members of a category to have individual differences. Stereotyping is a kind of destructive and evil gossip. It causes us to prejudge people before we even have met them. Examples include:

"Indians are lazy drunks."
"Jews are aggressive and greedy."
"Women are not good at math."
"Jocks are academic retards and poor writers."

Stereotypes may just be inaccurate, not negative, but still cause problems. For example,

"Blacks are wonderful dancers."
"American Indians love nature and are good hunters."
"People who have extensive subject matter background are good teachers."

OVERGENERALIZATION.   Prejudice and discrimination are based on overgeneralization (or overcategorization) and may result in self-fulfilling prophecies. An overgeneralization happens when a generalization or stereotype is broad to the point of distortion, prejudice, or discrimination (p. 9). It can be unjust and harmful. For example, a person in an affluent neighborhood sees a real estate agent take a minority-group family through a house. The person circulates a petition to be taken to the real estate firm to prevent the family from "depressing" the value of area property.

SELF-FULFILLING PROPHECY.   "Prejudiced people try to prove their invalid stereotypes and faulty generalizations by seeing in the world only what they want to see" (p. 7). This may become a self-fulfilling prophecy used as an excuse for neglect, cruelty, or attack. A self-fulfilling prophecy occurs when a "person acts or is a certain way because he or she is *expected* to act or be a certain way" (p. 9). Consider the following case. At one time authorities believed American Indian children to be unmotivated and less intelligent than white children. American Indian children were taken from their families and herded into residential schools. They were not allowed to speak their language and often punished if they did. This led the children to think they were savage, inferior, and dumb. We now know the damage to self-concept and academic achievement. Children do better in school and feel better about themselves when, in initial schooling, they speak and learn in the language of their family and community. American Indian children, on average, did not do as well as those whose first language was English. This allowed the authorities to say. "See . . . Indians are lazy and stupid." The scars from this ugly practice remain.

SCAPEGOATING.   Prejudice and discrimination are difficult to eradicate. Some people seem to need scapegoats for personal problems, mistakes or inadequacies. Scapegoating is the "process of singling out an individual, group or object, upon whom blame for the mistakes or crimes of others is thrust" (p. 16). For example, Hitler used Jews as scapegoats for Germany's economic problems. Politicians today routinely scapegoat, blaming the previous political administration for economic problems or as justification for use of patronage or nepotism.

The Alberta Human Rights Commission places the above terms together in a cycle (Figure 3.3) of attitudes and values, stereotyping, overgeneralization, prejudice, discrimination, and self-fulfilling prophecy (p. 10). The task of educators is to provide interven-

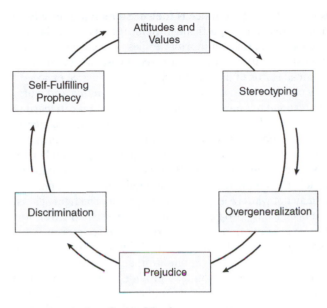

FIGURE 3.3 *Cycle of Racism*

Source: Alberta Human Rights Commission, 1978.

tions to derail the cycle. Instructional approaches, particularly experiential, can help combat discrimination on the basis of sex, handicap, or race. More will be said about this later.

Antiracist Education

Beads! Ukrainian Easter eggs! Flamenco dancing! Wooden shoes and tulips! Bar mitzvahs! Cultural diversity! It would be nice to confine discussion of cross-cultural teaching and learning to a rose-colored-glasses portrait of a beautiful "cultural mosaic"; however, multiculturalism and cross-cultural education must involve much more than foods, dress, customs, and habits.

DEFINING THE PROBLEM OF RACISM. Racism is a combination of stereotyping, prejudice, and discrimination. It is this combination that makes people from some races think they are superior. "Different" is seen as "worse." We can paint an unflattering picture that occurs in North America. In terms of ethnic heritage, different cultures often are not afforded the same value as the dominant culture. Theoretically, all groups should be able to follow and celebrate the norms and practices of their cultures and live their lives without hassle. However, not all groups (gender, class, race, or ethnicity) have equal economic, social, and political power. People do not have equal opportunity and equal access to education and jobs, so self-respect is robbed and gaining the respect of neighbors is unlikely.

The problems of racism and unequal power are reflected in every institution, including schools. The result is that students such as American Indian and African American children often are dead-ended. English, French, and Spanish languages are treated as more valuable than Cree, Punjabi, or Jamaican English. Children from Great Britain, European countries, or Canada "fit" better than those from Third World countries or American Indian reservations. What makes the problem of racism severe is that it is difficult to describe or prove except in blatant instances; however, the problem of unequal power and racism is prevalent and persistent.

CAUSES OF THE PROBLEM. Ignorance, stereotyping, and prejudice cause the problem. Institutional discrimination feeds prejudice and is nourished by it. When oppressed people fight back, they are labeled "extremist," "hard line," "radical," or "leftist." It is hard to fight racism. We need to probe how racism is rationalized and perpetuated to expose it if change is to occur. Antiracist education is needed.

APPROACHES TO CHANGE. The aim of cross-cultural and antiracist education is to change attitudes of people toward each other. Acquiring information about different cultures is not enough to increase tolerance. Though the intent is to increase understanding, students may learn more things to dislike and prejudice is fueled. Stereotypes have been taught by parents, peers, politicians, teachers, significant others, the mass media, and through observation of the socioeconomic status of minority peoples. If change is to occur, and stereotypes debunked, these must be identified and scrutinized. Reasons for continued unequal power, opportunity, and social status of different social groups must be exposed.

Education can help minority children learn the skills necessary for living and working. It can help them learn how to respond to oppressive conditions. Children can learn to communicate, work with others, seek complete information, think critically, and make unbiased decisions. Schools can teach attitudes of respect, cooperation, a sense of fairness, and a commitment to remedy injustices. Antiracist education should engage members of the dominant culture *and* those who experience racism. However, it must be recognized that some people resist engagement because of fear or a desire to retain the status quo. People who are in positions of power may not want to jeopardize their power. The fight against racism, understandably, has often been led by people who suffer its effects; however, it is difficult to influence individuals who are not offended or do not want to see racism.

Educators can study how some groups resist racism successfully. Teachers can bring community and world events into the classroom for examination and discussion. Racist jokes and remarks should be confronted. Support should be provided for those trying to rectify racism; students can learn to identify the symptoms and causes of racism, understand that efforts for change will be met by resistance, and discover how to deal with the resistance. Collaboration with parents and community members and leaders of different cultural groups is essential. Teacher associations, departments of education, and school board associations need to make eliminating racism a top priority.

Critical Beliefs

> When the voices of the school curriculum and of its teaching and learning are fully multicultural, then the appropriation of multiple voices—in dignity and without coercion, keeping a critical stance without despair—becomes possible for all students. (Banks & Banks, 2001, p. 54)

If you wish to teach well in a multicultural setting, be aware that your behavior and expectations are affected by your background. Brown and Kysilka (2002) assert that teachers need to be aware of the similarities and differences between their culture and the cultures of their students. This will be difficult for white middle-class teachers who have never experienced discrimination (p. ix). Become aware of your culture so you can learn and honor the culture of students. Your behavior can have dramatic effects on your students. Good intention is not enough.

- Recognize the cultural and linguistic differences in the class, and value that children's learning begins in their homes and community.
- Accept the validity of each child's learning/living environment, and build upon it.
- View cultural, racial, and linguistic differences as positive (not something to tolerate or change).
- Provide the means by which equal educational opportunity can be realized, and give children a positive view of themselves and their cultural heritage.
- Realize that culture is ever-changing (the culture of the past is different from the culture of the present or future).

- Be sensitive to the cultures and needs of students; learn about their backgrounds regarding:

    Home-family relations: Role definitions, family structure patterns, influences on learning style, and effects of child-rearing practices on behavior. These may not fit school expectations.

    Community culture(s): Structure and role of groups, functions of schools and the relationships to other institutions. Perceptions of these may not fit school expectations.

    Cultural heritage and contemporary lifestyles: Cultural and historical developments and the influence of culture, contemporary values, social and political activities, issues, leaders, and the effects of these on education.

    Personal awareness: Interpersonal effectiveness and personal development skills, dealing with conflict and the relationship to one's own culture and that of others.

Teachers may react negatively to children of another culture because of the way the children communicate (orally or nonverbally). Teachers may judge students' use of English language as "wrong" rather than as a valid form of communication. The challenge, when teaching the school "correct way," is to ensure that students do not feel backward, stupid, or inferior; that they do not believe their "home" language is wrong, bad, or inferior. Oral language is a valid means of communication, transmission of culture, and sociological identification. Language has developed differently in various parts of the world or a country. National and regional language differences should not be deemed good or bad; they are different but valid.

Importance of Empathy

A recurring theme in multicultural education literature is *empathy*—the ability to understand and communicate understanding of "where another person is coming from." It involves communicating, verbally and nonverbally, the feelings and content of what was said. It is a realistic, effective skill in cross-cultural teaching and in setting a warm and positive classroom climate.

Effective multicultural education is built on human relations. It has two components: human relations and ethics training. The richness and uniqueness of people are attributed, in part, to their ethnic background. Human relations is about the humanness and interactions of people while ethnic studies conceptualizes people as unique members of identifiable cultural groups. Multicultural education, thus, should integrate human relations and ethnic studies to increase awareness and capability, and diminish/eliminate racial and cultural prejudice and stereotyping.

Cross-Culturally Effective Teaching

The mix of cultures in your classroom can complicate communication. We perceive things the way cultural background has taught us to see, hear, smell, and touch. To illustrate, what we believe to be good to eat may be either beef or ants; what we believe moral may be one wife or more than one. In some cultures, children are expected to look at elders when being spoken to; in others, children are expected to look down.

Our perceptions may differ from those of some children in our classes. Realize *why* you act in certain ways and why some students might, quite naturally, act differently. Try to see things through the eyes of these students. This implies that respect for the cultures of others must be shown. It could mean, for instance, that though you prefer a structured, direct way of teaching, you should use an open discussion, movement-filled, or perhaps storytelling mode, if this is the culturally validated learning style of students and the community. A cross-culturally effective teacher demonstrates open mindedness, flexibility, genuine respect for and interest in the values and traditions of others, self-confidence, and (importantly) a sense of humor. Adapt curriculum to acknowledge and honor the cultural mix in the classroom. And, hands-on experiences are essential. Learn to live with ambiguity and how to cope with stress—trying to communicate and teach interculturally is stressful, particularly if the other cultures in your classroom are very different from yours.

Acquire the skills, attitudes, and abilities you will need to function within a range of cultural and ethnic groups and the ability to interact effectively with individuals who belong to diverse racial and ethnic groups. Teach all students about cultural diversity, not just students of racial or cultural minorities (Banks, 1999; Tiedt & Tiedt, 2006). Your cross- or multicultural teaching skills will help students develop cross-cultural awareness and sensitivity. Acquire the following abilities: communicating respect, being nonjudgmental, displaying empathy, having role flexibility, demonstrating reciprocal concern, and tolerating ambiguity.

The Hidden Curriculum

If schools are to become truly multicultural, the belief must prevail that all cultures are equal. Teachers must not enhance one and dilute others. We cannot assume the Western European culture is "correct" and more valuable, that other cultures have deficits, handicaps to be overcome. These, though different, have positive resources, vitality, and creativity. Ideally, equal attention should be allocated to the cultures represented in the classroom, be they immigrant or native. This can happen in teaching history, geography, art, literature, and every other subject. Many texts are written from a monocultural perspective with the assumption that this is superior. The "we" cultures tend to be Western European; the others (minority cultures) become the "they" cultures and tend to be ignored. Schools can do things to dramatically change this situation.

Become a Multicultural Teacher

Education is the key to overcoming discrimination. Tiedt and Tiedt (2006) stress a student-centered approach within an inclusive classroom. They advocate individualized instruction that addresses affective and cognitive goals. Even if you don't want to, you *have* an influence—make it informed and powerfully positive! The classroom is a forum within which constructive and positive multicultural education can occur, education that recognizes each child individually, that recognizes and celebrates diversity. The Council on Interracial Books for Children (Childcare, 1983) suggests activities to help students recognize and deal with racism:

Building Antiracism

Build cultural respect.
- Create a class book with a chapter on the family of each child.
- Use songs and play music from various cultures and in various languages.
- Invite musicians, artists, actors to talk to or perform for staff and children.
- Take children to events such as concerts, performances, displays that reflect various cultures.

Build community respect.
- Take "positive" pictures of scenes from *all* parts of the community. Invite community leaders to talk about how racism affects the community.
- Display pictures and hangings that show people from all cultures, ages, walks of life, and colors.
- Involve teachers and parents in building files on various cultural, racial, or national groups.

Deal with skin color.
- Have good pictures taken of the children in the class and display these in positive ways.
- Have children make attractive dolls depicting people of different skin colors.
- Use books about people with different skin colors.
- Use puzzles of people of different colors and features.

Deal with hair variations.
- Make a photo collage of different hair styles, colors, and textures.
- Use books and pictures that display the beauty of different colors and styles.

Build positive feelings about black and brown colors.
- Use the colors in positive ways and avoid negative usages.

Build respect for languages.
- Praise children who speak or learn other languages.
- Learn to use common words in languages children bring to school.
- Have children learn to count to ten in various languages.

Use holidays as teaching opportunities and create holidays to recognize various cultures.
- Create a calendar of the birthdays of leaders of various cultures and countries.
- Display and use books to celebrate birthdays of ethnic community leaders.
- Celebrate special days of the cultures of children represented in the classroom.
- Celebrate the birthdays of antiracist leaders.

Discuss racism and stereotyping with children.

The Childcare Council makes recommendations about responding to children's racial or cultural insults. We are often uncomfortable when we hear a racist remark or ethnic joke but say nothing. We should listen carefully, assess the remark, and immediately respond thoughtfully. Guidelines you can use include: (1) acknowledge that you heard the insulting remark; (2) make it clear that such remarks are not acceptable; (3) identify what was incorrect about the remark; (4) offer correct information; (5) offer support to the child who has been insulted; and (6) help children resolve any part of the conflict that had nothing to do with race or culture.

Learning about the Community

Putting multiculturalism into practice in a school requires cooperation, patience, and the will to make it work. A way to secure information about the ethnic composition of the community is through interviews. Suggestions for change can result so classrooms and school will be comfortable and enjoyable for students. Ask about the educational goals of parents, school subjects considered important, and extracurricular activities they find valuable. Discover important days the school could celebrate and how to do this. Learn the things deemed polite or impolite, how friendship or respect are shown, or things that are embarrassing. Among other things are ideas about time, how to use leisure, and awareness there might be conflict between what the home and the school teach children.

Bias in Books and Curricular Materials

Avoid materials that demonstrate bias. At least point it out. Passages that ethnic groups might find offensive should not be used. Books can contain distortions that affect the way children from majority and minority cultures feel about themselves and each other. The Manitoba Indian Brotherhood (cited by Goulet, 1987) identified seven distortions about Native people in texts:

- *Omission.* Failing to mention all the relevant facts; underrepresenting certain groups, which suggests they are of lesser value or importance in society
- *Defamation.* Calling attention to faults of a group, portraying a group in stereotypical ways, or assigning roles to a group that limit their abilities and potential
- *Validity.* Not ensuring that information was accurate, up to date, or unambiguous
- *Disparagement.* Belittling or denying the contributions of a group
- *Cumulative implication.* Only selecting information that reflects positively on one group and negatively on another; presenting one interpretation of a situation, issue, or group of people; or glossing over controversial topics and discussions about incidences of prejudice or discrimination that place the majority culture in an undesirable light
- *Obliteration.* Ignoring significant historical aspects
- *Disembodiment.* Using terms such as "menace" and "annihilation" as part of "progress," in a casual or depersonalized manner

Self-Concept and Integration versus Assimilation

Teachers need to stress *integration* and participation of students from other cultures as opposed to assimilation into the mainstream culture. *Assimilation* involves denying and downgrading minority cultures. The likely result is damage to the self-concepts of minority students. Schools should encourage students to develop positive attitudes toward others and build the self-concepts of all students. This can be fostered by providing opportunity for positive interactions and participation in the teaching and learning process. Techniques such as cooperative learning are effective. In cooperative learning, children are placed in groups mixed racially and ethnically; everybody's effort is required for the success of all, and interpersonal contact is maximized.

Knowledge, Action, and the Multicultural Teacher

You can help your students overcome a tendency to believe another culture is wrong because it is different. It is not uncommon in multicultural teaching to stress learning *about* other groups and talk about empathy, prejudice, and ethnocentrism, assuming that because you know about these qualities you will acquire them. Teach in a manner consistent with knowledge about these traits. Develop the attributes of high cross-cultural readiness, sensitivity to nonverbal behavior, and knowledge of the informal aspects of cultures with which you are in contact.

Importance of Nonverbal Behavior

Children from cultures different from the teacher's can develop disabilities in social perception that can lead to social and intellectual impoverishment. Further, more attractive students with "good" voice qualities in the teacher's view (the perception may be culturally determined) are considered more intelligent, enthusiastic, and academically successful.

Expectations and attitudes about students are shown in the nonverbal behaviors of teachers. For example, teachers may stand farther away from "low-ability" students, who may be placed in more distant regions of the room where it is harder for them to see, hear, and feel part of what is going on. Students placed close to the teacher are more involved in class proceedings, participate more, and behave more in accordance with the teacher's goals. Teachers tend to reciprocate the nonverbal behaviors of their students (positive and negative). Teachers may display more positive nonverbal behaviors toward children of their own ethnic background, but this is usually detectable only to persons of the same race. Racially prejudiced teachers tend to reflect their attitudes nonverbally.

Climate, Teaching Methods, and Student Activities

The classroom climate you establish and your approach to instruction should help students develop a positive self-concept. An effective multicultural teacher pays particular attention to: (1) establishing a positive climate; (2) modeling and teaching communication, interpersonal, and group skills; and (3) selecting teaching methods and activities that help overcome stereotyping, prejudice, and ethnocentrism. Chapter 4, on teaching for affective outcomes, discusses establishing a positive disposition or climate and teaching attitudes and values. Consider how content applies to multicultural teaching. Teaching methods that are effective include role playing, simulations, and small-group strategies (particularly cooperative learning).

The use of encouragement when working with minority students is powerful. Devitt (2004) notes that a study of seventh-grade students by Good, Aronson, and Inzlicht (2003) found that females and low-income minority students can improve their reading and math scores if children learn that intelligence is something they can develop over time. The findings suggest that if these students are given positive messages about their ability to learn, they are less likely to conform to the negative stereotypes they think others have of them regarding poor reading skills among minority students and poor math skills among girls. Students can be encouraged to attribute poor academic performance to their troubled situations, not to being female or part of a minority (Devitt, 2004). This changing of attitudes can stop the cycle of self-blame, anxiety, and underachievement. It is key for students to think that change is possible.

You can do several things to make sure your classroom has a positive climate and is truly pluralistic and bias free (Tiedt & Tiedt, 2006). Your language can be free from racist terms and labels. Recognize language and stereotyped perceptions that hurt people or limit potential. Emphasize that people are not less able because of, or limited by, variances in race, class, sex, or ethnic background. Without preaching or being hostile, gradually lead students to greater awareness by modeling appropriate behavior and language, initiating discussion of questionable language or practices, planning lessons that help break down stereotyping, and avoiding biased texts and materials.

Your teaching should reflect multicultural objectives. You will want students to appreciate and respect diversity and learn the contributions of the cultural groups in the country. Students can learn what is common to various peoples and universal behaviors and needs. Help students understand that group and individual differences are normal. And, students can learn to use critical thinking (see Chapter 14) to recognize prejudice, discrimination. and racism and the presence (though unintended) of these in their community, peers, family, and themselves.

Trimarco (1986) proposes that you: (1) discover how to integrate minority-group standards and priorities into affairs of the class; (2) strive to present a positive concept of all cultures; (3) involve children from subgroups in the dominant group's activities; (4) teach and celebrate the meaningful historical achievements of minority groups to counteract myths and stereotypes; (5) seek clues about each learner's self-image; (6) seek evidence of acceptance or nonacceptance of different cultures and lifestyles; and (7) watch for biases in textbooks and materials, particularly illustrations, that debase the worth of a cultural group (p. 80).

There are many excellent sources of multicultural and cross-cultural activities. Materials, many free, are available through commercial and public venues. Contact government and human rights agencies to see what is available to teachers regarding multicultural or antiracist education.

Development of Racial Awareness

The belief that racial attitudes are learned mainly from parents is not substantiated by research (Goulet, 1987). Goulet believes that children acquire racial attitudes from several interrelated social influences: people (other than family) children are in contact with; more subtle forms of communication such as children's books, movies, comics, radio, and television; and observation of practices in society such as lack of representation of minorities in positions of leadership, who have high-level jobs, who have the menial jobs, and who are unemployed. These develop children's understandings of what society expects and values about the majority and minorities.

Goulet says the school, as an institution, contributes to formation of racial attitudes. He observes that institutional racism is developed through:

1. *The success (or lack of it) of predecessors.* Some minorities have high dropout and failure rates. The real reasons are not examined.
2. *Prejudice in the school.* It is present in: testing (e.g., measuring English language fluency); tracking or streaming (e.g., vocational stream, opportunity rooms); and discipline practices (e.g., in a community where whites use parent control while Natives use community—not just parent—intervention, believe children learn more by making mistakes).
3. *The curriculum.* This tends to be ethnocentric, actually Eurocentric, with print and other resources geared for the white middle class and stereotyped and biased. Minorities tend to be represented differently and less favorably.
4. *Staff attitudes.* Teachers' backgrounds are largely middle class and European, and accepting and rejecting behaviors are based on their backgrounds.

You can acquire strategies to develop positive racial attitudes. Goulet suggests:

1. *Self-assessment.* Learn about your cultural values and attitudes and your attitudes toward other cultural groups. Provide opportunities for minorities to learn about the contributions of their cultures.

2. *Cultural celebration.* Get children to think about celebrations of other cultures. Recognize that differences are "O.K." Stress pride in diversity and things that are *similar* (underlying human values).
3. *Assess materials.* Look for evidence of racism, ethnocentric views.
4. *Variety of teaching styles.* Accommodate different learning styles; use cooperative and experiential teaching methods.
5. *Experience other cultures and reflect on and deal with racism.* To really learn, you need to experience, not just cognitively, but affectively.

Gloria Ladson-Billings (1994) suggests ways teachers can accommodate cultural diversity while maintaining the same standards for all. Her recommendations apply to all ethnic groups even though she wrote about teaching African American children. She studied eight exemplary teachers whose approach to teaching affirmed cultural identity but who differed in personal style and methods. She concludes that African American students' achievement levels are improved only when classrooms are desegregated. Culturally relevant teachers, she notes, believe teaching is an art. Effectives teachers "draw knowledge out" rather than "put knowledge in." They believe all students can succeed. They see themselves as part of the community and recognize the need to give back to that community and encourage students to do the same. Students are helped to make connections between themselves and their local, national, and global communities.

Accommodating Cultural Diversity in Your Classroom

You can become a teacher who accommodates diversity in your classroom. Addressing effective teacher education for cultural diversity, Zeichner (1993) identified key elements and in 1998, Zeichner et al. expanded on them. Based on these, the implications for you are to:

- Develop a clear sense of your own ethnic and cultural identity.
- Examine your attitudes toward other ethnocultural groups.
- Learn about the dynamics of prejudice and racism and how to deal with them.
- Learn about the dynamics of privilege and economic oppression and about school practices that contribute to the reproduction of societal inequalities.
- Learn about the histories and contribution of various ethnocultural groups.
- Learn about the characteristics and learning styles of various groups and individuals and the limitations of this information.
- Discover the relationships among language, culture, and learning.
- Discover procedures for gaining information about communities represented in classrooms in which you will teach.
- Learn about the relationships between methods used in the classroom and the preferred learning and interaction styles in students' homes and communities.
- Seek examples of successful teaching of ethnic- and language-minority students.
- Seek field experiences in a school or schools serving minority students.
- Live and teach in a minority community.

A reference to help you prepare for an ever-growing diverse population in schools is Gloria Ladson-Billings's, *The Dreamkeepers* (1994). It is a book of stories of her experiences as a teacher and teacher educator and stories of a group of her teacher education students. Her approach to teaching is a blend of academics, culture, and social justice.

CASE 3.1 Cross-Cultural Teaching

Climate of Acceptance

Ms. Kurtz works in a classroom in an inner-city school where the children who attend represent many different cultures. She worries that there doesn't seem to be the climate of acceptance and tolerance that should be found in such a school. The conversation in the staff room seems remarkably negative, with teachers expressing views that are questionable for educators anywhere, let alone in an inner-city school environment.

Similarly, the playground is a place of disagreements often based on racial differences. She knows that children in the middle to higher grades move in gangs after school, and about the increasing violence level in the community.

Recently, at a staff meeting, Ms. Kurtz brought up her concern that the school could be doing more to build pride, self-esteem, and positive relationships. Though the principal seemed receptive, most teachers rejected the idea. "These people have been fighting for centuries, we can't do much to change them," one said. "Since they've come to this country, we've had more and more trouble." "If they'd just become more like us," said another teacher. "They don't understand how we do things in this country." Ms. Kurtz suppressed her anger and frustration and said nothing.

Ms. Kurtz wants to make changes in the school, but is unsure how to proceed. What would you suggest? How, in a constructive, positive way, could this occur?

CASE 3.2 Cross-Cultural Teaching

Halting Discrimination

Ms. Gregory taught in a high school in which just over half of the students came from the homes of recent immigrant families. They had come from China, India, Japan, and Jamaica. Racial tensions were escalating. The school was rapidly developing a reputation among city teachers as being a tough place to teach. The staff was a committed and capable group of professionals but did not know how to be effective cross-cultural teachers. They realized that good intentions were not enough and that something needed to be done and as soon as possible.

Ms. Gregory knew what it was like to experience discrimination and self-doubt and believed students needed to be free to learn and teachers to be free to teach. Fundamental to this, she believed students needed to see themselves as competent and worthy human beings who could succeed. A major goal was to have the children from each ethnic group develop positive self-concepts. The secure person, she felt, was one who did not fear or scorn things that were different. Children, she knew, needed to learn to value diversity, particularly cultural and linguistic diversity. They needed school experiences where they could learn to: (1) think of themselves as worthwhile humans; (2) see their origin and cultural background as a strength; (3) respect and value the origins and cultural backgrounds of others; (4) interact in a positive and productive way with other students in the classroom; and (5) find ways of succeeding at school tasks. What suggestions do you have for Ms. Gregory and the rest of the staff to help students build positive self-concepts of self and others?

Special Needs Learners

Students with Exceptionalities (Special Needs)

The policy of free public education is universal in North America; there has been a trend to recognize diversity and increasingly to understand special needs students. Learners differ in learning style preferences, left or right brain dominance, and learning modality (auditory, visual, or kinesthetic) preference; and learners represent a variety of cultures and subcultures. The third dimension of diversity is special needs learners: those with learning problems or handicaps; the gifted, creative, or talented; the bilingual (or multilingual); the socioeconomically different or disadvantaged; migrants; and immigrants. Although these students may be limited in some ways in what they can do, they may not be "different" in other ways; teachers should concentrate on strengths, not handicaps, weaknesses, or differences.

Schools try to accommodate special needs learners in a variety of ways, but special learners are increasingly "mainstreamed" (placed in so-called regular classrooms rather than "resource rooms"). However, there is much to learn about working with special needs learners, and the current approach—mainstreaming—is controversial. Because the distinction between special education and regular classrooms is becoming blurred, additional demands are made on classroom teachers.

Preservice and inservice teachers need training in how to work with special students. Collaboration and consultation among teachers, resource teachers, specialists, parents, and perhaps students themselves is needed. Most teachers in mainstreamed classrooms agree that regular teacher training to work with special learners and to develop collaborative skills has been inadequate. How to work with special needs students should be addressed promptly and positively. In this chapter we merely "prime the pump," to begin the training process. We urge that you take at least one course in special education. A text that provides an excellent introduction to special needs education is A. Woolfolk's *Educational Psychology* (9th ed., 2004).

Disabilities and Learning Problems

Disabled children, those with learning problems, have the right to programs "consistent with their academic, social, and physical needs" (Hardman, Drew, & Egan, 2002, p. 29). You, as a teacher, need to approach potential problems positively. A team approach can aid planning, adapt curriculum, encourage, provide support, and evaluate. Peer support can be fostered to empower students with disabilities. All students can learn and contribute to society, and all are of equal value as human beings (SPDU/SIDRU, 1996, p. 32).

Special needs (exceptional) learners can be classified several ways, and different authorities use different approaches but may not always agree on the characteristics of categories. We cannot, in this text, cover the spectrum of exceptionality (special needs). We briefly consider the following: physical problems, communication (speech or sensory) disorders, behavior disorders, mental retardation and slow learning, multiple handicaps, and specific learning disabilities (see Figure 3.4).

PHYSICAL DISABILITIES.   Physical disabilities is a broad term that includes learners with neurological defects (e.g., cerebral palsy, which affects the ability to control muscles) or glandular defects, orthopedic conditions (e.g., clubfoot or the absence of, or damage to, one or more limbs), birth defects, and problems resulting from infection or disease (e.g., polio and bone tuberculosis). Students may have difficulty moving either themselves or body members or have limited vitality, alertness, or strength.

To work with physically disabled students, Turnbull, Turnbull, Shank, Smith, and Leal (2002) say that curricular goals need to depend on individual student needs. Goals may include:

- Increasing mobility (e.g., crutches, scooters, wheelchairs)
- Increasing communication (e.g., use of computers or robotic systems)

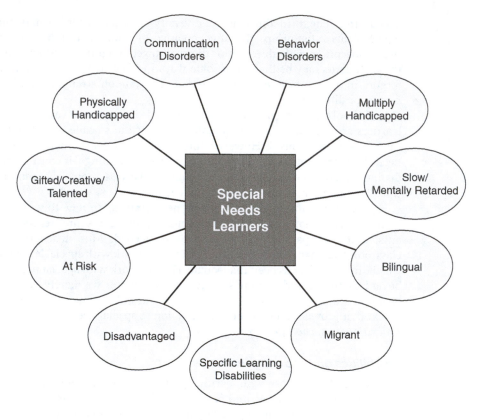

FIGURE 3.4   *Special Needs (Exceptional) Learners*

- Maintaining physical health (i.e., fitness regimens or medical technology assistance) involving a "mechanical device to replace or augment vital body functions"
- Helping students enhance self-determination and self-dependence (pp. 417–424)

Cooperation with professionals is needed to include accommodations and therapies into the class routine. Students need to know that, if needed, physical assistance is available.

COMMUNICATION DISORDERS.   Communication, the exchange of information and ideas, involves receiving, understanding, and expressing ideas (Turnbull et al., p. 482). Learners with communication disorders include children with speech (producing sounds) or language (expression) difficulties or sensory difficulties. These learners are often impaired to the point that communication is limited; they may be autistic or have severe speech and language disturbances. We include learners with sensory difficulties here, but they could be categorized separately. Sensory handicaps include auditory or visual impairments so severe that, even with auditory or optical aids, the learners have a critical loss of hearing or sight. Students should be allowed to make full use of visual and auditory cues. New material should be presented orally and in writing. A multisensory approach is important. For the visually impaired, a physical support system should be available so students know assistance is there when needed. Technology to enhance hearing or sight should be provided, as should materials such as "talking books."

SOCIAL, EMOTIONAL, OR BEHAVIORAL DISABILITIES. Behavior disorders include social maladjustment, psychoses, or emotional disturbances (Winzer, 1995, p. 269). Students may have one or more of the following characteristics: inability to learn (not due to health or intellectual problems), poor relationships with peers and teachers, unusual or overreaction to normal events, and unusual physical symptoms or fears related to school (Good & Brophy, 1995, p. 592). Some are aggressive and others withdrawn. Aggressive students tend to receive the most attention. With this disability, inappropriate behavior interferes with classroom teaching and learning. The problem is not the result of a particular event or context. The teacher needs to set clear, specific, classroom rules and enforce consequences consistently. The teacher may need support if the behavior causes interference in the classroom (SPDU/SIDRU, 1996, p. 39).

INTELLECTUAL DISABILITIES. Intellectually disabled (often called mentally retarded) "refers to substantial limitations in personal funtioning, characterized by significant subaverage intellectual funtioning, existing concurrently with related limitations in two or more of the following adaptive skills: communication, self-care, home living, social skills, community use, self-direction, health and safety, functional academics, leisure, and work" (Winzer, 1995, p. 270, quoting AAMR, 1993; see also SPDU/SIDRU, 1996, p. 38). In general, teachers need to state expectations clearly and to break down tasks and concepts into smaller parts or steps. Frequent feedback and reinforcement and frequent reviews should be provided.

Note that "slow learners" are not necessarily mentally retarded or students with behavioral problems. They are learners who cannot learn at the same rate as average students (Bloom, 1982). They tend to have deficiencies in basic reading, writing, and mathematics skills, a limited attention span, and may need many and varied repetitions when learning a task.

SEVERE AND MULTIPLE DISABILITIES. There is no single definition of "multiple disabilities." "Students typically have severe mental retardation and other accompanying disabilities, such as extensive physical and language impairments" (Turnbull et al., 2002, p. 302); some students, however, have average or better intelligence. A person with autism is also included under this heading. How to recognize, make placements for, and work with this category of learners is the subject of debate.

SPECIFIC LEARNING DISABILITIES. A relatively recent category is called specific learning disabilities. Woolfolk (2004) asks, "How do you explain a student who struggles to read, write, spell, or learn math, even though he or she does not have mental retardation, emotional problems, or educational disadvantages and has normal vision, hearing, and language capabilities?" (p. 124). An example might be chronic fatigue syndrome. Those afflicted with this condition seem to be always tired, lethargic, or experience unexplainable aches and pains. "Specific learning disabilities" are a group of disorders within an individual characterized by significant difficulties in acquiring and using listening, speaking, writing, reasoning, or mathematical ability.

BILINGUAL OR ESL LEARNERS AND MIGRANTS.   Definitions of the term bilingual-ism vary but generally refer to instruction in two languages, with the goal of making students proficient in both. In the United States the most common mix is English and Spanish; in Canada it is English and French. As another example, a person can be bilingual in English and ASL (American Sign Language). In a sense, one can even be "multilingual," if the mix, for example, is English and French while a person's original language is German or perhaps an Aboriginal language. Bilingual programs are used to help students make the transition from their original language to the official language, or the purpose may be to help students maintain or even restore their first language and culture. Other approaches are total immersion (e.g., English only) or structured immersion (the native language is used to speak to the teacher, but the teacher answers in English). English as a second language (ESL) programs are similar to bilingual programs because they are concerned with teaching English skills, but instruction takes place in English. ESL programs are most often provided for recent immigrants.

Although the percentages vary by region, over 10 percent of school-age learners in North America speak languages other than the official language—English (or French in parts of Canada and Spanish in parts of the United States). You will probably have some dual-language students in your classroom, and in some regions the number may be one-third or more. The percentage grows enormously when you include students who speak with a heavy accent or who use nonstandard English such as Black English, Jamaican English, Spanish English, East Indian English, or even Texas English. Many students chose to learn a second or even third language. Sometimes learning another language is required for graduation or college entrance. When schools have a large minority-language population (perhaps Spanish or Cree), the language of instruction during early schooling years can be in students' first language. Although there are benefits to speaking two or more languages, when the official language is not a student's first and other factors enter, the effect on self-esteem and pride can be devastating and damage academic achievement, perhaps permanently. This is particularly true when students are from poor families. The problem is compounded when children are from migrant families, for example, Mexico's migrant workers. Unless the school migrates with them, children change schools frequently and it is difficult to keep track of their progress or to establish a trusting student–teacher relationship. Children may not only miss school while traveling, they may also have a difficult time adjusting socially. Teachers contribute to the problem when they consider nonstandard English to be "improper" or "incorrect" and make students think their home language is shameful, needing upgrading or remediation. Another problem occurs when the children of immigrants have been bruised by the traumas of wars, violence, economic struggle, or racism.

Working with Special Needs Children

Grouping learners based on categories is fraught with problems. One learner may be both gifted and hearing disabled, another may be both "slow," and hearing disabled, still another may be disabled, "slow," and bilingual, and some are gifted in one subject but slow in another—the range of combinations seems endless. Obviously, when learners are tracked or grouped on one characteristic, they can differ markedly on many others; and placing individuals in one group may make them ineligible for another group and funded special services.

Many teachers are concerned about, even fear, working with disabled students. Woolfolk (2004) cautions educators about language and labeling. "A label does not tell which methods to use with individual students. . . . Everyone—teachers, parents, class-mates, and even the students themselves—may see a label as a stigma that cannot be changed" (p. 106). Those who work well with special students recognize they have spe-cial needs but make them "their own" in the same way as other students. These teachers are realistic and deal with handicaps matter of factly and realize special students share similarities with other students. Effective teachers plan carefully, establish a positive classroom climate with smooth management procedures and routines, and prepare other students to interact constructively with special students. Questions asked are congruent with ability. These teachers encourage, support, and provide positive feedback. They manage behavior and organize individual success experiences as they model, teach, and expect mutual respect, courtesy, and social acceptance in the classroom. Another approach is *differentiated instruction,* in which a lesson is taught to the entire class while meeting the needs of individuals. Students with exceptional needs have these met while taking part in the same lesson as their peers. This requires flexibility and use of a variety of in-structional techniques and manners in which individuals can choose to participate. Hamel (2004) describes how "Many school systems are moving toward an inclusion model for teaching special learners in which all students are included in general classrooms" (p. 33). She suggests several ways of adapting instructional methods and materials:

- Use overhead projector or computer enhanced image to enlarge materials.
- Allow hands-on experience of new materials when introducing a concept.
- Allow tape recording of lessons and oral response to assignments.
- Use computers for extra drill and practice.
- Limit the use of words not yet in the students' vocabulary (readiness level).
- Allow students to help plan their own learning and be a partner in the process.
- Vary the style of test items and provide accurate complete study guides.
- Use short tests at frequent intervals (brief assignments and frequent review).
- Vary the style of test questions used.
- Wait at least five seconds (+) for students to process your questions. (pp. 35–36)

Gifted, Creative, or Talented Learners

A group sometimes overlooked and poorly served is gifted, creative, or talented students. To most people the term "gifted" means that academic tasks are learned easily and quickly and the student has a high intelligence test score. Gifted students usually have above-average powers of concentration, are often more emotionally stable, and usually are larger, stronger, and healthier than the norm; but it is a mistake to think every gifted student has these characteristics. Because gifted students readily understand meanings and recognize relationships, they are more adept at critical thinking and tend to be far ahead in acade-mic achievement. "Creative" refers to the ability to solve problems in new and unusual ways; "talented" refers to exceptional performance in an area such as music or sports. Schools sometimes only recognize facility with words as giftedness. Verbal facility, how-ever, is only one kind of proficiency, and teachers should nurture other special abilities. Gardner, as discussed earlier (in Armstrong, 1994, pp. 338–341), believes students can be gifted in eight different ways (intelligences).

For several reasons, teachers may be uncomfortable working with gifted students. Teaching is less safe because, at times, gifted students come up with unexpected, though correct, answers. Sometimes a gifted child is "turned off" by the content and pace of instruction, and a teacher may not know how to handle this. Conformity to precise directions, unnecessary repetition or drill, inability to take creative "shortcuts," and inability to pursue interests may not be to the liking of gifted learners. When the interactive teaching strategy (particularly small groups) is not used well, a gifted student may be hard to handle or say, "I can do it better and faster myself." The student may fail to understand that interaction with peers promotes social growth, and performance may even be enhanced because they can hitchhike on ideas that would not otherwise have occurred to them. Although there are advantages when they teach peers, being used as "little teachers" may wear thin. On the flip side, the teacher may be so enamored with working with the gifted that the rest of the class is neglected.

It is easy for teachers to think that gifted students need little help. Gifted and talented learners normally do not experience school failure, but they often underachieve. Educational adaptations can, and should, be made. There is disagreement about how to teach the gifted. Some prefer "acceleration" (rapid progress through the grades) and others prefer "enrichment" (keeping students with their age group but providing additional, more challenging tasks). Suggestions range from full inclusion to complete segregation (Lewis & Doorlag, 2003). In mainstreamed instruction, students may be clustered in groups, get attention before or after class or both, be tutored within the regular class or allowed to do independent study. Segregation can involve special summer school, evening, or weekend programs, or enrollment in special schools. Aside from these alternatives, students can be placed in special classes in a school, take limited-enrollment courses, be assigned to resource rooms or clinical centers, or take limited-participation trips or take part in limited-participation events. In an inclusionary classroom, among other approaches, gifted students can be allowed choice in assignments and encouraged to access school and community resources.

Students Who Are Bullied

Bullied students also have special needs. In every elementary school, several students spend their day afraid. They do not feel safe at school. They avoid the restroom, cafeteria, playground, or hallways for fear of being picked on by bullies. Too often, they do not report the abuse for fear this will make matters worse; and too often no one helps them if they report being bullied. Many hide during the school day, some experience distress-related symptoms, and others refuse to go to school. As they get older, a danger is that some will carry weapons or join a gang for protection. Each year there are teachers who are threatened, their vehicles or property vandalized, or are physically attacked. Children being bullied need help and intervention from adults, and teachers can play an important role.

Garrity, Jens, Porter, Sager, and Short-Camilli (1994) cite some facts about bullies: (1) bullies can be male or female, (2) bullies are usually bigger and older than their victims, (3) they keep bullying for life unless the problem is dealt with at an early age, and (4) bullying is a learned behavior that needs to be treated with parents and child.

Garrity et al. suggest tips for victims of bullying. Children can be helped to know the "safe" people in the school to whom they can go when they are being bullied. They can be urged not to show strong emotions, which can excite the bully, making matters worse. Being assertive works best when the bully does not have an audience. The student can state that he or she does not like the bullying, it is not allowed, and will tell someone if it does not cease. Sometimes doing something unexpected can work, for example, turning the bullying into something humorous. Another tactic the child might use is to agree with the bully, because then the bully often does not know what to say or do next. A classroom role play of a bullying situation followed by debriefing can be effective. Students can be taught that those who observe an incident of bullying have a duty to assist the victim.

There now are excellent resources teachers can access to help them deal with bullying, and many school districts have resources or programs to help teachers.

CASE 3.3 Special Needs Learners

What to Do?

It is the beginning of the school year and Ms. Chavez, a first-year teacher, has a diverse group of students in her grade 4 class. She is particularly concerned about several of her students. She describes these students to you. What are your thoughts, realizing you are not an expert, about what you might do to help each of the following students if it were your classroom? Here are Ms. Chavez's comments.

Donald. Donald is a highly capable learner who reads at a grade 10 level. He has a broad range of interests and is a good athlete. He always seems to have the answers. Donald rapidly blurts out answers, often before the question is completed. His answers are always right. He frequently excitedly provides interesting, detailed explanations that are far beyond the level of the rest of the class. I find myself giving more and more attention to Donald; at times the lesson turns into a two-person discussion. Because of the danger that other students are being short-changed, I am beginning to cut Donald off before he can launch into a lengthy description of how he got his answer. Donald now does not complete his assignments or he halfheartedly tries. He often either sits and pouts or bothers the students around him. I am very concerned.

Leona. Everybody, including her classmates and her teachers from previous years, know that Leona is not very bright. Though very polite, she seems to be a loner. At a PTA meeting, I met her mother who, first thing, volunteered that Leona was slow and an embarrassment to the rest of the family. Leona clearly is having trouble with schoolwork. She has difficulty with the simplest math, can't read very well, and is always the last to finish seatwork if it is completed at all. She is overweight and has thick glasses but rarely wears them. I am hard-pressed to find something

complimentary to say to Leona. Leona does not act up at all in class. In fact, she sits near the back and is so quiet that I realize that I sometimes have not asked Leona a question for days. I wonder if I am subconsciously ignoring Leona.

Brigit. Brigit rides around in a motorized wheelchair. She was severely disabled at birth, and her body is short and twisted. She has minimum use of her limbs but can write well and has normal sight and hearing. She gets angry when somebody does something for her, testily remarking, "Leave me alone! I can do it myself." The rest of the class when they first saw her did not know what to make of her. They have been giving her a wide berth; some now are whispering and one big, loud, and boorish boy is starting to tease her. Her records indicate that she has been a good student. Her previous academic performance has been above average, but she is not living up to that record. I am worried.

Miguel. Miguel just arrived the other day, without lunch money or school supplies, and already has been in a fight. His parents are migrant workers who recently arrived to work the crops. Miguel has four older sisters and a younger brother. A group of boys had made fun of his ill-fitting clothes, unkempt appearance, and speech. The boys also made racial slurs. This, it seems, is what had prompted the fight. Miguel's first language is Spanish, and he speaks with a strong accent. I have not received a record of his previous academic performance or behavior. I have been checking his work and I am concerned that he is well behind the rest of the class in basic skills. Instead of completing written assignments in the prescribed manner, he constantly doodles. I notice, however, that his doodling often hinges around the work that I have assigned. I wonder what to do.

CASE 3.4 Special Needs

Maria's Math Test

Jean Warren is in the staff room marking papers. Raj Singh, the special needs teacher, comes in. "Jean, I want to talk to you about testing Maria in math, she's one of your students." "Yes, Raj, she didn't do well in the last test," says Jean, closing her marking file. "That's why I want to discuss her with you," says Raj taking a seat. "I'd like her to write her test in our special needs room." "Why?" replies Jean suspiciously. "So I can read the test to her and give her an additional fifteen minutes to answer the questions. Maria has been diagnosed with a reading difficulty, a visual impairment. She processes information slowly and needs extra time. In fact, reading the test and giving her time provides an equal opportunity with other students." Jean gets up to leave. "Sorry Raj. I think it will give her an unfair advantage." "Jean," replies Raj, as she moves away, "You wear glasses. Why don't you take them off and read the notice over there?" "I don't think I could," says Jean, then realizing, ". . . OK! I get your point. How can I help?" "Thanks, Jean," says Raj, smiling. "You've really been understanding. Maria will do much better on the test and you can discover what she knows."

CASE 3.5 Mainstreaming and Inclusion

The Adamant Parents

Jason is in grade 9. It is early in the semester, but there are signs Jason is having difficulties in some subjects, especially math and English. The school decided to have him tested by the special education department of the school and he is found to have difficulty processing information. Ms. Faro, the head of the special needs department, thinks he should take math and English with other special needs children, and have additional help with other subjects in the daily class designed for this purpose. Apart from math and English, this arrangement will permit him to be included in his other classes.

Ms. Faro calls Jason's parents and asks them to come for an interview. During the interview Ms. Faro goes over the test results and explains that Jason has a learning disability and that this will limit his ability to function in the regular math and English classes. She tells the parents that, with help, Jason might be able to rejoin mainstream classes in grade 10 or grade 11. The parents resist the arrangement. They are firm believers in inclusion and that Jason should be educated in the regular classroom. They insisted on this throughout Jason's education and have only agreed to special help for Jason at the end of the school day. They want no part of a situation where Jason goes to special classes. They don't want him to seem different from the other students.

Ms. Faro explains that all schools within the city have a policy of special arrangement and if testing reveals a learning disability, it is documented. This means the student is entitled to special education.

The parents are adamant. Jason must be educated in the regular classroom. It is up to the teachers to ensure that Jason succeeds. Parents are expected to be supportive.

Children of Poverty

Burden and Byrd (2003), in discussing children at risk, quote Redick and Vail (1991). Children at risk "include youth in poverty, youth in stress, youth without a home, abused and neglected youth, academically disadvantaged youth, youth from dysfunctional families, youth with eating disorders, chemically abusive youth, sexually active youth, homosexual youth, youth with sexually transmitted diseases, pregnant youth and young parents, delinquent youth, youth in gangs, drop outs, suicidal youth, youth members of Satanic cults, overemployed youth, mentally ill youth, disabled and handicapped youth, and lonely and disengaged youth" (Burden & Byrd, 2003, p. 107). A whole text could be devoted to these concerns, and no teacher could deal with all of these problems. An interesting development is that of making schools to some extent community schools. Rather than have the school and its staff alone deal with the range of concerns, schools reach out to experts within the community. The community school model is worth investigation.

The concept "at risk" means that something can be done; it is not too late, issues dealt with early will avoid serious problems in the future. Under the old adage, we teach children not subjects, teachers are at the front line of awareness. They can perceive potential concerns early and find the means of dealing with them.

Many at-risk situations link to low socioeconomic status, in particular, poverty. Woolfolk (2004), in discussing social class differences, defines socioeconomic status (SES) as "the term used by sociologists for variations in wealth, power, and prestige." She says, "Social class is a significant dimension of cultural differences, often overpowering other differences such as ethnicity or gender" (p. 157). In linking SES to in-school achievement, Woolfolk points out that "There are many relationships between SES and school performance. For example, it is well documented that high-SES students of all ethnic groups show higher average levels of achievement on test scores and stay in-school longer than low-SES students," and that "poverty, during a child's preschool years appears to have the greatest negative impact" (p. 158). There are more children living in poverty in North America than most people realize. Poverty rates are prevalent across ethnic groups including African American, American Indian, and Hispanic, although poor children come from all walks of life (McDevitt & Ormrod, 2002, p. 559). A disproportionally large number of minority children are placed in special education. Many of these live in poverty. Children living in poverty face additional challenges to those normally associated with physical, cognitive, and social development (p. 559). Children can be disadvantaged by a host of serious family and community problems, substandard nutrition and health care, inadequate housing, gaps in knowledge affecting readiness for schooling, lack of positive role models, and by dangerous surroundings. These students are subjected to chronically emotionally stressful conditions, causing them to function less effectively, and the probability of physical, mental, or socioemotional disabling conditions is increased (p. 560). These conditions are, in particular, a result of poor or inappropriate pre- or postnatal nutrition, substance abuse, or poor, harsh, and inconsistent parenting. For example, if the mother abused alcohol during pregnancy, the risk of a child being born with fetal alcohol syndrome (FAS) or fetal alcohol effect (FAE) is increased. Damage is characterized by low birth weight, heart problems, facial abnormality, small brain size, and developmental disabilities (Hardman et al., 2002, p. 296). FAS is the leading cause of developmental disabilities in Western civilization today (Kellerman, 1999, p. 1).

The Canadian Teachers' Federation (1989) reports that one child in six under the age of 16 is poor (the proportion is moving toward one in five). The situation in the United States is similar. Poor children, the federation says, are at increased risk of physical, psychological, social, cultural, behavioral, and educational problems. They suggest the potential effects of child poverty:

> *On physical health.* Infant mortality; death from birth defects; infectious disease; accidents (fire, falls, drowning, and motor vehicle accidents); low birthweight; sudden infant death syndrome; obesity; iron deficiency, dental caries; upper respiratory tract infections, chronic ear infections; mental retardation

On mental health. Higher suicide rates; higher homicide rates; increased narcotic addiction; increased drug and alcohol abuse; increased learning disability; increased child abuse; decreased school performance

On barriers to health care. Decrease in accessibility; decrease in availability; lack of coordinated care; lack of preventive health care; lack of comprehensive care; problems in communication

Low-income children are more likely to experience hunger; effects of inadequate child care; behavior problems; low self-esteem

Many will have difficulty in school. Less motivation to learn; delayed cognitive development; lower achievement; less participation in extracurricular activities; different types of teacher–student interactions; interrupted school attendance; lower university attendance; increased risk of illiteracy; higher dropout rates

School-related difficulties with long-term personal and social consequences. Illiteracy; delinquency; difficulties in personal adjustment; underemployment; unemployment (See www.campaign2000.ca)

McDevitt and Ormrod (2002, p. 559) offer suggestions for working with children from low-income families. Most of these also apply to working with special needs children.

- Identify and build on students' strengths.
- Create a sense of community in the school and classroom.
- Establish clear and consistent expectations for student behavior.
- Place a high priority on developing reading skills.
- Show the relevance of school activities and subject matter to students' lives.
- Communicate high (but achievable) expectations for students' success.
- Make sure students' basic needs (e.g., food and clothing) are met.
- Have compassion for the parents.
- Seek out good role models for students.

Accommodating Gender Differences in the Classroom

Literature on the Effects of Gender

To say that males and females are different is a truism. We should be aware of how they are, or should be, equal. Males and females *are* different in obvious and subtle ways. How people are viewed is determined by heredity and environment. *Sex differences* are biologically determined; *gender differences* are psychologically and socially controlled (Sternberg & Williams, 2002, p. 208). Trends about notions of gender and sex roles have changed significantly, particularly in recent years, and are continuing to change. In the past, gender roles were quite rigid. Notably, the horizons of females have been expanding, though acceptable role ideas for males have been much slower to change (Kantrowitz & Kalb, 1998, p. 56). Teachers must be sensitive to gender similarities and differences, avoid stereotyping, and contribute to reducing it.

Children develop images of themselves based on experiences in family, school, peer groups, and other social situations. Preschoolers tend to have more stereotyped ideas about sex roles than older children (Woolfolk, 2004). Elementary school children adopt beliefs about what it means to be male or female (p. 171). Up to about 1970, early childhood textbook portrayals of males and females were heavily stereotyped. More recently, publishers have tried to avoid stereotyping and be gender neutral.

Though gender roles now are not as rigid, gender discrimination, obvious and subtle, still exists (Woolfolk, 2004, Brophy & Good, 1995). In class, female students receive less attention and encouragement than male students (AAUW, 1992). Not too long ago, in many ways, girls were often at the bottom end of the gender gap, and the move to equity is not yet complete. Almost all efforts to reduce gender stereotyping have been directed toward improving the lot of females. However, as the twenty-first century begins, a more balanced approach to the issue of gender equity is needed.

Several studies have found no overall difference in scores of male and female students on intelligence tests (Sternberg & Williams, 2002, p. 209). Differences, though small, do emerge on different types of performance. Females score a little higher than males on many aspects of verbal ability; males do better on many visual-spatial tasks, and differences can be substantial (p. 209). Males outperform females on standardized quantitative tests—particularly at the high end of performance on math tests; boys normally do better at certain kinds of problem solving (p. 210). Oddly, public schools place twice as many boys as girls in special education (Vaishnev, 2002).

The experience of students in your classroom will affect how they assess their abilities. Have you thought about how you respond to male and female students during question-and-answer and class discussion? Loevinger (1994) says studies of classrooms, kindergarten through graduate school, have shown that teachers tend to:

- Call on male students more often than female students
- Allow more time for male students to respond to questions
- Make more eye contact with male students following questions
- Recall the names of male students better
- Use the names of male students when calling on them
- Attribute previous comments by male students in class discussion (e.g., "earlier, Joe said")
- Accept callouts from male students, but tell female students to raise their hands if they want their response to be recognized
- Interrupt female students before they are done responding
- Ask more higher-order or critical thinking questions of male students and coach male students to develop their thoughts by giving them more extended and specific feedback on the quality of their ideas
- Provide more specific information to male students on how to complete projects rather than doing it for them
- Praise male students who are assertive and vocal, but call female students with such qualities "rude," "aggressive," or "show off"

Good and Brophy (1995) suggest that there are "tendencies to reinforce assertiveness and achievement striving in boys but to reinforce conformity and responsibility in girls" (p. 567). The authors add, there are tendencies for "boys and girls to differ in patterns of interest and achievement in various subjects" (p. 574)—for example, mathematics and sciences and computers for boys, and French language and poetry for girls.

Early research on sex differences may have been flawed. Many early studies did not represent the population as a whole; more recently, better methods and more representative samples have been used (Halpern, 2000). In the past, girls got much more attention from researchers than boys. "Developmental research has been focused on girls; now it's their brothers' turn. Boys need help too" (Kantrowitz & Kalb, 1998, p. 55).

"An abundance of physical energy and the urge to conquer . . . are normal male characteristics" (p. 56). Boys are much more likely than girls to have discipline problems and to be diagnosed with attention deficit disorder. They are overrepresented in special education classes and are more likely to commit violent crimes (p. 55). Girls are more likely to use indirect methods of aggression, such as spreading rumors, excluding, and ostracizing (Crick, Bigbee, & Howes (1996). Recent media reports suggest that violence by girls is increasing.

Kantrowitz and Kalb (1998) say that, in early elementary school, the demands on boys can increase stress (p. 58). Boys and girls develop at different rates, and development of the fine motor skills of boys (e.g., holding a pencil) lags behind those of girls. Learning to read often occurs later in boys. They are more active, which is "not the best combination for academic achievement" (p. 58). Their exuberance, gross motor skills, visual and spatial skills—things they are good at—are not well rewarded. Boys enforce macho male stereotypes on each other, avoiding display of tenderness or compassion. Boys do want and need attention but may not know how to ask for it (p. 58). The authors (pp. 58–59) suggest characteristics of boys and girls that are normally present at various age levels (Table 3.2).

Eliminating Gender Stereotyping

What can you do to ensure that both boys and girls are not subjected to gender stereotyping? The needs of neither should take a back seat. Consider Woolfolk's (2004) guidelines for avoiding sexism:

- Check whether textbooks and other materials present an honest view of options open to both sexes (e.g., how are males and females portrayed at work, leisure, or the home? How are the sexes presented in the media?)
- Analyze your teaching for evidence of unintended bias (e.g., how do you group students for certain activities? Do you call on one sex for answers, such as boys for math and poetry for girls?)

TABLE 3.2   *Characteristics of Girls and Boys*

Period	Boys	Girls
4–6 years	Start of school is a tough time—boys have to curb aggression; lag behind in reading; may be hyperactive.	Well suited to school—calm, get along well with others; sensitive to social cues; reading and writing comes easily.
7–10 years	Good at gross motor skills; behind in finer control; many are among the best, but most poorest students are boys.	Very good years for girls—on average outperform boys; excel in verbal skills; hold their own in math.
11–13 years	Mixed bag—dropout rates climb; good students begin to pull ahead of girls in math, catch up in some verbal skills.	Puberty starts—most vulnerable time; many experience depression; as many as 15% may try suicide.
14–16 years	Entering adolescence—a rough time; drug and alcohol use and aggressive behavior, and rebellion may occur.	Eating disorders a major concern; anorexia can start as early as 8 but typical at 11 or 12, bulimia at 15.

Source: Kantrowitz & Kalb, 1998, pp. 58–59. From Newsweek, May 5, © 1998 Newsweek, Inc. All rights reserved. Reprinted by permission.

- Look for ways your school might limit the options open to males or females (e.g., what career choice advice is being given to males and females in the school? Are sports and other programs equally available for boys and girls?)
- Determine whether your language is gender free (e.g., do you say "mail carrier" rather than "postman"? Do you say "committee head," not "chairman"? (p. 174)

Suggestions for making classrooms gender and race equitable and appropriate are added by Scott and McCollum (1993, pp. 174–190):

- Challenge misconceptions about gender through class presentations and discussions.
- Model sex-appropriate behavior.
- Organize classrooms so students are not segregated by gender.
- Encourage girls to use equipment often reserved for boys.
- Structure cooperative learning group activities to occur across gender lines.
- Avoid assigning sex-stereotyped tasks (e.g., frog dissection by boys and taking minutes by girls).
- Don't overlook capable but quiet students.
- Give male and female students equal attention and equally specific feedback.
- Monitor classroom dynamic to ensure that discussion does not become dominated by more aggressive students.
- Vary the classroom structure to include more than just competitive modes of learning.
- Revise curricula to include female experiences in more than stereotypical ways.
- Increase the amount of time you allow students to formulate an answer to a question.
- Avoid sexist language in class discussions, lectures, and written materials.
- Do not ask female students to perform activities you would not request of male students or vice versa.

You and other teachers have an important role in reducing gender stereotyping. "Sound teacher training is key to reducing sex stereotyping," says Sandy Bernard, president of AAUW and a former Head Start teacher (in AAUW, 1992). We add that inservice training also should occur (see www.aauw.org/research/girls_education/hssg.cfm).

Sexual Orientation in the Classroom

Homophobia is a "force stronger than gravity in the lives of adolescent boys" (Kindlon & Thompson, 2000; Thompson, 1999).

> Under a barrage of homophobic attitude, and without positive reinforcement, many gay and lesbian teens will run away from home and turn to alcohol, drugs, prostitution, and suicide. These kids remain at risk as long as educators fail to recognize their unique needs and fail to find the courage to address those needs. (Dowler-Coltman, 1995, p. 12)

Whether to acknowledge the presence of gay, lesbian, bisexual, and transsexual students in schools and, if so, how to deal with differences in sexual orientation, remains an extremely controversial issue. Certain cultural groups think anything other than a heterosexual orientation is deviant. Some religious groups believe homosexuality is sinful. Some individuals call it unnatural. Homophobia is common, with many people rabidly so (Ramsey, 2004, p. 133). Attitudes of people are slowly changing, and the rights of nonheterosexual partners are beginning to be acknowledged by the courts and in other settings. Even in the most open-minded situations, homosexuals remain at risk as targets for discrimination (p. 134). In school, gay students are frequently marginalized. Even students who are not gay but who have gay parents or other family members may be hurt by homophobia—they face the same barriers, and choices, as students from racial, cultural, or socioeconomic minorities.

Not every teacher believes having a different sexual orientation is morally or socially acceptable. Almost all teachers, however, believe that *every child needs to be treated with dignity and respect.* With this belief, and by not engaging in, nor allowing, discrimination, they take an active step in eradicating homophobia from their classrooms (Frieman, O'Hara, & Settel, 1996). Schools can foster a safe environment for all students. This is not easy. It means "gay bashing," verbal and physical, open or subtle, cannot be tolerated. Schools hurt students who are gay or who have gay caregivers by not acknowledging differences in sexual orientation If homosexuality is not treated in the curriculum, if discussions about the topic are avoided, gay students may think they are unimportant or rejected, that they are a lesser and isolated group. Teachers need to realize that gay students may be struggling with, and agonizing about, their sexuality, and about whether they should "come out." They may experience self-doubt and depression, which can affect behavior and school performance. Shockingly, it is estimated that the suicide rate among gay, lesbian, and bisexual youth is four times higher than that of their heterosexual peers (Canadian Public Health Association, 1998, p. 6).

Erlandson (2005), in a study published by the Saskatchewan Teachers' Federation, provides suggestions that you may wish to follow. He says, don't assume all students in the class are heterosexual—some may be gay or lesbian. You can examine your homophobic and heterogenic assumptions (e.g., if a person is HIV positive, that person may not be gay). Educate yourself about homophobia. You can nurture an inclusive environment so each student can feel accepted and respected. The curriculum and materials can be screened for bias and be representative of diversity. The language you use can be inclusive, allowing for homosexual possibilities (e.g., "partner" instead of girlfriend or boyfriend). When minority issues are discussed, specific mention can be made about sexual minorities. Acceptance and tolerance can be modeled. Incidents of harassment, denigration, antigay jokes, and graffiti can be immediately addressed. General principles for working with diverse populations follow. These principles also apply to sexual minorities.

CASE 3.6 Gender

The Gap

James was doing well in his internship. He enjoyed his major, which was English. He was in an excellent school. He enjoyed the mix of students in the classes. He liked the challenge of teaching language arts to students from a range of ethnic backgrounds and appreciated the opportunity of teaching students of mixed ability ranging from gifted to those with learning difficulties. Currently he was teaching Shakespeare's *Midsummer Night's Dream* to grade 9. The play, with its very diverse list of characters, seemed to lend itself to a class of diverse needs.

Today he was expecting his faculty advisor, Dr. Witt. Because his lessons and units had been thoroughly planned with a variety of teaching strategies, he was confident the day would go well. The students had been well behaved and enjoying his classes, and his cooperating teacher was pleased and impressed. He looked forward to Dr. Witt and more feedback. So, he was surprised when into the class walked Dr. Helen Chang. "Hello, James," said Dr. Chang, "sorry for the sudden change. Dr. Witt has been called away, so he asked me to step in at the last moment." "I have grade 9 language arts first period. Then I have a planning period," James said. "Great," said Dr. Chang, "We can meet and discuss the class and then preconference the others you are teaching today. Dr. Witt speaks highly of you. I'm looking forward to the day."

James taught his class, which seemed to go very well. The students read their parts with energy. There were lively question-and-answer moments. This pleased James because his target was on questioning skills with particular focus on question distribution. His data sheet was his seating plan. He noticed that Dr. Chang was completing this and writing quite a lot of notes. Still, he was sure he was doing well. He was a little worried about the scene they were reading, which was the love scene between Demetrius and Helena. Helena was fawning on Demetrius with such lines as "I am your spaniel" and "Demetrius, the more you beat me I will fawn on you."

James hoped Dr. Chang would appreciate the exaggerated humor and that Helena and Helen were not too much of a coincidence! When the bell rang, he met with Dr. Chang. They discussed the lesson in general terms. Dr. Chang asked James how the lesson went; what he thought were its strengths, and areas he would change. James thought things went well and there were no major things to alter. He thought he would ask the students to read in the front of the room rather than from their desks. Apart from this, he was pleased with the lesson. Then Dr. Chang took up the data sheet and showed her notes on question distribution. "What do you think?" "I seem to have questioned most students," said James, "except for Jane and . . . Anita." Dr. Chang pointed to a column with her pen. "Do you notice anything else, the number of checks by each name?" "I see I asked more questions of some of the students," replied James, not clear what he was supposed to notice. "You don't notice that most questions are to boys," Dr. Chang said, with a hint of triumph in her voice. "Perhaps the boys had their hands up more," said James, not the least bit phased. "Maybe so," said Dr. Chang, pointedly, "but how would you get a more equal distribution?" "I guess," said James, realizing where Dr. Chang wanted to take him, "I should ask questions by name." "Well, let's try it for your next target," said Dr. Chang. "Research shows boys can dominate a class during questions, with some exceptions. A teacher must be conscious of this and ensure the fair participation of all."

James thought about Dr. Chang's comments. Certainly the evidence on the data sheet supported her comments. He wondered what Dr. Witt would have noticed.

Diversity Issues and Approaches

Mainstreaming and Inclusion

How can you and other teachers cope with the perplexing mix of backgrounds, state of health, abilities, dispositions, and behaviors in a typical school system? Students range from severely disabled to gifted and well adjusted. In particular, how can you provide quality instruction for students who are economically disadvantaged, disabled, or socially and educationally deficient? Should special students be grouped homogeneously in special classrooms, special schools, residential schools, regular classrooms with pullout programs, integrated but within-class special attention or tasks, or completely integrated in regular classrooms?

The term *mainstreaming* usually refers to selective placement of special education students in one or more "regular" classrooms (Rogers, 1993, p. 1). The student needs the opportunity to be mainstreamed by being able to keep up with other students in the work assigned. *Inclusion* refers to educating each child, as much as possible, in the school and classroom he or she would otherwise attend. Support service is brought to the child (the child does not have to move). The child does not have to keep up with other students (p. 1).

Hardman et al. (2002) provide an overview of educational service options for students with disabilities. These range from the most inclusive to the most restrictive, and responsibility taken on by general education to responsibility assumed by special education (p. 29).

It is believed that less able learners, regardless of disability, should be able to observe, interact, and develop friendships with the more able. Some call this "normalization." This means every exceptional learner should have an education and living environment that is as "normal" as possible. Increasingly, services are available within the mainstream of the school and special needs children are being educated alongside children who are not. Mainstreaming, sometimes called "educational integration," refers to "inclusion of special students in the general educational process. Students are considered mainstreamed if they spend any part of the school day with regular-class peers" (Lewis & Doorlag, 2003, p. 4). Creating a safe, warm, and accepting classroom is important if inclusion is to be successful. To accomplish this, the teacher needs to model treating others with dignity and respect, focus on strengths, speak directly to students (not around them), and demonstrate appreciation and acceptance of diversity. This teacher fosters social interaction in and outside of the classroom, and encourages participation while fostering independence. Students are encouraged, as appropriate, to assist those with exceptional needs.

Research on the effects of mainstreaming and inclusion paints a "murky" picture. Good and Brophy (1995) make three generalizations on the effects of mainstreaming: "most research has been on program labels and has addressed only simple questions; . . . one program label often means different things in different settings; . . . even when labels convey similar meanings, a particular philosophy may be implemented in various ways" (pp. 582–583). The authors add three generalizations from the research on mainstreaming: (1) "programs that take students with mildly disabling conditions from regular classrooms and place them in special rooms for instruction appear to have less positive effects on achievement than approaches in which students receive instruction in regular classrooms with nondisabled peers"; (2) "the quality of instruction that students with mild disabilities receive in regular classrooms is still low in too many instances"; and (3) "many special educators believe that educators need to reduce substantially the numbers of students who are given special-education labels and assigned to be taught in pull-out programs" (p. 583). The authors give four broad conclusions:

1. Pull-out instruction (instruction that occurs in the regular classroom) is overused.
2. Students who have mild disabilities learn in similar ways and generally benefit from the same type of instruction as other students.
3. Students with mild disabilities usually are best instructed in regular classrooms.
4. Considerably more research needs to be focused on the process of reintegrating students with learning disabilities. (p. 584)

Research on programs intended to supplement instruction, and compensatory and remedial educational (Chapter 1) programs, are often so poorly coordinated that learning may actually be impeded; teacher aides who may have little or no training, because this is less expensive, often serve as instructional staff; special needs students often spend too much time working alone at their desks; teacher expectations are often too low and teachers tend to teach at students' present levels of functioning rather than to the levels needed for success; programs are much less effective for students with severe problems; and when students achieve better skills they often are not moved and become "lifers," mainly because of the poor quality of instruction.

Most authorities agree that mainstreaming, or inclusion, while far from fail-proof, is desirable but, among other things, the adequacy of teacher preparation and resources is often criticized. Some argue that mainstreaming, like many innovations, is oversold and underfunded.

Tomlinson (1999) observes, "In differentiated classrooms, students begin where students are, not at the front of a curriculum guide" (p. 21). She compares traditional and differentiated classrooms (p. 26) as outlined in Table 3.3.

Curriculum Concerns

A concern in teaching for diversity is the design and delivery of the curriculum. What is to be taught is as important as how it is to be taught. The nature of the texts, materials, media, and today, web sites, affects the diverse students in the classroom. Curriculum selection can be controversial. What aspects of what cultures should be studied? What values and beliefs regarding family structure and sexual preferences can be examined? Once diversity in all its forms is accepted, the teacher has difficult choices. Some have been addressed earlier in this chapter. In terms of multiculturalism, Banks (2003) speaks of the "demographic imperative" and, although his main concern is with the growing ethnicity of North America, this is a world issue. He states, "Because of the growing ethnic, racial, language, and religious diversity throughout the world, citizenship education needs to be changed in substantial ways to prepare students to function effectively in the twenty-first century" (p. xxi). Curriculum planners need to take a broader look at what should be included. The social studies and literature, the sciences and the arts, physical education, and the languages need to adjust curriculum to meet the new imperatives.

Joyce, Weill, and Calhoun (2004), present the case that "children of poverty are stereotyped as inherently poor learners," and in order to address this, "the curriculum has been slowed down and watered down and very simple" whereas, by contrast, it should be

TABLE 3.3   *Traditional versus Differentiated Classrooms*

Traditional Classroom	Differentiated Classroom
Student differences are masked or acted on when problematic.	Student differences are studied as a basis for planning.
Assessment is most common at the end of learning, to see "who got it."	Assessment is ongoing and diagnostic.
A relatively narrow sense of intelligence prevails.	Focus on multiple forms of intelligence is evident.
A single definition of intelligence exists.	Excellence is defined by individual growth from the starting point.
Student interest is infrequently tapped.	Students are guided in making interest-based learning choices.
Relatively few learning profile options are taken into account.	Many learning profile options are provided for.
Whole-class instruction dominates.	Many instructional arrangements are used.
Coverage of texts and curriculum drives instruction.	Student readiness, interest, and learning profiles shape instruction.

Source: Tomlinson, 1999.

a "rigorous curriculum with challenging instructional strategies designed to improve the learning capacity of the students" (p. 360).

Lesson plans, unit plans, curriculum materials, and strategies and assessment approaches must address the diversity and the learning approaches of the students.

General Principles for Teaching Diverse Learners

You will want every student in your classroom to develop a knowledgeable and confident self-image. Students can learn to stand up for themselves and others in the face of prejudice. To accommodate diversity and foster equity, establish a comfortable, risk-free environment and provide a diverse-populations-balanced anti-biased curriculum. You can model acceptance and respect for *all* students. The Center for Teaching and Learning (2001) provides guidelines for inclusive teaching that you may find valuable:

- Get to know your students as individuals rather than as representatives of a particular group.
- Never ask a student to speak for a whole group (e.g., women, Hispanics, Muslims).
- Accommodate different learning styles and promote collaboration between students.
- Do not let injurious statements pass without comment.
- Allow students to disagree with you or others, but within guidelines that promote a safe learning atmosphere in the classroom.
- Reflect diverse backgrounds on your syllabus, in your readings, and in other materials such as visual aids.
- Depersonalize controversial topics and structure assignments to let students choose topics with which they are comfortable.
- Understand why you have designed your syllabus in the way that you have.
- Make your course goals clear to all students and give continual feedback on how students are meeting them. (pp. 11–12)

We would add:

- Select instructional (curriculum) material that accommodates the diversity of students.
- Select instructional approaches that address the range of learning styles of students.

LINKING PRACTICE TO THEORY

What has been your experience with diversity in the classroom? Why is respect for diversity more prevalent today? What is the social context of your location? Are there conflicting views on how teachers should approach classroom differences? Do your views conflict with majority or minority opinion? What is the teacher's responsibility to diversity?

Summary

Four dimensions contribute to diversity of learners in classrooms: learning approach preferences, cultural background, exceptionality, and gender and sexual orientation. Each student has a unique learning style, brain hemisphere, strength, and learning modality preference. Different preferences respond to different instructional approaches; teachers also have learning approach preferences but may teach the way they were taught. The implication for teachers is that a variety of instructional approaches should be used as they adapt to different learning styles; and students should be helped to learn how to "flex" from one approach to another.

Students' cultural backgrounds influence how well they do in school. One's values and beliefs may lead to prejudice, discrimination, and racism. Teachers must recognize that their values influence how they react to others. They must accommodate cultural background, recognize bias in materials, respect differences, recognize similarities, and become proficient in cross-cultural teaching. All have a duty to combat racism and help all learners achieve potential.

Inclusion is more and more common. Every classroom has at least some special needs or exceptional learners who may have learning problems or handicaps, be gifted, bilingual, socioeconomically disadvantaged, migrant children, or immigrant children. Working with diversity contributes to the complexity of teaching. Both preservice and inservice teachers need to learn more about coping with diversity.

The effect of schools on developing notions of gender and sexual orientation has been controversial. Most research and writing has focused on females. Recently, more attention is being paid to the effect of schooling on males and the impact of homophobia. A balanced approach to reducing stereotyping and discrimination is needed.

Activities

1. Have the class brainstorm ways in which students in a class may "differ" from each other.

2. Complete a learning style inventory such as the Kolb Learning Style Inventory (1976) or the McCarthy 4MAT System (1988). Divide students into groups mixed in terms of style type. Groups select lessons that learners of each of the four learning types would *not* like.

3. Complete individual hemispheric mode profiles using an instrument.

4. Complete a learning modalities inventory such as the Barbe and Swassing instrument.

5. Discuss the following: "What kind of learning experiences would be most suitable for me as a student?" "How might the stimulus be varied to respond to all configurations?" "What value is there in knowing more about learning style?" "Should we as teachers try to set up learning experiences that consistently match each student's individual learning style?" "What advantage is there in varying the teaching style regardless of the learning style?"

6. In subject area groups, develop a lesson plan for a class of learners predominantly of one style. The lesson plan should be shared with the total class together with the rationale for the chosen plan. The class should be invited to challenge the presenters and explore a variety of alternative approaches.

7. Use awareness-raising simulations like those by human rights or global education organizations.

8. Acquire the commercial Bafa Bafa simulation (available at www.simulationtrainingsystems. com; see also Hicks, 1981; Pike & Selby, 1999) or a similar cross-cultural simulation.

9. Prepare a lesson in a preferred subject area that has a multi- or cross-cultural major objective.

10. Join a group of four or five to discusses instances of racist remarks or behavior.

11. Invite community speakers who represent minorities to speak about racism and its effects.

12. Debate the following: (a) Resolved, that disabled students be taught separately from the more able students; or, (b) Resolved, that gifted students should be allowed to progress through the academic grades at their own pace.

13. Visit an elementary, a middle years, and a secondary school. Interview the principal or counselor about arrangements for special needs learners and, if possible, view facilities and speak with teachers who work with special learners. If classrooms are mainstreamed, ask a teacher how he or she works with special needs students.

14. Get in touch with your district, state, or national Council for Exceptional Children and Department of Education to discover and report the services available to teachers.

15. Seek permission to observe an exceptional learner in either a mainstreamed, resource, or accelerated classroom. Record everything the student says and does for half a day. Report your observations

to a group of five peers. With them, arrive at a tentative interpretation.

16. Many parents favor inclusion, especially in early childhood. They believe it is important to include young children with disabilities in classrooms with their typical peers. Divide the class into two groups, one in favor of inclusion and one not. (There are many web sites that will provide you information.) As part of the debate, provide a list of your sources.

17. Investigate the special education policies of your local school board.

18. Several school boards in the United States and Canada are including reading material for elementary students that reflects changes in family structures such as same-sex parents. For example, *Heather Has Two Mommies,* by Leslea Newman (2000), created much controversy. *My Two Uncles,* by Judith Vigna (1995), describes a young girl's close relationship with her Uncle Ned and his partner, Uncle Phil. Another well-known title is *Zack's Story: Growing Up with Same-Sex Parents,* by Keith Greenberg (1996). As potential teachers, discuss your views on including these and similar books in the elementary curriculum.

19. Bring in samples of texts currently used in elementary, middle years, and secondary schools. Examine them for sexual stereotyping as described in this chapter. Present your findings according to the subject groups in your class.

20. Review Loevinger's (1994) list of teacher behaviors toward male and female students. Discuss your experiences in school. Do you consider the list to be accurate today?

21. Research and discuss the benefits to special needs learners of computer teaching programs that use direct instruction and those that use a constructivist approach.

22. Brainstorm and discuss applications in technology that would benefit gifted children.

23. Have representatives from the class take two different sides. One group will present the case for inclusion and the other will present the case for special education separate from the "mainstream."

24. Have students read the following article from the *Washington Post* and, in groups, discuss its significance to teaching and schooling.

U.S. Counts One in 12 Children as Disabled Census Reflects Increase of Handicapped Youth

By D'Vera Cohn, Washington Post *Staff Writer, Friday, July 5, 2002, page B01*

Database editor Dan Keating contributed to this report

One of every dozen U.S. children and teenagers—5.2 million—has a physical or mental disability, according to new figures from the 2000 Census that reflect sharp growth in the nation's young disabled population over the past decade.

In the Washington area, the census reported that 87,000 young people, or one in 14, were handicapped. The disabilities captured by the census could range in severity from mild asthma to serious mental illness or retardation demanding full-time care.

The figures, which covered children ages 5 to 20, are the first collected on childhood disability in the decennial census in more than a century. But data from other sources have shown a rapid increase in the number and rate of childhood handicaps. Special-education enrollment rose twice as fast as overall school enrollment in the past decade. And a growing number of children receive federal Social Security payments because they suffer from serious disabilities.

The rising numbers come after a period of dramatic change in the nation's approach to disabilities. A vision of inclusiveness has been written into laws requiring equal access to services, including the 25-year-old federal law guaranteeing education to all handicapped children and the 10-year-old Americans With Disabilities Act.

While the extent to which society should accommodate people with disabilities is still being argued in courts and public discourse, the rising numbers already present a challenge to school systems and other public agencies.

Some reasons for the rise can be quantified. But it is difficult to know precisely how much is attributable to an increase in certain conditions and how much is explained by greater recognition, changing definitions or more willingness to report a handicap.

Improvements in medical care now can save low-birth-weight babies, whose greater risk of problems may explain some of the increase. Also, medical advances are allowing more people with spinal cord injuries or Down syndrome to live longer. Childhood obesity is rising, and with it the risk of disease such as diabetes. But there are more theories than answers for the sharp rise in autism, asthma and learning disabilities.

The definition of disability has broadened to include conditions such as attention deficit disorder, which decades ago was often not even recognized. Diagnosis of disability also has become more precise and aggressive. And some people with disabilities may be stepping forward because of lessened stigma or the availability of benefits.

Glenn T. Fujiura, a professor of disability studies at the University of Illinois at Chicago, said that although the reasons for the increase may not be clear, the results are. "More children are coming forward with needs and limitations that must be met," he said.

Steven Fine, a federal employee who lives in Columbia, has seen this firsthand as the father of a 12-year-old boy with severe autism, a neurological disease.

"Ten years ago, when my son was diagnosed, autism was a rare thing that no one had ever heard of," Fine said. "Every year since then, at parents' meetings, the number of diagnoses seems to have increased exponentially.

"Now doctors are much quicker—maybe a little too quick—to say your kid has autism," Fine said.

Poor children are more likely to be disabled, surveys have shown, but why that is true is still being debated. The District, which has the region's highest poverty rate, also has the highest rate of childhood disability, at 10 percent. The region's lowest child disability rate, 6 percent, is in Loudoun County, whose poverty rate is the lowest in the region.

Experts offer several possible explanations for the link between poverty and childhood disability, including a higher risk of premature birth or birth to a drug-addicted mother, poor nutrition or more exposure to lead paint, which can cause brain damage.

"If you look at children with disabilities, they are more likely to be in single-parent homes, they are more likely to be poor, they are more likely to be in homes where secondhand smoke exposure is a risk," said Dennis Hogan, a Brown University sociology professor who studies disabled children. "But the direction of the cause and effect is not certain. Single parenthood, per se, is not more likely to produce a disabled child, but poverty associated with being a single mom may well produce that result."

Among metropolitan areas, the Washington region's childhood disability rate ranks in the bottom quarter, and its household income is among the highest. The metro areas with the lowest childhood disability, according to 2000 Census figures analyzed by The Washington Post, are well-off ones such as Hunterdon County, N.J., Stamford, Conn., and the university areas of Charlottesville and Boulder, Colo. The metropolitan areas with the highest child disability rates—at least 10 percent—include Lewiston-Auburn, Maine; Huntington, W. Va.; and Dothan, Ala. All have above-average poverty.

For people of all ages, the census counted 50 million disabled nationally, and more than 740,000 in the Washington area. Specialists say the census numbers probably understate the disability rate by not including people with mild problems, such as a minor speech impediment. That is one reason the nation's special-education enrollment is higher than the census total.

As special education is expanding, so are other activities for disabled children. A Montgomery County soccer league for the handicapped expects to double in size this fall. Parents also increasingly are pressing to include their disabled children in standard summer camps, team sports and after-school programs.

At the Early Years Academy in Manassas, which operates Adventure Day Camp during the summer, "it used to be rare" that children needed to have inhalers and other equipment on hand to prevent or stop asthma attacks, said Samia Harris, school principal and camp director. "Now it just seems to be the norm."

Ellen Tuttle, a school administrator who lives in Herndon, enrolled her 12-year-old daughter who has multiple handicaps in after-school classes in gymnastics, swimming, ice skating and karate that are not just for handicapped children. She has found that most teachers are willing to help, and her daughter often finds one empathetic friend in each class.

"If I put her in a class that might have worse disabilities than she has, she would not have anything to reach for," Tuttle said.

Ruth Spodak, a suburban Maryland psychologist who is a special education consultant, said families who seek ordinary activities for their disabled children encounter everything from outright rejection to quick acceptance.

Some parents volunteer to coach teams or lead Scout troops to ensure that their disabled child can participate, she said. Spodak said children often have more success in "offbeat" activities such as nature camps or performing arts groups.

"Things are moving in the right direction," Spodak said. "I still think we have a ways to go in terms of educating the public and making this a routine kind of availability."

Another trend that special education experts have noticed—with an impact on their budgets—is that more children are arriving with multiple disabilities, which require more intensive services. "Although there has been growth in the number of students, what we see as more significant is the number of services that special education students are receiving," said Patricia Addison, Fairfax County's special education director.

Down the road, more challenges await. Fairfax social service agencies recently were approached by parents of middle school students with multiple disabilities and little hope of being able to work after graduation. County officials are discussing day-care options.

"Right now, if you say 'adult day care,' people think seniors," said John Hudson, director of disability services for the county's Department of Family Services. "They don't think about young people coming out of school."

4 Energizing Learners

The Affective Domain and Motivation

Taxonomies of Educational Objectives

Most teachers are familiar with the taxonomies of educational objectives. These are among the most influential developments in educational ideas. A taxonomy is a classification of the forms of learning from simple to the complex. There are three domains: the cognitive, dealing with levels of knowledge; the affective, concerned with the levels of values perception; and the psychomotor, addressing levels of physical skill. The cognitive domain was developed by Benjamin Bloom in 1956. The affective domain has received less attention. A classic source is that by Krathwohl, Bloom, and Masia (1964). Further work has been done by Dave (1975).

Experienced and novice teachers alike have found these domains useful in developing curriculum and instructional approaches. For example, if you intended to teach a lesson on Shakespeare's *Hamlet,* you could structure your questions in the class from the basic knowledge level, "Who did Hamlet's mother remarry?" to sophisticated synthesis questions on Hamlet's inability to act decisively. Similarly, through the affective domain, a teacher could take a class from awareness of an idea such as "justice" through to the higher level of organizing and conceptualizing a justice system. In teaching a psychomotor skill, the teacher could take students from the ability to imitate the skill to the ability to articulate and explain the essence of the skill to others and to use the skill naturally as an internalized ability (for example, using dancing steps to express an emotion in a ballet). The cognitive and psychomotor domains are discussed and explored elsewhere in the text. The affective domain, in the development of attitudes and values, is a critical foundation for motivating students to achieve the goals of education.

OBJECTIVES

You will be able to:

1. List principles for fostering attitude learning and demonstrate their use in a school classroom.
2. Discuss the importance of affective objectives in typical state or district statements of goals.
3. Include generic affective competencies, presented in this chapter, in your lesson plans.
4. Define motivation and describe three theories explaining motivation.
5. Describe attribution theory and apply it to a learner.
6. List guidelines for increasing motivation of learners.
7. State principles for personality integration and demonstrate use of these in lessons taught.
8. Describe strategies that can be used when working with at-risk learners.
9. State characteristics of and present a personal plan for establishing a positive classroom climate.
10. Teach a microteaching or school classroom lesson with an attitude or value outcome target.

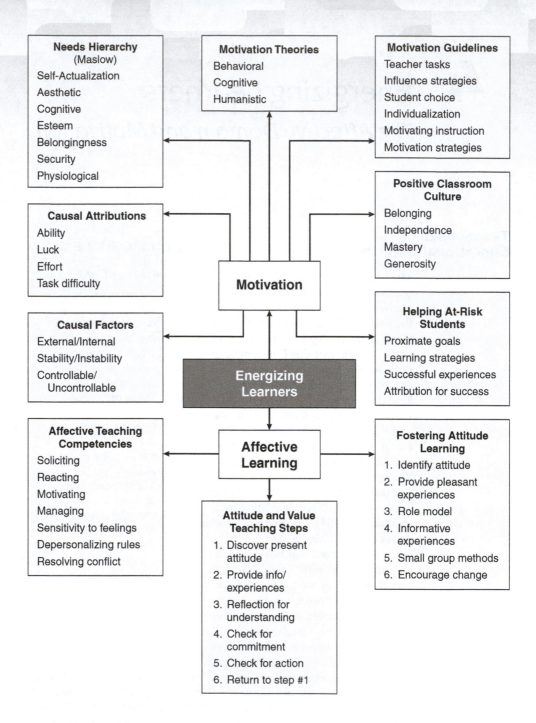

Needs Hierarchy
(Maslow)
Self-Actualization
Aesthetic
Cognitive
Esteem
Belongingness
Security
Physiological

Motivation Theories
Behavioral
Cognitive
Humanistic

Motivation Guidelines
Teacher tasks
Influence strategies
Student choice
Individualization
Motivating instruction
Motivation strategies

Causal Attributions
Ability
Luck
Effort
Task difficulty

Positive Classroom Culture
Belonging
Independence
Mastery
Generosity

Motivation

Causal Factors
External/Internal
Stability/Instability
Controllable/
  Uncontrollable

Energizing Learners

Helping At-Risk Students
Proximate goals
Learning strategies
Successful experiences
Attribution for success

Affective Teaching Competencies
Soliciting
Reacting
Motivating
Managing
Sensitivity to feelings
Depersonalizing rules
Resolving conflict

Affective Learning

Fostering Attitude Learning
1. Identify attitude
2. Provide pleasant experiences
3. Role model
4. Informative experiences
5. Small group methods
6. Encourage change

Attitude and Value Teaching Steps
1. Discover present attitude
2. Provide info/ experiences
3. Reflection for understanding
4. Check for commitment
5. Check for action
6. Return to step #1

The Affective Domain

We eat, play, work, and react with others as total persons—everywhere except in the classroom. Here we pretend, the mind floats suspended from the rest of the human system, at least temporarily. But the pretense serves poorly the aims of education and comes close to revealing what is most wrong with our schools. (Goodlad, 1983, p. 17)

While "verbal information, intellectual skills, and cognitive strategies are all part of the cognitive domain," attitudes and values are part of the affective domain (Driscoll, 2000, p. 355). Citing Gagné (1985), Driscoll states that attitudes are "acquired internal states that influence the choice of personal action, toward some class of things, persons, or events" (p. 355). When attitudes, according to Driscoll, are "organized into a consistent set, philosophy, or world-view that governs subsequent personal action," they are *values*. As a teacher you need to be aware that attitudes and values can serve as motivating forces, and teaching that fosters positive attitudes is part of your job.

Affective education deals with the attitudes and values that shape students' lives and whether students think of themselves as worthwhile, successful human beings. It deals with human meanings, human understandings, and human relationships and experiences, and focuses on attitudes and values (honesty, democracy, fair play), feelings and emotions (such as anxieties or frustrations), "character," personality, prejudices, personal philosophies, self-concept and self-esteem, personal and social adjustment, and mental health in general.

The Importance of and Teaching to Achieve Affective Objectives

Learning is not just cognitive. The affective aspect must be a vital part of the planning, delivery, and evaluation of instruction. The unambiguous mandate for schools to stress affective outcomes does not reflect what often happens in practice. Teachers and parents rank social and emotional goals as the most important, yet both (and the federal No Child Left Behind Act) overstress cognitive achievement. Programs should teach children how to understand themselves and others, how to make decisions, set goals, how to like themselves, how to cope with normal problems, how to clarify values, and how to understand their rights and obligations as human beings and citizens. Arguably, the affective domain is more important than the cognitive; traditionally, however, the focus of schools has been cognitive. Students and teachers are rewarded for academic gains, not affective or humanistic progress. Attention, often, is on information acquisition and low-level cognitive content. Federal and state exams and textbook questions tend to stress heavily the recall or comprehension level.

Learning (a very personal thing) is essentially a construction of personal meanings. It, unavoidably, is an affective experience that is a function of student need. It affects self-concept positively or negatively. If personal need is not met, it is unlikely that there will be a change in behavior. You, as a teacher, need to recognize that the tasks you present need to be challenging but not so difficult the learner feels threatened. As well, the classroom climate you establish should reinforce students' feelings of belonging and being cared for.

Schools' programs can help students become clear about who they are, what they want out of life, and how they can get it without hurting others. Students can have experiences to help them feel good about themselves, become aware of themselves and others, and develop communication and problem-solving skills to cope with things in general. Though it is not easy, teachers can identify and sequence affective content, judge its difficulty, relate it to the experience of learners, and construct appropriate evaluations. Affect and development of pro-social behavior can be built into the curriculum. It can be studied directly or integrated into subject matter. The teacher who is genuine, shows respect, and is empathetic will help further affective goals. Teaching and learning for affect need not be secondary or a hoped-for by-product. Appropriate affective content and teaching methods and student activities can be included. State and district goal statements indicate this is what we need to do.

Teachers can do much to systematically plan for and teach to achieve affective objectives. The Teacher Competence Profile introduced in Chapter 1 includes competencies the new teacher needs to master to help students understand attitudes and values and create a positive relationship with students.

TCP ATTITUDES AND VALUES

Helps students understand attitudes and values

Demonstrates love of learning and respect for others; helps students understand their attitudes and values; sets objectives and selects appropriate activities for the development of attitudes and values; helps students overcome negative attitudes and low self-esteem.

Models disinterest in learning and lack of respect for others; concentrates solely on cognitive and psychomotor objectives; oblivious of student attitudes and self-esteem.

Creates a positive classroom climate conducive to student-centered learning

Creates an enjoyable environment conducive to learning; fosters participation by all learners; deals quickly with interpersonal tensions; creates a positive attitude toward and excitement for learning.

Creates negative attitudes toward others and learning; allows interpersonal tensions to build.

Shows interest in individual students

Discovers individual student interests; promotes the development of specific abilities and interests of individual students; makes an effort to know students personally; establishes appropriate relationships to enhance student development.

Does not make an effort to discover individual student interests and abilities; does not establish a cordial relationship with each student.

Encourages and supports students

Encourages individuals and class to try their best and fosters development of a positive self-concept; fosters development of positive attitudes toward others and the school; sets challenging but achievable goals; shows confidence that students can achieve goals.

Does not encourage students to overcome barriers or to achieve potential; does not show confidence in students; is sarcastic or belittles and generally attacks self-concept of individuals; allows or encourages negative attitudes toward self, others, or the school.

Affective Teaching Competencies

Become aware of the learning needs of your students and strive to set and maintain a climate characterized by positive relationships. Certain teacher behaviors or competencies can be used to understand students, involve, motivate, manage the class, and provide instruction. Building your ability to use affective teaching competencies has powerful ramifications for good classroom management. Affective competencies can be grouped as soliciting, reacting, motivating, being sensitive to feelings, managing, and resolving conflict (Figure 4.1). Many of these are similar to the suggestions for motivation in the previous section, but focus more on the emotions of the students and the development of attitudes and values.

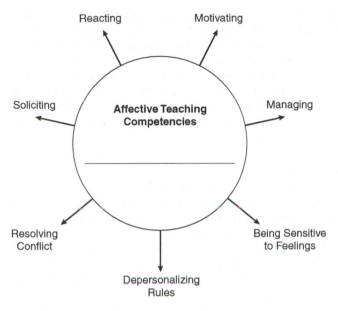

FIGURE 4.1 *Affective Teaching Competencies*

SOLICITING. Learn to give clear, simple instructions. Directions should be lucid and easily understood. Check for understanding; posting instructions or using a handout can help. State expectations briefly, to avoid the confusion of multiple orders or excessive language. Initiate dialogue with students who resist contact. Let students know you are open, nonjudgmental, fair, caring, and willing to help. Don't do things for students—this denies them the chance to succeed; however, an occasional push in the right direction is in order. Reinforce reasonable, sincere effort even though it may not be successful. Finally, invite, but do not force, communication. Show you are open to meeting students.

REACTING. How you react to students or incidents makes a difference. Use accepting, not rejecting language. Affective messages are communicated verbally through word choice and intonation. Facial expressions and body language are the two main ways to communicate feelings nonverbally. Recognize and acknowledge student efforts. Notice when they are working and encourage them. Reinforce work that is well done and reward positive effort. Give corrections without criticisms: for example, "That's not exactly right, but close," "Let me show you another way," "Have you thought of . . . ?," "How do you think this might work?," "You're doing better," "Here's another way of trying to get the answer." Accept and recognize feelings. Knowing feelings is critical. "I understand what makes you feel frustrated." Communicate confidence about a student's ability to learn and grow. Set high, achievable expectations and provide positive reinforcement. Show you are human, admit mistakes. Suppose, for example, you made an assumption about a student and decided to act in a certain way, but subsequent information causes you to change your mind. Explaining this to the student and, if appropriate, apologizing, can enhance your credibility.

MOTIVATING. A positive approach to motivation is critical. Plan for success by gearing expectations and activities to each student's potential level of achievement. Build on student strengths and level of functioning, and take a student from where he is, not where he is supposed to be. Make use of students' interests by picking topics and examples that motivate. Involve students in creating learning activities. Ask students what are fair assignments, interesting activities, and areas for study. Remind students of previous successes. Students want to discover and believe in their capabilities and strengths. This may require emotional "coaching" or support, for example, "Remember how well you did on . . . ?" It rubs off when you express enthusiasm about activities. Your feelings or moods affect student behavior—if you express apathy or tedium (not enthusiasm), student behavior may follow the principle of "contagion."

BEING SENSITIVE TO FEELINGS.   Establishing positive relationships requires that you be sensitive to student feelings and they to yours. You can focus on feelings and reflect them accurately. *Reflection* is a technique for mirroring another's behavior without expressing a positive or negative judgment. This can cause students, themselves, to reflect and reprocess the information. Reflective statements may begin like "You look . . ."; "You sound . . ."; "You seem. . . ." Although there is no need to reveal everything about your personal life, there is benefit in letting students know things such as your favorite season, color, how you feel about important issues, or how student behavior makes you feel—for instance, "I feel very uncomfortable when you. . . ."

MANAGING.   You need good classroom management skills to be free to teach and for students to learn. Structure the classroom and activities to facilitate group learning. Different learning activities may require different furniture arrangements, location of materials, or student groupings. Use questions rather than authoritative statements to remind students of limits. Students may react harshly to authoritative demands. If the goal is to help students learn self-control, provide opportunities for them to monitor personal behavior. Reduce hostility and reactiveness by asking questions. This leads learners to make sense out of what is going on at the time. It is better for learners to explain their behavior than for you to provoke further misbehavior.

ESTABLISHING A POSITIVE CLIMATE FOR LEARNING.   The conditions for learning must be favorable. Classroom settings are referred to with various terms: environment, ambiance, ethos, atmosphere, ecology, and climate. *Climate,* just as with instructional methods, is a matter of choice. A teacher can build a climate that encourages learning. The climate in the classroom needs to free students to learn and teachers to teach. It influences the manner and degree to which the teacher exercises authority, shows warmth and support, encourages competitiveness or cooperation, allows independence and choice, and motivates students. Students must feel important, valued, and that they can achieve. The term *climate* should not be viewed too narrowly. Whereas a classroom climate involves physical facilities and organization, interpersonal communications, and classroom management, it also is linked to the instructional modes used, school and teacher expectations, and evaluation schema. Classroom climate, along with classroom management, is discussed in detail in Chapter 6. For feedback on the climate in your classroom or practice teaching classroom you can use the data collection instrument in Appendix 4.1.

Motivation

In ideal classrooms, students pay attention, ask questions, and want to learn. They do their assignments without complaint and study without being coaxed or cajoled. But teachers don't teach in an ideal world. They often have students who are not motivated; more accurately, they don't seem motivated to work on the tasks their teachers set out for them. (Eggen & Kauchak, 2001, p. 411)

The Teacher Competence Profile stresses motivation as a key skill for the new teacher to master.

TCP MOTIVATION

Motivates students to participate

Student attention stimulated and maintained; uses a variety of stimulation variation techniques; accommodates student needs and interests; builds success experiences appropriate to individual and class; encourages and recognizes effort.

Uninspired approach to instruction; oblivious of student and class needs and interests; does not reinforce achievement by individuals or class; teaches only to the best students or "down the middle."

Experienced teachers realize that failure to motivate students can easily lead to control and discipline problems. A large part of a teacher's job is to create conditions and structure activities that motivate students to achieve their potential. Kauchak and Eggen (2003) note that in "a review of over 83 studies involving beginning teachers from nine countries . . . only classroom management ranked ahead of motivation as a beginning teacher concern" (pp. 11–12).

Defining Motivation

Motivation is usually defined as "an internal state that arouses, directs, and maintains behavior" (Woolfolk, 2004). Woolfolk says that motivation involves five aspects: (1) the choices people make; (2) when they get started in an activity; (3) the intensity of involvement; (4) what causes a person to persist or give up; and (5) what the person thinks or feels during the activity (p. 350). Motivation is not something we can see; we infer it by observing behavior. For example, when a student excitedly volunteers an anecdote related to the topic of a lesson, we say the child is motivated; or, when a student voluntarily selects another book written by an author studied in class, we believe the child is motivated. Motivation is internal—teachers do not "motivate," but they can create conditions that promote motivation.

"Some psychologists explain motivation in terms of personal traits or individual characteristics" and the "drives, needs, incentives, fears, goals, social pressure, self-confidence, interests, curiosity, beliefs, values, and more" (Woolfolk, p. 350). A teacher may, for instance, observe that a certain student has a strong fear of failure while another seems afraid of succeeding; or the teacher may discover a student does not want to be noticed while two others misbehave to gain attention.

Motivation may come from outside or within a person: it may be extrinsic or intrinsic. When a boy practices at the piano for half an hour because his mother promised him a piece of cake if he did, the motivation is extrinsic. *Extrinsic motivation* occurs when the possibility of reward or avoidance of punishment drives behavior. Woolfolk notes that "we are not interested in the activity for its own sake; we care only about what it will gain us" (2004, p. 350). If the boy sits down at the piano and plays without being told (he just enjoys it), motivation is intrinsic. *Intrinsic motivation* stems from factors such as interest or curiosity. Both kinds of motivation are important to teachers. They can make an effort to discover what students find intrinsically motivating and capitalize on the interest. However, there are situations when incentives and external supports are necessary. Teachers may use extrinsic motivation initially. However, students may come to associate the extrinsic motivators with learning, so the teacher should emphasize intrinsic motivation and withdraw extrinsic motivation before it becomes a crutch. The teacher should avoid the attitude of "What's in it for me? Why learn it?" You likely recall situations when a teacher used a game to teach a skill or a principle. This may have piqued your curiosity and led to an intrinsic interest in the topic.

Many factors affect motivation. It can be viewed from several perspectives. Educational psychologists use three major theories to explain motivation: *behavioral, cognitive* (Dembo, 1994; Good & Brophy, 1995; Borich & Tombari, 1995; Elliott, Kratochwill, Littlefield, & Travers, 1996; Sternberg & Williams, 2002); and *humanistic* (Dembo, 1994; Good & Brophy, 1995). You may wish to explore these approaches to deepen your understanding. For feedback on motivation you can use the data collection instrument in Appendix 4.2.

Attribution Theory

WHAT IS ATTRIBUTION THEORY?   Can you remember a time when everybody in your class did poorly on a test? The teacher may have said that the class should have studied harder, the students were not taking schoolwork seriously, or blamed the students in another way. You and your classmates may have said that the teacher included items on the test that had not been covered in class nor assigned as readings. Using the language of attribution theory, the teacher *attributed* poor performance to the laziness of students, but students *attributed* low marks to an omission by the teacher. In this situation, *attributions* by the teacher and students are quite different.

Attribution of motivation involves seeking the causes of events. It is an attempt to make sense out of what happened or is happening within and about an individual. *Attribution theory* is used to discover how people perceive the cause of their behavior and then look at the way their perception might affect later behavior. People seek reasons for their successes and failures. They like to do things for personal reasons, not because of pressure from outside. Attribution theory underscores the importance of providing students with feedback in ways that help build or preserve confidence that they can succeed if reasonable effort is expended. To keep trying, students need to be successful most of the time and to think that at least some of their success was due to *their* efforts.

ATTRIBUTION AND CAUSAL FACTORS.   Motivation of students is influenced by what they think caused past success or failure and what might influence future success or failure. That is, they tend to make *causal attributions.* They, for instance, judge how difficult the task was and whether success depended on ability, effort, or luck. For future tasks, students predict probable success or failure. This may be expressed as hope of success or fear of failure. The anticipation of success or failure even can become a "self-fulfilling prophesy." Causal factors to which people attribute success or failure are illustrated in Figure 4.2. Causal factors can be examined through three dimensions: *internal or external causes, stability,* and *controllability.*

External/Internal.   Research shows that there are four main reasons attributed to success and failure: (1) ability, (2) effort expended, (3) luck, and (4) the difficulty of the task. Ability, personal attractiveness or charm, and effort are *internal* to a person, but luck and difficulty of a task are *external.* Students who are high achievers tend to attribute their achievements to ability and effort and failures to not having tried hard enough. Low-achieving students, however, tend to attribute their achievements to luck and their failures to lack of ability (Rothstein, 1990, p. 143). Attributions are hard to change. The

Motivation is influenced by what students
think caused past successes and failures.

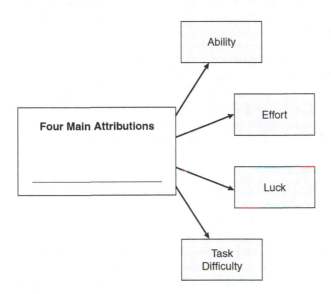

FIGURE 4.2   *Motivation and Attribution*

strong message is that teachers need to encourage students by being "organizers of success experiences," continually provide feedback, and
provide positive reinforcement for successes.

Locus of control refers to how people explain personal successes or failures. Those
with an *external locus of control* think their successes and failures are due to external factors
(e.g., "It was the teacher's fault that I didn't do
well"). Those who have an *internal locus of control* think performance is due to internal factors (e.g., "I did well because I am bright and
worked hard").

Stability/Instability.   We think some
tasks are easy and others hard. What we believe our general ability to be tends to remain
constant over time. However, the amount of effort put in and the luck we experience varies.
That is, ability is stable but effort is unstable;
task difficulty is stable but luck is unstable.
These influence students' expectations for future success and failure. A student who has always, for example, found mathematics difficult
does not expect to be good at it in the future; but a student who was sick and could not
study for a math test and did poorly will expect to be more successful on the next test.

Controllable/Uncontrollable.   Luck and ability cannot be controlled. The amount
of effort expended can be controlled. Success or failure can be attributed either to elements that are under a student's control or to those that are under someone else's control.
Students who think they are failing because of lack of ability are more likely to give up;
students who think failure was due to lack of effort can change.

THE TEACHER AND STUDENT MOTIVATION.   How students see themselves is critical. People avoid tasks that are too hard and situations in which they may fail or "look
dumb." Based on experience, some students believe they are bound to fail. Some students
believe that ability to succeed in school is fixed, so they often set goals and seek situations
in which they can look intelligent. Other students believe that intelligence is a set of characteristics and a body of knowledge that can be learned. When students think they cannot change ability, they set goals in keeping with what they think they *can* achieve and try
to protect themselves from failure. On the other hand, if they think they can improve, they
tend to set high learning goals and are likely to handle failure constructively. Students
whose perception of self-worth is low tend to play it safe and avoid potential failure situations. These students may blame external factors or other people for failures. They
avoid failure by, for instance, not participating, delaying work until the last minute, exerting only superficial effort ("I wasn't really trying!"), and setting low goals or picking
tasks that are easy to attain ("All I want is a pass!"). Avoiding failure usually doesn't
work and may lead to becoming "failure prone." Some students develop *failure avoidance
strategies* because of early home experiences or later because of competitive classroom

environments. In contrast, students with a high sense of self worth tend to seek ways to become even better.

Students like things at which they are successful and avoid things at which they fail. Success breeds success! *Ability cannot be controlled, but effort can.* Teachers need to structure success experiences for individuals.

DESIGNING INSTRUCTION THAT MOTIVATES. Keller (1983, cited in Good & Brophy, 1995, pp. 400–402) believes instruction can be designed that has one or a combination of four characteristics: (1) *interest* (to arouse and hold learner curiosity); (2) *relevance* (relate content to personal needs and goals); (3) *expectancy* (learners expect, through personal control, to succeed); and (4) *satisfaction* (employ intrinsic motivation or suitable extrinsic rewards). Guide and encourage students to ask questions.

Motivation: Common Sense Factors

The climate you foster in your classroom can make an enormous difference. What you say or do establishes that climate. The classroom needs to be a good place in which to live and learn. This has much to do with respecting your students and expecting respect toward you and their peers. Effective teachers are good at creating conditions that lead to positive self-image and interest in learning activities and content. They do not isolate themselves from their students. They move around the classroom and do not hide behind the safe barrier a desk provides. They "touch base" with individual students every day with a friendly word to help a student or to "catch somebody doing it right." They listen to what students say and have good interpersonal skills. Good teachers know that enthusiasm begets enthusiasm, and use humor (laughter makes learning better). Rapid feedback and contingent positive reinforcement occurs. Good teachers are well prepared for every lesson: they do not "wing it." Active involvement of students, where reasonable, in goal and curriculum setting, and in the process of learning, leads to accountability and intrinsic motivation, so liberal use is made of the interactive and experiential teaching strategies. Excellent ideas on motivational tasks you may wish to use are provided in some educational psychology books, for example, in *Looking in Classrooms* by Good and Brophy (2003).

At-Risk Students

Motivation is a major concern for classroom teachers, particularly motivating underachieving or at-risk students. These students are "tuning out." They are potential early school leavers. They usually have had a pattern of failure and do not expect to do well in the future. That is, there is a cycle of failure and low expectations. More and more students in North America are leaving school early. One of your greatest challenges will be to identify at-risk students and determine what to do to help. A downward spiral of low expectations and failure tends to occur with these students. This spiral, or cycle, which can be explained using attribution theory, is illustrated in Figure 4.3.

Attribution theory, discussed earlier, helped us understand the reasons for a pattern of failure:

1. *Lack of ability.* The belief that the ability is lacking ("I just can't do fractions")
2. *Lack of effort.* The belief that success would have occurred had the effort been expended ("I didn't really try")

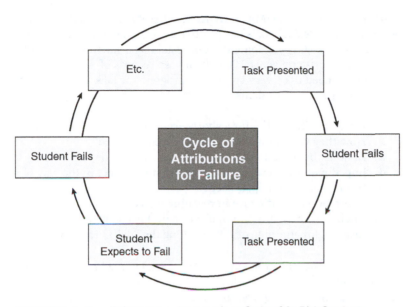

FIGURE 4.3 *Failure/Low-Expectations Cycle of At-Risk Students*

3. *Task believed to be too difficult.* The belief that the task was unreasonably difficult ("The test was unfair, it was too tough.")
4. *Bad luck.* The belief that bad luck was experienced when failures occurred or doing well was just good luck ("The test didn't ask questions about the stuff I knew" or "I was just lucky. I guessed right.") (Alderman, 1990, p. 27)

The concepts of *stable/unstable* and *internal/external* were discussed earlier. A student who has consistently failed in the past and believes he or she is to blame for the failures is at risk. At-risk students have internal/stable attributions for failure and feel helpless—failure becomes a self-fulfilling prophecy (p. 28). This presents a difficult motivational problem. Though they may experience some success, it is not enough to motivate internal/stable students. You can, however, help many at-risk students to begin to take responsibility for their learning and improve their performance.

Helping At-Risk Students

Alderman (1990) thinks teachers who are successful at helping at-risk students: (1) are confident in their ability to be of help and determined to help, and (2) have high but achievable expectations for at-risk students. These teachers are aware that learning problems exist, but they believe they can motivate students to put forth effort. They believe they can help students learn to believe in themselves, to believe that, with sufficient effort, they can succeed.

You have to do two things. The first is to structure a series of success experiences for at-risk students. The second is to help students understand that they contributed to the successes. Alderman says that four "links" need to be provided for "helpless" students to become successful and to increase their sense of self-worth.

LINK ONE: SET PROXIMATE GOALS.   Research shows that setting *proximate* (short-term and manageable) goals has positive effects on student performance at all grade and ability levels. Begin by helping students establish a starting point and then have them set achievable short-term goals. Have them keep records of progress.

Goals need to be very specific so progress, or lack of it, becomes very evident. Alderman suggests that students use a record form and state:

1. Their specific goal(s) for a short-term period (i.e., today or this week)
2. How they will know if the goal was accomplished
3. Actions that need to be taken to achieve the goal(s)
4. Impediments (internal or external) that might get in the way of achieving goal(s)
5. Who to go to for help, if needed
6. Their level of confidence in reaching the goal(s)
7. Their degree of satisfaction if the goal(s) is reached
8. Reasons for attaining or not attaining the goal(s) (pp. 28–29)

LINK TWO: LEARNING STRATEGIES.   Students who are low achievers usually make limited and inefficient use of learning and study skills and strategies. Good and Brophy (1995) note that learning strategies and skills include: rehearsal strategies (actively repeating material), elaboration strategies (making connections between the new and familiar—paraphrasing, summarizing, and creating analogies), organizational strategies (imposing structure on the material—concept hierarchy and diagrams), comprehension strategies (remaining aware of what one is trying to accomplish—objectives, sub goals, and self questioning), and affective strategies (motivation, concentration, managing performance anxiety, and time management) (pp. 324–325).

LINK THREE: SUCCESSFUL EXPERIENCES.   The question students must ask themselves is how much progress they have made toward the proximate goals they have set. They should *not* focus on how smart they are (ability). Remember, though low-achieving or at-risk students are successful in achieving a proximate goal, they may still have very low expectations for future success. Students must learn to attribute success to personal effort or personal use of a learning strategy (Alderman, 1990, p. 29). It makes sense for students to learn to view failures as "deferred successes," not as "sins"—students can learn from trials that were "not yet successful" to help them progress toward success. Mistakes should be viewed as a natural and important part of learning, not as lack of ability or finger-pointing catastrophes. Nonthreatening risk taking must be possible.

LINK FOUR: ATTRIBUTION FOR SUCCESS.   Students need to recognize the connection between effort and ability and personal achievement. The job of the teacher is to help students make the proper attribution (Alderman, 1990, p. 29). You can "model and give feedback about why the student succeeded or failed." Successes should be related to student effort, strategies, or ability (p. 29). Students need to recognize when successes can be attributed to ability and effort (internal factors) and when successes are to some extent attributable to luck and task difficulty (external factors). Students need to believe they have some control over successes and failures. They *can* control the amount of effort and the learning strategies they choose. They can find out that ability can improve over time (not stable) and that performance is affected by their approach to learning. A positive sense of self-worth is possible only if people believe they have ability and that, if they try, they can improve.

Initially, you may need to reinforce students *just for trying.* If progress was made, point out what students achieved because of their efforts. However, the converse is not desirable. You should not blame, that is, tell students they did not succeed because of lack of effort. Examples of successful student effort should be provided so that students believe their effort had an influence. Examples include completing homework, correcting errors, reviewing, redoing a task, or using a particular learning strategy. When students begin to have successes they begin to attribute these to internal, not external factors. They begin to feel self-confident, expecting (at times) to be successful, and indeed experience more success. The self-fulfilling prophecy is now reversed. Students can learn to deal with failure by either discovering the reasons themselves or recognizing them with the help of the teacher. Students can then try again, perhaps by using a different learning strategy suggested by the teacher (Alderman, 1990, p. 29).

The Circle of Courage and the At-Risk Student

We need look no further than traditional Native American child-rearing philosophies to provide a powerful alternative for establishing a positive classroom environment. Native American philosophies can be the basis for making your classroom a place where students want to be and where students have a positive attitude toward learning. Native philosophies of child management provide an approach that is holistic. A primary goal is to foster self-esteem. Without a sense of self-worth, a child is subject to social, psychological, and learning problems. Fostering a sense of self-worth for "normal" and for at-risk children needs to be a primary goal for all teachers.

Traditional Native practices, say Brendtro, Brokenleg, and Van Bockern (2002), address the four Coopersmith (1967) bases of self-esteem. The authors identify four interrelated central values as the "unifying theme—of positive cultures for education and youth work programs" (p. 45): (1) belonging (attachment), (2) mastery (achievement), (3) independence (autonomy), and (4) generosity (altruism) (pp. 46–59). These are contained in what is called the *circle of courage* (Figure 4.4).

Coopersmith (1967) said that self-esteem has four basic components: significance, competence, power, and virtue. *Significance* occurs through the acceptance, attention, and affection of others; if a person lacks significance, that person feels rejected, ignored, and not to belong. *Competence* is built as an individual masters the environment—success causes satisfaction, failure destroys motivation. *Power* is awarded when one controls one's

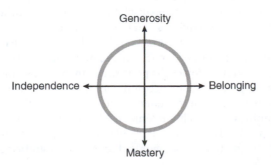

FIGURE 4.4   *The Circle of Courage: Four Central Values*
Source: Brendtro, Brokenleg, & Van Bockern, 2002, p. 54.

behavior and earns the respect of others; without a feeling of power, a person feels helpless and without influence. *Virtue* is judged by the values of one's culture and peers; without virtue, one's life is not spiritually fulfilling. We can note that:

1. *Significance* is expressed through belonging.
2. *Competence* is ensured by guaranteed opportunities for mastery.
3. *Power* is fostered by encouraging the expression of independence.
4. *Virtue* is reflected in the preeminent value of generosity. (pp. 40–41)

If, as a teacher, you foster these four values, you can help students build personal self-esteem. Students with positive self-esteem are likely to feel part of the classroom work community and to have a positive attitude toward learning. If students develop a clear sense of belonging in your room, if ample opportunity and encouragement are provided in their quest for mastery of the curriculum, if students develop a sense of responsible autonomy or power over their behavior, and if students learn to be unselfish and generous, you will have a class that is motivated, and a class that values and is excited about being part of a learning community.

Fostering the circle of courage is particularly important when working with at-risk students. Brendtro et al. (2002) outline approaches for working with what they call the "children of discouragement" (p. 70). This involves: (1) maintaining an environment that involves relating to the reluctant by "establishing positive relationships" with youth; (2) using alternative methods for structuring learning experiences that are "brain friendly"; (3) "mobilizing positive youth involvement" to counter irresponsibility and rebellion; and (4) having the "courage to care" by establishing programs that foster prosocial values and behavior (p. 70).

School Environment

Parents want a personalized atmosphere in their children's schools. A healthy environment features: trust, respect, warmth, caring and support, high morale, creativity, satisfaction, and high student and teacher involvement. Drefs (1989) reports that a school with an effective school environment displays several interrelated variables: (1) pervasive caring about individual students that permeates every aspect of school; (2) a positive physical climate (clean, well maintained, and attractive); (3) the ability to rise above the constraints of finite human and material resources (ways are found to free teachers to concentrate on instruction and professional development, extensive use is made of outside facilities and resources, and creative problem solving takes place); (4) the setting is orderly and well disciplined but definitely not oppressive (rules and consequences are clearly communicated and consistently enforced, teachers model desired behavior, and discipline is preventive rather than reactive); and (5) meaningful participation by students and the community occurs (pp. 18–23).

Achievements of effective schools, which are linked to a positive climate, are quite remarkable. These include: greater academic achievement, better attendance, reduced delinquency, greater staff stability, lower dropout rates, increased school pride and less vandalism, fewer discipline problems, and becoming more than cold dispensers of knowledge. Effective schools are places where students and teachers treat each other with respect. They are communities in which students are happy, confident, productive, and proud of their school (pp. 23–28). Hansen and Childs (1998), presenting the research of Purkey and Novak (1996), cite five key elements that can add significantly to school climate: place, policies, programs, processes, and people (p. 15). The school should be an attractive *place,* each expressing its unique personality; *policies* should "encourage and permit rather than restrict or direct"; *programs* should be "innovative and attractive"; *processes* should be participatory, with "group and collaborative effort"; and *people* should be partners, with many groups such as university and school working closely together and all individuals being recognized in "subtle but significant ways" (pp. 15–17).

Teaching Attitudes and Values

The notion of "value-free education," popular in some circles from about mid-century until fairly recently, harbors a contradiction in terms. . . . What we consider "good" or "bad," "right" or "wrong," "important" or "unimportant" constantly guides our practice . . . there is simply no denying the vital and influential presence of values in every facet of educational practice. (Carbone, 1991, p. 290)

You will recall that content can be conceptual (declarative), skills and processes (procedural), or affective (such as attitudes and values). All content has an affective aspect. All teaching and learning involves feelings and emotions as expressed through interests, appreciations, attitudes, and values. At times, affective outcomes are incidental to cognitive instruction. At other times, in keeping with curriculum objectives, you will be directly concerned with teaching affective content, principally attitudes or values.

Whether attitudes and values can be taught and whether schools should teach them have been persistent questions in the minds of many educators and parents. Some contend that values education should be left to the home and churches. However, federal and state and most district governments leave no doubt that the teaching of attitudes and values is key to the preservation of the best in society. Some educators argue that the learning of attitudes and values is more important than cognitive content. Although attitudes and values are learned, they are ultimately personal. If by "teaching" attitudes we mean "telling" students what they should believe and value, we are on shaky ground. For a person to have "internalized and accepted a value, that person must, of necessity have some experience, even a vicarious experience" of the conditions or event that evoke the value (Kizlik, 2002).

In the minds of many educators and political leaders, recent events have renewed interest in what now is often called *character education*—teaching moral values and character habits and traits directly. The incidence of in-school violence appears to be escalating. Bullying and racism are prevalent. Drugs, gangs, teenage pregnancy, and suicide are ongoing problems. Star (1999) asks whether character education is the answer to these many concerns.

Creating Conditions for Attitude Development

Character education is not simple. Character develops slowly, with many factors contributing to the development. However, teachers create conditions and provide experiences through which attitudes and values can develop. They can help students develop appropriate attitudes and values by the way they teach. First, if teaching is to "ring true," teachers need a clear sense of their own attitudes and values. Their impact as role models in altering or establish attitudes and values should not be underestimated. How teachers use reinforcement, or provide activities that are challenging but achievable, makes an important difference. Some attitudes are established because they are continually rein-forced. Being successful at tasks promotes positive attitudes toward the tasks, whereas continued failure leads to dislike. Also needed is awareness that attitudes and values are an inevitable part of everything that occurs in the classroom and school. Students will be favorably disposed to what is being taught in a lesson, dislike it, or have a neutral dispo-sition toward it (which is still a value position). Values are already present in the cur-riculum, obvious in the study of literature, social studies, and health and physical education. However, in some ways attitudes and values learning is part of every school subject, even math. What would be left after the study of poems, short stories, and novels if the affective dimension could be removed? Who would want to listen to a story that did not pique feelings and emotions? What would be the point of citizenship education if it were shorn of values? How do you divorce attitudes and values from learning about the effects of tobacco, alcohol, and drugs? Authorities agree that experiential, problem-based education is more effective than direct instruction (e.g., lecturing) for students to learn the values called for in curriculum guides. The challenge for teachers is to make instruc-tion authentic by having students collaborate in their studies and by using instructional methods and activities that allow students to solve problems and construct carefully con-sidered values that will be beneficial to themselves, their peers, and society.

Teaching for Attitude Change

Teaching attitudes and values can involve a sequence of steps (Figure 4.5). The first step is to discover students' present attitudes or values—the information and experiences about the desired attitude or value that should be provided. Allow time for reflection and understanding, and determine whether the desired change has occurred. If so, check for commitment or, if necessary, provide further information or experiences, time for reflec-tion and understanding, and checking for understanding. Discover the action with refer-ence to the attitude or value that students have taken. If needed, repeat the sequence.

You can discover the present attitude of students by observing them, collecting data on their behavior, and drawing inferences after analyzing the data. Once you have dis-covered their attitudes, provide information and experiences for students and ask them to reflect about and understand their atti-tudes, learn alternatives, and plan what they can do to revise their atti-tudes. This involves comprehension, analysis, synthesis, and evaluation. Re-vision can take place through concern, values clarification, and total aware-ness. Internalization of new attitudes involves a commitment to do so and an actual, relatively permanent change in behavior. A data collection sheet you can use when your professional target in a lesson is the teaching of attitudes is given in Appendix 4.3.

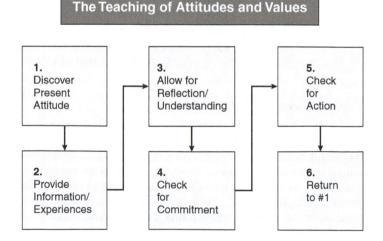

The Teaching of Attitudes and Values

1. Discover Present Attitude

2. Provide Information/ Experiences

3. Allow for Reflection/ Understanding

4. Check for Commitment

5. Check for Action

6. Return to #1

FIGURE 4.5 *Steps for Teaching Attitudes and Values*

CASE 4.1 Classroom Climate

Valuing Every Learner

Ms. Pleater teaches in a classroom of children with varying special needs. Several are children for whom English is a second language, and several are in grade 1 for the second year. Two children are hearing impaired, and several exhibit unusually high levels of anxiety and hostility. The school is in an economically depressed area, and many families struggle to maintain stability in spite of unemployment, rising costs, and the stress to families.

Ms. Pleater believes that classroom climate must be positive and welcoming, and that each child must feel special. She has arranged the desks so groups of four children sit facing each other, to allow easy interaction. At the beginning of the year, it is not unusual for some children to resist the close contact of a small group. Ms. Pleater allows time for them to get comfortable and does not insist they immediately join a group. A child may choose to work away from his or her group for a time.

At the beginning of each day, Ms. Pleater is in the classroom as the children come in. She greets each child by name and usually a personal comment. Children often hug her as they arrive, and she returns the hugs. She comments on new clothes, haircuts, and toys, asks about families, and welcomes those who have missed school.

Matthew comes in wearing his boots, sits on the floor, peels off his boots, and empties snow on the floor. Ms. Pleater says, "What a lot of snow, Matthew. How did you get so much in your boots?" He grins and says, "I walked in the deepest drifts I could find." She asks, "Where else could all that snow go before it melts?" "I'll sweep it up, Ms. Pleater," he says.

"Thanks, Matthew. Who can give Matthew a hand? (Helpee offers). Thanks, Helpee. You're a friend."

Occasionally, Ms. Pleater begins the day by asking if anyone has something kind they want to say to someone else in the room. Those who wish to, move to the person they are speaking to, shake his or her hand, and make the comment to them. Comments include, "I missed you when you weren't here yesterday," "I like your new shoes," "Thanks for sharing your popcorn with me this morning," "I saw when you helped the caretaker with those boxes." And "I like how fast you did your work yesterday." Ms. Pleater times these carefully so contributions are voluntary and the atmosphere comfortable. Initially, children were reluctant to participate, but more joined each time and they now are very attentive. The atmosphere has become relaxed, warm, and accepting. The children are natural in giving and receiving comments. There are lots of smiles.

Each table has a container of pencils, erasers, and crayons. The children share supplies freely. When all the class does the same work, Ms. Pleater spends extra time near students who need encouragement to finish tasks. A frequent arrangement for whole-class activities (such as stories, class discussions, receiving directions, or class meetings) is for the students to gather on a carpeted area at the back of the room, where they sit in a circle. Ms. Pleater also is part of the circle. At least twice a day, students gather in a circle at the back of the room. The time spent there has lengthened as the year has progressed and as students have become familiar with that setting.

CASE 4.2 Affective Education

Attitudes (Me Prejudiced?)

Mr. Enrich has just begun a unit on "Prejudice and Discrimination" in his grade 10 social studies class. He has prepared a one-page handout that contains two sets of questions, one on each side of the page. He says, "Page one contains questions to which you must underline one of two responses—Yes or No. You have

to choose the answer that is closest to the truth for you even though your Yes or No may not be 'cut and dried.'"

Yes No   1. Do you like dogs?
Yes No   2. Do you like raw oysters?

continued

Yes   No   3. Do you like bagpipe music?

Yes   No   4. Would you like to live in England?

Yes   No   5. Do you like to eat red or yellow peppers?

Yes   No   6. Do you like lizards?

Yes   No   7. Do you like to waltz?

Yes   No   8. Would you like to live in Russia?

Yes   No   9. Do you wrap silverware in newspapers before you store it?

"Now that you have all completed page one, turn the page and again answer the questions with either a yes or no."

Yes   No   1. Have you ever owned a dog for more than two months?

Yes   No   2. Have you ever eaten raw oysters?

Yes   No   3. Do you or anybody in your family listen to bagpipe music?

Yes   No   4. Have you ever been to England?

Yes   No   5. Have you eaten red or yellow peppers fairly frequently?

Yes   No   6. Have you ever had a lizard for a pet?

Yes   No   7. Do you know how to waltz?

Yes   No   8. Have you ever been to Russia?

Yes   No   9. If you saw a package wrapped in an old newspaper, do you think there would be something valuable inside?

When students had completed their responses, Mr. Enrich divided the class into groups of six. "Share your answers to each question, in turn. Then, as a group, decide the significance of this exercise." After students completed their sharing and had reported, Mr. Enrich asked the groups to seek consensus and report on the following questions.

a. Can you really judge something if you have had no, or little, experience with it?

b. What are the potential dangers in jumping to conclusions on hearsay evidence or on what a friend said about something or somebody?

c. Is there a difference between jumping to conclusions about something like an oyster or music and jumping to conclusions about a person or group of people?

d. People are like packages, they have an outside appearance but we can never be sure of what's inside. What do you think the effect is of judging a person by what that person wears, eats, or listens to, or where he or she lives?

CASE 4.3 Affective Education

Attitudes (Liking and Learning from Shakespeare)

Mr. Des has been thinking about his grade 11 *Macbeth* unit. He would like a more positive response than last year. Sometimes, as soon as he mentions Shakespeare, the whole class seems to turn off. How could he change their attitude?

He decides that he won't even mention Shakespeare at first. When he meets the class, he gives them a problem. "Suppose you met someone who said they could predict your future by using playing cards. And suppose they said that three things are going to happen, each thing better than the one before. What three things would you most want? Now suppose you laughed at the whole thing and then within a few hours the first thing became true."

The class was pretty excited about this, and an interesting discussion took place. When Mr. Des

asked how far students would go to get the other two wishes, there were many interesting responses. They were aware that life can give us interesting challenges, they were willing to explore the idea further, and there was no doubt Mr. Des had their attention.

Mr. Des then said he was going to show a movie clip of an ancient battle and of a brave soldier meeting three witches who promise that three special things will happen. The students were willing to give the scene a try and gained a lot of satisfaction in discussing the problem. The students enjoyed the brief scene and the discussion. When Mr. Des pointed out the promise that the man would become king and the problem of the existing king, some students even predicted the rest of the story.

At this point Mr. Des admitted the scene was from Shakespeare, but by now the class had accepted the idea that fate can be a powerful force and that drama, even Shakespeare, can be interesting. They want to know more, they are committed!

After the class leaves, Mr. Des reflects on how well things went. He realizes he had given personal meaning to the approach to Shakespeare. He had approached the play initially from an emotional and not an intellectual perspective. He had also met the students' need to be involved and that they saw significance in the content of the play. The students also had good self-concept and they did not feel that Shakespeare was above them. They felt good that they could understand the issues. Mr. Des felt confident about studying the rest of the play with his class.

CASE 4.4　Energizing Learners

More Than One Way

Mr. Kahn and Ms. Frisch each teach a grade 9 English class. Both are about to introduce the short story, *Miss Brill*. It is a story of a lonely old lady who likes to go to a local park and listen to the band music and then buy herself a small treat she takes back to her room. In her mind, she is happy, until she overhears a young couple talk about how odd she looks in her out-of-date clothes. Mr. Kahn and Ms. Frisch are, in their ways, excellent teachers. Mr. Kahn begins by going through the elements of a short story—plot, character, atmosphere, and so on. He gives detailed notes. He then explains the parts of a plot—rising action, climax, and denouement. The students read the story and, on a chart, begin to outline the plot of the story. There is some restlessness, so Mr. Kahn reminds students that the completed chart will be part of their final grade. The students learn a great deal and usually do well on tests. Mr. Kahn is considered a good teacher by the administration.

Ms. Frisch passes out cards to her students, who are in small groups. One card has "loneliness" written on it, another "old age," another "happiness," and another "poverty." She asks students to discuss what the words might mean to them and to share their ideas with the class. Soon a lively discussion is underway. Ms. Frisch is skilled at questioning, and she asks the class how could someone be happy if lonely and poor. One student thoughtfully answers, "Perhaps you make your own happiness in your mind." At that moment Ms. Frisch says she is going to read a story about just such a person, who enjoys her day in the park with the music and enjoys her small treat until something happens to take away her happiness. The students listen intently to the story. They are interested and curious about what is going to happen. After the story there is more discussion about how cruel young people can be sometimes. When Ms. Frisch asks the students to write about the story from the point of view of Ms. Brill, they have many ideas and are eager to write their thoughts.

Both are good teachers. How do they use extrinsic and intrinsic motivation?

CASE 4.5　Energizing Learners

Needs to Be Met

Mr. Papentropolous teaches in a large inner-city school. When he began teaching in this school he found it very difficult to motivate all the students. Some seemed to respond to the grades he gave; some didn't seem to care what their grades were. Some took pride in creative work and some seemed indifferent. Mr. Papentropolous struggled with his problem and was not getting anywhere. He then remembered his own schooling in a small village in Cyprus. There was a similar mix of children, some poor, some more affluent, some with learning difficulties, some very bright. His teacher was wonderful and took great care to find out all about the students. Mr. Papentropolous began to discover the needs of his students and find

continued

ways to see the needs were met. Some students seemed to be tired, while others he found had not had breakfast. Some seemed to need assurance that they were safe and secure in his class, while others seemed to need self-respect and were unsure of themselves. There were students who hovered around him because they enjoyed his care and attention. He realized that, somehow, he had to deal with basic needs before he could expect students to respond to the knowledge he wanted them to gain or to realize the pleasure pos-

sible from learning. He met with other teachers, the administration, and parents to obtain answers to many of his concerns. His class began to respond more and more, until he could see them approaching their potential. He gained the awareness that students' cognitive, aesthetic, and self-fulfillment needs cannot be met until their basic needs are dealt with. What things might a teacher do to discover students' needs and interests?

LINKING PRACTICE TO THEORY

Consider your experiences in school. What attention was paid to the affective domain? What excited and motivated you? What motivated you to become a teacher? What place will the formal and hidden curriculum have in your teaching? What place does emotion have? Consider the dichotomy between theory and practice as your build your experience. Reflect on motivation theory and how it works in practice for you.

Summary

The majority of the goals of education are affective or affectively toned, yet, for a variety of reasons, affective outcomes are understressed. Much of a teacher's job is to create conditions and structure activities that will motivate students to achieve their potential. Students who are motivated perceive the classroom to be a place that is "safe, fun, and at task." Motivation is what directs and activates behavior and affects what students will or will not do, like or not like doing. Motivation can be viewed from three perspectives: behavioral, cognitive, and humanistic. Attribution theory can be used to examine what students believe affects their success or lack of success—ability, effort, task difficulty, and luck. The teacher can do things to increase motivation, including: providing authentic learning tasks and strategies to influence students, allowing student choice, individualizing tasks to promote intrinsic motivation, providing interesting selection of

instructional approaches, and modeling. A primary concern for teachers should be maintaining a positive climate for learning. This involves: setting positive expectations; being enthusiastic, academically focused, businesslike, and encouraging; having a positive approach to management and expecting accountability; and ensuring a high rate of student success as learner ideas and interests are recognized. Teachers can intervene in the cycle of failure that is typical of at-risk students, helping them to set proximate goals, acquire learning strategies, assigning tasks at which students can succeed, and helping them to understand their effort can lead to achievement. Teachers have a duty to teach attitudes and values. Steps to follow when teaching attitudes are: discover the present attitude; provide information or experiences; allow for understanding and reflection; check for commitment; and check for action.

Activities

THE AFFECTIVE DIMENSION

1. Consider classes you attended in school that were an emotional experience, met some specific needs, and gave you a good sense of personal worth and

belonging. Make a brief list of these and share them in discussion with your classmates.

2. Form groups of five and brainstorm for ten minutes the things a classroom teacher can do, or en-

courage students to do, to foster a positive climate for learning. Then every group is to agree on a completion for the following stem: "A classroom that has a positive climate for learning is one where . . ." Groups report and debriefing occurs.

3. View the film *The Wave*. (A website that discusses the film in depth is www.geocities.com/Broadway/3145.wave.html.) This depicts a real-life social experiment in which an attempt was made to form a group identity and develop specific attitudes within a class. A fascist-like atmosphere and behavior pattern is established by a history teacher, which spreads throughout the school. If this film is not available, choose another or a story showing the influence of a teacher on his class. Discuss: (a) How are attitudes developed? (b) Are attitude objectives a legitimate concern of teachers? (c) What ideas, from the film, would help you in teaching attitudes? (d) How can students be involved in the choice of attitudes they are to develop? Should they have some choice?

4. Recall a teacher for whom you worked hard and who really made you feel good about yourself. List things the teacher did and said that made you and others behave in a constructive, positive way. Tell four other students about your teacher and listen to their descriptions. Arrive at a consensus about what teachers can do to establish a positive, productive classroom climate.

5. Using the data collection sheet on classroom climate (Appendix 4.2), observe a teacher, noting the things that person does and says that affect classroom climate (with the teacher's permission).

6. On the basis of information in this chapter, outline a plan for approaching a completely new class of students.

7. Consider some things to which you have a positive attitude. Make a list, for example: (1) love reading; (2) enjoy physical activities. Consider things about which you have a negative attitude. Make a list, for example: (1) dislike writing essays; (2) don't like math problems. Share what caused the positive and negative attitudes.

8. Debate the following positions: Character education can be taught in schools. Children come to school with most of their values already formed.

MOTIVATION

1. Consider subjects in which you were highly motivated. Was the motivation extrinsic or intrinsic?

2. Create a role-playing scenario in which a teacher attributes (a) a student's poor performance and (b) a student's excellent performance to various causes.

3. Using the various approaches discussed in this text, list the five best strategies to motivate (a) the gifted student and (b) the at-risk student.

4. Make a chart of the extrinsic and intrinsic things that motivated you when you were in school. Which were the more powerful motivation factors? Compare your findings with the extrinsic and intrinsic incentives discussed in this chapter.

5. Create a panel of expert psychologists. Have one argue the case for behaviorist psychology, one for cognitive psychology, and a third for humanistic psychology. The rest of the class poses questions.

6. As university students, discuss the reasons for what influenced your past successes and failures. Consider your ability, your effort, your luck, and the difficulty of the tasks. Which of the four could you control and which could you not?

7. Take a standard lesson plan and redesign it for maximum motivation. Consider the following factors: student interest, relevance, expectancy, and satisfaction. Consider as well the following: the learning environment, the level of challenge and difficulty, the learning objectives, and possible motivation strategies.

8. Examine the circle of courage chart (Figure 4.4). List ways in which students can show generosity, belonging, mastery, and independence.

9. Take a standard unit plan. Add to the plan a section on the adaptive dimension with focus on the at-risk student. Create the four links described in the text: proximate goals, effective learning strategies, successful experiences, and attributions for success.

10. If you are student teaching, to discover the interests of your students, have them complete the survey in Appendix 4.4.

APPENDIX 4.1   *Classroom Climate Professional Target*

PROFESSIONAL TARGET—CLASSROOM CLIMATE

Please describe what was said and done and how students reacted.

Behavior	Description
Kind of behavior modeled by the teacher	
Clarity of instructional objectives and reasons for these	
Specific behaviors that affect the climate	
Degree of active participation by students	
Behavior that affects self-esteem of individuals or class	
Use of student ideas and interests	
Use of reinforcement	
Provision for success by individuals and the class	
Use of competition and cooperation	
Behavior to reduce anxiety	

APPENDIX 4.2   *Motivation*

PROFESSIONAL TARGET—MOTIVATION

Please record what was said and done and how students reacted.

Behavior	Description
Preconditions that are apparent	
Supportiveness of environment?	
Appropriateness of level of difficulty?	
Relevance of stated or implied objectives?	
Advance organizers, objectives stated?	
Student awareness of effort/success connection	
Attention to underachievers?	
Directions clear and possible?	
Supplying extrinsic incentives	
Good performance rewarded?	
Improved performance rewarded?	
Competition used with care?	
Cooperation and mutual support stressed?	
Everyday and life value of content clarified?	
Student contributions valued?	
Appealing to intrinsic motivation	
Peer interaction occurs?	
Gamelike format used?	
Fantasies, simulations used?	
Tasks are completed?	
Feedback is given and immediate?	
Participation is active?	
Students have say in activities?	
Motivational strategies used	
Modeling by teacher?	
Students expected to succeed?	
Performance anxiety reduced?	
Teacher enthusiasm?	
Curiosity aroused, suspense used?	
Content personalized?	
Student interests discovered, used?	
Content seen as important, useful?	
Sensitivity to self-concepts?	

APPENDIX 4.3   *Teaching Attitudes Target*

PROFESSIONAL TARGET—TEACHING ATTITUDES

Please describe what was said or done and how students reacted.

Step	Teacher and Student Behaviors
Discovering students' present attitude(s)	
Providing information or experiences	
Allowing for reflection and understanding	
Checking for commitment	
Plans for attitude change	

APPENDIX 4.4   *Motivation Survey*

Name _____   Grade _____   Date _____

MOTIVATION: THINGS I AM INTERESTED IN

Please answer each question as completely as you can.

_____

Three things I like to do when I am at home?

If I had up to $100 to spend on anything I wanted, I would buy?

If I could take a trip anywhere I wanted, I would go to?

Three things I like to do at recess?

Three things I like to do when I have finished my seatwork?

The reasons for me doing well in an assignment or test are?

The reasons why I might not do well in an assignment or test are?

The person or persons who I like the most or are most important to me are? Why?

5 Assessment and Evaluation

Introduction

Given the variety of assessment and grading practices in the field, the increasing importance of assessment, the critical role each classroom teacher plays in determining assessment and grades, and the trend toward greater accountability of teachers... there is a need to more fully understand assessment and grading practices. (McMillan, 2001, p. 20)

Assessment and evaluation are important aspects of teaching and learning: (1) performance in school is used by society to sort people into occupational and other societal roles (for example, grades decide whether a person will be admitted to college); (2) grades are reward structures to motivate students; (3) parents want to know how their children are doing compared to others; (4) assessment can be used to judge the effectiveness of teachers and schools; and (5) other reasons for assessment will be explored in this chapter. Stiggins (2002) observes, "Politicians routinely ask, How can we use assessment as the basis for doling out rewards and punishment to increase teacher and student effort?" instead of the more important questions of: "How can we use assessment to help our students *want* to learn? How can we help them feel *able* to learn?" (p. 758). This is a critical part of assessment—not only assessment *of* student learning, but assessment *for* learning (assessment that helps students learn).

Teachers are responsible for assessing and evaluating students and reporting the results to school authorities, students, and parents. Material in this chapter will help you learn the basic concepts and skills. At the top of page 134 the sections on Assessment and Evaluation from the Teacher Competence Profile are included for your convenience.

Key Concepts

Several concepts need to be understood before meaningful discussion can occur. Assessment and evaluation are used by teachers to better understand students—to discover their abilities and interests, and what motivates. *Assessment* usually means collecting a full

OBJECTIVES

You will be able to:

1. Describe ways teachers seek information about students.
2. Define key concepts in assessment and evaluation.
3. Describe alternative (performance/authentic) assessment and the range of possible techniques.
4. Describe the various methods of recording assessment data.
5. Describe ways of preparing good test items.
6. Differentiate between good and poor test items.
7. Describe alternative marking systems.
8. Recognize bias in tests and ways to address diversity when assessing.
9. Propose ways to achieve balance in the use of testing procedures.

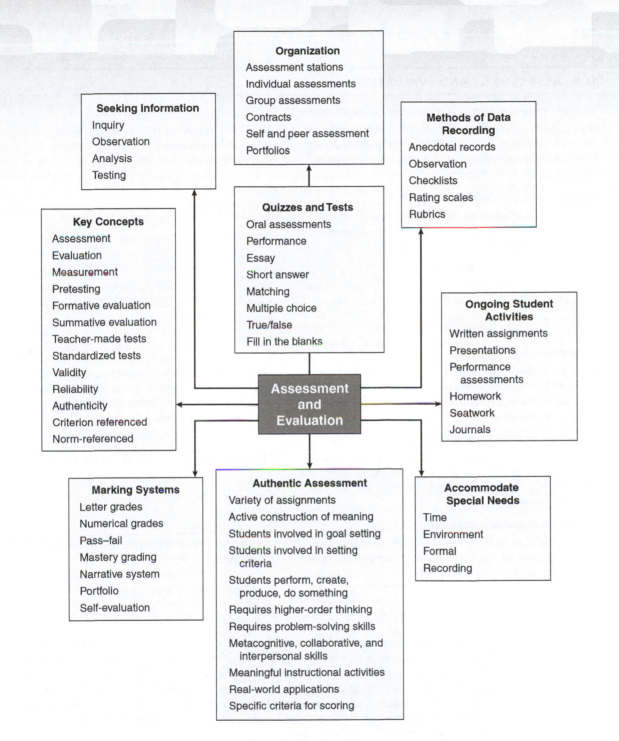

Seeking Information
Inquiry
Observation
Analysis
Testing

Organization
Assessment stations
Individual assessments
Group assessments
Contracts
Self and peer assessment
Portfolios

Methods of Data Recording
Anecdotal records
Observation
Checklists
Rating scales
Rubrics

Key Concepts
Assessment
Evaluation
Measurement
Pretesting
Formative evaluation
Summative evaluation
Teacher-made tests
Standardized tests
Validity
Reliability
Authenticity
Criterion referenced
Norm-referenced

Quizzes and Tests
Oral assessments
Performance
Essay
Short answer
Matching
Multiple choice
True/false
Fill in the blanks

Assessment and Evaluation

Ongoing Student Activities
Written assignments
Presentations
Performance assessments
Homework
Seatwork
Journals

Marking Systems
Letter grades
Numerical grades
Pass–fail
Mastery grading
Narrative system
Portfolio
Self-evaluation

Authentic Assessment
Variety of assignments
Active construction of meaning
Students involved in goal setting
Students involved in setting criteria
Students perform, create, produce, do something
Requires higher-order thinking
Requires problem-solving skills
Metacognitive, collaborative, and interpersonal skills
Meaningful instructional activities
Real-world applications
Specific criteria for scoring

Accommodate Special Needs
Time
Environment
Formal
Recording

range of information about students. It is gathered to make judgments about student progress and your instruction. *Performance assessment* provides information on the learning of tasks that require students to be actively engaged in a practiced behavior (e.g., playing a violin or taking part in a debate). *Evaluation* is the process of making judgments or

TCP—ASSESSMENT AND EVALUATION

Identifies student academic, personal, and social strengths

Uses formal and informal methods to identify students' strengths; shares assessment of strengths with students; incorporates knowledge of student strengths into planning for student assessment.

Tends to dwell on inefficiencies and weaknesses; does not assess student strengths or share them with students.

Assesses change in student development

Uses formal and informal methods to assess change in student development: maintains accurate and comprehensive records of each student's progress.

Does not document student development.

Involves students in assessment

Students are regularly given opportunities to set criteria for their work and to assess their progress; students are involved in individual conferences with the teacher; assessment is treated as a learning experience.

Students are not given the opportunity to assess their own work; no dialogue with students regarding progress.

Evaluates student progress

Various assessments are interpreted to evaluate student progress; the basis for evaluation is clearly and regularly reported to students and parents; evaluation is used to set goals for future growth.

Student evaluation is not based on regular formal and informal assessment; evaluation is reported as marks, with little or no reference criteria or interpretation.

Keeps thorough, well-organized records

Record keeping thorough, well organized, and accessible (e.g., attendance, marks, student progress, assignment and test schedules, record of professional targets, progress in essential learning).

Little or no evidence of usable record keeping.

Provides diagnosis and remediation

Uses and acts on standardized and teacher-made evaluation techniques for remediation or enrichment; refers to other professionals when appropriate.

Does not diagnose or provide remediation or enrichment.

decisions about achievement of learning objectives or the degree of value or merit of a particular program, activity, or approach. It usually involves assessing information against some standard. *Measurement* is the way data are provided for making judgments or decisions. It involves collecting data on the frequency or magnitude of something. When teachers take attendance, they engage in measurement; but assessment occurs when they decide that English usage is important in learning; evaluation occurs when teachers decide a test was too difficult or too easy.

Evaluation can be formative or summative. *Formative evaluation* happens before or during instruction and the learning process. It is used to plan and make adjustments to promote learning. It includes observation by the teacher of students and their work, questions during instruction, homework, pretests, and checkup tests. Formative evaluation should not be used to decide grades. Frequent *en route* (formative) evaluation may be used to increase comprehension and to provide repetitions to increase retention. *Summative evaluation* occurs after instruction, to discover the extent of student learning or the effectiveness of instruction. It is often used to decide grades. Summative evaluation may occur after an instructional unit has been completed or at the end of a course. It should measure student learning against the intended learning outcomes of a unit or course. It may include teacher-made, end-of-chapter or other tests, completed projects or papers, homework, portfolios, self-evaluation, and even standardized achievement tests. Summative evaluation is used to decide grades.

Tests can be teacher made or standardized. *Teacher-made tests* are created by the teacher to discover student achievement and teaching effectiveness. They should measure exactly what was taught *and only* what was taught. When built properly, test items reflect classroom objectives and the teaching methods and classroom learning activities used. *Standardized tests* are usually commercially designed. They sample performance under uniform procedures (directions, time limits, and methods for scoring), and they are usually meant for broad (often nationwide) use and include norms. *Pretesting* is used to discover students' knowledge or skill about a topic or performance before a lesson that requires these as prerequisites. If teachers are to design curricula and assessments appropriate for their classes and individuals within them, they need to take students from *where they are—not from where they are supposed to be.* Discovering "where students are" in their development is the critical beginning point in the teaching–learning enterprise. Teachers can try to discover students' prior knowledge and capabilities both formally and informally. Formally, they can administer pretests, both teacher made and norm- and criterion-referenced standardized tests. Informally, pretesting can occur through observation, class assignments, person-to-person interactions, and class discussions.

How good is a test? Tests need to be valid, reliable, and authentic. *Validity* refers to the ability of a test to measure what it says it will measure. For example, if it is supposed to measure ninth-grade reading skills and does, then it is valid. *Reliability* refers to the consistency of a test (or another version of a test with similar items) to yield the same score or rank repeatedly when given to the same individuals under similar circumstances. *Authenticity* means the degree to which tests are congruent with reality—do they deal with important content, "real problems" that are transferable to life situations?

Evaluation may be criterion referenced or norm referenced. A *criterion* is a standard against which something is compared. *Criterion-referenced evaluation* involves comparing student performance to an absolute criterion (standard). It is used to help decide if a student needs more instruction or practice. For example, the criterion may be 7 out of 10 correct; or, to pass a course, students may have to score 80 percent or better on a test. *Norm-referenced evaluation* involves comparing each student's results to those of others in the group—either the class or another group. A norm-referenced test is a standardized test that evaluates a student's performance relative to that of a large representative sample of learners (called the *norm group*).

Assessment Techniques

Assessment techniques can be categorized into four groups: methods of organization, methods of data recording, ongoing student activities, and quizzes and tests. The discussion that follows uses this arrangement (Figure 5.1).

FIGURE 5.1   *Student Assessment Techniques*

Methods of Organization	Methods of Data Recording	Ongoing Student Activities	Quizzes and Tests
Assessment stations	Anecdotal records	Written assignments	Oral assessments items
Individual assessments	Observation checklists	Presentations	Performance test items
Group assessments	Rating scales	Performance assessments	Extended open-response items
Contracts	Rubrics	Homework	Short-answer items
Self- and peer assessments	Multiple-choice items	Journals	
Portfolios	True–false items		

Source: Adapted from Saskatchewan Learning (1991). *Student evaluation: A teacher handbook.* Regina, SK: Saskatchewan Department of Education.

Methods of Organization

ASSESSMENT STATIONS.   An assessment station is an area, in or outside the classroom, set by the teacher for assessment. Students, individually or in groups, go to this area to be assessed on academic or attitude achievement. Having such a spot allows students, during regular class time, to work with ideas or materials. At a station, they can, for example, demonstrate ability to use a zoology display to classify a specimen, prepare a chart on a computer, write a story, or perform a gymnastic skill.

INDIVIDUAL ASSESSMENTS.   Individual assessment involves examining individual student progress. In doing this, the teacher decides whether to use norm referencing (a group standard of students of the same age or grade), criterion referencing (a predecided standard), or self referencing (a student's previous level of achievement).

GROUP ASSESSMENTS.   Group assessment is a way to collect information about students working in groups; it accounts for group progress. The teacher awards the same mark to every member of the group, assigns individual marks, or uses a combination of group and individual marks. Each has advantages and disadvantages. The *individual* mark procedure is traditional, and some assessments are best done individually, but it encourages competition and it is difficult to measure an individual's contribution to a group project; the *group* procedure encourages cooperation and the teacher only has to assign one (not several) marks, but students and parents have come to expect individual marks. A compromise is to use a combination of individual and group assessments.

CONTRACTS.   A contract is an agreement between a student or group of students and the teacher about what is to be done, who will do it, how it will be done, when it is due, and how it will be marked. Students are involved in planning what the product is to be and how it is to be evaluated. Examples of products include written assignments, displays, models, and portfolios. Students may need to be taught how to plan contracts and encouraged to become self-directed learners.

SELF- AND PEER ASSESSMENTS.   When students evaluate their work, *self-assessment* occurs. When another student, or group students, evaluate a student's work, *peer assessment* occurs. Checklists or rating scales can be used for self- or peer assessment, though assessment can be written or oral. Self- or peer assessment is best used when student self-knowledge is important. Self- and peer assessments lend themselves to project work or group work. Ideally, students are involved in developing the criteria. When a teacher uses peer assessment, both the person being evaluated and the person doing it can benefit. Students should be taught how to assess peers in a descriptive, nonjudgmental way. It may involve the use of rubrics, which students may even help in designing.

PORTFOLIOS

> If you want to appear accountable, test your students. If you want to improve schools, teach teachers to assess their students. If you want to maximize learning, teach students to assess themselves. (Stiggins, 1993)

A *portfolio* is a chronological collection of student work over an extended period. Paulson, Paulson, and Meyer (1991) say it "is a purposeful collection of student work that exhibits the student's efforts, progress, and achievements in one or more areas. The collection must include student participation in selecting contents, the criteria for selection, the criteria for judging merit, and evidence of student self-reflection" (p. 60).

Teachers increasingly use portfolios of student work so that students gain the "real" information needed to assess progress and set learning goals. Portfolios can empower the teacher and learners. Achievement tests measure outcomes that can be tabulated or counted. Portfolios allow teachers to observe students in a more complete way and encourage students to be creative, take risks, and learn how to self-evaluate. A major purpose is to help students become self-directed learners. Portfolios, many teachers believe, are better ways to report student progress to parents or guardians.

Effective learning occurs when students have control over and take responsibility for learning. Doing a portfolio is a way to promote self-directed learning. It can have the added benefit of improving self-esteem, as students take pride in their work and share portfolios with others. Opportunities for sharing can occur during student-led conferences or as students share portfolios with peers. It occurs when portfolios are presented to the teacher and parents. By examining their children's work, parents form a clearer image of what occurs in classrooms. This can lead to genuine relationships with their children and the teacher. That is, portfolio assessment may be "authentic" in that it can communicate student learning in a very authentic way.

Regularly collected, dated, samples of student work provide an "image" of the learner over time. Because learning is continuous, standardized tests provide an imprecise snapshot of a student's knowledge on a given day. Assessment should reveal more. Students and teachers can jointly put together *a complete collection portfolio.* A *showcase portfolio, assessment portfolio,* or *parent conference portfolio* can be drawn from the student's portfolio.

Though using portfolios can have positive results, some educators cite disadvantages. Time and administration demands increase, and scoring and recording student performance is subjective and difficult. Critics add that deciding what should be included can be a problem.

Methods of Recording Data

Information about student progress, including tests and quizzes, or participation in ongoing activities, can be recorded in several ways. The technique selected should be easy to use, accurate, and represent fairly what occurred.

ANECDOTAL RECORDS.   Anecdotal records are written day-to-day accounts of student progress. They are based on observations of students and are usually collected in a folder or book. Most often, records consist of dated, descriptive, open-ended, and unstructured notes. The use of forms, with headings and space under which observation can be recorded, is common. *Formatively,* narrative records inform the teacher about how a student is progressing and areas that might require immediate attention. In the latter respect, they can be used for *diagnosis. Summatively,* anecdotal records detail student development over a period.

OBSERVATION CHECKLISTS.   Observation checklists focus on a teacher's observations of a student on critical behaviors or key things. They measure the presence or absence of desired concepts, skills, processes, or attitudes. They are usually completed during class time. Each entry is a formative picture. A longitudinal profile of progress may emerge if a checklist is used several times and evaluated. Examples of things recorded are problem-solving skills in mathematics, handwriting samples, spelling, ability to use information, an essay or report, attitudes and values about an issue, and participation in group or project work.

RATING SCALES.   Rating scales are used to judge the quality of performance or end product. They assess the extent to which students attain concepts, skills, processes, or attitudes. They provide a scale of values describing what is being evaluated whether a person, a group, or an object. We can, for example, use a 1–5 scale to rate students on nonverbal communication (facial expression, movement, gestures, mannerisms, eye contact, and use of silence) as they give presentations. Other examples are performance at a piano, doing technical work in a science laboratory, and a product in a woodwork shop (e.g., a bird house).

A variation is holistic rating scales. A *holistic rating scale* combines global and analytic scoring methods. Portfolios can be a good way to assess investigations reported in oral or written assignments in language arts and for long-term or extended problem solving in mathematics. Further discussion of rating scales is provided later in this chapter.

RUBRICS.   When we wish to assess how well a student has completed a task such as a performance, product, or something written, we look at two parts: the *task* itself and the *criteria* necessary to achieve the task. A *rubric* is a set of guidelines for assessment that states the characteristics being assessed with clear performance criteria and a rating scale (Scarborough Board of Education, 1997, p. 22). A rubric includes (1) the criteria or key elements of a piece of work, and (2) a scale or gradations of quality for each criterion. An example of a map rubric is given in Table 5.1.

Rubrics can be used to assess a wide range of work, including essays, presentations, portfolios of assignments, book talks, displays, projects, music performances, and physical education performances. As well as specifying expectations, they can be marking tools and make assessment *authentic.* A rubric form can be attached to student work and the degree of quality achieved for each criterion highlighted or circled. It is suggested that a *comments* section be added to the form, because the form alone may seem impersonal.

Rubrics are increasingly popular with teachers and students alike. Teachers like them because they provide a clear set of criteria or standards, and students like them because they clarify expectations. A rubric is learner centered. It openly lays out what the teacher expects

TABLE 5.1 *Criteria Descriptors*

	Excellent (4)	Very Good (3)	Good (2)	Fair (1)
Content	All labels included and accurately placed; details careful and accurate	All labels included, most accurately placed	All but one or two labels included, somewhat accurately placed	Several labels not included, many not accurately or carefully placed
Visual appeal	Very nicely colored, clean looking, labels easy to read	Some color, generally clean, a few labels not easy to read	Little color, labels somewhat difficult to read	Little or no color, labels very difficult to read
Map elements	Clear title, date, compass rose, scale key, source line, latitude and longitude lines	Most standard map elements, most accurate, easy to read	Several standard map elements are missing	Most standard map elements missing

and provides clear feedback to students about their achievement. Not only can a rubric be used by a teacher to assess student work, it can be used to do self-assessment or peer assessment. Parents like rubrics because they provide clear descriptions of what their child needs to do for a particular assignment (Goodrich, 1997). A rubric can reduce grading subjectivity. Huba and Freed (2000, pp. 170–171) give ways in which we can educate students by using rubrics:

- We can reveal to students the standards of our disciplines.
- We can inform students about the many qualities that comprise good—and poor—work.
- We can involve students in setting standards.
- We can involve students in describing the criteria in the rubrics.
- We can open channels of communication between us and our students.
- A variety of individuals give feedback to students about their work.

Goodrich (1997, pp. 14–15) gives five major reasons for the appeal of rubrics to students and teachers:

1. They are powerful tools for teaching and assessment—to improve and monitor student performance, make teachers' expectations clear, show students how to meet expectations.
2. They help students become thoughtful judges of their own and others' work.
3. They reduce the time teachers spend evaluating student work (teachers can circle an item in the rubric rather than write an explanation).
4. They can accommodate heterogeneous classes because of the range of quality in the descriptors (they also can accommodate gifted students and those with special needs).
5. They are easy to use and to explain to students and parents.

Although rubrics have much appeal, they have disadvantages. They are time consuming to design. Writing good criteria for each level of achievement is not easy. It is suggested that rubrics should be created by teacher teams and that students be involved. Involving students provides a sense of ownership in their assessment.

CASE 5.1   Assessment

Rubrics and Great Expectations

Mr. Polski's class is getting ready for the local history fair. The class has been divided into groups of two and three and each group has selected a history project to be researched and displayed. Sean and Hassim chose "The Oregon Trail," while Zillah, Maria, and Tiffany are doing "The Underground Railway to Canada." Mr. Polski is explaining the rubric by which work will be assessed.

Mr. Polski tells students there are four criteria: (1) originality of research, (2) quality of display, (3) clarity of writing, and (4) quality of interview with the judges. "What does 'criteria' mean?" Maria asks. Mr. Polski comments on the four criteria. Regarding research, he says there are four levels of quality and asks Hassim what they might be. "Well, the best would be 'excellent,' and the next . . . would be 'very good,' then 'good,' and then 'lousy' " says Hassim, grinning. The class laughs. "Not bad, Hassim," says Mr. Polski indulgently. "A better word might be

'poor.'" Mr. Polski reads the criteria for excellent research. "Students find high-quality evidence from several sources such as encyclopedias, textbooks, and a variety of print and audiovisual sources. All sources, including the Internet, are acknowledged. Primary sources such as print, pictorial, visual, and oral material will be considered." Mr. Polski asks Maria to explain what that all means. Maria thinks for a moment, knowing Mr. Polski waits for them to think their answers through. "It means that you just didn't get your stuff out of one encyclopedia or book, but took some trouble to find really interesting material." "Good, Maria, well thought out." Tiffany is asked what "primary" means. She answers, "For our project on the underground railway, we might find a photograph or a letter telling how some slaves fled to Canada." "Excellent," says Mr. Polski, pleased with the quality of his students' responses. "Let's discuss the other criteria."

Ongoing Student Activities

Students engage in a variety of activities during a school day, week, and term. Activities may involve the class as a whole, a group, or individuals, during a lesson, after a lesson, and in or outside of the classroom. Some activities are routine, others vary with the content and the judgment of the teacher.

WRITTEN ASSIGNMENTS.   Teachers can have students, individually or in groups, plan, complete, and submit a written product. The written product can be accompanied by an oral presentation. Examples of written assignments include essays, reports, journal entries, poetry, articles, short stories, interviews, analyses, observation reports in science, or research of some kind. Written assignments can be assessed with a rubric, checklist, or rating scale, or become part of a portfolio. Assessment may be done by the teacher or combined with self- or peer assessment.

PRESENTATIONS.   Presentations can be made by individuals or groups. They can be supplemented with audiovisuals or activities. A written report may accompany a presentation. Presentations can be used in any school subject and on a wide range of topics. For example, the class may be divided into groups to investigate topics that are part of a teaching unit on the environment. Different groups investigate different aspects (e.g., natural resources, pollution, conservation, energy sources, and land use and reform). Assessment can be at the end of a unit or course (summative) or as the course progresses (formative). The teacher can do the assessment or involve student self- or peer assessment. Stations, contracts, or portfolios can be used. Information can be sought, recorded, and assessed in various ways.

PERFORMANCE ASSESSMENTS.　Many things students should learn are more complicated than identifying, naming, or listing. *Performance assessments* are techniques to gather information about students as they actively engage in learning. Examples are manipulating materials (e.g., a basketball or a baton) or their bodies (e.g., dance or tumbling), doing a skill (embroidering or charcoal sketching), solving a complicated problem, giving a speech, or engaging in a debate. Some performances are assessed as they occur (e.g., operating a microscope); others by examining the product (e.g., a water color painting). The criteria used to measure achievement normally should be limited to important facets, and students should be informed about these.

HOMEWORK.　Homework is work students are to do beyond regular classroom presentations or activities. Frequent and systematic teacher monitoring of homework is important. It helps teachers identify students' strengths and weaknesses and the effectiveness of instruction. Homework can be teacher, self-, or peer assessed. Homework and seatwork are discussed in Chapter 8.

JOURNALS

> How can I know what I think until I read what I wrote? (Scotty Reston, Bureau Chief, *The New York Times*)

The use of journals for assessment is relatively recent. Journals are popular with many teachers. They can be a way to gain insight into student abilities and enhance student–teacher communication (Robinson, 1995). Teachers can use journals to help students construct concepts treated in class, promote critical thinking, and foster student self-assessment. Journals provide valuable information about the effectiveness of instruction. When they are done thoroughly, they make assessment an ongoing process for student reflection, teacher–student dialogue, continuous feedback, valuing of student ideas, encouragement, and they "enrich face-to-face interaction" (Heinmiller, 2000).

Students need to be taught how to use journals. They need to know why they are writing, and how to go about it. Journals provide opportunities for one-to-one conversations with their teacher, which helps the teacher monitor progress and enhance students' personal development. A conscious effort is needed to make journal writing nonthreatening. To encourage meaningful description, good analysis of learning, and expression of feelings, students need to know that there will be no undue emphasis on the quality of writing, grammar, and spelling. Rather, emphasis should be on good description, critical analysis, expression of feelings, and justification of responses. Students can be encouraged to express themselves in ways they feel comfortable. For example, some may wish to use pictures, diagrams, concept maps, or lists. A common format for journals is: (1) describe learning about what occurred in class, what was read, or experienced elsewhere, about an event, a lesson, or learning unit; (2) analyze the impact on personal understanding and feelings; and (3) propose what is intended to be done in the future as a result of what was learned and feelings about what was learned. With the increased use of computers, students may opt to submit journals by e-mail or as attachments. When it is done well, journal writing is a powerful way to construct meaning.

Although many teachers use journals extensively, some have stopped or cut back because: (1) they can consume much teacher time; (2) when several teachers assign journals, the workload for students may be too heavy; (3) students who are good at writing tend to like journals, but poor writers may dislike them; and (4) when journals are graded, free and honest expression may be inhibited.

Quizzes and Tests

Quizzes and tests present common situations to which students respond. Each quiz or test has common instructions and rules for grading. Quizzes differ from tests in that quizzes are usually shorter and limited to material studied in a lesson, a previous lesson, or recent lessons. Quizzes often are used to find whether students are ready to move to new material. The major use of quizzes and tests is to measure academic achievement. Most subject-matter quizzes and tests measure the degree to which students have achieved intended learning outcomes; they allow students to show what they know or can do at the time of the quiz or test.

PREPARING GOOD TESTS.   Good tests should be valid and reliable. They seek information about what was treated, and the way it was treated. Tests should consist of items appropriate for the learning outcomes to be measured. These may be recall, understanding, application, or higher-level outcomes that call for analysis, creativity, or reasoned judgments.

Testing and grading, particularly paper-and-pencil tests, have been fraught with controversy as long as they have been used. The arguments pro and con have changed little over the years. A summary of the criticisms and reasons for the use of testing are presented in Figure 5.2.

You, as the teacher, may know what you wanted to ask with a test item—students might not. Students need to understand what was asked and how to respond. Items should be free from clues, and the level of difficulty should be appropriate. Also, tests should be used to improve learning; though an important purpose is diagnosis of achievement and teaching effectiveness, *tests should also be teaching and learning tools.* Students deserve to receive clear feedback about how they did. This lets them check what they know and to turn "deferred successes" into "successes." In addition, tests should deepen understanding. Recall is enhanced because of this, and because material is reviewed while the test is written, and reviewed again when taken up. Tests can be learning experiences

FIGURE 5.2   *Testing and Grading: Criticisms and Reasons for Use*

Criticisms	Reasons for Use
• Dehumanizing	• To sort people for jobs and other roles
• Unduly emphasizes competition	• Used as rewards to motivate
• Promotes cheating	• To judge whether a teacher is or is not doing a good job
• An extrinsic reward system that discourages intrinsic interest	• So parents can judge how their children are doing compared to others
• Often tests the wrong things (recall rather than thinking and application)	
• Preparation and marking are very time consuming	

in themselves. They can be arranged so that less difficult items precede the more difficult ones. Short-answer questions in the early sections can provide knowledge that might be used in later long-answer sections. Initially, simple recall can be required, followed by questions that require analysis and synthesis. There are science and experience behind creating good test items. It is worthwhile to examine the testing approaches for Advanced Placement and The International Baccalaureate.

The types of test items you select should require the same performance of students, and the same conditions or "givens," identified in the instructional objectives, and be congruent with the activities students engage in to achieve the objectives. The types of test items available include: oral assessment, performance, extended open response (essay), short answer, matching, multiple choice, true/false, and variations of these. A first step is to decide what it is that you want to test.

ORAL ASSESSMENTS. Oral assessment is done on what students say rather than write. It can be used when written assessment is not feasible or appropriate. It can supplement written assessment or check its validity. More questions can be asked, because written responses take longer than oral responses. Oral assessments can assess students' ability to express themselves orally or to check ability to "think on one's feet." Rating scales or checklists may be used to record judgments about student performance. If you use oral assessment, try to reduce the level of tension most students experience. Private sessions may be less stressful. The teacher can use oral assessment to recognize differences in culture or language background. Oral assessment may be used if a student has a physical handicap such as blindness or paralysis. When you use oral assessment, be wary of the tendency to provide prompts that are not available to every student. A variation is to use oral questions but require written responses. Oral assessments can be used in courses in which development of auditory comprehension skills is an objective. A major use of oral assessment can be to balance testing approaches and accommodate various learning styles.

PERFORMANCE TEST ITEMS. Normally, performance tests are used to assess how well a student performs a behavior that has been practiced to achieve an objective or objectives. It include processes such as "working with others" or skills in physical education (e.g., tumbling). Usually, performance tests measure direct performance, such as operating a computer, giving a speech, playing a musical instrument, or operating a lathe. Assessment can occur on performance in simulations, for example, the simulated operation of an automobile. Clear criteria need to be set, and students need to be aware of them. The use of rubrics for grading has become common. Usually, both product (the "correct" answer) and process (how something is done) should be assessed. Avoid undue emphasis on product.

EXTENDED OPEN-RESPONSE (ESSAY) ITEMS. Most people call extended open-response items *essay* items. Students are asked to compose a comprehensive, lengthy, or complex response on a topic. Students provide, rather than select, answers. No single response or pattern is correct. More than recall should be involved. Good items test complex cognitive processes or skills. Students have to "pull things together" (organize), use information to solve problems, express what they know, or be creative. Examples of outcomes that can be assessed through essay items are: seeking a solution to a problem, synthesizing data from two or more sources, comparing and contrasting, examining cause-and-effect relationships, developing an argument to support a position, and critically examining assumptions.

When items are prepared, be sure students know what is expected (e.g., to compare and contrast, to predict, to judge the merit of something using certain criteria, or to provide original examples). Avoid items that are "as broad as all outdoors," leave students guessing, require students to have memorized reams of information, and choices when you may want every student to write the same test. Importantly, *test only what was taught!*

Extended responses are time consuming to grade and the course content sampled is restricted, so important content may not be tested. Though only a few items have to be prepared and marked, marking may be long, laborious, and lack objectivity. Objective tests (e.g., multiple-choice) allow greater coverage of what was taught. Bluffing and writing skill can influence the score, so the test may not help you discover what students know. There is a tendency for teachers to grade essay items higher than objective items. Some authorities believe that extended response items should be restricted to term papers or take-home tests.

RESTRICTED RESPONSE (SHORT-ANSWER) ITEMS.   Restricted response items have students supply, or complete, short written responses to specific questions. Answers to short-answer items may be a single word, a phrase, or a paragraph or two. The question should specify response limitations, and evaluation criteria for scoring should be provided. Short-answer items are good for testing students' ability to recall. Many facts can be tested in a short time. Test construction is relatively easy. Fewer items are required than in other objective tests. Guessing is less than when other objective items are used, but less content can be surveyed than with, for example, multiple-choice items.

It is not easy to measure complex learning through restricted response items. As in other rapid response items, rote recall may be stressed and students may take time to memorize trivial details. It is difficult to construct clear, unambiguous items, and scoring can be difficult.

It is a good idea to develop a bank of short-answer and other items. If you want to use items in future tests, have tests returned. When you reuse items, make sure they are still appropriate.

MATCHING ITEMS.   When matching items are used, students are presented with two lists of items. Tell them to select an item from one list (the *premise* list) that most closely matches an item in the other list (the *response* list). Matching questions can test knowledge of facts, relationships, or associations. Arrange items in a list randomly and have the response list longer than the premise list. To avoid confusion, make sure the material is homogeneous (or related), avoid making the lists long, keep both lists on one page, and provide clear directions. Matching items are not suitable for assessing achievement of higher-level objectives. Constructing lists that are free from clues takes time and is difficult. Guessing may occur as the process of elimination takes place.

MULTIPLE-CHOICE ITEMS.   Multiple-choice items consist of a question or statement (the *stem*) followed by a list of possible *answers*. Provide four possible answers. Each answer should be plausible, and students should be told to pick the "best." Many think multiple-choice questions are the best type of objective test items. They are versatile and easy to mark. Learning at all cognitive levels can be evaluated, and items can be reliable and objective. A large knowledge base can be tested in a short time. Multiple-choice items probably should be used in conjunction with other testing formats.

Multiple-choice items, normally, are not suitable for measuring organization or composition capability. Measuring higher-level thought processes (though possible) is not easy. Constructing good items is time consuming and difficult. Great care must be taken to word items carefully and to avoid clues. It is hard to construct higher-cognitive-level items; therefore, tests sometimes include an inordinate number of low-level items. Many more items are required than in essay tests. Multiple-choice tests may promote guessing. Students with above-average reading ability may have an advantage, though students with less reading skill may know as much.

TRUE–FALSE ITEMS. True–false (alternate response) items require students to indicate whether a statement is correct or incorrect. True–false items can test the most facts in the shortest time and are the easiest to score. They *seem* easy to prepare. While they are usually used to test recall, they can measure a range of thinking abilities. True–false questions should rarely be the sole testing technique in a test. A way to increase the value of true–false tests is to have a large number of items.

Guessing is a problem, so care must be taken to reduce the effects of guessing. A variation to reduce guessing is to have students explain their choice or to revise statements that are false (providing credit only if the revision is correct). Guessers tend to select "true" more often than "false," so have more "false" items than "true." True–false tests are good ways to pretest or diagnose. A short true–false test can be used as a set or preview of what will be learned.

ESSAY VERSUS OBJECTIVE TEST ITEMS. A question you have may be whether to use essay or objective test items when you are testing. Table 5.2 may help you decide.

TABLE 5.2   *Whether to Use Essay or Objective Test Items*

	Essay	Objective
Competency measured	Ability to express oneself in own words using own background and knowledge. Taps high reasoning levels. Inefficient for measuring factual information.	Student selects answer from options provided, or supplies answer in one word or phrase. Can tap high reasoning levels. Efficient for measuring fact knowledge.
Content coverage	Only a limited field of knowledge in one test. Questions take long to answer. Good writers have an advantage. Questionable reliability measurement.	Broad field of knowledge can be covered in a test. Questions can be answered quickly, so there can be many questions. Broad coverage helps provide reliable measurement.
Encouragement to learn	Encourages students to learn how to organize ideas and clearly express them.	Encourages students to develop broad background and knowledge.
Preparation ease	Only a few questions per test. Tasks need to be clear, general enough for some leeway, specific enough to set limits.	Need to write many questions. Wording to avoid ambiguities and giveaways.
Scoring	Time consuming to score. Teacher can provide written feedback on test paper. Grade awarded.	Easily and quickly scored. Answer usually either right or wrong. However, scoring very accurate and may vary widely. Different markers may use different criteria.

Preparing Test Items

Writing Good Assessment Items

Make sure your assessment items measure the instructional outcomes intended. Good objectives specify behavior, conditions, and degree. Good assessment items measure the exact performance identified in the objectives. If assessment items ask for the same performance as the objective, and if the conditions or givens are the same as in the objective, the item will likely be good. Assessment items must not only be appropriate, they need to be well written. Consider the following good matches between the givens and the performances specified in instructional objectives and the performances required in assessment items.

1. (a) *Objective:* When presented with a newspaper or magazine advertisement, the student will be able to correctly identify the psychological influences on the consumer.
   (b) *Assessment item:* The teacher provides clippings of magazine and newspaper advertisements and students are asked to identify which psychological needs are being appealed to in each ad.
2. (a) *Objective:* Given a map of North America and a list of latitude and longitude coordinates, students will be able to identify the names of nine out of ten cities that match those coordinates.
   (b) *Assessment item:* Using their atlases, and given the coordinates for ten cities with a blank space beside each coordinate, students are to write the name of the city that matches. You will notice the performance in the objective is the same as that required in the assessment. Also, the way students are to do the performance is identical.

Now, look at examples of poor items.

1. (a) *Objective:* Given a mannequin, the student will demonstrate the correct procedure for mouth-to-mouth resuscitation.
   (b) *Assessment item:* The test item requires the student to, from memory, provide a written description of mouth-to-mouth resuscitation.
2. (a) *Objective:* The student will, for items in a list of foods, write the correct name of the food group to which each belongs.
   (b) *Assessment item:* Students are shown a picture that displays different types of foods and are asked, under the headings "milk," "meat," "vegetable," "fruit," and "bread–cereal," to name three foods that appear in the picture.

In the first poor example above, in the objective, a given was that a mannequin be present and the student was to simulate mouth-to-mouth resuscitation. However, in the assessment item, a mannequin was not present and the student had to describe, rather than do, mouth-to-mouth resuscitation. In the second poor example, in the objective, students were expected to name the food group to which items in a list belonged. The assessment item, however, asked students to select three examples for each food group, the names of which were provided.

If objectives specify, and learning activities involve, performance at one cognitive level, but assessment is at another, the assessment is inappropriate. Here is an example:

suppose the objective is for students to name different types of levers, a lecture is provided on different types of levers, and students then practice identifying levers. The test item, however, requires students to choose the types of lever to use in different situations and to justify their choices. A mismatch between objectives and learning activities and assessment has occurred. Students at all levels find mismatching objectives and testing to be unfair.

Writing Clear Assessment Items

Items should state clearly how students should respond. Avoid test items that allow more than one interpretation of the performance expected. Higgins and Sullivan (1981) say that lack of clarity occurs when directions are too complicated, or several answers may be correct, or students are asked to put things in sequence without telling them the sequence, or students are to describe something without knowing the kind of description expected. Examples of each of these follow.

1. *Unnecessary details*

   There are four factors of production, and combinations of these factors, that economists consider when they analyze the productive capacity of a geographic region. Name them.

   It takes too long to ask students to name the four factors of production.

2. *No basis for ordering things*

   In correct order, list the planets in our solar system.

   What order is wanted? Distance from the sun? Date of discovery? Size? Number and kinds of satellites? Alphabetical?

3. *Several correct answers possible*

   Geese migrate in _____ .

   Correct answers include: "the fall," "the spring," "flocks," "V-shaped formations."

4. *No basis for providing a description*

   Describe the cities, towns, and villages in Mexico.

   Students do not know whether to sort these by size, location, political status, goods produced, etc.

5. *Insufficient clues—the item is mutilated*

   The _____ calendar contains _____ and is based on calculation of the earth's orbit _____ .

   There are too many blanks and key information is missing—the missing words are "Gregorian," "365 days," and "around the sun."

6. *Confusing word choice*

   T   F   It is not correct not to fly the flag after sundown.

   This can confuse the student because of the double use of the word "not."

Avoid Prompted Items

Testwise students look for prompts or clues to correct answers. Tests laden with prompts are poor indicators of what students have learned. Instances of prompts are grammatical clues, equal-length lists in matching questions, specific determiners, and illogical alternatives in multiple-choice tests. Look at the prompted items below.

1. *Grammatical clues*

   Copper is an: (a) rare metal; (b) common metal; (c) alloy.

   The article "an" only fits the response, "alloy." Use "a/an." Avoid other prompts by, when appropriate, using combinations such as: "his/her," "is/are," and "was/were."

2. *Equal number of items*

   Match each metal with its category:
   ___ Gold   1. Alloy
   ___ Brass   2. Common
   ___ Aluminum   3. Rare

   The student who has two correct answers automatically will be correct on the third.

3. *Specific determiners*

   T   F   Aspirin should be taken with care because it always causes stomach problems.

   Test-smart students immediately circle "F" because words such as "always," "only," or "never" are usually false, and words such as "sometimes," "may," "could," or "usually" are normally true. In multiple-choice items, the longest response to a stem is most often the correct one.

4. *Illogical choice*

   A union may use a boycott as a tactic. A boycott is: (a) withholding of services; (b) a place where males sleep; (c) members don't buy the employer's product.

   Item (b) is ridiculous, so those who are unsure of the answer have a better chance of guessing the correct response.

More Ideas on Constructing Good Items

In true–false tests, every statement should be completely true or completely false. Statements should be concise, and trivial details should not cause a statement to be true or false. Normally, in true–false tests, there should *not* be a pattern of correct answers (e.g., every item false, every item correct, or a pattern of two correct answers followed by a false answer).

In multiple-choice tests, the stem items should clearly state the central problem. Choices should be grammatically consistent and concise, and repetition of lead words in possible answers should be avoided. Though a pattern of responses for multiple-choice items may ease scoring, avoid patterns (e.g., repetition of a pattern of "c," "b," "d," and "a" as correct responses). Test takers can tumble to the pattern. Each choice should be plausible. Begin with clear directions and keep the lists of premises and responses homogeneous.

For matching tests, the list of responses should not be too long nor too short (i.e., between five and fifteen).

No matter how well a test is written, unless students have learned how to take tests, it may not assess what was intended. After all, shouldn't you discover what each student knows? "Dry run" tests can be given and taken up to teach students how to read questions and provide appropriate answers. Students who have not taken many essay tests during their schooling may not know how to respond. They can, for example, learn to prepare and use an outline before they respond. Students can also be taught how to take objective tests.

After the Test Is Administered

After you have administered a test, before you file it, evaluate whether each item does the job for which it was designed. Examine the level of difficulty and the *discrimination index* of each item (the degree to which students who know the work answer the item correctly, more often than those who do not know the work well). Good items should be filed in a test bank; however, when you teach the course again, you probably will have to write new items to reflect how the course was taught. Many references describe how you can analyze test items. Examples include Stiggins's *Student-Involved Classroom Assessment* (2005) and McMillan's *Classroom Assessment: Principles and Practice for Effective Instruction* (2004).

Marking Systems

Grading and marking systems have long been sources of controversy. Differences of opinion exist on whether letter, percentage, or other symbols (e.g., stanine, which is a 9-point scale), or pass–fail systems should be used. More and more educators believe that alternative forms of assessment and reporting should supplement grades, even replace them. Some authorities prefer systems such as narrative reports, mastery reports, or portfolios, because these can make assessment more *authentic*. More and more authorities argue that instructional approaches such as cooperative learning, whole-language, outcome-based, or authentic instruction require approaches that are more flexible. To overcome objections to using a single marking system, some school districts have adopted multiple marking systems or *standards-based grading*. Though combinations, when used well, may be reasonable, the number of grades to report is doubled or tripled, and explaining the systems to parents is more difficult.

In any given school you may be required to use the marking system agreed upon, but you may have some flexibility. Whichever system or combination of systems is chosen, report cards should explain clearly what is used. Students and parents, not just school personnel, have a right to understand the method(s) chosen.

Letter Grade System

The letter grade system is the most widely understood. People are generally aware that A is the top mark, D denotes marginal performance, and F is failing. Letter grades that record and summarize performance over a period or a term are easy to record. The number of signs is as few as four or five, or as many as fifteen if plus and minus are used. Meaningless ranking of students is reduced (e.g., a student with a grade of 70 percent is ranked below a student with 71 percent); and unfair award decisions are less common (e.g., the student with an average of 96.29 percent does not get a scholarship because a classmate with an average of 96.56 percent is the winner). Some believe that letter grades (and for that matter, numerical grades) are needed as extrinsic motivation, arguing that students will not work hard enough if there are no objective grades.

The advantages of letter systems are balanced with disadvantages. Different school jurisdictions use different marking systems, so interpretation is difficult when a student moves from one school to another (e.g., performance awarded a B in one school may earn a C in another). Also, letter grades are arbitrary, gross indicators of a student's level of mastery—there may be much difference between a low C and a high C. For that matter, differences can occur between one teacher and another in the same school or department. Little information about a student's strengths and weaknesses is communicated. Some teachers think differentiation between the achievements of different students is necessary and so prefer a numerical system.

Numerical Grade System

The numerical grade system is not as widespread as the letter system. The most common numerical system uses percentages. Numbers are convenient ways to record a summary statement of work over a period or term. Scores or percentages are easy to average, and ranking is more discriminating. Many parents think numerical grades are meaningful and easy to understand, and some parents and teachers believe they are extrinsic motivators. Disadvantages include the impossibility of making, for example, 50 valid and reliable distinctions between 50 percent and 100 percent. Grading is arbitrary, and little information about student strengths and weaknesses is communicated. As with letter grades, numerical grades are not keyed to a common standard, so considerable differences occur in the meaning of the designations between one school or district and another (a grade of 88 percent in one jurisdiction may be 68 percent in another). And, remarkable differences occur between grades awarded by teachers in the *same* school or department.

It is not uncommon for school systems that use letter or numerical systems to supplement these with checklists or brief comments. Symbol systems do not describe a students' strengths or weaknesses, nor what a student can or cannot do. Checklists also may be used to describe nonacademic aspects such as social skills, responsibility, organization, or conduct.

Pass–Fail System

Another approach is the pass–fail system. Variations are *pass–fail–incomplete* and *satisfactory–unsatisfactory*. The pass–fail system is not as common as some other systems. It sometimes is used for subjects with a high performance or finished-product component. It can be argued that it is silly to use letter or numerical grades in performance-oriented, dance, drama, or visual arts classes or for products in vocational classes. An advantage is that the negative effects of competition and test anxiety are reduced, so students are not afraid to take risks and are more prone to help each other. Cheating on letter and numerical tests is more common than many educators care to admit. Some argue that students will do only what it takes to pass; others say that the opposite is true—students actually learn more and are more likely to improve interpersonal and social skills. Ranking and discriminating between one person's performance and others is difficult, but parents may want to know how their child did compared to other children.

Mastery Grading System

Mastery grading can be used for all or part of a course. Usually, the assumption is that virtually all students can master learning objectives if given enough instruction and time. Content is broken into parts with specific objectives and criteria for meeting objectives for each part. If, when tested, a student does not achieve a certain grade (e.g., 80 percent), more instruction and time are provided and, when a learner is ready, retesting takes place. Grading usually is pass–fail, but performance can be converted to marks. A variation of mastery grading, often used with individualized instruction, is *contract grading*. A contract, for example, specifies the type, quality, and amount of work required to earn an A, B, C, and D. Learners choose the grade they will work to achieve and will know exactly where they stand.

Narrative System

In the narrative system, teachers describe and comment on students' learning in writing. Narratives can provide much more information than letter or numerical grades. Diagnostic information can be included to help teachers consider how best to help students. Some believe that rubrics or checklists of competencies are easier to prepare and are as good as narrative reports. However, it is difficult to prepare checklists that adequately describe a student's level of performance or mastery. Narrative reports may be used for more than academic progress, such as work habits and level of effort, conduct, social skills, organization, and responsibility. *Anecdotal reports* may be included—brief, presumably objective descriptions of incidents or events involving students. Narrative systems can reduce test anxiety and the negative effects of competition. It is difficult to institute a narrative system, however, because of potential opposition from parents and politicians who use grades to rate teachers.

Portfolio System

Many school systems either use, or are considering using, portfolios as the major assessment tool or for use with other techniques. Many teachers are excited by the progress of their students and have become advocates of the portfolio approach.

Portfolios were described earlier. They are collections, in a binder or container of student work, to be reviewed and judged against preset guidelines. Ideally, students are involved in selecting work to be included, deciding how it should be rated, and evaluating it. This can motivate students. They can be useful for reporting to parents and to supplement report cards and standardized test results. "When using portfolios, students should be involved in deciding what will be included and how it will be evaluated" (Kauchak & Eggen, 2003, p. 412). The best portfolios contain evidence of student self-reflection, for example, through free-expression logs or journals. Common ways to check work are rubrics, checklists, and rating scales. Portfolios provide good information about students' strengths and weaknesses. They can reduce testing trauma, encourage cooperation, increase motivation, and free students to risk and be creative.

Teachers must not ignore parental, business and industry, and political objections to the use of portfolios, particularly if they are used as the main assessment technique. Critics, at least initially, object to portfolios, though they may be aware of the possible devastating effect of failing on some when a letter or numerical systems is used, sometimes with life long consequences. Portfolios can be very time consuming to examine and assess, record, and report results. Fine discriminations between the work of one student compared to others are difficult. In spite of criticisms, portfolio use is growing in popularity. This seems to parallel acceptance of the notion of *authentic instruction*.

Self-Evaluation

Increased emphasis is occurring in many school systems on self-directed learning. Self-evaluation is an important aspect. Students have input in determining their grades. This may be done through guidelines set by the teacher or by students in cooperation with the teacher.

Motivation may increase because students develop ownership and accountability for their learning. A potential shortcoming is that students may over- or underrate themselves.

Self-evaluation can occur in partnership with, or supplement, other grading techniques. It is argued that students are natural self-evaluators. If they are to learn to think critically and make sound judgments, they should have experience with self-evaluation (Bowd, McDougall, & Yewchuk, 1994). Self-reporting can occur on checklists, rating scales, self-report forms, or be included in a journal or log. Learning logs or journals, as self-monitoring aids, are increasingly popular, particularly in language arts. They are records, by students, of their reflections about themselves as learners, their learning, feelings, and goal setting. Teachers should encourage students to be constructively analytical about their successes and "deferred successes." Instruction on how to do meaningful reflection and self-evaluation is needed, as is frequent feedback on the process of reflection.

Other Forms of Assessment

Performance Assessment

The trend today, congruent with a desire for active learning and for student learning while being assessed, is the use of *performance assessment, alternative assessment,* and *authentic assessment.* Some educators use the terms interchangeably, saying students are required to perform a task rather than complete a paper-and-pencil test (Office of Educational Research and Improvement, 1993). Others distinguish between the terms. Arends (2004) says, in *performance assessment,* students are to demonstrate certain skills and behaviors, while in *authentic assessment* students go a step further, asking that the demonstration occur in a real-life situation (pp. 245–248). Another view is that performance assessment is an umbrella embracing both alternative and authentic assessment (Wangsatorntanakhun, 1997). Some use *alternative assessment* to differentiate between paper-and-pencil tests and most other tests. Regardless of the definition, students have to do something, whether over an extended time such as several weeks or a short time such as five minutes, for instance: write an essay, play a melody, paint a picture, prepare a report, interpret a problem, or demonstrate a ballistic stroke in badminton. Performance assessment has two parts: a clearly stated task and explicit criteria for assessing a product or performance. The purposes for using performance assessment are so (1) students will be better motivated because they must organize experiences and actively construct personal understanding, (2) teachers will glean valid information for improving teaching, and (3) learning will be improved because students perform better when they know the goals they are working toward and how their performance compares to criteria to be met.

Alternative Assessment

Alternative assessment methods can foster authentic learning; opportunity is provided to foster critical thinking skills, depth of knowledge, and to connect learning to student's daily lives (Muirhead, 2002). More and more educators use alternative assessment methods. The shift began because of frustration with the limitations of conventional evaluation. There are two main differences between traditional educators and those who use alternative assessment. The traditional educator depends on fewer assignments to evaluate performance, stressing tests and term papers (Muirhead, 2002). Teachers using alternative procedures use a variety of assignments requiring active construction of meaning, and moving beyond heavy reliance on passive recitation of information (McMillan, 2004). Critics of alternative assessments point out that they take much time to design and grade. Nevertheless, they offer opportunities for teachers to prepare relevant work so individualized learning opportunities can be provided and achievement promoted.

The shift in preference by educators from traditional paper-and-pencil testing has been made to increase relevance and meaningfulness for students as emphasis moves to contextualized problems without single correct answers. Individual pacing for student growth is a characteristic. In shifting attention to cognitive processes, how students learn is more important than the product. Active construction of meaning is the goal, aided by student self-monitoring. Emphasis is on the use or application of knowledge. Multiple approaches to assessment are used to recognize students' abilities and talents and to provide opportunities for students to develop, and demonstrate, diverse abilities. Assessments such as portfolios and journals provide an ongoing thermometer of developing understanding, skills, successes, and difficulties encountered, and students' feelings about their learning and themselves. Journals and portfolios encourage meaningful self-assessment. By including collaborative products to develop a profile of each individual's progress, the socioemotional dimension is included.

Several threads can be seen to link alternative assessments:

- Students are involved in setting goals and criteria for assessment.
- Students perform, create, produce, or do something.
- Tasks require students to use higher-level thinking and/or problem-solving skills.
- Tasks often provide measures of metacognitive skills and attitudes, collaborative skills, and interpersonal skills as well as the more usual intellectual products.
- Assessment tasks measure meaningful instructional activities.
- Tasks are often contextualized in real-world applications.
- Student responses are scored according to specified criteria, known in advance, which define standards for good performance. (Dietel, Herman, & Knuth, 1991)

Critics of alternative assessments point out that they take much time to design and grade. Nevertheless, they offer opportunities for teachers to prepare relevant work so individualized learning opportunities can be provided and achievement promoted.

Authentic Assessment

You likely will try to make your assessment *authentic,* as close to "real life" as possible. Proponents of authentic assessment argue that achieving fairness does not mean that assessment has to be impersonal and the same for every student. Instead, they say, assessment needs to be "appropriate." That is, it should be personalized and flexible to examine specific abilities and structured at the right level of difficulty. Authentic assessment is criterion referenced to identify strengths and weaknesses of students without comparing or ranking them. Students are asked to demonstrate their learning in a way *they* find appropriate. Authentic assessment is more labor intensive for a teacher but is nevertheless desirable. As you can understand after thinking about the various approaches to testing, each form has advantages and disadvantages. Differences of opinion exist and will continue to exist about the best approach. Some strongly favor the letter or numerical grade approach, others would jettison that approach and do away with standardized testing. The best approach may be a combination.

Educators who are reform minded should realize that meaningful contexts and authentic assessment can occur regardless of the technique or techniques used. That is, instruction and assessment contexts can be meaningful, authentic, and relate to the concerns and problems faced by students, as a combination of procedures is used. Jacqueline Brooks and Martin Brooks (1993) exhort us to "abandon the mimetic approach to learning and implement practices that encourage students to think and rethink, demonstrate and exhibit" (p. v). This can happen as we select a mix of assessment techniques and thereby reap the benefits of each.

Accommodating Special Needs Learners

Should students of different cultures, ESL learners, special needs learners, and learners with differing learning-style preferences be assessed in the same way as "mainstream" learners? If diverse learners should be treated differently, how can this reasonably occur? This is an issue you will face.

As a caring teacher you will try to understand all students in your class. What are their backgrounds? How proficient are they in the use of standard spoken and written English? Any physical or mental disabilities? Are any gifted? How do these factors affect how the students learn and how they can be meaningfully assessed? What are your students' sociocultural values, customs, and mores? Does gender or sexual preference affect performance? What stereotypes are typical for each diverse learner category? Maker, Nielson, and Rogers (1994) stress the need for a change in assessments within a diverse setting. To do this they rely on Gardner's theory of multiple intelligences. They designed a model to discover each student's particular problem-solving style and strengths. Each individual's preference is stressed while means for remediation are sought. Teachers need to be flexible in their formal and informal assessment practices so that every student can display what he or she knows and can do.

Have you ever heard someone say it is unfair for athletes, during competition, to wear eyeglasses or contacts? Glasses and contacts allow athletes with visual disabilities to perform as though they did not need help. The purpose is to reduce the influence of the disability on performance. Teachers need meaningful achievement information on *every* student and what might be done to help make assessment fair. Standard testing procedures may yield useless information about student progress (Iowa Testing Programs, 1999). Students with certain learning disabilities or physical limitations should have a "level playing field." They need the opportunity to show what they know and can do. "Let them wear glasses"—special arrangements, modified administration procedures, or the way students can respond to an assessment can provide a more authentic indication of achievement. Accommodations, however, should not compromise the validity of assessments.

Many school districts and departments of education have policies or guidelines regarding test accommodations for students with disabilities. The Wisconsin Department of Public Instruction (2001) provides examples of accommodations.

1. *Time accommodations*
   - Administer the test in shorter sessions with more breaks or rest periods.
   - Space testing over several days.
   - Administer the test at a time most beneficial to the student.
   - Allow the student more time to complete the test.

2. *Environment accommodations*
   - Administer the test at a time most beneficial to the student.
   - Allow the student to work in a study carrel.
   - Place the student in the room where he or she is most comfortable.
   - Allow the special education teacher or aide to administer the test.
   - Provide verbal praise or tangible reinforcers to increase motivation.
3. *Formal accommodations*
   - Use a Braille edition of the test for students with visual impairments.
   - Administer practice tests or examples before the date of the test.
   - Use sign language for directions and items for students with hearing impairments.
   - Allow use of equipment or technology that the student uses for other tests and school work.
   - Read directions and items for tests.
4. *Recording accommodations*
   - Have someone record the student's responses.
   - Use a computer board, communication board, tape recorder, etc., to record responses and then transfer these to the test booklet.

Assessment Issues and Trends

Bias

Teachers need to be fair and impartial, *and to be seen to be fair and impartial*. A huge range can occur in the grades awarded by different teachers on a test or assignment. Be aware of how easy it is, even with the best of intentions, for assessment to be biased. There has been extensive research on bias. The term *bias* refers to unequal treatment of students because of gender, culture, race, socioeconomic status, or other reasons. Each student is the product of his or her unique background. Previous experiences affect how students approach problems and how they respond to questions. Students from different cultural, linguistic, and socioeconomic backgrounds have different experiences and prior knowledge. Ask yourself whether students in your classroom have enough background knowledge to be successful in the assessment items you intend to use. Students should have had the opportunity to learn the test-taking knowledge and skills required for success.

Classrooms contain diverse populations—something to celebrate. Students are different by virtue of (1) learning style, (2) ethnic and cultural background, gender, and socioeconomic background, and (3) exceptionality. Because of diversity, it is easy to use biased tests. Kauchak and Eggen (2003) believe that bias can be reduced by accommodating diversity in assessment. Differences in background can be responded to, they say, by providing test-taking practice, teaching test-taking techniques, avoiding the use of language that may be confusing or unfamiliar, and making provision for non-native English speakers (p. 413).

Bias in content can occur in several ways. Consider a few examples. If you ask questions that include baseball or hockey illustrations, you may bias the test in favor of boys; if the illustrations include activities typically associated with girls, you bias the test in favor of girls. If you have items that speak of winter activities in the snow, you bias the test against recent immigrants who have never experienced winter snow. An item that speaks of a "touque" may be understood by a Canadian but not by an American, who would call the headgear a "stocking cap." If you ask students where the sun rises, the typical answer is "in the east." A student who was born near the North Pole would know that this is not always true, but the answer could be marked wrong.

Bias in testing procedures or test use occur because minority students, or those from another culture, respond to a test differently than expected. Metaphors and idioms common to people native to Canada or the United States may leave students who have recently immigrated totally confused. Severe problems with assessment procedures can occur with students who have limited command of English or who speak nonstandard English. Views of the role of testing can be another source of trouble. In North America, African American, Hispanic, and Indian heritage students, and in Britain certain ethnic group students, may have quite a different perspective of the role of testing and of the competitive nature of some assessment practices. Another problem can occur when students come from a culture that stresses oral rather than written communication. Tests with time limits may be a problem for people who believe it is best to do things when one is ready, rather than rushing through something and doing it poorly.

Discrimination can occur because tests do a poor job of measuring performance of students from minorities and nonstandard-English-speaking and non-English-speaking backgrounds. Inappropriate test scores can affect entrance into postsecondary programs or success in seeking employment. Problems such as the above provide a strong argument for using alternative methods of assessment. Students from minorities or nonstandard or non-English-speaking backgrounds should not be denied opportunities to achieve their potential. Some may come from cultures that emphasize testing and examinations and so may be more successful in taking tests than the majority school culture, especially tests that stress knowledge and recall.

Popham (1999) observes, "During the past couple of decades, educators have increasingly recognized that the tests they use are often biased against particular groups of students. As a consequence, students in these groups do not perform as well on a test, not because the students are less able, but because there are features in the test that distort the nature of the students' performances" (p. 67).

If you are aware your beliefs and practices are the products of your experience, and if you try to become more knowledgeable about the value systems and beliefs of other cultures, you can become a good cross-cultural teacher. Know where bias can occur and what you can do to make assessment less biased. Preparing students for tests, using problem situations and stems that are familiar to students, accommodating nonstandard-English or non-English-speakers (e.g., let a student who speaks Spanish answer questions in Spanish), taking up the tests in class, and use of alternative tests (e.g., an oral test), are among the things you can do.

Bias may be subtle, so teachers may not be aware of unintentional bias in the way they grade students. Marzano (2000), in discussing problems with the current approach to assessment, says, "Virtually all of the criticisms focus on one or more of three problem areas: (1) teachers consider many factors other than academic achievement when they assign grades, (2) teachers weight assessments differently, and (3) teachers misinterpret single scores on classroom assessments" (p. 3).

Assessment Trends

An examination of the literature on assessment reveals international trends: authentic assessment, emphasis on the cognitive rather than the behavioral view of learning, continuous assessment rather than written assessment, more student involvement and choice in assessment, self-assessment ability understanding of process at least as important as product assessment, use of technology in testing, use of multiple alternative assessments (including portfolios, journals, interviews, and documented observations), and group as well as individual assessment. A good source on international trends is provided by Brown, Bull, and Pendlebury (1997) in their book, *Assessing Student Learning in Higher Education.* An excellent U.S. reference is Stiggins's (2005) *Student-Involved Assessment for Learning.*

Effects of No Child Left Behind (NCLB) Legislation

One must wonder whether, in the United States, there will be a reversal of at least some of the trends described above because of pressure from politicians at the state and federal levels and given the effects of the federal No Child Left Behind (NCLB) legislation and state assessment and achievement standards. School districts in the United States must now respond to the call for accountability in assessment, use standardized tests, and meet achievement standards. State-imposed requirements differ from state to state, which further complicates matters. Another complication is that NCLB sets specific criteria for whether a teacher is "highly qualified," and every state helps define the benchmark.

Ylan Q. Mui (2004) of the *Washington Post* summarizes NCLB legislation. Under NCLB, enacted in 2001 as the core of President George W. Bush's education policy, U.S. schools must test student performance each year in grades 3 to 8 inclusive and once during students' last three high school years. Test results are sorted into subgroups by race or ethnicity, English proficiency, and special education class placement. Students with limited English now are included in that subgroup for two years after becoming fluent in English. All subgroups must be proficient in reading and math by 2014. If a school does not attain test-score benchmarks for two years in a row, students can transfer to a school that is performing better. A school could, ultimately, face being taken over by the state. The federal law has been, and is, sharply criticized by many educators, parents, and politicians as being too stringent, with too much weight placed on one test.

NCLB has had a strong impact on the teaching profession and what is expected of teachers. Amrein and Berliner (2003) believe that high-stakes testing has had a significant impact. NCLB "aims to make high-stakes testing more pervasive than ever before" (p. 32). The authors explore the extent to which such tests improve student motivation and raise student achievement. Their conclusion, based on several studies, is that motivation and learning are not increased and have negative results: students' intrinsic motivation to learn is less, they are not as likely to use critical thinking, teachers are more controlling in selecting learning experiences, teachers do not encourage students to explore content that interests them, becoming life-long learners is obstructed, students are alienated from their learning experiences, student motivation is decreased and the number of dropouts is increased, and more students do not progress to the next grade (pp. 32–34).

Classroom, and thus school climate, say Amrein and Berliner, is a key factor in motivation and learning. Schools, they claim, as a whole, suffer under external testing. Schools emphasize drill activities, use district funds to buy test preparation materials, narrow the curriculum taught, and keep language-minority and special education students from taking the tests (p. 34).

It should be noted that state backlashes and continuous criticism of NCLB throughout the country by educators and parents has, not surprisingly, caused the federal department of education to announce new flexibility for states regarding teacher quality, special education assessments, assessment for English Language Learners (ELL), and assessment participation rates (ASCD, 2004).

Standardized tests have taken on great importance in many North American jurisdictions. Although it appears that students are being tested, the real use appears to be to evaluate school and teacher quality. Popham (2003), in a discussion of the use and misuse of standardized achievement tests, argues that standardized achievement tests are first-rate tools when used for an appropriate purpose but are currently misapplied to assess educational effectiveness. He believes the tests do not assess the most important things that teachers try to teach. He observes that some of the items on standardized achievement tests are highly related to a student's socioeconomic status (SES).

- Most items on standardized achievement tests are concerned with qualitative, verbal, and spatial aptitudes and do not account for multiple intelligences.
- Tests include too many items that ought not to be used to measure the quality of instruction.
- Standardized achievement tests don't do a very good job of measuring what students have learned in school through their efforts and the efforts of their teachers.
- There are better legitimate ways to evaluate instructional quality. (pp. 122–138)

Assessment of and for Learning

If we want to foster improved student achievement in North America, says Stiggins (2002), we need to pay more attention to improving classroom assessment. He argues that the route to improvement lies in assessment, not only *of learning,* but also assessment *for learning.* While both are important, more attention is needed on the latter. He states, assessment *of learning* is done to seek evidence of achievement for reporting purposes; assessment *for learning* is done "to help students learn more" (p. 761). This involves gathering evidence to revise instruction and involving students. A continuous flow of information is needed to advance student learning. Teachers, Stiggins observes, do this by:

- understanding and articulating *in advance of teaching* the achievement targets their students are to hit;
- informing their students about those learning goals, *in terms that students understand,* from the very beginning of the teaching and learning process;
- becoming assessment literate and thus able to transform their expectations into assessment exercises and scoring procedures that *accurately reflect student achievement;*
- using classroom assessments to *build students' confidence* in themselves as learners and help them take responsibility for their own learning, so as to lay a foundation for life-long learning;
- translating classroom assessment results into frequent *descriptive feedback* (versus judgmental feedback) for students, providing them with specific insights as to how to improve;
- continuously *adjusting instruction* based on the results of classroom assessments;
- engaging students in *regular self-assessment* with standards held constant so that students can watch themselves grow over time and thus feel in charge of their own success; and
- actively involve students in *communicating* with their teacher and their families about their achievement status and improvement. (pp. 761–762)

An important part of assessment to help students learn is *formative assessment*. Formative assessment is increasingly important because of standardized testing and the pressure to have students succeed. Formative assessment "of learning," then, can be an enhanced, functional teaching and learning tool. Stiggins (1999), being interviewed on the theme of "assessment without victims," says for formative assessment to be most effective, teachers need to:

- Clearly state the achievement targets for students regarding knowledge, reasoning proficiency, performance skills, and product development capabilities
- Be confident, competent masters of the targets set for their students
- Transform valued achievement targets into quality, day-by-day indicators of achievement
- Provide evidence of things their students can now do they could not do before
- Ensure that formative assessment surfaces evidence that students are progressing
- Along with students, feel in control, not victimized

For formative assessment to be done well, teachers should be provided with, and take advantage of, an opportunity to increase what Stiggins calls their "assessment literacy." They need to know which assessment strategies to use in various situations, and how self-assessment and peer assessment can strengthen formative assessment. Students, he says, should be deeply involved in the assessment process (with no surprises, no excuses). Teachers, he adds, should build a portfolio of increasing competence with the use of formative assessment. Stiggins (2005) identifies three key factors in assessment. The teacher needs to articulate the standards of good assessment practice, meet these standards by accurately assessing student achievement, and have practical options for communicating assessment results. He stresses the importance of "the use of classroom assessment as a confidence builder for your students, as a motivator to keep them striving to learn, and as a strong foundation for unprecedented achievement gains for them" (p. 1). He adds, "We achieve excellence in classroom assessment when we balance a continuous array of assessments used to help students learn (assessment FOR learning) with periodic assessments used to verify that they did, in fact, meet prescribed academic achievement standards" (p. 1).

Technology and Assessment

"Technology can make the job easier and more efficient" (Heroman, 2003). You will want to enhance your proficiency and comfort with the use of technology in assessment. Kauchak and Eggen (2003) believe that technology (particularly computers) can provide important, time-saving functions. They can help you plan and construct tests, analyze data (particularly from objective tests), and keep student records (p. 422).

Most teachers have access to, and make frequent use of, computers in designing assessments and recording results. Computerized grading is common in many school systems. With this approach, a range of assessment items can be entered and weighted by importance in assessment of student progress. At the press of a button, the final mark can change significantly according to the weight given an item, but the programs do not make the grades generated "more accurate, honest, fair, or objective . . . in the end, teachers must still decide what grade offers the most accurate and fairest description of each student's achievement and level of performance" (Gusky, 2002, p. 780).

Integration

Assessment is a complex process that must be considered at all stages of the teaching process. Assessment, an aspect of learner-centered teaching, is the process of seeking information about student development. It is not just an add-on that happens after instruction—it is a key part of teacher decision-making and is closely integrated with instruction (McMillan, 2004).

Wiggins and McTighe (1998) present the idea of *backward design*. The implication of backward design for assessment is that we need to plan assessment early in the unit and lesson-planning process and not as an add-on at the end. Backward design involves the following stages:

1. *Identify desired results.* What should students know, understand, and be able to do? What is worthy of understanding? What enduring understandings are desired?
2. *Determine acceptable evidence.* How will we know the students have achieved the desired results and met the standards? What will we accept as evidence of student understanding and proficiency?
3. *Plan learning experiences and instruction.* With clearly identified results (enduring understandings) and appropriate evidence of understanding in mind, educators can now plan instructional activities. (pp. 9–13)

Assessment design should normally occur early during planning. "When planning to collect evidence of understanding, teachers should consider a range of assessment methods":

- Informal checks for understanding
- Observations and informal dialogue
- Traditional quizzes and tests
- Open-ended prompts
- Performance tasks and projects

"The assessment of understanding should be thought of in terms of a collection of evidence over time instead of an event—a single moment-in-time test at the end of instruction—as so often happens in current practice" (pp. 12–13).

CASE 5.2 Assessment

A Parent–Teacher Interview

It is parent–teacher interview night and Mr. Polski, the history teacher, is discussing Hassim's work with Hassim's parents, who, in looking at his report card, are surprised how well he has done. They note that English and history are not his best subjects. "I used to give a lot of written assignments," Mr. Polski says, "and most of my testing was done with essays and quizzes. I went to a workshop that opened my eyes. I realized, to be fair to every student, I had to assess in a variety of ways and provide more choices to students so I could discover their real ability." Hassim's mother looks puzzled. Mr. Polski, warming to the topic, explains that he always thought Hassim and several others were more intelligent and capable than his original testing revealed. He adds that Hassim is not a great writer, and has to work on that, but when he asks questions in class, Hassim knows what he's talking about. Hassim's parents smile at each other, knowing how much Hassim likes to talk. "We've been studying the American Civil War," continues Mr. Polski, "and usually I test through essays and a quiz. This time I included a portfolio, which includes all Hassim's class work and homework for the unit." He opens Hassim's portfolio. It includes written work, material found in different sources with a section on Civil War weapons, and maps of key battles, and Mr. Polski tells Hassim's parents that he is a very good artist. He explains that he gave credit for presentations and that Hassim did a great job on the significance of the Gettysburg Address. Hassim's parents

smile even more proudly as they remember how excited their son was. Mr. Polski continues, explaining that in the final exam he tried several approaches, including an essay on the part that slavery played, and students could write an essay, journal, or a short play, as long as it answered the question. Hassim had written a remarkable imaginary diary of a freed slave— what a slave might have written if he could write. While there were style problems, it was very powerful. "We're very pleased, Mr. Polski," says Hassim's father, carefully folding away Hassim's report card. "We don't want any special treatment." "I understand," says Mr. Polski, "I think, this time, I found Hassim's true abilities. He needs to work on writing, but, as you can see in his portfolio, it's getting better and better. You have a very intelligent son."

LINKING PRACTICE TO THEORY

You have had much experience in being assessed. Now you are about to assess others. Try the approaches suggested in this chapter. Consider the difference between assessment of and for learning. What are the responsibilities and possibilities involved in assessment? What are the multiple perspectives in which assessment is used? How much do you have to conform to societal expectations? What are the possibilities?

Summary

Assessment is the process of seeking and obtaining information about student development and the effectiveness of instruction. Students' progress should be reported systematically from the beginning of the school term and be a regular professional activity. Student performance in a wide range of activities provides ample material for teachers to observe, record, and assess.

Assessment, evaluation, measurement, and testing are key aspects of promoting and recording students' performance. Inquiry, observation and analysis, and avoiding bias and discrimination are important characteristics. Assessment techniques can operate through an individual or group approach that involves

teachers and students. Instruments of assessment vary widely and may be used singly or in combination. Data may be recorded in a variety of formats, from grading systems using letters or numbers to narrative reports and portfolios of student work. Bias and discrimination in testing, assessing, and grading students' work are not always easy to identify, but a strong and continual effort should be made to avoid them. Accommodations, when testing, can be made for special needs learners. Using a variety of approaches to testing, assessment, and grading probably is the fairest approach. Assessment should be considered early when planning lessons and units, and assessment needs to be continuous.

Activities

1. List things you liked or disliked about the way your performance was tested during your K–12 and post-high schooling.

2. In groups of four or five, identify what you consider the most important points a teacher should convey to parents when reporting student progress. Report the three or four most important points.

3. Ask your cooperating teacher (or other teacher) how he or she tests, assesses, and grades. Ask why this approach was taken and what alternative approaches he or she might take.

4. If, currently, you have a field experience in which you teach a short unit, construct a test to assess student performance. In groups of three, discuss your units and testing. Ask for questions about what you intend to do.

5. Pick a unit from a school subject you intend to teach. Assume you have taught that unit and now must prepare the test. You wonder whether to make the test an extended response test, an objective test, or a combination. Agree on a solution.

6. Using the key terms in this chapter, have the class create an assessment and evaluation wall chart.

7. Have members of the class bring in a unit or a series of lesson plans they have designed. Using the principles in the chapter, have them attach effective assessment procedures.

8. In subject groups, discuss, then present to the class, the most common forms of assessment in their subject areas.

9. Present Gardener's multiple intelligences theory. Debate whether all students should have some choice in how they are assessed.

10. In subject groups, select a standard test item you have used before and redesign it giving choices based on multiple intelligences.

11. Get together in subject groups. Select an item of instruction for which you have a standard form of testing. Redesign the testing using a multiple intelligences approach.

part II

Mastering the Fundamentals

Classroom management is the number one concern of novice and experienced teachers. In Part II, this and other fundamental issues are treated:

- Establishing and maintaining appropriate classroom management and discipline
- Identifying common management problems
- Establishing and maintaining preventative, supportive, and corrective approaches
- Planning resource and instructional units that foster the learning of all students
- Being aware of the cognitive affective and psychomotor aspect of lesson planning
- Engaging learners through questioning, discussion, seatwork, and homework
- Teaching students to learn and analyze concepts, and to construct and use conceptual relationships and hierarchies
- Teaching cognitive, affective, and psychomotor skills
- Using deductive and inductive approaches in teaching skills
- Explaining and demonstrating

In summary, an effective teacher manages knowledge, materials, strategies, and people. A key element of management is how teachers engage students in learning. A teacher needs skill in questioning and giving directions and in using preventative, supportive, and corrective management. Teachers need to become proficient in teaching concepts and skills. Knowing how to run an interactive classroom is important, as is the ability to help students conceptualize and construct knowledge.

6 Classroom Management

Background for Classroom Management

Because one of the first and most basic tasks for the teacher is to develop a smoothly running classroom community where students are highly involved in worthwhile activities that support their learning, establishing an effective classroom management system is a first priority. (Emmer, Evertson, & Worsham, 2003, p. xiii)

No other aspect of teaching is as much of a concern to prospective and inservice teachers as classroom management and discipline. Gallup polls of the public's attitudes toward public schools have consistently identified "lack of discipline" as the most serious problem of the nation's educational system (Cotton, 1990; Rose & Gallup, 1999). In 2002 and again in 2003, *Phi Delta Kappa* identified lack of financial support as the biggest problem facing schools. However, in 2003, "lack of discipline" was the next most serious concern (p. 43). Eighty-four percent of parents believed that lack of discipline contributed much to why students fail to learn. Also in 2003, lack of home or parental support (93 percent), and lack of interest by the students themselves (90 percent), were first and second (Rose & Gallup, p. 51). Marzano, Marzano, and Pickering (2003), based on a meta-analysis of research, argue that, of the three roles of the teacher—using instructional approaches, designing curriculum, and using classroom management techniques—classroom man-

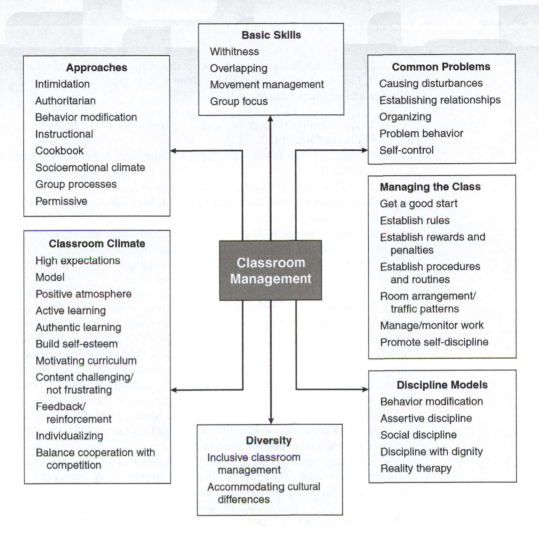

Basic Skills
Withitness
Overlapping
Movement management
Group focus

Approaches
Intimidation
Authoritarian
Behavior modification
Instructional
Cookbook
Socioemotional climate
Group processes
Permissive

Common Problems
Causing disturbances
Establishing relationships
Organizing
Problem behavior
Self-control

Classroom Management

Managing the Class
Get a good start
Establish rules
Establish rewards and penalties
Establish procedures and routines
Room arrangement/ traffic patterns
Manage/monitor work
Promote self-discipline

Classroom Climate
High expectations
Model
Positive atmosphere
Active learning
Authentic learning
Build self-esteem
Motivating curriculum
Content challenging/ not frustrating
Feedback/ reinforcement
Individualizing
Balance cooperation with competition

Discipline Models
Behavior modification
Assertive discipline
Social discipline
Discipline with dignity
Reality therapy

Diversity
Inclusive classroom management
Accommodating cultural differences

agement is the foundation. Good management is critical for effective instruction and learning—*it frees teachers to teach and learners to learn.* Involved are the complex set of behaviors teachers use to establish and maintain classroom conditions that will help students achieve instructional objectives efficiently. The more effective teachers are at motivating students, the easier it will be to manage behavior and the less need to discipline (see Chapter 4). Woolfolk (2004) highlights the dimension of *classroom environment.* The aim, she says, "is to maintain a positive, productive learning environment" (p. 397). She gives three reasons for working hard to manage classrooms: (1) *more time for learning*—time can be critical, and out of allocated time for learning there must be significant time on task and increased academic learning time when there is real learning and understanding; (2) *access to learning,* with an awareness that each task has its rules for participation—different expectations for a reading task compared with a group discussion task; and (3) *management for self-management*—the shift from demanding obedience to teaching self-regulation (pp. 397–399).

Management issues are a greater concern today because of changes of attitude. Jacobsen, Eggen, and Kauchak (2002) claim that management is a concern for both preservice and beginning teachers:

- Unquestioning respect for authority figures has been replaced by questioning, doubt, and hesitancy.
- Faith in schools as instruments of socialization has been replaced by criticisms of education.
- Attitudes toward child rearing have changed.
- The student population has changed dramatically. Learners won't sit quietly through dull presentations, and motivation is an important consideration; students spend much time in front of television sets; many urban classrooms have a majority of students with first languages other than English.
- An alarming number of students come to school with home environments and other experiences that place them "at risk." (p. 259)

While many authorities include "discipline" within their definition of management, some differentiate between management and discipline. Management, they say, is preventive; discipline is reactive. *Instruction* includes actions such as diagnosing learner needs, motivating, planning lessons, using instructional skills (which include management) activities, using teaching strategies, and assessing student progress. *Management* activities are intended to create and maintain conditions in which learning can take place. They include setting a positive and warm climate, establishing classroom group norms, and establishing classroom routines and procedures. *Discipline* refers to setting rules and consequences (rewards and punishments) and enforcing them. Good instructional and management skills reduce the need to discipline.

Smoothly running and productive classrooms in which students are highly involved in learning activities, where there is little disruption and off-task behavior, do not happen by accident. You can create a well-managed classroom and prevent disorder.

The Perspective of Students

What we read or hear about classroom management is usually from the perspective of teachers. It may be useful to look at management from "the other side of the desk." How do students feel? What are their goals? What coping strategies do they use? If we cannot put ourselves into the shoes of students, instruction may not be as effective as it should be. A study by Allen (1986) provides insight. He found that students tend to use six strategies to achieve two major goals: socializing with peers, and passing the course. Students behaved differently with different teachers because teachers vary in their approach to instruction, management, and discipline. Strategies students used during classes reflected their agenda at any given time:

During the initial events of classes:	1. Figuring out the teacher
During routine classroom events:	2. Having fun
	3. Giving the teacher what s/he wants
	4. Doing the minimum amount of work to get by
During critical classroom events:	5. Reducing boredom
	6. Staying out of trouble

Allen found that in classroom situations where there were few academic demands, students concentrated on socializing by "having fun" and finding ways to reduce boredom. In classes where academic demands were high and instruction was fast paced, students gave the teacher what was wanted so they could pass the course; however, when bored, they used socializing tactics to reduce boredom. In this latter case, students often did not enjoy the course because it was mostly an individual, nonsocial experience. Students believed classes that allowed them to socialize *while learning something interesting* were classes they liked best.

The message from the Allen study is that management should foster learning in a sociable environment. Learning does not have to be like taking bitter medicine. Teachers can select instructional approaches that promote student learning and allow students to achieve socialization objectives.

Common Management Problems

The results of a University of Regina (Saskatchewan, Canada) study illustrate common management problems (McBeath, 1989). Classroom management concerns of third-year secondary teacher education preinternship students that arose during their practicum experiences are reported. By category, and in order of frequency of mention, the concerns were as follows.

1. *Causing disturbance*—talking, not paying attention, not working at assignments, crude remarks, students moving around at will, smart remarks, constant socializing during preparation for home, not listening to instructions, and making trouble for others
2. *Establishing relationship*—establishing positive relations with students and enforcing discipline), getting respect as a teacher, getting respect as a woman, authority of student teacher being tested, concern with joking with students because they take advantage of it, not being too hard on students, how to act when patterns are already established, and handling a poor attitude
3. *Organizing*—how to work with entire class while an individual wants attention, the teacher directs attention to a few students and the others talk
4. *Motivating*—keeping up interest during class. Controlling students who are excited about what they are doing without dampening spirits
5. *Recognizing problem behavior*—odd behavior, e.g., students who had been drinking, "spaced out," refusing to participate, students not following a direct order, students refusing to answer questions, students refusing to do homework, cheating, absent previous period, and not bringing books
6. *Controlling self*—controlling my temper when I am triggered, and having to follow my cooperating teacher's pattern of management

Lang (1990) investigated classroom management concerns of secondary teacher education students that arose during their preinternship practicum. Findings are summarized in Figure 6.1. *Minor disruptions* included students disrupting the class, using profanities, testing the limits, and seeking attention. *Student teacher authority/personal style* included showing a lack of respect for the student teacher, determining the limits of student teacher authority, differences in approach by the student and cooperating teacher, and development of a personal discipline style. *Apathy* involved lack of interest in the school, class activities, or a school subject, keeping students on task, and sleeping in class. *Defiance*

FIGURE 6.1   *Major Classroom Management and Discipline Concerns of 94 Secondary Teacher Education Pre-Interns*

1. Minor disruptions	36
2. Student teacher authority/personal style	27
3. Apathy	26
4. Defiance	22
5. Suspected substance abuse	15
6. Keeping students of differing abilities on task	12
7. Major disruptions	7
8. Absenteeism and tardiness	7
9. Handling group work	6
10. Miscellaneous	12

Note: Students selected at least one but no more than two concerns.

behaviors were students refusing to pay attention, participate, or do assignments. *Keeping students of differing abilities on task* included some students finishing tasks early and others working slowly. *Major disruptions* ranged from students throwing objects, being physically aggressive, and terrorizing other students, to having a class completely out of control to the point of near-chaos. The concerns *absenteeism* and *tardiness,* and *handling group work* are self-explanatory. *Miscellaneous* concerns: dealing with students of different cultural backgrounds, recognizing and dealing with misbehavior resulting from family problems or pressure, a student who is isolated or rejected by peers, and cheating during a test.

Aspects of Effective Classroom Management

When one reads the literature on classroom management, common topics emerge such as those presented by Emmer, Evertson, and Worsham (2003) and by Evertson, Emmer, and Worsham (2006). The topics, in no particular order, are (1) getting off to a good start; (2) organizing the classroom and supplies; (3) choosing, establishing, and maintaining rules and procedures; (4) managing student work (grading, feedback, monitoring, and assignments); (5) using rewards and penalties; (6) maintaining good student behavior; (7) organizing and conducting instruction; (8) managing special groups; and (9) evaluating classroom organization and management. Emmer, Evertson, and Worsham (2003) add (10) managing cooperative learning groups and (11) communication skills for teaching. The novice teacher can be easily overwhelmed by management concerns. A useful structure would be to see management in terms of *preventive approaches* (getting off to a good start to minimize concerns), *supportive approaches* (maintaining good order), and *corrective approaches.*

Preventive Approaches

Just as you plan your lessons and units, you need to plan management. Preventing problems before they occur is best. This involves getting off to a good start, establishing clear rules and procedures, and being aware of effective teacher characteristics—knowing before classes even begin what works. This will reduce stress, make teaching pleasurable, and prevent teacher burnout. Management concerns form a major section of the Teacher Competence Profile introduced in Chapter 1.

TCP—CLASSROOM MANAGEMENT

Creates a positive classroom climate conducive to student-centered learning

Creates an enjoyable environment conducive to learning; fosters participation by all learners; quickly deals with interpersonal tensions; creates a positive attitude toward and excitement for learning.

Creates negative attitudes toward others and learning; allows interpersonal tensions to build.

Communicates and monitors expectations

Consistently provides clear and achievable directions; models and fosters appropriate behavior norms; clear standards; checks for understanding: monitors behavior expectations; immediate attention to behavior, i.e., feedback and correctives as appropriate; checks up periodically as needed.

Poor direction giving; does not model or promote appropriate behavior; inconsistent or inappropriate standards; does not check for understanding: does not notice (or allows) inappropriate behavior that often escalates; does not reinforce appropriate behavior.

Establishes and uses effective classroom routines and procedures

Maximizes on-task behavior through establishment of appropriate routines and procedures.

Routines and procedures nonexistent or inconsistent; high proportion of off-task behavior.

Handles minor disruptions in a positive way

Is aware of and unobtrusively and immediately deals with minor disruptions; watches for recurrence.

Is unaware of, does not respond to, or responds inappropriately or inconsistently to minor disruptions.

Uses a problem-solving approach to misbehavior

Uses a constructive problem-solving approach to discipline; involves the student and, as appropriate, others; ensures understanding of consequences of actions; sensitive to student self-concept and promotes student accountability.

Autocratic, teacher-centered, punishment oriented; insensitive to student self-concept; lack of student accountability.

Uses consultation when necessary

Recognizes personal limitations for dealing with unique needs or situations; provides appropriate documentation and involves others as needed (i.e., cooperating teacher, principal, guidance counselor, medical doctor, social services, parents, etc.).

Does not recognize personal limitations in dealing with unique needs or situations; fails to involve appropriate personnel.

Anticipates problems and plans for successful (preventive) management

Anticipates and plans for potential problems, which helps maximize on-task behavior.

Does not anticipate or preplan responses to inappropriate behavior; much off-task behavior occurs.

Uses management skills (Kounin) effectively

Consistently demonstrates awareness of off-task student behavior; plans for and monitors a consistent flow of meaningful activities; makes smooth transitions from one activity to another; is able to deal with minor problems without disrupting classroom routines.

Often unaware of off-task student behavior; does not plan for organized classroom; transitions often disrupt the classroom; ineffective use of time.

continued

TCP—CLASSROOM MANAGEMENT *(continued)*

Involves students in formulating classroom rules and consequences

Promotes student self-discipline; involves students in both setting and monitoring classroom rules and consequences; rules and consequences are appropriate to grade and age level.

Sets rules and consequences that are inappropriate; relies on punishment rather than rewards; does not involve students in setting and monitoring classroom rules and procedures.

Exhibits understanding of student behavior

Always able to anticipate problems and identify sources of classroom problems; uses cues to control behavior without interrupting entire class; clearly established behavior standards, can distinguish between major and minor disruptions and responds appropriately; reprimands are consistent with infractions, reacts quickly and decisively in handling discipline cases.

Is hesitant and indecisive when dealing with discipline cases; generally does not identify problem source; interrupts entire class to reprimand both major and minor infractions; behavior standards are not established or are seldom adhered to; reprimands are not consistent with infractions.

Practices fairness and is consistent

Is, and perceived to be, fair and consistent in enforcing rules and promoting positive behavior; positive behavior is rewarded and rule violation results in suitable consequences.

Is inconsistent in applying consequences or rewarding appropriate behavior; relationship between behavior and consequence is not congruent.

Getting a Good Start

Effective management begins with motivation and problem prevention. There is no substitute for starting the term by displaying a professional attitude that gives the message, "I care about you; I know that you can behave; I want to help you be a *better* you," and by quickly showing that your lessons are meaningful, interesting, and relevant. You can show that you believe each student is important and can grow academically and socially. Right at the beginning, they should know you mean business, care about them, will be firm but fair, expect them to behave and succeed, will be consistent, will not have favorites, have a sense of humor, and that you will do your best to provide excellent lessons. At the outset, remind students of the unequivocal "given" that misbehavior cannot be tolerated because it interferes with the rights of other students to learn and grow and your right to carry out your professional duties.

Students learn quickly whether a teacher will consistently enforce rules and make sure procedures and routines are followed. *Follow through!* If you say that something will occur, it usually should. Importantly, don't fall into the trap that imprisons many beginning teachers—the "nice guy syndrome." Those afflicted want students to like them and avoid applying the consequences of misbehavior or late assignments; worse still, sometimes consequences are applied, and at other times not. The almost inevitable result is that the teacher loses the respect of students and misbehavior escalates. Rules, procedures, and routines should be carefully thought out and communicated; ideally, students are involved in establishing rules. Students should discover very early that when they misbehave, the teacher will not allow the misbehavior to continue, but also will not hold a grudge or resort to "put-downs" or sarcasm that damages self-concept. Student misbehaviors should not be taken as personal attacks. Problems should be handled professionally. As well as a good start through well-planned classroom organization and instruction, Emmer et al. (2003) stress the need for being "actively involved in maintaining student cooperation and compliance," but note that "readiness alone, however, is not sufficient to sustain good behavior throughout the year" (p. 129).

Establishing Rules and Procedures

DEFINING AND SETTING RULES AND PROCEDURES.   Effective classrooms have reasonable rules and procedures. Students need to understand and see the behaviors expected of them as fair. *Rules* specify expected and forbidden behaviors; *procedures* prescribe the steps to accomplish activities. Nothing is more important than maintaining classroom rules and procedures that are understood and accepted by both students and teacher. *In successful classrooms, rules and procedures are taught explicitly* (not just stated). Effective teachers spend up to one-third of the first few days of school teaching rules and procedures. Even high school teachers should teach them explicitly and discuss consequences.

RULES.   Rules are statements of standards. They should be phrased positively, suggesting what "should be done," not what "should not be done." Authorities, such as Emmer et al. (2003), generally agree there should not be a proliferation of rules and that a few, say five to eight general precepts, are generally sufficient (p. 20). An example of a general rule is, "Respect others and their property." This covers a multitude of specifics, is easy to remember, and is easily accepted. Good rules are based on the golden rule: "Do unto others as you would have others do unto you." Some rules are quite specific, for example, "Only one person, the person who is recognized, can talk during a class discussion or in answer to a question."

Many teachers believe that students should be involved in rule setting, to promote "ownership" and responsibility. Students are more likely to accept and respect rules they helped design (Schimmel, 1997). This helps students understand reasons for rules and allows them to share in, and learn about, decision making. If students are involved, teachers must differentiate between rules that have to be accepted and those for which students can have a say. You could begin by setting the "givens," i.e., school rules that must be followed by everybody. Commonly accepted rules are

- Respect the rights and feelings of others.
- Respect the property of others.
- Bring all necessary materials and be ready to start when the period begins.
- Be attentive, only one person at a time can talk during presentations.
- Follow all school (or building) rules.

Rule making can be a learning experience if the teacher and students work together. The rule creation process becomes a critical thinking endeavor as students reflect and solve problems while negotiating with their peers (Castle & Rogers, 1994; Latham, 1998). As a caution, while all students need to be seen to be treated fairly, teachers should be flexible enough to meet the needs of individuals, and rules should be reviewed as needs of the classroom and school community change.

PROCEDURES AND ROUTINES.   Students need to know what is expected of them. Procedures are activities that are to be done and ways of getting things done in class. They are not aimed at prohibiting certain behaviors. To be "caught," procedures and routines need to be "taught" and practiced. A surprisingly large number of procedures and routines are used in the typical classroom (Figure 6.2). It is suggested that, in the first few days of school, teach only those needed to make the classroom operate smoothly.

Preventing Behavior Problems: General Considerations

Effective classroom managers engage in "preventive medicine." Many authors, including Weber, Roff, Crawford, and Robinson (1983, pp. 47–60), describe attributes of effective teachers. Consider the following distillation of their views:

- They work hard at establishing an environment, or ecology, that is pleasant, warm, caring, supportive, businesslike, and task oriented.
- They know their subject-matter content well, are enthusiastic about it, and organize it into "success experiences" for students.
- They set high, but achievable, standards of achievement and behavior with their students.
- They are encouraging, fair, consistent, and do not have favorites.
- They use a variety of instructional strategies, methods, and skills, recognizing learning styles, individual differences, developmental level, and the multicultural composition of their classrooms.
- They model, set, and consistently enforce reasonable, broad rules (and the logical consequence of breaking them) founded on mutual respect and the Golden Rule.
- They don't take student misbehavior personally; rather, they handle disruptions in a professional manner.
- They model, teach, and expect interpersonal skills such as paraphrasing, perception checking, behavior description, and feelings description.

FIGURE 6.2   *Typical Classroom Procedures and Routines*

- Behavior during morning opening events
- Handling attendance and tardiness
- Entering and leaving the room
- Beginning and ending a period
- Obtaining quiet in the room
- Talk during presentations
- Participation in questioning/class discussion
- Getting/putting away equipment and references
- Taking out/putting away books and supplies
- Distribution of materials and supplies
- Behavior during seatwork
- Getting help from the teacher/peers
- Notices, information about assignment
- Consequences of late assignments
- Handing in and returning assignments

- When an assignment is done early
- Participation in groups
- Moving from one area to another
- Changing classes
- Sharpening pencils
- Going to the bathroom
- Using the waste basket
- Homework
- Working in the library
- Visiting the local museum
- Behavior when guests are in classroom
- Interruptions—knock on door, intercom
- Behavior during emergencies
- Safety routines in the gym or labs
- Emergencies—fire and other disaster drills

- They have good conflict-resolution skills.
- They never do things to hurt the self-concepts of students. Sarcasm, belittling, blaming, and embarrassing are not used, and confrontation in front of the class is avoided.

Supportive Approaches

After a teacher has had a good start with a class, maintaining a positive learning environment or climate is important. Although much needs to be established at the outset (*preventive approach*), maintaining an atmosphere of positive learning must be ongoing. Key concepts include monitoring, facilitating, and motivating. Also significant are basic management skills as developed in Jacob Kounin's (1970) classic study, how to deal with the rules that were established, how to react to minor disruptions, and giving clear directions. The result of good supportive approaches will be more active learning time (ALT) and more effective learning and teaching.

Classroom Climate

The elements that make up a school climate are complex, ranging from the quality of interactions in the teachers' lounge to the noise levels in hallways and cafeterias, from the physical structure of the building to the physical comfort levels . . . of the individuals and how safe they feel. Even . . . opportunities for students and teachers to interact . . . add to or detract from the health of the learning environment. (Freiberg, 1998, p. 22)

Conditions for learning need to be favorable. The *climate* of the classroom is a matter of choice, just as instructional methods are a matter of choice. A teacher must build a climate that encourages learning. This involves the physical facilities and organization of the classroom, interpersonal communications, and the classroom management techniques used. The combination of these elements creates an environment in which students are motivated and encouraged to learn.

Classroom climate is the atmosphere in which students and teachers work and interactions between the teacher and students occur. It "can be a positive influence on the health of the learning environment or a significant barrier to learning" (Freiberg, 1998, p. 22). Climate influences how and the degree to which the teacher exercises authority, shows warmth and support, encourages competitiveness or cooperation, allows independence and choice, and motivates. Students must feel that they are safe, that they are valued, and that they can achieve. As well, climate is strongly linked to the instructional modes used, school and teacher expectations, and the evaluation schema used.

CHARACTERISTICS OF EFFECTIVE CLIMATE.   Effective teachers communicate positive expectations and demonstrate that they believe their students to be capable, and will try to achieve. Emmer et al. (2003) emphasize "the importance of keeping a positive perspective and avoiding overdwelling on student misbehavior or inadequacies" (p. 134).

The goal should be to establish a classroom that is conducive to learning, in which students feel good about themselves and others. The ambiance should be positive, where students are encouraged to engage in learning activities they find interesting, challenging, and relevant. Students should use communication, interpersonal skills, and group skills, listen to others, and be listened to by others. When the climate is good, students care about others and are cared about by others. They support one another, take risks, and learn from both successes and "deferred successes." Students move from being dependent to interdependent and then independent learners. For this to occur they need an empathetic, caring, and credible teacher-model who values and enjoys learning, is knowledgeable and skilled, and earns respect.

ORGANIZING THE PHYSICAL ENVIRONMENT.   The physical environment of the classroom affects how easy or difficult it is to manage students and how well they learn. It affects the intellectual, social, and emotional climate. The classroom should be a pleasant place in which to live and work. Ideally, the room allows different seating arrangements, accommodates different teaching strategies, and takes traffic patterns into account. Logical arrangement of furniture, equipment, and supplies can conserve class time and reduce interruptions and delays. Suitable room and materials arrangement is part of "preventive management." Answers to the following should be sought:

- Can everybody easily see the presentations and visuals? Not being able to see and understand invites inattentiveness and misbehavior.
- Can you, the teacher, see every student, and can they all see you? If you can see all the students, you can be aware of what is going on and students will not be as tempted to be inattentive or misbehave.
- Are high-traffic areas separated and uncongested? If high-traffic areas are separated and easily accessible, there will be less jostling and misbehavior, traffic will move quickly, and it will be easier for you to see and keep control.
- Are teaching materials and student supplies easily accessible? If materials and supplies are easily accessed, time is saved when they are brought out and put away.

CLASSROOM ENVIRONMENT AND INSTRUCTION.   The physical and affective environment should be pleasant with an academic emphasis. The teacher organizes success experiences—nothing succeeds like success; nothing stultifies like continued failure. People like to do things at which they are proficient and stop doing things they do not do well. They do not like situations that damage self-concept. This does not mean students must always be successful; but students who put forward reasonable effort should usually be successful. Learning tasks and expectations should be challenging but achievable. Successful teachers believe their students (capable and less capable) can master curriculum objectives and that they, the teachers, can support students' instructional needs. If necessary, they augment, even replace curriculum content to meet student needs. You can foster a positive attitude or mind set toward academic achievement.

Successful teachers create a positive classroom and school atmosphere as they interact frequently and positively with students, parents, and colleagues. They model positive attitudes and behaviors, handle incidents patiently, calmly, nonjudgmentally, and kindly. They avoid actions that may have adverse effects. They communicate information, explanations, opinions, and feelings to students, parents, and colleagues in a positive and constructive way. They raise self-confidence and self-esteem through encouraging and reinforcing, rewarding and praising good work and behavior, finding a balance between positive and negative feedback, seeking opportunities to make students feel liked, valued, special, accepted, included, supported, successful, and emotionally secure, and ensure that the classroom is safe, harmonious, and orderly.

Content quantity and pacing is linked to achievement, and achievement is highest when teachers expect students to master the curriculum. Early establishment of rules and procedures, an appropriate level of challenge in assignments, and consistent accountability procedures are important. Students need to know how to behave during seatwork, understand what they are to do, and when and how to get help. They need to know what to do when work is finished. The work expected should suit students' current achievement levels and needs. Success rates should usually be at 75 percent and up, to 100 percent for seatwork.

Classroom climate should be convivial, promote student engagement in academic tasks, promote cooperation, encourage, and foster self-sufficiency. Teachers who motivate encourage, are energetic and exciting, and stimulate. Sternberg and Williams (2002) say that lessons are interesting when teachers generate enthusiasm and use a variety of instructional approaches (pp. 392–393). Moore (1989) suggests guidelines:

1. Expect the best from students.
2. Model desired behavior.
3. Inform students what is expected (and why) and procedures for reaching objectives.
4. Establish a positive atmosphere.
5. Involve students actively.
6. Make learning seem worthwhile.
7. Cultivate self-esteem.
8. Capitalize on student interest.
9. Capitalize on student ideas.
10. Capitalize on curiosity.
11. Challenge students
12. Use reinforcement.
13. Individualize instruction to meet needs, interests, and abilities.
14. Use competition and cooperation when appropriate.
15. Reduce anxiety. (pp. 201–203)

CLIMATE AND SCHOOL ENVIRONMENT.   Parents want a personalized atmosphere in their children's schools. A healthy environment requires trust, respect, satisfaction, creativity, warmth, caring and support, high morale, and a high degree of student and teacher involvement. Drefs (1989), who reviewed literature on school climate, reports that an effective school environment has several interrelated variables. It displays: (1) pervasive caring about individual students that permeates every aspect of the school; (2) a positive physical climate (clean, well maintained, and attractive); (3) the ability to rise above the constraints of finite human and material resources (teachers are free to concentrate on instruction and professional development, extensive use is made of outside facilities and resources, and creative problem-solving occurs); (4) a school that is orderly and well disciplined, not oppressive (rules and consequences are clearly communicated and consistently enforced, teachers model desired behavior, and discipline is preventive, not just reactive); and (5) meaningful participation—by students and the community (pp. 18–23).

Drefs notes that the achievements of effective schools are remarkable, including greater academic achievement, better attendance, reduced delinquency, greater staff stability, lower dropout rates, increased school pride and less vandalism, fewer discipline problems, and more than cold dispensing of knowledge. Effective schools, he notes, are places where students and teachers treat each other with respect. They are communities in which students are happy, confident, productive, and proud of their school (pp. 23–28).

Managing and Monitoring Student Work and Behavior

Effective management and monitoring ensures that resentment, anxiety, or confusion will not occur. Teachers can and should: set a positive climate, accept student ideas, clearly state work requirements and assignments, monitor behavior and achievement, establish and follow through on consequences, promote student accountability, pace instruction appropriately, keep students on task, use interesting and success-oriented teaching techniques, and provide feedback to students on their behavior and work. Later chapters include things teachers can do as they manage and monitor student behavior.

Grading criteria must be congruent with well-thought-out and clearly communicated objectives. Criteria must be seen by students to be fair. Work in progress should be monitored, and regular feedback on student behavior and progress should be given. Descriptive, accurate record keeping that reflects progress and completion dates needs to be established.

Consistency is important. Rules and procedures must apply to *every* student on all occasions. Violations normally should not be ignored or misbehavior will spread ("ripple"). Be calm, reasonable, and never overreact. The personal worth or self-concept of individuals must never be attacked. Violations should be handled discretely, calmly, and usually one-on-one. Avoid interrupting the flow of presentations or class activities. Infrequent, short-duration, insignificant misbehaviors can be safely ignored rather than cause undesirable attention. Exercise judgment: Has the misbehavior occurred frequently in the past? Is it likely to persist? Has it interrupted the flow of the class? Was it an accident (e.g., a book inadvertently dropped)?

Basic Management Skills

"An ounce of prevention is worth a pound of cure." Do you want to establish and maintain classroom conditions that promote positive student behavior? Do you want to be free to teach well? Do you want every student to be free to learn? Then make these *basic management skills* part of your repertoire (Figure 6.3): (1) withitness (awareness), (2) overlapping, (3) movement management, and (4) group focus. These were identified by Jacob Kounin and his associates (Kounin, 1970; Kounin & Doyle, 1975; Doyle, 1977; Charles, 2005). In a classic study, they compared teachers who had relatively trouble-free classrooms with teachers whose classrooms were besieged with behavioral problems. Their studies and those of others, including Emmer et al. (2003), Evertson et al. (2006), and Weber and Roff (1983), confirm the effectiveness of these skills. The number and severity of problems you face can be greatly reduced.

WITHITNESS BEHAVIORS.   The word "withitness" has caused English language purists to shudder, but it expresses an important teacher capability. Withitness refers to quickly identifying and acting on potential behavior problems (Marzano, Marzano, & Pickering, 2003, pp. 66–67). Teachers who are "withit" seem to have "eyes in the back of their heads"; they are very much aware of what students are doing (or not doing), and students know the teacher is aware. Withitness refers to the degree of *teacher and student awareness* of everything happening in a classroom. Teachers who are aware can "nip problems in the bud"; and students who know they will be caught are less likely to misbehave and more likely to be on task. Withitness allows you to "time" interventions so you do not wait too long before taking corrective action, and to avoid blaming the wrong person for a misbehavior or punishing a group for the misbehavior of one or a few. If you are "withit," you can take corrective action before misbehavior spreads or "ripples."

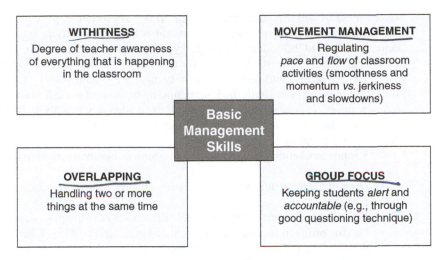

WITHITNESS Degree of teacher awareness of everything that is happening in the classroom	**MOVEMENT MANAGEMENT** Regulating *pace* and *flow* of classroom activities (smoothness and momentum *vs.* jerkiness and slowdowns)
OVERLAPPING Handling two or more things at the same time	**GROUP FOCUS** Keeping students *alert* and *accountable* (e.g., through good questioning technique)

FIGURE 6.3 *Kounin's Basic Classroom Management Behaviors*

Examples of teacher behavior that increases withitness include the following.

- Stand in places that allow you to see each student when you are presenting. Maintain frequent eye contact. Make a practice of glancing at all parts of the room.
- When you present, don't stay frozen in one spot (when appropriate, circulate).
- When helping individuals, place yourself so you can see as many students as possible.
- When writing on the chalkboard, angle yourself so you do not lose withitness. Use a "stage" turn (keeping sight of the class) when you move to the chalkboard (this allows you to maintain eye contact).
- Arrange classroom furniture (your desk and student desks) and equipment in a way that allows you to see and have ready access to each student.

OVERLAPPING BEHAVIORS. Overlapping refers to handling two or more situations or activities simultaneously. Skilled teachers avoid becoming so immersed in an activity they neglect another that needs immediate attention. Overlapping behavior allows the flow of productive classroom activity to continue uninterrupted. It ensures that undue attention is not drawn to, for example, a minor disruption. Teachers who use overlapping behavior well have mastered withitness.

Examples of effective overlapping behavior include the following:

- Making eye contact with a misbehaving student
- Moving closer to, or standing beside, a misbehaving student or group of students
- Asking a student who has not been paying attention a question
- Acknowledging raised hands with a nod or other nonverbal signal
- Picking up something a student is playing with without interrupting your presentation
- Gesturing at a misbehaving student
- Monitoring or directing group work and independent seatwork simultaneously

MOVEMENT MANAGEMENT BEHAVIORS. What moves in a classroom? . . . *people, things, and the flow of a lesson.* Movement management refers to regulating the pace and smoothness of classroom activities. "Dead time" should be kept to a minimum, lessons should move at a proper pace, and transitions from one activity to another should be smooth and rapid (but not rushed or jerky). Teachers who can do this manage movement well. They get activities started promptly, smoothly move students from one activity to another (*smoothness*), and keep the activity moving (*momentum*). The counterpart of smoothness is *jerkiness* (with the lesson moving in fits and starts), and the counterpart of momentum is *slowdowns* (e.g., taking too long to start a new activity or having interruptions). Teachers who maintain instructional momentum and make smooth transitions have fewer disruptions.

Examples of effective movement management behavior include the following.

- Having demonstration materials, teaching aids, or learning stations ready for effective use.
- Giving clear, concise, and achievable directions (see the preceding section).
- Having efficient routines for distributing materials and supplies. Ensuring that students take out their books or materials rapidly and are quickly ready to begin work.
- Establishing routines for moving students efficiently from one part of the room to another or from one room to another.
- Pacing the lesson slowly enough so all can follow but rapidly enough to keep wasted time to a minimum. The pace should be rapid, yet unhurried.
- Moving efficiently from one segment of a lesson or activity to another.

A data collection instrument you can use when practicing these basic skills is given in Appendix 6.1.

GROUP FOCUS BEHAVIORS.   Group focus is the process of keeping everybody in the class "actively involved, alert, and accountable for their performance" (Weber & Roff, 1983, p. 25). Avoid narrowing in on one or two individuals, making the rest of the class wait. Every student should be paying attention (on task), helpful in the development of the lesson, and responsible for his or her own and peer learning. Students should be actively, or at least covertly, participating in class activities. The teacher who uses group focus effectively is "withit," uses overlapping behavior, and manages movement (ensures smoothness and momentum). You can foster group focus through (1) "group alerting" (getting students' attention and quickly letting them know what they are supposed to do; and keeping students "on their toes" by, for example, making every student feel that she or he could be asked the next question); and (2) expecting accountability (holding students personally responsible for positive participation and achievement).

Examples of effective group focus include the following:

- Tell students you expect them to be responsible for their growth, that they have responsibility for the development of the lesson, and that they have responsibility for the learning of their peers.
- Phrase a question, pause, and look around the room before you ask a specific student to respond (rather than naming the student first, which lets others "off the hook").
- Phrase questions clearly, avoiding repeating the question. Frequently repeating the question encourages inattentiveness and wastes time.
- Normally, require students to raise their hands if they think they have the answer to a question.

- Have students address the whole class, not just you.
- Avoid asking questions such as, "Does everybody understand?" or "Do you have any questions?" Instead, ask individual students to show they understand.
- Make sure students understand and are learning. Circulate during seatwork and make sure work is handed in and that feedback and reinforcement are given.
- Normally, accept responses only from students who have been recognized. Do not accept chorus answers or those that have been "blurted out." This is a major cause of classroom management problems, and attention must be given at the beginning of the year by you to make sure it is not allowed. Chorusing, however, does have a place with shy students or situations, for example, where the sounds of a language are practiced.

Minor Disruptions

Any group that is productive but caring must live by rules. Classrooms are no exception. If rules and procedures are to be followed, they have to be understood and students need to know how to obey them. Merely stating rules and procedures is not enough. Rules need to be explained, illustrated, and practiced—*they need to be taught.* Marzano et al. (2003) emphasize the importance of *emotional stability.* This refers to being able to interact with students in a matter-of-fact, businesslike way even when you are upset, particularly when you apply the negative consequences of unacceptable behavior. Know how to deal with the minor disruptions that will inevitably occur. Three techniques for dealing with disruptions of a minor nature are (1) *deterring* (stop) the unacceptable behavior; (2) *maintaining* acceptable behavior through *checking up;* and (3) encouraging and *reinforcing* desirable behavior.

DETERRING.   Although positive motivation is the real key to classroom control, when a student disrupts others, you need to intervene, either verbally or nonverbally. That is, you must "issue a desist" and turn the behavior in a positive direction. Of course, accidental disruptions sometimes can be ignored or handled with sympathy or humor. Reacting to them interrupts the lesson. When a minor disruption occurs, the approach should be positive and the message should be, "Your behavior is not acceptable, and although it must stop, I still like you!" Reprimands, if they must be used, should be firm, calm, clearly indicate the behavior to stop, and (importantly) indicate the desired behavior. Deviant behavior should be handled in a calm, matter-of-fact, and objective way. Angry and attacking ways of punishing may backfire, resulting in further disruption.

Do you remember what can happen when one person starts to giggle and soon another person giggles, then another, and the giggling "ripples" to still others? How you handle a minor disruption can spread to other students. This is called the ripple effect. Ripple can be positive or negative. It is *positive* when you deal effectively with a student who breaks a rule and this causes other students to observe the rule. It is *negative* if you let a student get away with an infraction. This can lead others to try to get away with the infraction or cause the rule breaker to do it again. Minor disruptions should be dealt with before they ripple. Based on suggestions by Emmer et al. (2003, pp. 172–174), procedures for dealing with minor disruptions or interventions include the following:

- *Use nonverbal clues:* Make eye contact and give a signal . . . to issue a desist.
- *Get the activity moving:* Get the next activity underway and cue students to desired behaviors.

- *Use proximity:* Move closer to students.
- *Use group focus:* Use group alerting, accountability . . . to draw students back into a lesson when attention has begun to wane.
- *Redirect the behavior:* Remind students of inappropriate behavior.
- *Provide needed instruction:* Check student work. If many students can't proceed, stop the activity and provide whole class instruction.
- *Issue a brief desist:* Tell the student(s) to stop the undesirable behavior.
- *Give the student a choice:* Tell the student that he or she has a choice to behave appropriately . . . (or) receive a consequence.
- *Use an "I-Message":* An I-message is a statement that describes the problem and its effects on the teacher, the student, or the class.

Lang (1990), in a study of secondary teacher education student management concerns, found that the major weakness student teachers need to overcome is what he called the "nice guy (or gal) syndrome." When teachers want to be liked and are afraid to issue desists, the ripple effect begins. Before they know it, control is lost. Once it is lost, it is hard to regain. Failure to nip minor disruptions in the bud results in the very thing student teachers fear the most. Students do not respect, nor particularly like, teachers who cannot control the class. Desists are needed! Be firm to be kind. Students must learn you care about them, like them, want them to learn, but mean business. Consequences must be understood by students and enforced dispassionately.

CHECKING UP.   The above procedures normally should work and cause little interruption to class activities. Misbehaving, off-task students will usually return to task quickly. Students may, however, resume disruptive behavior when you look away or later in the period or school day. To ensure that students remain on task, *check up,* and be sure *students know you will check,* to see they remain on task. Be withit. Checking up should usually be done in an overlapping way, so that activities are not interrupted.

REINFORCING DESIRABLE BEHAVIOR.   Why not catch students doing it right? Not just when they are doing it wrong. Students can be encouraged and complimented when they are behaving constructively and can be congratulated for improvement. People tend to behave in ways that yield rewards. Encouragement and praise are powerful. However, praise should usually be qualified, indicating what was praiseworthy. Effective praise is sincere, delivered contingently, and indicative of the value and particulars of the accomplishment.

Positive reinforcement for desirable behavior can be used (1) whenever a disruptive student returns to the desired behavior, or (2) to reinforce students who are behaving appropriately and by emphasizing the correct behavior with the misbehaving student.

A PROCEDURE FOR HANDLING MINOR DISRUPTIONS.   A sequence of actions when dealing with misbehavior is suggested by TeacherNet (1995–2003). (1) Divert misbehavior, for example, by asking the misbehaving student a question, starting a new activity to boost interest, or removing materials with which the student might fiddle. (2) If diversion does not work, move closer to the student, use eye contact, use verbal cues such as naming the student, reminding the class they should be engaged or attending, or praising a student or group of students who are well behaved. (3) If the misbehavior continues, issue a more severe warning, or apply the consequence the student has chosen. A data collection instrument you can use when dealing with minor disruptions is given in Appendix 6.2.

Increasing Academic Learning Time

Academic learning time (or engaged time) is the time "students are actively and successfully engaged in learning" (Cruickshank, Bainer Jenkins, & Metcalf, 1999, p. 354). To state the obvious, the more time students spend working diligently, the more they learn. Studies have shown that the number of minutes lost through interruptions, disruptions, late starts, and inefficient transitions is significant. The time students are engaged in constructive, interesting, and meaningful work should be high, though there should be some "play" time. Students should be on task as much as possible, to learn more and have less time to misbehave.

The main goal for using active teaching and learning is to increase the time students spend on academic tasks, and thus increase academic achievement (Educational Research Group, 1995). A way to increase academic learning time (ALT) is to be aware of things that will detract students. Potential detractors include students waiting while the teacher is organizing materials or searching for something, waiting for materials to be passed out, getting materials out at the beginning of class, students finishing assignments early, transitions that take too long, and students falling off task when a peer is being helped during seatwork.

ALT can be increased by planning interesting lessons appropriate for your students. Having challenging but achievable activities that actively engage students can reduce disruptions and the time needed to deal with them. Materials for instruction should be prepared in advance and sequenced in the order they will be used. Teaching aids, such as a videotape or DVD, should have been previewed and ready to switch on. Begin the class promptly, and teach students how to prepare for the start of the lesson. The time taken to handle instructional visuals and to distribute materials and supplies should be well thought out. Transitions from one topic or activity to another or to move students from one spot to another should be smooth and short. During seatwork, circulate to ensure that students are promptly provided with correctives or reinforcement. If several students require help during seatwork, design a procedure to keep all working. Students should be instructed about what to do when they have finished an assignment. Reasonable rules and efficient management procedures and routines need to be understood and followed—these must be explained, illustrated, and practiced.

The NWREL (2000) provides ideas for designing activities that are more engaging to increase the amount of time students spend on task:

- Make sure course materials are authentic, relevant to students' lives, and teach how these materials can apply to their lives.
- Allow some student control over learning (e.g., choice of assignments, less supervision, and letting students evaluate progress).
- Select tasks that are challenging but achievable for all students (including disabled, remedial, and at-risk students).
- Stimulate student interest in topics being studied (e.g., choose topics that require problem solving or letting students discover for themselves).
- Pick projects that let students share their knowledge with others (e.g., use cooperative learning methods such as jigsaw or group investigation).

Use Appendix 6.2 to help you analyze the cases that follow. Your instructor may pose specific questions for your response.

CASE 6.1 Minor Disruptions

Easy to Bear

Ms. Bear's class is working on Christmas wreaths made from clothes hangers and colored plastic. Students are working in pairs to complete the project. Ms. Bear has given instructions and is circulating around the room while students work. She nods to Sharim and Joseph, who are sharing the tasks involved. To Janice and Peter, she says, "Good work. I like how you're tying the pieces close together. Can I show the others how you're doing it?" The partly finished wreath is shown to the other students. Ms. Bear spends more time in the area of the room where children are having difficulty sharing the task. Occasionally she asks a question or makes a suggestion to a pair about how the task might be shared. When everyone is on task, she says, "I wish everyone in the school could see how well you're all working. You are sharing, taking turns and deciding together how to

finish the wreath. Give yourselves a pat on the back." Giggling, the children give themselves a pat on the back and then they carry on with their work.

Julia quickly loses interest in the task and makes threatening gestures toward her partner with her scissors. Ms. Bear says, "Julia, will you take the waste basket around and collect the scraps, please?" When Julia returns with the wastebasket, Ms. Bear says, "It's your turn to cut now, Julia. Please be careful with the scissors. If you wave scissors around, someone might get poked." She accompanies Julia to her desk and helps her get restarted on the task, demonstrating proper procedure. "That's the safe way to use scissors." She has Julia begin as she watches. "Good for you." As she moves away, she positions herself so that she can see Julia, to monitor her behavior. Julia notices and says, "See, I'm still cutting nice."

CASE 6.2 Minor Disruptions

Managing Giddy

Miss Prentice's grade 11 social studies class was to be taught by Mr. Chernyko, the intern. As part of a unit on collective bargaining, he was introducing a section on devices used by labor as bargaining tools. Mr. Chernyko began, "Both management and unions use tactics to help them bargain. For example, if things are not going well for the union, it may initiate a boycott. Do you know what that is?" Jason, the class clown, being smart, responded, "Oh I know, it's the place where the men rest when they're on strike." This

caused several of the class to laugh. Not to be outdone, Herman, on the other side of the class, countered with, "Yeah, and the women rest on girlcotts." More of the students laughed and the class was now thoroughly giddy. For the rest of the period, whenever Mr. Chernyko asked the class a question, the same kind of smart cracks emerged. At the end of the class, when he was discussing what had occurred during the lesson with his college supervisor, his eyes were filled with tears of frustration and dismay.

Giving Directions

Many teacher skills are involved in good management. A fundamental skill is direction giving. Whether written or oral, directions need to be concise, clear, have a positive orientation, and set the stage for success.

Giving directions is a critical activity to create and maintain conditions for learning. It occurs many times each day. Directions are given for distributing materials and supplies, completing assignments or activities, doing seatwork, moving individuals or groups, changing from one activity to another, and describing rules and procedures. Effective explanations and demonstrations involve giving clear directions.

When directions are given correctly, the confusion that sometimes plagues beginning teachers is avoided. Students cannot do what they do not understand. If they do not understand, they become confused, angry, indifferent, or belligerent. Self-concept can be damaged when students think they are too stupid to understand the directions. The result may be (1) working on the wrong thing or in the wrong way; (2) off-task behavior (daydreaming or working on something other than what was expected); or (3) misbehavior—students lose valuable opportunities for learning.

Directions are given to establish and maintain rules and procedures. Directions should be positive and stress what should be done—not what should not be done. Good classroom management is founded on students understanding the behaviors expected. When students misbehave, it is not enough to say, "Stop it." Students need to know what is expected to replace the disruptive behavior. Clear directions promote student accountability for positive behavior.

Giving directions is fundamental to good classroom management. If students know what to do, they are less likely to be off task or misbehave. Good direction giving involves securing attention, alerting, being clear, checking up, and anticipating (Figure 6.4).

SECURE ATTENTION. Begin your presentation only after you have secured the attention of all students. You should not have to repeat yourself because some students were inattentive. This wastes time and is an annoyance to those who were paying attention. Most students are willing to meet a teacher's expectations if they are clear and they know the signal that requests immediate attention. Signals that alert students include: statements such as "Can I have everybody's attention please?", standing silently at a certain spot in the room, raising a hand, clapping hands, ringing a bell, and flicking the light switch. While you are waiting for complete attention, look around the room and make eye contact with nonattending students.

ALERT. A request for attention may interrupt students' activities. You can alert students that directions for an activity or assignment will be coming shortly. To respect the students' concentration on the task they are engaged in, give notice they should be finishing their task or to organize themselves to be ready for an interruption. For example, you might say, "In five minutes I'll tell you how to complete your graphs."

FIGURE 6.4 *Steps for Giving Directions*

1. **Gain attention.**
   Secure the attention of *all*.
2. **State.**
   Give the directions clearly and concisely.
3. **Prior checkup.**
   Make sure directions are understood *before* students begin to work.
4. **In progress checkup.**
   When students are working, monitor to make sure directions are understood and followed.
5. **Anticipate.**
   In advance, have a plan for handling problems that could emerge.

BE CLEAR. "Clear teachers," compared to "unclear teachers," are concerned that their students understand. They *want* students to succeed! Research shows that student achievement and student satisfaction are closely related to teacher clarity and that students, to a large extent, judge teachers based on clarity (Cruickshank, 1985a, pp. 44–45). Students are willing to meet reasonable instructor expectations. Learn to express yourself clearly.

When planning—good direction giving involves careful planning—consider whether your directions will be: (1) concise, (2) easy to understand, (3) well organized, and (4) positive.

A good practice is to routinely post directions in a special place on the chalkboard. For example, the homework might always be entered in the upper right-hand corner of the chalkboard; or the page and question numbers of seat assignments may be recorded in the center chalkboard. Complex directions might be provided in a handout. Using the chalkboard or a handout should often be accompanied by an oral explanation.

At times, when directions are complex or lengthy, break them into "chewable pieces." A piece can be presented followed by student work, the next piece added, and so forth. This could be preceded by an advance organizer (or overview) of the whole task, and concluded with a review. When directions are given for a new activity, it may be a good idea to begin with one or more teacher-guided step-by-step whole-class examples, checking up after each step. This allows a smooth transition to seatwork. If direction giving is for completion of assignments, students need to be clear about all requirements and features of the assignment. Tell them about the standards for form, neatness, accuracy, and legibility. Students need to know due dates and penalties for lateness or noncompletion. A model completed assignment can be useful.

CHECK UP.   Don't take it for granted that students will understand directions. Have you ever seen the blank faces, a barrage of questions after directions are given, students nudging each other and talking, or misbehavior? If one or some of these has occurred, the directions were likely unclear (however, it is normal to give individual attention to special-case students). Problems can be avoided if you check for understanding *before* students are expected to begin to work by themselves or in groups. *Check up by:* (1) Asking a particular student (or students) to review the directions for the class. At times, the student selected may have had difficulty in the past understanding directions; care must be taken not to embarrass. (2) When students begin to work, circulate to ensure they are "getting off on the right foot." (3) After work has been in progress for a time, circulate to see if students are following directions and how they are progressing.

ANTICIPATE.   Good direction giving avoids annoyances and anticipates student difficulties. Students should not have to ask, "What do I do now? I'm finished," or "Where do I put this assignment. I'm finished?" Anticipate the words or phrases or procedures students may have difficulty understanding and find ways of simplifying language or explaining the procedures. Perhaps suitable synonyms or examples can be used.

A data sheet for information on your direction giving skills is given in Appendix 6.3. Use this to help you analyze the cases that follow. Your instructor may pose specific questions for your response.

CASE 6.3 Giving Directions

Going to the Gym

Jenny Smith's grade 2 class had returned from their last gym period in such excitement that they had run up the two flights of stairs to their classroom loudly jostling and pushing past each other. They made so much noise that several teachers came out to see what was causing the commotion. One child, who had fallen on the stairs and badly skinned his knee, came into the classroom sobbing. He accused another student of pushing him.

Jenny wants to make sure this doesn't happen again. She walks to the lights and flicks them briefly. The children become quiet and look toward her.

"In a few minutes we are going to be leaving for the gym," she says. "When we go down all those stairs, we have to be careful that no one gets hurt. It is very dangerous to run or push others on the stairs. Someone could get knocked down and be seriously hurt. And, you must also think about the other children in the school who are still working. If they hear loud noises, they will not be able to work. You don't want that. Let's see if we can think of a list of things to remember when we go down the stairs and to the gym. If we make a chart, we can go over it each time before we go to the gym."

The children prepare a list:

Walk in line.
Keep your voice low.

Keep hands by your side.
Walk quickly but don't run.
Stay in order.

Jenny asks several children to repeat the list of items before they go. As they walk, their teacher walks along, making comments such as "Good for you, Josh!" "That's right, Guy!" "You're a good leader, Star!"

When the class gets past the long hallway, she stops them and asks, "How do you think we're doing?" The children think that, so far, they have kept all their rules. The teacher commends them and they carry on to the gym.

CASE 6.4 Giving Directions

Class Beginning Procedure

It is the beginning of the term and Mr. Hersch wants to make sure that students will use each period of his grade 10 keyboarding class productively. He wants them to begin working the moment they enter the room rather than waiting until all are seated and he provides directions or begins his presentation.

He begins, "When you enter the room, place your books neatly under your chair. Turn on your computer. Look at the front upper left-hand corner of the chalkboard. Your warm-up and review assignments will be written there. Open your text to the page indicated and begin to work. When I ring the timer bell, stop work immediately. Do not finish the word or sentence. Do not correct or save what you have been working on." He then asks students to check that the printer has enough paper for their computer assignment.

The next day, the class trickles into the room. About half the class follows the directions given the previous day regarding storing books, turning on the computer, looking at the chalkboard, and beginning to work. A group of five students engages in a conversation; the rest sit silently, waiting to be told what to do. Mr. Hersch moves toward the five who are talking and says, "Get to your seats and do what I told you to yesterday." They move uncertainly to their desks. Then Mr. Hersch says to the ones who are sitting and not working, "Get to work! You can't learn if you aren't practicing!" Jillian, one of the group that has been quietly waiting, shyly asks, "What are we supposed to be doing?"

CASE 6.5 Giving Directions

Magnetism Lab

Mrs. Blair-Jones' grade 9 science class is about to do a laboratory on magnetism. They get up, several at a time, to wander slowly to their laboratory stations. In the middle of the confusion, though not all are at their benches, Mrs. Blair-Jones tries to get their attention.

She provides a brief lecture about the experiment they are about to perform and expectations about how they are to proceed. Some listen and some don't. After a few minutes, Mrs. Blair-Jones finally gains their attention. At this time, she asks the students to return to their

continued

desks to get their lab books. Instant confusion! Though some students had not yet picked up their lab books, she asks the students to come to her desk to pick up a set of magnets and some iron filings. They all start to come up though they are working in pairs and she runs out of magnets before she discovers the problem. Further delay occurs as time is taken to make sure that each pair has a set of magnets. When students begin to work, some pairs follow the manual, write something down, and return to their seats. Others ignore the manual and play with the equipment. As the bell rings, Mrs. Blair-Jones wonders what went wrong.

Corrective Approaches

You have taken careful steps to get your classroom management off to a good start, your class is well run, rules and procedures are understood, and you are maintaining a good environment for learning. However, management crises will happen. What can you do? Have corrective approaches in place! This will involve: applying consequences, knowing how to present both penalties and rewards, the ability to deal with disruptive behavior in a variety of situations and with different students, understanding the nature of discipline, and having specific strategies for dealing with serious rule violations.

Resolving Conflict

Schooling is not all "sweetness and light." Some conflict is inevitable. Handle it calmly and constructively. Maintain a positive problem-solving approach. It is easy to respond with anger or the desire to punish; instead, use a positive, alternatives-and-consequences, solution-seeking approach. Conflict can be an opportunity for growth. When a student shows recurring conflict-promoting behavior, help the student gain insight into the dynamics and consequence of that type of behavior. Control impulses and choose the most effective response to deescalate conflicts. When a conflict occurs, keep your "professional cool" and take "cool-off" time to think things out calmly. Impulsive actions often are regretted. Detach yourself from arguments and avoid power struggles. "Power struggles" might be a "game" in which one person tries to benefit at the expense of another to satisfy a feeling or belief about control, mastery, security, or superiority. Avoid the game by: (1) simply withdrawing from the argument (e.g., "I'm not going to argue with you about this") or (2) stopping the game by not playing (e.g., "I'm not going to play. Find someone else.").

Be aware of your limitations. Nobody's perfect! Recognize when you need help and your areas of intolerance and ineffectiveness. This is fundamental to professional growth. You can, however, model effective alternatives for students to use when coping with conflict. Students are probably watching to see how you respond to provocation. If you want students to control impulsive behaviors, demonstrate control yourself. Convey calm confidence (be shockproof during conflicts and do not blame). In short, avoid impulsive reactions. "Touch base" with a student once a conflict has subsided. After a student–teacher conflict, residual feelings may be present (e.g., anger, shame, fear). It is helpful to "clear the air." You could use humor to neutralize stressful situations, to "lighten the mood." Tension and stress affect learning and increase anxiety—laughter relaxes.

Consequences of Behavior

Why have rules and procedures if students do not follow them? Teachers need to establish and enforce consistent positive and negative consequences of actions (ideally, in consultation with students). Students must see consequences as fair. An effective consequence system includes a positive, caring climate and excitement with, and curiosity for, learning. Rewards and penalties should encourage engagement in learning tasks and build a sense of personal worth.

A *reward* is something desirable that students earn for suitable achievement, effort, or behavior. A *penalty* is something undesirable that occurs because of inappropriate behavior. Rewards should be attainable after reasonable effort—not too easy or too hard—or they lose motivational value. Penalties "should fit the crime," neither trivial nor harsh. The concept of individual "choice" and accountability is critical. It is the student who chooses to work and behave or to not work and misbehave. In so doing, the student chooses the consequence (the reward or punishment), *not you*! Penalties, when the need arises, should be administered "without malice," in a matter-of-fact, nonblaming way: "I still like you, but the consequence you have chosen will happen."

Rewards that teachers might use include: grades or other symbols (e.g., gold stars); public or private teacher approval; recognition through certificates, posting of student work; material goods such as money, equipment, games, or books; or privileges such as socializing time, reading what they want, or playing a game. Penalties that teachers might administer include: reduction of grades, demerit systems, loss of privileges, confiscation, referral to an administrator, isolation (in class, the hallway, or study hall), restitution (e.g., replacement of stolen or damaged material or cleaning up a mess that was made), suspension, and expulsion.

Disruptive Behavior in Inclusive Classrooms

In general, teachers can use the same management practices with students with disabilities as they use with students without disabilities—much undesirable behavior is similar for both groups (Daniels, 2000). The difference may be in the kind of intervention chosen, considering the kind of disability and ensuring the strategy will help the student develop. As a teacher, learn the policy regarding discipline of special needs students in your district and state, and the resources available. Furthermore, if you teach in the United States, become familiar with the Individuals with Disabilities Education Act (IDEA) as enacted into law in 2004. It lays out safeguards for students with disabilities. A good idea is to seek training in working with special needs learners. If you do not have specialized training, consult trusted professionals before you implement management or discipline techniques or therapies. The good news is, studies show that when teachers receive appropriate training, intervene in a timely manner, and have good in-class supports, the inclusion of students "is greatly enhanced" (Hardman, Drew, & Egan, 2002, p. 270).

No one plan fits all situations. Daniels suggests that teachers begin by establishing classroom rules and consequences, defining limits, setting expectations, clarifying responsibilities, and setting up a curriculum that accommodates individual differences. She suggests questions to help you analyze situations that foster disruptive behavior in students with disabilities:

- Is the behavior the result of inappropriate curriculum content or instructional approaches?
- Is the behavior the result of the student not understanding the concepts presented?
- Is the behavior the result of a student's disability (or is the student just misbehaving)?
- Is the behavior due to other factors (e.g., physical arrangement of room; frustration; boredom; poor transitions)?

- Are the causes of misbehavior something you can control (e.g., can you address learning style preference, provide more positive feedback, change the way you communicate)?
- Can you teach students to self-manage or self-regulate behavior?
- Do you use reinforcement techniques suitable for the student, to reduce disruptive behavior?
- Is it appropriate to use punishment (which may suppress the behavior but not teach desirable behavior)?

Disciplining Majority and Minority Students Fairly

Carolyn Bower (2004) of the St. Louis *Post-Dispatch* provides a compelling analysis revealing that, in St. Louis area districts, the suspension rate for black students can be as much as two to three times that of white students. The situation in the rest of the country is not dissimilar. She reports that Indiana University researcher Russ Skiba says school systems can resolve the problem by training employees in how to manage classrooms and deal with students of different cultural backgrounds. Excerpts from her column follow.

Discipline Policies Vary

Carolyn Bower, St. Louis Post-Dispatch, *March 28, 2004*

African-American students are suspended at higher rates than other students. Some metro districts report suspensions of black students at two to three times the rate for white students. . . . Researchers and parents place much of the blame on cultural misunderstandings between white teachers or administrators and black students. They also say black students may act out if they perceive racism at school or if they don't get the academic help they may need. . . . A statistical analysis two years ago by the Seattle *Post-Intelligencer* found that explanations such as living in single-parent families or poverty or qualifying for special education also fell short of accounting for the disparity between white and black suspension rates . . . the average suspension rate for all public school students in St. Louis County last school year was 2.47 for every 100 students. The rate for black students there was 4.48, compared with 1.36 for white students. . . . School districts vary widely in how they handle suspensions. Some have zero tolerance for misbehavior. Others use suspensions as a last resort. . . .

Bridging the Gap. Russ Skiba, an associate professor in counseling and educational psychology at Indiana University, has studied the discipline issue extensively.

"What is promising is that we are seeing more and more places such as the St. Louis region become aware of the issue," Skiba said. "Taking the data seriously is the first step. This data is a sign that we have a problem."

Studies in which Skiba participated show minority students are likely to be punished more severely for less severe behavior, Skiba said.

In a study called "The Color of Discipline" done four years ago, Skiba and other researchers found white students were referred for objective discipline infractions such as smoking or vandalism, and blacks were more likely to be referred for suspension over disrespect, loitering or threats.

Skiba said the solutions to disproportionate suspensions lie in making sure school employees are trained to deal with students from different cultural backgrounds and in how to manage behavior and classrooms.

In many ways, the discipline gap is linked to the achievement gap, said Jody Stauffer, director of student discipline for Parkway. Stauffer said African-American students might misbehave because of frustration over lack of school success.

When Darlynn Bosley became principal at Jackson Elementary in St. Louis two years ago, she decided suspensions were running too high. She reduced the number of suspensions by half to 60 in the 2002–2003 school year.

Bosley did that by talking with students about self-discipline. She told them to look at themselves with respect and dignity and pride. She asked students to suggest the type of school community they would like.

Bosley offered incentives such as notebooks, pens and movie tickets for good behavior and for attendance. She set up an in-school suspension room overseen by an African-American man to serve as a male role model. She got parents involved at school.

"Reducing suspensions is a matter of building relationships," Bosley said. "A willingness to delve and find out what is actually causing misbehavior will make a difference."

Charles Arms of the *Post-Dispatch* contributed data analysis, and Alexa Aguilar of the *Post-Dispatch* contributed information for this report.

Reprinted with permission of the St. Louis Post-Dispatch, copyright © 2004.

Dealing with Misbehavior and Rule Violations

It is easy to oversimplify how to handle disruptions or to believe there are prescriptions or recipes a teacher can follow. Every classroom is different and every teacher is unique and needs to establish a personal management style. It is important for the teacher to have the flexibility to accommodate a host of variables. As well, the teacher should try to understand *why* a student is disruptive and the circumstances that triggered the disruptive behavior. An approach for dealing with disruptions that follows is provided by Cipani (1998). It is one approach among many.

Misbehavior disrupts! It reduces attending and on-task behavior and thus the quality and amount of learning that occurs. It interferes with the teacher's ability to teach and students to learn. The teacher has no choice but to deal with disruptive behavior, hopefully in a proactive and positive way. A student's behavior may be inappropriate and need to change, but the student needs to understand that he or she is a valued and respected member of the classroom community. Both the teacher and student need to be aware that it is the misbehaving student who chooses to be disruptive, and thus chooses the consequences. The teacher is responsible for maintaining a safe, at-task learning environment and must deal with those who are disruptive in a prompt, firm, but caring way. This rarely is easy.

Disruptive behavior can occur in many ways. It ranges from unauthorized talking or leaving seats during a presentation to endangering welfare or safety such as destruction of property or striking or hitting. Rule violations range from leaving the room without permission or jumping the leaving-the-room queue to throwing pencils or books or swearing at another student or the teacher. Violating rules is disruptive and so are deviations from procedures and routines.

Disruptive behavior, says Cipani, can be dealt with in several ways (pp. 80–81). One approach is to *remind the student of the rule*. For example, when a student, for the second time, calls out an answer to a question without being recognized, the teacher says, "Joan, the classroom rule is that you raise your hand if you have a question." The teacher may remind the student of the reasons why hand raising is important during presentations. If the student continues to ignore the rule, the teacher might *tell the student that if the behavior continues, a consequence will be applied*. "Joan, the rule is that you raise your hand, if you call out again your name will be added to today's 3:30 club." If Joan's callouts continue, *the teacher applies the consequence* and writes her name on the board under the heading "3:30 Club" and has Joan stay after school.

Another tactic is to *establish incentives* to handle misbehavior, "Joan, if, for two weeks, you raise your hand when you want to respond to or ask a question, for a whole week you can be the first person at the door at recess and you pick the row that will leave first." Incentives that work with some students may not work with others; and, with some students, rewards need to be immediate. A final approach is *out-of-class isolation*. This can range from isolation just outside the classroom to the principal's office or to suspension or expulsion from school.

Cipani believes that, at first, the focus should be on *reinforcing appropriate behavior* so that attending and on-task behaviors are increased. If the student discovers that positive behavior is positively reinforced and academic achievement is improved, disruptive behavior may be reduced, even eliminated. He describes techniques to promote on-task behavior and assignment completion: the good behavior game, behavioral contracting, individual disruptive incident barometer, signal time out, removal time out, and relaxation training.

GOOD BEHAVIOR GAME.   The teacher assigns each student to a team. Teams are given names and posted on a chart on a bulletin or chalkboard. A behavior standard is established (e.g., three or fewer misbehaviors). Teams compete against this standard. Students try to avoid violating the behavior standard. When a student does something that disrupts or violates a rule during a class period, the student (and thus the team) is docked a point. At the end of a preset time—a class, several classes, or longer—every team whose point level matches or is better than the behavior standard is eligible for a lottery to pick the winner of a big prize (e.g., playing a special game or free time). Teams that often are eligible for the lottery can, over time, have a better chance to win the big prize.

BEHAVIORAL CONTRACTING.   When a class is in general well behaved but a few students are of concern, the teacher may need special approaches for these students. A *behavioral contract* is an agreement linking a student's behavior with long-term incentives or rewards. The contract period usually is in force over several weeks. The behavior of the child is evaluated each day against a daily standard that specifies behavior that is acceptable on a given day and specifies the duration of the contract. It may take time to reach the goal of eliminating misbehavior. For example, a student may strive to meet a standard of having three or fewer disruptive behaviors per day for a week. If this is met, a new contract for the following week may be two or fewer disruptive behaviors per day. If this is achieved, the standard may be one disruption per day, and the following week, no disruptive behaviors. When the goal is achieved, the reward is earned.

SIGNAL TIME OUT.   The technique called the *signal time out* is used to address minor disruptive behaviors. Children are not removed from their areas or the classroom. They remain in their seats but cannot earn points during time out. During time out, children cannot earn points for appropriate behavior. A badge or card (the "signal") is placed on the student's desk or a tag board for a designated time. If misbehavior continues, the signal time-out period can be extended; or, another tactic may be used if more severe behavior occurs. A tally is kept of the incidence of targeted behaviors (e.g., talking or leaving the seat without permission). The badge or card is removed only if the disruptive behavior has ceased. When the signal time period is over, the child can start to earn points for being attentive or on task.

REMOVAL TIME OUT.   *Removal time out* is used to decrease very disruptive and aggressive behavior. This is done to preserve the safety of another student or other students and maintain a healthy learning environment. The student who is disruptive is removed from the area or class for a specified period. During this time, the student cannot earn points. If the student continues disruptive behavior while in the area established as time out, removal time out is extended. The hope is that the student will become motivated to behave. Some students may welcome removal time out as a way to get out of work, so it is recommended that it be combined with a reinforcement plan for being on task, attending, and completing assignments. Time out continues until the student shows readiness to behave appropriately.

RELAXATION TRAINING.   When some students get upset they rapidly progress to violent, verbal or physically aggressive behavior. Others hyperventilate dangerously. Long-term behavior management therapy is necessary to deal with these conditions, but a short-term tactic is needed. This should be something that gets a student to calm down and avoid escalation to violence. One tactic is *relaxation training*. As the name implies, the student is shown how to relax. When a stressful situation occurs, the student is urged to initiate a procedure for relaxation (e.g., tensing and relaxing muscle areas, or deep, slow breathing). Importantly, the student needs to be taught by someone who is trained in relaxation techniques. A key aspect is discovering the conditions that trigger stress or cause the student to become upset. This therapy works best with older children. If the unacceptable behavior is controlled, the student is provided with a prespecified reinforcer. How, when, where, and how much of the reinforcer is provided is specified. When a contract has been met, a new contract can be written for another period. Over the school term, several contracts may be written, perhaps with the contract period extended with each renewal.

INDIVIDUAL DISRUPTIVE INCIDENT BAROMETER.   If a teacher wants to monitor the occurrence of a student's specified disruptive behaviors, these can be plotted on a *disruptive incident barometer*. This is a visual display using a line or connected boxes with a set number of levels (e.g., ten levels with level 10 at the top and level 1 at the bottom). Each level indicates a disruptive act. The level (behavior standard) deemed acceptable is specified (e.g., level 6). When a student is disruptive, the teacher marks the next level, moving the student closer to the point at which the reinforcer is lost (e.g., between level 6 and 7). If, at the end of the period (or day, week, etc.) the child remains or is below that level, reinforcement occurs. The barometer can be kept on the chalkboard, teacher's desk, or student's desk. "A positive learning community with a shared responsibility and cooperation does not merely happen, you will create it by teaching, responding to, and modeling the kinds of behavior you expect from every member of your class" (Erlandson, 2002, p. 12).

Guidelines for Classroom Management

Common Guidelines

Data collection instruments you can use to practice the professional targets presented in this chapter are provided in Appendices 6.1, 6.2, and 6.3. In conclusion, a set of practical guidelines will be useful for all three stages of management (preventive, supportive, and corrective) that we have discussed in this chapter. A review of literature on effective management and discipline raises common guidelines. Read these before you begin practice teaching and review them often. A summary follows.

1. The community and parents or guardians expect the classroom to be a learning-oriented place that is safe, fun, orderly, and at task.
2. No student has the right to interfere with the learning of another student or your right to teach. This needs to be expressed the first day of classes.

3. Thoughtful rules, procedures, standards, and behavioral expectations need to be set.
4. Rules should be firmly, calmly, and promptly enforced. Avoid the ripple effect. If misbehavior is not checked, the student and others will notice and misbehavior will recur and spread. Chaos may follow.
5. Encourage students to be involved in rule and consequence setting so that a safe, orderly, democratic, and at-task classroom can be maintained.
6. When a student chooses to break a rule or interfere with teaching and learning, he or she also chooses the consequences. You, as the teacher, have no choice but to enforce the consequences.
7. While misbehavior is never acceptable, a student is always acceptable and worthy of respect. Separate the "deed" and the "doer."
8. Handle misbehavior in a professional manner. "Professional cool" must be maintained. The teacher has not been attacked personally. A medical doctor does not get angry with a patient who is ill, he helps deal with the problem. In like manner, the teacher must not get angry with a learner but should calmly stop the misbehavior, apply the consequences, seek the causes, and find ways to prevent it from recurring.
9. Involve parents in student discipline when a problem persists, and know when to refer. Seek counseling for students to help them with persistent problems. Consult colleagues for ideas on how to help misbehaving students. Keep parents involved and informed. For example, letters about your class, its objectives, and expectations are invaluable.
10. Avoid public censure of a misbehaving student. Deal with most problems on a one-to-one basis. Never argue with a student in front of the class. You can't win. Animosity escalates.
11. Never ridicule, embarrass, or use sarcasm with a student. You lose respect, and the self-concept or self-worth of the student is damaged.
12. Every student must be treated fairly and equally. There must be no appearance of favoritism.
13. The punishment must fit the crime. Apply consequences consistently and uniformly.
14. Don't punish all for the transgression of one. This builds resentment and damages climate.
15. Catch them doing it right. Encouragement and positive reinforcement work. Compliment a student for improved behavior. To avoid embarrassment, usually do this privately.
16. The foundation for good management is motivating instruction and a caring, positive climate. Have positive expectations, get to know students as persons, and show you respect them.

Reality Therapy: An Approach for Working with Problem Students

Many approaches to dealing with problem students are described in the literature. One you may wish to consider is that of William Glasser (1969, 1984, 1993), called *control theory/reality therapy*. Glasser believes there are four basic human needs (love, control, freedom, and fun) that are needed for healthy psychological balance. People need to feel in *control* of their lives. He thinks people who misbehave need to be helped to admit their behavior is irresponsible and learn to act in a more logical and acceptable way. Students need to learn they have choices, learn to be responsible for their actions, and satisfy their needs in ways that do not interfere with others. Excuses for bad behavior are not accepted. Instead, students are asked to identify the choices they had, why they chose the one they did, and what was learned. If their behavior was inappropriate, they can learn to accept the consequences and vow to act more responsibly toward others. Reasonable consequences, which can be developed in classroom meetings, should always follow good or bad behavior. These meetings can be effective for diagnosing problems, seeking solutions, and maintaining positive class behavior.

Reality therapy involves steps to help students understand that they have choices, the choices they made, and the consequences. The teacher helps the student identify appropriate behavior. Then, the student is helped to become aware of the consequences. The teacher does impose consequences—the student must identify them. Then, the student needs to devise a plan to stop inappropriate behavior. The student is either helped to implement the plan successfully or the consequences are allowed to occur (Edwards, 1994, pp. 340–346). The steps of reality therapy are popular with many teachers and school systems.

Reality therapy is intended to help the student change. You have a conference with the student, confront the student by describing behavior, help plan a better course of action, and help the student become more responsible (Weber & Roff, 1983, p. 39). The steps are as follows.

1. Describe the student's disruptive behavior and typical teacher reactions.
2. Analyze the list and determine what does not work and what works. Avoid repeating reactions that do not work.
3. Attempt to improve personal relationships with the student. Take the initiative to show concern and provide encouragement.
4. Encourage the student to analyze his or her behavior. Ask the student to describe what he or she is doing. Then, ask the student to stop the disruptive behavior.
5. If the problem continues, hold a short conference with the student and again ask the student to describe the disruptive behavior. Ask whether it is against the rules, reasonable, or an unstated expectation. Have the student state what should be done instead. Be warm and supportive but persistent and firm.
6. If the disruptive behavior persists, call a conference with the student and have the student focus on the behavior and call for a specific plan to solve the problem. Arrive at an agreement about what the student will do and how she or he will go about doing it. Have the student state the positive actions that will be taken to eliminate the problem.
7. If step 6 does not work, isolate the student (away from others). While isolated, give the student responsibility for devising a commitment and plan to ensure that rules will be followed. Isolation is continued until the plan has been formulated and agreed on.
8. The next step is in-school suspension. The student must now deal with the principal or person responsible for school discipline. The student can only return to the classroom when a workable and agreed-on plan is made. Parents should be notified if suspension continues for longer than one day.
9. If students remain out of control and in in-school suspension, parents take the student home. The next day, the student returns and the process begins again.
10. The last step is removal from school and referral to another agency. Even now, students can continue if specific plans and a clear commitment are forthcoming.

Models of Management and Discipline

Teacher personalities vary. Diversity of students, schools, and districts is common. Approaches that work with some may not with others. There are many models of management and discipline. One or more may be useful to you. Teachers are expected by society to "control" their classes. The validity of this view, in the minds of many teachers, is reinforced when administrators measure the quality of a teacher by the amount of control the teacher has (Van Tassell, 1999). The degree of teacher control and how much, if any, student autonomy should exist has been and will continue to be controversial. An ongoing question is whether the teacher should be a "coach" or a "leader." The problem is compounded because the teacher can never abrogate responsibility for creating a learning environment that fosters learning.

Models you may wish to investigate include:

- The Skinner model—*Behavior Modification* (Skinner, 1971, 1976)
- The Canter model—*Assertive Discipline* (Canter, 1988a, 1988b)
- The Dreikers model—*Social Discipline* (Dreikers, 1968; Dreikers, Grunwald, & Pepper, 1982)
- The Curwin and Mendler model—*Discipline with Dignity* (Curwin & Mendler, 1980, 1997)
- The Albert model—*Cooperative Discipline* (Albert, 1989)

Classroom management is one of the biggest challenges you will face as a new teacher. In order to get off to a good start, we recommend two valuable books: if you are teaching elementary students, Evertson, Emmer, and Worsham (2006); if you are teaching secondary students, Emmer, Evertson, and Worsham (2003).

Use Appendix 6.1 to help you analyze the cases that follow. Your instructor may pose specific questions for you to consider.

CASE 6.6   Basic Management Skills

Volcanic Management

Mr. Agropolis is presenting a lesson on volcanic action to his grade 6 class. He is using a model of a volcano and is explaining the causes and effects involved. He has placed the model on a table at the side of the room where all students can see. Students are in a semicircle around the table. He stands on the other side of the table so that he can see all the students while he explains. While he is explaining, Beulah begins to speak to her neighbor, Yoko. Mr. Agropolis catches Beulah's eye and, without stopping his explanation, raises his finger to his lips. Beulah stops talking, and both Beulah and Yoko pay attention. Derrick puts his hand up to ask a question, and Mr. Agropolis, without interrupting his presentation, signals that he

should wait to ask the question. Later he asks the boy for his question.

Mr. Agropolis keeps the students' attention by varying his voice pattern, asking questions of the students in a random pattern, and occasionally drawing their attention to the model for clarification of some detail. When asking questions, he phrases the question first, looks around for a few seconds, and then asks a specific student to respond.

When the demonstration is over, Mr. Agropolis motions to John and Shasha, who are near the front of the class. They begin to distribute the worksheets that are on the side table. He tells the other students not to begin working until after he has given directions and then signals them to return to their desks. When everyone is seated and has a worksheet, he calls for attention, waits briefly until all are quiet and looking at him, and explains the assignment. As he does this he moves around the room, moving nearer to nonattending students, sometimes pointing at work or staying nearby until a student is attending again. He unobtrusively gives a "thumbs up" signal to a shy student who is attending carefully.

CASE 6.7 Basic Management Skills

Ask the Class

It is three weeks into the term, and Ms. Benedictine d'Havier is concerned about classroom management in her grade 10 science class. There is a constant hum of people talking, though she often asks them to stop. Sometime she just talks above the hum when presenting. Her directions frequently need to be repeated. People visit each other, and assignments are often poorly done or not done at all. She stated classroom behavior rules on the first day of class and feels she must enforce them. She wonders if students should have been involved in setting the rules and suggesting consequences. Ms. d'Havier knows she must do something, and quickly.

She plans to have a meeting with her class to discuss the problem and arrive at solutions. She also wants to emphasize preventive management and wants a plan for doing this.

There never has been, nor ever will be, a classroom in which no disruptions occur. The effective teacher knows how to keep disruptions to a minimum. Handling them is the major concern of beginning and even many experienced teachers. You can learn to handle minor disruptions. If you do, the likelihood of major disruptions occurring is greatly reduced. There are preventive things to do and steps to follow to handle the minor disruptions that will occur.

LINKING PRACTICE TO THEORY

What worked for you as a student in school? What was conducive to learning? Think of classrooms you have observed where there is excitement for learning. What did the teacher do to achieve this? What would work for you? How successful are you at communicating and monitoring expectations? Why is it critical for classroom management? As you observe effective classrooms, what is the place of routines and procedures. What is your management style? As you try management skills, what works for you? Ask questions about management that gives meaning to your experience as a new teacher.

Summary

Together with motivation and wise choice of teaching strategies, good classroom management frees teachers to teach and students to learn. When students feel safe, cared for, and have fun, they remain at task and learn. Approaches to classroom management range from intimidation to permissive. Getting off to a good start is critical. Classroom routines and procedures must be taught to students. About five to seven broad rules and consequences for violation should be established, preferably in consultation with students. These must be enforced, and the teacher must avoid the "nice guy (or gal) syndrome." Teachers should master effective direction giving and withitness, overlapping behavior, movement management, and group focus. A positive, supportive classroom climate must be established and minor disruptions must be deterred, checked to avoid reoccurrence, and good behavior reinforced.

Hold regular classroom meetings. This gives students an authentic voice and opportunities for problem solving; it can help create a democratic learning community that is caring and positive. Varying your choice of teaching strategies and methods and becoming proficient at using basic instructional skills helps make it possible for all students to succeed. Students who are succeeding rarely misbehave. Teach procedures and routines. Students need to know and observe procedures that allow lessons to flow smoothly with a minimum of delay or off-task time. Plan lessons

carefully and ensure that materials are ready and transition times flow smoothly. Clarify what is expected. Be clear about what is and is not a behavior problem. Be consistent about the definition, the consequences, and the application of the consequences. Know when to seek assistance. When faced with challenging behaviors, think about what has been happening. Be objective and record what occurred without interpreting or judging. Make an effort to understand what is happening. Seek patterns. Ask yourself which students are involved and the context in which misbehavior occurs. Then, try to identify techniques you might use to avoid repetition of the misbehavior. Finally, if these do not work, talk to someone who may have ideas for addressing the problem.

Activities

MANAGEMENT BACKGROUND

1. Think of a teacher or instructor who had very good classroom management. Record the things this person did or said that kept students on task and learning. Then, have students pick two partners, telling them about their teacher. The trio should agree on five characteristics. Pairs or trios join to agree on five characteristics. Groups report to the whole class.

2. Think about your philosophy or approach to classroom management and discipline and then record the major principles in which you believe. Compare your philosophy with the ideas in this text. What are the essential similarities and differences? Share your thoughts with another student.

3. After the material in this topic has been covered, join a group of five. Suggest ways in which the concerns of the preinterns identified by McBeath could have been handled.

4. On file cards, write two personal classroom management concerns. Students in the class will write one concern on the chalkboard or on newsprint (duplications are not allowed). Students examine the concerns recorded, add any not yet mentioned, and place a check mark beside ones already written. A frequency count will be done. In order of frequency, in your group, problem solve and report suggested solutions. Debrief.

5. The next time you are in your student placement, make a list of all the procedures used by the cooperating teacher. Interview the teacher to discover the rules established and why and how they were established.

FUNDAMENTALS

1. After your instructor has introduced the basic skills of withitness, overlapping, movement management, and group focus, join four or five others. In turn, each person provides examples of what she or he has noticed teachers use to achieve each of the basic management skills.

2. As a culminating activity, join a group of seven. Each group composes and delivers a skit that illustrates each of the four basic management skills. A student from each group role-plays the "teacher" and the others the "class." While skits are being presented, the rest of the class uses the data collection instrument in Appendix 6.1 to collect data on use of the four skills.

MINOR DISRUPTIONS

1. Recall a teacher whom you believe handled minor disruptions well. Join five others to list and categorize effective behaviors for handling minor disruptions. Groups report. Debrief. Join six others to compose and perform a skit illustrating ways of handling minor disruptions effectively. Each

group performs and class members use the data collection sheet in Appendix 6.2.

2. Respond to the following: (a) Think of an example of a minor disruption that occurs periodically in a classroom. (b) Describe the class situation that is present when it occurs. (c) How does the teacher react? What does she or he do or say? (d) When the teacher reacts, how does the misbehaving student(s) react? (e) What is the effect on other students in the class? (f) What happens later? In ten minutes; twenty minutes; next period; next day? (g) Are the teacher's actions (desists) effective? Why? If not effective, what should the teacher try? (h) How could the disruption have been prevented from occurring in the first place?

GENERAL CONCERNS

1. In groups, brainstorm what you consider to be the main classroom management concerns of teachers. Compare the groups' findings with what is presented in Figure 6.1.

2. On cards, write out the main norms, routines, and procedures needed for a well-managed class. Also on cards, list the main discipline problems of an ill-managed class. Place the management cards under one column and the discipline cards under another. Decide, by placing cards side by side, which discipline strategies might eliminate the problems.

3. Divide the class into two groups. Call one the "few academic demands class" and the other the "high academic demands class." Groups list what they might do during a typical lesson.

4. You are about to teach a class for the first time. Prepare your "Classroom Management" notes for a teaching binder. Use the material presented in this chapter. Write notes under the headings in this section of the text.

5. Select one of your lesson plans. Rewrite the lesson using as your professional target the charts and materials presented in this chapter.

6. Have a volunteer teach the whole group. Distribute minor disruption cards to selected class members. Have cards contain instructions such as "Write a note and pass it to your neighbor," "Tell the teacher you don't have a pen," "Blurt out loud the answer to the teacher's questions," etc. Also on the cards should be such instructions as "Stop after being told by the teacher," "Stop after being warned twice," "Stop if the teacher stands close to you or gives you an eye-contact warning." Data are collected using the data sheet in Appendix 6.3.

DIRECTIONS

1. As a set activity, join a group to consider the following. Begin a unit involving gymnastics with a grade 8 class of twenty-four students. As a matter of routine, you want students to help you set up mats and then move rapidly into place for instruction. What directions should you give? Consider the steps needed and what you will say and do. Groups report. After reporting, groups reconsider their plans in light of what they have heard. Join the class for a debriefing.

2. Join a group of four. Two engage in an exercise where they sit back to back; one gives the other directions for tying a shoe. The other must follow the directions literally. The other two are observers and report what they saw and how they think participants were feeling. Debrief.

3. As a culminating activity, join a subject-interest group. Each group selects a topic from a subject area and determines the directions that should be given. Each group has ten minutes for one of the group to give directions to the class on the activity. Class members, using Appendix 6.3 collect data on how directions were given.

4. Have volunteers give "Giving Directions" lessons. Have other volunteers collect data on the sheet in Appendix 6.3. Discuss the findings after the lessons.

APPENDIX 6.1 *Basic Management Skills Target*

PROFESSIONAL TARGET—BASIC MANAGEMENT SKILLS

Please describe what was said or occurred and student reactions.

Management Behavior	Descriptive Notes

Withitness
Teacher aware/students know it
Examples:
   Using eye contact
   Gesturing at student
   Positioning to be able to see all
   Seeing student while at board
   Positioning while helping individual

Overlapping
Teacher attends to student or minor disruption
   without interrupting flow
Examples:
   Seeing and acknowledging hand raised
   Moving toward disruptive student(s)
   Standing beside disruptive student
   Asking question of disruptive student
   Attending to needs of several groups

Movement management
Reducing "dead time" by smooth transitions
   from one activity, part of lesson, to another
Examples:
   Having demo materials or aids ready
   Giving clear directions
   Rapid distribution of materials
   Rapid taking out of materials
   Rapid movement to parts of room or in and out of room
   Smooth transition activities/to groups
   Appropriate pacing of lesson

Group focus
Students kept alert/accountable
   Getting and holding attention
   Making sure all know what to do
   Question posed before student asked
   Wait time provided
   Students raise hands
   Questions not repeated
   Chorus and unsolicited answers avoided
   Responses directed to entire class
   Unsolicited responses not permitted
   Question distribution
   Volunteers/nonvolunteers asked to respond
   Repeating of question/answer avoided

PROFESSIONAL TARGET—HANDLING MINOR DISRUPTIONS

Please describe what was said or occurred and student reactions.

Management Skill	Nature of Disruption	Teacher Response	Effects on Student(s)

A. Deterring
Firmly stopping
  unacceptable behavior
Examples:
  Pausing
  Raising eyebrows
  Gesturing
  Using eye contact
  Walking toward
  Reminding
  Telling to stop
  Asking what should be
    done
  Talking one-to-one
  Other			

B. Checking up
Letting student(s) see you
  are checking up so
  disruption doesn't restart
Examples:
  Gesturing
  Circulating
  Asking question			

C. Reinforcing desired behavior
Verbally/nonverbally
  reinforcing desired
  behavior:
Recognizing desired
  behavior of individuals
Recognizing desired
  behavior of a group or
  whole class			

APPENDIX 6.3   *Giving Directions Target*

PROFESSIONAL TARGET—GIVING DIRECTIONS

Please describe what was said or done and student reactions.

Behavior	Descriptive Comments
Giving signals (using voice, body language, to get students to attend)	
Securing attention (Making sure that all are listening *before* starting)	
Timing (giving right amount of time; telling how much time left)	
Giving clear directions (brief, understandable, complete; putting on board or handout)	
Checking up (determining if students understand, are doing it right; asking; observing while students do; etc.)	
Anticipating/attending (anticipating problems; telling students what to do when done; keeping students on task; helping, reinforcing)	

7

Facilitating Learning
Lesson and Unit Planning and Delivery

It is the supreme art of the teacher to awaken joy in creative expression and knowledge. (Albert Einstein)

Being an educated person means being guided by values and beliefs and connecting lessons of the classroom to the realities of life. (Boyer, 1995, p. 16)

The Teacher Competence Profile criteria on lesson and unit planning can be found at the top of page 203. The key ideas are addressed in this chapter.

Planning Approaches

Teachers are accountable for lesson, unit, and yearly planning to district, state, and national standards, curriculum guides, and expectations of students, administrators, and parents. They think about how to attain the goals of education and student development.

Although effective teachers do not begin a course, unit, or lesson without careful planning, they realize that plans are not always followed to the letter. Changes occur because of emerging interests and needs. Good plans include alternative activities. Effective teachers are flexible and revise plans to help students achieve intended outcomes. They know subject matter, have a bank of instructional methods, and draw on a storehouse of activities. Content, and the mix of experiences, need to be carefully selected, well organized, and sequenced. They should motivate students and match their needs. Planning requires reflection and must be continuous.

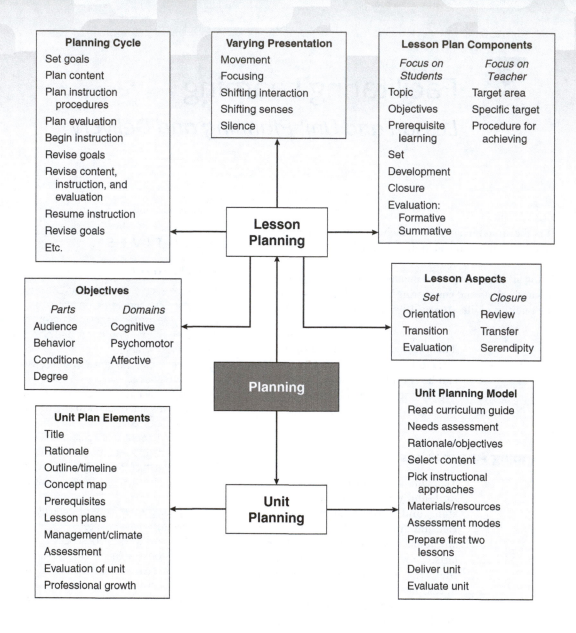

There are three interrelated levels of planning: (1) a year or semester course; (2) a sequence of instructional units or themes (a few days to two or three weeks); and (3) a series of lessons within a unit, from about twenty minutes to two or three classes.

Planning Phases

Planning and decision making usually occur during three phases: before, during, and after instruction.

During the *first phase* (preinstruction), teachers chose the content to be studied and a variety of teaching strategies, methods, and student activities. They think about the content, how rapidly to cover it, the time allocated to each topic, classroom management ex-

TCP—LESSON AND UNIT PLANNING

Integrates skills common to all subjects and adapts curriculum to individual needs

In planning units and lessons, incorporates the skills common to all subjects; adapts curriculum plans to individual needs.

Unaware of common essential skills; does not incorporate skills common to all subjects; does not adapt curriculum plans to individual needs.

Plans varied learner-centered activities

Plans enable students to be actively involved in a broad range of motivating activities congruent with objectives and evaluation; development level and student needs and interests recognized; activities often learner selected; aware of the need to adapt to individual and group needs.

Prescriptive activities randomly chosen and sequenced or inappropriate to developmental level and student needs and interests; often incongruent with objectives and evaluation; activities always teacher selected; unaware of the need to adapt to individual and group needs.

Outlines long-range plans to guide student development

Logically sequenced; variety in presentation and student activities; addresses student readiness; plans adaptable to a variety of student needs; provides for evaluation; plans available prior to teaching.

Generally fails to plan units or drafts or series of lessons with little coherence, variety or attention to student needs; plans not available in advance.

Plans interdisciplinary thematic units

Plans units that focus on a specific theme/problem/issue, that integrate several areas; themes are realistic, relating to student interests and abilities.

Units always subject area specific.

Involves learners in the planning process

Learners are involved in planning units.

Students are never consulted or involved in unit planning.

Includes classroom management in plans

Unit plans contain detailed plans for classroom management.

Unit plans do not incorporate classroom management.

pectations, routines, and procedures. A key consideration is how to set a positive climate for learning and how to motivate while having high but achievable expectations.

In the *second phase* (the developmental or interactive), teachers make instructional decisions. They think about whether presentations and student activities are effective, how they can help students, whether transitions from one part of a lesson to another or from one lesson to another are smooth, and if pacing is appropriate. They are aware of classroom climate and the suitability of routines and procedures. Formative evaluation (on the progress students are making) is occurring continuously, and thoughts are given to summative evaluation.

In the *third phase* (postinstructional), summative tests or other measures are given and marks assigned, recorded, and reported. Testing may be through paper-and-pencil examinations, papers, projects, or portfolios (a combination technique). Tests provide feedback and an opportunity for teaching. Evaluation should inform students how they are doing—what they know well and what they still need to master. Follow-up is critical. Conscientious teachers provide guidance so students will be successful with work that was initially difficult and help turn deferred successes into successes. Importantly, *it is not just students who are being evaluated*. The effectiveness of the teacher's instruction and the appropriateness of evaluative measures also should be examined. The teacher needs to reflect on what went well during the teaching and learning process, what should be modified, and how it should be modified.

Linear and Nonlinear Approaches

Much research has been done on teacher planning. The traditional view is that the process is *rational-linear*. This begins by establishing goals and objectives, moves to planning instructional actions to promote achievement of objectives, and concludes with measurement of achievement. However, instructional planning is often nonlinear and teachers may, for good reason, deviate from plans. It is unrealistic to believe that a unit plan should consist of carefully preplanned lessons and be closely followed. The first lesson or two can be planned but may or may not be executed exactly as planned. It is more realistic to gather a selection of introductory, developmental, and culminating activities from which to choose in the light of what occurs from day to day. Of course, other activities may be added. Arends (2004, p. 99) claims the nonlinear approach is how many experienced teachers approach some of the aspects of planning.

As can be seen, there are four major sources for planning: (1) *goals and objectives* (examples of sources: department of education, school districts, and texts); (2) *subject matter* (i.e., knowledge of content; content-specific information, concepts, generalizations, skills, and processes; ordering of content for instruction); (3) *knowledge of teaching models, strategies, methods, and skills* (i.e., selection and use of these based on their effect on motivation, classroom management, and factors such as student motivation, at-task orientation, and rate of success); and (4) *learner characteristics and differences* (i.e., aptitude, past achievement, personality [anxiety, motivation, and self-concept], home life, and peer influences).

The Backward Design Approach

Wiggins and McTighe (1998) developed an approach called *backward design*. This, they note, is close to the way experienced teachers often plan. The backward design approach has three stages (pp. 9–13).

Stage 1. *Identify desired results.* What should students know, understand, and be able to do?

- Consider goals, examine established content standards (national, state, and district), and review curricular expectations.
- Make content choices. What is of enduring understanding (the big ideas and important understandings)? What is important to know and do (the facts, concepts, principles, and skills needed for students to accomplish key performances)? What is worth being familiar with? What do we want students to hear, read, view, research, and otherwise encounter?

Assessment

Stage 2. *Determine acceptable evidence.* How will you know students have achieved the desired results and met standards? What will be accepted as evidence of student understanding and proficiency?

- Think like an assessor before designing units or lessons.
- Consider how you will determine whether students have attained the desired understandings.
- Consider the range of assessment methods to use.

Instructional strategies

Stage 3. *Plan learning experiences and instruction.* With clearly identified results (enduring understandings) and appropriate evidence of understanding in mind, educators can plan instructional activities.

- What activities will equip students with the needed knowledge and skills?
- What needs to be taught and coached? How should it be taught in the light of performance goals?
- What materials and resources are best suited to accomplish these goals?
- Is the overall design coherent and effective?

The Standards Movement

Many content areas now have standards that are helpful in planning content, strategies, and materials. Because most have web sites, unit planners can readily examine what subject councils and associations consider important.

"The standards address what should be taught, and the performance assessment indicates the level of performance that students should demonstrate. The goal of these new standards is to benchmark or match these assessments to those of other countries whose students achieve highly on international assessments" (Burden & Byrd, 2003, p. 30). What is essential can change over time and according to world events. They reflect national values, which in our postmodern society are subject to change. An examination of the standards of the National Council for the Social Studies (NCSS) web site is an example of the value of the standards movement to planners. Learner and teacher expectations descriptors in this text are an excellent source of planning ideas.

- *Learner expectations.* The realities of global interdependence require learners to understand the increasingly important and diverse global connections among world societies. Analysis of tensions between national interests and global priorities contributes to the development of possible solutions to persistent and emerging global issues in many fields: health care, economic development, environmental quality, universal human rights, and others. Analyzing patterns and relationships within and among world cultures, such as economic competition and interdependence, age-old ethnic enmities, political and military alliances, and others, helps learners examine policy alternatives that have both national and global implications.

- *Teacher expectations.* Teachers of social studies at all school levels should provide developmentally appropriate experiences as they guide learners in the study of global connections and interdependence. They should guide learner analysis of the relationships and tensions between national sovereignty and global interests in such matters as territorial disputes, economic development, nuclear and other weapons deployment, use of natural resources, and human rights concerns.

DIFFERENCE BETWEEN STANDARDS-BASED AND NORM-REFERENCED SYSTEMS.
The Disney Working Partnership (2004) quotes Mitchell, Willis, Crawford, and Chicago Teacher's Union Quest Center (1997), who provide a useful comparison between norm-referenced and standards-based systems.

Norm Referenced	Standards Based
Believe some students are naturally smarter than others.	Believe virtually all students can "get smart" through effort.
Content subject matter varies with different groups of students.	Content subject matter is the same for all groups of students.
Assessments compare what students know to what other students know.	Assessments compare what students know to standards and benchmarks.
No objective criteria to deploy resources—who need the most often get the least.	Resources are deployed as needed for all students to meet student standards—students who need more get more.
Professional development episodic—workshops.	Professional development focuses on improving instruction one-time so all students meet standards.

WHAT ARE THE BENEFITS OF ACADEMIC STANDARDS?   The Disney Working Partnership points out that standards provide focus for reform efforts. All students must reach the standards. By viewing progress students make toward standards, teachers can judge the effectiveness of their instruction.

The greatest benefits of standards are focus and publication. All can see what schools aim to teach and students must learn. This is not a secret privy to a small part of the student population. Standards can be an equity tool. If all students must meet the standards, then all schools must strive to get children to reach them—not just schools with a majority of middle-class, college-bound students.

Because they provide a focus, standards are a yardstick for all aspects of schooling. For example, does the textbook provide opportunities to meet standards? Is the staff development workshop worthwhile because it is likely that teachers will learn things to help students reach standards? All resources, materials, schedules, and personnel assignments can be judged by the criterion, "Will students achieve the standards?"

WHAT DO CRITICS OF STANDARDS HAVE TO SAY?   Critics of standards, the Disney Working Partnership says, tend to fall into three camps: one camp worries that standards force teachers to "teach to tests" and stress rote learning, not creative and individualized education. Another group worries that if standards are set too high, low achievers (particularly in disadvantaged communities) will become discouraged and drop out; if standards are too low, high achievers will not be challenged. The third group thinks standards should be set locally, not federally or by the state.

Those who object to "teaching to tests" say that this measures test-taking ability, not real-life skills, and is biased against those from disadvantaged backgrounds; it stresses memorization rather than creative thinking. Although these concerns do fit some standardized tests used as benchmarks, it should be noted that standards-based teaching does not rely only, or even primarily, on these kinds of tests. Achievement of standards can also be measured through writing skill or other assignments.

Fears about the levels of standards are common. For example, Richard Rothstein (1999) argued that holding schools with largely poor populations to the same standards as suburban schools penalizes students in disadvantaged districts for factors they cannot control and causes students in suburban schools to be insufficiently challenged. Also, holding students to standards—especially where promotion is the issue—will increase dropouts, especially in schools with heavy minority populations.

Planning Variables

Content

Content is more than facts, information, and motor skills. It includes concepts and generalizations, and interpersonal and social skills. It involves creative and critical thinking, problem solving, decision-making capability, attitudes, appreciations, and values. Content (and therefore objectives) can be declarative, procedural, or conditional and can be product or process. It can be cognitive, psychomotor, or affective.

Declarative content and objectives include the facts, concepts, or generalizations that students are to learn. *Procedural content and objectives* include the skills or processes—cognitive, affective, or psychomotor—that students are to learn and be able to do. *Conditional content and objectives* refer to the conditions and contexts associated with knowledge—knowing where, why, and when to apply declarative and procedural content. *Product objectives* ask that students acquire the knowledge, get the right answers, or acquire facts or information (what, where, or when); and *process objectives* ask students to acquire the processes of getting knowledge or knowing how to get the right answers or appropriate facts or information (how or why).

Cognitive objectives refer to information acquisition, comprehension, analysis, synthesis, and evaluation capability; *psychomotor objectives* refer to the manipulation and use of objects or the body; and *affective objectives* consider such things as attitudes, values, and emotions.

Objectives

IMPORTANCE OF CLEAR OBJECTIVES.   You, as the teacher, must have a clear idea of what students should know or be able to do as a result of a lesson, unit, or course. Student achievement can be improved if instruction is directed toward specific outcomes and if students know what is expected without sacrificing flexibility in the light of emerging contextual needs.

Although writing good objectives is hard work, the advantages are that (1) instruction is more focused; (2) learning is more efficient; (3) evaluation is fairer; and (4) students are better at evaluating themselves. To prepare good objectives, think about what the outcomes should be in keeping with the broad objectives of the unit and course under study. Consider the instructional procedures that can best help students achieve expected outcomes, and the kinds of evaluation suitable to see whether or not the hoped-for outcomes have been attained by students. Congruence is needed:

Course Objectives ◄──► Unit Objectives ◄──► Lesson Objectives

◄──────────────── CONGRUENCE ────────────────►

Lesson Objectives ◄──► Instructional Procedures ◄──► Evaluation Procedures

Objectives should specify the content students are to learn and the circumstances under which they are to show their learning. It is often more important to know how to do something than to get the right answer. Acquiring independent learning skills is also critical.

Initial planning involves setting goals and objectives, deciding on instructional approaches and activities, and devising evaluation congruent with objectives. Planning provides direction, should be continuous with preinstructional, during instruction, and postinstructional phases, and include the elements illustrated in Figure 7.1.

Professional teachers begin with aims or goals that may be adapted from a curriculum guide and from the school's statement of goals. Content and instructional approaches and student activities and evaluation schema are selected. How specific this planning is, and the sequence in which it occurs, varies by individual teacher and the school and district. However, effective teachers know, "Teachers who fail to plan, plan to fail."

If you want to be an effective professional, plan well ahead and think of adaptations that can be applied if needed. Many things can cause plans to change. A few examples are:

- You give a pretest and discover students either are more advanced than anticipated or do not possess the needed knowledge or skills.
- The time budgeted for a topic is either too short or too long.
- An activity you planned does not secure or hold student interest.

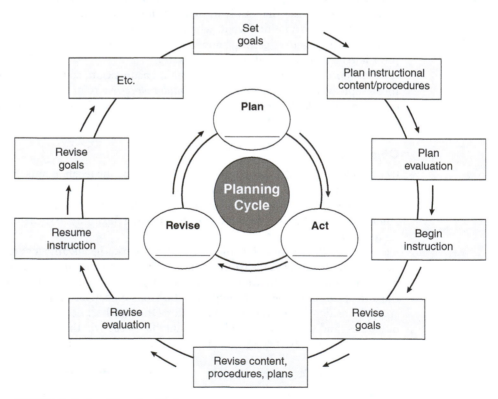

FIGURE 7.1 *Planning Cycle*

- A serendipitous happening provides a teachable opportunity to treat a topic out of the order planned.
- A golden, unanticipated opportunity presents itself (e.g., a television program is announced that is ideal for your language arts class; a surprise call for an election fits neatly into your social studies course).
- A resource you planned to use is no longer available or arrives too late. What resources are available? What adaptations can be made?

WRITING OBJECTIVES. When students understand what they are to learn, they are more likely to have successful learning experiences. What are students to accomplish? What should students know, be able to do, or be like through their learning experiences? The success of programs, courses, units, or lessons depends heavily on how well thought out this is.

Teaching and evaluation of student progress is effective when there are clear and observable objectives that may be modified in the light of classroom events and student needs.

Well-thought-out objectives describe behavior you can observe. Compare the following. The first examples are vague and the second examples are clear.

> *Vague:* Students will understand why Hamlet was called the melancholy Dane.
> *Clear:* By referring to excerpts from *Hamlet,* students will be able to write a brief paper explaining why Hamlet has been called the melancholy Dane.

> *Vague:* Students will be good at doing basketball set shots.
> *Clear:* Each student will be able to sink at least seven out of ten set shots.

PREPARING LESSON OBJECTIVES. Course or unit objectives are too general for specific lessons. Lesson objectives need to specify what learners are to know, be able to do, or value about what was learned. These express expected learner behavior. Objectives do *not,* for instance, include listening to a lecture, taking part in a discussion, or watching a film or demonstration—these are *activities* that may lead to the achievement of objectives.

When you prepare objectives, ask yourself, "How can students show me what they know or can do?" Objectives call for evidence of one of three things: (1) the *information* (concepts or generalizations) you want students to know or use; (2) the *skill or process* you want students to perform or display; or (3) the *value or feeling* you want students to experience.

ACTIVITIES VERSUS OBJECTIVES. *Activities* are the learning experiences in which students participate to achieve objectives. *Objectives* describe the knowledge, skills, or attitudes students should display as a result of participating in a lesson. That is, activities are the *means* to achieve objectives, whereas objectives are the *ends.* Try the following exercise.

> *Activity:* Students will view a filmstrip about the significance of nonverbal communication in a Native American culture.
> *Objective:* After viewing a filmstrip on the use of nonverbal communication by Northern Cree people, each student will be able to list five ways in which Canadian Northern Cree people may use nonverbal signals.

Which of the following are parts of good objectives that are activities?

1. Students will solve square-root problems.
2. Students will read Chapter 3 in the text.
3. Students will write a good business letter.
4. Students will take a field trip to the museum.
5. Students will practice cutting and pasting on computers.
6. Students will discuss the causes of pollution.
7. Students will name three advantages and three disadvantages of "free trade."

Items 1, 3, and 7 are parts of good objectives.

DESCRIBING STUDENT PERFORMANCE.   Objectives specify the performance expected of students because of the lesson. Based on the objective, you should easily be able to evaluate the achievement or nonachievement of the objective. The key to describing performance is to use specific, observable verbs. The verbs should be active, not vague.

> *Vague (broad) verbs:* understand, know, comprehend, learn, remember, evaluate, feel, enjoy, value, and appreciate.
> *Action (specific) verbs:* list, name, select, write, draw, outline, match, pronounce, solve, and form.

Which of the following are good objectives because they include good verbs and observable student performance?

1. Students will list the countries through which the Danube River flows.
2. Students will appreciate the painting, *Mona Lisa.*
3. Students will be able to add two-digit numbers.
4. Students will match the names and pictures of Canadian animals.
5. Students will know the difference between the bass and treble clefs.
6. Students will list the causes of the Battle of the Plains of Abraham.
7. Students will remember what causes lightning.

Items 1, 3, 4, and 6 are observable.

CONDITIONS OF PERFORMANCE.   Not only should the behavior expected be clear, the *conditions* under which it is to appear also should be clear and specific. Ask yourself, "Under what circumstances is the behavior to be performed?" Conditions often include materials or information students will be given. A common way to express conditions is to use the term "given."

> *Conditions included:* Given a three-page essay, students will be able to underline each simile and circle each metaphor.
> *Conditions absent:* Students will recognize the difference between similes and metaphors.

Which of the following identify the conditions (or givens)?

1. Students will know how to prepare a Caesar salad.
2. Given advertising slogans, students will be able to name the product being advertised.

3. Students will identify different figures of speech that writers can use.
4. When provided with an unlabeled map of the United States, students will write in the name of each state.
5. Students will appreciate the complexities of the rules of baseball.
6. As they prepare the reference page of a manuscript provided, students will follow the rules in the APA style manual.
7. Students will underline each adjective in the list of words provided.

Conditions are identified in items 2, 4, 6 and 7.

Following the "B, C, D's" will help you write good objectives. "B" is the *behavior* expected of students as they provide evidence of what they have learned—specific verbs are needed. "C" is the *conditions* (or "givens") under which the student behavior is to occur. "D" is the *degree* to which students are expected to achieve what they have been studying—it is an estimate of how well students will do or how many of the class will be able to do something. Consider the following.

1. *Behavior:* Students will hit a golf ball into an area five yards in diameter,
   Conditions: on the practice range, using a nine-iron and the Vardon overlapping grip,
   Degree: seven out of ten times.
2. *Behavior:* Students will name the pieces used to play chess,
   Conditions: when shown a diagram of a chessboard containing randomly arranged pieces,
   Degree: in ten minutes or less; 28 of 30 students will correctly identify all the pieces.
3. *Behavior:* Students will be able to circle the capital cities of European countries,
   Conditions: when shown an outline map of Europe,
   Degree: and correctly identify at least 8 capital cities.
4. *Behavior:* Students will write a paper explaining factors that led to the fall of the Third Reich,
   Conditions: after viewing a sixty-minute film on PBS;
   Degree: 25 of the 30 members of the class will satisfactorily describe at least four factors.

TAXONOMIES AND OBJECTIVES. Objectives express educational intentions. The taxonomy approach developed by Benjamin Bloom and his colleagues (1956) has stood the test of time and is the most common. Bloom et al. classified learning intentions into three domains: *cognitive, psychomotor,* and *affective.* Each domain has levels of learning in a hierarchy from simple to complex. When you become aware that various levels exist, you will be sensitive to where learners are in their development. Understanding taxonomies helps you to adjust learning experiences to match learner needs.

Although you can write objectives for behaviors that are cognitive, affective, and psychomotor, in real life, behaviors from each domain often occur simultaneously. Considering each aspect separately sharpens your awareness of student progress and the experiences learners need.

It is not our purpose here to provide a detailed description of each taxonomy of Bloom et al. (1956), Krathwohl, Bloom, and Masia (1964), and Harlow (1972). You will be given information and practice with the cognitive taxonomy and information about the affective and psychomotor taxonomies. More information about the taxonomies is provided later. It is likely you will learn more about the other two elsewhere in your teacher education program.

The Cognitive Domain (Bloom et al., 1956).   Ms. Boyko teaches a unit on physical geology to her grade 7 students. Today's lesson is "rock families." She asks students the following:

- What are the names of the two main classifications of silicates?
- Can you think of an example of an igneous rock?
- What is one major difference between sedimentary rocks and metamorphic rocks?
- Look at samples of sedimentary rocks. What do they all have in common?
- What is a way we can make economic use of the rocks in this area?
- Can you think of new ways in which we could make use of the rocks in this area?
- What do you think of the practice of digging out and selling most of the rocks in an area?

Ms. Boyko's questions range from simple recall to requiring considerable understanding and thought. Bloom's cognitive taxonomy categorizes learning into six levels (below). Into which level do you think each of her questions fits?

BLOOM'S COGNITIVE TAXONOMY

Knowledge	Recalling information in the way it was presented, but not necessarily understanding it (i.e., recalling, recognizing, memorizing).
	To learn and remember information (how many, when, who, where, locate, tell, name, list, point to, repeat).
Comprehension:	Understanding, or ability to state content in your words, not necessarily applying or relating it to something else (i.e., describing, give an example, interpreting, why, explain, summarize).
	To understand information (reword, define, discuss, paraphrase, explain, give an example).
Application	Applying information to a new situation, or using a general concept to solve a problem (i.e., problem solving).
	To use information (try, employ, relate, put into action, follow steps).
Analysis	Breaking down, or subdividing, a situation into its parts (i.e., finding structure, identifying motives, discovering relationships).
	To take information apart or discover the parts or organization (dissect, test for, examine, inspect, "what makes it tick").
Synthesis	Coming up with something new, or organizing something in a new way (i.e., creating, inventing, composing, designing).
	Note: It need not be "new to humankind"; it may just be new to the learner.
	To create new ideas or things; doing something new with the information (build, make, create, formulate, develop, invent).
Evaluation	Judging using criteria, using a rationale or standards that decide the value of applying materials or methods (i.e., judging, resolving conflicts, reasoned choosing among alternatives).
	Based on criteria, making judgments about information (judge, appraise, assess, decide, rate, rank, evaluate).

The cognitive domain is the domain that is best known by teachers. It places ability in the sequence: knowledge, comprehension, application, analysis, synthesis, and evaluation. Though it is not rigidly followed, many teachers believe the cognitive taxonomy helps ensure that learning progresses well beyond memory work into the domain's higher levels, which are compatible with constructivist approaches to teaching and learning. Jill Slack (2002) notes that Bloom's taxonomy can be used to improve students' thinking and comprehension.

During the 1990s, Lorin Anderson (a former student of Benjamin Bloom) and a team reworked the cognitive taxonomy in an attempt to modernize it (OZ Teachers Net, 2004). The names of the six major categories were changed from noun to verb forms. The subcategories were replaced by verbs, and some were reorganized. This version (Anderson, Krathwohl, Airasian, et al., 2001) is preferred by some educators. A search of the literature reveals that extensive use is still made today of the original version of the cognitive taxonomy.

Instructional Variables

The effective instructor has a host of instructional approaches in his or her toolbox. These can be selected to match the context of any class or topic.

TCP—INSTRUCTIONAL VARIABLES

Demonstrates competence in basic instructional skills

Provides motivating lesson introduction (set); gives clear explanations; words questions clearly; provides for review and practice; checks for student understanding; provides lesson summary (closure).

Lessons introduced in unmotivating, vague ways; explanations are confusing; questioning skills are poorly developed; no effective closure.

Teaches for holistic development (physical, social, emotional, cognitive)

Lessons consist of activities that address physical, social, and emotional as well as cognitive needs.

Lessons are primarily cognitive.

Varies teaching approaches and activities

Consistently uses a variety of teaching strategies and methods appropriate for the content and students; experiments with a variety of ways of teaching.

Uses only one or two teaching strategies and methods; tries new methods only when urged to do so.

Ensures the participation and success of all

Assesses ongoing individual student development; modifies activities for active participation to ensure success of all students.

Little individual assessment; students expected to engage in the same activity regardless of level or ability.

Engages students in instructional dialogue

Engages students in dialogue about their experiences and learning; debriefs the processes of learning with students; teaches specific learning strategies, monitors the use of learning strategies.

Learning activities seldom debriefed; learning processes not taught to students; learning strategies not monitored.

continued

TCP—INSTRUCTIONAL VARIABLES   *(continued)*

Provides motivating set and closure

Always provides a motivating set for lessons and units that facilitates transfer from previous to new learning; always provides closure to lessons and units that reviews and provides transfer.

Begins lessons and units without a set; lessons end abruptly, without review or transfer.

Orders and sequences content to meet learner needs

Orders and sequences content to meet learner needs; recognizes when text organization is inappropriate. Uses advance organizers and in progress and post organizers well; fosters student capability in recognizing structures and patterns in content.

Rigidly follows the text or curriculum guide without consideration of learner needs; content is a smorgasbord of information; absence of use of organizers; students not helped to discover structures in patterns of content.

Provides for transfer of learning

Deliberate provision for transfer (bridging) within the subject, across subjects, and to life; examples used are relevant and interesting to students.

No attempt to bridge previous and new learning, or transfer learning within the subject, or to other subjects or life.

Varying the Presentation

Effective teachers, research suggests, make presentations varied and interesting (Good & Brophy, 1995, p. 283) so students pay attention, are motivated, and so they are more likely to learn and remember. The teacher appeals to a variety of senses, moves around the room, uses visuals, has students write or handle materials, varies speech, uses pauses, asks questions, and has students interact. In interesting lessons, stimulus variation occurs because of careful planning; at times it is spontaneous. Just using multiple senses—sight, touch, sound—has been shown to increase learning, as has greater involvement of, and participation by, learners (Diem, 1998). Shostak (1982) defines *stimulus variation* as teacher actions "designed to develop and maintain a high level of student attention during the course of a lesson by varying the presentation" (p. 121). A more complete definition would add that stimulus variation facilitates learning and retention.

Literature on learning styles, brain hemisphericity, learning mode preferences (visual, auditory, and kinesthetic), and multiple intelligences supports the need for variation in instructional approaches and learning activities. The skillful teacher uses stimulus variation techniques to direct and keep student attention on the lesson, emphasize key points or certain features, and provide a refreshing change of pace (Shostak, 1982, p. 123).

Why Vary the Presentation?

Varying the mode of presentation and choice of learning activities is important because students only tend to listen, watch, or do something, and remain interested for a limited time. Although this is particularly true of young children, it also applies to adults. A wise old sociology professor used to say, "If you can't strike oil after five or ten minutes, quit boring."

Information is received through all the senses. Murgio (1969) tells us that, of what we know, we have learned about 1 percent through taste, 2 percent through touch, 4 percent through smell, 10 percent through hearing, and 83 percent through sight.

Retention is increased if a multisensory approach is used. According to Murgio, of what we learn, we retain 10 percent of what we read, 20 percent of what we hear, 30 percent of what we see, 50 percent of what we hear and see, 70 percent of what we say, and 90 percent of what we say as we do. For several reasons, including previous experience and culture, we have preferred learning styles. Individual preferences vary. By varying the presentation, you reach more students.

Depending on the background of learners, at times presentations should be very concrete or "hands on," sometimes pictures or other visual representations can be used, and at still other times words (spoken or written) or other symbols may be sufficient. Keeping to a single mode of representation may be ineffective; using a symbolic mode before students have had concrete, or at least pictorial, previous experience may be a waste of time. These three "levels" of learning are similar to the learning processes (*enactive, iconic,* and *symbolic*) proposed by Bruner (1960), which are closely related to those described by Piaget (1929; see also Piaget & Inhelder, 1969).

Variety for the sake of variety is not productive in many life situations; however, when it comes to selection of teaching strategies, it pays dividends. Although research does not clearly demonstrate the superiority of one teaching strategy or method over another, use of a variety of strategies and method results in greater learning. Students are bound to get bored in an unchanging environment.

Techniques for Varying the Stimulus

How can you vary presentation in your lessons to attract and hold student attention? Shostak (1982, pp. 124–129) describes five *stimulus variation techniques* that should be part of your repertoire: (1) focusing, (2) kinesic variation, (3) shifting interaction, (4) pausing (silence), and (5) shifting senses. Descriptions of these techniques are presented below. We begin with focusing because it needs to be emphasized; as you will discover, all the other stimulus variation techniques are variations of focusing.

FOCUSING.   Learning takes place only through mental or physical activity. You use a stimulus so learners can focus on, and attend to, whatever is to be learned. Gain and hold attention to avoid boredom and loss of attention. Focusing can be done

- *Orally:* voice emphasis, variation, audio equipment and questions
- *Nonverbally:* gestures and pointing, physical movement, facial expressions
- *Visually:* variations in print, chalkboard or other visuals, films, etc.
- *With teaching materials:* blocks, rods, models, displays, and other teaching materials (many can be looked at, handled, smelled)
- *By varying interactions* (described below)
- *With silence* (described below)
- *By shifting senses* (described below)

The teacher who deliberately controls the direction of students' attention uses the skill of focusing. Among ways you can focus are

- *Using gestures.* Examples include pointing with your hand or an object, expressively motioning with your hands, nodding, raising your eyebrows or shoulders, and by smiling or frowning.

- *Making a statement.* Say things such as "Look at the map," "Listen for three main points," "Notice the differences in size," "Watch carefully when I add sulfuric acid," "Now, the next step is really important."
- *Supporting statements with gestures.* Examples include using a pointer on an overhead projector and saying, "This is the direction the water will flow"; holding up two fingers and saying, "There are two things you should remember"; tapping at a spot on a chalkboard diagram and saying, "This is where water will flow"; holding up two fingers and saying, "There are two things you should remember"; tapping a spot on a large map, saying, "This is where the attack took place"; bringing your hand gently down from above your head and saying, "The glider gently followed the air currents and eventually landed."

KINESIC VARIATION. The eye tends to be attracted to, and follow, movement. Skillful directors make effective use of movement in plays or movies to draw attention, hold interest, and emphasize aspects of plot development. Good teachers move smoothly and freely and purposefully to various parts of the room. This is called kinesic variation. It causes students' attention to be focused on you.

SHIFTING INTERACTIONS. Students are more actively involved when you use question and answer. They pay attention if they may be asked a question and can feel good about adding to the development of the lesson. Also, students like to interact with each other. Peers sometimes explain things to each other better than you can, and at-task socializing with peers can be motivating.

When you lecture without involving students, there is no overt interaction; when you ask a question of the group (rather than specific students), interaction is teacher centered; when you ask specific students questions to involve them in the development of the lesson, interaction shifts to being teacher directed rather than teacher centered; and when you redirect a response from one student to another, interaction shifts to become student centered.

PAUSING (SILENCE). You have heard the expressions, "Silence is golden" or "Eloquent silence." Many teachers seem to feel they should not get paid if they don't constantly fill the air with words. People in the dramatic arts have long known the value of the dramatic pause. You may recall the story of the old couple in a small town where the train went through at 2:00 A.M. every morning. It never woke them. One night the train did not go through and the couple woke up, startled. The pause can be used effectively during the course of a lesson. Among the ways silence can be used are

- To emphasize an important point; to let it "sink in."
- To break a passage or information into smaller parts to promote comprehension.
- For dramatic effect, for instance, to create suspense.
- To provide time for students to think something through before they respond.
- To promote student participation through encouragement and opportunity to add comments or ask questions.
- To draw attention by contrasting speech with silence.
- To give a student time to think before finishing a response.
- To give students time to take notes before continuing with the lecture or dictation.
- To show disapproval of student misbehavior.
- To recognize the multicultural nature of the class. Some cultures make much more use of silence than white Americans, Canadians, or British.

SHIFTING SENSES. Unfortunately, teacher talk is the dominant mode in most classrooms—about 70 percent of the time (Shostak, 1982, p. 128). Students' ability to take in and process information is increased significantly when the senses of sight and sound are used alternately (p. 127). We learn through all the senses and remember best when we use variety and combine senses.

Examples of ways that you can shift senses during the course of a lesson are:

- Explaining a dance step; demonstrating it; then having students try it.
- Showing a transparency on a screen; turning the projector off and commenting verbally; then, showing the transparency once more.
- Telling students about the difference in texture between wool and silk; having students feel actual samples of wool and silk; then, verbally clarifying the differences further.
- Flashing a slide on the screen; turning the projector off and commenting on the slide; turning the slide back on; then, after turning the projector off, having students draw what they have seen.
- Giving a lecture about sound; doing a demonstration using a tuning fork and a pith ball on a string; then, explaining the principle involved while pointing to a diagram on the chalkboard.

Use the data collection instrument in Appendix 7.1 to help you analyze the cases that follow. Your instructor may pose specific questions for your response.

CASE 7.1 Varying Presentation

Counting by Hand

Ms. Chadwick is teaching a lesson to a grade 2 class on counting by fives. She asks everyone to move to the carpeted area at the back of the classroom. There she has set up a stand that displays a 1–100 chart. She makes sure everyone can see the chart.

She tells the students what the lesson will be about and explains why it is important to know how to count by fives (telling time and counting money).

Ms. Chadwick checks to see if everyone can see the chart and shows how, when counting by fives, the fifth number is the one that is used. Pointing to the chart, she begins to identify the numbers by finding and circling each fifth number. She asks the children, "What number comes next? How do you know?" When the first several numbers have been identified, she says, "I'm going to ask you a question. I want you to think hard and put up your hands when you know the answer. Close your eyes and listen. Listen to me read the numbers we have circled. Listen to see if you can hear a pattern." She reads "5, 10, 15, 20, 25, 30,

35, 40, . . ." Hands begin to go up. After pausing a few seconds, Ms. Chadwick asks Manuel to identify the pattern. Manuel responds that the pattern is numbers ending in 5, then 0, then 5, then 0. "How many of you agree with Manuel?" The children raise their hands in agreement. Several also nod. "Can anyone guess what the next number will be?" Tanya is selected from many raised hands to provide the answer. Then, the rest of the numbers to 100 are identified.

Ms. Chadwick asks the students to let their left hand be the "5 numbers" and their right hand be the "0 numbers." As they count by fives to 100, they raise their hands alternately, keeping time as they count in unison. Then the children are asked to move into a circle and each becomes a living part of a "counting by fives" procedure by putting up his or her left and right hand, in turn. One says "5, 10," the next says "15, 20," the next says "25, 30," etc., to 100.

Ms. Chadwick asks the children to form pairs. "I can see you can count by fives. In your pair, think

continued

of a way to count by fives so each partner is doing some counting. It's important to count correctly— help each other with that. See if you can think of a way to share the counting."

One pair alternates numbers, another does two numbers each, another pair does a pattern of three numbers, then one ("5, 10, 15," "20"; "25, 30, 35,"

"40") and so on. After a few minutes, Ms. C. asks children to show the class the ways they shared the counting.

As a final activity, the children work at their desks on a dot-to-dot activity that provides individual practice in counting by fives.

CASE 7.2 Varying Presentation

AttenSHUN!

Mr. Sargent, the grade 11 algebra teacher and a retired military man, was highly organized. Just by looking at his desk and the way he was dressed, you could tell. The school year was planned with precision. So much time, no more and no less, was devoted to each topic, and the pages to be covered in the text were identified in advance. His schedule of tests was strictly followed. Nothing could make him deviate from his schedule. His teaching was a study in the use of precise routines. Each day he would take up the last day's questions,

going up and down the rows and beginning with the student after the one with whom he left off the previous day. This took twenty minutes. The next twenty minutes were used to present three (and always three) examples of the new material on the chalkboard. Next, questions for seatwork and homework were assigned. He would always have everybody do the first three questions and odd-numbered questions thereafter. Then Mr. Sargent circulated to help individuals as the students began their assignments.

Lesson and Unit Planning

Lesson Planning

In the following paragraphs you will be introduced to the elements of a basic lesson plan. Written plans are aids to teaching. First lesson plans should be detailed and in writing. Planning is not always linear. When you plan, you do not have to start with objectives and work your way down to the evaluation. Frequently, you will begin with the need to teach a certain topic or specific skill. Then you may ask yourself how you will know if students are learning what you hoped. Planning can start anywhere, for example, with information students need to learn or skills they need to develop, and then turn attention to writing specific objectives.

Lesson plan data collection instruments are given in Appendices 7.2 and 7.3. Elements of a lesson plan are shown in Figure 7.2.

LESSON PLAN MODELS.   Lesson plan models can range from an unstructured approach (going with what appears to meet the needs or interests of the students and teacher at a given time) to a rigidly structured and followed approach. The Gagné instructional model, Hunter direct instruction approach, and a constructivist approach are some popular models.

The Gagné Instructional Model.   The classic Robert Gagné (1985) nine-step model for lesson planning can be used for most models of instruction (Figure 7.3). Although some argue that it is not sufficiently learner focused, it is widely used. The Gagné model begins with gaining learner attention and motivation. Then, learners are told the objec-

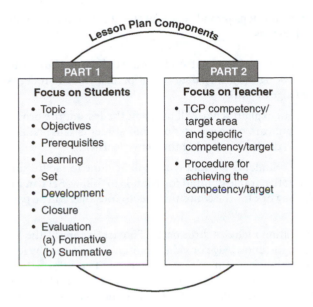

FIGURE 7.2   *Elements of a Lesson Plan*

tive of the lesson to provide a framework for what is to follow. Recall of prior knowledge is stimulated as a foundation for new learning. An appropriate amount of new material is then presented (Bloom's taxonomy can be used to sequence content). Following this, guidance for learning is provided, with the teacher simplifying and making the content easier to grasp. Next, learners practice using the new behavior, skills, or knowledge, followed by descriptive feedback using a test, quiz, or verbal comments. Performance is assessed to discover whether the lesson has been learned. Finally, provision for transfer of the learning to new contexts occurs.

The Hunter Direct Instruction Lesson Approach. Madeline Hunter's (1984) direct instruction lesson plan model may be considered a behavioral approach. Some authorities believe that behavioral approaches should be avoided. It

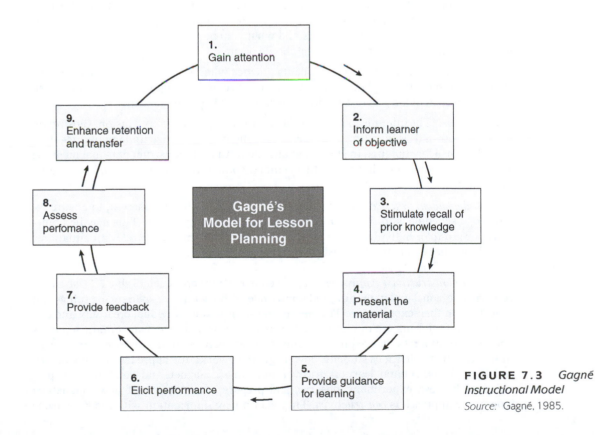

FIGURE 7.3   *Gagné Instructional Model*
Source: Gagné, 1985.

was Hunter's intent, however, that lesson steps provide a useful structure for many kinds of lessons, including nonbehavioral lessons.

1. *Objectives (intentions).* The teacher decides what students are to know or be able to do as a result of a lesson. Decision making includes a determination of whether students have the needed prerequisite knowledge or skills.

2. *Standards.* The teacher needs to explain what will occur in the lesson, the procedures to be followed and what students are expected to do, what students will achieve through the lesson, and how they will demonstrate what they have learned.

3. *Anticipatory set (set induction).* Students are told what will be done to secure student attention and put them in a receptive frame of mind for what is to follow. Set can include an "advance organizer" or framework for the content and activities that will be part of the lesson.

4. *Teaching/presentation.* Presentation includes three parts. The first is *input*—the information needed by students to gain the knowledge or skill is presented, whether by lecture, videotape, PowerPoint presentation, computer, or other means. The information could be drawn out of students through questioning or gleaned through research by the students. The second part is *modeling*—"how to do it" is modeled. Students are shown examples of what is expected and an end product of what their work will be like. Key aspects can be explained in a variety of ways. Students need to visualize what they will be expected to know (e.g., how to solve a problem or perform an operation). The third part of the presentation is a *check for understanding*—before students begin to work, a check is made to discover whether they understand what is to be done. They need to "get it" before they begin. If necessary, reteaching should occur.

5. *Guided practice/monitoring.* Students practice what was modeled. The teacher circulates to observe the level of mastery being achieved and, as appropriate, provides positive reinforcement for progress made, remediation, and encouragement.

6. *Closure.* The intent is to bring the lesson to an appropriate conclusion. Closure involves review and clarification and should consolidate or organize understanding—that is, make sense for students. In short, it should help students construct personal meaning and understanding. Furthermore, it lets students know they have achieved something important.

7. *Independent practice.* When the content or skill has been mastered, to ensure retention, a schedule is initiated for repeated reinforcement practice. This may be homework, or group or individual work in class. Provision for transfer to relevant situations, including other contexts, also needs to occur (pp. 175–176).

The Constructivist Approach.   In the constructivist approach (Table 7.1), students construct personal understanding and knowledge of the world by experiencing things and reflecting on their experiences. This approach can promote individual creativity and collaboration if students are to discuss and exchange ideas. A lesson can contain activities and involve resources that require students to engage actively in the discovery process. If, in science, the teacher tells students how magnetism works, the approach is *explicit* or *direct.* If, on the other hand, learners discover they can use magnets and iron filings, are provided with these, experiment, observe, and prepare a description of how magnetism works, the approach is *constructivist.* They act on new information with the knowledge

TABLE 7.1   *A Constructivist Lesson Plan*

Invitation	Setting the stage—students' prior knowledge, ideas, and beliefs in the lesson surfaced and engaged using, for e.g., a question, demonstration, event, or interesting challenge. Includes objectives and materials needed.
Exploration	Describes the activities students will do to explore the concepts, phenomena, or ideas of the lesson.
Explanation	Students share. They discuss and reflect on findings, data, and analyses and compare ideas of peers and authorities on the topic.
Taking Action	Students take part in an activity to help them take personal or social responsibility for the ideas researched. They ask themselves what they learned and how this knowledge might help them solve a problem.

they bring to the activity. At this stage you are only introduced to constructivism; more will be said about it in Chapter 11. A useful description of constructivist theory and teaching practice you may want to read is by Fosnot (2005).

The role of the teacher, in the constructivist approach, is to pose questions and guide students to assist them in finding their own answers. A constructivist approach, though it may be more demanding on teacher planning and class time, allows learners to gain a deeper understanding and result in better recall. Students, it is said, are more motivated because they are actively involved and activities are "real world" (authentic) and social and communication skills are fostered.

A lesson plan template is provided to plan a constructivist lesson in Table 7.1. A constructivist lesson plan guide (author unknown) is provided on the following web sites: http://cied.gsu/Hassard/mos/con9.html, and www.gsu.edu ~ mstjrh/webbasedtemplate. html.

SET, DEVELOPMENT, AND CLOSURE.   Instruction needs to be organized logically, normally beginning with an outline ("advance organizer") or preview, by pointing out connections (transitions) between parts, and by summarizing. Figure 7.4 reflects the theories of psychologist David Ausubel (1963, 1968, 1978), who helped develop the notion of constructivism, on concept mapping. Advance organizers (a concise structure or overview of what is to follow) are very useful. Post organizers (at the end of a lesson) also can be useful. Organizers are particularly important in lessons that use an expository (direct) format, when the teacher presents information, concepts, and principles in a logical, sequenced manner. Post organizers may be particularly significant when lesson presentation is inductive (indirect), by which students are led to discover the ideas, concepts, or principles and how they are linked. Expository and inquiry teaching is discussed later.

Well-designed lessons usually have three parts: (1) they begin with a memorable focusing event and preview what is to come; (2) they logically present and link new materials, and check for understanding; and (3) they close with an event that summarizes, "pulls things together," and points out what students have achieved. We shall call the beginning event *set* and the ending event *closure* (Figure 7.4).

Set.   You want students to have favorable view, or positive set, for learning. In the context of a lesson, set is the predisposition to react in a certain way to the presentation and activities to follow. How you begin lessons (or lesson segments) has an important effect on the set that students will have.

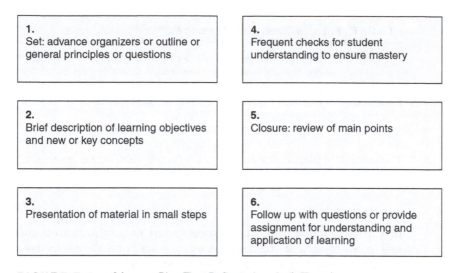

1.
Set: advance organizers or outline or general principles or questions

4.
Frequent checks for student understanding to ensure mastery

2.
Brief description of learning objectives and new or key concepts

5.
Closure: review of main points

3.
Presentation of material in small steps

6.
Follow up with questions or provide assignment for understanding and application of learning

FIGURE 7.4   *A Lesson Plan That Reflects Ausubel's Theories*
Source: Good & Brophy, 1995.

Set has four purposes: (1) focusing student attention on the lesson; (2) creating a framework for the forthcoming information, ideas, concepts, or generalizations; (3) furthering understanding and application of abstract ideas by using examples or analogies; and (4) promoting student interest and involvement in what is to follow. The first purpose is likely a part of the other three.

There are three basic kinds of set (Figure 7.5) that teachers can use: orientation, transition, and evaluation (Shostak, 1977, p. 128).

1. *Orientation set.* Orientation set is used to introduce the lesson and leads to motivation. It focuses attention on new learning, using a motivating activity, event, puzzle, anecdote or joke, object, or something that students have interest in, or experience with. It can provide a structure to help students visualize the content or activities, or it can help clarify the objectives of the lesson. Use can be made of orientation to ready students for the lesson.

2. *Transition set.* Transition set links what already is known or covered to that which is about to be learned. Reliance is on analogies, examples, or activities that students have interest in or with which they have had experience. It can also alert students about the content of future lessons.

3. *Evaluation set.* Evaluation set involves evaluation of students' understanding of previous material, or a review of previous material before going to new material. It relies on questions, examples, quizzes, and activities that are heavily student centered or generated, so the degree of understanding of previous content can be determined. Evaluation set also leads to a focus on the lesson ahead (pp. 128–130).

Development.   After the set, development of the lesson occurs. You provide experiences that guide and support students' efforts. For students to achieve planned or emerging instructional objectives, choose content that is meaningful, logically organized, and

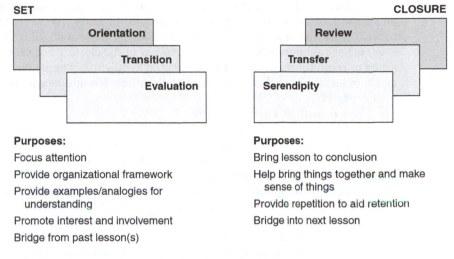

FIGURE 7.5   *Set and Closure and Their Purposes*
Source: Shostak, 1977.

sequenced. Content should be challenging, not frustrating. During the lesson, students should be as actively involved as possible and should feel good about themselves and their accomplishments. Establish a warm, positive, but businesslike climate. So students can experience success, choose appropriate:

- Instructional skills
- Management procedures
- Resources and aids
- Teaching strategies and methods
- Student activities
- Checking-up procedures

Instructional skills, among others, include explaining and demonstrating, varying the stimulus (auditory, verbal, and tactile), and questioning technique. The teaching strategies chosen can be direct, indirect, interactive, experiential, or individual study. Teaching methods choices range from lecture to group problem solving, from seeking answers in a textbook to simulations requiring students to discover the answers. Choices include a variety of interaction patterns from independent study to small groups to the whole class. Teaching strategies are dealt with in detail in Part III of the text. Examples of classroom management procedures are the establishment of routines and procedures, a positive climate, and ensuring that acts are followed by consequences. Student activities range from viewing a film to conducting an experiment, completing a project, playing a game, copying notes from the chalkboard, or doing seatwork. A wide range of resources and aids is available. Resources include texts, reference books, newspapers, laboratory equipment and supplies; aids are things such as flip chart paper and smart boards. Checking-up or assessment and evaluation procedures include asking questions, student reports, circulating around the room to view student work, worksheets, homework, and tests.

Closure.   Closure includes the statements or actions you use to "bring a lesson to an appropriate conclusion. . . . To help students bring things together in their own minds, to make sense out of what has been going on during the lesson" (Shostak, 1986, p. 128). Students should normally be actively involved in the closure. For example, they can be asked to recall the main ideas. Closure should highlight key ideas, reinforce, synthesize, and summarize. Good closures normally take at least ten minutes, particularly at the elementary level.

There are three kinds of closure.

1. *Review closure* concisely "ties up" a lesson or lesson segment. It uses techniques such as drawing students' attentions to a lesson's or segment's closing point; drawing attention to the major points, and their sequence; summarizing discussion that took place; or relating the lesson to the original concept or generalization can occur.
2. *Transfer closure* is used to reinforce or consolidate learning. Learning should be available for use in new contexts. Transfer closure draws students' attention to a closing point and facilitates transfer by reviewing the new learning, immediately practicing it, and asking students to extend the new learning to other contexts or to develop new knowledge from what has been learned.
3. *Serendipity closure* refers to a "natural" but unplanned opportunity for closure. You can take advantage of an opportunity to close that arises spontaneously near the end of a lesson. This might arise because of a student response, a key student question, an unusual event, or because of a sudden insight or idea.

The three major phases of the lessons that effective teachers follow—set, development, and closure—should flow naturally one to the other. This does not come about by accident. It requires planning. Smooth transition from one phase to the other is affected by the teaching methods and student activities chosen. Each time a group of students is being taught, whether for ten minutes or an hour, the elements of set, development, and closure should be present. A data collection sheet for microteaching lab and classroom lessons is shown in Appendix 7.4. You can use the data collection sheet to help you analyze the cases that follow. Your instructor may pose specific questions for your response.

CASE 7.3

Set and Closure

Mr. Jacobs was planning a learning experience on "pairs" for his first-grade class as preparation for counting by twos. He waited until all the children had returned to the classroom from physical education, then he entered the classroom, conspicuously wearing a shoe on one foot but just a sock on the other. He walked around the classroom busily as children got settled to give the children opportunity to notice his feet.

Soon there was snickering and whispered comments from many youngsters. Several asked questions: "Where's your other shoe, Mr. Jacobs?" "Did you forget something, Mr. Jacobs?" Mr. Jacobs pretended not to know what they meant. He asked, "What do you mean? What's the matter?"

Erin explained patiently, "Mr. Jacobs, you have a shoe on one foot and only a sock on the other. Teachers always wear two shoes, don't they?" "Yeah," added Sarah. "Two feet means you have to wear two shoes."

"Do shoes always come in twos?" asked Mr. Jacobs. Most children agreed. "What do we usually call a set of two shoes?" The children were thoughtful and several had ideas. "Boots." "Sandals." "Sneakers."

"Those are different kinds of footwear," said Mr. Jacobs. "But I'm still wondering what a set of two shoes is called. Two boots or two sandals or two sneakers would be a set or a . . . ?" "*Pair!*" shouted the youngsters. "A *pair* of sandals. A *pair* of sneakers."

"That's the word I was thinking of," said Mr. Jacobs. "So you think I should have a *pair* of shoes on, instead of just one?"

The activity proceeded with the children thinking of as many kinds of shoes as they could, telling where they might wear each pair. As a way of leading into counting by twos, Mr. Jacobs had the children put their gym shoes in a row, count them, and try to think of a counting pattern that would help them count

faster. There were several ideas for how this might be done, but Mr. Jacobs noticed it was just a few minutes before the children had to prepare for the noon break. "We'll work on this more tomorrow," he said. "But, before we stop today, someone explain what we were learning. Can you think of how to say it in a short way?" The children had been practicing summarizing (saying things in a short way), and several tried to summarize the discussion and activity. Mr. Jacobs encouraged responses, making sure, through questioning, that the idea of "pair" as two matching items and the fact that there are several ways to count pairs of things were mentioned. "Good summaries, and good thinking," he said. "Tomorrow we'll do more on finding a counting pattern to speed up our counting." Then Mr. Jacobs put on his second shoe.

CASE 7.4

Set and Closure

Ms. Holmberg began her lesson on stereotyping, discrimination, and racism in her grade 11 social studies class by writing the headings "Black," "Indian" (North American), "Japanese," "Spanish," and "White" on the chalkboard. Then the class was divided into five groups of six. She began, "You remember the rules for brainstorming. Just state whatever comes to mind. I am going to assign one of the headings on the chalkboard to each group. Your group will, for ten minutes, brainstorm all the characteristics that come to mind. These will be recorded under the appropriate chalkboard heading by the recorder in your group." Jason raised his hand and asked, "Should you avoid saying not nice things, like, uh, lazy or smelly?" "I'm glad you asked," Ms Holmberg replied, "it shows you are a very sensitive person. At this stage you should not judge whether the characteristic is true or

false or good or bad. The next step, however, is to select the statements that are merely descriptive and those that are generalizations that do not apply to all, or even most, people in your category."

After students completed the initial stage of the exercise, Ms. Holmberg gave a presentation about beliefs, attitudes, stereotyping, discrimination, and racism. She reminded the class about what they had learned about critical thinking, particularly their learning about checking assumptions. She then asked the class to rejoin their groups to discuss the lists on the chalkboard, to see which of the characteristics they would now categorize differently. Then each group reported the characteristics they had placed under each category. Finally, with the help of the class, Ms. Holmberg summarized their learning about discrimination.

Unit Planning

Unit planning, or long-range planning, at its simplest, is the decision to teach a series of related lessons on a particular theme. For example, a teacher might decide to teach about the fur trade. Such a theme could take from several days to several weeks to teach. At the most basic level the teacher, when planning such a unit, would consider the major or foundational objectives of the unit, the best instructional approaches for the various lessons, how many lessons, what resources might be needed, and, finally, the best means of assessing the students' learning during and after the unit. There are, of course, other considerations, such as learner characteristics and subject matter, but the basic elements of a unit are not difficult.

When thinking of the major objectives, the learner-centered teacher asks, "What do I want students to know and be able to do?" and "What attitudes, values, and appreciations are desirable?" Very often the objectives are laid out in the state curriculum guide. It is advantageous to have a range of instructional strategies. Some lessons in your unit might require direct instruction through lecture or video. Other lessons will need an interactive, constructivist approach, with the teacher building knowledge with the students. Other choices might involve group work such as cooperative learning or experiential learning, with simulations and role playing. There may be times when the students work individually. A variety of approaches is normally best. Consideration must be given to the nature of the learners, their academic backgrounds, and any special needs. After instruction is carried out, the teacher determines if the students have met the objectives and if the planning and instruction were effective. Unit planning essentially involves a three-step process of planning, implementing, and evaluation.

Good planning improves classroom management. It produces interesting attainable goals and higher student achievement. It is a good idea to inform students of the plans. Instruction is most efficient when the objectives, content, and the way it is presented and evaluated are congruent, and when a course is divided into units and then structured and sequenced into individual lessons for clarity and ease of learning and to avoid confusion. Designing units and lessons to achieve educational objectives is both an art and an applied science as decision making occurs. A professional doesn't "wing it."

WHY PLAN UNITS?   A bridge is not built without a blueprint; a diamond is not cut without a careful plan. A professional teacher needs to plan. It is simply not sufficient merely to follow the chapters and pages of a text or workbook. What does the curriculum guide suggest? What is the grade level? What are the ages, capabilities, needs, and interests of the students? How much can be done in a semester, a month, a week, a lesson? What teaching methods and student activities are best? What materials and resources should be used? There are no short cuts. Research shows the relationship between student achievement and teachers who plan and are organized. Lessons do not spring out of thin air. Instead, they should arise from the broad objectives of units that are planned to achieve course objectives.

WHAT IS A UNIT?   A course should flow from one topic to another to promote integrated student understanding and performance capability. *Units* are centered on a topic, theme, or major concept and organize the course into manageable, cohesive divisions that focus learning; units center learning and instruction on course objectives. Units may be either *interdisciplinary* (integrating more than one subject area) or *subject focused* (staying within a specific subject area).

Courses are typically divided into several units (themes), consisting of a series of from three to twenty or more lessons that tie together into a whole. Just as lessons are to achieve unit objectives, units are to meet course objectives. A unit is based on a broad problem or area of investigation and is an arrangement of content (product and process), materials, and activities around a central topic. A good unit plan replaces blind acceptance of the text as the basis for curricular organization (and day-to-day planning based on expediency) with a series of meaningful, internally unified learning experiences. Some people think a unit plan is an outline of the content to be covered, but much more is involved.

Good unit planning considers the myriad of variables you must face to foster student "success experiences."

By now you may have developed some proficiency in planning and delivering lessons. Units and lessons are similar in several ways. In a sense, a unit plan is like a large lesson plan. Both have objectives (unit objectives are broad); identifiable content; introductory, developmental, and culminating activities and teaching methods; and ways of assessing student progress. Good lesson and unit plans are based on knowledge of course objectives, learners, subject matter and organization of these for instruction, suitable teaching methods and student activities, and tacit knowledge picked up from daily classroom experiences. Units are different from lessons in that lessons must link together to achieve unit outcomes. The first lesson hooks to the next and subsequent lessons, the second lesson hooks to the following lesson and subsequent lessons, and so forth.

Good unit planning follows the basic steps of effective decision making for teaching:

1. *Needs assessment:* Student readiness and needs
2. *Objectives:* Knowledge, skills, and values
3. *Presentation:* Content; instructional strategies and methods; materials and resources; communicating expectations and classroom management
4. *Assessment* (formative and summative) and *evaluation* of the unit.

Sensible but creative choices can be made through careful course, unit, and lesson planning. Berliner (1984) describes the preinstructional, during instruction, postinstructional, and climate decisions that should be made (Figure 7.6).

FIGURE 7.6   *Decisions in Instructional Planning*

Preinstructional Factors

Content decisions: What goals and objectives? What will be taught and content emphasis?

Time allocation decisions: How much time will be given to subjects and topics?

Pacing decisions: How rapidly should the content be covered?

Instructional decisions: What instructional strategies and methods will be used?

Activity structure decisions: What student activities will be used?

Climate Factors

Communication of expectations: How will expectations of students be communicated?

Developing the environment: What will be done to have a safe, orderly, academically focused environment?

Managing deviancy: How will discipline procedures be sensibly managed?

Developing cooperative environments: How will cooperative and interpersonal relationships be fostered?

During-Instruction Factors

Engaged time: How much on-task time will be used?

Time management: How much time will be given to each subject, topic, and transitions?

Monitoring success rate: How will success rate be monitored and ensured?

Academic learning time: How much time will learners be in activities related directly to learning outcome measures?

Monitoring: How will students be monitored, including during independent study? What individual teacher–student interactions will occur?

Structuring: What kind of organizers and summaries will be provided?

Questioning: What type and levels of questions will be posed?

Postinstructional Factors

Tests: How can the desired learning be appropriately tested?

Grades: What kind of grading and reporting system will be used? How can grading used be objective and fair?

Feedback: How can substantial corrective feedback and praise contingent on appropriate behavior be provided and student ideas used?

Source: Berliner, 1984, pp. 51–77.

Arends (2002) presents three phases of teaching and thus three phases of teacher planning and decision making: preinstructional, instructional (or interactive), and postinstructional. Phases are useful in simplifying planning. Other chapters examine elements of unit planning in detail. For example, Chapter 5 deals with assessment and evaluation (postinstruction), whereas Parts II and III of this text deal with teaching methods and instructional approaches.

Renner (1983, pp. 97–99) has a useful 10-Step Planning Model you could use. Start anywhere and shift back and forth as ideas come to mind. The important thing is that all the steps be completed. Teachers, when they plan, usually consider instructional approaches and content *before* they write objectives. An experienced teacher might first decide what to do (content), how to do it (strategies), consider the broad goals (objectives), and, finally, how to evaluate (assessment). Following is another ten-step planning sequence.

A Ten-Step Unit Planning Sequence

1. Select the *unit topic* and decide which *course objectives* (taking into account school, district, and department of education guidelines) the unit is to address.
2. Do a *concept hierarchy and task analysis* of the concepts and skills to be learned (this could be called a concept map or web).
3. Prepare a *content outline* and sequence the topics (facts, concepts, principles, skills, and processes) to be learned.
4. Beginning with brainstorming, select suitable *teaching methods* and *student activities* and organize these under the headings of introductory, developmental, and culminating.
5. Identify appropriate *resources and materials.*
6. Ensuring they are congruent with course objectives, write appropriate *unit objectives.*
7. Prepare the summative *evaluation,* making sure this is congruent with unit objectives and student activities.
8. Decide which personal *professional targets* you will work on and the data collection instruments you will likely use.
9. Determine *prerequisite student learning* and how you will know whether students have the necessary background to proceed.
10. Prepare *lesson plans* for the first one or two lessons of the unit. (pp. 97–101)

Note: You will likely be returning to previous steps to make additions or changes (going back and forth) as you plan.

ELEMENTS COMMON TO MOST TEACHING UNIT STRUCTURES.   Unit plans involve advance thought about what will be taught and how. Plans should not be "cast in concrete." Alternate selections, emphasis, choice of teaching methods and student activities, and expansion, addition or deletion should be possible. However, most good unit plans have common elements. The main ideas of unit planning we have been discussing are illustrated in Figure 7.7.

CONSIDERATIONS IN PLANNING.   The general goal or purpose for the unit should be written. This is explained in a *rationale statement* that, in one or two paragraphs, overviews the content to be covered, outlines the major outcomes to be met, and explains why it is important that students achieve the outcomes. The rationale should communicate the nature

FIGURE 7.7 *Elements That Most Unit Plans Have in Common*

I. A. Unit title
   B. Subject and grade level
   C. Rationale (justification and the broad purpose) for unit
   D. Foundational objectives: knowledge; skills; and attitudes and values
   E. Curriculum link
II. A. Timeline/content outline
   B. Concept map
III. A. Prerequisite learning
IV. A. Lesson plans (introductory, developmental, and culminating)
   B. Instructional approaches and activities
   C. Resources (print, nonprint, and human)
   D. Adaptive dimension
V. A. Management plan
   B. Classroom climate
VI. A. Assessment (diagnostic, formative, and summative [congruent with objectives])
   B. Evaluation of unit
VII. A. Professional growth targets

and substance of the unit and help you select and organize content and write and sequence objectives.

The *content* and its sequence must be decided and reflected in a content outline. Discover curriculum guide requirements and how much time you can allocate. A good content outline is based on knowledge of the concepts, skills, and processes involved. Therefore, before the outline is written, a hierarchy of concepts should be created, and, an analysis of the skills and processes in the unit should be conducted. This information is vital for sequencing content.

Consider the essential cross-curricular content of all learning and integrate this into the planning. These should include oral and written communication skills, creative and critical thinking, technological literacy values, and independent learning skills.

Decide the *prerequisite learning* students need. A *pretest* (formal or informal) may need to be selected or constructed. Consider the interests and backgrounds of students, and their level of development, expectations, cultural background, and learning styles.

Broad *objectives/goals* should be written. Later, objectives for each lesson must be prepared (congruent with unit objectives/goals). Unit objectives/goals express the reasons for the unit and guide the specific objectives chosen for lessons. Whereas course objectives are stated in broad terms, unit objectives are a step closer to specificity, and lesson objectives should be very specific. Each objective should contribute to the achievement of the general objectives of the course and the goals of schooling. Every unit objective should suggest expectations of behavioral change in the learner as a result of the experiences students would have. Unit objectives should be (1) stated in terms of some recognized need; (2) learner, not teacher oriented (they are not a list of activities); (3) specific and measurable; (4) achievable by most learners; and (5) descriptive of desired functional learner behavior, not the subject matter to be covered (i.e., what the learner is to be able to do or know or feel). Of course, unit objectives may need to be modified as the unit is delivered.

TEACHING STRATEGIES, METHODS, AND STUDENT ACTIVITIES. When selecting teaching methods and student activities, consider the topics, ideas, concepts, skills or processes, and affective content to be covered; lesson presentation skills, instructional techniques, methods, strategies, or models; classroom routines and management; and interpersonal relating and group skills (including establishing the teaching/learning environment) to be used. Learner readiness, background, and interests must be recognized. Planning, too, must be in keeping with sound learning psychology principles and the developmental stage of the learners.

While "teaching methods" refers to the instructional approaches chosen, "activities" are what students will be doing. Think of more activities than you can use, so good choices can be made as the unit unfolds. Plan to use a range of teaching methods; variety helps maintain interest and meet diverse student needs and learning styles. Once a concept map and skill analysis have been done, the content, teaching methods, and student activities should be planned for subsequent sections.

1. *Introductory.* This part should set the stage, provide motivation, or provide orientation to the problem or area of investigation. The first thing that might be done is a pretest (written or oral) to discover the knowledge and abilities of each student about the topic to be studied. This section can be part of one, two, or more lessons.

2. *Developmental.* This is the "heart" of the unit. It is where the topic is studied. It is one to fifteen or more lessons. Normally, a variety of teaching strategies and methods and student activities should be used. Data are analyzed, generalizations drawn, and conclusions made. Student participation should be as active as possible and lead to success. Activities should be varied to suit individual abilities, interests, and learning styles; activities should be challenging, and methods and activities should consider the facilities and time available.

3. *Culminating.* Learning should be unified. Students need to tie understandings together, recognize interrelationships, and examine the problem or topic in retrospect. They should recognize what was gained, unsolved problems, and needed further study of related problems or topics. The culminating section may dovetail with the introductory section of another unit or units. Summative testing is usually included. In short: Conclude! Review! Summarize! This section may be the last part of a lesson or be two or more lessons.

4. *Materials and resources.* Materials and resources should reinforce the teaching methods and student activities used. They are aids to, not substitutes for, teaching. Models, strategies, methods, activities, rules and procedures, and materials and resources are vehicles through which learning occurs. Materials and resources may include the assigned text, workbooks, manuals, books, the Internet, reference materials (both for use by students and to be used by you), newspapers, games and simulations, models, charts, maps, films, recordings, transparencies, bulletin boards, TV, community resources, and so forth.

5. *Assessment.* Assessment should measure the degree of student achievement. It also should measure the effectiveness of instruction and the unit. Checklists, formative and summative tests, and anecdotal records can be used to evaluate achievement. Examples of assessment techniques are standardized or teacher-made tests, student assignments, case studies, conferences with other teachers and parents, diaries or logs (kept by students), rating scales, anecdotal records, and self-analysis by students.

6. *Professional growth.* Student teachers should plan for professional growth. Planning and delivering units involves many teacher competencies: the actual planning, use of a variety of instructional strategies and methods, assessment ability, and self-evaluation. Student teachers should use data sheets for the collection of descriptive data on their unit planning capabilities.

7. *Concept map or web.* Prepare a concept map or web to help you sequence the content and learning activities of a unit. This instruction device can foster student success, since it is easier for you to arrange the content appropriately, decide the important concepts, and break the content into logical divisions.

Concepts can be arranged into a hierarchical (or other) structure that illustrates the relationships of concepts to each other. A concept map is a means for representing the conceptual structure of a unit or units of knowledge. When you prepare a concept map, you have something that can be used with students as an advance organizer, an in-progress organizer, or a post organizer. Imagine that you intend to teach a unit on systems of the human body. The concept map of "Systems of the Human Body" (in Figure 7.8) shows a possible approach.

A concept map is a sophisticated advance organizer. Students can see the whole picture as well as the details to be covered. It may be a good idea to post the concept map on a bulletin board so students and teacher can refer to it as knowledge is constructed.

A unit plan uses all aspects of the educational palette to create an overall picture. Different modes of representation have been considered. Some elements of the plan will involve concrete experiences, others may be visual or symbolic. Objectives, sequence, and degree of control have been examined. The learning styles of the students have been taken into account as well as the kinds of outcomes required. Careful attention has been given to incorporating the major teaching strategies and methods. The unit reflects a sophisticated teaching approach after careful thought to the learning of the students. It is more than the content outline or textbook chapter headings. Appendix 7.5 is a checklist to help you plan units, and Appendix 7.6 is a data sheet that can be used for feedback on your unit. A unit planning model is shown in Figure 7.9.

INTEGRATED THEMATIC UNITS.   Thematic instruction occurs when instruction is organized around macro "themes." It is based on the belief that people acquire knowledge

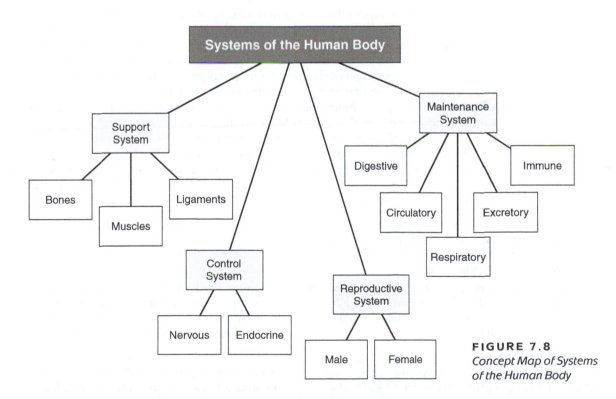

FIGURE 7.8
Concept Map of Systems of the Human Body

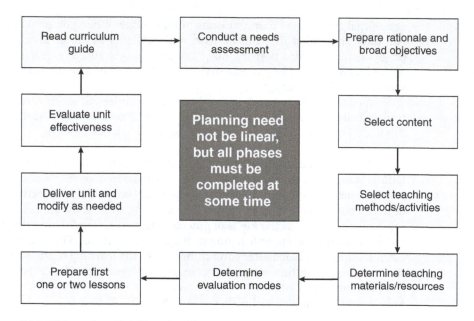

FIGURE 7.9   *Unit Planning Model*

best when learning occurs in the context of a coherent "whole" and when learners can connect it to the real world. Thematic instruction integrates basic disciplines such as reading, math, and science by exploring a broad subject, such as communities, pollution, rain forests, or use of energy. These topics can be placed in the context of an authentic subject that is practical but broad enough to allow creative exploration. Reasons put forward for using thematic units are that their use eliminates the isolated, reductionist nature of teaching around disciplines rather than experience, compacts the curriculum, recognizes the reality and value of interdisciplinary learning, increases student interest and time engaged, and is a powerful way to reintegrate the curriculum.

Thematic instruction most often occurs within a grade level of students. Teachers work together as a team to design curriculum, instruction, and assessment around a theme. It tends to be used more in elementary grades than in high school, where vertical planning tends to dominate.

TCP—CURRICULUM KNOWLEDGE

Adapts curriculum to student needs

Selects material appropriate to learner needs and interests; sets curriculum goals taking into account learner differences and interests; can restructure content for various ability and interest levels.

Uses prescribed curriculum without adjusting for learner needs and interests; cannot restructure content for various ability and interest levels; rigid application of curriculum guidelines.

Knows subject matter

Has an excellent grasp of the subject area content (concepts, information, skills, theories); can articulate the

Treats subject content as a body of disjointed information; unable to construct relationships

---

TCP—CURRICULUM KNOWLEDGE *(continued)*

---

structure of different subject areas; can see interrelationships among different subject areas; rich in breadth and depth; presents information, skills, and methods of the subject accurately and in appropriate sequence; uses teacher and student resources appropriately.

within individual subject areas; unable to build relationships among different subject areas. Inaccurately, poorly used, poorly sequenced information; superficial skills and methods; inadequate use of sources.

Exhibits knowledge of local and state curriculum

Understands local and state core curriculum requirements; uses local and state curriculum guides effectively.

Not aware of the value of local and state curriculum guides in planning.

A SUGGESTED PLANNING APPROACH.   The discussion above has presented the essential elements of unit planning. You need an approach that works for you. Parsons (1992) has practical suggestions you can easily adapt. He stresses that although "it may seem easy to pick up another teacher's unit, . . . you must make your own units of study. . . . If you don't you will never really be comfortable" (p. 10). He gives helpful, practical tips for the novice and experienced teacher (pp. 10–13).

1. Start fresh. You do the initial planning and structuring. Find the curriculum guide for your area, for both legal and practical reasons. Legally, you are required to teach the state or provincial curriculum. Practically, curriculum guides are full of useful ideas. See the curriculum guides as resources, not laid-out plans.

2. Break research into two areas, content and methods.

3. Photocopy the part of the curriculum guide you will be teaching. Highlight and list the things you believe students should know. Decide how important the unit is and what its length will be.

4. Look at the learning activities in the curriculum guide. (The guide is usually more than a list of topics.) List the activities in no particular order. This will be your resource of ideas.

5. You are now ready to look at other resources. (Remember, you are teaching children, and you do not need to know everything before you begin to teach.)

6. To find appropriate content, you need appropriate resources—many small sections from several books may be better than a large section from one book. More detailed content can be suggested later. Reading in depth should come later, not at the planning stage.

7. As you read the resources, note the major things, ideas, and generalizations the resources repeat. What content do all the resources mention?

8. Write out the key content elements. These, along with the specific content from the curriculum guide, become the core content you want students to know.

9. Check these and other state or provincial resources and teaching units for ideas for activities. List those that might be helpful. Check especially for stimulating activities for students and crucial content you may have missed. Modify the activities and ideas for your use.

10. Take the material and ideas you have gathered, and cut and paste your unit together.

11. Take a big, current, empty calendar and jot down what will happen each day. Put this up in the class so students can see what is happening. Organize according to the scope of the unit, variety of activities, chronology of topics, holidays, and whatever else is important.

12. Construct a finished product that is tight, well organized, and justifiable.

13. Finally: think skills (work toward students' learning); think success (work toward mastery of content); be sensitive to students' reactions (plans are absolute if nothing better happens in class); ask yourself, "What will students be doing when I am doing what I am doing?" (How will the class respond to the approaches and activities?); don't worry if things don't go as planned—it's better to fill lessons with good learning and not just get through the material.

Gregory and Chapman (2002) ask questions that aptly summarize the key ideas of planning.

- What do I want students to know or be able to do as a result of this learning experience?
- How will we judge success?
- What do they already know and are able to do?
- How can attention be captured and sustained?
- What will be the emotional "hook" for the learners?
- How will new information and skills be required?
- How will students practice and rehearse to make new meaning and understanding?
- How will they receive ongoing feedback during and after the learning? (p. 84)

LINKING PRACTICE TO THEORY

Note the many elements of planning. Were you aware of the planning involved in your school and university classes? As you plan, what influences you the most—the subject or the student? Do you teach to promote the status quo, or to bring change? How do your values influence your approach to planning? How much freedom do you have as you plan? Should you plan alone or with others? How did your plans change as you taught your students?

Summary

Successful lessons do not just happen. Think about what learners should know or be able to do as a result of a lesson, and how you will begin, develop, close, and evaluate the lesson. Have a plan for personal professional development—a target—for every lesson. There are three different kinds of set (orientation, transition, and evaluation) and two kinds of closure (review and transfer) you can plan, or a serendipitous event may become an excellent closure. Students should be as actively involved as possible. You can maintain interest by varying your presentation through focusing, kinesic variation, shifting interaction, using silence, and shifting senses. Conscious attention to transfer should occur.

Activities

OBJECTIVES USING THE COGNITIVE DOMAIN
For each objective (items 1–11): (a) Indicate the B, C, and D; and (b) name the level of the cognitive domain.

1. Given an outline map of Canada (showing province borders), each student will be able to write the name of each of the ten provinces and two territories in the appropriate area of the map.

2. Upon completion of a study of the book, *North and South,* each student will be able to list at least three factors that led to the outbreak of the U.S. Civil War.

3. Given ten shots in basketball, each student will be able to sink at least five.

4. When given six major events that contributed to the outbreak of World War II on September 1, 1939 (in random order), each student will be able to list the events in chronological order and write an analysis on how each event contributed to the conflict.

5. In hockey, using twenty-five pucks lined up on the nearest blue line, and using the slap shot, the student will be able to shoot at least twenty of them into the open net.

6. Using the guitar chords C, G7, and D, the student will compose a simple song (including lyrics).

7. Given the hypothesis that your state wants to make a sales tax increase of 15%, each student will write a document outlining at least four pros and four cons of this proposal. The student will defend each pro and con with at least one argument.

8. Given five poems, each student will be able to identify and list at least three poetic devices common to the five poems. He or she will write the examples found in each poem.

9. After studying six painting elements, each student will paint a picture and will state how she or he has used each element in the picture.

10. After watching a videotape of the baseball World Series game in 1989 during which an earthquake struck San Francisco, the student will write a reflection on how she or he would have felt had she or he been present.

11. The class will meet at 9:00 P.M. on October 15 outside the Brown Farm gate. After gazing at the sky, each student will point out the constellations Orion and Ursa Major, and the following stars: Betelgeuse and Rigel. Then, the class will meet at Ernie's Pizza Palace and each student will draw a picture of the two constellations and name the stars mentioned above (while eating pizza).

12. Join four classmates whose grade and subject-level interests are similar to yours. In turn, each person describes a lesson he or she has taught or observed. The group agrees on well-stated objectives for each lesson.

13. In the same groups as in Activity 12, agree on a topic of interest in a school subject of the group's choosing and design an objective for each level of the cognitive domain, each level of the affective domain, and each level of the psychomotor domain.

14. Turn to a classmate and (a) agree on the difference between an activity and objective, (b) what makes an objective "well written," and (c) how you typically would go about planning a lesson.

15. Participate in a class discussion on the value of careful planning, things that might cause plans to change, and what can be done to prepare for possible changes and the unexpected.

SET AND CLOSURE

1. Your instructor may model a lesson that has a clear set, development, and closure. Determine the parts of the lesson and critique it in terms of the principles discussed in this chapter.

2. Join a subject specialization group. Brainstorm examples of set inductions under the headings Orientation, Transition, and Evaluation.

3. In the same group, brainstorm closures under the headings Review, Transfer, and Serendipity.

4. Join a subject specialization group. Pick a topic and design a lesson plan that has an appropriate and motivating set, an interesting development, and an appropriate closure. The plan must flow smoothly and appropriately from one phase to the next. Groups tell the class about their plan, and the class has to identify the kind of set and kind of closure chosen.

5. Every member of the class is to prepare a lesson plan having an appropriate set, development, and closure. Share plans in subject specialization groups. Group members are to identify the kinds of set and closure and comment on the flow from one phase of the lesson to the next.

6. Teach a microteaching lesson and field classroom lesson that has the professional target of appropriate set, development, and closure.

7. Try the activity that follows.

RECOGNIZING LEVELS IN BLOOM'S COGNITIVE TAXONOMY

Write the level of Bloom's taxonomy for each statement in the exercise below.

K = knowledge; C = comprehension; AP = application; AN = analysis; S = synthesis; E = evaluation

1. _____ From memory, recite a stanza from a poem.
2. _____ Put a statement into your own words.
3. _____ Name the states on the West Coast.
4. _____ Discover how a lawn sprinkler works.
5. _____ Classify flowers.

6. _____ Find the area of a triangle.
7. _____ Debate the pros and cons of. . . .
8. _____ Demonstrate how to fold a letter.
9. _____ Draw a map of a room.
10. _____ Categorize all the clothes you own.
11. _____ Name Donald Duck's nephews.
12. _____ Insert the correct jigsaw puzzle piece.
13. _____ Predict the outcome of a murder mystery.
14. _____ Critique a play.
15. _____ Choose the best option.
16. _____ Solve an algebra problem.
17. _____ Give an example of a hero.
18. _____ List all the Presidents of the United States.
19. _____ Design a house.
20. _____ Plan a family reunion.
21. _____ Adjudicate in a music festival.
22. _____ Compare cars of the years 1950 and 2002.
23. _____ Which Greek god was the god of war?
24. _____ Find a way to make poison ivy edible.

KEY: 1 – K; 2 – C; 3 – K; 4 – AN; 5 – AN; 6 – AP; 7 – E;
8 – K; 9 – AN; 10 – AN; 11 – K; 12 – AN; 13 – AN; 14 – E;
15 – E; 16 – AP; 17 – C; 18 – K; 19 – S; 20 – S; 21 – E;
22 – AN; 23 – K; 24 – S

In review, the six levels of Bloom's cognitive taxonomy are

Knowledge: To recall specific information, terminology, and generalizations and to know methods of organizing and criticizing facts

Comprehension: To understand the material or data; to translate, explain, or summarize and extend the idea

Application: To use general ideas, procedures, or principles in concrete situations

Analysis: To break down information into its component parts, identify the parts, and understand their relationships and organization

Synthesis: To put together parts of experiences with new material into a well-integrated whole to provide creative behavior for the learner

Evaluation: Based on criteria (or standards), to make judgments about the value of ideas, methods, solutions, etc.

These and other uses of the taxonomy can be found in Bloom et al.'s classic (1956) work. Ideas on Bloom appear in many modern educational texts and articles.

LESSON PLAN COMPONENTS

Read the case that follows—twice. The first time, get an idea of how the teacher intends to teach a lesson. The second time, see if you can pick out the parts of a lesson plan. Each paragraph focuses on a different decision that must be made—decision descriptions follow the case.

1. Mr. Messer intends to teach a lesson on planets as part of a unit called "Our Solar System." He has been asked by another middle-school science teacher, Ms. Schmidt, what he intends to do. He says he wants students to know the parts of the solar system. More specifically, after the coming lesson, he wants students to be able to look at an unlabeled chart of the solar system and, based on their knowledge of the characteristics of planets, pick out the planets.

2. The teaching aids he intends to use are a large chart of the solar system, a three-dimensional model of the planets, sun, and moons, a twelve-minute film, and an unlabeled one-page diagram of the solar system. He realizes the lesson will spill over into the next day's science period. He knows that some lessons will take only fifteen minutes, whereas others may take two or three periods.

3. Students have been taught procedures for learning new concepts and are familiar with concept hierarchies and concept mapping.

4. Mr. Messer thinks students already know something about planets but he is unsure how much. He plans to begin the lesson by asking how many have seen the *Star Trek* movies or the television series by that name. Using questions, he wants to discover what students know about planets. Then, he will show a big chart of the solar system and provide an overview of what students will learn.

5. He tells students they are about to see a film and to pay particular attention to the planets. After the film, he will ask students to name the planets mentioned, and why they are all called planets. Using the three-dimensional model of the planets, sun, and moons, Mr. Messer, while occasionally referring to the film, intends to review how planets orbit the sun and how moons orbit planets. Then, he wants to form heterogeneous groups of five to agree on the critical attributes of planets. Groups will list and display these on newsprint. Once this is done, he wants to draw a definition

of "planet" from the class. Using question and answer, he wants to help the class learn the characteristics that are part of all planets and those characteristic of some but not others. He wants to draw a definition of the concept "planet" from the class. Now, using the unlabeled chart of the solar system, he intends to point randomly at planets, the sun, and moons and ask students to tell which are planets and which are not. The students have to justify their answers based on the definition and their knowledge of the critical attributes of planets.

6. To close the lesson, Mr. Messer will use question and answer to review the critical and noncritical attributes and the definition of the concept "planet." He intends to ask students how their learning about planets can be useful. After showing students how to go about it, he will distribute an unlabeled diagram of the solar system and prepare students for the next lesson. For homework, they are to label the planets and, in writing, explain their decisions.

7. During the lesson, Mr. Messer intends to watch students carefully for signs of uncertainty. He will ask questions and, if necessary, reteach portions of the lesson using an alternate activity. He will get further evidence of understanding through the homework assignment and, later, through the unit test.

8. Mr. Messer has a personal professional development plan for each of his lessons. Lately, he has been working on improving his questioning technique. He discovered that most of his questions have been directed to six or seven students. His intention for this lesson is to spread questions evenly. To help him achieve his target, he will ask one of the students to insert a check mark on a seating plan beside the name of every student asked. This will provide objective data on how he spread questions during the lesson.

During practice teaching, before you teach a lesson, your cooperating (sponsor) teacher will expect you to present and discuss your written lesson. Your plan will have two components: (1) *learning by students*—plans to help students achieve the intentions (objectives) of learning the subject matter and developing positive attitudes; and (2) *professional development*—plans by the teacher to achieve a professional target or competency.

Does the inclusion of component 2 surprise you? Think about it. Professional teachers, no matter how good, are always seeking ways to improve. *After ten years of teaching you will want to have had ten years of experience, not one year of experience ten times.* It is unlikely that much improvement will occur without a systematic approach. What better way to improve than to target an aspect of your teaching every time you teach?

How well did you do in identifying the parts of a lesson? A paragraph-by-paragraph analysis of Mr. Messer's lesson plan follows.

Paragraph 1. The *topic* of the lesson is identified, and intentions or *objectives* students are to achieve are stated. How the teacher will know whether they have achieved objectives is specified.

Paragraph 2. A list of teaching *aids and resources* that the teacher intends to use is given.

Paragraph 3. The background students are expected to have is identified. This is *prerequisite learning.*

Paragraph 4. This is the introductory or *set* portion of a lesson. Mr. Messer wants the interests of students to be piqued. Teachers want students to be positively disposed (have a positive mind set) toward, and be encouraged to be involved in, the lesson. The set of a lesson often includes a preview or overview of what is to be studied "Today we will . . ." or "After today's lesson you will know . . . and be able to. . . ." "You will enjoy learning about. . . ."

Paragraph 5. The next part of a lesson is the body or *development.* The teaching methods and student activities to be used, and the sequence of these, to help students acquire the knowledge and skills intended are specified. How interactive the lesson will be and how actively students will be engaged in learning tasks is outlined. (Although they are not mentioned in this scenario, classroom management plans also can be stated. Sometimes, to ensure clarity, questions that will be asked are written out. Sometimes, more activities than will actually be used are listed. If the teacher finds something is not working, he or she will not be at a loss for what to do.)

Paragraph 6. The *closure* portion of a lesson is intended to bring the lesson to a successful end. It often involves review to "tie up" a lesson, and frequently, a bridge is built to subsequent learning ("Today we did. . . ." "What you now know or can do is. . . ." "Tomorrow we will. . . ." That is, a summary of what has been learned is provided, and the students become aware of how learning will connect to future study.

Paragraph 7. The teacher needs to know whether students have learned what is intended. The intentions (objectives) are constantly kept in mind—sometimes, in the light of what is occurring, they are modified. This portion of a lesson plan is the *evaluation.* Evaluation is formative *and* summative. *Formative evaluation* occurs during every part of the lesson (e.g., paragraphs 4 through 6). This happens as the teacher looks around the room and notices nonverbal behavior such as a puzzled look, or (verbally) by how students respond to questions. Another way is to give several spot quizzes (written or oral) during segments of the lesson. *Summative evaluation* occurs when, at the end of the lesson, a test is written or students have to perform something. You may have noticed that summative evaluation may also be used to do closure.

Paragraph 8. The set, development, and closure portions of a lesson plan include a record of what the teacher intends to do to help students achieve learning objectives. The focus is on students. In this paragraph the focus is on the *professional development* of the teacher. The *target* area, and specific aspects of that target, are specified (e.g., the distribution aspect of Mr. Messer's questioning technique). Plans of how this is to be done are stated.

GENERAL PLANNING

1. Join a subject group. Brainstorm examples of each of the five kinds of stimulus variation.

2. In the same group as in "Activity 1," write and present a skit illustrating stimulus variation. The rest of the class observes and collects data using the data collection instrument shown in Appendix 7.1.

3. Planning is a critical part of many ventures. In groups, consider things that are frequently planned, such as going on a trip. Create a planning cycle that includes planning, carrying out the plan, and reviewing and revising the plan.

4. You and your classmates have been taught by teachers. Reflect about a favorite lesson. Explain what was taught and consider the components the teacher had to consider and carry out. Compare your findings with the lesson outline in the text.

5. Things "happen" in school classrooms. However, some teachers, when planning, confuse activities with objectives. Teachers might write in their planning books: today we will have a discussion, or today we will watch a film. Consider things you have learned in your major. In a chart, compare the activities you did and the learning objectives (what you were expected to learn).

6. Think again about your major subject area. What cognitive, psychomotor, and affective knowledge have you mastered? Share your learning with students from another discipline.

APPENDIX 7.1   *Stimulus Variation Professional Target*

PROFESSIONAL TARGET—VARYING PRESENTATION

Please describe what was said or done to vary the stimulus and how students reacted.

Presentation Skill	Descriptive Notes
Focusing Pointing, gesturing, making statements to draw attention to aids being used or for emphasis	
Shifting interaction Using different interaction patterns: teacher–class; teacher–student; student–student	
Pausing (silence) Pausing to: gain attention; emphasize; provide time to think; create suspense; stop a minor disruption	
Shifting senses Having students use different senses: looking; listening; feeling; tasting; smelling; doing	

Describe student reactions to the stimulus variations:

APPENDIX 7.2   *Lesson Plan to Achieve Objectives and Targets*

LESSON PLAN

Date _____   Subject _____   Name _____

Planning for Student Learning

(a) Topic:

(b) Content:

(c) Objectives:

   (1)

   (2)

   (3)

(d) Prerequisite Student Learning:

(e) Presentation (teaching methods and student activities):

   Set:

   Development:

   Closure:

(f) Materials and Aids:

(g) Evaluation:

Planning for Professional Development

Date _____   Name of Data Collector _____

(a) Target:

(b) Specific target:

(c) Descriptor elements:

(d) How I will go about trying to achieve the target:

(e) Data collection method: Check one.
   _____ Please use the attached sheet from the target topic.
   _____ Please use the attached sheet other than the target topic sheet.
   _____ Please collect data as described below.

APPENDIX 7.3 *Lesson Plan Elements Professional Target*

PROFESSIONAL TARGET—LESSON PLAN ELEMENTS

From your observations of the lesson presented, please describe what you perceive to be the lesson element or the things that were said and done.

Lesson Element	Descriptive Notes
Topic	
Content	
Objectives	
Set	
Development	
Closure	
Materials and aids	
Evaluation	
Professional target	
Plans for achieving the target	

APPENDIX 7.4 *Set and Closure Professional Target*

PROFESSIONAL TARGET—SET AND CLOSURE

Please describe how these were done: (a) *set* at the start of the lesson, and (b) *closure* at the end of the lesson.

Set and Closure Options	Descriptive Notes

A. Set:

Orientation Set (focusing attention through motivating activity)

and/or Transition Set (smooth transition from known to new material)

and/or Evaluation Set (determining what students know about previous material before going on to new material)

B. Closure:

Review Closure (reviewing material just taught)

and/or Transfer Closure (providing practice, and/or alerting students about future use of, or link to, material covered)

and/or Serendipity Closure (taking advantage of unique, unexpected situation that provides ideal closure)

On the reverse side of this sheet, please list and briefly describe each of the activities and instructional skills used in the development of the lesson.

APPENDIX 7.5   *Unit Planning Professional Target*

PROFESSIONAL TARGET—PLANNING THE TEACHING UNIT

Unit Title
Grade Level and Subject Area   Time Estimate

Rationale statement adequate for explaining why is it important for students
to study the teaching unit?   Yes _____   No _____
Comments:

Unit objectives clear and measurable?   Yes _____   No _____
Comments:

Content outline clear and in appropriate sequence?   Yes _____   No _____
Comments:

Appropriate concept map completed?   Yes _____   No _____
Comments:

Prerequisite student learning identified and provision made,
as appropriate, for pretesting?   Yes _____   No _____
Comments:

Sequence of lessons, Introductory, Developmental,
and Cumulative?   Yes _____   No _____
Comments:

Variety and balance of appropriate teaching methods and
student activities?   Yes _____   No _____
Comments:

Suitable variety of resources and materials listed?   Yes _____   No _____
Comments:

Formative and summative assessment congruent with objectives?   Yes _____   No _____
Comments:

Additional observations?

APPENDIX 7.6   *Unit Plan Feedback Sheet*

UNIT PLAN FEEDBACK SHEET

Requirements met: **1** Most definitely,   **2** Quite well,   **3** For the most part,
4 Partially,   or **5** Little Evidence

1. Planning and Organization   Comments

    1 2 3 4 5   Rationale statement
    1 2 3 4 5   Prerequisite learning; entry knowledge
    1 2 3 4 5   Concept/skills/processes map
    1 2 3 4 5   Declarative/procedural/affective objectives

2. Selection of Teaching Methods/Student Activities   Comments

    1 2 3 4 5   Use of competencies presented in text
    1 2 3 4 5   Choice of teaching methods/student activities
    1 2 3 4 5   Selection of routines/procedures

3. Meeting Student Needs   Comments

    1 2 3 4 5   Motivation
    1 2 3 4 5   Varying interactions/control
    1 2 3 4 5   Recognizing learning styles
    1 2 3 4 5   Recognizing cross-cultural needs
    1 2 3 4 5   Evaluation

4. General Assessment

    1 2 3 4 5   Provision of appropriate teaching methods and learning activities
                for student growth in all three domains
    1 2 3 4 5   Meaningful sequence of experiences and components to accomplish
                the central purpose of the unit
    1 2 3 4 5   Interesting, relevant, and challenging, but achievable
    1 2 3 4 5   Holistic understanding of the teacher as a decision maker evident

5. Personal Professional Development

    1 2 3 4 5   Target/competencies (selection and data collection targets identified, a
                plan for achieving each is stated, and a suitable data collection method
                and instrument for each target are selected or designed)

8 Engaging Learners

Questioning, Discussion, Seatwork, and Homework

Students across the educational spectrum understand studied material better, retain it longer, and enjoy their classes most when they learn actively rather than passively. (Shenker, Goss, & Bernstein, 1996)

Questioning

What's in a question, you ask: Everything. It is the way of evoking stimulating responses or stultifying inquiry. It is, in essence, the very core of teaching. (Dewey, 1933, p. 266)

Questioning Trends

Teachers ask an incredible number of questions. They use them to check recall of and increase retention of information, to interpret information, to guide the development of concepts or skills, to promote thinking, evaluate learning, and to review. Questions are used to discover what students know before beginning a lesson or unit, to motivate and to discover what interests students. During a lesson, questions are asked to see if students recall and understand what was presented. Questions increase student involvement in the development of the lesson. They keep students attentive and on task.

Effective teachers ask more questions than less effective teachers, they phrase questions clearly, avoid run-on questions, and specify the conditions for the response. They probe for clarification and nudge students to higher levels of thinking. Although responses are acknowledged, praise is used with discretion.

Many questions require rote memory for a correct response. Perhaps, because questions that require recitation of facts take less time, teachers sometimes avoid asking

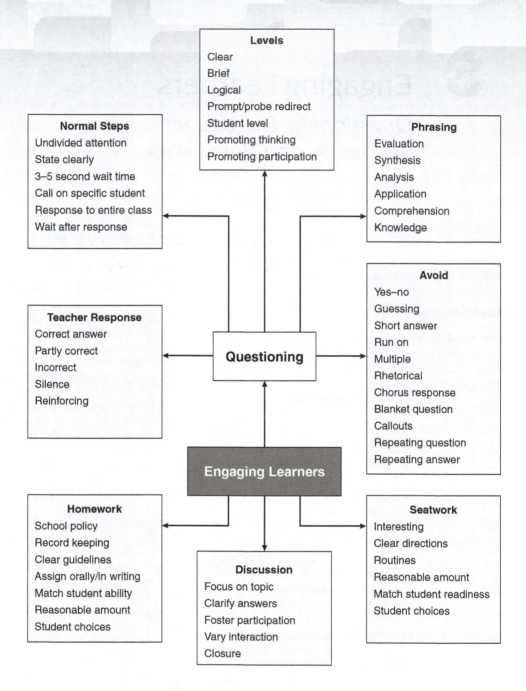

Levels
Clear
Brief
Logical
Prompt/probe redirect
Student level
Promoting thinking
Promoting participation

Normal Steps
Undivided attention
State clearly
3–5 second wait time
Call on specific student
Response to entire class
Wait after response

Phrasing
Evaluation
Synthesis
Analysis
Application
Comprehension
Knowledge

Teacher Response
Correct answer
Partly correct
Incorrect
Silence
Reinforcing

Questioning

Avoid
Yes–no
Guessing
Short answer
Run on
Multiple
Rhetorical
Chorus response
Blanket question
Callouts
Repeating question
Repeating answer

Engaging Learners

Homework
School policy
Record keeping
Clear guidelines
Assign orally/in writing
Match student ability
Reasonable amount
Student choices

Discussion
Focus on topic
Clarify answers
Foster participation
Vary interaction
Closure

Seatwork
Interesting
Clear directions
Routines
Reasonable amount
Match student readiness
Student choices

higher-level questions. Both elementary and secondary teachers ask many questions, but, elementary teachers ask more. Sadker and Sadker (2003) report that the typical teacher asks between 30 and 120 questions an hour. According to Kathleen Cotton (1998), research reveals that questioning follows lecturing as the most commonly used teaching method, with teachers spending from 35 to 50 percent of instructional time in questioning sessions.

Sandra Feldman (2003), discussing teachers and questioning, notes that "many teachers feel inadequately prepared in this critical component of effective teaching. Teacher education and induction programs sometimes gloss over questioning strategies. This is a disservice to both teachers and their students" (p. 8).

TCP—QUESTIONING SKILLS

Has effective questioning skills

Excellent use of questions: choice; steps in; conducting; wait time; cognitive level; prompts, probes, and redirects; and distribution.

Rarely uses questions; unaware of effective steps, use of wait time, and cognitive level; up-and-down rows distribution; repeats questions and student answers; accepts chorus responses and callouts.

Questioning Procedures

The way questions are asked is important (see Figure 8.1). CTE Home (2003–2004) recommends that teachers ask clear, specific questions; use suitable vocabulary level; ask questions ranging from the lowest to the highest levels of Bloom's taxonomy; and use questions to help students connect important concepts.

"The act of questioning has the potential to greatly facilitate the learning process, it also has the capacity to turn a child off to learning" when done poorly (Brualdi, 1998).

NORMAL STEPS.   Teach students how to participate in questioning, explaining why it is important for them to normally follow the routine you wish to establish. As part of your explanation, tell the class you value the contribution of everybody as a member of the class. Tell them that nobody knows everything and it is OK to risk: no sincere answer or question is "dumb" or something to be ashamed of—sincere questions present opportunities for learning. Having students observe the questioning pattern that follows can increase participation and learning and is an important aid to classroom management.

1. *Get the undivided attention of the entire class.* All students should feel a part of the teaching/learning process and think they personally are being addressed. This is supported by eye contact and body movements.

2. *State the question clearly.* Direct the question to the entire class rather than a specific student. Each student in the class should think he or she could be asked for the response. Eye contact and body language can help achieve this goal.

3. *Pause for three to five seconds.* Wait for at least three seconds before calling on a specific person to respond ("wait time" will be discussed later in this chapter).

4. *Call on a specific individual to respond.* Requests for responses should be spread among volunteers and nonvolunteers, matching question difficulty with student likelihood to respond successfully. Normally, callouts and chorus responses should not be accepted, and questions should not be posed in an up-and-down-the-rows manner (this limits participation to those being asked, lets others "off the hook," and invites control problems).

5. *Require students to respond to the whole class.* Because all students should feel ownership for the development of the lesson, responses should be directed to you *and* the

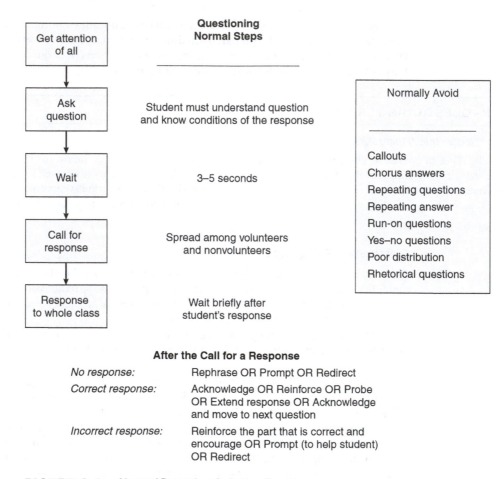

FIGURE 8.1 *Normal Procedure in Asking Questions*

entire class. A student's answer may lead to the next question, or a redirect, and be part of the development of the topic. Exercise patience in letting students complete their answers. Jumping in too quickly may cut students off from giving a more complete answer.

6. After a student is asked and responds, you can: (a) acknowledge the answer if correct and provide reinforcement if appropriate; (b) if the answer is incorrect or incomplete, you can recognize what is correct and use a prompt, rephrase the question, or redirect the question; (c) probe for clarification or for a higher-level response; or (d) simply move to the next question. If the student does not respond, you can encourage and prompt the student or redirect. Questions should be asked of volunteering and nonvolunteering students. This helps ensure that all remain attentive. Teachers should normally help students with incorrect responses, acknowledge the part that is correct, and help them get the correct answer. A data sheet you can use to practice this target is given in Appendix 8.1.

PHRASING QUESTIONS.   All thinking is driven by questions. "Good questions generate good thinking. Deep questions, deep thinking. No questions, no thinking" (Paul,

2002). Phrasing questions is important to what goes on in a class discussion. You set the stage and make statements that provide information, challenge, summarize, and help organization and development. The statements you make are as important as the questions posed; and the questions or comments that come from students help the discussion.

The questions you ask should be:

1. *Clear.* Students should know what is asked and how they should respond.
2. *Brief.* Long questions can tax memory (students can easily forget what was asked and therefore be embarrassed). Run-on, or a series of questions, should be avoided.
3. *Logically sequenced.* Early questions provide background (for review). Follow with questions that increase understanding and then application to solving problems. Concluding questions can lead to new insights or be used to evaluate.
4. *Match the level of students.* The language used should not interfere with learning. If new or complex words must be used, define these before the question is asked.
5. *Designed to promote thinking and participation.* Use questions that emphasize why and how, rather than what, where, and when. Build on lower-level questions with higher order questions. Move students along by using *convergent questions* (bringing things together to get a "right" answer), *divergent questions* (those with "no right answer," leading students to a new perspective, to synthesize, or be creative), and *evaluative questions* (students make carefully considered and substantiated judgments).

Education is more than filling a child with facts. It starts with posing questions. (D. T. Max, *The New York Times*)

Good questioning is not something that works in isolation. It occurs within the structure of a classroom and exemplifies the key elements of high-quality teaching. Weiss and Pasley (2004) say that teacher questions are crucial in helping students make connections and learn concepts, and that effective questions monitor students' understanding of new ideas and encourage them to think more deeply. High-quality instruction, they say, takes place:

- When the teacher's questioning strategies are likely to enhance the development of student conceptual understanding/problem solving (e.g., the teacher emphasized higher-order questions, used wait-time appropriately, and identified prior conceptions and misconceptions).
- When the teacher encourages and values participation by all.
- When the climate of the lesson encourages students to generate ideas, questions, conjectures, and/for propositions.
- And not when teachers use low-level "fill-in-the-blank" questions asked in rapid-fire fashion with an emphasis on getting the right answer and moving on rather than helping students make sense of the concepts. (pp. 24–28)

PRACTICES TO AVOID
- *Yes–no questions.* They encourage guessing and have little diagnostic value.
- *Questions that encourage guessing.* They have low diagnostic power.
- *Leading questions.* These contain a portion of the answer or suggest the answer and may encourage dependence on you.

- *Short-answer questions.* Except when drilling or preparing for higher level questions, avoid questions largely restricted to narrow, short answer, memory, or recall—we want to help students improve their ability to think.
- *Run-on or interrupted questions.* These add confusing and unnecessary detail or are lengthy and may cause students to forget or wonder what was asked.
- *Multiple questions.* These may cause students to forget what was asked, wonder which question to answer, or what you are really asking.
- *Rhetorical questions.* These are questions for which you do not expect a response; although they occasionally have emphasis value or cause students to participate covertly, overuse may cause students to be inattentive and not respond when actually asked.
- *Questions that ask for chorus responses.* Although chorus responses have value for reviewing or drilling facts or practicing foreign language vocabulary, they can lead to control problems and should normally be avoided; they have little diagnostic value.
- *Blanket questions.* Questions such as, "Does everybody understand?" or "Do you have any questions?" usually waste time and have little or no diagnostic value. After asking a question, it is better to ask a specific individual to respond to discover if that student understands.
- *Allowing callouts.* When students call out an answer without being asked, management problems can result; you lose control of appropriate distribution of questions, and many students will not have had enough wait time. Of course, when you call for a free-flowing discussion, it is normal to have unsolicited responses.
- *Repeating the question.* This may just encourage inattentiveness, interrupt the flow of discussion, and center the interchange more on you. However, if the question was poorly phrased or too complex, it may need to be rephrased or broken into sub-questions.
- *Repeating a student's answer.* This usually wastes time and causes students to be inattentive and ignore the contributions of peers. If a response was unclear, ask the student to rephrase it, or use a redirect. On occasion, for emphasis, another student can be asked to repeat the answer, or you may do this.

DISTRIBUTION OF QUESTIONS.   When a few eager or aggressive students dominate question-and-answer sessions, others tend to "tune out" or participate passively. All students should have the chance to contribute and think they may be asked to participate.

The climate should be positive and encouraging. Effective teachers encourage a high rate of correct responses and help students with incorrect responses. They use "wait time" to encourage broad participation. When you distribute questions, consider student ability and the likelihood of a correct response. Question sequences should be thoughtfully planned; normally, begin with questions that review the information needed for success with subsequent higher-level questions. A data collection instrument for question distribution patterns is shown in Figure 8.2.

Using "Wait Time"

The concept of "wait time" was developed by Mary Budd Rowe (1972). Wait time, the time from the end of the teacher's question to when a student is called to respond, has been extensively researched. Authorities agree that wait time should be three to five seconds (Cotton, 1988; Stahl, 1994; Sadker & Sadker, 2003) or more, particularly when

Professional Target—Question Distribution

Enter student names in boxes. Place a check mark or the question number in the appropriate box as questions are asked.

> Descriptive observations about the nature of question distribution:
>
>
>
>
>
>

Note: This observation form can also be used for recording eye contact, teacher movement, student off-task behavior, etc.

FIGURE 8.2   *Question Distribution Target*

higher-order questions are asked. The benefits are impressive (Berliner, 1987; Stahl, 1994; Sadker & Sadker, 2003): students tend to give longer answers (up to 700 percent longer); the number of supported and logical responses increases; failures to respond are reduced; more students volunteer to respond; higher-order responses are given more frequently; students rated as slow by teachers respond more often and ask more questions; more confidence is shown in responding; students ask more questions; student–student exchanges increase; students are more willing to risk because the number of speculative responses increases; and the need to discipline decreases.

In summary, Cotton's review of literature on questioning led her to conclude that increasing wait time could result in: higher student achievement, retention, more higher-level responses, greater response length, more unsolicited responses, decreases in failure to respond, more and better-quality support for responses, more contributions by students who participate infrequently with short wait times, expansion of the variety of responses, more student–student interactions, and more questions asked by students.

Some authorities prefer the term "think time" over "wait time." Stahl (1990), who initiated the term think time, says the purpose of wait time is to allow students and the teacher to do on-task thinking, and there are places in a lesson where periods of silence are as important as wait time. He adds, sometimes less than three seconds of uninterrupted silence is appropriate.

When wait time is increased, students have time to think an answer through, rehearse it, and build up courage. Teachers make better use of questions and answers. They have time to scan the room and encourage students to feel accountable, consider the next question and its phrasing, sequence questions, make distribution decisions, and think about how to handle responses. When wait time is increased, teachers are more flexible, make fewer errors, and have better continuity in the development of ideas. Teachers ask fewer questions, make more requests for clarification or elaboration, and become better at using student responses. With sufficient wait time, teachers revise their opinions of some students favorably. For example, minority students may now participate or increase the quantity and quality of their participation (Rowe, 1986, p. 45).

Levels of Questions

Jill Slack, in an interview in Blair (2002), says, "Questioning is one of the missing pieces in teacher training. Teachers often ask closed-ended questions that don't allow the students to demonstrate their level of knowledge or lack of knowledge." She explains, "The quality of response is affected by the quality of the question's content and how the question is asked. The pacing of the question also comes into play" (p. 1) Richetti and Sheerin (1999) observe that teachers who are constructivists share "a fundamental belief in the potential of a child's mind, in the need to challenge and refine students' thinking, and in their ability to make curriculum come alive" (p. 58).

When using questions and answers, you can help students progress well beyond a low level. Use probes and questions that are open ended or require analysis, synthesis, or judgments and support. This stimulates thinking, moving beyond rote memory. Asking higher-cognitive-level questions (requiring thought, not just memory) increases student achievement. The best pattern for younger and lower-ability students is simple questions with high success rates; for high-ability students, harder questions should be asked and more critical feedback given.

Bloom's taxonomy was introduced earlier. It is one way to look at levels of questions as student readiness and appropriate objectives are considered. Examples of key words or phrases in each category are given below.

Knowledge level (recalling or recognizing information):

Recall	How many?	Where?
Define	Who?	When?
List	What?	

Comprehension level (describing, putting in own words, giving examples):

Describe	Summarize	Interpret
Give an example	Explain	Paraphrase
Rephrase	What's the main idea?	

Application level (applying to a new context; using a concept to solve a problem):

Classify	Operate	Demonstrate
Select	Solve	Relate
Prepare	Use	

Analysis level (Discover, or break down into, the parts; find the structure):

What are the causes?	Analyze	Subdivide
What is the order?	Diagram	Infer
Outline	What are the reasons?	

Synthesis level (organize in a new way, or into a new whole):

Plan	Produce	Devise
Construct	Design	Combine
Create	Rewrite	

Evaluation level (judge based on criteria, a rationale, or standards):

Judge	Which is better? Why?	Discriminate
Criticize	Appraise	Do you agree?
Support	Justify	Why?

Note: As a caution, Bloom's taxonomy should not be used rigidly nor used as a linear and inflexible hierarchy. It is a guide to varying questions and to moving from low to higher levels. There is little point, however, in arguing about exactly where in the taxonomy a given question fits. Furthermore, you may prefer another classification system.

A data instrument you can use to practice this target is in Appendix 8.2.

QUESTIONING AND COGNITIVE LEVEL.   Cotton (1988), in a Northwest Regional Laboratory report, cites research on cognitive level questioning.

- About 60 percent of questions are lower cognitive, 20 percent are higher, and 20 percent are procedural.
- Higher-cognitive questions are not always better in getting higher-level responses, fostering learning gains.
- Lower-cognitive questions are more effective than higher-level questions with primary-level children, particularly disadvantaged children, and better when the teacher's purpose is learning factual knowledge and helping students commit it to memory.
- When asking many lower-level questions is appropriate, the greater the number of questions, the greater the student achievement.
- When lower-level questions are predominant, the level of difficulty should result in a high percentage of correct responses.
- Beyond the primary-grades level, a combination of higher- and lower-cognitive questions is more effective than exclusive use of one or the other.
- Students whom teachers perceive as slow or poor learners are asked fewer higher-cognitive questions than students perceived as more capable learners.
- Above the primary level, particularly for secondary students, increasing use of higher-cognitive questions considerably above 20 percent results in higher learning gains.
- Asking higher-cognitive questions alone will not necessarily result in higher-cognitive responses.

- Teaching students how to draw inferences and providing practice leads to higher-cognitive responses and greater learning gains.
- Increases in the use of higher-cognitive questions in recitations do not reduce student performance on lower-cognitive questions on tests.
- For older students, increasing use of higher-cognitive questions to 50 percent or more is related to increases in on-task behavior, student response length, relevant volunteered contributions by students, student-to-student interactions, use of complete sentences when responding, speculative thinking, and relevant questions asked by students.
- For older students, increased use (up to 50 percent) of higher-cognitive questions is positively related to higher teacher expectations about children's abilities, particularly for students teachers habitually have thought to be "slow" or "poor" learners.

Handling Responses

Teachers tend to fall into a pattern of calling mainly on higher-ability students to answer questions; the questioning pattern should have all students called upon as equally as reasonable (Good & Brophy, 1995, p. 277). Having equitable distribution is a demanding but important challenge (Kauchak & Eggen, 2003, pp. 167–168).

How you handle student responses makes a difference. Discussion and participation can be enhanced. Allowing sufficient *wait time* is fundamental to encouraging responses. You can use *prompts* or clues if the initial question was too difficult or you want to encourage a student. Cueing is an important skill. You can learn how to guide students to the right answer without giving it to them (overuse of prompts, however, can cause dependence). *Probes* can be used to elicit clarification, more detail, or higher-level responses; probing encourages students to move just ahead of where they are and is part of the essence of good teaching. *Redirects* shift the question to another student to confirm a response, invite comment, stimulate discussion, or when a student originally asked did not respond.

Normally, only accept responses from those recognized. This lets you control distribution, allows wait time to be used, and leads to better diagnosis. Responses should be addressed to the whole class. This helps students feel accountable for the development of the lesson. Effective teachers encourage the student who has been asked to respond. This shows they want all to participate and learn. To this end, prompts or probes can be used and unanswered questions can be redirected. Students achieve best when they have high success rates (from 70 to 80 percent), and students giving incorrect answers should be helped (Wilen & Clegg, 1986, p. 157). Give time for a complete answer. A student may need time to complete a response; and providing postresponse time allows other students to think and to consider volunteering (Stahl, 1994). Don't jump in or nod quickly after a response—rapid reinforcement may distract and block development of ideas. Use reinforcers selectively; an endless stream of teacher "OK's" or "right's" becomes a meaningless "part of the woodwork." Not every correct answer need be reinforced. Moving to the next question implies that the response was correct and keeps discussion moving. Building on a student's response, immediately or later, is a good way to reinforce. When you reinforce, be sincere and use a variety of expressions instead of repeatedly saying, for example, "good." Add *why* the answer was good.

When you are responding to a student answer, if the answer is correct and confident, you often can simply accept it and move on. If the answer is correct but hesitant, surface why the answer was right. This provides an opportunity to explain the content again (students may need the review). If the answer was partly or totally wrong, but the student did honestly try, then probe, prompt, rephrase the question, or reteach. Interpret sincere attempts to the student's advantage. Return later, with a similar question, to a student who gave an incorrect or hesitant answer. Use answers to earlier questions as a basis for later questioning. Normally, students should reply with complete statements and good English (encourage this in a nonblaming, nonthreatening way). Finally, promote constructive inter criticism among students (ideas can be challenged, but personal attacks cannot be permitted).

LINKING PRACTICE TO THEORY

How you ask questions is influenced by your experience and philosophy. If you see knowledge as compartmentalized and able to be transmitted without considering the learner, your questions may deal only with basic content. If you see content as closely linked to your teaching approach and knowledge and to your and your students' interests, your questioning may be more complex. Why is asking questions not as simple as it might seem? How does questioning affect learning?

Use the data collection instruments in this chapter to help you analyze the cases that follow. Your instructor may pose specific questions for your response.

CASE 8.1 Questioning

Making Haystacks

Ms. Lepage's grade 2 class has been working on a "Farm" theme for a few days. Today, Ms. LePage gathers students at the back of the room on the carpeted area. She says, "I have something for you to think about. I'm going to ask some questions to help you think." She pauses until everyone seems ready. "I want everyone to have a turn answering today, so I'll ask you to put up your hands instead of calling out the answer. I'm going to give you time to think before I call on anyone, to help us get some high-quality answers. I will ask somebody to respond. The answer should be loud and clear so all in the room can hear and keep up with what is going on. Listen carefully, because I usually will not repeat the answer that was given.

"This afternoon, we're going to make haystacks. What do you think we'll need?" Children's hands begin to go up. Ms. LePage acknowledges hands by smiling, but waits for more hands. She calls on students by name. Answers include, "Hay," "Straw." "Think about what haystacks look like," Ms. LePage prompts. "What else could we use?" Again a few

hands go up, then more, and finally most hands are up. Ms. LePage calls students by name for their answers. "Grass," "Weeds," "Corey's hair" (all laugh, including Corey), "String," "Twine," "Bullrushes," "Cattails." "Good answers!" Ms. LePage says. "You really do remember what haystacks look like. Now, I'm going to give you another clue that will change things quite a bit. We're going to be able to *eat* the haystacks. What do you think we'll use to make them?" The children wave their hands. Again Ms. LePage waits until many hands are raised. A student blurts out an answer and Ms. Lepage shakes her head with a smile, looks at the student, and puts an index finger to her lips. The students are very anxious to be chosen. Answers include "Spaghetti," "Fettucini," "Linguine," "Cotton candy," "Noodles." "Oh, that's close," says Ms. LePage. "What kind of noodles?" The children guess several kinds of noodles, but no one guesses chow mein noodles. "Have you ever seen this kind of noodles?" Ms. LePage holds up a box of chow mein noodles. She shows the recipe on chart paper, and preparations are made for cooking.

CASE 8.2 Questioning

There Should Be a Law

Mr. Njika's grade 12 social studies class has been studying the idea of "free trade" between Canada, Mexico, and the United States. As the class opens, Mr. Njika reviews the last day's lesson on different kinds of trade barriers, including tariffs. This is done through recall questions. He goes on, "Class, what are examples of products that we import?" The class supplies answers that Mr. Njika writes on the chalkboard. "What products do we export?" He records these on the chalkboard and adds items that students had missed. "Which of our imports do you think come from the other two potential free trade partners, and to which partners do we export our products?" Students respond, some just guessing. Mr. Njika receives their answers, making sure that they are accurately entered on the board.

The next part of the lesson is a brief lecture on the law of comparative advantage. To summarize, students learn that economic theory states the country that should produce a product or service is the one that can do it in the most cost-effective way. Each country should produce those goods and services at which it has an advantage compared to other countries, and these goods and services should be traded for ones for which they do not have a "comparative advantage."

"Let's try to discover if the Canada–Mexico–United States free trade idea is a good one. How do you think we should go about making such a decision?" One student responds that there must be an economic advantage for all countries. Another student adds that it's important to retain national identity. With some prompting, probing, and redirecting, students advance most of the arguments pro and con that they had learned in their study of tariffs. The class concludes with small groups beginning to discuss a question posed by Mr. Njika: "What do you think the long-term effects, on each country, of the three-way free trade agreement, if it is passed, will be?" The groups are to finish their discussions next day and report. They are told to think about the problem overnight and to ask others, or read about it.

CASE 8.3 Questioning

To Be or Not to Be . . .

Mr. Schmidt is taking up Shakespeare's *Hamlet*. He is a substitute teacher fresh out of university. The regular teacher is on sick leave. Mr. Schmidt looks about the room at faces that are sizing him up and says, "Your regular teacher tells me you were just doing the *Hamlet* soliloquy." "Yeh," calls out Henrico from the front row. Mr. Schmidt looks at his seating plan and says "Let's talk a bit about Hamlet. Jan, who is he?" "I guess he's the son of the king, he's . . . the prince of Denmark," replies Jan. "Pretty good. Can you explain why he's unhappy?" "I guess it's because someone killed his father," replies Jan with more confidence. "Great answer," says Mr. Schmidt, smiling. "Can you relate the death of his father to other scenes in the play? Take your time. None of you has to answer at once." "Would that be where the ghost told Hamlet he should get revenge?" asks Andrea. "Andrea, why doesn't he get revenge right away?" queries Mr. Schmidt. Andrea thinks deeply. "Could it be because his uncle killed the king?" "And what did his uncle do next?" asks Mr. Schmidt. José holds up his hand. "José, what do you think?" Mr. Schmidt walks toward José. "The uncle married Hamlet's mother, which complicates things," says José. "Then," says Mr. Schmidt, "what are the reasons for Hamlet's hesitation?" "I guess he loves his mother and doesn't want to make her unhappy," José confidently offers. "Great," says Mr. Schmidt, moving to the front. "How does all this link to the soliloquy?" Andrea eagerly gets back into the discussion: "Could it be that he's so unhappy he's thinking about suicide?" "All of you," Mr. Schmidt says, "what do you think of Hamlet so far"? Praveen, usually a quiet student, joins in: "It's great how you got us thinking for ourselves without telling us the answers." "Yeh!" adds Andrea, "That was fun. I liked the way you ask questions." "You get us thinking," says Praveen, as the bell rings.

Discussion

> One implication of Vygotsky's theory of cognitive development is that important learning and understanding require interaction and conversation. Students need to grapple with problems in their zone of proximal development, and they need the scaffolding provided by interaction with a teacher or other students. (Woolfolk, 2004, p. 333)

TCP—DISCUSSION SKILLS

Conducts effective class discussions

Conducts effective classroom discussions; helps class focus on topic; fosters participation; varies interaction so all participate; brings closure and summary; conducts guided and open discussions.

Discussions have no apparent structure; little evidence of planning; a few students dominate; no satisfactory summing up and closure.

How do you like sitting through a typical lecture, dutifully taking notes? Although there is an important place for lecture and other direct and expository approaches, your participation as a student is passive. You know that the more actively you are involved in learning, the more you are motivated, the easier it is for you to master the content, and the better you remember it. In highly teacher-centered instructional approaches, teachers select the objectives, content, and the teaching and learning strategies and methods—students sit and listen. In contrast, in student-centered (constructivist) approaches, teacher and students make decisions together. Effective teachers involve students actively. They use a variety of interaction patterns, particularly question and answer and discussion, to promote interaction and reflective discourse. They also involve students in meaningful seatwork and homework.

Discussion (small group and whole class) is a major part of this chapter because it involves all the targets (instructional skills) studied in previous chapters: lesson planning, communication, interpersonal and group skills, classroom management skills, varying presentation, and questioning. Seatwork and homework are examined at the end of this chapter.

Purposes of Discussion

Discussion can be used for several purposes (Cruickshank, Bainer, & Metcalf, 2003, pp. 185–186) to: review and extend what students have studied for mastery of a subject, to provide an opportunity for students to examine opinions or ideas, to solve a problem and to improve problem-solving capability, and to help students develop communication, interpersonal, and group skills. One or more of these four goals might be part of a lesson using discussion. Discussion is usually more effective than a more direct method for higher-level outcomes and retention. Most students enjoy discussion and are motivated by it. It fosters attitude change and enhances moral reasoning.

Conducting Discussion

> Discourse can be thought of . . . as exposing one's invisible thoughts for others to see. Through discussions, then, teachers are given a window for viewing the thinking skills of their students. . . . Thinking out loud also provides students opportunities "to hear" their own thinking and to learn to monitor their own thinking processes. (Arends, 2004, p. 428)

Learning and understanding are enhanced through interaction and conversation. "By thinking together, challenging each other, and suggesting and evaluating possible explanations, students are more likely to reach a genuine understanding" (Woolfolk, 2004, p. 451). Discussions are particularly effective when multiple answers are possible (Gage & Berliner, 1998).

Discussions are characterized by: (1) recognition of a common problem or topic, (2) introduction, exchange, and evaluation of ideas and information, (3) seeking an objective or goal, and (4) student–teacher or student–student interaction (Orlich, Harder, Callahan, Kauchak, & Gibson, 1994, p. 224).

Discussion can be with the whole class, the teacher or a student as the leader, or in small groups of students. Whole-class discussion requires teacher and students to interact verbally. Much knowledge can be gained through creative inquiry and active student participation. Discussion can be adapted to many classroom situations. It can be *guided* or *unguided* (open). It can help build classroom climate and lead to intrinsic student interest in the subject.

GUIDED DISCUSSION.   When you conduct a discussion by interjecting and using thought-provoking questions, you are using guided discussion. This is effective for promoting understanding of important concepts. In guided discussion, you are the discussion leader and authority source, and (when needed) the information source. Guided discussion is used to guide students as they review what they have been studying, or to promote understanding or develop the ability to apply learning—you draw out needed information and make frequent use of convergent (who, what, where, and when) questions. You prompt, probe, and seek wide participation. Guided discussion is similar to guided discovery or inquiry.

OPEN DISCUSSION.   Discussion can be completely free and consist largely of student–student interchange. This is unguided or open discussion. It is an exciting way for students to engage in high-level, creative thinking. Open discussion may be risky and more difficult to conduct, but can be exciting and rewarding. It is more free flowing than guided discussion. You are a facilitator, not an authority source or figure. Your role involves focusing, setting boundaries, encouraging participation (but, unlike guided discussion, not necessarily wide participation), and promoting positive interaction. You listen, paraphrase, perception-check, ask open-ended questions, and probe, without pushing the class toward predetermined conclusions. Avoid intervening too often, because it may get in the way. Divergent ideas and originality are welcomed, and high-level and critical and creative thinking is sought.

Guidelines for Effective Discussion

Discussion should be "businesslike," on-topic conversations. There is much more to it than first meets the eye. You need to plan, conduct, and summarize. Skills include interpersonal exchanges, motivation, questioning, and reinforcement.

Effective discussions normally need to be based on material that is familiar to students. Students should not "pool ignorance." The discussion topic can be a problem or issue that does not have a "correct" answer. It may be desirable to have students discover the answer. The issue should be of interest to the class. You set the stage, stress that opinions must be supported (based on evidence), and ensure the terms and concepts needed are understood. Students need to understand that although consensus may be sought, arriving at consensus is not mandatory—it is OK to "agree to disagree." Good discussion is student centered. Normally, interject only to encourage, keep discussion on track, mediate, spread participation, provide needed information, or reinforce. The rules of common courtesy must prevail. Ideas can be challenged; personalities must never be attacked. If possible, students should be seated so they can easily see and hear each other. Discussion should usually conclude with consensus, a solution, insights gained, or a summary (preferably provided by students). Students need a clear understanding of the major points and application to other situations. A summary of considerations for conducting discussions follows.

Teachers who are good at conducting class discussions demonstrate certain behaviors. They are aware that good discussions have certain characteristics:

- Based on material familiar to students
- Terms and concepts needed are understood
- Opinions reflect sound critical thinking
- Encourage, paraphrase, ask for clarification
- Discussion kept on track
- Rules of common courtesy honored
- Students easily see and hear each other
- Time for thought
- Summary of arguments, insights, decisions
- Discussion leader mediates, spreads participation, provides needed information, reinforces
- Issue to be discussed of interest to class
- Students briefed on rules and behavior
- Student centered
- Welcome diverse suggestions
- Unsupported opinion giving avoided
- OK to challenge ideas, no personal attacks
- Consensus sought but not demanded
- Use of prompts, probes, redirects
- Transfer of learning to other situations
- Discourage self-serving behaviors (e.g., blaming, storytelling, showing off)

Encouraging Participation

You can do much to make discussion meaningful to students when you encourage positive and productive participation. Students need to appreciate the importance of, and be directly taught how to: listen, take turns, encourage others to participate, and speak clearly and to the point. Arends (2004) provides some interesting approaches to encouraging participation and to promote discussion. For participation he suggests:

- *Time tokens.* If a few people talk most of the time and some never talk, time tokens can be distributed. Each student is given some tokens designating a time (i.e., 10 or 15 seconds). Students who have used up their tokens can say no more.
- *High-talker tap-out.* In most classes, if you do not intervene, a few students will do most of the talking. Balanced participation can be encouraged by assigning a student to act as participation monitor. The monitor can pass a note or use a "limited number of entries" system to have the "high talker" suspend participation until all have had a turn (p. 379).

For discussion he recommends:

- *Think-pair-share.* After a discussion topic is introduced, have student pairs exchange ideas and practice listening. An alternative is to have students write about the topic before they share. The advantage is that individuals are more likely to participate because they will have something to say and participation is less risky. This technique might also be used in the middle of a discussion.
- *Buzz groups.* To encourage listening to each other, insist that during some discussions (those in which objective is to learn listening skills), before students can speak they have to paraphrase what the previous speaker said.
- *Beach ball.* Beach ball is particularly effective for younger students. A beach (or other) ball is given to a student to start the discussion. Only the person with the ball can talk. Other students raise their hands and are passed the ball when they want to talk. A variation is to have to continue to pass the ball to somebody who has not yet spoken. The procedure can begin again when all have spoken (p. 446).

The Talking Circle

You can learn how to respect the needs of diverse learners when you include students from cultures different from your own in class interactions. As one example, many indigenous traditions use a process for coming to a group decision or understanding. It is called the *talking circle.* The Four Worlds Development Project (1982) describes how talking circles work. Each person, when it is his or her turn, can speak as freely and passionately as he or she wishes, without interruption (but is not required to speak or can speak later). Comments are restricted to the issue or question—not to what another person has said. Participants receive the contributions of all other speakers with respect, even when disagreement occurs. They are allowed to speak without interruption. Each speaker's ideas are to be acknowledged and built upon. Participants need to believe that what they say will be accepted without criticism. Comments need to be descriptive and nonjudgmental—positive and negative comments are to be avoided. Everybody needs to feel safe, so moral or ethical issues can be dealt with without offending anyone. Good talking circles make it possible for rich thought to be accumulated so common ground and consensus can be sought. The goal is for group members to stand together and move forward in a cooperative spirit.

Talking circles are particularly useful when people need to share feelings or when a topic does not have a right or wrong answer or when a risk-free environment is desired. Your class does not have to be aboriginal for you to use talking circles. They can be a valuable part of your instructional repertoire. When you use them, teach guidelines for their use. Learning needs to be a shared endeavor and cooperative experience. The Four Worlds Development Project (p. 30) presents guidelines for the use of talking circles:

- All comments should be addressed directly to the question or issue.
- Only one person speaks at a time.
- Silence is an acceptable response.
- At the same time, everyone must feel invited to participate.
- It is often better to hold talking circles in groups of ten to fifteen, not a large group.
- The group leader facilitates the discussion by acknowledging contributions in a nonjudgmental way.
- No comments that put down others or oneself should be allowed.

- Speakers should feel free to express themselves in any way that is comfortable.
- Some groups have found it useful to encourage participants to pray silently for the one who is speaking.

A mechanism is needed to ensure that a few vocal students do not dominate. An atmosphere of patience and nonjudgmental listening can help shy students speak out and bolder students to moderate participation. A way to signify who has the floor can be established. Going around the circle from one person to the next can be used. Another way is to use an object (such as a feather), which is held by the person speaking, who, when finished, passes it to another person who has indicated the desire to speak or to the person next to him or her.

A data instrument you can use to practice conducting discussions is given in Appendix 8.3.

Interaction Patterns

Discussions involve a range of interaction patterns. You may wish to discover your pattern of interaction with members of a class. Some students tend to monopolize a discussion. You can use a simple data collection instrument to discover: (1) which students tend to monopolize discussion and (2) how the discussion moves from one person to another. At five-second intervals indicate, by tallies or arrows, where the discussion is centered, and, by means of arrows, show lines of interaction. Two simple ways of analyzing teacher–student interactions are shown in Figures 8.3 and 8.4.

Planning Class Discussions

As with any teaching method, advance planning is a must. Although some discussions occur spontaneously, planning ahead allows flexibility and spontaneity. As you plan, think about the purpose and whether discussion is appropriate for the lesson. Consider whether students have the background or skills needed for a worthwhile discussion. How will you handle situations such as the silent student or a student who verbally attacks another (ideas can be challenged, but persons never attacked)?

Decide the approach, for example, guided or unguided, or exchange of ideas after a reading or experience versus a problem-based interchange. Make a lesson plan (a concept map or web of the information, ideas, and feelings that may surface in the discussion can be included). Consider room arrangement—circular or semicircular works best. Decide the *set* to stimulate interest and participation. Review discussion etiquette, what is appropriate and inappropriate behavior. Decide what you will do to ensure orderly exchanges, wide participation, and elicit formative summaries, a concluding summary, and the closure you intend to use.

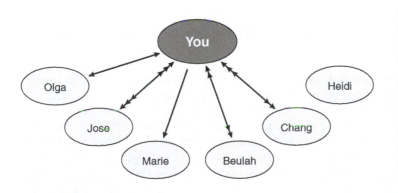

Student–Teacher Interaction:

- What was the nature of the discussion and interaction?

FIGURE 8.3 *Interaction Pattern One*

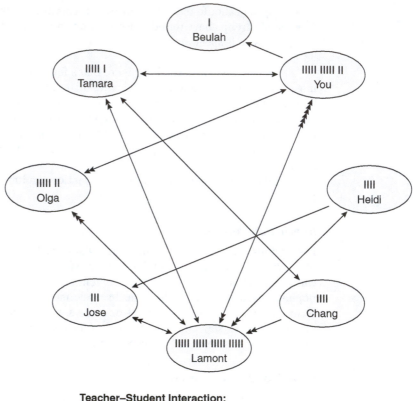

FIGURE 8.4   *Interaction Pattern Two*

Teacher–Student Interaction:

- What was the degree of teacher control?
- Who did not participate?
- Who received the most attention?
- How many tallies were there?
- How much student initiation of interaction was there?
- How many are the same persons?

Guidelines for designing teacher led class discussions are suggested by Allan and Nairne (1984):

1. *The topic.* When you plan, begin by focusing on the topic and getting everyone involved. The topic should be: (a) positive in focus (what *should* occur, rather than what should not occur) and (b) narrow in scope. This does not mean negative thoughts and feelings should not come out (especially during the exploration stage), but movement must be toward, and toward clear emphasis on the goal, new and adaptive things, or behaviors.

2. *Introduction and warm-up.* Explore the problem area. You can begin with a warm-up or "icebreaker" activity or presentation that readies students for the discussion. Questions requiring "yes" or "no" or closed answers about the topic could be asked. For example, "Have you heard about . . . ?" or "How many of you . . . ?" Then announce the discussion topic and, if possible, tie it to previous work. The warm-up might provide clues about students' feelings toward the topic.

3. *Exploration.* Open questions, those that move from general to specific, should be asked during the exploration phase. For example, "What does the term racism mean?" Then move to more specific questions, such as, "Have you ever witnessed a situation where you think somebody was being racist?" Questions here should help students explore the problem by coming to know and verbalize their thoughts and feelings about the topic.

4. *Understanding.* The goal in this phase is to help students objectively understand the problem area by moving their frame of reference from themselves to other people and to see other perspectives. Use questions that foster insight or greater awareness and help students understand the dynamics involved in an issue. Use questions such as, "For what reasons do racism occur?" or "What would make somebody act in a racist way?" or "How do you think the other person would feel?"

5. *Action steps.* In this stage, activate a sense of responsibility and encourage students to move into action. The kind of question to use is, "What can you do to deal with the problem?" or "What can governments do to improve matters?"

6. *Termination.* In this phase, help students organize and summarize their thoughts and feelings. Ask questions such as, "What have you learned from the discussion?" and, moving a step further, "What do you think you will do the next time you witness a racist incident in the school yard?" These questions provide feedback about what students have learned.

Effective discussion can involve many different approaches. Try the approaches suggested until you have several models that work for you and your students.

CASE 8.4 Discussion

Born or Made to Order?

Professor Gomez wants to model running a discussion with his class. As the students come in they notice the VCR/DVD player.

JOHN: So, Professor Gomez, do we get movies today?

PROF: Very perceptive, John. OK, everyone, today we are going to explore running a discussion. The topic is "Is teaching an art or a science?" In other words, are teachers born to teach, or do they need to be trained? I'm going to begin by showing two clips from the film, *Dead Poets Society.* The first one shows teachers in the school beginning their lessons. The next one shows the way Mr. Keating begins his first English class. Here is a data sheet on running a discussion. I want you to describe what happens in our class.

JOHN: So, running a discussion is our professional goal.

PROF: Right. (They watch the videos.)

LUIS: Hey, that's a great film.

PROF: Thanks, Luis, for your enthusiasm. Now, how many of you think teaching is an art, just comes naturally with no training needed? *(Ten hands go up.)* Great! How many think teaching is a science and training is needed? (Eight hands go up.) Good! I guess the rest of you are on the fence or think teaching is a bit of both. *(The remaining seven nod.)* OK, get into your three groups and each group brainstorm why you think teaching is an art, a science, or both. Write your responses on the newsprint I have provided. *(The groups get to work.)* We will hear both sides and use the third group to come to a conclusion.

PROF: All ready? Right? Each group can present in turn; then we'll have an open discussion with each group defending its position.

continued

GROUP 1: We think teaching is an art. People are born with a natural instinct for teaching; we think skill without passion is not effective; knowing skills does not mean you can teach well. You need an intrinsic feeling for teaching to teach well. You need humor and empathy; you have to have personality and need intuition. The best place to learn is *with* the students.

GROUP 2: We think teaching is a science. There are steps and rules to follow; there are goals and targets that you work toward. You need to experiment (like scientists) with new techniques and need lesson-planning skills and knowledge about learning and teaching styles. There are so many theories on teaching, it must be science based. Many of the skills must be learned.

GROUP 3: We think it's a mix, like Yin and Yang. Yes, you need passion, but you need skills to deliver the passion. You need empathy for kids, but if you don't have knowledge, the empathy won't do much good. Teaching is a bit like theater. You need the innate feeling for acting, but the best actors go to acting school, just as dancers go to dancing school.

PROF: Great stuff! Tell me, was Keating a natural teacher?

GROUP 1: Yes, he had a real instinct and passion.

PROF: Do you think he planned ahead to take the students into the hall?

GROUP 2: Yes, that was his set. He thought the whole thing out. He knew how to motivate.

PROF: So John, share with us what you wrote.

JOHN: The topic was "Is teaching an art or a science?" You introduced it with the film *Dead Poet's Society.* You said the aim was to look at both sides of the issue and come up with a synthesis. After each group, your questions brought about a summary of the positions. For clarity, you made us paraphrase what we said, and I guess you probed quite a bit and challenged our assumptions. There was a lot of student participation in our groups, and when we presented you waited quite a bit while we thought out our answers. You allowed us to come to a summary so we agreed on some of the main points.

PROF: Well, thanks, John, that was great.

CASE 8.5 Discussion

Getting Them to Talk!

In the staff room, Ted, a social studies teacher, is having coffee with Sophie, who teaches English. Ted closes his teaching notes with frustration. "My discussions don't seem to work," he comments. "I put the kids into groups and have them discuss topics I give them. They always get off task." "Well, there are guidelines," says Sophie. "What kinds of topics do you discuss?" "It varies," says Ted, sipping coffee, "usually topics like the causes of war, the nature of revolution, and people's basic rights." "Wow, those do sound interesting," says Sophie, "but it's important that students know something about the topic, understand the terms and concepts, and the subject should be something students are interested in." "You mean, topics close to their lives," says Ted, thoughtfully. "Yes," continues Sophie, "because they must be able to support what they say. So, either the topic should be familiar, they should have knowledge of it, or both." OK," comments Ted, opening his notes, "I can appreciate that. What else?" "First," replies Sophie, "students need practice in how to think critically so that not only do they give sound opinions, they learn how to discuss intelligently. For example, you can help them see the difference between a fact and an opinion—they should separate what's relevant from the irrelevant and detect bias." "I see," says Ted, "I need to teach them quite a few skills. How about running a discussion? My students seem to ramble." "Well," replies Sophie "keep the discussion on track and summarize the arguments from time to time. Students should be taught to respect each other's points of view. Most important, they can challenge someone's opinions but not the person." So," says Ted, thoughtfully, " I have to teach students new skills in discussion and critical thinking. Thanks Sophie, I'll give it a try."

Seatwork and Homework

> The intense feeling homework arouses may be proportionate to its important role in a child's education. Numerous studies testify to the powerful link between homework and improved student achievement. Homework has also been shown to help teach students to work independently, encourage responsibility and develop good study habits. (Feldman, 2004, p. 6)

TCP—ASSIGNING SEATWORK AND HOMEWORK

Sets meaningful seatwork and homework

Seatwork and homework assignments follow a clear school or classroom policy; guidelines clear to the students; assignments match student ability or challenge reasonably; students given some choice; prompt and meaningful feedback.	Little consistency or policy to the seatwork and homework assignments; haphazard setting of homework; no clear guidelines; care not taken to match student ability; no choice in the assignments; inadequate feedback; assignments returned late.

Both seatwork (in-class individual study) and homework (out-of-class individual study) usually involve independent learning but can occur in pairs or small groups. Studies by Weinstein and Mignano (1993, pp. 149–150) revealed students spend over half the time working independently. School policies often require teachers to assign homework regularly. The time students are expected to spend on homework may vary from 15 minutes a day for young students up to 60 minutes per class for older students Time spent on seatwork often is a sizable portion of each subject period. This means that seatwork and homework should be structured and monitored to increase learning and help students become self-regulated learners.

Student practice, through seatwork or homework, often is needed after material (particularly a skill) has been presented. When done well, practice allows students to deepen understanding of content, retain (overlearn) what was presented, and gain speed and accuracy (Kaplan, 1990, p. 390). Some skills need to be practiced to the point of automaticity. Practice provides opportunity for students and you to become aware of what students know and do not yet know. The main reasons for seatwork and homework are to provide practice, enrichment, or remediation when students have difficulty learning content or a skill (Montague, 1987, p. 258). Independent practice gives students the repetitions needed to integrate new and previous knowledge or skills, to become automatic in the use of skills, and to overlearn content (Rosenshine & Stevens, 1986, p. 386). Unless overlearning occurs (particularly in math and elementary reading), material will likely not be retained (p. 386).

Seatwork

The activity elementary students engage in most is seatwork. Seatwork can be defined as independent, supervised classroom desk work. It is even plentiful in junior high school and high school. *Seatwork,* or supervised individual study, is used to provide students with opportunity to gain appropriate practice and feedback on a variety of academic tasks. It is normally used to provide practice after instruction, but it can be used to develop inquiry abilities. It should not be the main approach. Woolfolk (2004) cautions that seatwork requires careful monitoring. Teachers need to be constantly on the move to help students who need it and to catch students "doing it right" (p. 446).

THE NATURE OF SEATWORK.   Most seatwork consists of work that is designed for students to perform independently as practice after they have learned the work. Two kinds of seatwork are common. The most common is whole-class supervised study; the other occurs when you work with one group while another works independently. Students should be told the purpose and relevance of seatwork that follows directly from instruction. It should be carefully chosen and sequenced, clearly explained and monitored, and specific feedback provided. Seatwork assignments may be prepared by the teacher or assigned from a text or workbook.

PURPOSE OF SEATWORK.   Although seatwork in school classrooms is usually assigned to extend knowledge, not just to keep students busy, much seatwork is unlikely to succeed in meeting its intentions. This is true of both teacher-made and workbook assignments. Seatwork needs to be a meaningful extension of lessons and students need to see the connection between a lesson and seatwork. Assignments may coordinate poorly with the preceding instruction and do little more than confuse, mislead, or be busy work. Make sure students understand and do not just want to get it over with, that they do not just daydream, walk around, or socialize. What can happen is the assignment is "just right" for a few students but too hard or too easy, too short or too long, or boring for the rest. Most difficulties with seatwork can be corrected. For best results, the work assigned should be individualized. It can be more effective when individualized and when it is used to diagnose problems or solidify learning, but it must be used correctly.

ASSIGNING SEATWORK.   As stated above, assignments should be tailored to meet individual needs and interests through the content involved and the exercises available. Student choice is desirable. Directions for seatwork should be clear, and teachers should move about during seatwork to react to the work being done. Students should not practice errors! They should be able to do at least 80 percent, even 100 percent, of seatwork correctly. As mentioned earlier, "catching students doing it right" is as important as tactful correctives. Time "up front" (before seatwork begins) reduces the time needed for explanations to individuals at their seats. Clear directions increase at-task behavior and eliminate misbehavior because students do not understand, or cannot do, what was assigned.

Before you ask students to begin seatwork, make sure they understand the concepts and skills involved and know how to do the work. A good procedure is to begin the seatwork as a whole-class endeavor. If, for example, students have been assigned questions, you should do the first one or two questions, step by step, with the whole class. Then, it may be a good idea to do one or two more questions asking individuals to tell you and the class "what to do next." After "guided practice" has taken place, students can work independently. Following this, monitored seatwork can begin. A data sheet on direction giving is included in Chapter 6.

MONITORING SEATWORK.   Move about the classroom during seatwork. Do not spend too long with one or two students. When you discover a student is doing an assignment incorrectly, do not just tell the student what to do next, nor just have the student tell you what to do next. Ask "how" and "why" questions. Although repetition for retention is important, understanding needs to be promoted.

Content that is difficult or complex should be broken into parts. Several segments of instruction, each followed by practice, may be necessary. If you find that many students are experiencing the same problem, halt the seatwork and reteach the troublesome material.

You may have one group (or grade, in a two-grade classroom) work independently while another is being instructed. Be positioned and have seats arranged so both groups can be observed. A routine should be set up and followed. For example, for students who need help, the routine may be to have them write their names on a certain place on the chalkboard and then work on another question or other material until you can get to them. A good practice is to signal while students are working. For instance, you can say, "You should have about half of the questions done now," and later, "You have five minutes left." When work has been completed, students must know how to turn it in and what to do next (for example, other assignments, free reading, or to check work with designated peers).

ALTERNATIVE USES OF SEATWORK.   The evidence suggests that less time should be devoted to individual seatwork and more to techniques such as teacher-led whole-class practice (e.g., question-and-answer sessions and repetition drills). Other alternatives include having students work in pairs, cooperative group activities, and competition between groups.

Borich (1998, p. 432) notes that research offers guidelines for seatwork (below).

GUIDELINES FOR USE OF SEATWORK
- Select and teach interesting content until students are likely to get 80 percent of seatwork correct.
- Provide clear directions and establish routines for doing the work, its format, handing it in, and correcting it.
- Do guided teacher-led practice; check comprehension as well as knowledge of "what to do and how to do it."
- Assign work that is differentiated to suit individual needs.
- Monitor in-progress seatwork, stress understanding and skill, provide feedback, correctives, and reinforcement. Have the work handed in, provide feedback, and return it.
- Have sufficient appropriate materials available to students.
- Students need to think the seatwork has real learning value and believe that self-regulated learning is important (not just busy work).
- Clear instruction is needed on what to do and how to do it.
- Best suited for (a) practice of previously taught material, or (b) preparation for a lesson.
- Teachers need to monitor student progress and ensure the work is being done correctly.

CASE 8.6 Seatwork

The Seat of Learning

Ms. Desai's English class is getting ready for a seatwork assignment on Greek mythology. This is their first seatwork assignment so she wants them to understand her guidelines for seatwork.

MS. DESAI: OK, class, we've examined several Greek myths. Now I want you to work on your own myth of Prometheus. I have a handout for you, so let's go over the assignment. Mark, will you read the first section?

MARK: In your own words, write out the story of Prometheus in one paragraph.

MS. DESAI: Fine. Abdul, what is the story basically about?

continued

ABDUL: Well, Prometheus feels sorry for humans so he steals fire from the gods on Mount Olympus and gives it to humans to use.

MS. DESAI: Great. OK, Sharma, will you read the next section?

SHARMA: Do a drawing of the story. It can be one drawing or done as a cartoon strip.

LEE: Ms. Desai, I can't draw!

MS. DESAI: That's OK, Lee, you can do stick figures. They can be very effective. Maria, will you read the next instruction?

MARIA: Make a list of things the fire that Prometheus took could represent in Greek times and today.

MS. DESAI: Thanks, Maria. Could you give an example?

MARIA: Fire could represent knowledge.

MS. DESAI: Anything else?

ABDUL: It could be technology.

MS. DESAI: Great, you all have the idea. Does everyone know what to do and how to do it? [Class members nod in agreement.] And, what's our routine, Mark?

MARK: We do a rough copy, have you check it, and then do a good copy on white typing paper.

MS. DESAI: I think you're all ready to go. Check with me if you have any concerns. You know where the crayons and typing paper are kept. Enjoy!

Homework

THE RESEARCH ON HOMEWORK. There are five kinds of homework: practice to master skills and reinforce material learned in class; preparation for upcoming lessons; extending learning beyond what was treated in class; transfer of ideas and skills to new situations; and practicing creativity, critical thinking, and problem solving (Burden & Byrd, 2003, p. 181). Homework needs careful planning, and students need to be taught how to make it meaningful.

Whether homework should be assigned and how much and the kind have been, and still are, issues among students, teachers, and parents. Many school personnel and parents think homework is a good way to extend learning. To be most effective, students "should feel responsible for doing homework and should understand that homework is crucial to learning" (Kauchak & Eggen, 2003, p. 416). Homework use, however, varies from district to district and from school to school. It can be a useful supplement to in-class instruction and increase achievement (at least for secondary students), but we know little about how much and the kind to assign. Research on homework suggests that if teachers assign homework to increase achievement, the odds are that homework for elementary students will have little effect, five to seven hours of homework per week for middle-grades students will have moderate results, and students in high school who do large amounts of homework have higher achievement than those who do little. Cooper (1989) reports that the effects of homework are substantial for high school students, positive for junior high students, but negligible for elementary school students (p. 88). More recently, Kauchak and Eggen (2003) report that homework significantly increases achievement, but "to be effective, it must be a logical extension of classroom work" (p. 375). They add that research has "found that in addition to amount, the frequency of homework is important" (p. 375), with five problems each night, not twenty-five once a week (Cooper, Lindsay, Nye, & Greathouse, 1998). Homework should be an extension of instruction. Cooper (1989) says homework to practice previously taught content or preparation for forthcoming lessons is more effective than homework related to new materials. Kaplan (1990) observes that most studies questioning the value of homework were done on assignments of routine practice, not preparation for new lessons (p. 393). Cooper (1989) concluded that homework works best if material is not too complex or completely unfamiliar (p. 88). Cooper (2001) reviewed findings that younger students do not benefit from homework as much as older students.

He concluded, "Studies indicate that younger students have limited attention spans, or more specifically, limited abilities to tune out distractions," and that "younger students haven't yet learned proper study skills" (p. 36). He provides the following homework policy guidelines, which "can make homework an effective teaching tool."

- *Coordinate policies.* Districts, schools, and classrooms should coordinate policies.
- *State the rationale.* The broad rationale for homework should be stated (why mandatory, time requirements, and coordination of assignments among classes).
- *Assign homework.* Homework should be assigned, but the amount depends on developmental level and the quality of home support. It should not be just for knowledge acquisition. In younger grades it can develop good study habits, help students realize they can learn at home as well as at school, foster independent learning, and show parents what is going on at school.
- *Use other approaches.* Homework is only one approach to show children that learning takes place other than in school. (pp. 37–38)

Cooper stresses that teachers should have "flexible homework policies" to "take into account the unique needs and circumstances of their students" (p. 37).

Guidelines for the frequency of homework by students are provided by Cooper (2001): grades 1–3, one to three assignments no longer than fifteen minutes each; grades 4–6, two to four per week; grades 7–9, three to five; and grades 10–12, four to five. Teacher discretion can be used for additional voluntary assignments.

When effective teachers use homework, they grade it and provide correctives and reinforcement (Walberg, 1990, p. 472). Cooper agrees, saying that homework should be included in the grading system. The U.S. Department of Education (1986) notes, "Homework is most useful when teachers carefully prepare the assignment, thoroughly explain it, and give prompt comments and criticism when the work is complete" (p. 42). Research suggests that students need to be taught to organize their assignments (Kaplan, 1990, p. 393).

PURPOSE AND CHARACTERISTICS OF HOMEWORK. Most students think homework is valuable, even if they do not always do it. Parents also think it is valuable and expect it. Inform parents of your homework policy as well as when it is done well and when it is not done. Parents can be asked to check homework, although some of it may have been completed at school. In some jurisdictions, especially in disadvantaged economic areas, it may be unrealistic to assign homework or expect it to be checked by parents. Homework, like any school work, should *never* be used as punishment. This leads to a dislike of the subject, teacher, and schooling.

Many of the characteristics of effective seatwork apply to homework used for practice. If homework is for students to preview material, students should be taught how. Ideally, when homework is for practice, it is individualized. This may be difficult to do if a class is large. Homework should be of reasonable length and difficulty, and should match student ability to work independently. It should be monitored and an accountability system established to ensure it is done on time. It should be marked, and students should correct mistakes and turn the work in again. If needed, reteaching should occur.

"Effective homework assignments do not just supplement the classroom lesson; they also teach students to be independent learners" (U.S. Department of Education, 1986, p. 42). That is, when homework is used well, students gain experience in "following directions, making judgments and comparisons, raising additional questions for study, and developing responsibility and self-discipline" (p. 42). Stress positive reinforcement. Emphasize what was done well and why.

Homework can have value beyond student achievement. Ideally, parents need to know, in general, what is happening in the classroom, the homework expected, and what they can do to support the learning of their children. Providing homework and emphasizing its benefits can help students develop responsibility for studying outside the classroom. It can extend opportunities for students to expand assignments, let students respond to classroom instruction in individualized ways, prepare students for upcoming classroom activities, and provide opportunities for students to practice what they have learned.

If teachers use homework as an instructional tool, it must be part of what happens in the classroom and not an afterthought to keep students busy at home. Homework, normally, should be addressed first thing, before the day's lesson begins. Also, if homework is to be effective, teachers must assign it based on some objective other than simply on the belief that homework is useful.

PROVIDING FEEDBACK ON SEATWORK AND HOMEWORK

- *Rapid feedback.* Provide feedback as soon as possible, to avoid practice of errors and to avoid impeding learning at subsequent levels.
- *Specific feedback.* Students need to know, specifically, what was done satisfactorily and what is needed to achieve success. "Very Good" with little or no comment is not helpful. What was "good," and what made it so should be said in writing or orally.
- *One-on-one as much as possible.* Get around to each member of the class to personalize feedback and leave the messages, "You are important" and "You can succeed."
- *Match learner readiness.* Try to tailor assignments to accommodate individual needs.
- *Stress positive reinforcement.* Emphasize what was done well and the reason why; for areas needing improvement, help students do "even better."
- *Deferred success—not failure.* Avoid the notion of "failure." Instead, emphasize that students "have not yet succeeded" and encourage them to keep trying.
- *Stress discovery of how to perform correctly.* Encourage students to constantly improve by checking their own work or by getting feedback from peers.
- *Stress process during formative stages.* During the formative stages of learning, stress the "how to" and the "why" instead of putting inordinate emphasis on a correct product.
- *Feedback on total class performance on assignments.* Tell the class how the group did on an assignment. What went well, why, and what needs attention? Accept part of the responsibility, telling them you will do some reteaching to help them help themselves.

ACADEMIC INTEGRITY.   An important consideration for seatwork and homework is *academic integrity.* Increasingly, students are doing seatwork and homework with the aid of computers. The availability of the Internet has increased the possibility of plagiarism. The following guidelines can help.

- Expectations of academic honesty must be made clear to all students.
- Students welcome clear guidelines on integrity in their assignments.
- Guidelines must not be ambiguous or unrealistic.
- Periodically review the guidelines and expectations.
- Deal with and discourage the "everyone does it" perception.
- Assess students' work fairly and promptly.

- Have assignments that are well planned to encourage creative and original work.
- Build preplans into assignments, so students show their intended approach and ideas.
- Ensure effective classroom management and examination security.
- Model integrity and honesty. Do not ignore or trivialize dishonesty.

A CAUTION.   Homework can have a negative effect on family life and worsen the disparity between social classes; it can punish children from families with fewer resources (e.g., owning a computer) or in a nonsupportive home environment (CPSER, 2004). The quality, amount, and timing of homework have frequently come under criticism by parents. Schools need a reasonable, fair homework policy that is clearly communicated to students and parents. Responding to the effects on students of poverty and the effects of nonfunctional family settings is an issue that school staffs need to address.

CASE 8.7 Homework

The Dog Ate It!

Ms. Desai has just finished marking homework assignments. She wants to acknowledge what the class accomplished.

MS. DESAI: Good morning, class. I've marked your homework. Because this is your first homework assignment, I want to say how well you have all done. Samuel, what is our homework policy?

SAMUEL: I can't remember exactly.

MS. DESAI: Well, it's posted on the wall over there. Will you read the first line?

SAMUEL: Homework shall be given out no more than three times a week, and should take no more than one hour each time.

MS. DESAI: How much time did I give you for this assignment?

SAMUEL: You gave us two nights, one night to find modern examples of Greek or Roman myths in magazines and so on, and one night to write our accounts.

MS. DESAI: What did you find, Abdul?

ABDUL: I looked in the Yellow Pages and I found lots of stuff like Midas Mufflers and Ajax Cleaners.

MS. DESAI: Wonderful. And what did I ask the class to write, Maria?

MARIA: We had to write out the story of the myth in a few words, telling how the modern example matched.

MS. DESAI: Did I give you choices?

MARIA: Yes, you said we could do pictures instead of a written write-up or we could paste an example from a magazine.

MS. DESAI: So, did everybody have enough time?

SEAN: I took more than an hour to find examples, but it was kind of fun, so I didn't mind.

MS: DESAI: How about the rest of you . . . enough time? *(Nods and smiles from the class.)* OK. I'm going to pass out the work. Then I'll come around and have a word with each of you while you read the story of Demeter. What's her other name?

MARK: I know, . . . it's "Ceres." I know 'cause it reminds me of cereal.

LINKING PRACTICE TO THEORY

What was your own experience of homework and seatwork in your schooling? Try the approaches suggested in this chapter. To what extent can they apply to your current teaching situation? Did you enjoy discussions when you were a student? Were they effective to your learning? Can discussions play a significant part in your classroom approach?

Summary

Much is known about effective questioning. Normally, good questioning involves a sequence of gaining attention, addressing the question to the whole class, waiting, asking an individual to respond, having the individual respond, and waiting briefly. How you phrase questions makes a difference. Avoid questions and questioning practices that discourage students or that have low diagnostic value. Distribute questions evenly, and take into account learner ability and readiness. Using wait time increases the amount and level of learning. Use more open-ended and higher-level questions. Handle responses sensitively, making effective use of prompts, probes, and redirects. Students should not be afraid to risk answers, and their questions should be encouraged. You can use the data collection instrument in Figure 8.2 for lessons with the target of questioning.

Discussion can be used for four purposes: to review and extend what students have studied for mastery of a subject; to provide an opportunity for students to examine opinions or ideas; to solve a problem or to improve problem-solving capability; and to help develop communication, interpersonal, and group skills.

Teachers can learn techniques to make discussions effective. A particularly effective form of discussion is the talking circle. Students like the guideline that encourages participation *when ready* to contribute. Complex issues can be handled with dignity.

It is useful for teachers to examine interaction among students and between teacher and students. Critical thinking is an important part of engagement. It is enhanced through effective questioning, especially through higher-level questions and the use of wait time.

Seatwork and homework can extend learning time, produce investigative work, and help students become independent learners. Monitoring seatwork is important. Seatwork needs purpose and relevance. It should not be assigned to keep students busy. It should meet individual needs and, when appropriate, involve student choice. Homework can be a way to create positive relationships with parents, informing them of their children's learning. Take care to ensure that your students have the at-home resources to do homework. Both seatwork and homework need prompt feedback.

Activities

QUESTIONING

1. Recall a teacher who made effective use of question and answer. How did this teacher go about questioning? Join four or five peers to agree on principles for effective question and answer.
2. The instructor teaches a brief model lesson (about fifteen minutes) on a topic using questioning that systematically moves through the levels of the cognitive domain of Bloom's taxonomy and using as many of the techniques presented above as possible. Debrief, commenting on the behaviors used and the sequence of questions.
3. Join a subject group of five. Pick a topic that lends itself to question and answer. Compose a series of questions that move students through the levels of Bloom's cognitive domain.
4. On cards, list practices to avoid. In class, discuss why they are ineffective. Then, compare the findings with those stated in the chart.
5. Have a volunteer teach a lesson to the class that involves questions. Have the volunteer practice

good wait time. Discuss the results with the class. Use Figure 8.2.

6. Take a typical lesson from your files. Rewrite the plan, include questions at each level.
7. Research technological software programs that foster thoughtful responses to questions. A good example is the CD, *Sophie's World,* based on the book by Jostein Gaarder (1996), in which a young girl responds to questions on philosophic issues.
8. The summary of the book, *Sophie's World,* states, "One day Sophie comes home from school to find two questions in her mail. 'Who are you?' and 'Where does the world come from?' " Try the questions on young children during your field experience. Share the results.
9. Groups of four play a game that is a variation of "Tic Tac Toe" ("X's and O's") devised by Sadker and Sadker (1979). Two people act as players, the other two as judges. Disputes are settled by the teacher—the appeal court judge. The player who begins announces the cognitive domain level (see

diagram below) at which he or she will attempt to phrase a question. The question is posed. Judges rule on whether the question is at the level proposed. If the answer is correct, the player can enter an X. The next player then attempts to phrase a question after announcing the chosen domain. If this player is successful, an O is entered. There is a winner when a player has a series of three vertical, horizontal, or diagonal correct answers. When the game is over and if there is a winner, the winner wins the right to be a judge and a former judge becomes the other player; the loser continues to play. If the result is a draw, players and judges switch roles.

Tic-Tac-Taxonomy		
Synthesis	Knowledge	Analysis
Analysis	Synthesis	Evaluation
Evaluation	Application	Comprehension

DISCUSSION

1. Small groups explain how you might deal with problem individuals during a whole-group discussion: (a) students who never participate; (b) students who monopolize the conversation; (c) students who begin to argue with each other; (d) "smart Alec" students; and (e) students who play the part of class clowns.
2. Interview your supervising (or other) teacher, asking when and how he or she uses whole-group and small-group discussion.
3. Select a controversial topic, e.g., "Is teaching a science or an art?" (See 7.) Divide each group into three groups: those who support the topic, those who oppose the topic, and those who have mixed feelings. Have each group prepare a defense of

their point of view, listing reasons on a blank transparency. Conduct a discussion. Debrief using Figure 8.5. On the Internet, find some highly recommended discussion group sites for students. Consider the value of such sites for helping young people to discuss.

4. Discuss in class: on the spaceship *Enterprise,* what/who would be the perfect electronic teacher?
5. Design a questionnaire that would be useful to rate a school's technological capability.
6. Discuss, in class, the advantages and disadvantages of guided and open discussions.
7. Select a discussion topic (e.g., teaching as an art versus teaching as a science). Create three groups. One group presents "teaching as an art," one "teaching as a science," and one "teaching as a mix of art and science." Following the third presentation, encourage open discussion on the ideas raised.
8. Divide the class into four groups. Following the guidelines presented in this chapter, each group presents a teacher-led discussion.

SEATWORK AND HOMEWORK

1. Select one of your lessons. Following the guidelines presented in this chapter, add a seatwork assignment.
2. Create pairs. Half the class sets a homework assignment that the other half must do. The next class, in pairs, has the homework "marked" according to the guidelines presented in this chapter.
3. Visit the web site, "Ask Jeeves" (www.ask.com). Rate the value of such a site in terms of helping students ask questions and in terms of homework help.
4. Design homework assignments for your discipline (e.g., English or social studies), requiring students to use electronic sources such as online or CD-ROM encyclopedias. Build in a variety if choices.
5. Many schools now have web sites on which homework is posted. Have groups of five consider the ways in which you as a teacher would use such a site.
6. Have students investigate the question of how a teacher might deal with the problem of plagiarism by students using the Internet?

APPENDIX 8.1   *Questioning: Steps, Prompts, Probes, and Redirects*

PROFESSIONAL TARGET—QUESTIONING STEPS, PROMPTS, PROBES, REDIRECTS

1. Record the steps used: attention of all secured (record an "A"); phrase question ("Q"); wait ("W"); name student ("N"); student responds ("R").
2. Enter the number of seconds of wait time allowed after question is asked.
3. Enter a check mark if a prompt, probe, or a redirect is used.

Question Number	Steps Followed (e.g., of correct steps: A, Q, W, N, R).	No. of Seconds of Wait Time	Prompt Used	Probe Used	Redirect Used
1.					
2.					
3.					
4.					
5.					
6.					
7.					
8.					
9.					
10.					
11.					
12					
13.					
14.					

APPENDIX 8.2   *Question Patterns Target*

PROFESSIONAL TARGET—QUESTIONING PATTERNS

Please record the question asked (or the substance of it). Later, (a) classify questions as: knowledge: facts or information, (enter a "K"); comprehension ("C"); application ("Ap"); analysis ("An"); synthesis ("S"); or, evaluation ("E"); (b) decide whether the question was clear, repeated, "yes–no," run-on, leading, blanket; or, (c) classify questions as convergent (single correct answer expected), divergent (unexpected or differing from the standard answer) or evaluative (seeking significance or worth).

No.	Question	Level
1.		
2.		
3.		
4.		
5.		
6.		
8.		
9.		
10.		
11.		
12.		
13.		
14.		

Analysis of questioning patterns (by student teacher or teacher):

APPENDIX 8.3

PROFESSIONAL TARGET—DISCUSSION

Record what was said and done by the teacher and the reaction of students.

Discussion Skill	Observations

A. Focusing on topic
  Way topic was introduced
  Establishment of aims
  Restating of aims
  Irrelevancies redirected?
  Stage summaries emerge?
  Dealing with off-task behavior

B. Clarification of answers
  Paraphrasing
  Summarizing
  Probing
  Elaborating
  Analyzing

C. Promoting participation
  Use of students' ideas
  Use of silence
  Challenging
  Key questions
  Providing information

D. Varying interaction
  Setting of ground rules
  Use of eye contact
  Encouraging participation/interaction
  Seeking agreements

E. Summarizing
  Evaluation of discussion effectiveness
  Proposal(s) for follow-up

F. Other teacher interventions/actions
  to ensure all are attending

9 Teaching Concepts

The Nature of Concepts

Understanding Concepts

From the womb to the tomb, concepts provide meaning and are vital to the way we organize and structure our world. It would be impossible to think about anything without concepts. Concepts help us live and learn and see things in generalized patterns. In this chapter, we look at the kinds of concepts, their importance to learning and personal understanding, and the nature of attributes, prototypes, and exemplars. The value of concept mapping in giving meaning and structure, and the need to consider learner diversity and readiness, are examined.

WHAT IS A CONCEPT?   If we had to, we could tell somebody what concrete objects such as desks, hats, or cups are. We could give understandable definitions of ideas such as friendship, or democracy and dictatorship. We likely could define events such as wars and conferences or classes of people such as Caucasians or Aboriginals. Each is a concept. These words are labels under which we categorize objects, ideas, events, or people—they are *concepts*.

Have you ever said, "I haven't any concept of what you're talking about?" or "Can you conceptualize my tripping over the out-of-bounds line?" Popular usage of the term *concept* is different from pedagogical usage. In education, a concept is a category or set of objects, conditions, events, or processes, that can be grouped together based on similarities and represented by a word or other symbol or image. When we encounter something—for example, a desk—we recognize it because of its key characteristics, or attributes, though that particular desk may differ in some ways from other desks we have seen. We know it is something to sit at while we attend school, study, read, or write. The particular color, height, or material it is made of is not important for us to recognize it is a desk. When we say, "Somebody is sitting in my desk," the person to whom we are speaking knows what

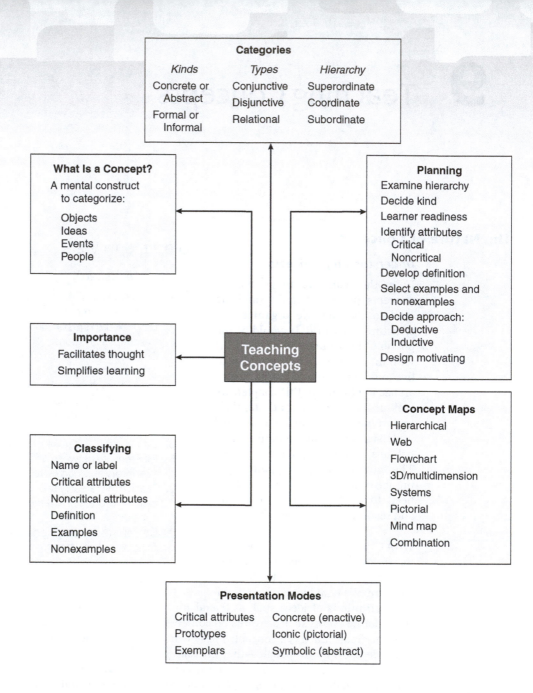

a desk is. This aids communication. Concepts have labels or formal or informal definitions represented by a word, symbol, or mental picture.

IMPORTANCE OF CONCEPTS.   Concepts help us cope with living and learning. They are mental constructs or images that simplify our learning efforts and facilitate thought and communication (Martorella, 1986, p. 183). Concepts are essential to comprehension, promote recall, are functional shortcuts to communication, and aid the transfer of learning.

We are inundated by countless bits of information and knowledge in our personal worlds. Suppose every individual chair had a separate name (or category), and the word *chair* did not exist. How could we learn and remember the name of every single chair we encounter? How could we communicate efficiently without concept names? When we tell someone to "take a chair," he or she knows what we are talking about. We do not have to name each object in the room that can be used for sitting and provide the option of selecting and sitting on one. Besides, would that person have had experiences with, and the same label for, each individual object? Further, communication breaks down when two people have different understandings of a concept, or when one person does not have a concept that is essential to a conversation. Mutual knowledge of the same concepts is essential for efficient communication. For example, the "light" might "go on" for you when somebody from Paris says *chaise* and you catch on that he means the concept of *chair*. Thought and learning are aided immeasurably by grouping, or organizing, all chairs under the same label—*chair*. After all, they all have the same essential characteristics. We need societally accepted word meanings and labels for things and beings. Concepts are basic building blocks for thinking, higher-level thinking in particular.

Generalizations are based on concepts expressed in a relationship, but they are more complicated than their component concepts. Generalizations are rules, regulations, principles, laws, conclusions, inferences, axioms, proverbs, mottoes, propositions, and hypotheses. They are relationships of broad applicability; for example, "A stitch in time saves nine" is a generalization composed of several concepts (stitch, time, saves, nine), meaning it is more efficient to take time do it now, or right, and so to save the time needed for undoing or redoing—it is much easier to do it right the first time. It is important that students understand the component concepts of generalizations. For instance, in the rule, "Water freezes at 32° Fahrenheit," students must understand the concepts water, freezes, degrees, and Fahrenheit, or they will not understand the generalization and learning is reduced to rote memorization. True learning requires making connections between concepts.

CONCEPTS AS PERSONAL UNDERSTANDINGS. Concepts are *personal* understandings of a symbol, an individual's unique way of acquiring meaning from experience. Each person has a history with concepts and will have different experiences with concepts. How often has somebody asked you to clarify, or define, what you meant when you used a word or expression? How often have you had a misunderstanding or argument, because a word had a particular meaning to you but a different one for the other person?

A four-month-old baby has a limited range of functional concepts and responds to a limited number of "words." When children grow older and begin to speak, they acquire many verbal labels for concepts that, initially, are based on one or a few instances. At first, the word *chair* may be used by a child for a single chair, perhaps a highchair. Slowly, the child says and understands *chair* for other objects used for sitting. As the child grows older, many other objects are labeled *chair*: an easy chair, a rocking chair, a reclining chair, and so on. As an adult, the term *chair* will likely extend to things such as to "chair a meeting," and to "chairperson."

Concepts develop slowly from facts and information, moving from specifics to abstractions. They are constantly open to change through experience and insights, and they develop at different rates for different people. They have somewhat different meanings for different people and mean different things as new experience is gained.

TCP—TEACHING CONCEPTS

Provides effective teaching of concepts and explanations

Prior analysis; students learn critical and noncritical attributes and appropriate definitions; effective examples and nonexamples and understanding extended over time; effective selection of the number and sequence; concepts presented in a lesson or unit interrelated: appropriate choice and use of inductive and deductive approaches.

No prior analysis; definitions often "muddied" with noncritical attributes; definitions presented without emphasis on understanding; relationships not identified; poor selection of examples and absence of nonexamples; approach always deductive.

Kinds of Concepts

Concepts can be categorized in several ways, as shown in Figure 9.1. Some are harder to learn than others because of learner background or developmental level and because it is easier to find examples or prototypes for some, and different kinds of concepts may require different teaching approaches. We can examine the kinds of concepts, such as concrete and abstract concepts, and whether concepts are acquired in formal or informal contexts. We can distinguish different types of concepts and we can examine how concepts relate to each other in a hierarchy. Figure 9.2 shows an example analysis of a concept.

CONCRETE/ABSTRACT.   *Concrete* concepts (e.g., wheels, reptiles, and levers) can be perceived through the five senses. *Abstract* concepts (e.g., democracy, beauty, and truth) are concepts that are only acquired indirectly or through inference.

Abstract concepts are harder to learn than concrete concepts. Different teaching approaches may need to be used. For example, analogies (comparisons) may be used to teach abstract concepts such as *nationalism*. Students are told that the concept *nationalism* is somewhat like the concept *family*—families are groupings of people that have common at-

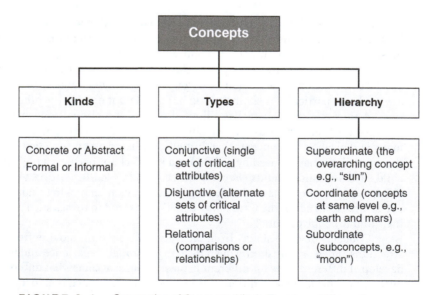

FIGURE 9.1   *Categories of Concepts: Kinds, Types, and Hierarchy*

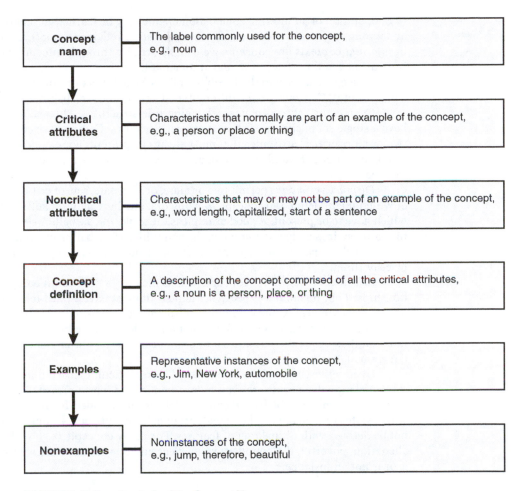

Concept name	The label commonly used for the concept, e.g., noun
Critical attributes	Characteristics that normally are part of an example of the concept, e.g., a person *or* place *or* thing
Noncritical attributes	Characteristics that may or may not be part of an example of the concept, e.g., word length, capitalized, start of a sentence
Concept definition	A description of the concept comprised of all the critical attributes, e.g., a noun is a person, place, or thing
Examples	Representative instances of the concept, e.g., Jim, New York, automobile
Nonexamples	Noninstances of the concept, e.g., jump, therefore, beautiful

FIGURE 9.2   *Analysis of the Concept* Noun

tributes. Some of the critical attributes of family are also nationalism attributes. Then, another analogy can be used, and still another, pulling out attributes of nationalism. This is done until students can distinguish between good analogies and inappropriate analogies (a streetcar full of people is not an example of nationalism) and grasp the definition of nationalism. Although some concepts are learned informally and others are learned formally, many concepts are learned through a combination of formal and informal experiences—for example, truth, justice, morality, or "good music."

Another approach is to consider examples of the behavior of people who are nationalistic and, from this, infer the meaning of nationalism. An alternate way to teach abstract concepts is to provide instances (and noninstances) of acts and consequences (or before and after, or cause and effect). Attributes are inferred and definitions derived. This approach could be used for concepts such as pollution, waste, or war.

FORMAL/INFORMAL.   Concepts acquired in *formal* contexts are acquired through some form of systematic instruction in, for instance, schools, job training, or from parents (e.g., operation of an internal combustion engine may be learned in school; rules of right and wrong may be learned in Sunday school or other religious school). Concepts acquired in *informal* contexts are concepts we usually acquire through informal life experiences (e.g., using a radio, refrigerator, and automobile).

Concepts can vary in the flexibility of rule structures or in the relationships of critical attributes. Concepts can be differentiated as conjunctive, disjunctive, or relational.

Conjunctive concepts have unchanging rule structures. Phrased another way, they have a single set of characteristics or critical attributes. Conjunctive concepts must have two or more critical attributes that must always be present. For example, a *lake* is always a body of water surrounded by land, and a *square* is always a quadrilateral with all four sides equal.

Disjunctive concepts permit two or more, or alternate, sets of critical attributes, each of which might define the concept, *and* any one attribute alone is sufficient, *or* not all of which have to be present. A good example is the strike in baseball. A strike is called when the batter swings and misses *or* when the batter hits a foul ball *or* when the umpire judges that the ball has passed through the strike zone (Martorella, 1986). A noun is a person *or* place *or* thing.

Relational concepts are concepts whose meanings depend on comparisons or relationships. They do not have special attributes but must have a fixed relationship between or among attributes. A line cannot be called parallel *unless* there is another line to compare it to (Martorella, 1986); a man is not an uncle *unless* he has a nephew; a woman is not a mother *unless* she has at least one son or daughter. Other examples are pollution, large, small, heavy, time, ugly, and rapid.

Disjunctive concepts are complex and more difficult to learn than conjunctive concepts. Relational concepts are even more complex and hard to learn. Disjunctive and relational concepts do not fit the concept definition provided for conjunctive concepts, which states that there must be a single set of defining attributes. Some concepts just cannot be defined with a single set of features. For many concepts (e.g., social class, justice, alienation, poverty), the boundary is not clear and one cannot state with certainty what is or is not an instance.

RELATIONSHIPS TO OTHER CONCEPTS AND HIERARCHIES.   Learners should be aware of how the concepts they are learning are related to other concepts. A *hierarchy* of related concepts can be developed that can be helpful in planning and delivering instruction. Consider the, albeit incomplete, hierarchy of minerals in Figure 9.3.

Components of a hierarchy can be described in terms of superordinate, coordinate, and subordinate concepts. A *superordinate concept* in the example in Figure 9.3 is minerals. All the other concepts are part of this generic concept. Similarly, metals are superordinate to rare, common, and alloy; rare is superordinate to gold, platinum, and silver; and so on. *Coordinate concepts* are coordinate to one another: metals and stones; rare, common, and alloy metals; rare and precious stones; gold, platinum, and silver rare metals; and so on. Coordinate concepts share common critical attributes, but have to be differentiated from one another—each shares the critical attributes of the concepts to which it is coordinate, but also has one or more unique critical attributes. *Subordinate concepts* explain a hierarchy. Metals and stones are subordinate to minerals; rare, common, and alloy are subordinate to metals; gold, platinum, and silver are subordinate to rare metals; and so on. Subordinate concepts share common critical attributes and have one or more unique critical attributes.

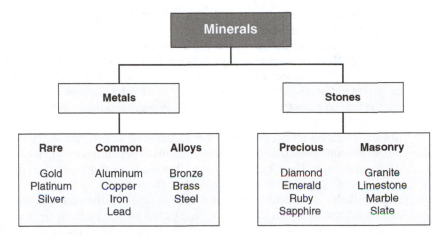

FIGURE 9.3 *Hierarchy of Minerals*

Not all concepts lend themselves easily to placement in a hierarchy. There are unclear cases. To illustrate, is a tomato a fruit or a vegetable? For many concepts, it is difficult to identify and articulate critical attributes. Concept analysis is still useful, however, whether we use the traditional attribute approach, the prototype approach, or a combination.

Teaching concepts so they make sense to learners means taking hierarchies into account. Instruction should be in a logical sequence, recognizing and taking advantage of groupings and relationships (vertical or horizontal). An advance organizer (e.g., a chart or table depicting the key ideas and relationships in a unit) may be presented representing the hierarchy of concepts to be learned. This helps, particularly when direct instruction is being used. Presenting concepts that are part of a hierarchy in a hit-and-miss fashion makes little sense. Usually, an advance organizer should be used when teaching deductively, and a postorganizer may work well when teaching inductively. As each concept is introduced, its place in the organization can be pointed out, and, finally a postorganizer should be used.

Learning Concepts

ATTRIBUTES AND PROTOTYPES OR EXEMPLARS.   As stated earlier, we can recognize a concept because of its key characteristics or critical attributes. Concepts such as *hat, envelope,* or *tree* each have key attributes. In a class discussion of the concept *tree,* students would have little trouble giving example attributes such as having leaves or being a living thing. Teaching of concepts through critical attributes is discussed below.

Some authorities prefer to stress prototypes (sometimes called *exemplars*) of concepts rather than critical attributes. *Prototypes* are the best representatives of a category. For instance, cats and dogs are prototypes of mammals and, even though a whale is also a mammal, it is not a prototype. Kauchak and Eggen (2003, p. 258), Woolfolk (2004, p. 276), and as far back as Medin and Smith (1984) describe the prototype approach, which is based on the belief that students learn concepts by forming mental prototypes after being exposed to *best examples.* Those who emphasize the prototype approach point out that, particularly for more complex concepts, it is difficult to identify clear and unchanging attributes. They believe attributes may only be probable of class members and cannot be stated on an all-or-none basis; and better examples of a concept have more characteristics than poorer examples.

Exemplars, say Sternberg and Williams (2002), are "highly typical instances" of a concept (p. 312). Some examples, says Ashcraft (2002), are better examples of concepts than others. A student's memories, for example, of specific dogs provide the basis for recognizing examples not previously seen. The pet dogs in a student's town may be the exemplars that are the basis for categorizing other animals as dogs seen in another town or on TV.

McKinney, Gilmore, Peddicord, and McCallum (1987) compared the traditional approach (concepts taught through critical attributes) and the prototype approach (concepts taught through presentation of best examples). They found no difference in achievement between groups. They found, however, that students taught by the critical attribute approach could generate more examples than those taught by the prototype approach. You should likely not take an either–or stance in favor of one approach or the other. In any case, it is important that the first examples presented to learners be "pure" or clear representatives of the concept to be learned; and selection of examples should be based on familiarity to learners. A rule might be to present examples in the order of "pure to obscure." In other words, they should be prototypes that learners know about. Less prototypical examples should not be introduced until learners have a good understanding of the critical attributes of the prototype or exemplar. For example, when teaching about "birds," begin with birds such as robins, which students have seen, before introducing birds such as ostriches, which do not fly, or penguins, which do not fly but do swim.

Two approaches to teaching concepts are the *deductive* and the *inductive* approaches. Some teachers prefer the deductive approach (providing the definition, and then listing attributes), but Joyce, Weil, and Calhoun (2004, pp. 62–64) argue that this runs counter to much current practice. They prefer the inductive approach, what they and some others call *concept attainment*. This involves a sequence of presenting students with data in sets of items (both positive and negative exemplars), students comparing these exemplars, students developing hypotheses about the nature of a category, having them identify positive exemplars, perhaps having students provide examples, students sharing hypotheses and describing how their understanding developed, having the teacher supply the technical label of the concept, and finally, having students search for more items of the class of concept.

Helping learners acquire concepts is one of the greatest challenges teachers face, whether in kindergarten or graduate school. There is no substitute for careful planning and sensitive, methodical instruction. If you plan and teach effectively, learners can master concepts. Mastery involves the ability to tell whether something is or is not an example of a concept and the ability to find or create an example of a concept and tell why it is an example. It includes the ability to modify nonexamples to make them examples and justify the changes made, and to use a concept name, or label, correctly and justify the choice through critical attributes.

A good coach devises a "game plan" and helps team members acquire the knowledge and skills needed to execute the plan. If the coach is to have an effective game plan executed well, he or she must have a thorough knowledge of the concepts and skills involved. This knowledge is used when the coach does the planning needed before instruction and practice occurs. Careful planning must precede effective and efficient concept instruction and learning. "Winging it" normally just does not work. A Concept Analysis Form that may be helpful is shown in Appendix 9.1. A *Ten Step Model* for planning to teach a concept is discussed below. It is *not* intended to be rigidly linear and sequential for either planning or teaching concepts.

Connecting Concepts through Concept Maps

Where does a concept being learned fit into the scheme of things? The ability to understand, recall, and use a concept is enhanced when students can see visually how a concept is related to other concepts as a hierarchy or ideas that are related. Concepts can be mapped as a hierarchy of relationships. A visualization of a *concept map* is given in Figure 9.4.

Students' understanding of a concept is not complete unless it is linked to other related concepts (Kauchak & Eggen, 2003; Hall, Hall, & Saling, 1999). It is easier for students to make meaning of what is being taught when concept maps are presented or created. When concept maps are used, relationships between concepts are depicted visually, either as a graph presented by the teacher, or as one designed by students themselves. Concept maps can be used in several ways. By constructing a map you become more aware of the key concepts and their relationship. Also, you will not be as likely to leave out or misinterpret some concepts. You become more sensitive to how concepts can best be presented. Concepts can be used as an advance organizer and referred to as the lesson or unit progresses. This helps students get "the bigger picture," notice the relationships between individual concepts, and develop a better understanding of the definitions of individual concepts. A concept map can also be used at the end of a lesson or unit to review and consolidate learning. Alternatively, you can have students construct concept maps, thereby allowing them to become active learners and attain deeper personal meaning. A further possibility is for you, as an assessment strategy, to have students make concept maps. This makes assessment more meaningful and authentic.

Figure 9.4 is a concept map showing the hierarchy of bodies in our solar system. By viewing the parts of the solar system as a hierarchy, students can see the connections between concepts within the hierarchy. This enhances learning. In the map of the solar system, concepts are named. Later in the chapter a complete lesson is built around the concept of a solar system. Novak and Gowin (1984) show a concept map made by a student on "water" (Figure 9.5). In this concept map, linking words are used to make relationships obvious.

Concept maps come in a variety of formats, including hierarchical, web or spider, flowchart, systems, and 3D or multidimensional (Table 9.1). Regardless of background, it

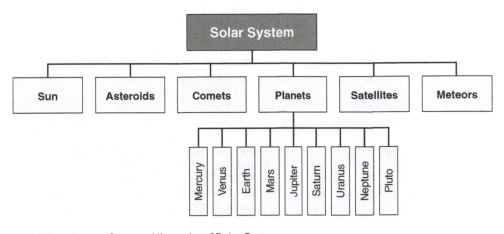

FIGURE 9.4   *Concept Hierarchy of* Solar System

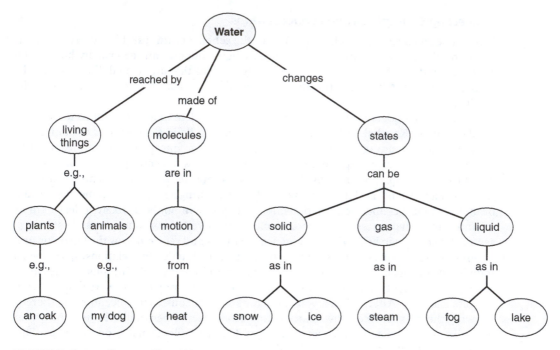

FIGURE 9.5   *Concept Map: Water*

Source: Based on ideas from Novak, 1991, and Novak & Gowin, 1984, p. 16.

is always desirable to have the "real things" or at least pictures available for handling or viewing. Even when learners are mature, there still are times when learners lack readiness and enactive or iconic examples should be used. Abstract concepts, of course, are learned indirectly through the senses and inference. For these, instruction may need to be heavily verbal, or symbolic, as in, for example, algebra or sentence structure.

TABLE 9.1   *Concept Map Formats*

Hierarchical	Information presented in order of importance, with the most important information on top.
Web or spider	Information organized with the central theme in the middle and subthemes arranged around the center.
Flowchart	Information or steps organized in a linear way.
3D or multidimensional	Information too complicated to be shown in two dimensions, so three dimensions are used.
Systems	Like a flowchart, information organized in parts, one part flowing to the next, each with an input, process, and output. The output for one becomes the input for the next part.
Pictorial	Information presented as pictures, landscapes, or symbols. Also, word ideas can be arranged in the shape of a tree, a wheel, a snake, or other design.

Diversity: Recognizing Learner Background

When concepts are introduced, consideration must be given to the previous experiences and developmental levels of learners. The medium through which concepts are presented (concrete, pictorial, or symbolic) should depend on learner developmental level. A teacher could largely talk about a concept, but learners may not have the necessary linguistic comprehension to benefit. The examples presented should, in this case, be concrete or hands-on. At the next level, learners may have had day-to-day experience with the examples, but it may be desirable to provide visual representations of the concept—for example, pictures. At still another level, it may be sufficient to use verbal or other symbols. Furthermore, learners differ in preferred learning style or cultural background (e.g., a student who recently arrived from Thailand may have no idea of how hockey is played). Abstract concepts, of course, are learned indirectly through the senses and inference. For these, instruction may need to be heavily verbal, or symbolic, as in, for example, algebra or sentence structure. Metaphors and analogies may not be familiar to all learners, so teachers need to consider the background of students in their classes. It now is more common for teachers to stress connections with prior knowledge. Bulgren, Deshler, Schumaker, and Lenz (2000) call this *analogical instruction.*

Learner Readiness: Modes of Presentation

The examples used, defining attributes noted, and definitions used should vary with the developmental level of learners. The concept *plant* is introduced early in a child's schooling and returned to many times with increasing degrees of complexity as the child progresses through the school grades, and with even more complexity with college study of the concept. The first grappling with a concept is at a simplified level. With successive reintroductions, the examples or exemplars (prototypes) used become more complex, the defining attributes more detailed and varied, the definition more encompassing and complex, and the hierarchy to which the concept belongs becomes more specific and inclusive. That is, there is a vast difference between the definitions studied and the way they are studied by a grade 3 student in a science class and a graduate student in biology. Graduate students are at an advanced level at which discussion can take place about what may or may not be critical attributes.

A useful and classic way to think about presentation mode is *Dale's Cone of Experience* (Figure 9.6), which shows the progression from direct, first-hand participation to pictorial representation and on to purely abstract symbolic expression (Wiman & Mierhenry, 1969). The Cone of Experience is similar to Bruner's (1960) three major modes of learning (enactive—doing; iconic—seeing, observing; and symbolic—reading, hearing).

Concepts and Teaching Approaches

So far we have discussed the nature of concepts. We now look at some practical teaching approaches. These include doing a concept analysis, examining a specific lesson model, teaching concepts through both deductive and inductive approaches, and a suggested teaching cycle.

Planning Guide for Analysis of Concepts

Concept learning involves the skill of *classifying*—putting things into a class and then being able to recognize members of that class. It involves ability to list or, when presented,

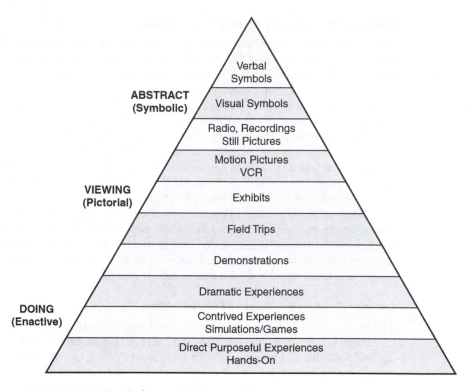

FIGURE 9.6   *Dale's Cone of Experience*
Source: Based on the research of Edgar Dale, 1969.

recognize examples of a concept when asked. When teaching concepts, you need four components: (1) the name of the concept; (2) examples and nonexamples; (3) relevant and irrelevant attributes, and (4) a definition. Joyce et al. (2004) present a concept attainment model. In this approach there are two phases. In phase one, the concept is identified and the teacher presents examples; students compare attributes in positive and negative examples, generate and test examples, and state a definition. In phase two, the teacher confirms hypotheses, names the concept, and restates definitions; the students generate additional examples (p. 72). You can play a major role in helping learners through these operations by analyzing the concepts to be learned before they are taught. As a first step, when planning to teach a concept you can identify:

- Names or labels
- Critical attributes (or characteristics)
- Noncritical attributes
- Definitions of concepts to be learned
- Examples
- Nonexamples

Before teaching a concept, it is advisable to do a concept analysis. The format illustrated in Appendix 9.1 may be used to help you analyze concepts. While the sequence of analysis can be done as illustrated, planning need not be linear. Let us examine each aspect.

CONCEPT NAME.   Most concepts can be named. The name or label of a concept is the symbol under which all instances of that concept are grouped or categorized. We use names to think and to communicate concepts such as *wheel, lake,* or *reptile* (we also use words to communicate concepts such as *democracy* or *love*).

CRITICAL ATTRIBUTES.   We should be able to identify concepts rapidly and easily. This can be done based on their key common characteristics—the critical (nonvarying) attributes. Consider these examples:

Concept name	Critical attributes
wheel	circular frame; hard material; can turn on an axle
lake	large; body of water; surrounded by land
reptile	cold-blooded; egg-laying; air-breathing; moves on belly or on small short legs; vertebrate; scales or bony plates

NONCRITICAL ATTRIBUTES.   Much of the confusion when students try to learn concepts occurs because of noncritical attributes (which can vary) that can be associated with a concept. For example, a young child may first associate the word *chair* with the yellow chairs in the kitchen. All chairs, then, must look like those yellow kitchen chairs. Chairs in the living room, because they are a different color and shape, are not yet *chairs*. The child has not learned that color and shape are noncritical attributes of *chair*. Some noncritical attributes are particularly befuddling. For example, a child may believe that all birds fly, but there are birds that cannot fly. Flying is a noncritical attribute of the concept *bird*. Noncritical attributes are attributes found in some, but not all, members of a class. Consider the following:

Concept name	Noncritical attributes
wheel	color; size; whether or not it has spokes
lake	depth; size; location; vegetation
reptile	size; coloration; length of tail; habitat

CONCEPT DEFINITION.   Concept definitions contain all the essential or critical attributes and express the relationship of these attributes to each other. Consider these examples:

Concept name	Definition
wheel	a circular frame of hard material capable of turning on an axle
lake	a large body of water surrounded by land
reptile	an air-breathing vertebrate that moves on its belly or on small short legs, and is covered with scales or bony plates

CONCEPT EXAMPLES AND NONEXAMPLES.   Simply defining a concept is not sufficient. It is essential that we have experience with both examples and nonexamples of concepts (exceptions will be discussed later). Gold is an example of a rare metal and a nonexample of an alloy; and a diamond is an example of a precious stone and a nonexample of a common metal. Examples are *positive instances* of a concept. Nonexamples are *negative instances* of a concept. Examples and nonexamples of some common concepts are

Concept name	Examples	Nonexamples
wheel	wagon wheel; car wheel; game show wheel	pie; frisbee; Chinese checkers board
lake	Lake Superior, Windemere Lake, and Lac LaRonge	Amazon River, Pacific Ocean, and Juan de Fuca Strait
reptile	snake, lizard, alligator	beaver, seal, and duck

There are exceptions to the example approach to teaching concepts. Sometimes it may not be possible to consider examples. For example, have you ever observed an atom (even with a microscope)? An amp, ohm, or erg? Nationalism? An angel? Models and diagrams are often used to teach these, analogies might be used, or act-and-consequence instances might be used. Examples are only such if they are part of the learners' backgrounds.

USING EXAMPLES AND NONEXAMPLES.   When you teach a concept, we recommend that you start with a few well-chosen familiar examples (four or five are sufficient), emphasizing the defining attributes. Learning complicated concepts and being able to generalize to recognize new instances requires a larger number of examples; younger or less able learners require even more examples. Then, nonexamples should be presented, discovering why they are not examples. Following this, learners can practice differentiating between examples and nonexamples, giving reasons for their selections. Examples are more effective when they differ widely in a number of noncritical attributes—for example, plants can be of different sizes, shapes, and colors—and nonexamples are more effective when they exhibit few critical attributes—for example, a plant is alive, but so are the nonexamples rabbits and trout. Woolfolk (2004, p. 279) says that nonexamples should be very close to the concept but miss by one or just a few critical attributes (e.g., a circle-like line that is not completely closed is a nonexample of a circle, or a drinking-glass-like object that does not have a bottom is a nonexample of a drinking glass. This, she feels, should be done to avoid *overgeneralization*. Perhaps the truth is that, initially, nonexamples should have few critical attributes, and when students have a grasp of the definition, nonexamples that differ only on one or a few critical attributes should be introduced. Begin by presenting very pure and common examples before moving to the more obscure. *Undergeneralization* should be avoided. For example, learners should realize that the concept *mammals* includes whales and dolphins. These kinds of examples should not be introduced until students have had experience with pure instances (or prototypes) of the concept.

Concepts and Textbooks

A serious weakness in some textbooks is that the authors too frequently provide a definition of a concept, provide an explanation, and then support the explanation with only one example or too few examples. Often, a key defining attribute is underemphasized or even missed entirely. The problem is compounded by definitions that do not include all the critical attributes, definitions that do not clearly state the relationships of attributes, or definitions that are too sophisticated for the learner level. What often is missing is careful prior concept analysis. Small wonder students have difficulty and that learning then is reduced to a kind of rote search for contextual clues.

The message is, do not unduly (or undeservedly) rely on textbooks. They are teaching aids, not "the course." Do an analysis, yourself, of the concepts students are to learn.

An Example Approach

TEACHING THE CONCEPT *SOLAR SYSTEM.* See the *Ten Step Model* in Figure 9.7.

1. *Examine the concept hierarchy.* Emerging research has found that concepts "typically are not learned in isolation" but are assimilated into knowledge organized into networks (Good & Brophy, 1995, p. 251). Concepts are part of a hierarchy that can provide important information that should be used to control the sequence in which the component concepts

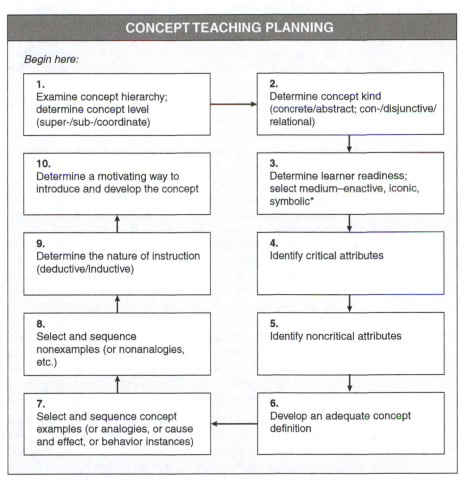

CONCEPT TEACHING PLANNING

Begin here:

1.
Examine concept hierarchy; determine concept level (super-/sub-/coordinate)

2.
Determine concept kind (concrete/abstract; con-/disjunctive/relational)

10.
Determine a motivating way to introduce and develop the concept

3.
Determine learner readiness; select medium–enactive, iconic, symbolic*

9.
Determine the nature of instruction (deductive/inductive)

4.
Identify critical attributes

8.
Select and sequence nonexamples (or nonanalogies, etc.)

5.
Identify noncritical attributes

7.
Select and sequence concept examples (or analogies, or cause and effect, or behavior instances)

6.
Develop an adequate concept definition

*In step 3, *enactive* refers to the use of hands-on learning, *iconic* refers to learning through the use of images such as pictures, models, diagrams, and drawings, and *symbolic* involves learning through, for example, words, numbers, or codes.

FIGURE 9.7 *Ten Step Model for Teaching a Concept*

are presented. Determine the place in the hierarchy the concept occupies. Assume that a teacher is about to begin an astronomy unit in science on the solar system, and consider the partial hierarchy in Figure 9.4 shown earlier.

The concepts *sun, asteroid, comet, planet, satellite,* and *meteors* are subordinate to the superordinate concept *solar system.* The concept *planets,* however, is superordinate to the concepts *Mercury, Mars, Pluto, Earth, Venus, Uranus, Neptune, Saturn,* and *Jupiter.* These nine planets, therefore, are subordinate to the concept *planets.* Though they have an identity and unique attributes, they also are coordinate concepts because they have common critical attributes.

A likely first step is to prepare a concept hierarchy (see Figure 9.4). This can be an advance organizer and part of the set for a unit. The complexity of the hierarchy should depend on the previous experience and age of the learners. A sequencing decision has to be made. What will help learners understand and recall the concepts in the hierarchy and the relationship of these concepts to each other? In what order should the concepts be introduced? Proceed from the top and work down? Vice versa? Probably during the development of the unit, coordinate concepts should be introduced and then presented individually. If the coordinate concepts of the nine planets are being treated, in what order should they be presented? Smallest to largest? Vice versa? Most to least familiar? Closeness to sun? Other?

2. *Decide the kind of concept.* Once a concept has been selected from the hierarchy, a decision has to be made about the kind of concept, whether concrete or abstract, or conjunctive, disjunctive, or relational.

- Is it a concrete concept (one that can be perceived through the five senses), or is it an abstract concept (one that can only be acquired indirectly or through inference)? A rabbit, as an example of a mammal, can be observed and is a concrete concept; socialism is an example of an abstract concept. Specific planets can have both concrete and abstract attributes. If the concept is the planet Venus, it can be observed without a telescope, but Pluto is so distant and small, the technology needed to observe it is normally not available. The concept Venus is less abstract than Pluto, because Venus can be viewed more readily.

- Is it a conjunctive concept (one with an unchanging rule structure or single set of critical attributes), or a disjunctive concept (one that permits two or more, or alternative, sets of critical attributes—one attribute alone may be enough or not all the attributes need to be present), or a relational concept (one whose meaning depends on comparison or a relationship)? The concrete concept of the metal *copper* is a conjunctive concept. The abstract concept *citizen* is a disjunctive concept (one can be a citizen of a country *or* a city *or* a state or province, and one can be born a citizen *or* become one after immigrating). The concept *moon* (a satellite) is a relational concept because each moon has a relationship to, or must circle, a specific planet.

3. *Decide learner readiness.* What background, previous experience, do learners have with the concept and the hierarchy to which it belongs? Some concepts (and their hierarchy) are presented to learners several times, with increasing complexity, during schooling. How old are the learners? What are their developmental levels? Slow or fast? Preferred learning styles? The kind of concept to be learned should influence the medium chosen to teach it.

If learners are young or "slow," presentation should, as much as possible, be at the enactive (hands-on or concrete), or possibly at the iconic, level (pictures, diagrams, models). If the concept is abstract and good analogies are hard to find, the presentation may need to be largely symbolic (words or other symbols). A rule of thumb is that it is often appropriate to support symbolic presentations with "the real thing" or visuals—at least at the introductory stages. Readiness influences: (1) the kinds and number of examples that should be used; (2) the specificity and complexity of the concept definition to be learned; and (3) the pacing and number of repetitions (practices) needed for mastery.

The first thing you may have to do is clear up misconceptions that can impede the use of a term in the subject being studied. The popular use of the term *concept* is different from a professional teacher's use of that term. For example, the popular use of the word *credit* is different from that of an accountant. The accounting instructor must point out (and periodically reinforce) the difference.

4. *Identify critical attributes.* The key common characteristics of the concept must be identified. These are the defining, or critical attributes, sometimes called "nonvariable" attributes. *Large, body of water,* and *surrounded by land* are critical attributes of the concept *lake.* You can use several sources to begin to decide what these attributes are, and how they can be presented. Two common sources are a dictionary and the textbook for the course. An important caution is that these are just starting points! The critical attributes identified as part of the concept definition or description may not be complete and/or may be misleading or at an inappropriate level for the class. In other words, because it is in the dictionary or textbook is no assurance the information is accurate, complete, or appropriate.

Let us examine an example to find critical attributes. Imagine a science text stating, "Comets are balls of ice and dust that orbit around the sun, but usually have elongated, elliptical orbits." This definition reveals that two attributes ("balls of ice and dust" and "orbit around the sun") are critical. Some confusion could be caused because the textbook definition states the orbit is usually elongated and elliptical; therefore, you need to decide whether to include this in the definition used by students.

5. *Identify noncritical attributes.* The next step is to find the characteristics that may be, but not need be, part of a given instance of the concept to be learned—the noncritical attributes. These attributes are normally not needed to define the concept. Including them in the definition can be confusing and interfere with learning and transfer. For example, the size of a triangle is a noncritical attribute and has no bearing on whether a given figure is or is not a triangle. The ring around the planet Saturn is a noncritical attribute of planet. A comet does not have to have an orbit that is elongated and elliptical—though that is the usual shape. Clearly identifying noncritical attributes helps ensure that learners will understand the concept.

6. *Develop an adequate concept definition.* Once you have clearly identified critical and noncritical attributes, select or compose a suitable definition. The definition must include the critical attributes and the relationship of attributes to each other. Including noncritical attributes most often provides a "muddy" definition that is hard to understand. A lake is a large body of water that is surrounded by land. The attributes—all must be present—are "large" *and* "body of water" *and* "surrounded by land." A comet, in the definition provided above, is a "ball of ice and dust" that [*and*] "orbits around the sun," but [*and*] "usually has an elongated and elliptical orbit."

7. *Select and sequence concept examples.* Suitable examples must be selected and sequenced if learners are to understand a concept. Good examples, presented in the sequence of obvious to less obvious, help learners discover critical attributes, and help

prevent undergeneralization. Examples must be sequenced. The first example should be "pure"—a "best example" (prototype or exemplar) of the concept and contain few non-critical attributes. If possible, at least three to five examples should be given. Young learners, or slow learners, may need additional examples. You point out—better still, learners discover—the critical attributes of the concept from the examples presented. If, for example, the topic under study is the planets in our solar system, begin with the better-known planets Venus, Earth, Saturn, and Mars and defer introducing the planet Pluto.

8. *Select and sequence concept nonexamples.* Based on the definition, particularly through critical and noncritical attributes, learners will need to be able to distinguish between examples and nonexamples of a concept and should be able to give reasons for the distinctions. Your task, as teacher, is to select and sequence nonexamples. Probably, the first nonexamples should be obvious and contain few critical attributes. For example, *sun* and *stars* could be nonexamples of *planet*. To prevent overgeneralization, later nonexamples should be close to the definition and differ in, say, one attribute—for example, *asteroids*. With very young learners, less stress should be on nonexamples and more stress on examples.

9. *Decide the nature of instruction.* You now must decide the instructional approach to use. This should be based on the information gained through doing the above eight steps. Should the approach be deductive or inductive? Should an example and nonexample (from which attributes can be observed or deduced) approach be used? Should analogies be used from which inferences can be drawn and attributes identified? Cause–effect and inference? Behavior and inference?

The *deductive* (or *expository*) *approach* begins with the presentation of a concept definition, then is illustrated with examples and nonexamples. This uses a rule → example sequence, and, as a memory jog, can be called the *rule–e.g.* approach. The *inductive approach* involves presenting examples followed by student discovery of the definition. The sequence is from specifics to the general, or *e.g.–rule.*

10. *Find motivating ways to introduce and develop concepts.* Learning concepts can be productive and enjoyable when it touches the personal lives and needs of students. Recognize learner interests and lead them through exciting adventures. Learner developmental level must be recognized and instruction should be varied, interactive, and involve as many senses as possible. Learning styles and cultural background need to be considered. Challenge learners but still "organize for success experiences." When a student asks, "Why do I have to learn this?" give a good answer from the student's point of view. Statements such as, "You may need this later in life," or "Astronauts need to know this," or "It's going to be on the exam" are not good enough.

If you have planned well, you will be armed with knowledge that will let you: (1) provide different kinds of well-sequenced examples students can understand and use and that avoid undergeneralization; (2) provide well-sequenced nonexamples that avoid overgeneralization; (3) help learners identify or infer the critical attributes of the concept; (4) help learners identify or infer the noncritical attributes of the concept; (5) help learners understand a concept definition that contains the critical attributes and the relationship of these to each other; and (6) provide practice so learners will be able to recall and use the concept correctly.

EXAMPLE OF A LESSON PLAN.   Using the format provided earlier, a lesson plan for teaching the concept *planet* follows.

Lesson: Planet

I. *Topic*   Planet

II. *Content Identification*   The topic "Planets" in a unit on "Our Solar System"

III. *Objectives*
 A. Given a diagram of examples and nonexamples of a planet, each student will be able to identify each planet.
 B. Given the above items, each student will be able to write a suitable justification for the selections made.

IV. *Prerequisite Student Learning*
 Familiarity with the solar system concept hierarchy and exposure to the concepts of solar system and sun. Familiarity with the notions of critical and noncritical attributes and super-, sub-, and coordinate concepts.

V. *Presentation Activities*
 A. Introductory
   1. Ask students whether they heard about the recent meteor shower and what they know about it.
   2. Questions to discover students' knowledge of the solar system they have gained through watching the television series or movie *Star Trek*.
   3. Using a large, unlabeled chart of the solar system, provide an advance organizer and state the objectives.
 B. Developmental
   1. Show a short film on the solar system, asking students to pay particular attention to the planets.
   2. Ask students to name the planets that were mentioned in the film.
   3. Using a large three-dimensional model of the planets, sun, and moons, demonstrate how planets orbit around the sun.
   4. Divide students into groups of five to agree on the critical attributes of planets; groups report to the class and then agreement is reached.
   5. The same groups agree on and report what they believe to be noncritical attributes.
   6. Using questions and discussion, draw the concept definition from the class.
   7. Using the unlabeled chart of the solar system, with the class as a whole, randomly point to stars, planets, satellites, etc., asking students to say whether items are examples or nonexamples of planets, requiring that students' responses be justified.
 C. Closure
   1. Using question and answer, review critical and noncritical attributes and the concept definition.
   2. Draw super-, sub-, and coordinate concepts of "planet" from students, and how their learning about "planet" can be useful.
   3. Assign an unlabeled diagram of the solar system for homework. Students are to label the planets and, in writing, justify their choices and show why other items were not chosen.
   4. Foreshadow the topic of the next lesson.

VI. *Materials and Aids*   Large chart of solar system; short film on solar system; one-page diagram of solar system.

VII. *Evaluation*   Questioning; reports by groups; homework assignment; unit test.

Teaching Using Deductive and Inductive Approaches

Your approach in a lesson may be deductive, inductive, or a combination. You can learn when each approach is appropriate.

Deductive (expository) teaching may work better in some situations, and inductive teaching in others. The deductive approach, being teacher centered, tends to be direct and closed; the inductive approach, being learner centered, tends to be open, indirect, and emphasizes helping learners to think.

Expository teaching is suitable for teaching the relationships among several concepts. Older learners are better able to benefit from an expository approach because they have a larger bank of concepts they can mentally manipulate. An advance organizer should precede the deductive approach. It can be time efficient for teaching large numbers of facts and simple, concrete concepts. It can be used if rapid attainment of basic familiarity with background concepts is needed for what is about to be taught. The deductive approach should begin with a discussion about the concept before the definition is provided. For instance, some ideas or anecdotes about, or characteristics of, the concept can be surfaced. Then the definition can be provided and examples and nonexamples used to understand the definition based on critical attributes.

Learners are more intrinsically interested when an inductive approach is used. They achieve higher-cognitive-level outcomes and are better able to transfer their learning. Proponents of problem-based and active learning believe learners should learn through active involvement with concepts and be permitted to discover concepts themselves.

Whether the approach is deductive on inductive, the question "Why?" should be asked. "Why is this an example?" "Why is this a nonexample?" Most students recall concepts only through examples and not through definitions. Insistence on rote memorization of definitions is questionable—do stress understanding.

Many authorities argue that the definition should never be given before examples are provided. They believe the definition-first approach may be suitable for formal reasoning, but only in a few cases. Presenting the definition first can court disaster because it promotes rote learning, not understanding. It is critical for most young students that the definition come last and that learners put definitions together themselves to prove understanding. A summary of the deductive and inductive approaches to concept teaching is presented in Figure 9.8.

Deductive and Inductive Approaches to Teaching a Concept		
DEDUCTIVE "rule–eg"	Establish set and then:	INDUCTIVE "eg–rule"
1. Concept label and definition given by teacher		1. Learners discover critical and noncritical attributes through examples
2. Examples, then nonexamples, given, and critical and noncritical attributes pointed out		2. Further learner discovery through nonexamples
3. Definition reviewed		3. Concept labeled and defined by learners
4. Examples and nonexamples presented simultaneously		4. Examples and nonexamples presented simultaneously
5. Practice		5. Practice

FIGURE 9.8   *Deductive and Inductive Approaches to Concept Teaching*

Steps normally followed in the deductive approach are

1. Establish the set and introduce the concept definition, drawing attention to the critical attributes and their relationship(s) to each other.
2. Introduce examples and nonexamples, drawing attention to the critical and noncritical attributes.
3. Review the definition, pointing out critical attributes and their relationship to each other.
4. Present examples and nonexamples simultaneously; draw attention to reasons why examples are instances and why nonexamples are not instances of the definition.
5. Provide practice that requires justification of choices.

Steps often followed in the inductive approach are

1. After establishing the set, introduce examples, helping learners "discover" the critical attributes and noncritical attributes. Learners can provide additional examples.
2. Introduce nonexamples, helping learners strengthen their understanding of the critical and noncritical attributes. Learners can provide other nonexamples.
3. Help learners label the concept and "discover" an appropriate definition that includes the critical attributes and their relationship(s).
4. Present examples and nonexamples simultaneously and have learners distinguish between them, justifying their choices.
5. Provide practice that requires justification of choices.

A Concept Teaching Cycle

Helping learners acquire concepts involves a cycle of preparing and motivating learners to learn; presenting advance organizers; delivering the body of the lesson in an efficient, well-organized, and interesting way (using a variety of media, providing for transfer, and reviewing and providing meaningful practice). Display enthusiasm and explain (and demonstrate) the inquiry approach and questioning techniques. Good concept lessons often follow the teaching cycle in Figure 9.9. A data sheet you can use for feedback when teaching a concept lesson is shown in Appendix 9.2.

1. *Planning.* Before instruction begins, the content is chosen in keeping with the curriculum. The text and other references should be reviewed. The previous experiences and readiness of learners must be considered. Study the hierarchy of which the concept is a part and prepare an advance organizer (concept map or web). Then select the appropriate instructional approach and learning activities.

2. *Presenting objectives and advance organizer.* Normally, at the outset, explain the instructional objectives and how the new learning ties in with what has been studied before and what will be studied in the future. Provide the advance organizer. Presenting objectives and using advance organizers aids understanding and retention.

3. *Engaging in learning activities.* In this phase, learners participate in learning activities. Instruction should include examples and nonexamples and help learners recognize and understand the concept's critical and noncritical attributes and definition.

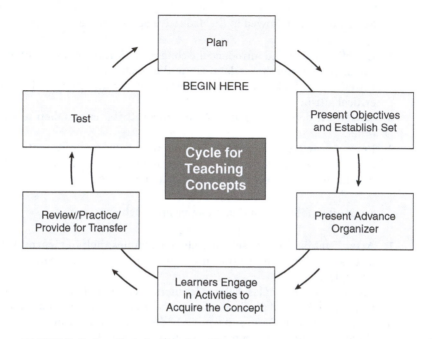

FIGURE 9.9   *Cycle for Teaching Concepts*

Motivation is increased if you show enthusiasm and have high, but achievable, expectations. In this phase, learner participation should be active. Learning is increased by skillful use of question and answer, discussion, clear explanations, and by using a variety of media. During a good concept lesson, students need the thinking skills of data gathering and retrieval (to surface and report examples), contrasting and comparing (to discover differences and similarities), summarizing (forming the concept definition), and classifying (to decide if new items are examples or nonexamples).

4. *Providing for review and transfer.* If the concept is to be remembered and used, practice opportunity is needed. Learners can be asked to distinguish between simultaneously presented concept examples and nonexamples. Lesson closure should include a review of the concept definition. Ideally, the critical attributes and their relationships should be drawn from the learners rather than recited by you. Learners should show they know the superordinate, subordinate, and coordinate concepts related to the concept. If you want learners to *transfer* learning (generalize to new or related examples or use learning in higher-level operations), teach for transfer.

5. *Testing.* The final step is testing. This lets you and learners know how well learners have mastered the concept *and* how effective your planning and instruction have been. If necessary, reteach and retest. Testing can be informal and formative (e.g., teacher observation or use of question and answer) and formal and formative or summative. Formal testing may occur later.

Use the appended data collection instrument in Figure 9.10 to help you analyze the cases that follow. Your instructor may pose specific questions for your response.

FIGURE 9.10 *Concept Analysis Form*

Concept name: Peninsula

Kind of Concept (please check as appropriate):

    __X__ Concrete   _____ Abstract

    __X__ Conjunctive   _____ Disjunctive   _____ Relational

Presentation Medium or Media: _____ Observing/doing   __X__ Pictorial   _____ Symbolic

Examples of Concept (in sequence of presentation):

Chart showing geographic features of the earth. Overhead transparencies (maps) of areas of North America, with peninsulas circled. Sequence of examples would range from coastal peninsulas of moderate size with clear land links to larger land mass, to those of varying sizes, shapes, and locations.

Nonexamples of Concept (in sequence of presentation):

Maps and pictures of plains, lake, and islands.

Critical Attributes (in sequence of presentation):

Area of land; linked by land to a larger land area; almost surrounded by water

Noncritical Attributes:

Size; shape; location (whether jutting into ocean, lake, sea); man-made or natural

Concept Definition:

"A land area, almost surrounded by water, with a narrow link to a larger land area."

Relationship to Other Concepts:

A peninsula is a geological land feature on the surface of the earth. Geographic features are natural or man-made. Each geographical feature has attributes that make it different from other features.

Name of Superordinate Concept: Geographical (land) features of the earth.

Names of Some Subordinate Concepts: (Kinds of peninsulas.)

Names of Some Coordinate Concepts: Island, valley, plateau, delta, isthmus

CASE 9.1 Concepts

What Is Cazoptopin?

Consider the following excerpts from hypothetical lessons.

Excerpt One

It is very important that you learn about cazoptopin. Cazoptopin is a newly discovered form of quanoptopin. It is extipated in Bratislava. Bratislavians plescalate cazoptopin by salinking quants and then pasking these to prube cazoptopin. Cazoptopin may become one of our most used quanoptopins because it is very effective and relatively easy and inexpensive to pask.

Using complete statements and correct English, please answer the following questions:

1. What is cazoptopin?
2. Where is cazoptopin extipated?
3. How is cazoptopin plescalated?
4. Why is it important to know about cazoptopin?

If you think the above example is a little ridiculous, consider the next one, putting yourself in the place of a grade 7 or 8 student subjected to the following example.

Excerpt Two

It is very important that you learn about the nervous system. The nervous system is the body's "telephone system." In response to stimuli, it receives and transmits messages about the welfare of the total organism through interoceptors and exteroceptors. Anatomically, the nervous system consists of the cerebrum, the pons and medulla, the spinal cord, twelve pairs of cranial nerves, and thirty pairs of spinal nerves.

The nervous system functions as a storage system and has an environment interpretive system. The peripheral nervous system senses and responds to stimuli and works with the central nervous system to keep the organism alive and well.

Please answer the following:

1. To what can the nervous system be compared? What is the reason for the comparison?
2. Through what does the nervous system transmit messages?
3. Besides receiving and sending messages, what functions does the nervous system have?
4. Why is it important to know about the nervous system?

The above are examples of an all-too-common teaching approach in which a presentation is made or a reading assigned, then questions are asked to see if students can recall what was presented. The teacher may wonder why students have difficulty or are so unmotivated.

CASE 9.2 Concepts

What Is a Peninsula?

Mr. Lewchuk is continuing a series of lessons on geographical concepts, using the form shown in Figure 9.10. He begins by reviewing the concepts covered so far: *continent, coast, island, harbor,* and *gulf.* He asks students for definitions in their own words and to tell whether each is a land or water feature. He then asks individuals to find examples of each concept on a large wall map in the classroom.

Mr. Lewchuk introduces today's topic. "We are going to examine another kind of land feature this af-

ternoon. I will show you examples of this feature; we'll describe each carefully and see if we can generate a definition for this new concept." From the front of the room, he shows a chart drawing of physical features. Pointing, he says, "See this part right here? This is called a peninsula. What can you tell about it from this picture?"

Students volunteer answers that include "it's hooked onto the land," and "it has water around most of it." Mr. Lewchuk jots responses on the board

continued

Chart Example	Map Example #1	Map Example #2	Map Example #3	Map Example #4	Map Example #5
• hooked on to land • water nearly all around • a land feature • large in size • long straight sides • smooth coastline • an area of land	• water on 3 sides • small narrow shape • made of land • not wide anywhere • curved shape • is joined to a larger body of land • shaped like a sheep's head	• narrowest where it joins the land • large rounded shape at the end • water almost all around • irregular coastline	• small in size • water nearly surrounds • a land area • connected to other land	• long, narrow shape • smooth coastline • an area of land • hooked to other land • water almost all places, wide at end	• water on 3 sides • a land feature • large, L-shaped • uneven coastline

as answers are supplied. Keeping in mind the definition he want students to discover, he asks, "Is it land or water?" Students respond that it is land. "What can you say about the shape? How about the size? Does it extend into an ocean, a lake, or a bay?" Mr. Lewchuk continues to record responses.

Showing an overhead transparency of the Maritime provinces of Canada, Mr. Lewchuk shows areas (peninsulas) that have been circled. He asks the students to describe each example. For each example, he begins a new column of descriptive notes. When all the examples have been examined, there are six columns of descriptive notes, side by side, as shown above.

Mr. Lewchuk asks students to look at the notes on each example. "Are there some things, some descriptors that are present in every example?" Students select the common descriptors: joined to other, usually larger, land, a land feature, and, almost surrounded by water (except for the land link). Mr. Lewchuk explains that, because not all peninsulas are the same, they may vary in size, shape, type of coastline, length, and width. "But to be a peninsula, it must be joined to another land body, must have water nearly all around, and must be made of land."

"We need to think of a way to define 'peninsula' so that we are clear about what it is and is not. A good definition will include all the things a peninsula *must* be. What could we say, in one sentence, about a peninsula?"

Jerry begins, "A peninsula is almost surrounded by water." "I think there's more," says Natasha. "A peninsula is a land feature that is nearly surrounded by water, that is connected to other land." "Good," says Mr. Lewchuk. "We've included all the common descriptors. Can we tighten that up a little?" Jean-Paul concludes, "A peninsula is a land feature, joined to a larger body of land, that is nearly surrounded by water."

"Very clear," says Mr. Lewchuk. "Let's see how the definition works on other examples." He shows two more examples, saying, "Is this a peninsula? Why do you think so? What characteristics does it have?" He then shows a picture of an island. "Is this a peninsula? Why not?" Students respond although it is made of land, it is surrounded entirely by water and does not have a link to another land body. They work through another example and two nonexamples. By comparing the feature to the definition, students decide whether they are peninsulas.

Finally, Mr. Lewchuk asks students to think where they would rather live, on an island or on a peninsula. "Think of being the first inhabitants. Which would have the most advantages? What would be some disadvantages?" After a lively discussion, Mr. Lewchuk asks the students to explain, in writing, reasons for their selection and the advantages and disadvantages of their choice.

CASE 9.3 Concepts

What's in a Contract?

Mr. Yanski's grade 11 law class is studying the law of contracts. The class has been told that there are five elements to a binding contract. One of the elements is "consideration." "A valid contract" Mr. Yanski says, requires 'consideration.' Do you know what that is?" After a long pause, Damon volunteers, "Well, before you sign anything, you should consider things carefully." Mr. Yanski replies, "What you say, Damon, is certainly true, but the legal definition of 'consideration' is a bit different. Let me give an example. When you buy a camera for a friend that has a price tag of $210, the camera is consideration and so is the $210. If the person who had the camera agreed to take a pair of car wheel mags for the camera, the mags also would be consideration. You could even promise to paint his car in exchange for the camera. The service you promise to provide is consideration too. Are you getting the idea?" Upon Mr. Yanski's request, students begin to volunteer other examples. Freda says, "I heard of cases where people bought something really valuable, like a house, for one dollar. Is that legal?" Mr. Yanski replies, "Consideration does not

have to be of equal value in a contract. The one dollar also is consideration." Students discover that consideration need not be adequate, that both parties need not benefit personally (for instance, a donation to charity can be made or a person can promise to stop doing something like cutting a lawn at five in the morning).

Mr. Yanski draws the essential features of consideration from the class. Based on the examples the teacher gave and those that students provided, students prepare a definition of consideration. The definition states that consideration is money or money value. The courts won't enforce a promise to do or give something unless the person benefiting does or gives something in exchange (or promises to do so). Mr. Yanski provides a handout containing ten cases. Students are to figure out whether consideration was present and justify their answers. He does the first case with the class and assigns the rest as seatwork. He takes up the cases the next day, using probing questions to see if students understand the definition and critical and noncritical attributes of "consideration."

LINKING PRACTICE TO THEORY

How does your approach to teaching concepts reflect your views on how learning takes place? Should you do a concept analysis before teaching a concept? Do you prefer to build knowledge with your students, or to guide them on a predetermined path? How does this chapter tie in with the chapters on communication and questioning? Are you and your students more comfortable with a "doing," pictorial, or symbolic approach? Try the strategies suggested in this chapter to provide an analytical framework for you to think about your experience with concept teaching.

Summary

We cannot think or function without concepts; concept teaching and learning are fundamental to effective schooling. Before teaching a concept, the teacher needs to be sure of its critical and noncritical attributes, examples and nonexamples, and definition. Concepts, which are declarative content, can be classified as: con-

crete or abstract; formal or informal; conjunctive, disjunctive, or relational; and superordinate, coordinate, or subordinate. Presentations of concepts in textbooks are often inadequate. Concepts can be taught, and attained, deductively or inductively. A systematic approach to planning and teaching should normally be followed.

Ample pure examples of concepts should be presented, followed by less obvious examples and nonexamples. Students should normally be asked to discover the definition of a concept themselves. Overgeneralization and undergeneralization should be avoided.

Concepts can be explained in terms of their purposes: to show a cause-and-effect relationship; to show an action is governed by a general law or rule; to illustrate a procedure or process; or to reveal the intent of an action or process.

Activities

CONCEPTS

1. As an initial exercise, review Case 9.1. Discuss the following: Is a cazoptopin a label or a term? How would you categorize it? In what ways is a cazoptopin a mental construct? Why does seeing a cazoptopin as a concept simplify learning, facilitate thought and communication, and act as a building block for the future? In what ways has teaching about the cazoptopin as a concept been more effective than the contextual clues to answer questions approach?

2. Select several concepts that are common to a school subject of your choice. Analyze each in terms of critical attributes, noncritical attributes, definition, examples, and nonexamples.

3. Select a text from a subject you will teach, or hope to teach, and find examples of: (a) concrete and abstract, (b) formal and informal, and (c) conjunctive, disjunctive, and relational concepts.

4. The instructor may model two short lessons on the same topic to illustrate the deductive and inductive approaches to teaching a concept. Point out the components of each lesson.

5. Join a subject interest group. Brainstorm examples of concrete and abstract concepts, then classify these by degree of difficulty of analysis. Then, select three concrete and three abstract concepts and agree on the critical attributes, noncritical attributes, and concept definitions.

6. In your group, brainstorm, agree on, and justify the selection of examples for conjunctive, disjunctive, relational, and connotative concepts.

7. In your group, using the concept analysis form provided in Appendix 9.1, analyze a concrete concept and an abstract concept.

8. Select a concept and prepare two lesson plans, one illustrating a deductive and the other an inductive approach to teaching that concept.

9. Teach a microteaching lab and a field classroom lesson with the professional target of teaching a concept, using the data collection form in Figure 9.10. Attach a completed concept analysis form (Figure 9.8) to each lesson.

10. In groups, create learner background charts showing how you would teach concepts using concrete, iconic, and symbolic approaches.

11. In subject groups, select a concept from your discipline and create a hierarchy of the concept. Share this with the rest of the class.

12. In pairs, create a lesson plan for teaching a concept from your discipline.

13. Divide the class into four groups. Have one group teach the concept of *chair* from a deductive approach and the other teach it from an inductive approach. Similarly, have the other two groups teach the concept *teaching*.

APPENDIX 9.1 *Concept Analysis Form*

CONCEPT ANALYSIS FORM

_____

Concept name: _____

Kind of Concept (please check):   _____ Concrete   _____ Abstract

                                      _____ Conjunctive   _____ Disjunctive   _____ Relational

Presentation Medium or Media: _____ Observing/doing _____ Pictorial   _____ Symbolic

_____

Examples of Concept (in sequence of presentation):

_____

Nonexamples of Concept (in sequence of presentation):

_____

Critical Attributes (in sequence of presentation):

_____

Noncritical Attributes:

_____

Concept Definition:

_____

Relationship to Other Concepts:

_____

Name of Superordinate Concept:

Names of Some Subordinate Concepts:

Names of Some Coordinate Concepts:

APPENDIX 9.2   *Concept Teaching Target*

PROFESSIONAL TARGET—CONCEPT TEACHING

Kind of Concept: _____ concrete   _____ abstract   _____ conjunctive   _____ disjunctive   _____ relational

Presentation Mode: _____ active   _____ graphic   _____ symbolic

Procedure Used: _____ deductive   _____ inductive

Please describe what was said and done and how students reacted.

Aspect of Concept	Descriptive Notes
Examples or analogies or cause-and-effect or behavior	
Nonexamples or nonanalogies or . . .	
Critical attributes identified and/or stressed	
Noncritical attributes	
Relationships identified (e.g., CAR—wheels *and* body *and* steering wheel)	
Concept rule defined (critical attributes and relationships?)	
Related concepts identified? Use of concept? (Sub-? Super-? Coordinate?)	
Practice and transfer	

10 Teaching Skills

The Nature of Skills

A student has struggled with language arts and English in school. He was assigned an essay but received a low mark, and tried to write the required critique of one of the short stories the class had studied. He enjoyed the stories, but failed. He took the class again in summer school and, this time, did well. The summer school teacher taught not only the content of the literature, but the skills needed to read for ideas and to write essays and reports. The teacher taught stages of essay writing and, for critiquing a short story, she taught the skills of finding ideas, writing thesis statements, and supporting statements with evidence and comment. The teacher was encouraging and supportive, and gave feedback on each stage of the assignments. Incidentally, this is a true story. A similar example could be found for other subjects. Everything students do in school requires skills. The *how to* (the skills) is as important, if not more so, than the *what* (the content).

Skill Domains

Many people, when they hear the word *skills,* assume what are referred to as *psychomotor* skills, such as playing tennis or using a computer. Some skills, however, are predominantly *cognitive* (for example, categorizing or comparing and contrasting), others have strong *affective* purposes (for instance, paraphrasing, or checking for feelings). Psychomotor skills also have cognitive and affective aspects. Skills fall under the rubric of *procedural knowledge*—knowledge and ability to do something, as contrasted with *declarative knowledge* about something (though, most often, both are needed).

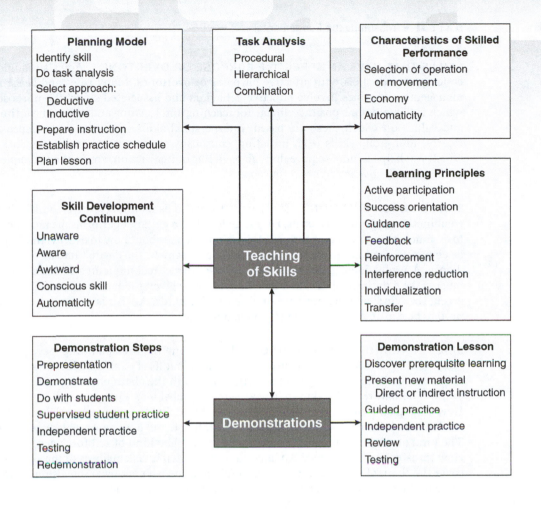

Planning Model
Identify skill
Do task analysis
Select approach:
　Deductive
　Inductive
Prepare instruction
Establish practice schedule
Plan lesson

Task Analysis
Procedural
Hierarchical
Combination

Characteristics of Skilled Performance
Selection of operation
　or movement
Economy
Automaticity

Skill Development Continuum
Unaware
Aware
Awkward
Conscious skill
Automaticity

Learning Principles
Active participation
Success orientation
Guidance
Feedback
Reinforcement
Interference reduction
Individualization
Transfer

Teaching of Skills

Demonstration Steps
Prepresentation
Demonstrate
Do with students
Supervised student practice
Independent practice
Testing
Redemonstration

Demonstrations

Demonstration Lesson
Discover prerequisite learning
Present new material
　Direct or indirect instruction
Guided practice
Independent practice
Review
Testing

TCP—SKILLS AND DEMONSTRATIONS

Provides effective teaching of skills and demonstrations

Prior analysis of skills; developmental level of students accommodated and desired skill level determined; demonstrations clear and systematic; effective guided practice and feedback before independent practice; appropriate choice and use of inductive and deductive approaches.

No prior analysis; readiness of students ignored; absence of or ineffective demonstration; absence of guided practice and feedback; approach always deductive.

SKILLS THAT ARE MAINLY COGNITIVE. We can use a language arts example. If the intention is for learners to develop the cognitive skill of writing paragraphs with topic sentences, several subskills are required: spelling, usage, topic selection, sentence construction, punctuation, and capitalization. Another example, this time in social studies, is map reading, which also involves subskills. Thinking, problem-solving, and decision-making skills are important cognitive skills that must be taught to be learned.

SKILLS THAT HAVE AN AFFECTIVE PURPOSE OR OVERTONE. You also should be concerned with skills with affective purposes or overtones. Many rules and classroom management routines involve affective behaviors and associated skills, the purpose of which is to maintain a positive climate for teaching and learning and reflect the attitudes and values on which these are based. Interpersonal skills (e.g., listening or speaking clearly) and group skills (e.g., initiating, consensus seeking, and conflict resolution), which you help learners acquire through modeling or instruction, are further examples of skills with affective overtones or purposes.

SKILLS IN COMBINATION. Skills are not isolated as motor, cognitive, or affective. A combination and interplay exists. For example, when a guitarist performs, he must be able to do much more than pluck strings. A decision is made about how to express the feelings or emotions involved, using techniques learned to achieve the desired impact on the audience. A professional golfer must not only use correct technique in striking a ball, she must make a decision about the kind of shot to play given the layout of the fairway and green, the wind, and the presence or absence of hazards. As this is occurring, emotions need to be controlled and concentration maintained.

SKILL TEACHING AND PLANNING. Skill teaching requires planning. Several questions need to be asked before instruction begins: What level of skill do learners possess? Learners' readiness? The place of a particular skill in the chain of skills to which it belongs? The nature of the skill to be learned? The subskills? The sequence of subskills? How the lesson is to be presented? The degree of learning (or overlearning) desired? The kind of, and how much, practice needed? The kind of, and how much, guidance needed? The kind of, and how much, feedback to be given? The kind of reinforcement desired? How transfer can be fostered? An important initial step is task analysis of the skill to discover the chain of subskills involved. Careful planning isn't enough. You also need to become proficient with the demonstration-and-practice lesson format.

Learning Principles

The effective teacher recognizes the learning principles to be brought into play while helping learners acquire skills. A brief description of these follows (Figure 10.1).

ACTIVE PARTICIPATION. Active student participation is needed. Participation should be as overt (observable) as possible. Some skills can only be learned this way. Covert (not observable) practice can be used to advantage—for example, silently thinking through the steps of solving an algebra problem, or mentally practicing phrases or short sentences on an imaginary keyboard.

SUCCESS AND FAILURE. Nothing succeeds like success, and nothing stultifies like continued failure. Failure, in itself, is not necessarily damaging; continued failure can be. Nobody likes doing things at which they are not very good! Learners need tasks at which they can succeed *after reasonable effort.* "Organize success experiences." The climate should encourage risk taking and emphasize learning from "deferred successes" (not *yet* succeeding). Errors are clues for further learning, not sins.

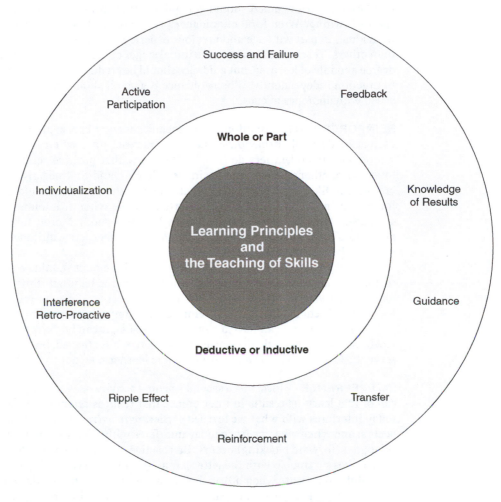

Success and Failure

Active
Participation

Feedback

Whole or Part

Individualization

Knowledge
of Results

**Learning Principles
and
the Teaching of Skills**

Interference
Retro-Proactive

Guidance

Deductive or Inductive

Ripple Effect

Transfer

Reinforcement

FIGURE 10.1   *Learning Principles and the Teaching of Skills*

FEEDBACK AND KNOWLEDGE OF RESULTS.   Practice is critical to the development and maintenance of skills. To be most useful, feedback must be provided. Knowledge of results (KR) is essential for speedy and efficient learning. Doing something over and over without feedback is inefficient and often unproductive. Joyce, Weil, and Calhoun (2004, p. 316) say that the kind of feedback students receive during practice has much to do with later success. Feedback helps students discover how well they understand new material and discover their errors. To be effective, they say, "feedback must be academic, corrective, respectful and deserved." Good feedback, they add, involves telling the students their correct actions; praise, when given, must be deserved. The more immediate and descriptive (precise and specific) the feedback, the more helpful and the more rapid will be the improvement. When feedback is delayed, students may practice incorrect responses.

GUIDANCE.   How much should you guide a learner as a skill is being learned? What speeds learning? What kind of guidance? How much? The answers lie in part with the individual, in part with age and previous experience. Some learners need more guidance than others. Teacher guidance, at the initial stages of instruction, can greatly increase the degree and rate of learning, but guidance should be gradually withdrawn so students learn to function independently. When guidance is given it should be positive, concise, and focused with appropriate cues.

REINFORCEMENT.   Reinforcement means showing approval or issuing rewards for correct or desirable behavior. Some teachers react only when learners do something wrong, not when learners do it right. We know that positive reinforcement (pleasant tones) strengthens correct and desirable behavior, and that negative reinforcement increases the likelihood of behavior that removes the negative reinforcer. Positive reinforcement in skill learning is particularly effective when it is immediate, earned, and contingent (specifies what was good and why it was good). Merely telling a learner what *not* to do is not particularly effective (and can lead to a negative attitude); the learner must be clear about what to do.

Ideally (not always practical), positive reinforcement should be immediate for correct performance of a skill or subskill until behavior is habitual (this is *regular reinforcement*); *intermittent reinforcement* can also be effective. Regular reinforcement speeds learning; subsequent intermittent reinforcement improves retention.

Reinforcement can have a *ripple effect,* that is, it can be "vicarious." The ripple effect occurs when not only the learner who receives it is affected, but so are others who observe it. However, what is motivating for one learner may not be motivating for another.

INTERFERENCE.   Inserting a second learning activity between original learning and recall of that learning results in interference that reduces retention. When what we learn today interferes with what we learned earlier, *retroactive inhibition* (backward blocking) occurs; and when what we learn today interferes with what we will try to learn, *proactive inhibition* (forward blocking) occurs. Retroactive inhibition occurs, for example, when a student has no trouble with the letter *p* until *q* is introduced. A classic example of proactive inhibition occurs when a British national rents a car in Canada, and having learned to drive on the left side of the road in Britain interferes with driving on the right side.

Be aware that learning some things helps the learning of others. For example, having learned to keyboard on a typewriter will greatly help you learn to use a computer, or having learned Spanish first will help you learn Italian.

The way learning experiences are organized aids or hinders skill acquisition and retention. Students can be helped to discover meaningful organization by having elements of the skill placed, and learned, in a logical way; and each part must be seen to fit the whole. Past experience can be used, and instruction must be pitched at the learners' level of ability and insight. You can help reduce interference. The more thorough the earlier and later learning, the less the interference. The things most easily forgotten are those not well learned in the first place. In learning keyboarding, the letter *m* can be practiced for some time before the letter *n* is introduced and practiced. You can teach a memory aid (mnemonic device), telling students the two letters are on the keyboard in the same order as in the word *name.* Learners should do *response differentiation* practice using words that contain both letters. This requires them to differentiate between stroking an *m* and stroking an *n.*

INDIVIDUALIZATION. Successful skill teaching and learning requires that individual differences be considered. Some students need more practice than others, and the focus of practice for each person will vary. The wise keyboarding teacher will not tell the whole class to do a timed writing with the objective of simultaneously improving both speed and accuracy. This is confusing and frustrating! The learner cannot focus on both. A student who makes ten or more errors per minute should be working on accuracy; a student who makes two or fewer errors per minute can work on speed; and another who has flaws in stroking technique should work on particular aspects of technique, not accuracy or speed. Although this example is principally psychomotor, the need for individualization is as important for cognitive or affectively toned skills. You can individualize practice through the objectives set and the exercises assigned, checking up during seatwork. Many cognitive skills, and those with affective purposes, can be taught using cooperative group strategies or peer teaching. These provide ample opportunity for individualization.

TRANSFER. Education is predicated on transfer. It occurs when training in one activity affects a student's performance in other contexts. For example, if a student has learned the steps of problem solving in social studies and applies these to a language arts problem, positive transfer has taken place. Thinking skills learned in one context should be taught so they are likely to be used in other subjects and daily life. Transfer is at the core of problem solving and higher mental processes, innovation, and artistic achievement.

If you want transfer to occur, teach for it! It is not likely to happen by itself. For example, math teachers may recall students learning to do algebra problems using x, y, and z to represent unknowns. When the students were given the same problems but the unknowns were represented by a, b, and c, some couldn't do them—no transfer!

You can facilitate transfer. Hunter (1971) presents four things teachers can do:

1. Point out the *similarities* of past learning to what is about to be learned and the similarities of what is being, or has been learned, to what will be learned. If past learning can interfere, point out the *differences*.

2. Use *associations* students can make between things not necessarily related. For example, when a science teacher teaches astronomy, associations formed by students through having watched a television series on space adventure may stimulate learning. Or a teacher can use a game as a teaching method. Students associate games with fun, and so the new learning likely also will be fun. A field trip used as part of another unit can be *associated* in future units. The perceptive teacher knows the power and transferability of associations. It is not enough for students to learn a skill in isolation—they should apply it to new material in a course, other subjects, and life.

3. The greater the degree of original learning, the greater is the likelihood of transfer. Highly overlearned skills transfer more readily than those half-learned. The teacher needs to provide opportunities for transfer, pointing out how transfer can be affected.

4. The more learners are aware of *essential unvarying elements* (the main concepts and processes and their organization), the greater is the possibility of transfer. Stress these elements and help learners become aware of how they apply to new contexts. For example, a correct stroke in tennis involves a smooth, continuous motion from backswing through follow-through. Don't "hit at the ball," "hit through the ball." This is called a "ballistic stroke," and it applies equally to squash, racquetball, golf, and even striking the keys of a computer. It is an essential unvarying element.

Performance Skills

Effective performance has certain characteristics. The teaching of skills requires an awareness of key stages.

CHARACTERISTICS.   Although all skills involve cognitive, affective, and psychomotor elements, performance skills may involve many psychomotor characteristics. Have you ever heard a seemingly flawless musical performance by a solo guitarist, pianist, or singer? Watched top-ranked tennis players playing a match? Seen somebody rapidly editing a document on a computer? A teacher quickly solving a complex algebra problem on the chalkboard? Someone performing incredibly acrobatic and proficient break dancing? Each is an example of "expert" performance. What features do they have in common? What is expert performance? Bloom (1986) notes that mastery of a skill, from a routine daily task to the highest level of artistry, "depends on the ability to perform it unconsciously with speed and accuracy while carrying on other brain functions" (p. 70). If you study the above examples you will discover that the characteristics of expert performance include selection, economy, and automaticity. Consider golfing:

* *Selection.* The expert rapidly selects and initiates the appropriate response or operation needed. For example, as the golfer walks to her ball on the fairway, she sizes up the shot needed, and by the time she gets to the ball she knows exactly what she is going to do. Among other things, she has considered distance, wind and grass conditions, slope of the fairway and green, placement of the flag, club selection, and the kind of golf swing needed.

* *Economy.* An expert accurately performs a skill with optimum economy of effort, movement, and time. When an expert golfer swings a golf club, each subskill is performed unhesitatingly, smoothly and rapidly, in the appropriate sequence, without a single unnecessary movement or operation, and with just the right amount of effort. Many of the same characteristics are true of an expert musician or a person who rapidly solves a math problem.

* *Automaticity.* An expert performs a skill so that it is totally appropriate and seems to be effortless. The golfer seems consistently to do things without having to think about them. However, the golfer is performing a cognitive skill (thinking) while using a psychomotor skill that has been automatized.

STAGES FOR TEACHING MOTOR SKILLS.   Hellison and Templin (1991) provide the following stages for teaching motor skills:

1. Set
   * Students may not be ready for a demonstration and drill.
   * Play the game or do the activity first to create interest.
2. Modeling or visual clues
   * Demonstrate one of the motor skills involved in the activity they have participated in.
   * The teacher or a student models or demonstrates.
   * Give a few cues or tips.
3. Specific behavioral objectives or challenges
   * Give students a specific behavioral (or performance) objective that challenges them to develop a specific motor skill.
   * Specify what has to be accomplished.

- Challenge but within the students' range.
- When an objective is met, do not continue doing the task (unlike typical drill).

4. Extensions
- Students who complete a specific objective are given more difficult challenges with the same motor skill.

5. Applications
- Modify games so the skill being practiced is the focus of attention.
- Research shows that the old "demonstrate, drill, play the game" accomplishes little skill learning.
- Practice within a gamelike component.

6. Close
- Leave students with something to think about.
- Cue, reminder of the role of the skill in the game.
- General reinforcement.
- What to look forward to in the next lesson. (pp. 55–59)

The principles of learning a skill must not be forgotten when working with the levels. Judith Rink stressed, "Tasks must be appropriate in order for students to learn them," and "If students do not have the prerequisites to learn a skill, they could practice forever and probably not make a great deal of progress" (in Silverman & Ennis, 1996, p. 175).

The Deductive versus the Inductive Approach

A skill can be taught either *deductively* (the teacher tells and directs) or *inductively* (learners discover the steps and relationships). Burden and Byrd (2003, p. 167) argue that students learn basic skills more rapidly when they receive most of their instruction directly from the teacher. Others argue that the choice of approach, deductive or inductive, should depend on the nature of the skill and how important it is for students to understand the concepts and principles involved.

DEDUCTIVE APPROACH.   The pure deductive approach to teaching skills (for example, directly teaching math or directly teaching a dance routine) is very teacher centered. You direct and monitor each step. The skill is modeled, using verbal and nonverbal input. Statements are made such as "First you do this, second you . . ." or "Watch as I. . . ." The first try by students is also directed, "Everybody do this . . . don't go on until I tell you to," and then, "Now do this. . . ." You tell students the principles involved and summarize. In short, you do the showing and telling and students do the listening and doing. Practice is guided, and erring students are told what to do.

Some of the literature discusses skills teaching under the heading of *direct* teaching. Other terms are *explicit* or *active* teaching. A systematic, check-for-understanding, small-step, and active-learner-participation, success-oriented approach is involved. Note that direct instruction has been thought to be indispensable for mastering content and overlearning facts, rules, and action sequences that are essential to later learning. Direct instruction can be used for procedural knowledge (how to do something) for simple and complex skills, and for declarative knowledge (about something) that can be presented in a step-by-step way. Indirect instruction promotes understanding of the conceptual aspects of a skill.

The traditional approach to the teaching of most skills has been the deductive, or directed, method of teaching, whereby the teacher shows or tells what to do. If the teacher notices what a student is doing is wrong, a correction is given. Emphasis for the teaching of *complex skills* is shifting toward discovery, perhaps guided with suggestions, because some now believe skills are learned more permanently this way.

INDUCTIVE APPROACH.   When you stress *discovery* by students of the principles, processes, or steps involved, you use an *inductive approach.* Before the skill is modeled or demonstrated, students watch and think about how it is performed. Questions or cueing can be used to help students discover the steps, processes, or principles. Students summarize. When students practice, you help individuals by asking what should be done and why. When the skill is reviewed, or after students have practiced independently, stress is on *how* and (particularly) *why,* to help students construct personal understanding and meaning.

WHOLE VERSUS PART LEARNING.   The *whole approach* can be used for skills that are not too complex and where subskills are closely knit. This has the advantage of including an overview of the total skill and the relation, or associations, of parts to each other. Skills with many subskills should probably be broken into parts or "chewable pieces." A good practice is to work with as small an amount as possible, while retaining meaning and not wasting time. Proceed in small steps, check for student understanding, and have active and successful participation by all.

For some skills, practice of parts (or subskills) occurs while performing the whole. For example, a student can concentrate on the subskill of the golf grip while swinging a golf club; or a student may concentrate on punctuation while writing sentences.

If the decision is to use the *part approach,* decide the order to introduce parts (subskills). Selection will be based on the nature of the skill and dependence of the parts (subskills) to each other. Probably the most-used approach is the sequence of occurrence of the parts in the total task; another approach is to begin from the end and work in reverse order. Still another approach is to move from the simplest to the most complex subskill. If successful performance of one subskill depends on proficiency in another, then the foundational skill should be learned first.

Sometimes the elements of a skill chain can be learned independently and then put together. Sometimes it matters which part is taught first; in other cases it does not. For example, the parts of speech in a sentence can be learned separately, but you likely will present verbs before adverbs, nouns before pronouns, nouns before adjectives, and so on. Conjunctions and definite and indefinite articles do not normally have to be taught in any particular order. In any case, integration of the components into a smooth sequence must happen eventually.

Skills and Responsibility

Skill development has cognitive, psychomotor, and affective implications. Students may need to learn self-control and responsibility. Many skills are learned within a team or group context—not only in physical education, drama, and music, but also when learning any skill. A way of teaching skills and responsibility popular in physical education programs is Hellison's Awareness Levels. Skills learning is placed within the context of "awareness of and interaction with a loose progression of four values" (Hellison, 1986, p. 27). Hellison's levels are as follows.

> *Level IV, Caring:* Students at Level IV, in addition to respecting others, participating, and being self-directed, are motivated to extend their sense of responsibility beyond themselves by cooperating, giving support, showing concern, and helping.

Level III, Self-Direction. Students at Level III not only show respect and participation but also are able to work without direct supervision. They can identify their own needs and begin to plan and carry out their physical education programs.

Level II, Participation. Students at Level II not only show at least minimal respect for others but also willingly play, accept challenges, practice motor skills, and train for fitness under the teacher's supervision.

Level I, Respect: Students at Level I may not participate in daily activities or show much mastery or improvement, but they are able to control their behavior enough that they don't interfere with the other students' right to learn or the teacher's right to teach. They do this without much prompting by the teacher and without constant supervision.

Level Zero, Irresponsibility: Students who operate at Level Zero make excuses, blame others for their behavior, and deny personal responsibility for what they do or fail to do. (Hellison, 2003, p.28)

Students learn both skills and self-responsibility. "Unless responsibility is internalized as part of a student's belief and value system, it is much less likely to be transferred to settings beyond the gym" (Parker & Hellison, 2001, p. 25).

The Teaching of Skills

Preparing to Teach a Skill

Figure 10.2 shows a *Seven Step Planning Model* that is useful as a planning guide for teaching a skill. The steps do not have to be followed rigidly.

1. *Identify the skill.* The skill that is to be learned must be part of the curriculum for the course. Be clear about the context of the skill in the unit being covered; you may need to refer to the curriculum guide, the textbook, or other references. Know what was previously learned, the learning to follow, and the time that can be allocated for acquiring the skill.

2. *Task analysis before teaching a skill.* Preinstructional planning should include task analysis. This involves analyzing and ordering content as it relates to: (a) the sequence of steps or operations involved (for example, when you open a pop-top can, first you place your finger in the ring, then you lift the lid with the ring, and finally you twist the lid off), or (b) the order in which steps or operations should be learned (for example, before students can find a location on a city map, they have to know how to read the index and use the vertical and horizontal block systems). The latter requires discovery of the sequence of skills prerequisite to acquisition of a higher-order skill. Both kinds of task analysis involve identification of the subskills and the relationships and sequence of the subskills. Task analysis will be treated more fully later.

3. *Desired degree of proficiency and learner readiness.* Consider the age and developmental level of learners and their previous experiences with the skill or a related one. If the skill is cognitive, what cognitive readiness do learners have? If the skill has affective overtones, what is the learners' moral development level and what previous formal or

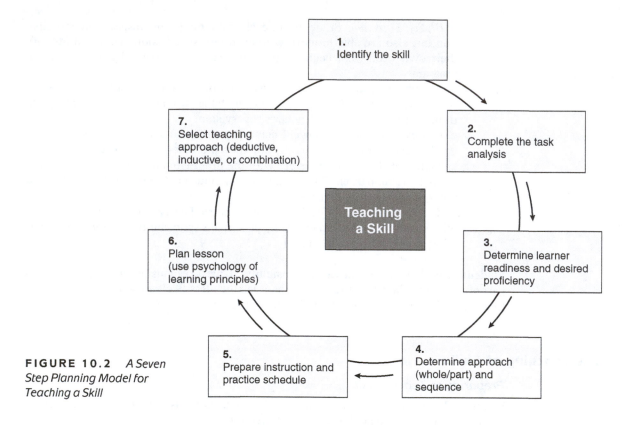

FIGURE 10.2   *A Seven Step Planning Model for Teaching a Skill*

informal learning experiences do they have? If the skill is psychomotor, what is the level of maturation and degree of physical readiness?

An important consideration is the degree of proficiency desired. How well must learners know the skill? Be aware that learners tend to move along a *skill development continuum:* (1) Unaware (2) Aware (3) Awkward (4) Conscious skill (5) Automaticity.

- *Unaware stage.* The learner begins by not being aware of what is involved in the performance of a skill and, perhaps, where and how it is to be used.
- *Awareness stage.* Before a skill can be acquired, the learner must become aware of it, discover its purpose, and be made aware of why it should be learned.
- *Awkwardness stage.* When the learner is aware of, and has knowledge of, the components of the skill, the learner can try it. First efforts tend to be inefficient, awkward, and full of errors.
- *Conscious skillfulness stage.* Conscious skillfulness develops through numerous tries, guidance, and feedback. The learner becomes proficient but must think consciously about what he or she is doing. The learner lacks complete spontaneity, and performance is still somewhat mechanical.
- *Automaticity stage.* The final stage is the integrated stage. Eventually, with much correct practice, behavior becomes habitual and the learner reaches an automatized phase. The skill can be used comfortably and creatively where and how it should be used.

When you plan to teach a skill, identify where learners are along the skill development continuum. Then, decide the level of skill, or degree of proficiency, learners are to acquire (awareness, awkwardness, conscious skillfulness, or automatization). If learners only need to be familiar with the skill, a portion of a lesson may be sufficient; if students will be expected to perform the skill automatically while doing other things, much practice over several weeks may be needed.

4. *Select the approach (whole or part) and the sequence of presentation.* When is it more efficient to break a skill into parts (or subskills), with separate instruction for each part? When is it better to teach the whole task? Age, previous experience, preferred learning style, and complexity must be considered. Decide how compact and meaningful the task is. Regardless of the approach, whole or part, identify the order in which subskills should be taught.

5. *Prepare the instruction and practice schedule.* If a skill is to be learned and retained, a suitable instruction and practice schedule must be set. The classic approach is to review previous learning, establish set, explain and demonstrate (and check up), guided practice (and check up), and independent practice (and check up).

After a new skill has been presented, to be retained and used, and for it to transfer to new contexts, it must be practiced. How much practice, whether in short or longer sittings, and how many sittings, are things you must decide.

6. *Consider the learning principles to be included in the lesson.* Several principles of the psychology of learning must be taken into account as you plan and deliver a skill lesson. Examples include having learners participate actively, being aware of the effects of success and failure, giving feedback and providing knowledge of results, providing guidance, providing reinforcement, dealing with the effects of interference, individualizing teaching and learning, and facilitating transfer of training.

7. *Select the teaching approach.* The approach chosen may be direct (explicit) or guided discovery—it may be deductive or inductive. The deductive approach is satisfactory if skills are straightforward or not too complex, but the inductive approach may be better if students are to understand the principles and processes involved and to speed learning and promote transfer. Skillful modeling or demonstration is important to both the deductive and inductive approaches.

Both approaches require modeling and usually involve demonstration. We all have learned much by watching someone perform a skill and imitating what we saw, whether this be a psychomotor skill (e.g., using a Bunsen burner in the chemistry lab), a cognitive skill (e.g., solving a geometry problem), or an affectively toned skill (e.g., manners at the dinner table). Become proficient at modeling and demonstrating. When you model and demonstrate, make sure learners can see what is going on, and accompany the demonstration with concise explanations. Discussing the skills and their uses helps later performance.

Task Analysis: Procedural, Hierarchical, and Combination

Whether the skill is motor, cognitive, or affective, ask yourself what is involved in performing it proficiently. What background knowledge or previous experience do students need? What steps or operations are involved? Is a there a sequence of steps or events to follow? You may need to do a task analysis. The operations of physical tasks can be observed and recorded; cognitive tasks, however, require analysis of the knowledge and thought processes needed to perform the tasks (Hanser, 1995). Although task analysis is often associated with special education and vocational education, it has much wider application. It is an important instructional strategy for every teacher. It is done to identify the specific details of tasks, including the knowledge, subskills, attitudes, and personal characteristics needed for successful performance (Brown, 1998).

Task analysis of skills can be approached in terms of the sequence of *procedures* (or steps) to be followed, the *hierarchy* of skills and concepts involved, or a *combination* of the two. You will need to choose between, or combinations of, three kinds of skill analyses:

- The procedural approach: step-by-step
- The hierarchical approach: the hierarchy of subskills needed
- The combination approach: a combination of step-by-step and hierarchical

Be able to use each approach to instructional analysis to identify the subskills and their relationships. This is needed in planning for efficient presentation and learning to be possible.

PROCEDURAL TASK ANALYSIS.   The procedural approach involves identifying the chain of events or operations to be performed (in sequence) to achieve an instructional goal and listing these step-by-step (Dick & Carey, 2005, p. 67). This analysis is useful for pinpointing where instruction should be focused—identifying chain elements and spots where elements must be linked for smooth performance. Analysis of a procedure for folding and inserting a letterhead business letter into a business envelope is illustrated in Figure 10.3.

If these procedures are followed, the final product is a letter inserted into an envelope. When following the procedural approach, steps can be taught independently of each other; however, they do follow a sequence. Each step involves stages: (1) The *input* of one step initiates a (2) *process* followed to reach an (3) *output* of that step. Dick and Carey (2005) recommend that after "you have identified the instructional goal, you will determine step-by-step what people are doing when they perform that goal. The final step in the instructional analysis process is to determine what skills, knowledge and attitudes, known as *entry behaviors*, are required of learners to be able to begin the instruction." (p. 6). Diagrams are an important part of instructional analysis (Dick & Carey, pp. 71–72). In pro-

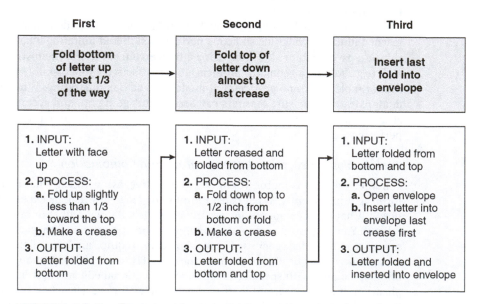

FIGURE 10.3   *Procedural Analysis: Folding and Inserting a Letter into an Envelope*

cedural analysis the diagram is a continuous line (envelope example). In hierarchical task analysis sub-skills must be identified (job interview example). Combination task analysis requires both the step-by-step and hierarchical stages (dictionary example).

HIERARCHICAL TASK ANALYSIS.   A hierarchy is a set of component skills to be learned before the complex skill of which they are a part can be learned. Hierarchical analysis is used to discover what students must know and be able to do before they can successfully learn a skill. For example, students need to know how to write sentences before they can learn to write paragraphs. It identifies the skills (or subskills) needed to perform a higher-level skill. Subskills can be called *enabling* skills, those needed to achieve a "terminal" skill objective. For instance, if the terminal objective is subtracting whole numbers of any size, students need to be able to subtract when several borrowings are required, and before this, they need to have learned single borrowing. The list could be extended downward through other subskills to the ability to do simple subtraction and knowledge of simple subtraction facts.

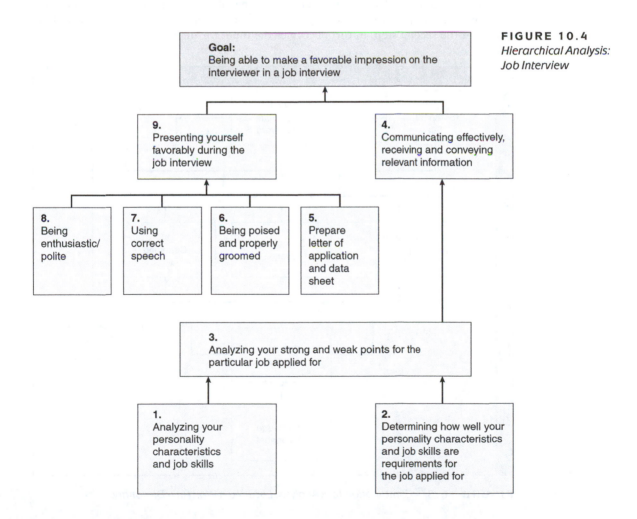

FIGURE 10.4
Hierarchical Analysis: Job Interview

Study the example on preparing for a job interview in Figure 10.4. It identifies the sequencing of enabling skills (subcompetencies) and the terminal objective of making a favorable impression in a job interview. You will see that hierarchical task analysis objectives can be accomplished by: (1) having a good knowledge of the behaviors that are effective for a successful interview, and (2) identifying and arranging the subskills into a logical order (showing the sequence of those that might be prerequisite to others).

When you do hierarchical analysis, you may need numerous revisions before you are satisfied. However, it will provide valuable information about the kinds and sequence of enabling skills students must have or master before the overall skill can be acquired.

Procedural analysis is appropriate for psychomotor skills. Complex skills, cognitive skills in particular, normally require hierarchical analysis. For a detailed description of hierarchical analysis by Dick and Carey, refer to the sixth edition of *The Systematic Design of Instruction* (2005).

COMBINATION TASK ANALYSIS.   Many tasks require a combination of procedural and hierarchical analysis. Consider locating a word in a dictionary (Figure 10.5). The steps to be followed to locate a word are: locate the tab, locate the guideword, and locate the word. The output of the first step is the input for the process of the second; and the output of the second step, in turn, becomes the input for the third. This requires proce-

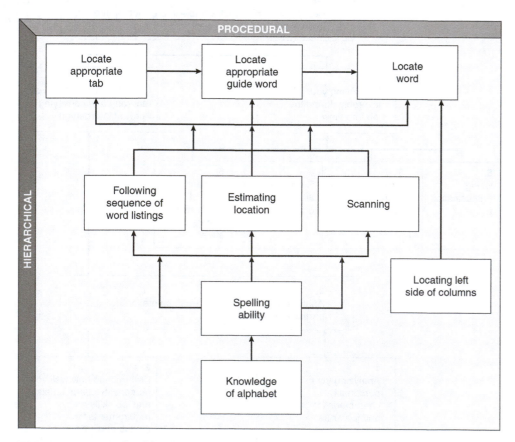

FIGURE 10.5   *Combination Task Analysis: Locating a Word in a Dictionary*

dural (horizontal) analysis, with each step examined in terms of input, process, and output. Prerequisite subskills are shown vertically—selecting and ordering these requires hierarchical analysis. The combination approach is used to analyze a relatively complex psychomotor skill or linear chain of cognitive tasks.

Skills Lesson Planning

Thorough planning precedes effective skill teaching. Steps for planning a skill lesson were presented earlier. You may wish to study these before you proceed. Authorities on the direct teaching of skills agree on essential procedures: orientation, presentation, structured practice, guided practice, and independent practice.

When setting foundational objectives, many states and provinces now specify skills as well as knowledge and affective objectives. Consider the following examples of knowledge, skills, and values requirements in a social studies unit on global issues (Saskatchewan Learning, 2004).

Knowledge Objectives

1. Know that some challenges or issues are global in nature because they affect the entire earth and will require global involvement to find solutions.
2. Know that human rights are rights to which an individual is entitled simply because he or she is human.
3. Know that the acquisition and utilization of technological and scientific knowledge have given humans the power to change the world's environment significantly.

Skills/Abilities Objectives

1. Learn and practice using criteria as a basis for analyzing information.
2. Learn and practice selecting and applying the abilities of problem solving, dialectical thinking, decision making, and conflict resolution to the issue.
3. Learn and practice defining the main parts, describing cause-and-effect relationships, and describing how the parts of the whole are related to each other.

Values Issues the Student Will Discuss

1. Whether there are acceptable and nonacceptable methods available to individuals and groups seeking to secure their rights.
2. Whether humans and societies will continue to demonstrate a willingness to use force and violence to achieve goals.
3. What criteria are to be used to determine how the earth's resources and species should be used.

It is the role of the teacher to present these objectives in specific terms in lesson plans. However, note how the teaching of skills enhances knowledge and values objectives. A six-step framework for skills teaching designed by the authors of this text is presented in Figure 10.6. Following is an eleven-step procedure for the teaching of skills.

1. *State objectives and provide set.* The effective teacher begins by explaining the objectives, establishing a learning set, and, often, providing an overview. Students should know why it is important to them to be able to perform the skill.

2. *Review and check previous day's work.* Daily review is important for material needed for subsequent learning. The purpose of review and checking assignments is to emphasize the relationships between lessons, ensure that students have the prerequisite

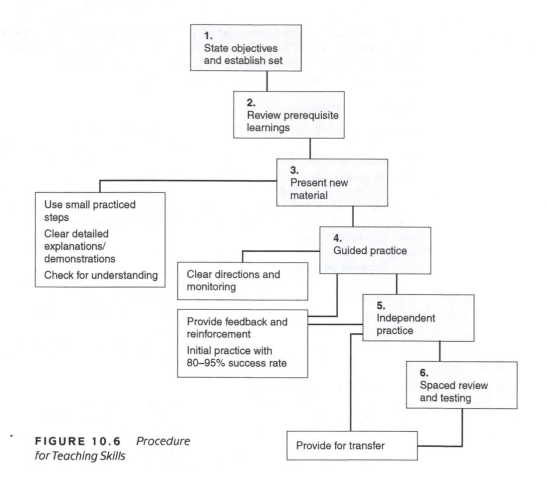

FIGURE 10.6   *Procedure for Teaching Skills*

knowledge or skills, and ensure they see the new material as an extension of content already mastered.

3. *Present new material in small practiced steps.*   Good teachers spend more time presenting new material and guided practice than less able teachers. Make purposes clear and teach in small portions, using step-by-step directions. Make sure each step is mastered before the next is given. Use clear, pure, simple-to-complex demonstrations and examples. Do not skimp on examples or demonstrations. Stress understanding.

4. *Provide clear explanations and demonstrations.*   As the skill is explained, modeled, or demonstrated, make sure students know the execution and flow of skills and subskills. All must see what is being modeled or demonstrated. Make explanations interesting, to the point, and complete. Check for understanding. Reteach if necessary.

5. *Check for understanding.*   Students must do more than memorize steps or operations. They should understand how and why steps fit together. After each step, make sure each student understands and performs the step correctly. Doing a poor job of assessing the progress of individuals is a major reason for poor skill development. Ask one or more students to show they can understand and perform. Assuming everyone can do it is common. Evaluating the progress of every student and record keeping are necessary.

6. *Provide a high level of guided and active practice.* Practice does not always make perfect—correct practice can. Have students do initial practice, step by step, with you as you demonstrate. Observe carefully whether it is being done correctly. At the initial stages, practice should focus on process (how to do it) rather than product (doing it right). Stress technique. You do not want students to practice incorrect procedures that must be unlearned.

7. *Provide feedback and reinforcement.* Provide specific and descriptive feedback, correctives when needed, and reinforcement for each student's guided practice, seatwork, or homework. Feedback should focus on process. Reinforcement must be supported by an accurate description of what was good. Just telling the student, "That was good," is not helpful. Tell the student what was done well and add, in a supportive way, tips for improvement.

8. *Provide clear directions and monitor seatwork.* Provide clear directions before guided seatwork. Circulate, to give feedback and correctives for those who need it. Effective teachers provide sufficient practice when students learn new material. Students must be able to perform a skill well before practicing independently. Practice should emphasize process with a high rate of success. Decide the nature and quantity of further practice. This depends on the level of learning desired—awkwardness, conscious skillfulness, or automaticity.

9. *Work toward high initial practice success rate.* Students should achieve a success rate of from 80 to 95 percent in initial practices. Assignments should challenge but not be too difficult or complex. Students must "get it right" before engaging in independent practice.

10. *Provide for transfer.* Students must see the relevance to what they studied before and will study later. Ensure transfer. Practice should be as close to an actual situation as possible. After monitored practice, practice can be assigned as homework or done in class the next day. If transfer is wanted, practice it.

11. *Provide spaced review and testing.* If the skill is to be retained, it must be learned very well in the first place; spaced review should occur to ensure retention and consolidate learning. Test often to provide clues for reteaching and the nature of further practice. Testing should disclose present performance capability, understanding, and the ability to transfer.

Practicing a Skill

Practice is important. It is used to overlearn and maintain a skill so it can be used in other, or new, contexts. Simple or isolated behaviors may require little or no practice (for example, locating the space key on a computer). Practice becomes more important as learning becomes more complex, and prolonged practice is needed to polish skills such as touch keyboarding, reading, writing, and computing. Basic skills normally must be overlearned, that is, brought to the automaticity level. The kind, amount, and distribution of practice must be decided and a distributed practice schedule set that includes drills, reviews, and testing. Consider whether practice should be *massed* (in one or a few lengthy sessions) or *distributed* (in a larger number of short sessions). Usually, when motor skills are being learned, it is better to distribute practice with rest intervals between. If time is limited, rest intervals reduce the time available for practice, so rest intervals may be reduced or even eliminated. These affect performance, but not learning, of motor skills. Rest intervals may not be as important for cognitive or affectively toned skills if a high interest level is maintained, but it is generally better to distribute practice unless breaking it up interferes with the flow or degree of learning. It is difficult to generalize about practice schedules and whether practice should be whole or part, massed or distributed. Decisions about these depend on the skill to be learned and the learners.

Example Lesson Plan

Study the lesson plan presented below. Task analysis should be done before the skill lesson is taught. A procedural task analysis for folding and inserting a business letter into an envelope was provided earlier. The lesson below is based on that analysis.

Lesson Plan

I. *Topic:* Business letters

II. *Content:* Folding a standard business letter and inserting it into a standard business envelope

III. *Objective:* After a demonstration of the correct procedure for folding an 8½-by-11-inch business letter and inserting it into a business envelope, each student will be able to do the procedure in one minute or less.

IV. *Prerequisite learning:* None

V. *Presentation activities*

    A. *Introductory:* Tell students they will be learning an efficient procedure for folding and inserting business letters and that this is useful and important personal and occupational information. Have them watch as you remove an actual business letter from an envelope and show them the creases on the letter.

    B. *Developmental*

        1. Tell students to watch carefully as you demonstrate the correct procedure for folding and inserting; conduct the demonstration in three stages: (a) folding bottom of letter up almost one-third of the way; (b) folding the top down almost to the last crease; and (c) inserting the last fold into the envelope. Repeat the demonstration.

        2. Distribute three business letters and an envelope to each student; demonstrate and have students copy what you are doing, one stage at a time. They are not to go ahead on their own. After each step, ask students to hold up their letters so you can see if they are doing it correctly and provide help if needed. Repeat the guided practice with a fresh letter.

        3. Call a student to the front of the room; call on other students to tell this student how to do the three steps.

        4. Ask students to practice folding and inserting with letters they had previously printed. Circulate as students practice to provide feedback, correctives if needed, and reinforcement.

    C. *Closure*

        1. Tell students you will be timing them as they fold and insert a business letter. Inform them they should be done in one minute or less. Students are to hold up their inserted letters when done. Time the students. Repeat the procedure until everybody in the room is doing it in one minute or less.

        2. Compliment students about their accomplishment. Tell them that for every business letter they handle in future assignments, they will be required to fold and insert the letter into an addressed envelope.

VI. *Materials and aids:* Standard business letters and envelopes

VII. *Evaluation:* Observation as students hold up completed materials and one minute timed practice results.

You can use the data collection instrument to help you analyze the cases that follow. Your instructor may pose specific questions for your response.

CASE 10.1   Teaching a Skill

A Great Skill Teacher

You might use the following case as an introduction to this chapter. As you read the following case, note the steps being followed by the instructor and ask yourself what principles of effective teaching are being used.

> Bill Duffer had bought a set of used golf clubs and had played for about two months. Though he had good eye–hand coordination, Bill realized that if he was to improve to the point where he could play a "respectable" game, he needed to take lessons. He booked a set of lessons with golf professional Lee Palmer, who, he was told, was a very good instructor.

It was Monday, and Lee and Bill began the first lesson with the two playing three holes of golf together. This was a surprise to Bill. He thought the first lesson would be on the practice range, but Lee explained he wanted to observe Bill play so he could decide where instruction should begin and the sequence of instruction for future lessons.

The two then went to the practice range. On the way, Lee presented Bill with a diagnosis of Bill's current capability and a projected improvement schedule that was to take place through ten lessons over a period of ten weeks. Bill's putting did not need attention, but he could benefit significantly by improving his golf swing, chipping to the hole, and planning strategy for playing differing golf holes. Lee told Bill that because golf is so complex, a learner cannot concentrate on every aspect simultaneously. He said the golf swing takes about three seconds and there are dozens of parts to an expert swing. A learner can concentrate effectively only on one or a few things simultaneously. Lee said he'd pick the really important aspects first, give a lesson on an aspect, and then Bill needed to practice that aspect to the point where he no longer needed to think consciously about it.

Lee then demonstrated the proper golf grip, telling Bill that this was the foundation of the golf swing, that the two hands must act as a unit, and that holding the golf club was like holding a bird—tight enough so that the bird could not escape but loose enough so that the bird would not be hurt. Lee guided Bill's hands into the proper position. Bill then hit several balls as Lee helped Bill make minor adjustments, until Lee said, "Very good, you look like you have the idea." Bill stated that the grip felt awkward. Lee said that this was normal, and that during the rest of the week he should not worry about his score. With practice, the new grip would feel natural and, after some initial awkwardness and perhaps a very temporary drop in proficiency, improvement could be dramatic. The lesson ended with Lee asking Bill to review the elements of the golf grip. The next lesson, Lee said, would concentrate on the body turn as the club was taken back, the ball struck, and the follow-through was completed.

CASE 10.2   Teaching a Skill

Using the Alphabet

Mr. Aftahi planned to teach his grade 1 class how to organize information alphabetically and put words into alphabetical order. Though the children read at varying levels and several have been using primary dictionaries and other reference books, the skill has not been formally taught.

continued

Mr. Aftahi obtained several dictionaries, telephone directories, encyclopedias, reference books, and enlarged copies of index pages. Children enter the classroom after recess and Mr. Aftahi has displayed the books so everyone can see. The students are interested in the large number of books and other materials and become quiet as they watch.

Finally, Jay asks, "What are we going to do with all those things, Mr. Aftahi?" Mr. Aftahi, who has finished displaying the materials, looks around to make sure he has everyone's attention. He asks, "Let's see if we can answer Jay's question. What do you see on these tables?" The children answer, "Books," "Dictionaries," "Encyclopedias," "Papers," and "Telephone books."

"What is in these books?" asks Mr. Aftahi. The students respond, "Names," "Words," "Sentences," "Stories," "You can find out stuff you want to know," "I saw maps in one of those books," and "My mom looks up telephone numbers in the telephone book."

"So there are words, names, sentences, stories, maps, and telephone numbers in these books? Would you say people use these books to find things out?" The children agree. "If I wanted to find a telephone number in this book, what would I do?" Mr. Aftahi gestures toward the telephone directory. "You'd look it up," says Danny. "OK, what does that mean?" asks Mr. Aftahi. Danny explains, "Look for the name of the person you want to phone and the right number is beside his name."

"All right, let's look up Mr. Jessop's number. You say I look for his name and his number will be right there?" Danny nods vigorously and Mr. Aftahi begins at the first page and reads the first few names. "Danny, can you help me here?" Danny comes to help. He studies the page, looks at the name on the board and back at the page. "I don't see it yet," he remarks. "Do you notice anything about the names here?" asks Mr. Aftahi. Students begin to wave their hands. "These names all start with 'A,'" Danny says. "Is the whole book like that?" asks Mr. Aftahi. Danny looks at successive pages. "No," he announces. "There are lots of other letters at the start on other pages."

"What else has 'A' at the start?" "My name," says Andrea. "Yes, it does, but I'm thinking of something bigger than a name," responds Mr. Aftahi. "The ABCs," answers Tuan. "Right. The ABCs, or

the alphabet, starts with 'A.' I wonder if the rest of the book is anything like the alphabet. Tuan, come and work with Danny to see if the telephone book is like the ABCs." Tuan and Danny pour over the book, turning pages, and saying the names of the letters as they come to them. "Yes," they report. "First come the 'A' names, then the 'B' names, and the 'C' names, and so on. The 'Z' names are at the end."

"So where will we look for Mr. Jessop's name?" asks Mr. Aftahi. "In the 'J' names," answer several children. Danny and Tuan turn to the "J" section and find Mr. Jessop's name and number. "See how easy that was once we knew how the names were organized? What is it that tells us what comes first or last, or helps us to know where names are found?" "We can look at the alphabet on the wall, or we can just say the ABCs," says Yvette. "Right, the alphabet can be our guide." Mr. Aftahi then assigns three or four children to each resource to see if the information is organized in the same way. The students are excited to discover the same pattern in the resources they examine. Some say, "I knew it all the time."

"Putting things, like words or names, in ABC order, or alphabetical order, is an important thing to be able to do. It helps us understand the way to find information more quickly and it is a way that many people understand. Today we will practice arranging some word cards in alphabetical order. What will we use as our guide?" "The alphabet." "That's right. Now look at these three words and try to decide which would come first, second, and third if we put them in alphabetical order." He shows the words *cat, apple,* and *ball.* The children easily put them in order.

"How did you do it? What did you do first?" Tara explains, "I just thought of A, B, C and matched up the words." Matt says he looked at the letters on the wall to help him put the words in order. "Both ways are good," says Mr. Aftahi. "Let's try these." He shows word cards saying *Candice, Ewen,* and *Dominique.*

The students arrange these words and do two other examples Mr. Aftahi presents. Finally, each child is presented with a set of three words and asked to arrange them in alphabetical order. "When you have finished, look around for someone else who is finished, get him to check yours and you check his. Look at the alphabet on the wall if you're not sure. Then trade your cards with someone else who has had theirs checked. Then, do the same thing again. Try to do three sets of cards, and check three sets of someone else's. Don't do the same set twice."

The children work busily at their desks, the floor, and a large table. Mr. Aftahi circulates.

CASE 10.3 Teaching a Skill

Being Interested in Interest

Ms. Atwater had just taken up yesterday's homework questions on calculating interest in her grade 11 business math class. "Today," she said, "We are going to learn something that is going to be a real benefit to you in the future. You or another member of your family have at times buy something, for instance, a stereo or car, by making a down payment and then paying the rest in monthly installments. As you know, credit is not free. Let's say you buy a boombox for $135.00 and make a $35 down payment. You are told the interest rate will be only 6 percent and that you can pay in 12 monthly installments. How much do you think you will pay in interest?" Maria answers, "That's easy, six dollars." "No way," Orest interjects. "You'll get ripped off for much more." "You're right, Orest. The rate is not calculated as a simple annual interest rate. The truth is that you will pay about twice that. Today you will learn how to calculate true interest rates so you can easily test what you will pay and you won't have a surprise or so you can choose to shop elsewhere if you can get a better deal."

Ms. Atwater then wrote the formula for calculating true interest rate on the chalkboard.

$$\frac{2PC}{A(N+1)} = R$$

where A = amount of cash or credit received
 N = number of payments in the contract
 P = number of payments per year
 C = total charges including service charges
 R = interest rate in terms of simple annual interest

"Let's see how much that boombox is really going to cost. Watch me use the true interest formula."

$$2 \times 12 \times 6 = 144 = 11.08\%$$
$$100 \times (12 + 1) = 1300$$

"So, you can see, as we said, you are paying almost twice as much as a simple interest rate would lead you to believe. You pay $11.08 in interest rather than $6.00."

Ms. Atwater then did two more examples on the chalkboard. She asked individual students to tell her each step. Then she sent six students to the chalkboard to do a problem. When they were done, she asked them to explain what they had done. The six went back to their seats and she said, "Turn to page 196. Do problems 1, 2, 3, 4, 5, 7, 9, 11, 13, and 15." Next, she did the first problem, step by step, with the entire class. Then, she circulated as students began their assignment. She stopped to talk to several students. To some she made comments such as, "Why don't you try this . . . ?" To others she said, "That's right. Can you tell me how you got the answer?"

With two minutes left in the period, she gained the attention of the class, saying, "You are well on the way to acquiring a very important 'smart consumer' skill. Please do the rest of the problems for homework. Do one more thing. If you have recently purchased something on credit, calculate the true interest rate on that purchase. Alternately, find out if somebody at home has purchased something on credit recently. Perhaps you can calculate the true interest rate on that purchase."

Demonstrations

Have you ever bought something you had to assemble that included an "easy" explanation for how to do it? Was it easy? Were you frustrated? Didn't you wish that the explanation was clearer, or, better still, that somebody would show you? How often did you memorize something without understanding it because the teacher did not explain it or did so in a confusing way? Were there times you could not solve a problem or complete an operation even after a teacher demonstrated it and you did not want to appear stupid so you did not ask for a redemonstration?

While *explaining* relates largely to the teaching of concepts, generalizations, and principles, *demonstrating* (showing how) applies to skills and processes (cognitive, psychomotor, or interpersonal or social). Demonstrations can be used to help students learn a procedure, process, or illustration. Direct teaching makes extensive use of demonstrations because many of the things we learn come through observing others. A demonstration can provide a critical observed-action experience that transcends verbal explanation. As a teaching method in its own right, demonstration normally involves both a visual part and a spoken explanation. Watching demonstrations saves students unnecessary and time-consuming trial and error. Demonstrations may require concrete performance of actions, skills, or processes. It is the link between "knowing about" and "being able to do." Demonstrations can stimulate interest and provide the advantage of having students use several senses. When demonstrations are done well, ideas and concepts are presented clearly. The result should be increased student attentiveness, learning, and performance. Examples of demonstrations include watching a tennis stroke, a dance step, magnetic attraction or repulsion, solving a quadratic equation, or mixing water colors. Demonstrations can be used to enhance aspects of every school subject.

Procedure for Effective Demonstrations

Before you begin a demonstration, decide whether you will permit students to ask questions during the demonstration. Ask yourself whether a handout is a good idea or whether students should take notes.

1. *Analyze.* Analyze what is to be demonstrated before you begin (i.e., procedural, hierarchical, or combination skill analysis).
2. *Practice.* Do a "dry run" (rehearse). Ask, "What are the key steps to be followed?" "What words should I use?" "Where will students have the most difficulty?"
3. *Set up.* Before the class begins, set up demonstration materials so class time will not be wasted. Make sure all can see. Remember that when one faces the class, right and left are reversed; if possible, demonstrate so students will not have to make right/left transfer. Have ready any materials that students will need. Plan how materials can be distributed quickly (or, in advance, place them at student stations).
4. *Establish the set.* State the objectives for the demonstration and establish the set. If necessary, review prerequisite knowledge or skills. Provide an overview. Students must be informed (and believe) it is important for them to know what is to be learned. With some demonstrations, highlight the aspects students are to observe.
5. *Get and maintain attention.* Secure undivided attention before beginning. Watch for nonverbal clues of inattentiveness or lack of understanding. Check up if necessary.
6. *Demonstrate.* Use well-defined, clearly presented steps. Do not move too quickly. For some demonstrations, do them at normal speed first and repeat the steps in "slow motion." If the procedure is complex, break it into steps and demonstrate these separately. Use clear, concise, oral descriptions. Stress key aspects.
7. *Record key aspects.* It may be useful to record important steps or points for review on the chalkboard, a transparency, or handout.

8. *Redemonstrate.* For understanding, repeat the demonstration (or steps) as necessary. This means check to see if students know the "how" and "why" and if they are ready to try it themselves.

9. *Provide practice.* Have students do it with you, step by step, as often as necessary. Then provide individual practice. Initial practices must be monitored and have a high rate of success (80 to 95 percent). Provide immediate feedback, correctives, and reinforcement. Assign independent practice after you are sure the students know how to do it.

A data collection instrument for use with the target of demonstrating is given in Appendix 10.3. Normal demonstration steps are shown in Figure 10.7. After you have done your demonstration, do a self-evaluation. You can ask yourself:

1. During the introduction, did you get the attention of the class? Tell why what is being demonstrated is important.

2. Did you communicate clearly, make eye contact, encourage feedback, use appropriate language, and pause when appropriate? Could everybody easily see and hear?

3. Where you aware of whether students were following, that you were not moving to quickly or too slowly? Did you respond clearly to questions?

4. Was the quality of the materials used attractive, suitable, easily seen?

5. Did you review the key points, ask for questions, and provide feedback and reinforcement during student practice?

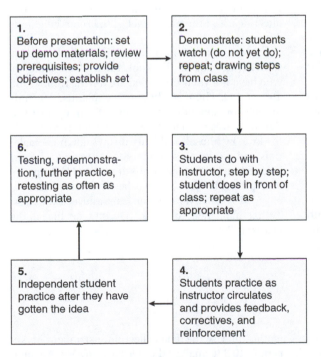

FIGURE 10.7 *Steps in Demonstration*

Demonstration Principles

Modeling (demonstration) by the teacher is most often part of a skill lesson. The purpose is to give students a clear idea of what is expected. This is true whether the skill is psychomotor (e.g., doing a set shot in basketball), cognitive (e.g., estimating an answer in mathematics), or affectively toned (e.g., paraphrasing).

Students need to see and hear each substep. The demonstration must not be hurried. Verbal explanations must be to the point and focus on key aspects. If a skill involves several steps, it may need to be demonstrated several times. Steps may have to be isolated and demonstrated. Students should try the skill (or subskill) "with you." Monitored individual practice should not begin until students are ready. Data collection instruments for use with the professional target of teaching a skill are given in Appendixes 10.1 and 10.2, and for demonstrating in Appendix 10.3.

Common mistakes in giving demonstrations include: (1) students try a skill before they are ready to do it without guidance, (2) too many details are given in an explanation, or too many directions, steps, or details are included (more than a beginner can possibly assimilate at one time), and (3) feedback is not given on "with-the-teacher" attempts.

Use the data collection instruments in Appendixes 10.1, 10.2, and 10.3 to help you analyze the cases that follow. Your instructor may pose specific questions for your response.

CASE 10.4 Demonstrations

Macramé Getting Planted

Mr. Santez has talked with his grade 6 class about making macramé plant holders as Christmas gifts. Not one of the students knows any of the knot-tying techniques, and Mr. Santez intends to demonstrate the half-hitch first. When the students have mastered this, he plans to teach them other knots. Mr. Santez worked at a summer camp in charge of crafts, and he feels sure he can quickly teach students to tie a half-hitch.

After recess, Mr. Santez begins to explain how to tie a half-hitch. Though several students are not attending, he describes the procedure verbally. He soon realizes that several students seem to be having trouble following the directions. He looks in his desk drawer for cord and finds a length of string. He goes through the procedure again at the front of the room, noting he inadvertently omitted a step in his explanation. He points out the change in procedure. Some students look anxious, some seem confused.

The string is rather small, and soon the students are fidgeting and muttering about not being able to see. Mr. Santez tells them to pay closer attention and that if they had been watching in the first place, they would know how to do the knot. He says, "I will show you once more. Then you'll have to do it yourselves."

Mr. Santez goes through the procedure again and leaves the classroom to fetch the macramé cord stored in the art supply room. When he returns with two colors, the students are arguing noisily about the

correct procedure. He calls for attention and asks the students to choose a color and to each cut off an arm's length of cord. They begin to follow these directions but are unable to continue because no one can find scissors. Mr. Santez remembers that, because of the last budget cuts, scissors are kept in the principal's office, so he sends a student to get them. Students are quickly losing interest in the project, and begin to make disparaging remarks about the idea.

When the scissors arrive, only a few children seem interested. The others have to be encouraged, and in a few cases ordered, to begin the task. There is general confusion and many students call out questions, and the noise level in the room heightens dramatically.

Mr. Santez works with one individual at a time, showing how to tie the knot. Most of the students who have not yet been helped are having trouble and are waiting. There is a hum of complaints, demands for help, or demands for a change of activity. Frustration increases until a boy who has been trying to tie the knot by himself suddenly throws down his materials and, for a few seconds, sits glowering. The girl behind him laughs and points at him and he leaps up, overturning his desk, and rushes from the room.

Mr. Santez notices him leave and asks the class, "What happened to Mark? Doesn't he like doing macramé?"

CASE 10.5 Demonstrations

Business Math

Look again at Case 10.3, describing a business math lesson. The teacher, Ms. Atwater, demonstrates a

math skill. Use the data collection instrument in Appendix 10.3 to analyze the steps used by Ms. Atwater.

LINKING PRACTICE TO THEORY

To what extent do we teach students "what" but not "how" or "why"? Do you find teaching the "what" easier than teaching "how" or "why"? As you plan lessons and units, how should you incorporate the procedural and hierarchical skills involved? How skill-based are the subjects you teach? Try the guidelines suggested in this chapter. How important is it to analyze a skill before teaching it?

Summary

Effective skill teaching requires that teachers recognize the attributes of skilled performance. Planning for teaching a skill should, as appropriate, include procedural, hierarchical, or combination task analysis. Decisions are needed about whether to use a part or whole, a deductive or inductive approach, and the skill-teaching principles involved. The basic steps for good skill teaching are orientation, presentation, structured practice, guided practice, independent practice, rapid feedback, and spaced reviews. Most skills need to be demonstrated within a framework of planning and preparation, demonstration by the teacher, students "doing with" as the teacher demonstrates, monitored student practice, independent practice, testing, and redemonstration as required.

Activities

1. The instructor or a student might model short lessons to illustrate the steps and elements of skill teaching and the deductive and inductive approaches. Point out the components of each lesson.

2. Join a subject area group and brainstorm examples of procedural skills, hierarchical skills, and skills that are a combination of procedural and hierarchical. Do task analyses of a procedural skill, hierarchical skill, and combination skill, and prepare lesson plans for the skills analyzed.

3. Have a class discussion in which class members tell about skills at which they are at an automaticity level.

4. Pass out sheets of letter paper and envelopes and take the class through the steps given in the example of procedural analysis in Figure 10.3.

5. Have the class brainstorm the preparation needed for a successful job interview and then compare their findings with the chart in Figure 10.4.

6. Using a large dictionary, invite selected members of the class up and have them look up preselected words from the front, middle, and back of the dictionary. Ask the class what subskills were needed before the words could be found quickly.

7. Have two volunteers give a skill lesson while the remainder of the class completes the data gathering sheet in Appendix 10.1.

8. Reread the Bill Duffer case presented at the start of the chapter; analyze it in terms of what you have learned.

9. Join a subject group of five. Select a task in the subject, then apply your learning about the teaching of skills and prepare a suitable lesson plan.

10. Examine a can of pudding that has a pop-top opening. Do a procedural analysis of opening the can. Following this, by subject-area interest, join a group to select and analyze a subject skill

11. Obtain a city map. Given an address to find, do a hierarchical analysis of the skills involved. Then, by subject interest, join a group of five or six to select and analyze a subject skill.

12. In a subject-area group, brainstorm examples of demonstrations that can be given in that subject. Categorize these under the headings of skills, processes, procedures, or illustrations.

13. In your group, prepare a demonstration and present to the class. Class members are to provide feedback using the data collection sheet in Appendix 10.3. Debrief.

APPENDIX 10.1   *Teaching a Skill Lesson Target*

PROFESSIONAL TARGET—TEACHING A SKILL LESSON

Lesson Elements	Descriptive Notes

A. Deductive Lesson

Set

Gaining attention?
Reviewing prerequisite skills?
Describing context for use of skill?
Giving skill objective "Today you will . . . learn to. . . ."

Development

Modeling/demo'ing skill step by step?
Cueing ("First you do," "second")?
Visual or verbal input?
Highlighting terms or steps?
Modeling again?
Leading students through skill, cueing?
Checking students' tries?
Modeling again?
Supervised practice?
Feedback?

Closure

Reviewing steps—by student? by instructor?
Reviewing context in which skill is used?
Assigning practice?
Bridging to next step or lesson?
Provision for transfer?

B. Inductive Lesson

Set

As above, *except* skill is introduced in general terms only
("Today you will learn a skill that will help you. . . .")

Development

Present/develop, e.g., visually, concrete, on board, etc.
Examples used?
Discovery by students of steps involved?
Summarizing?

Closure

Reviewing steps—by student? by instructor?
Reviewing context in which skill is used?
Assigning practice?
Bridging to next step or lesson?
Provision for transfer?

APPENDIX 10.2   *Teaching a Skill Target*

PROFESSIONAL TARGET—TEACHING A SKILL

Name of Skill: _____

Procedure Used: _____ Procedural   _____ Hierarchical   _____ Combination

Teaching Elements	Descriptive Notes

Major subskills identified

Subskills of major skills identified

Relationship of subskills

Practice of subskills and/or whole skill

Feedback to students

Use of skill identified

List steps of
    Presentation or Demonstration

Check procedures for the direct teaching of skills as used:

1. _____ Objectives and set provided   4. _____ Guided practice provided

2. _____ Prerequisites reviewed   5. _____ Monitored practice

3. _____ Skill modeled   6. _____ Independent practice assigned

APPENDIX 10.3 *Demonstrating Target*

PROFESSIONAL TARGET—DEMONSTRATING

Please describe what was said or done and how students reacted.

Procedures	Descriptive Notes

Before demo
   Preparation
      Materials/equip ready
      Students able to see

Establishing set
   For demo
   Review prerequisites

Conducting the demo
   Gaining and maintaining attention
   Oral description clarity, language usage
   Nonverbal cues
   Emphasis on key elements/points
   Use of materials, concrete/visual

Check steps used: Comments:

1. _____ Set
2. _____ Instructor demo
3. _____ Instructor repeats demo
4. _____ Instructor repeats drawing steps from class
5. _____ A student is asked to do demo
6. _____ Students practice under supervision
7. _____ Testing
8. _____ Redemo
9. _____ Further practice
10. _____ Retesting
11. _____ Individual practice assigned (e.g., homework)

Practice of skill or procedure
   Directions given
   Feedback: checking up, reinforcing

Provision for transfer

Selecting Instructional Approaches

The range of instructional strategies and approaches that are a key part of the teacher's repertoire are examined in Part III. Discussed in this section are

- The nature of direct instruction
- Approaches to individual study
- The role of the teacher in indirect instruction
- The inquiry method as an important aspect of indirect instruction
- Experiential learning and the experiential learning cycle
- Collaborative learning and its various methods
- Working with groups
- Cooperative learning, its possibilities, and effectiveness in teaching diverse classes
- Thinking skills and processes (approaches and models)
- Problem-based learning

One of the key aims of teacher training is to prepare the teacher in a broad range of instructional strategies and methods. This chapter is designed to provide the foundation.

11 Direct Instruction and Individual Study

Before direct instruction and individual study are examined, it is useful to place these strategies into a broader context. Figure 11.1 provides an overview of the five main strategies, the teaching methods that are part of each, and the skills the teacher needs to teach the strategies and methods effectively.

> Knowledge for practice is perhaps the most widely accepted perspective on teacher learning. . . . This perspective holds that the more teachers know about subject matter, instructional strategies, effective interventions, and so forth, the more effectively they will teach . . . the new image of teacher learning and related professional development has moved to a more constructivist model of instruction, and away from a transmission model. (McLeskey & Waldron, 2004, pp. 5–6)

As the quotation suggests, the strategies and methods as examples of good practice described in Part III cannot be learned in the college classroom alone. Skilled use is developed over time through classroom experience, interaction with peers, and reflection.

    The literature on instruction is inconsistent in its use of the terms *strategies, methods,* and *skills.* We use these terms in a hierarchy of broad (strategies) to specific (skills). An *instructional strategy* is a general approach (e.g., direct or experiential); an *instructional*

OBJECTIVES

You will be able to:

1. Describe the direct instructional strategy and its methods and skills.
2. Describe procedures for effective lecturing, assigned questions, practice and drill, and other direct teaching methods.
3. Suggest the best uses and the limitations of the information presentation or acquisition methods of lecture, assigned questions, and practice and drill.
4. List tips for note taking and decide when note taking might be appropriate and when handouts might be the best approach.
5. Design lessons that involve use of the direct (explicit) instruction strategy.
6. Demonstrate initial competence in the use of direct study methods in microteaching or school lessons.
7. Describe the individual study instructional strategy and selected individual study methods.
8. List advantages and disadvantages of individual study.
9. Discuss effective use of learning centers and computerized learning.
10. Demonstrate initial competence in the use of individual study methods in microteaching or school lessons.

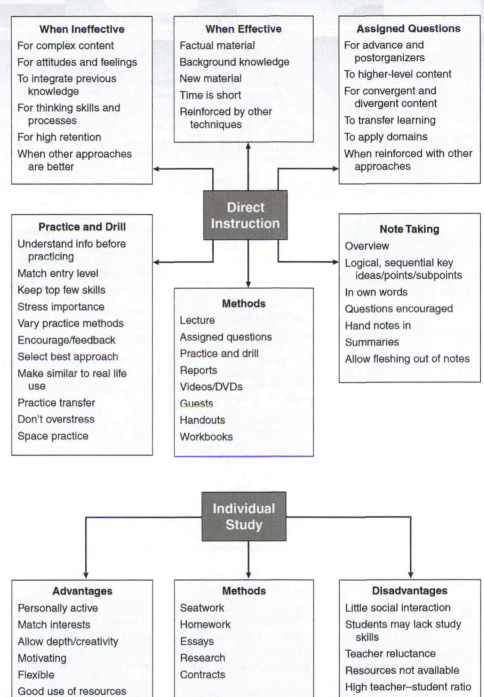

When Ineffective
For complex content
For attitudes and feelings
To integrate previous knowledge
For thinking skills and processes
For high retention
When other approaches are better

When Effective
Factual material
Background knowledge
New material
Time is short
Reinforced by other techniques

Assigned Questions
For advance and postorganizers
To higher-level content
For convergent and divergent content
To transfer learning
To apply domains
When reinforced with other approaches

Direct Instruction

Practice and Drill
Understand info before practicing
Match entry level
Keep top few skills
Stress importance
Vary practice methods
Encourage/feedback
Select best approach
Make similar to real life use
Practice transfer
Don't overstress
Space practice

Methods
Lecture
Assigned questions
Practice and drill
Reports
Videos/DVDs
Guests
Handouts
Workbooks

Note Taking
Overview
Logical, sequential key ideas/points/subpoints
In own words
Questions encouraged
Hand notes in
Summaries
Allow fleshing out of notes

Individual Study

Advantages
Personally active
Match interests
Allow depth/creativity
Motivating
Flexible
Good use of resources
Develop individual responsibility
Life-long learning

Methods
Seatwork
Homework
Essays
Research
Contracts

Disadvantages
Little social interaction
Students may lack study skills
Teacher reluctance
Resources not available
High teacher–student ratio
Costs of computers

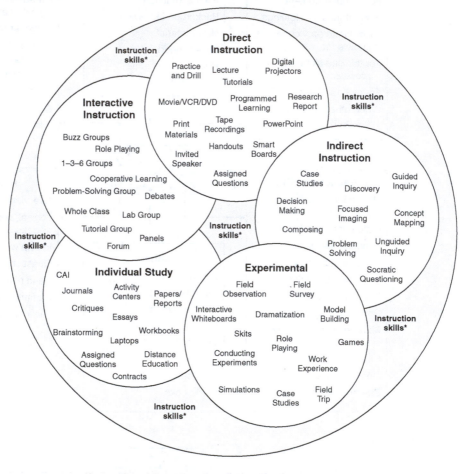

*Instruction skills: skills that are part of many methods (e.g.,
giving directions, demonstrating, using an overhead projector,
focusing, establishing set or closure, and managing).

FIGURE 11.1   *Teaching Strategies with Methods and Skills*

Source: Saskatchewan Learning (1991).

method is a specific approach (e.g., delivering a lecture or small-group report); one or more
methods can be part of a strategy; and an *instructional skill* is a specific teacher behavior
such as giving a demonstration, asking questions, giving directions, varying presentation,
using set, using closure, or using technology such as an overhead projector or PowerPoint
presentation.

The strategies are direct, indirect, experiential, collaborative, and individual study—
the "big five." You decide which strategic approach, or combination of approaches, to use
in a given unit or lesson, and the methods and skills you will use.

Instructional approaches can be selected to match the purposes, whether information acquisition, skill acquisition, high-level cognitive capability, values or attitude development, or a combination of these. Effective course and unit plans normally include

several teaching strategies, an array of teaching methods, and numerous instructional skills. Good lessons often include two or more strategies and several methods. No one strategy or method is equally effective for all students.

You, as the teacher, decide whether the strategy should be *direct,* with material transmitted by the teacher or another source. Ask yourself whether the strategy (approach) should be *indirect,* in that as students are asked to discover the meaning of a concept or generalization or how to go about learning or doing something. Should an *experiential* strategy be used, in which students are personally engaged in doing and reflecting about what they do? Should the strategy be collaborative (interactive), in which students work with others as they explore topics or share experiences about what is occurring or has occurred? Finally, should students be asked to be self-directed, to engage in *individual study* and learn and work on their own? Whatever strategies and methods are followed, specific skills are needed. To teach through cooperative or collaborative strategies, for example, skill in working with groups is essential.

The Nature of Direct Instruction

TCP—DIRECT INSTRUCTION

Effective direct instruction/deductive/expository methods

When used, fit content and learner needs; effective principles of lecture and assigned question methods demonstrated; stimulates pupil participation; makes effective use of audiovisual aids, discussion, and question and answer.

Exclusive use of expository approach; instruction highly abstract and not learner centered; students passive; no use of audiovisual aids, discussion, or question and answer.

What Is Direct Instruction?

Traditionally, direct instruction has been associated with "chalk and talk," and, more recently, the overhead projector. Today, direct instruction by overhead projector is being increasingly replaced by techniques such as PowerPoint or smart board presentations.

Instructional strategies need to be learned. Direct instruction can be effective. Its use does not deny building knowledge with the students. However, it is most effective when its subskills are mastered. In the hands of a knowledgeable and skilled instructor, direct instruction is powerful when used with certain content and in the right context.

Using new technologies can help. Weinert and Helmke (1995) report that many studies provide testimony that the direct instruction strategy is effective for certain goals. Direct instruction can even involve and help students learn actively, rather than passively (Leinhardt, 2001).

Paik (2003) presents an interesting synopsis of direct education. She states, "Effective direct instruction, which is still expected in the modern classroom, should consist of: (1) clear teaching, daily review, and homework checks; (2) presentation of new content and skills; (3) teacher monitoring and guided student practice; (4) corrective feedback and instructional reinforcement; (5) independent practice in school and at home with a 90 percent success rate; and (6) weekly and monthly evaluations. The skills and attributes of teachers employing effective direct instruction should include organization, clarity, task orientation, enthusiasm, and of course, flexibility" (pp. 83–84).

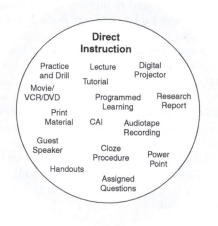

FIGURE 11.2 *Examples of the Direct Instruction Strategy*

Source: Saskatchewan Learning (1991).

Joyce, Weil, and Calhoun (2004) observe that the intention of direct instruction is for there to be "a predominant focus on learning and in which students are engaged in academic tasks a large percentage of the time and achieve a high rate of success" (p. 314). Direct instruction is teacher centered. It normally is not very effective for teaching the skills and processes required in thinking skills, critical thinking, creative thinking, interpersonal or group skills, and learning attitudes and values. Direct teaching is deductive. That is, the rule or generalization is presented and then illustrated with examples. Though this strategy is thought to be easy to plan and use, there is more to it than first meets the eye. It can be effective if careful planning occurs, the content is suitable, and if it is used in conjunction with other approaches. It can be effective for acquiring information or step-by-step skills, introducing other teaching methods, or as parts of other methods. Examples are lecture, assigned questions, didactic questioning, explicit teaching, research reports, workbooks, audio, videotape, DVD, or PowerPoint presentations, library research, and practice and drill. Lecture and assigned questions are the two most common methods. Figure 11.2 illustrates direct instruction.

Lecture and assigned questions should pique student interest and attention, include advance organizers or pattern guides, invite participation—overt (through questions and discussion) or covert (silently to oneself)—through higher-level and open-ended questions, through use of rich examples, and illustrated with audiovisual aids. Direct instruction should include provision for transfer and be combined with, or followed by, other teaching methods.

Direct Instruction and Constructivism

Although direct instruction and constructivist approaches are sometimes presented as opposites, this view is inaccurate because teachers often blend the approaches. Direct instruction can be constructivist. However, this idea is often the subject of heated debate. There are many different names for the approaches. Direct instruction has been called "the training model," "the active teaching model," "the mastery teaching model," "explicit instruction," and "expository teaching." Constructivist teaching goes by such names as "guided discovery," "authentic instruction," "teaching for understanding," "student-centered instruction," or "constructivist teaching." It is worth examining what some see as distinct elements of each approach.

DIRECT INSTRUCTION.   Those who support direct instruction see it as effective in improving student achievement. In particular, it is considered valuable for at-risk children. Parents, teachers, and students who want high performance on standardized tests often prefer direct instruction. Supporters claim that systems of knowledge have been developed over time and it is the role of teachers to pass this knowledge on in an organized and systematic way. This suggests that "teachers teach and students learn." The teacher's responsibility is to follow the curriculum and adapt it to student needs. To best achieve this, teachers design lesson and unit plans based on clear objectives, structured instructional approaches, and formal testing. Teachers should teach focused knowledge in a systematic way (Smerdon, Burkam, & Lee, 1999, pp. 5–34). Advocates believe that knowledge and skills are mastered quickly and with high academic gains, and that students will do well in school and university. It is, they think, the proved, classical, and tested approach. Swanson (2001) suggests that a mixed range of strategies is a sound approach. Kozioff, LaNunziata, Cowardin, and Bessellieu (2001) see direct instruction as highly beneficial to students, teachers, and the social structure of the school as a whole. They are critical of the focus on having students doing most of the discovering and believe that learning occurs best through proven instructional units and explicit teaching. Contrary to what some opponents claim, those who support the use of direct instruction, where appropriate, recognize the importance of having students learn and use higher-order thinking skills, research skills, analysis skills, and problem-solving skills.

Those with negative views of direct instruction label it traditional, teacher centered, and didactic (students are passive receptors of knowledge). The most-used direct instruction method is lecture, with teachers teaching as they were taught. Teachers talk, write notes on the chalkboard or overhead, and pass out worksheets for students to complete. Teachers are authority figures; they are active, students are passive.

CONSTRUCTIVISM.   Supporters of constructivism say that it is student centered— students explore and experiment with ideas. Students are active and the teacher is more of a guide or coach. Students construct knowledge linking new information to previous knowledge.

In constructivist teaching and learning, knowledge is actively constructed and reconstructed. It is claimed there are no received and fixed sets of knowledge systems. Students explore ideas and learn research and analysis skills. Earlier knowledge is important, as are higher-order thinking and problem-solving approaches. Students raise questions, test ideas to build understanding, and develop skills. The approach is not as new as it may seem. Some say that good teaching has always involved so-called constructivist elements and, of course, students learn new knowledge on a base of past learning. John Dewey, in 1902, argued for the end of traditional rote learning, saying that students should be active participants in building their knowledge and skills. Sizer states "a prominent pedagogy will be coaching, to provoke students to learn how to learn and thus to teach themselves" (1992, p. 226, in Smerdon et al., 1999). According to the NAASP and the Carnegie Foundation, teachers should be "adept at acting as coaches and facilitators of learning to promote more active involvement of students in their own learning" (NAASP, 1996, pp. 22–23, in Smerdon et al., 1999).

Smerdon et al. (1999) state several assumptions about constructivism. "(1) Some of our notion of what constitutes 'knowledge' may be culturally constructed, rather than truth or fact; (2) knowledge is distributed among group members and the knowledge of the group is greater than the sum of the knowledge of individuals; and (3) learning is an active, rather than passive, process of knowledge construction" (p. 8). They add, "In constructivist classrooms students are encouraged to pose hypotheses and explore ways to test them" (p. 8). Through this approach, students develop transferable problem-solving skills. The views gained become theirs, not necessarily those of their teachers. Using science as a model, Smerdon et al. present five instructional practices as examples of a constructivist classroom: students "(1) make up their own problems and work out their own methods to investigate the problems; (2) design and conduct experiments and projects on their own; (3) make their own choice of science topic or problem to study; (4) write up reports of laboratory and practical work; and (5) discuss career opportunities in scientific and technological fields" (p. 16).

Those who are skeptical about constructivism believe that it relies too much on inefficient time-consuming student discovery and trial and error rather than acceptance of bodies of knowledge. They argue that students may not master important knowledge bases in the disciplines and skills essential to their educational development. They consider it a vague and watered-down approach in which teachers, at times inappropriately, ignore their responsibility as purveyors of knowledge.

CONCLUSION.   Why is constructivism currently so much in vogue? Dalgarno (2001) sees it as the result of the cognitive view of learning replacing the behaviorist view. Behaviorism, he claims, stresses repetitive practice by the student until the required knowledge and skills are mastered through direct instruction. A cognitivist approach has students construct knowledge. Under constructivism, learners build personal representations of knowledge through active individual experiences within the social context of the classroom. This latter, interactive approach to constructing knowledge is based partly on the views of Bruner (1960, 1967) and Vygotsky (1962, 1978).

As stated earlier, direct instruction and constructivism are not necessarily opposites. Students can construct personal knowledge or meaning through direct instruction. Direct instruction could be used for presenting general background information, what Kameenui and Carnine (1998, pp. 8–9) call "the big ideas," followed by the constructivist approach focusing on particular applications and problems. Students could, for example, be presented with the general principles of rocketry, then work on solving the problem of creating and launching their own rocket models. This would fit well with the Smerdon approach.

At times you may need to have students memorize information or master well-defined performance skills (e.g., students must learn the alphabet and how to add and subtract). The approach to be used for these has been called *explicit teaching*. It involves direct instruction methods and has high levels of student time on task. Goals are made clear to students, and sufficient time for instruction and extensive enough content coverage should occur. Careful monitoring of progress and appropriate pacing is needed, and many low-level questions that elicit a high level of correct responses followed by prompt and academically oriented feedback should be used. The major features of direct and explicit instruction are (1) teaching in small steps, (2) providing guidance during initial practice, (3) having students practice after each step, and (4) ensuring a high level of success. Hall (2002) observes that certain components are essential in explicit instruction: pacing, processing opportunity, frequent student responses, monitoring responses, and feedback. When effective teachers teach a body of information or well-defined performance skills, they tend to use an approach such as the Madeline Hunter (1985, 2004) plan that is recommended in some school districts (Figure 11.3). A description of how to use the Hunter approach in basic lesson planning was presented in Chapter 7.

The direct instruction procedure should *not* be rigid. Gradually transfer responsibility from yourself to students. Teach students to observe, activate prior knowledge, construct meaning, monitor their understanding, organize and relate ideas, summarize, and extend meaning. That is, help students develop *meta-cognitive ability* (thinking about what they know, how they are learning, and how to control their learning). When possible, use interactive approaches including student/teacher discussion and peer teaching.

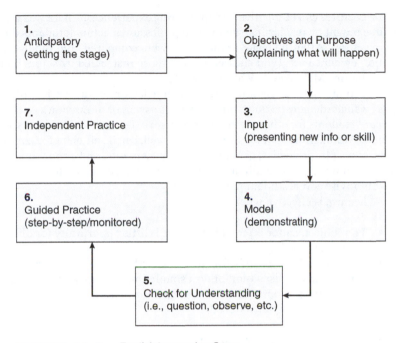

FIGURE 11.3 *Explicit Instruction Steps*
Source: Adapted from Hunter, 1985.

This latter approach, particularly when used to teach higher-order thinking, leads to higher achievement by all, including low-achieving students.

The information presentation/acquisition methods are not the only ones available to the innovative teacher to vary or individualize instruction. Techniques that can be used include programmed learning materials, computer-assisted instruction, learning contracts, group tutorials, workbooks, panels, debates, brainstorming, CDs/DVDs, outside speakers, video- or audiotapes, individual or group presentations, and the Internet.

Direct Instruction Teaching Methods

Lecture

Typically, the proportion of instructional time devoted to lecturing increases with grade level. Lecture is a valuable part of your repertoire if it is not overused and if it is not used when other approaches would be better. It may be a waste of time if it is used to present information that will not be needed later in a school subject. Lectured information normally is rapidly forgotten.

Students typically are passive, sit, listen, answer low-level questions, and are often bored (Goodlad, 1983). Lecture is teacher centered, and the attention span of students is limited. Remember, many students—because of learning style preferences and developmental levels—do not readily assimilate lectured content. Other instructional strategies should be used as well, especially if the goal is thinking skills or processes or affective outcomes.

Lectures can be positive and interesting experiences. There was an experiment of a course taught by regular instructors and professional actors (students did not know they were actors). After the term, exam results were compared, and the overwhelming, "dramatic," evidence was (you guessed it) that those instructed by actors had acquired more information (McLeskey & Waldron, 2004).

You may use "straight lecture," combine lecture with a variety of other methods or aids (visuals, demonstrations, question and answer, or discussion), or use "lecturettes" to prepare students for other methods or seatwork. Lecture–discussion is a frequent combination. Although straight lecture, delivered well, can be efficient for communicating basic facts, concepts, principles, generalizations, viewpoints, and arguments about a particular area of knowledge, normally it is best to combine lecture with other techniques and at least to invite covert student participation.

Lecture is effective when:

- The subject matter is factual and there is little opportunity for difference of opinion or problem solving.
- "Firepower" is needed before another method is used (for example, you may wish students to use discussion or do a simulation or role-play) and to make sure they do more than "pool ignorance" or use misinformation.
- A subject is being introduced.
- Time is limited.
- It is later reinforced by another technique.

TIPS FOR EFFECTIVE LECTURING.   A good lecture is like a good speech. Tell them what you are going to tell them; tell them; and then tell them what you told them. Relate past learning to what is being presented, and what is being presented to what will later be learned. Do not present too many points—five or six major points are enough in an hour. Use (or ask for) summaries at the beginning, during the presentation, and at the end. Use pauses to give listeners a chance to catch up and summarize for themselves, or for emphasis. Invite covert participation, use rhetorical questions, challenge students to think, summarize, or formulate questions they can raise later. Supplement lecture with visuals, demonstration, or discussion. Support major points with visuals (including the chalkboard, overhead, charts, or visuals). Show enthusiasm, interest in the topic, and color. Be aware of students' developmental levels—"what they can handle." Incorporate ample examples (verbal or visual) to illustrate points. Select examples that motivate, things students have had experience (or success) with or will be interested in. Draw examples from the class. Use a rate of speaking and choice of vocabulary that suits the class. Speak loudly enough to be heard easily, but not so loud as to irritate. Seat students so all can hear and see. Use stimulus variation techniques: move around the room, use gestures, focus attention ("Listen carefully," "Look at the diagram," etc.), vary interactions, vary volume and tone of voice, and use silence. Create the impression that every student, personally, is being addressed. Use eye contact, position in room, and statements such as "What do you think the result will be?" Do not read from notes or text. Put "key ideas" on a card, chalkboard, or visual. Data collection forms to obtain feedback on the above approaches are provided at the end of this and the following chapter.

Decide if you are going to ask students to take notes, provide a handout, or the information is in the text. If note taking is to be used, teach and provide practice in note taking. Note taking needs teacher pacing and pausing to allow students to take proper notes.

Lectures can be used effectively when time is short, if you have a large class, and it is well supplemented, but be aware of how you can handle potential shortcomings.

Cruickshank, Bainer Jenkins, and Metcalf (2003) suggest the following visual aids through which a presentation can be enhanced:

- Printed material that serves as advance organizers: handouts, outlines, "questions to think about"
- Overhead transparencies: outlines, drawings, charts, diagrams, maps, cartoons, quotes, key words and ideas
- Pictures and prints: photographs, paintings, posters, slides
- "Clips" on CD or videotape
- Maps, wall charts, and globes
- Concrete objects (manipulatives) (p. 179)

The above ideas can make a presentation exciting. Advance organizers help focus attention on the material to be covered. The advance organizer can be a concept map, chart, outline, or simply key words. Transparencies for lectures often are poorly prepared. They can be dramatically improved by using different font sizes, colors, or illustrations such as pictures, drawings, or cartoons. A powerful quotation or key words can add emphasis, focus, interest, or humor. Pictures or posters, a few slides, and video or CD clips can change the pace, add dramatic effect, and bring the lecture to life. A bulletin board or maps or wall charts can be effective. Students can get up and point to significant information. Finally, concrete objects can be viewed or passed around and touched. Imagine the creativity, power, and interest, depending on the topic, that is possible by, for example, bringing in a human skeleton or a live animal.

A data collection instrument you can use for feedback on your use of lecture is provided in Appendix 11.1. Lecture is often accompanied by use of a chalkboard or overhead projector. Data collection instruments to help you use and get feedback on these techniques are provided in Appendixes 11.2 and 11.3.

Handouts

More material can be covered when handouts are provided. Students are freer to think about the presentation, formulate questions, and get the pertinent and correct information. Also, you do not have to pace yourself as for note taking. A disadvantage is that students' minds may wander because they don't have to concentrate to take notes; or they may not attend because they are getting a handout. Students remember better if they write it down themselves. Note taking promotes comprehension and retention because students must understand if they are to select pertinent material, organize, and summarize.

Tips for Effective Note Taking

When you lecture, foster effective note taking by:

- Providing an overview, or outline, of what is to be presented
- Presenting your lecture logically, sequentially, teaching students to be aware of structure
- Teaching students to listen for key ideas, points, and subpoints—using verbal and nonverbal clues and appropriate pauses or tonal/volume variation

- Teaching students to record ideas in their own words, defining the concept for themselves—this requires comprehension
- Encouraging students to ask questions
- Avoiding verbatim dictation—if used, limit it to confirm important features such as summaries or definitions
- Having students hand in notes to discover if they are complete and accurate, or having them check notes against the text or other reference (alternately, have students periodically "play back" what they have taken down)
- Making sure you provide (or elicit) stage and closing summaries
- At times, asking students to take abbreviated notes that can be "fleshed out" later

Note taking is a specific skill. Don't assume students know how to do it. Like any other skill, it must be taught and practiced. You may have heard of a teacher telling students not to copy notes verbatim but to record the highlights of the information. The teacher wonders why this was not done well or not done at all. The answer is that the skill may not have been taught.

Assigned Questions

Teachers, particularly in multigraded situations, often assign questions as seatwork or homework. These are usually taken up the next class period. *Assigned questions* is a teacher-centered method in that the teacher structures the questions and is in control of taking them up. Questions may be written on the chalkboard, dictated, provided in a handout, or assigned from a text or workbook.

Questions can be used to introduce facts, concepts, generalizations, argument, and points of view. To foster comprehension, students should answer in their own words. Ensure that questions are not trivial and that students have independent study and research skills. Because learning styles differ, some students do not benefit greatly from this method. If questions are assigned as seatwork, circulate to reinforce correct work, encourage, or supply correctives. Good assigned questions stimulate high-level thinking, problem solving, decision making, and affective outcomes. Questions can move beyond information acquisition and promote comprehension and use of thinking skills. To use assigned questions well, have students do sample questions in class to ensure a minimum of 80 percent success during seatwork and of 95 percent for homework; normally it is best to combine this method with others.

WHEN THE ASSIGNED QUESTIONS METHOD IS EFFECTIVE.   Assigned questions are effective when the questions are well phrased and answering involves more than mechanical "search and copy" from a reference or other source. Assigned questions can be effective when rapid information acquisition is necessary (time is limited) or when "firepower" is needed before another method is to be used (for example, you want students to acquire background information before engaging in a group discussion) and if the questions are later reinforced by another method. Assigned questions can be used for basic facts, concepts, principles, generalizations, viewpoints, and arguments. Students should have been taught independent study and research skills, particularly if sources beyond the text (e.g., the resource center) are used. The method is useful when you want to attend to individual students during seatwork. It can be used to advantage if the text is well written and structured.

TIPS FOR USING THE ASSIGNED QUESTIONS METHOD

- Use advance or postorganizers and introduce material in a motivating way for a positive mindset for learning—if students see the worth of questions, they are more likely to do them, and do them well.
- Select questions well: (a) make sure students focus on important information or thinking skills, (b) go beyond low levels—ask students to apply information, seek out relationships, assumptions, or implications, combine information in new ways, or evaluate information using sound criteria; (c) use a mix of *convergent* (single correct answer) and *divergent* open-ended (several correct answers) questions.
- Teach summarizing skills. Have students learn information acquisition skills and how to use the resource center and community resources.
- Ask students to phrase responses in their own words rather than mindlessly copying.
- Circulate during seatwork, helping students learn research and reporting skills, and providing encouragement and positive reinforcement.
- When taking up questions, apply the skills presented in Chapter 8 (avoid an up-and-down-the-rows procedure, use probes and redirects, and challenge students to stretch their minds).
- Build bridges ("transfer") between present learning and past and future learning, between your subject and others, between present learning and life.
- Help students use and apply the conceptual, skills and processes, and affective domains.
- Think about how you can overcome the shortcomings of this technique (which are similar to those of lecture); and reinforce learning through other teaching/learning methods.

A data collection instrument you can use for feedback on your use of assigned questions is provided in Appendix 11.4.

Practice and Drill

The old saw has it that "practice makes perfect." Lecture and assigned questions (and other teaching methods) are often followed by practice and drill. After knowledge has been presented, students may need to overlearn the material to remember and use it in new contexts. The practice-and-drill method is used so that students can repeat information or do a skill or process almost automatically. Practice should stress understanding and students should have learned how to transfer to another aspect of a subject, other subjects, and life. This, too, requires practice.

The effectiveness of practice depends on how it is conducted. If it is done well, it extends or polishes a skill or habit or enhances the ability to recall and apply information. The word *drill* has negative connotations, and sometimes extensive and better-quality practice may be needed. Rote practice and drill usually have little value. For practice and drill to be valuable, original learning must be thorough, and learning must be a problem-solving process (in that a learner, with your help, explores ways of making personal connections).

WHEN PRACTICE AND DRILL ARE EFFECTIVE.   Students develop a personalized understanding of the skill, habit, or information when time is allocated to overlearn content. Practice and drill promote long-term retention and automatization (instantaneous recall or application). It is effective when students link past and future learning and feelings of accomplishment are generated.

TIPS FOR USING PRACTICE AND DRILL

- Make sure the information or activity is clearly understood, to avoid practice of errors.
- Match students' entry skill/recall and set a practice schedule.
- Only a few skills can be effectively drilled simultaneously.
- Make sure students realize why they need the skill.
- Avoid boredom—use a variety of enjoyable practice situations.
- For initial practice, encourage and provide feedback and positive reinforcement.
- Decide which practice approach is best: review of previous work, extensive or intensive practice, short or longer periods of practice, learning by part or whole, practice of new with the old, and point of diminishing returns.
- To aid transfer, conduct practice under conditions as similar as possible to actual use situations of the skill or information.
- Provide regular, and sufficient, opportunity to apply (transfer) what has been learned.
- Avoid having students become unduly product conscious. Focus may need to be on process or technique—don't impose summative criteria at a formative stage.
- Some pressure is desirable, but too much is counterproductive. Stress self-competition, not other competition.
- Space practice (close together at the start) and provide reviews.

Precede practice with clear demonstration and directions. This usually needs to be followed by guided (often teacher-led) practice. Proper materials and working conditions are needed. Conditions should be as similar as possible to later use situations. It must be carefully monitored and feedback, correctives, and reinforcement provided. Practice should be individualized to focus, as needed, on technique, accuracy, and speed.

A data collection instrument you can use for feedback on your use of practice and drill is provided in Appendix 11.5.

Didactic Questioning

In didactic questioning, the teacher is in control. Questions tend to be convergent, low cognitive, and often begin with *what, where, when,* or *how.* A danger is that questions may be simplistic, encourage guessing or waving of hands to gain approval, and discourage insightful answers or creativity. Questions can be used to diagnose student recall and comprehension, previous learning, decide the extent to which lesson objectives were achieved, or drill students for retention of information or skills. Effectiveness can be increased by frequent "why" questions and occasional "what if" questions. The didactic questioning method has the same limitations as lecture and assigned questions.

Use the data collection instruments in Appendices 11.1 to 11.5 to help you analyze the cases that follow. Your instructor may pose specific questions for your response.

CASE 11.1 Direct Instruction

Sounds Interesting!

Mr. Braun planned to begin a series of lessons on sound and hearing with a grade 8 class. The human ear and its structure had been studied in previous years, but Mr. Braun thought a review lecture on the nature of sound should precede project work by the class. Mr. Braun decided that work on individual and group projects would strengthen students' research and independent study skills.

During recess, Mr. Braun assembled charts and other materials. When the class resumed, he began, "I mentioned yesterday that you were going to choose a project that has to do with an aspect of sound and hearing. This is a fascinating area to study, and many interesting projects could be picked. First, though, let's review the basic information you need before we can go on.

"Suppose you are about to step off the curb of a busy street. You look left and right but don't see any cars. Just as you are about to step into the street, you hear the blare of a car horn. You jump back, saved by your ears. Your ears are very special equipment. They gather information from every side; they continuously keep you in touch with the world around you."

Mr. Braun went on to explain that sounds we hear are caused by motion. Motion causes sound waves to go out in every direction. He took out a metal ruler and held it tight against the edge of the table so about eight inches stuck out. He twanged the free end, which caused the ruler to vibrate and make a low humming sound.

Mr. Braun asked, "What is causing the sound you hear?" Miriam responded, "The ruler is moving up and down." "Why does that make a sound?" Miriam answered, "I think it has something to do with molecules." "That's right. Does anyone know how sound is related to molecules?" He paused, but no one volunteered.

Getting a piece of chalk, Mr. Braun drew a series of diagrams on the board showing the effect on air molecules when a ruler moves up, down, and up again. He used the terms *compression* and *expansion.* "While the ruler continues to vibrate and push the air into a pattern of compression and expansion, you hear the disturbance as a humming noise. The air molecules push against other molecules nearby, transferring the force of the disturbance across the air. The disturbance—the sound—moves incredibly quickly, 1,120 feet each second." He drew a wavy line to represent the sound and showed it reaching a human ear.

Next he demonstrated that plucking a guitar string made it vibrate, though the vibration was harder to observe, causing a sound. The sound was higher pitched as well. Mr. Braun explained the differences in compression and expansion between higher-pitched and lower-pitched sounds.

"Remember learning about the human ear?" Mr. Braun put up a large diagram of an ear. "How is it that we 'hear' sounds?" Marc recalled the project he did last year on sound and hearing, and, using the diagram, showed how sound waves are "heard." After a discussion, Mr. Braun asked the students to get pen and paper and join work groups. When each group was settled in its area, Mr. Braun gave instructions. "There are many things about sound and hearing we have not talked about today. There are questions that haven't been answered. Let's prepare a list of the questions you think need to be answered. Questions will provide ideas for your group's research topic. Record all questions that are mentioned. We'll put them together so you can choose a topic and start work."

CASE 11.2 Direct Instruction

What's Bugging You?

Mr. Johnson's grade 10 health lesson is on the agents of infection. He gains the attention of the class, tells them they will need to take notes, and begins to write on the chalkboard saying, "There are four main causes of infection: bacteria, viruses, fungi, and animal parasites. First, bacteria are microscopic plantlike, single-celled organisms that can be classified by their shapes." He then, in turn, describes bacilli, spirilla, and spirochetes. Following this he describes and de-

fines generation time, botulism, and tetanus. He continues, "Most bacteria, like *Escherichia coli* that live in our intestines, are not harmful and are actually necessary for our existence; others, like Staphylococci, can be present on our skin without causing much of a problem but once infection starts can lead to serious complications and need to be treated with antibiotics." He describes how staph problems occur. He asks, "Remember when you had a sore throat? This was likely

continued

caused by Streptococci." Then he tells the class about these bacteria and the problems they can cause.

When he has finished his presentation of bacteria, in a similar way he presents information to the class about viruses, fungi, and animal parasites. With eight minutes left in the period he says, "Close your notebooks. Who can name the four agents of infection?" He continues reviewing until the bells rings.

CASE 11.3 Assigned Questions

Mapping It Out

Ms. Perez has a mixed grade 6 and 7 class. Nineteen of the students are in grade 6 and eight are in grade 7. On this day, she wants to begin a study of Paraguay with the grade 7s. She also must spend time with the grade 6s to finish teaching the map reading skills they need for their group projects. She decides to assign questions for the grade 7 students to work on while she spends the first part of the period with the younger students. She wants the questions to do more than simply keep the grade 7s busy; she hopes the questions will both provide valuable background information and engage the students in thinking about Paraguay.

Ms. Perez assembles copies of maps showing the physical features, population distributions, and annual rainfall of Paraguay. She includes world maps and two globes. Questions are on the board:

1. What are the physical features in this country?
2. Where are the areas of dense population?
3. Which areas are dry and which have heavy rainfall?
4. Judging from the names of cities, towns, and rivers, what language might be spoken?
5. What might the climate be like? Give reasons for your answer.
6. What might be some ways of earning a living in Paraguay?
7. Can you suggest reasons for the way the population is distributed?
8. Can shipping and trading with other countries take place easily? Why or why not?

At the beginning of the period, Ms. Perez asks the grade 6 students to get their materials ready while she gives instructions to the seventh graders. "As you know, we are about to begin a study of some South American countries. It is possible to tell many things about a country from maps. I have copies of maps of Paraguay that show the physical features, population distribution, and annual rainfall in different areas. Remember, as we learned about African countries, the way people earn their living is influenced by the climate, the amount of rainfall, access to cities, and access to transportation routes. I want you to build on what you've learned earlier and see how much information you can gather from these maps. Feel free to guess, but have good reasons for your answers. We'll check our information later. You may work in pairs or threes. Discussion will help you select the best answers, but try to work quietly." Ms. Perez has the students read the questions, makes sure they understand them, and turns to work with the sixth-grade students.

The seventh graders move to tables at the back of the room where the maps are placed, and begin to work through the questions in pairs and threes.

CASE 11.4 Technology and Direct Instruction

Teaching with Power

In the corridor of the local elementary school, Chan, a grade 6 teacher, notices his friend John pushing a cart, with new-looking equipment, into his grade 7 room. "John," he asks, "What's that you're wheeling into your room?" John pauses and replies, "I went to this workshop on 'The Computer in the Classroom.' Most was on PowerPoint. I'm going to try it." "Well, John," comments Chan, "Give me the chalk and overhead any day. That's all I need. I don't want the board to force me to try all this stuff in the classroom. I'm busy enough and don't have time for the training." "It doesn't take that much time," observes John, looking at his colleague's slim folder of teaching material. "Look," argues Chan "I put in about sixty hours a week in this place and don't have time for fads. Chandra got into technology and tells me she spends hours on Web searches for materials. Time is a teacher's most precious resource."

Noticing that students are beginning to gather in the hall, John wheels the cart into his room. Chan follows. "I know," says John, "it took me longer last night to make my PowerPoint presentation than if I just wrote it up. But it's terrific, the kids'll love it, and I can use it over and over or adapt it for future classes." Chan argues, "I never make the same presentation. I always vary the pace or focus. That's how I reach students, and chalk or transparencies give me flexibility. If I use PowerPoint, I'd be controlled by technology. Kids are never quite the same. They vary in ability and personality. I adjust like an actor with different audiences! There's no need to change my methods." John points at the board and says, "The chalkboard was once technology. Kids learned 'cause they got what was said or taught by at least copying our notes. Think of PowerPoint and the Web as new, improved, colorful chalkboards. You can't fight technology."

Chan moves toward his room. He motions John to follow. An impressive computer system is on the desk. "Look," he says, indicating the computer, "I don't fight technology. I use the computer to do marks. The spreadsheet is easy and helps keep my grades in order." "Well, then" comments John, "how about letting the kids work at computers in the classroom? The computer can give them much of the stuff you do." "Sure," says Chan, "kids can find information on the computer, but to really learn, they need to interact with a person. It's a question of time. The best use is having kids learn with my guiding them. Computers take too much time, training, and resources. They're not worth the trouble. The computer spreadsheet saves me time, so I use it. But what you're doing *adds* work. Computers help administration with attendance, grading, and getting supplies. They don't save time and work for the teacher in the classroom. Education is a people thing, not a tech thing. Anything that takes me away from teaching kids weakens education. Get me a computer that grades papers and I'm on your side!" "Chan," says John, "you're a lost cause!" "No," says Chan, writing notes on the board, "most teachers think like me. Technology isn't a natural part of how teachers work. I like technology, but it doesn't really help me be a teacher."

CASE 11.5 Direct Instruction

To Be Told or to Discover

A heated argument has been taking place in the staff room of Harbor High School. It began when one of the teachers asked if the teacher in the class next to his could keep the noise down. The other teacher had said that it wasn't "noise," it was "discussion." Eventually the whole group in the staff room were involved in a lively debate on direct instruction versus a constructivist approach. Both groups seemed to have powerful points. The direct side argued that teacher-directed instruction was much more structured, efficient, and systematic. It was, after all, the teacher's job to teach and transmit the needed knowledge and skills to students—*teachers teach and students learn.* Constructivist learning is too vague and time consuming. The constructivist side retaliated by saying that learning isn't given out, it must be built by the students through meaningful activities. Students

should work together and the teacher must not be the sole source of learning. Direct instruction is rigid, with a single point of view dominating. Students need to learn how to learn.

If you were a member of the staff of Harbor High School, what side might you have leaned toward? Should teaching be a mix of both strategies, or is one approach better than the other?

Though direct instruction is often perceived negatively, it can be a powerful way to teach. What has been your experience as a student in school and university classes? Was it positive or negative? To what extent has your experience shaped the kind of teacher you would like to be? Try the approaches to direct instruction suggested in this chapter. Reflect on your attempts. What worked for you and your students? Do you see the strategy in a new light?

The Individual Study Strategy

TCP—INDIVIDUAL STUDY STRATEGY

Effective use of the individual study strategy

Students are taught specific research skills and effective use of computer technology; homework and seatwork well planned and monitored: students encouraged to develop individual responsibility and lifelong learning skills and interests; students taught to think carefully about their academic tasks.

Limited use of individual study approaches; students rarely do meaningful homework and seatwork; individual research and computer skills rarely taught.

Employs resource-based teaching/learning and a wide variety of media and resources

Students involved in research; students are involved in individual and group research projects; school resources used beyond classroom include community resources; students taught how to use resources; inquiry oriented climate promoted; students involved in planning and assessing their learning.

Bound to prescriptive materials; lesson formats are stereotypical; students not taught to process information; lack of variety in resources used; direct instruction orientated; students not involved in planning and assessing their learning.

Uses instructional technology to enhance student learning

Uses computers effectively to enhance student learning; effectively uses a range of audiovisual technology and approaches; teaches students to use technology and the Internet with skill and awareness; uses a variety of nonprint material.

Computer and Internet illiterate; seldom uses nonprint materials; does not teach students to use available technology and resources.

What Is Individual Study?

The term *individual study* has several synonyms: independent learning, self-regulated learning, self-directed study (or learning), self-teaching, and individualized study. The term *individual study* is used in several ways. Broadly, it can include anything a person does independently, ranging from supervised seatwork on mathematics in a classroom to a personal trip to Italy to study Roman ruins. For our purposes it is an individual educational pursuit carried on by a person to self-improve. Individual study may be self-initiated or teacher initiated, but the focus here is on study under the guidance of a teacher. This involves identification of a topic, problem, or project through to evaluation based on course objectives. Feedback and correctives are as important to individual study as they are to other strategies. Feedback can come from you, be built into materials, or be a combination of the two.

The Importance of Individual Study

One of the joys of a good education is to gain a love of learning for its own sake. The child who can learn alone has the gift of independence. There is immense satisfaction in following your interest or hobby. Independent learning encourages responsible decision making through problem analysis, reflection, and decision making. Life-long learning and the ability to respond to change are developed. The teacher who encourages individual study fosters skills and attitudes of immeasurable importance. Figure 11.4 presents the strategy and some key methods.

FIGURE 11.4 *The Individual Study Strategy and Methods*
Source: Saskatchewan Learning (1991).

Students need to learn how to learn. They need to be able to work independently to become self-sufficient, responsible citizens. A major purpose of schooling is to teach students how to learn independently—how to teach themselves. Independent learning must be taught and practiced. Use should begin as early as kindergarten and be used throughout schooling.

Much of what students learn can be learned through other teaching strategies, but students must acquire life-long independent learning skills. Mastery of the basic knowledge in a school subject does not automatically increase independent learning. New knowledge can easily be lost if students do not use it in new contexts. Specific efforts, by students, need to be made to bridge the gap between possessing knowledge and using it to learn on their own.

Kinds of Individual Study Methods

Bear in mind that a *strategy* is a broad label for a specific teaching approach. Each of the five strategies presented in this text has its methods. When you decide to use the individual study strategy, a choice can be made from many methods. Examples range from supervised study in the classroom or library to self-directed learning separate from, or instead of, course requirements. Alternatives include:

Essays	Interviews	Individualized assignments
Reports	Brainstorming	Programmed learning
Projects	Problem solving	Computer-assisted instruction (CAI)
Models	Decision making	Independent research
Journals	Learning centers	Acceleration (individual progress
Inquiry	Learning units	through text)
Games	Learning activity packets (LAPs)	Correspondence courses
Fantasies	Learning contracts	Distance education

SELECTING AN INDIVIDUAL STUDY METHOD. The individual study instructional strategy can be the major instructional strategy in combination with other strategies or with one or more individuals while another strategy is used with the rest of the class. Ask yourself which will be effective for the class as a whole and for individuals. How much control are you willing to relinquish? When direct instruction is used, high teacher control is normal and learning outcomes and pacing are predictable and safe. Unintended learning outcomes—sometimes desirable, sometimes producing outcomes you may not like—and inappropriate pacing can result when individual study is used. This is a risk that must be taken if students are to improve their independent learning capabilities.

It is possible to run an entire course effectively using individual study methods. Courses that emphasize mastery learning may be set up this way. In this situation, you become a resource person rather than a presenter. On the other hand, you can use the direct instruction approach and explicit instruction but provide opportunity for independent learning through assignments or asking students to apply (using an independent learning technique) the content learned through explicit instruction.

THE TEACHER'S ROLE.   Butler (2002) outlines the importance of the teacher's role in fostering independent (self-regulated) learning:

> To promote self-regulation teachers must assist students to engage flexibly and adaptively in a cycle of cognitive activities (i.e., task analysis, strategy selection and use, and self-monitoring). Further, key instructional targets include promoting students' construction of (a) metacognitive knowledge about academic work, (b) strategies for analyzing tasks, (c) metacognitive knowledge about task-specific strategies (e.g., for managing work, history reports, reading text books, writing paragraphs, learning math), (d) skills for implementing strategies, and (e) strategies for self-monitoring and strategic use of feedback. (p. 82)

What is implied here is that for students to be successful at independent learning, they need skills to think about their academic tasks, to be aware that different tasks require different strategies, skills in getting tasks done and the needed skills to work independently, and to be open to constructive feedback.

For such an approach to be successful, teachers need to: (1) provide an environment that allows growth of learner independence (one that is supportive and encourages curiosity, the desire to learn, and self-confidence); (2) provide a continuum of increasing student responsibility for decision making; (3) transfer control as students take greater responsibility; and (4) provide an appropriate student/learner relationship.

Advantages of the Individual Study Strategy

- Students personally and actively, not passively, interact with the content to be learned.
- The interests and needs of individual students within the prescribed curriculum can be matched; the curriculum can be supplemented and enriched.
- Students can pursue topics in as much depth as they like and exercise as much creativity as they like.
- Motivation is higher when students are involved in selecting what is studied.
- It can be used in any subject and allows flexible choice of time, place, and other elements.
- Many individual methods are inexpensive and do not require additional equipment.
- Students feel their studies are relevant and important when a reason for its use is to bridge school learning and community reality.
- Resources available to students are broadened when the out-of-school community is used. It lets students develop knowledge and skills that cannot be obtained in the school.
- Emphasis is placed on individual student responsibility and accountability.
- The study skills learned contribute to life-long autonomous learning capability.

Independent Study Methods

Independent study methods can empower students as control is increasingly shifted, as earned, from teacher to student.

Teacher-directed learning   Student-directed learning

➤ ——▶

Well-designed methods personalize learning and are motivating. They add flexibility and variety to your instructional repertoire. What follows is a description of a selection of teaching methods within the independent study instructional strategy.

INDIVIDUALIZED INSTRUCTION AND TECHNOLOGY. Current technology, especially computers, can enhance opportunities for individualized instruction and prepare young people for technological developments. Today's young people need technological skills and critical-thinking and problem-solving abilities. DuBosq (2002) observes that individualized instruction through technology "gives students choice in and control of their learning" (p. 29). He adds that students "can evaluate their own performance through a rubric" (p. 30). Good software, for example, will give direct feedback to the student. And the computer has endless patience! A concern of some educators is how to both individualize instruction and bring everyone in a class to the desired level of achievement. Roth (1999) sees the computer as the means to do this (p. 27). Previously we discussed the issue of direct instruction as a means of disseminating information. The problem is that the teacher has to present information to the whole class. Roth says the role of the computer is to present information to individuals at their computers. He says, "this responsibility can be shifted, for computers are generally better than humans at disseminating the desired information" (p. 28). He presents advantages: (1) Students gain individual attention. (2) Students can progress at their own rate. (3) Subjects can be better integrated. (4) Feedback is immediate. (5) Mistakes are private and positive, not negative learning experiences. (6) Encouragement is always provided. (7) Class level boundaries are eliminated so there is no limit to the possible level of achievement. (8) Students compete against themselves, not each other (pp. 27–30).

Individualized instruction does not mean working alone. Students can work in small groups with the computer or interact with other students, in different locations, who use computers. Students enjoy working together at the same computer, but they can work with students in another part of the world.

The most influential item of technology in the past was the written word and later the printed book. The student, for instance, could be guided by another person through reading. That person need not be present and in fact could have died centuries earlier. Today the most influential item of technology is the computer. Just as the printing press freed information for all to peruse, so the computer is becoming the great democratizer of knowledge, changing the teacher to a facilitator, not a disseminator of information.

Teachers still like to control the flow of information, once through chalk, then through the overhead projector, and, more recently, thorough PowerPoint presentation. Perhaps the computer with its sophisticated software will introduce a new mindset and new opportunities for individualized instruction. The computer can dramatically shift the focus from teacher-directed to student-directed learning.

The chalkboard has returned in a new and dramatic form. A BBC broadcast on March 7, 2002, in a report called *Digital Change at the Chalk Face,* discussed "digital whiteboards" or "smart boards." At Queniborough School in Leicestershire (England), the head teacher purchased one for every classroom. These permit teachers to project the Internet in real time and use it with DVD and videotape. The "smart board" can record up to twelve hours of information, written in the teacher's handwriting, which can later be converted into print as class notes. Students enjoy the technology. "It is wonderful for children to look at a large piece of text, and for that text to become interactive is amazing. The children say it has helped them remember things and they are very focused. It makes learning so much fun." So, the chalkboard, albeit digital with many new possibilities, is alive and well.

Computers in the Classroom

Because most computers in the classroom are used individually, the role of computers deserves attention. Computerized instruction brings novelty and variety and can be more fun than the usual seatwork. Three levels of involvement are possible: drill and practice (the computer gives questions, scores answers, and provides immediate feedback), tutorials (applications range from simple recall or knowledge level to problem solving), and simulations (for involvement in gamelike or near-real applications). Research on the effectiveness of computerized instruction is largely positive. Some studies found that learning time was reduced and others that the time used was about the same as with traditional instruction. Student attitudes about using computers for instruction were improved.

TERMS.   Cotton (1991) presents definitions of terms that are helpful in understanding the varied uses of computers in the classroom (not all terms apply to individualized instruction).

Computer-based education (CBE) and *computer-based instruction* (CBI) are broad terms that can refer to almost any kind of computer use in educational settings, including drill and practice, tutorials, simulations, instructional management, supplementary exercises, programming, database development, and writing using word processors. These terms may refer to stand-alone computer learning activities or to activities that reinforce material introduced and taught by teachers.

Computer-assisted instruction (CAI) most often refers to drill-and-practice, tutorial, or simulation activities offered either by themselves or as supplements to traditional teacher-directed instruction.

Computer-managed instruction (CMI) can refer to the use of computers by school staff to organize student data and make instructional decisions or to activities in which the computer evaluates students' test performance, guides them to appropriate instructional resources, and keeps records of progress.

Computer-enriched instruction (CEI) refers to activities in which computers (1) generate data at the students' request to illustrate relationships in models of social or physical reality, (2) execute programs developed by the students, or (3) provide general enrichment in relatively unstructured exercises designed to stimulate and motivate students.

BENEFITS OF COMPUTER-ASSISTED INSTRUCTION.   Cotton says the best-supported research is that use of computer-assisted instruction to supplement traditional, teacher-directed instruction results in achievement superior to that with traditional instruction alone. In general, this is so for different ages and subject areas. Cotton suggests advantages of CAI over traditional approaches:

- The use of word processors in writing programs leads to better writing outcomes than the use of paper and pencil.
- Desirable outcomes are obtained when computers are used as part of a holistic, writing-as-a-process approach.
- CAI enhances learning rate.
- The retention of content learned is superior.

- The use of CAI leads to more positive student attitudes.
- CAI students have more of an internal locus of control/sense of self-efficacy.
- CAI students have higher rates of time on task.

STUDENTS LIKE COMPUTERS.   Cotton's list of why students like computers offers insight into student attitudes to learning. Students say they like working with computers because computers: are infinitely patient; never get tired; never get frustrated or angry; allow students to work privately; never forget to correct or praise; are fun and entertaining; individualize learning; are self-paced; do not embarrass students who make mistakes; make it possible to experiment with different options; give immediate feedback; are more objective than teachers; free teachers for more meaningful contact with students; are impartial to race or ethnicity; are great motivators; give a sense of control over learning; are excellent for drill and practice; call for using sight, hearing, and touch; teach in small increments; help students improve their spelling; build proficiency in computer use, which will be valuable later in life; eliminate the drudgery of doing certain learning activities by hand (e.g., drawing graphs); and work rapidly—closer to the rate of human thought.

POSSIBILITIES AND PITFALLS OF COMPUTER USE.   Based on an extensive range of literature, Gibson (1999) lists the possibilities and pitfalls of computer use.

Possibilities
1. *Enhanced learner motivation* (excitement and novelty; computers more engaging to students than texts; motivated to explore; polished-looking products; seen as personally relevant)
2. *Increased access to information* (quicker and easier access to information; students can learn to manage information rather than memorize; increases student acquired information)
3. *Perceived authenticity* (first-hand information; direct data gathering perceived as more relevant)
4. *Increased individualization* (information in a variety of modalities—auditory, visual; computers accommodate different learning styles; students can work at their own pace; students can choose and determine the direction for their learning)
5. *Expanded interactions* (students can be more active in their own learning; simulations allow students to direct and vicariously experience events; the teacher no longer the primary dispenser of information but a facilitator of students' explorations)
6. *Opportunities for collaboration* (computer technology can provide a more meaningful "workshop" atmosphere)
7. *Expanded representation of ideas* (students are provided with multiple ways of representing their ideas)
8. *Increased productivity* (students often more productive, with some children better able to express their ideas)

Pitfalls
1. *Mindless fact gathering* (students will need instruction in how to critically examine and make informed choices about the material)
2. *Poor curriculum coverage* (computer programs may be a poor match with curriculum objectives and guidelines)

3. *Reduced reading development* (concern over reduced development of reading skills; computers very visual, with reduced text)
4. *Diminished writing skills* (although computers may encourage some, students lose interest in the key stages of writing such as first drafts; work may be disjointed and lack cohesion. Prewriting note form stage neglected)
5. *Neglected research skills* (the abundance of sources can get students off task; easy to cut and paste rather than synthesize, sequence, and analyze information)
6. *Need for critical thinking* (computer seen as the "truth" or as neutral; need critical thinking as with any other source)
7. *Absence of real-life experience* (the computer cannot promote the same learning and deep understanding that comes from real-life experiences)
8. *Reduced direct interaction* (potential isolation from others; working cooperatively on computer projects can counter isolation) (pp. 227–230)

Learning Centers

Though "open education" has largely disappeared as a significant movement, it has left the legacy of a more flexible approach to instruction. Learning centers that let students work "hands on" independently or with peers are part of that legacy.

A learning center is a self-contained, self-directed learning environment where students interact with materials; the center may provide immediate feedback about learning. Learning center assignments make it possible to individualize a portion of the curriculum. They can be used by individuals, pairs, or small groups. Learning centers provide students with choices in keeping with their interests. They are a constructive academic alternative for students who have finished assigned tasks. They allow students to interact directly with materials and can even allow concrete, hands-on experience.

Learning centers can be used at all grade and subject levels and for a broad range of assignments. Assignments can be subject specific or multidisciplinary. The duration of tasks can be five minutes to several weeks. Centers may be inexpensive, requiring minimum materials and space, or may require much space, extensive equipment, and expensive supplies.

For learning centers to be effective, they must be well planned and able to operate with minimum teacher direction. Preassessment of learners' knowledge and skill should occur. Ideally, students have a say in selecting and constructing centers, with student choice of activities possible. Activities should motivate students so they remain on task. Monitoring and feedback systems should be established. Ideally, a student progress record-keeping system is needed, and continuous, nonpunitive feedback should be built in. Paired or small-group work can be used effectively and is a desirable alternative.

Mastery Learning

Mastery learning is a common form of individualized instruction that may be done with or without a computer. You would like to have all your students achieve 100 percent success. How realistic is this? Though it might be argued that this technique is dated, no discussion of the individual study instructional strategy is complete without attention to mastery learning. It is an individualized method that lends itself to use in traditional settings. Advocates of mastery learning believe that if by success one means achievement of well-defined goals, expecting a rate of 80 percent or higher may not be unrealistic.

Mastery learning is based on the belief that differences in achievement are at least partly due to differences in the time needed to learn (Bloom, 1968), the appropriateness of the task for a learner, and the kind of instruction chosen (Hart, 2002; Motamedi & Sumrall, 2000). Bloom emphasizes clear directions, active learner participation, and reinforcement based on success, feedback, and correctives. Mastery learning programs can be for the class as a whole, a small group, or an individual. They have several things in common:

- Objectives are determined.
- The curriculum is divided into small chunks of knowledge and skills to be learned.
- Preassessment is used to determine if students have the necessary skills to begin or if they already have some or all the skills to be studied.
- Students take different lengths of time to complete a task (self-pacing).
- Formative evaluation (progress checks) such as daily or weekly tests, that are not part of the grading system, is used extensively.
- Correctives (or remediation), as many as necessary, are provided.
- Evaluation is criterion based.

Key considerations are the amount of active learning time, the feedback and correctives provided, and the nature of instruction. Mastery learning uses a cycle of teaching, testing, reteaching, and retesting. It can result in a higher level of performance and achievement compared to traditional instruction because students learn at different rates and need different materials. Some believe that mastery learning does not have a proper conceptual base, takes from advanced students and gives to the poorer students, and not all students are equally capable.

Focused Imaging

You help students' tap into their personal creative ability when you provide opportunities for them to use their imaginations. A wonderful teaching method for this is *focused imaging*. It can be used for something to be pictured, heard, sensed, or felt. It is fun, motivating, and inspiring for students and teacher. An example of focused imaging occurs when students are told to close their eyes and imagine they are the lead singer performing in front of an adoring audience, followed either by writing a paragraph describing the experience or sharing feelings with peers.

Focused imaging, which can be used in any school subject, is the use of personally developed images applied to curricula. It is like daydreaming that is used to explore the content of a lesson or unit. The process is free flowing, unique to each individual, with no incorrect answer. Self-esteem is fostered through safe, successful personal imaging. The teacher needs to make sure the classroom atmosphere is relaxed and to be open to a variety of (sometimes unexpected) responses. When students engage in focused imaging, they build a bridge from external sensations to internal awareness. It helps them assimilate new information. Another use is mental rehearsal before trying something "for real." Also, students can mentally come up with and try alternate approaches to a problem, imaging what would happen given different scenarios. Students can use focused imaging before they begin creative writing, a visual art project, a badminton strategy, or even before they attempt an answer to a test question.

Study Skills

To learn efficiently through independent study methods, students must understand what they have experienced and comprehend what they have read. They should be able to retain and use the information and ideas studied. The techniques students use to study can be put into two categories: (1) knowing how to find information needed for an assignment, and (2) techniques for learning the material presented. Teachers need to be aware of common study problems. Many students do not budget time effectively. They cannot estimate how much time to allow, nor do they set up a regular study schedule. Physical conditions may be unsuitable, finding a good place to study may be difficult, lighting may be inappropriate, or noise may interfere. Some students are disorganized and either do not know how, or are not sufficiently motivated, to organize well. Students may be deficient in reading skills and find it hard to read with comprehension; or note-taking skills (from written material or classroom presentations) may be weak. Finally, students may not have learned specific techniques for studying.

The ways children study influence how much they learn. Teachers can often help children develop better study skills.

- Adjust study according to the complexity of the material, time available, what is already known about a topic, purpose and importance of the assignment, and standards to be met.
- Space learning sessions over time rather than cram or study the same topic continuously.
- Identify the main ideas in new information.
- Connect new material to what is already known.
- Draw inferences about the significance of new information.
- Assess how well study methods are working by appraising personal progress. (U.S. Department of Education, 1986, p. 39)

How well students learn depends on academic potential, motivation, academic skills, and personal management skills. *Academic skills* refer to how new information and ideas are gathered, connected to those already known, organized and understood, committed to memory, and used. *Personal management* refers to how students manage time, their emotions, and their relationships with other people. Students can be taught academic skills and helped with personal management. In short, students can acquire effective learning strategies.

CASE 11.6 Individual Study

Wild Animals

Ms. Perez plans to have her grade 5 class develop reports on "Wild Animals in the Tropics." She wants the children to experience and learn basic things about research projects. They will need to generate ideas, organize topics, find and record information from resource materials (note taking), organize information, and present it in a clear way. Ms. Perez intends to review and teach the research skills needed as students work on the project. She thinks the project will take about two weeks.

First she gets the children to choose the animal they will research. To work toward an outline or concept map of their topic, she has the students, in threes, brainstorm questions about their choices of animals. She suggests everyone should have at least one hundred questions. Questions become more specific, and many more are generated. That afternoon, students who had fewer than one hundred questions take their materials home to add to their lists.

Next class, Ms. Perez reviews concept mapping as a way to show relationships among categories. Each child spends the period categorizing his or her questions into groups of related information. The next period is used to tentatively sequence the question categories.

In a subsequent class, Ms. Perez distributes 3 × 5 cards on which students are to record their information. She has found that using cards encourages students to summarize instead of copying long passages as they take notes. There are enough resource books in the room for everyone. The children have, in the past, practiced looking for and recording information. They spend class time and some out-of-school time to find and record information. To stay on topic, they are encouraged to keep checking over their categories of questions.

Later, Ms. Perez gets the students to sort their information and notes into question categories. Over the next few days they work on the categories, one at a time, deciding what to include and putting information in order. For this project the students are to develop a set of notes for an oral report to their classmates.

CASE 11.7 Individual Study

Spoon Feeding

Mr. Wang and three of his colleagues in the English Department of Beacon High School had a discussion after school one day that started with a long-time department member, Ms. Traut, saying, "Students nowadays just seem to want to be spoon fed. Their attitude seems to be 'Tell me what to memorize and then don't bother me.'" The discussion got Mr. Wang thinking. "Perhaps," he thought to himself, "there are two things the matter. One, teachers haven't taught students learning strategies; and second, teachers don't allow students to act as independent learners."

Mr. Wang resolved that he had an obligation to his students to do something about the two problems. He had read that it was possible to improve students' study skills, that learning strategies such as reading comprehension skills could be learned and could transfer to other subjects.

What would you suggest that Mr. Wang do to help students acquire learning strategies; and how could he release control to his students in such a way that they would rise to the challenge of becoming independent learners?

LINKING PRACTICE TO THEORY

The individual study strategy has changed considerably, especially with school use of computers and the Internet. Compare your schooling experience with the expectations of students today. What new skills need to be taught? Compare the skills in this chapter with skills teaching in Chapter 10. How can individual study approaches be given realistic significance? Compare the effectiveness of your approach to teaching with the expectations of the strategy described in this chapter.

Summary

The "big five" instructional strategies are direct instruction, indirect instruction, interactive instruction, experiential learning, and individual study. The most common approach is direct instruction. It is deductive and teacher centered. The two most common methods in direct instruction are lecture and assigned questions. It often involves note taking and practice and drill and is effective for information or skill acquisition. Direct instruction can be an exciting and valuable teaching approach when presented with the creative use of media and other techniques. Direct instruction should be balanced with other strategic approaches. Individual study involves teaching students specific research skills and the effective use of computer technology. Individual study encourages students to develop individual responsibility and life-long learning skills and interests. It is an approach that encourages meta-cognition, in which students think about their learning.

Activities

DIRECT INSTRUCTION

1. Join a subject group to discuss: (a) what you think to be a proper mix of teaching methods; (b) when it is appropriate to use lecture, assigned questions, and practice and drill; and (c) how these methods can be best used in subject specializations.
2. Teach a lesson that has effective lecture as a professional target. Using the data collection instrument in Appendix 11.1, have someone observe and give you feedback or complete the instrument yourself after you have taught the lesson. If teaching a lesson is not practical, observe a lesson (or film of a lesson) and analyze it using Figure 11.4.
3. Teach a lesson with assigned questions as a professional target. Use Appendix 11.4. Have somebody collect data or complete the instrument yourself. If teaching a lesson is not practical, observe a lesson (or film of a lesson) and analyze it.
4. Observe a teacher using practice and drill. Use Appendix 11.5. Do a class survey on the following (circle the appropriate response): SA, Strongly agree; A, Agree; D, Disagree; or SD, Strongly disagree.

> Direct instruction was an effective part of my education.   SA   A   D   SD
>
> Direct instruction was an enjoyable part of my education.   SA   A   D   SD

5. In subject groups, take up a topic suitable for direct instruction. Design a PowerPoint presentation. Share with the class the pros and the cons of using PowerPoint in your discipline. You should show samples of your presentation to the class.
6. The overhead projector is used frequently by teachers. (a) In your next field experience, discuss with your cooperating teacher its possible uses. (b) In class, discuss the most effective ways of using an overhead projector.
7. Marshall McLuhan (1994) said, "The medium is the message." Discuss this statement in the light of technology and education. Do chalkboards, overhead projectors, and PowerPoint presentations give different messages?

INDIVIDUAL STUDY

1. Form pairs. Research and do a two-page write-up of an independent-study teaching method. Use the headings: "What is the (name the method)?" "How does it work?" "What are its advantages?" "What are its disadvantages?" "How can the disadvantages be overcome?" "For what kind of subjects or content is it particularly suitable?"
2. The next time you are in a school setting, if appropriate, ask one or more teachers which independent study methods they use and how they go about seatwork and homework and if the school has a policy regarding these.
3. In a subject-area/grade-level group, discuss and then report to the whole class how the teaching of learning strategies can be incorporated in the delivery of the subject(s) you hope to teach.

APPENDIX 11.1   *Professional Target: Lecture*

PROFESSIONAL TARGET—LECTURE

Describe what was said and done and student reactions.

Lecture Considerations	Observations
1. Organization (advance organizer, structure, postorganizer)	
2. Relating present to past or future learning	
3. Using summaries (by teacher or students)	
4. Stimulating students to think, participate covertly	
5. Using stimulus variation	
6. Supplementing with visuals, discussion, question and answer	
7. Showing enthusiasm, interest in topic, color	
8. Examples used to illustrate key ideas (verbal or visual)	
9. Appropriateness of delivery for note taking	
10. Creating feeling each student is being addressed	
11. Use of handout	
12. Appropriateness of time for amount of material covered	

APPENDIX 11.2   *Professional Target: Chalkboard*

PROFESSIONAL TARGET—USING THE CHALKBOARD/WHITEBOARD

Describe what is done and student reaction.

Chalkboard/Whiteboard Plan

Chalkboard/Whiteboard Observed

Examples of Skills	Descriptive Comments
1. Easy to follow organization?	
2. Writing in a straight line?	
3. Writing large enough?	
4. Organization—left to right top to bottom	
5. Clarity/quality of writing	
6. Movement to and from board	
7. Position while writing	
8. Movement while writing	
9. On board in advance? As part of presentation?	

APPENDIX 11.3 *Professional Target: Overhead Projector Use*

PROFESSIONAL TARGET—USING THE OVERHEAD PROJECTOR

Please use descriptive statements.

1. *Simplicity*

   (a) Using point form (not sentences)

   (b) Normally having no more than six points per transparency

   (c) Using LARGE print

2. *Focusing*

   (a) Using a pointer (pen, pencil, bar stick, etc.)

   (b) Turning projector off when not in use to return attention to the teacher

3. *Progressive Disclosure*

   (a) Showing one point/line at a time; blocking out others until you get to them

4. *Visibility*

   (a) Having the screen in a corner of the front of the room

   (b) Having the projector far enough for its light to fill the screen

   (c) Making sure the images are clearly focused

   (d) Facing the class but not blocking students' view of the screen

   (e) To focus attention, pointing at the transparency, not the screen

5. *Appeal of Presentation*

   (a) Spacing, use of pictures, cartoons, borders, boxes, etc.

   (b) Motivational impact

APPENDIX 11.4   *Professional Target: Assigned Questions*

PROFESSIONAL TARGET—ASSIGNED QUESTIONS

Describe what was said and done and student reactions.

Assigned Questions Considerations	Observations
1. Way topic was introduced	
2. Directions on how to go about getting/recording answers	
3. Advance organizer or postorganizer use	
4. Nature of questions: domain, levels, convergent or divergent	
5. Circulation during seatwork; nature of help	
6. Procedure in taking up; use of probes, redirects	
7. Tie in to past/future learning	
8. Integration of domains	
9. Use of encouragement, reinforcement	

APPENDIX 11.5   *Professional Target: Practice and Drill*

PROFESSIONAL TARGET—PRACTICE AND DRILL

Practice/Drill Considerations	Observations
1. Determination of entry capability	
2. Provision for understanding	
3. Need for information/skill established	
4. Provision for practice variety	
5. Provision of feedback, reinforcement, encouragement	
6. Similarity to actual use conditions	
7. Emphasis on product or process	
8. Use of competition; self–competition	
9. Length and spacing of practice	
10. Linking or application of skill to other content	

12 The Indirect and Experiential Instruction Strategies

The Indirect Instruction Strategy

What Is Indirect Instruction?

Learning can be more meaning-ful, thorough, and usable when learn-ers seek and discover knowledge. Students benefit when they draw conclusions from information they find themselves or have been given. Indirect instruction comes under many headings. Terms that are some-times used interchangeably are in-quiry, induction, problem solving, action research, decision making, and discovery. We group these under the heading of indirect instruction. The kinds of methods to achieve this are in Figure 12.1 on page 370.

In contrast to the direct in-struction teaching strategy, indirect instruction is student centered. Ex-amples of indirect teaching methods are debates, panels, field studies, re-search reports, group investigation, brainstorming, simulations, guided in-quiry, and unguided inquiry. In indi-rect instruction, a high level of student

OBJECTIVES

You will be able to:

1. Define direct and indirect inquiry, and deductive and inductive learning/teaching.
2. Demonstrate the use of inductive behaviors while using a direct teaching method.
3. Describe guided and unguided inquiry.
4. Demonstrate initial competence in the use of indirect and individual study methods in microteaching or school lessons.
5. Describe mastery learning and considerations in using it.
6. Describe indirect learning strategies and places in the curriculum where they can be used.
7. Define the experiential instructional strategy and list its characteristics.
8. State the purposes of experiential education.
9. Name and describe the experiential instruction methods presented in this chapter.
10. Describe the experiential cycle and apply it to a school subject.
11. List advantages and limitations of experiential teaching and learning.
12. Apply learning about experiential learning to in- and out-of-school learning experiences and in a microteaching or school classroom lesson.

TCP—INDIRECT INSTRUCTION STRATEGY

Provides effective use of indirect/inductive/inquiry methods

Use matches content and learner needs; instruction highly learner centered; pupil discovery fostered; appro-priate learning materials available; sensitive to learners' experiential backgrounds; learners presented with prob-lems or issues to be explored and solved.

Instruction exclusively teacher centered and expository or deductive; information-centered instruction.

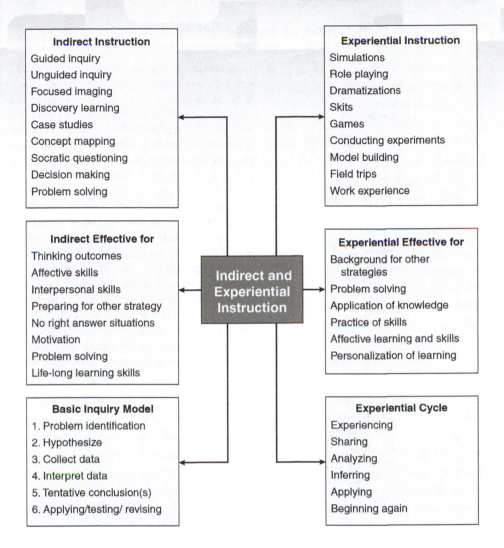

Indirect Instruction	Experiential Instruction
Guided inquiry	Simulations
Unguided inquiry	Role playing
Focused imaging	Dramatizations
Discovery learning	Skits
Case studies	Games
Concept mapping	Conducting experiments
Socratic questioning	Model building
Decision making	Field trips
Problem solving	Work experience

Indirect and Experiential Instruction

Indirect Effective for	Experiential Effective for
Thinking outcomes	Background for other strategies
Affective skills	Problem solving
Interpersonal skills	Application of knowledge
Preparing for other strategy	Practice of skills
No right answer situations	Affective learning and skills
Motivation	Personalization of learning
Problem solving	
Life-long learning skills	

Basic Inquiry Model	Experiential Cycle
1. Problem identification	Experiencing
2. Hypothesize	Sharing
3. Collect data	Analyzing
4. Interpret data	Inferring
5. Tentative conclusion(s)	Applying
6. Applying/testing/ revising	Beginning again

involvement is sought. It is flexible, frees students to explore diverse possibilities, reduces fear of incorrect answers, fosters development of creativity, and promotes development of interpersonal skills. On the other hand, indirect instruction is a slower way to expose students to content than direct instruction, and it requires expertise in indirect methods and skills.

Although much indirect instruction is a combination of inductive and deductive teaching, the inductive approach is predominant. For example, it occurs when students are asked to identify basic information, encouraged to explain data by determining cause-and-effect relationships, or infer or make a hypothesis that goes beyond the information at hand.

What Is Inquiry?

Indirect teaching fosters student participation through observation, investigation, drawing inferences from data, or forming a hypothesis. When indirect instruction is used, you

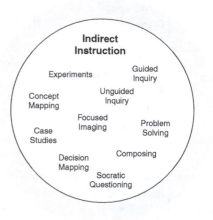

FIGURE 12.1   *The Indirect Instruction Strategy*

Source: Saskatchewan Learning (1991).

take advantage of students' natural interest in discovery, suggesting alternatives, or solving problems. Your role shifts from lecturer/director to facilitator/supporter/resource person. You relinquish control, and outcomes are often unpredictable and less "safe." You arrange the learning environment, provide opportunity for student involvement, and provide feedback on student responses. Students conduct an inquiry rather than passively receive information.

Webster's dictionary defines the word *inquire* as "to ask about," "to search into," or "to make investigation." Importantly, the investigative process of inquiry should involve the student not only in seeking answers but also in formulating questions and deciding the best methods to use, and then conducting the study. Some people think the inductive method of inquiry is the traditional "scientific method." Inquiry is no longer viewed this way. Scientists use inductive methods, but modern science goes beyond pure inductive logic. Inductive reasoning is a basis for inference building, and scientists rely on theories on which to base experiments.

Basic steps in using inquiry teaching are illustrated in Figure 12.2. The basic processes of inquiry are

1. Observing
2. Classifying
3. Using numbers
4. Measuring
5. Using space–time relationships
6. Predicting
7. Inferring
8. Defining operationally
9. Formulating hypotheses
10. Interpreting data
11. Controlling variables
12. Experimenting
13. Communicating

Inquiry processes should be learned and practiced systematically. Provide time for conceptual skill building. Every student can, and should, learn the skills (even the "slow" students). This opens doors to learning things that just might not be in the textbook. Some of the skills will be stressed in Chapter 14.

Guided Inductive Inquiry

We can approach inquiry in two ways. In the first way, the teacher carefully guides students toward a specific discovery or generalization; in the second, inquiry is more casually supervised (free discovery), and students are involved in setting up the problem and seeking its solution. Descriptions of guided and unguided inductive inquiry follow.

In *guided inductive inquiry,* students are expected to arrive at generalizations because the learning activities, classroom recitations or discussions, learning materials, and visuals

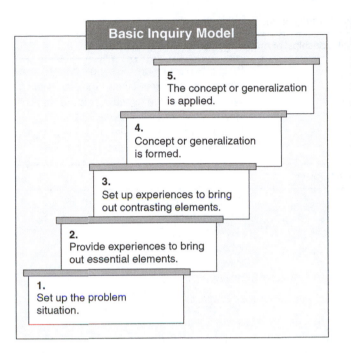

Basic Inquiry Model

5.
The concept or generalization
is applied.

4.
Concept or generalization
is formed.

3.
Set up experiences to bring
out contrasting elements.

2.
Provide experiences to bring
out essential elements.

1.
Set up the problem
situation.

FIGURE 12.2   *Basic Steps in Using the Inquiry Teaching Method*

are arranged so everything is available for students to arrive at the generalizations you have determined. Students are to develop the habit of being systematic and use a process of making observations and drawing inferences. An observation is recorded and inferences drawn (inferences are generalizations about certain objects or events). Years ago, but as relevant today, Womack (1966) presented classic steps for arriving at a generalization through guided discovery:

- Decide on the generalization(s) students should discover from a particular unit of study.
- Organize the learning activities and materials in a way that exposes the strands or parts of the generalization(s) to the students.
- Ask students to write a summary of the content that contains the generalization(s).
- Ask students to identify the sequence of the pattern of events comprising the content, omitting any reference to any particular people, place, or time.
- Ask students to synthesize the various parts of the pattern of events into one complete sentence that purports to be a generalization.
- Ask students to offer proof that their generalization is suitable by citing examples that it existed and operated in other periods, places, and among other peoples. (p. 13)

QUESTIONING AND GUIDED INQUIRY.   As you know, questioning is important in inquiry. You become a question asker, not a question answerer. Much time is spent interacting with students, but you provide few answers. See Figure 12.3 for stems for questions that can be used in inquiry.

USING GUIDED INQUIRY.   Beamon (2002) describes the elements of guided inquiry as

- Guided questioning
- Linking content to issues, themes, and problems
- Social interaction
- Active exploration
- Authentic assessment
- Helping learners to make meaningful connections among the big ideas of a discipline and their personal experiences, conceptions, and beliefs

Beamon stresses that when we teach adolescents we need to understand how they think, learn, and feel and that we need to be aware that the curricular and instructional decisions we make affect the nature of the adolescent's learning experiences. Central to Beamon's writing is the *adolescent teaching model,* which has four components: (1) emphasis

FIGURE 12.3   *Examples of Inquiry Stems*

Examining Cause-and-Effect Relationships, or Analyzing Events

---

What is happening?	What took place before this happened?
What has happened?	Where have you seen something like this happen?
What do you think will happen now?	When have you seen something like this happen?
How did this happen?	How could we make this happen?
Why did this happen?	How does this compare with what we saw or did?
What caused this to happen?	How can we do this more easily (or quickly)?

Stems for More Static or Nonliving Objects

What kind of object is it?	What can you do with it?
What is it called?	What is it made of?
Where is it found?	How was it made?
What does it look like?	What was its purpose?
Have you ever seen anything like it?	How does it work or operate?
How is it like other things?	Where?
When?	How can you recognize or identify it?
How is it different from other things?	What other names does it have?

Note: These prompting questions help students understand all kinds of relationships, which is a goal of inquiry. The questions can be used with pictures, models, and other visuals (particularly when teaching younger children or children without first-hand experience with something).

on student understanding of the essential concepts of the discipline in question; (2) strategies to motivate students and to promote student inquiry; (3) suggestions for guiding students to become progressively self-directive; and (4) opportunities for student self-evaluation, reflection, and application of learning.

The key to the inquiry approach is active, not passive learning. In, for example, the teaching of science, students "are introduced to science methods and use them to engage in hands-on, 'minds-on' activities that inspire them to discover scientific knowledge rather than being told answers by the teacher or textbook" (Jorgenson & Vanosdall, 2002, p. 602). These authors condemn what they call the "drill and kill" model of teaching science, with emphasis on the text, videotapes, or end-of-chapter questions. They observe, "The inquiry approach was founded on the premise that children learn actively, not passively" (p. 602).

Inquiry-based learning requires students to find a topic, create questions, and gather, sort, and analyze information. A crucial next stage is to do something with the information. This "is what distinguishes inquiry-based projects from typical school research projects" (Owens, Hester, & Teale, 2002, p. 617). It links inquiry-based approaches to constructivism and authentic instruction. The authors claim that the "most successful inquiry projects emerge from topics that are of real interest to the students" (p. 617). They say that teachers should be models and demonstrate for students how to (1) formulate questions that move beyond the literal level of understanding, (2) collect information from a wide variety of resources, and (3) use the information in a meaningful way (p. 618). Science is particularly suited to inquiry:

The hallmark of science learning . . . is independent student inquiry. . . . Inquiry-based approaches to science instruction invite learners to investigate the world around them in order to pose and solve problems, construct mental models of phenomena, and understand procedures that scientists use in their work. Students practice inquiry at varying levels of sophistication, ranging from guided investigations of elementary concepts to independent explorations in which learners generate and refine hypotheses, design ways to systematically test complex relationships, evaluate evidence, and internalize the epistemological assumptions of the inquiry enterprise itself. (Windschitl, 2000, p. 81)

Windschitl sees the value of computer-supported learning environments, including software, to enhance inquiry approaches and experiential learning.

Drayton and Falk (2001) note that a key question in inquiry-based learning is "Who is doing the intellectual work?" (p. 28). Although they see the value of direct instruction, they say there must be student-to-student talk, activities in which students need each others' results, and times in which they need to test arguments and evaluate their methods (p. 29).

Unguided Inductive Inquiry

As you can see, in guided inductive inquiry you play the key role by asking questions, prompting, structuring materials and situations, and in general being the major organizer of learning. This is a good way to begin a gradual shift from direct teaching to teaching that is less structured and is open to alternative solutions. Unguided inductive inquiry is predicated on inductive logic, but it is open ended and students take responsibility for examining data, objects, or events.

The basic processes in unguided inductive inquiry are observation, inference, classification, communication, prediction, interpretation, formulation of hypotheses, and experimentation (as in guided inquiry). Your role is reduced and that of the student is increased. The major elements of unguided inductive inquiry are that:

- Learners' thought processes are a progression of specific experiences and observations to inferences and generalizations.
- The purpose is to learn procedures for examining occurrences, objects, or data to draw inferences and arrive at generalizations.
- You, as teacher, control only the materials and pose questions such as "What does this mean?" Students interact, work, and ask many questions with no further teacher guidance.
- Students discover meaningful structure or patterns through observations and inferences.
- Appropriate resources and materials are needed.
- The number of generalizations that learners will generate may be unlimited.
- Students should share inferences and generalizations so class members can benefit from each other's perceptions.

Inquiry permits greater learner creativity. Learning is enhanced because learners "find out for themselves." You may need a new set of behaviors. You act as a "clarifier," helping when students make gross errors in logic, generalize too broadly, take too much inference from data, assign cause–effect relationships where there are none, or assign single cause–effect relationships where there are several. Use a nonthreatening manner in

---

Guided Inquiry

Teacher carefully guides students toward a discovery or generalization

---

Unguided Inquiry

Supervision more "casual" (free discovery and students are involved in setting up the problem as well as seeking the solution)

Steps for Both

1. Problem identification
2. Tentative research hypothesis/objectives
3. Data collected; tentative answers tested
4. Data interpreted
5. Tentative conclusions/generalization
6. Applying or retesting conclusions, revising original conclusions

---

FIGURE 12.4 *Overview of Guided and Unguided Inquiry*

verifying conclusions and generalizations. If there are errors in logic or inferences, point them out, but do not tell what the correct inference is because this defeats the purpose of the inquiry episode. Concrete evidence should be required for generalizations; thus, comprehension and analytic skills are reinforced. Practice is given in making and testing hypotheses. Inquiry can stimulate classroom discussions in every school subject.

As you have discovered, inquiry processes can be used in daily lessons as part of almost every teaching strategy and method. If students are to be involved (overtly or covertly), if you tell less and ask more, if you stress thinking skills and processes, your teaching will be more inductive or inquiry oriented. An overview of guided and unguided inquiry is provided in Figure 12.4.

Using Inquiry Methods

WHEN TO USE INQUIRY METHODS.   Inquiry methods can be effective when:

- Thinking skills and processes, or affective skills or processes should be stressed.
- Learning "how" to do something is more important than just getting the right answer; or when "why" is more important than "what."
- Students need to experience something rather than just hear or read about it.
- Several "right" answers are possible, or when "right" can change with circumstances.
- The content should focus on discovering solutions to problems or making decisions.
- The focus is on development of creativity.
- The focus is on concepts, attitudes, or values.
- You wish students to become more ego-involved and thus self-motivated.
- An objective is for students to develop life-long learning capabilities.

TIPS FOR USING INQUIRY METHODS.   Begin by discovering the experience your students have had with inquiry techniques. If necessary, teach, and provide practice in, inquiry skills and processes. Use open-ended and higher-level questions, solicit and accept divergent responses, and use probes and redirects. Encourage and reinforce as students develop responsibility for discovering "answers." Avoid telling the answers and what to do next. Act as a helper or facilitator. Be supportive of student responses, ideas, differing views and interpretations, and recognize that inquiry techniques are harder to do well and take more planning. Have adequate facilities and materials, including data sources, so inquiry can occur effectively. Make full use of school and district resource centers and staff. In using guided inquiry, ensure that the problems are suitable; in unguided inquiry, ensure that the investigations students select are manageable. Require students to support their comments with evidence and reason. Teach how to write or phrase the concepts, principles, or generalizations to be tested. Elicit student–student interaction and sharing; stress support and cooperation, not competition. Encourage the attitude of acting on the current verified "best answer," knowing that additional evidence may lead to a new "best answer," rather than not acting until the final, ultimate truth is found. Teach the difference between "healthy" and "negative" skepticism. Remember that the "content" of inquiry is the "process," and that the product or solution may be less important. A goal is to develop students' abilities to learn how to learn and to take responsibility for planning, conducting, and evaluating.

Summary

The term *inquiry* is sometimes used interchangeably with *discovery* and *problem solving.* Whatever the term, the emphasis in this method is on questioning and actively engaging students. As a teaching method, it is used to encourage students to recognize and state problems, ask questions that lead them to seek answers, recognize whether the answers are reasonable, and for "answers" to point to further study.

TEACHER BEHAVIOR AND INDIRECT INSTRUCTION.   Students' backgrounds need to be discovered and, if necessary, they should be taught suitable skills and processes (e.g., data gathering techniques, data interpretation, and critical thinking). Reason and evidence are stressed. The attitude to be fostered is that what seems the "best answer" may not be best in the light of evidence. Students are encouraged to make informed guesses and helped to realize the difference between healthy skepticism and negativism. Teachers who use the indirect strategy well make sure the problem is manageable and that students understand the purpose of an activity. Adequate references, materials, and facilities should be available, and full use made of the resource center. Students are encouraged to accept ownership for learning and are helped to select and use investigation techniques and thinking skills. The teacher avoids "telling" and uses "asking." Open-ended questions and prompts and probes are used and divergent responses accepted. Students are encouraged to risk. Creativity and independent, resourceful thinking are valued and transfer to new situations fostered.

Importantly, the effective teacher accentuates the positive, deemphasizes competition, encourages exchange of ideas, and encourages students to cooperate and support each other. Ideas can be challenged, but people cannot be attacked. The teacher provides feedback on students' use of inquiry, decision-making, and problem-solving skills.

WHEN ARE INDIRECT INSTRUCTION METHODS EFFECTIVE?   You can use indirect instruction processes every school day and with almost every lesson. It is effective when:

- Thinking outcomes are desired.
- Value, attitude, or interpersonal or group skills outcomes are desired.
- Process (learning "how") is at least as important as product (getting "the right answer").
- Students need to experience something in order to benefit from later instruction.
- There are no "right" answers.
- The focus is personalized understanding and long-term retention of concepts or generalizations.
- Ego involvement and intrinsic motivation are desirable.
- Decisions need to be made or problems need to be solved.
- Life-long learning capability is desired.

BASIC FORMAT FOR INDIRECT TEACHING.   You can use the examples of indirect teaching strategies shown in Figure 12.1. Examples of indirect instruction methods vary from use of question and answer as part of a lecture to use of full-blown unguided inquiry. In the basic model for indirect teaching, a problem is posed, students inquire, and a discovery is made.

The Inductive Approach

In the previous chapter you were introduced to the use of teaching strategies categorized as direct or expository (i.e., lecture, assigned questions, and practice and drill). Direct strategies tend to be teacher centered, deductive, and closed, often based on the view that bodies of knowledge (the "content") are both a means and an end. This is the traditional approach (though many teachers do not use it exclusively). Indirect strategies tend to be student centered, inductive, and open, often exploring and building the knowledge with students.

It may be useful to review the definitions of the terms *inductive* and *deductive*. In the *inductive approach,* learners move from the specific to the general. You, for example, may provide experiences in which students organize several facts or details into a major concept or principle. Alternatively, you may first introduce the concept or principle and then show how a set of known facts fit. Here, students are guided from the general to the specific through direct teaching. This is the *deductive approach.*

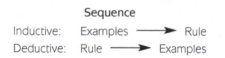

Sequence

Inductive: Examples ⟶ Rule

Deductive: Rule ⟶ Examples

The teacher's role is to create situations in which students can learn on their own rather than provide prepackaged information. The fundamental goal should be to make students self-sufficient. Students should often learn through active involvement with concepts and principles and be permitted to discover concepts and principles themselves. Students need to learn to think for themselves, to take part in the knowledge-getting process.

Instructional experts agree that learning should be much more experiential (and interactive). This is an inductive inquiry approach. Initially, you may experience difficulty and frustration with some aspects, and want more structure—to some extent, we are all "prisoners" of our own experience. This chapter will help you learn more about inquiry and set the stage for further experience so that the inquiry or inductive approach can become a more comfortable part of your repertoire.

INDUCTIVE TEACHING.   Inductive teaching encourages development of the academic skills of reasoning and theory construction. It encourages students to work either from evidence they discover themselves or from material handed out by the teacher for concept and principle learning. An example of the inductive process is when students are required to identify basic information (data), encouraged to explain the data by relating one point to another (drawing cause-and-effect relationships), and when they make inferences and form hypotheses that go beyond the information at hand. For example, students given pictures of various nationalistic activities and objects (a flag, a group of soldiers, an anthem) might hypothesize on the meaning of nationalism.

Inductive instructional strategies usually are soliciting skills. "Inductive teaching consists largely of systematic movement from fact recall questions to conceptual questions and finally to opining and valuing questions" (Martin, 1983, p. 85). Reacting skills are used to encourage student responses. The three kinds of inductive instructional skills (Table 12.1) are (1) structuring—arrangement of the learning environment; (2) soliciting—provision

TABLE 12.1 *Inductive Teaching*

Component Skill	Example
Structuring Skills (A very simple overview usually suffices)	"Today's discussion will concern the Cold War balance of power that existed among the nations of the world."
Soliciting Skills Fact-recall questions	"How many countries did we classify last time as Western, Communist, Third World, and Neutral?" "Which countries, if any, within each group might have been considered major military powers?"
Conceptual questions	"How did the political ideologies of each group related to their international policies?" "Why were the United States and the Soviet Union involved so often in other countries' problems?"
Opining or valuing questions (In inductive teaching, such questions ask pupils to speculate and theorize as well as state their own opinions.)	"What general principle concerning the role of superpowers would you be prepared to make in this regard?" "Can you imagine what would have happened if Cuba joined the Western Bloc? What would our theory say about this?"
Redirection (A great deal of redirection of the previous questions will occur in any good inductive teaching strategy, in order to involve many pupils.)	"All right, can somebody else carry that idea a bit further?" "Tom, you don't agree. Tell us why." "What do you think, Bert?" "Brenda?" "Carl?"
Positive questioning	Ask questions; pause; call on reciter.
Reacting Skills Descriptive praise	"That's one good reason why the United States resisted such a move."
Incorporating student responses into lesson	"You're saying that each superpower must be viewed as being equally strong as all other superpowers. Let's see whether we can work with your idea for a few minutes."

Source: Adapted from Martin, 1983, pp. 85–86.

of opportunities for student involvement; and (3) reacting—provision of feedback or instructional responses to student involvement (p. 63).

The indirect, inductive teaching strategy makes many demands of the teacher. It can be one of the most satisfying approaches. Why? To what extent do you need to know your students and subject matter well? Think of all the skills and competencies it draws upon—communication and interpersonal skills, awareness of the learning abilities and values of students, classroom management, and planning. How did you find the inductive experience? Is it more risky than direct instruction, where *you* control the variables? Reflect on your experiences. How is knowledge structured in the classroom? Can discovery be fostered? How satisfying is the approach for you and your students? What insights did you have?

A data collection instrument you can use for inquiry is provided in Appendix 12.1. Use this data collection instrument to help you analyze the cases that follow. Your instructor may pose specific questions for your response.

CASE 12.1   The Inquiry Approach and Computer Software

An Ant Community

Mr. Stein's grade 6 class is studying the behavior of ants. First Mr. Stein placed an ant hill simulation software program on the computers. With the simulation, he thinks, he can have students study the behavior of ants—where they live in the ant hill, their hierarchical relationship to one another, how they forage for food, and how they interact with the world outside the ant hill. By changing the variables in the simulation, students try various interesting experiments—including

what happens when the population is dramatically increased or decreased, or the temperature changes, or there is a decline in the food supply. The students have many questions and try variations to find the answers. Mr. Stein also obtained an ant hill in a glass case so the students can conduct inquiry with real materials as well as computer-based models. This study of the real ant hill helps students see the limitations of science and learn respect for the complexity of science.

CASE 12.2   Indirect Instruction

An Awareness Lesson

Ms. Jacques was a student teacher in a grade 4 class. The youngsters were enthusiastic participants in most activities. In their enthusiasm, they could become very competitive. Ms. Jacques had tried to use small-group learning, but the children found it difficult to follow the instructions and the structure of group learning. They appeared to lose interest before the task began. Ms. Jacques was not happy with the way she found herself enforcing basic expectations. She decided to try a more indirect approach.

She assigned the class to three groups in three different locations and gave instructions for the task. This time, she did not tell them how to work together in groups. As the groups began, the cooperating teacher and Ms. Jacques's student teaching partner each attached themselves to a group, leaving Ms. Jacques to work with one group. Both of the other groups received direction and coaching as they worked. Disagreements were resolved and the groups kept on task.

In Ms. Jacques's group, however, things did not go smoothly. The children quarreled over the materials, couldn't agree on the task, and three children competed strongly for leadership. While this was going on, in keeping with her plan, Ms. Jacques managed to keep from intervening. At the end of the period, her group had not completed the task. The other two groups had finished products of which they were proud. With

prompting from their respective adults, they explained how they had worked to complete their tasks.

Ms. Jacques gathered her group together and asked them how they felt about their group work. They said they wished they had finished so they'd also have had something to show. "I wonder why we didn't finish," said Ms. Jacques. "Did we understand the task we had to do?" The group agreed they knew what had to be done. "Did we have the materials?" she asked. "We had everything, we just didn't do it right," volunteered Jesse. "That's right," added Jeremy. "We should've started working instead of arguing." "If we'd decided who would be leader, that person could've made sure everyone's idea was listened to and we could've decided how to do our project sooner," offered Amanda. "And better," Pat broke in, "I still have a great idea for how to start." "I wanted to be the one that drew our invention," Joan said, "but I should have shared instead of keeping the markers myself." "We wasted our time," said Simon.

"I wish we could do the project," Jeremy said. "I'd miss recess if we could." The others agreed. "Well, I think that's possible," said Ms. Jacques. "It sounds as if you have good ideas of how to work as a group now. Maybe it wasn't a waste of time if you have learned ways *not* to work in a group. Let's list the things we want to do as we work on the project. Then we'll decide when we can get together to have another go at it."

CASE 12.3 Indirect Instruction

Getting the Point

Mr. Haggar found that the students in his grade 10 language arts class did not know how to use the colon and semicolon. He decided to take time out to teach the use of these to his class. He began, "I've just finished reading your essays and noticed that you have difficulty distinguishing between and using colons and semicolons. We'll take time today to help you understand the difference between these useful punctuation marks and provide practice to help you remember them. After today, I'm sure you will find it easy to use these helpful writing tools."

The class was divided into groups of six. Then, Mr. Haggar distributed a handout that consisted of three parts: (1) ten examples of the use of colons, (2) ten examples of the use of semicolons, and (3) ten sentences that required, as appropriate, insertion of either a colon or a semicolon. "There are rules for the use of the colons and semicolons in written English. You are to do a three-stage exercise. First, go through

part one of the handout to study examples of the use of a colon. Discuss what you observe and agree on a definition of a colon. Second, study the sentences that contain semicolons and then arrive at a definition of a semicolon. We will then take time out to hear the definitions you have discovered and to agree on a common definition. The third step will be for you to go through the sentences that do not contain the necessary mark, colon or semicolon, and agree on which mark to use and where to place it."

Mr. Haggar circulated as groups were working and listened to reports of their definitions. A common definition was derived from those provided by the groups. He circulated again as they did the third part of the exercise. He was pleased with what he saw and heard. In conclusion, he had each student, privately, write a definition in his or her own words, of the two punctuation marks. Finally, several students read their definitions to the rest of the class.

The Experiential Instruction Strategy

> The teacher's task . . . can be supported by a wise use of a wide variety of devices that expand experience, clarify it, and give it personal significance. (Jerome Bruner, 1960, p. 91)

TCP—EXPERIENTIAL LEARNING STRATEGY

Uses experiential learning regularly to encourage active learning

Able to design experiences that facilitate active participation in learning; debriefs student experiences; gets students to discover generalizations from experiences; gets students to apply learnings to new situations.

Students seldom engaged in actual experiences to generate active learning; does not debrief student experiences.

The Nature of Experiential Learning

As you decide the approach to teaching to use to meet the needs of your students, choices will need to be made based on the readiness of learners, their learning styles, the nature of the content, learners' previous experience, and the degree of overlearning desired. Teaching and learning can be approached in the following ways:

Actively doing ← Observing → Hearing or reading about

Action ← Representing → Abstract

The first continuum depicts a range of experiences from being actively involved through observation to listening or reading. The second continuum is the range of abstraction of a learning experience. You can pick learning experiences that are at an *abstract level* (verbal or visual) *or* representational *or iconic level* (recordings, movies, slides, pictures, exhibits, models) *or* action or *enactive level* (games, simulations, or direct experiences). The approach can be structured, rigid, artificial, and direct, or less structured, real, integrated, holistic, and indirect. *Experiential learning* (or teaching) is at the left side of the continuum. All the modes along the continuum can be used at one time or another. The purpose of this section is to discuss what *experiential education* is, when to use it, and how to use it.

WHAT IS EXPERIENTIAL LEARNING?   Webster's defines *experiential* as the actual living through of an event or events. Experiential learning is an action strategy. Instead of hearing, talking, or reading about something, students participate in the context to be studied. Although there is some disagreement on the meaning of the term, many definitions emphasize the same thing. In experiential learning, the learner is directly in touch with real things and people or is involved in activities that simulate real activities and people. For example, students might role-play the 1919 Versailles Peace Conference or enact the trial of Galileo. It involves direct encounter with the phenomenon being studied, instead of just thinking about it or only considering the possibility of doing something with it. The process is normally inductive, learner centered, and activity oriented. Personalized reflection about an experience and plans to apply learning to other contexts are critical. This is a critical part of the debriefing process in which students reflect on or discuss what they have learned. Experiential learning occurs when learners: "(a) participate in an activity, (b) critically look back on the activity to surface learning and feelings, (c) draw useful insight from analysis, and (d) put learning to work in new situations" (Pfeiffer & Goodstein, 1982).

Australia's RMIT Teaching and Learning Unit (2004) defines experiential learning as "experiences that are designed and chosen for their ability to extend and challenge student thinking in a broad range of capabilities." The characteristics, they say, are that (1) students are actively involved in the process of learning; (2) the problems they work on are realistic, as are the situations; and (3) the learning can be used to develop many different capabilities, such as acquiring, assimilating, or creating new knowledge and deeper understanding; personal development; problem-solving capability; interpersonal skills; planning ability; assessment skill; assessment by peers; and learning how to learn. Additional information can be found at the RMIT web site, www.rmit.edu.au. Go to "Our Organization" and then to the Teaching and Learning section for additional ideas for teachers.

The experiential learning model is learner centered and activity oriented. Learners must work cooperatively with varying degrees of teacher direction to make curriculum decisions. The mode tends to be self-directed, unstructured, self-paced, and personalized. When using experiential learning, flexibility in the developmental process may be necessary. Feelings, attitudes, values, and (importantly) experiences are critical content. An assumption is that people really learn only that which has personal meaning. The needs of learners and their psychological and cultural characteristics are considered.

Self-control of one's educational experiences is critical. Students feel better about themselves and the value of educational experiences if they have a hand in identifying learning experiences that affect their growth and development and their progression toward self-integration.

Experiential education involves a first-hand "encounter" or "directness" or "involvement" or "participation" with the "context" to be studied and reflection on that episode. This results in a change in learners' understanding, skills, and attitudes. It is integrated and holistic and necessarily has an affective component. Students tend to become more emotionally involved in experiential learning approaches. In role playing, students take a considerable degree of personal ownership. Field trips and work experience also involve a high degree of affective learning. Experiential learning occurs when a learner takes part in an activity, reflects critically on it, draws insight from the analysis, and puts the results to work in new contexts. It is an inductive process that proceeds from observation.

PURPOSES OF EXPERIENTIAL EDUCATION.   Because experiential education is a direct encounter with the phenomenon being studied, it is more realistic and therefore is more meaningful. Indirect encounters, like "academic" learning, are also needed and should, based on experience, be woven into development.

It is reasonable to believe that higher-order skills—and indeed intelligence, understanding, and wisdom—develop through experience and reflection. Therefore, it is logical that schools provide opportunities for students to engage in experiences with real (authentic) problems and opportunities that include the variables likely to be encountered in real-world situations.

Further justification for using the experiential teaching/learning mode has come through studies of learning style. Some people prefer a direct, action-oriented style; they, probably, are among those who learned at home by watching and trying what was modeled. Cultural background also influences learning-style preference.

Another purpose of the experiential mode—described some time ago by Jean Piaget—is to aid student cognitive development. For students to be able to think at the highest cognitive development level (formal operations), they must have had some experience, or direct contact, with the substance they bring to bear on mental operations. This applies to any learner who has not proceeded through concrete experience. You, in studying experiential learning, will find that experience is necessary for you to really understand the meaning and use of the experiential mode. Academic knowledge is often a very critical part of experiential learning.

It can be posited that learning is not complete unless the learner moves beyond "knowing about" and "knowing how" into "doing." The ability "to do" fosters transfer of learning. Indeed, the argument goes, "doing" deepens understanding of what something is and knowing how something is (or was) done. Put in another way, theory informs practice and practice informs theory. Struggling with experiences using the experiential mode or applying learning in a "real" context yields completeness of learning.

THE KOLB MODEL OF EXPERIENTIAL LEARNING.   No discussion of experiential learning would be complete without the classic Kolb model. David Kolb (1984) defines learning as "the process whereby knowledge is created through the transformation of experience" (p. 38). The emphasis of experiential learning is on the process of learning and not the product. Because of experience and reflection, knowledge is constantly being transformed (created or recreated) within the learner. Kolb observes that experiential learning theory assumes "ideas are not fixed and immutable elements of thought but are formed and reformed through experiences" (p. 26). According to Kolb, learning is a *process* (not an outcome) by which concepts are constantly modified by experience. He developed an approach to experiential learning that involves conflict between opposing ways of dealing with the world. He emphasizes conflict between concrete experience and abstract concepts and generalizations and between observation and action.

Kolb believes that learners need four abilities or learning modes:

1. *Concrete experience.* Learners must involve themselves fully in new experiences.
2. *Reflective observation.* Learners must observe these experiences, or obtain observations on these experiences, as well as analyze and reflect on these observations. This reflection will bring a previous background, and thus previous experiences (firsthand and second-hand), to bear on these observations.
3. *Abstract conceptualization.* Learners must develop abstractions that, in turn, create concepts and generalizations that are logically sound.
4. *Active experimentation.* Learners must use these new theories to take action, such as making decisions and solving problems. (p. 30)

The Kolb thesis has two dimensions. The first involves "concrete experiences" at one end and "abstract conceptualization" at the other. The second has "active experimentation" at one extreme and "reflective observation" at the other. Kolb argues that conflicts among the four modes must lead to integration for the highest level of creativity and growth to occur. "It involves the integrated functioning of the total organism—thinking, feeling, perceiving, and behaving" (p. 31). The four-stage cycle can be explained as the interaction of two dimensions. The first, the *concrete to abstract,* reflects two different ways of "taking hold" of experiences: (1) reliance on conceptual interpretation and symbolic representation (Kolb calls this "comprehension"); and (2) reliance on the tangible, felt qualities of immediate experience (called "apprehension") (p. 41).

The second dimension, from *action to reflection,* is the manner in which the first dimension is transformed, through either internal reflection or active manipulation of the "external world." The first is called *intention,* and the second is called *extension.* Therefore, "learning is the process whereby knowledge is created through the transformation of experience" (p. 41).

Kolb (1984) says that experiential learning has six characteristics:

1. It emphasizes how learning takes place, instead of what is to be learned.
2. Learners continuously gain and test knowledge through, and in terms of, their experiences.
3. Learners need abilities that are opposites. Choices are made among opposites—concrete experience or conceptualizing abstractly; actively experimenting or reflectively observing.
4. Learners are asked to adapt, in a holistic way, to their social and physical environment.
5. It is an active, self-directed process involving transactions between the learner and the "real-world" environment.
6. Knowledge is created within learners. (pp. 25–38)

Terry (2001) presents an excellent example of how the Kolb model can enhance learning, and its value as a teaching tool. Terry describes how the learning modes can be used in learning situations such as group work, essay writing, and assessment to appeal to different learning style preferences, be matched to student abilities, and the design and application of "diverse examination formats" (p. 7). The idea is that the experiential learning model must consider different learning styles in deciding objectives, planning activities, and assessment. Terry believes the Kolb model is a useful way to increase student learning performance.

A data collection instrument you can use to get feedback on your use of experiential learning is provided in Appendix 12.2.

BENEFITS AND LIMITATIONS OF EXPERIENTIAL LEARNING.   It is common to believe in the superiority of first-hand experience. People speak of "being there," "doing it," and "seeing for oneself" as a valuable way to learn. Buchmann and Schwille (1993), however, say that relying on first-hand experience may delay student teacher development. Previously (1982), they claimed that the notions behind these expressions, and the belief in the value of "common sense," tend to conceal problems and connections and might lead to incomplete understanding or misunderstanding. They say that first-hand experience tends to emphasize only the senses (p. 1), observing that, for those who believe in the superiority of first-hand experience, the "mind is visualized as a container to be filled by whatever comes from the various sense organs" (p. 4).

Sight, sound, and touch can convey misinformation, and a sample may not be an adequate basis for generalizations. First-hand experience may limit learning to practices and standards already established. Much learning requires imagination, and one cannot assume that the present condition is all that is possible. To get beyond the present, learners must develop abstract categories derived from collective experience that can then be used in second-hand experiences. First-hand experience can close avenues to conceptual and social change. Knowledge, too, can be acquired independently of practical action by using resources such as print, visual materials, and other persons.

> Unlike firsthand experience, secondhand information . . . lends itself to a consideration of what is typical, what is generalizable, and what can be found that is different from what is already known. It enlarges the number of cases that can be considered, can include rare occurrences of high value for learning, and represents more adequately than firsthand experience the distribution of events in the real world. (p. 22)

The limitations and fallacies of first-hand experience can be overcome if one plans experiences carefully, anticipates what they have to offer, and selects experiences that vary in some systematic fashion.

Although the limitations of experiential learning must be recognized, there are things students cannot really understand or appreciate just through reading, hearing, or viewing. Experiential learning is an effective strategy if direct or "hands-on" experience is needed before teaching methods that involve iconic (e.g., looking at pictures) or symbolic (e.g., listening to the teacher talk) approaches are used. Experiential education greatly increases retention over methods that stress talking, reading, or even viewing. Students are more motivated when they actively do something or, even better, teach one another by describing what they are doing. Experiential learning helps move education to a personalized, life-enriching process. If you have a choice between two methods, choose the one that involves students the most actively.

There is much truth in the old saying, "If you really want to know something you have to experience it." Obviously there are limitations. It is a bit impractical to have yourself blown up in an atomic explosion to learn about it. When students have the background, much can be learned from print and other materials and other people. Effective teachers decide when to use first-hand and when to use vicarious or second-hand learning experiences.

Teaching Approaches to Experiential Learning

ACTIVE LEARNING AND EXPERIENTIAL LEARNING.   Because in experiential learning the learner is directly in touch with real things and people or involved in activities that simulate real activities and people, students develop many capabilities. *Active learning* is a specific experiential learning approach with its own advocates, publications, and web sites. Bonwell and Eison (1991), in an analysis of research, say that active learning has certain characteristics: students must read, write, discuss, or be engaged in solving problems; they must engage in higher-order thinking tasks such as analysis, synthesis, and evaluation; and instructional activities should involve students in doing things and thinking about what they are doing.

Actions suggested by Bonwell and Eison include:

- Pause three times for two minutes each during a lecture.
- Insert brief demonstrations or short, ungraded writing exercises followed by class discussion.
- Create a supportive intellectual and emotional environment that encourages students to risk.
- Use more visual-based instruction.
- Incorporate case studies, cooperative learning, debates, drama, role playing and simulation, and peer teaching.

As can be seen, active learning ranges from making traditional lectures more interesting and active to role playing and simulation. In essence, experiential learning is a form of active learning at the engaged, complex, and risk-taking end of the continuum. If teachers incorporate active learning elements in the classroom, students can acquire the attitudes and skills needed to gain the most from field trips and simulations.

Chickering and Ehrmann (1996) assert that learning is not a spectator sport. When students just sit in class listening to teachers, memorize assignments, and spit out answers, they do not learn much. They need to discuss what they are learning, write reflectively about it, relate it to past experiences, and apply it to their daily lives. What they learn must become part of them. Active learning enlivens teaching as it complements the rationale and framework of experiential learning.

EXPERIENTIAL LEARNING METHODS IN AND OUTSIDE THE CLASSROOM.   A teacher can use experiential learning as a teaching strategy both inside and outside the classroom. Inside the classroom, students can, for example, build and stock an aquarium or engage in a simulation; in the community, they can, for example, observe a courtroom as the legal system is being studied. A wide range of experiential learning methods is possible:

|—————————————|—————————————|
Classroom Game/Activity   Field Trip   Direct Experience

THE EXPERIENTIAL LEARNING CYCLE.   There are five phases to the experiential cycle (Figure 12.5). A discussion of these five phases, based on the thinking of Jones and Pfieffer (1979), follows.

1. *Experiencing (an activity occurs).* The first stage in the cycle is to have an experience (an individual or group activity) that includes interaction with the environment and with others. This generates information and leads to feelings. Students usually find this

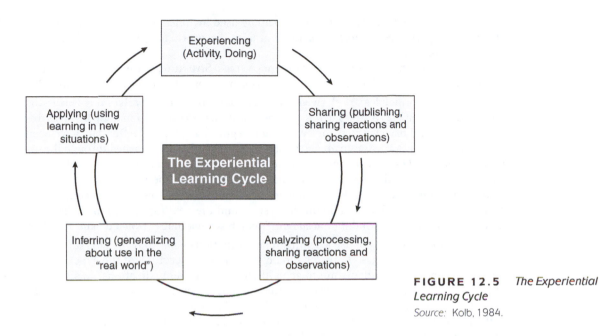

FIGURE 12.5 *The Experiential Learning Cycle*
Source: Kolb, 1984.

stage to be like a game and fun. When you use the experiential learning strategy you can choose from, among others, the following:

Game	Writing	Simulation
Manipulating symbolic objects	Case study	Field project
Conducting an experiment	Fantasy	Field interview
Making a model	Role playing ·	Field observation
Creating an art object	Skit	Field trip
Making a product	Improvisation	Work experience

The purpose of this stage is, from whatever happens, to develop a common database for the discussion and reflection to follow. The "answer" derived or the product obtained is far less important than the process experienced. In a sense, the process is the product.

Unfortunately, what often passes for experiential education stops with this step, so much of its potential value is lost. For example, students go on a field trip with little follow-up. Typically the follow-up is students completing a prepared factual answer sheet or the teacher later making occasional reference to some aspect of the trip. A successful field trip needs very thorough planning with clear objectives, activities that meet these objectives, and follow-up activities that assess the success of the objectives.

2. *Sharing* (reactions and observations shared—*publishing*). In this stage, students re-call what was experienced, reporting everything they saw and how they felt. This is shared with members of the group or class. The purpose is to provide a database for later analysis. Observations and reactions can be recorded in several ways: a written report, posting on newsprint or a chalkboard, an oral report, an e-mail report or web page, a free discussion, or interviews.

3. *Analyzing* (patterns and dynamics are determined—*processing*). This is a key stage. It involves "talking through" the published experiences and feelings. Data are processed.

This must be systematic. Techniques that can be used include: seeking common themes, classifying experiences, completing a questionnaire, discovering key terms or skills, or discovering patterns of events or behavior.

This is *not* an interpretation or inference stage. Structure, patterns, or key aspects of what was experienced are sought. The focus is on dynamics rather than "meaning."

4. *Inferring* (principles are derived—*generalizing*). Inferring involves answering the question, "So what?" Principles, rules, or generalizations are sought. This step involves discovery of "What I have learned" or "What I am beginning to learn." After data have been analyzed, inferences are drawn about the significance of what was learned through the experience as it applies to new contexts (preferably to life). Ways to infer generalizations include: students record generalizations and how learning can be used in new contexts; students tell what was generalized and potential application; or students post conclusions on newsprint or chalkboard. The inferring stage and the next (applying) make learning practical. They move beyond the "academic," which is sometimes "isolated" and "sterile."

5. *Applying* (planning to use learning in new situations—*the future*). This stage is the reason for the other stages. Transfer should take place for learning of the experience to have optimum value. Students are to apply their learning (generalizations) to situations in which they are currently involved. Techniques that can be used include group planning for application, individual or group contracting, and practice (or simulated) applications. This step involves, "What I intend to do tomorrow is. . . . " If statements of intent are written or made publicly, the likelihood of follow-through is enhanced. (pp. 18–25)

In summary, experiential learning occurs when students (1) engage in an activity, (2) publish what occurred, (3) look back at it critically, (4) gain useful insight from the critical analysis, and (5) put the results to work. For full impact, ensure that *all* the steps are carefully followed. The cycle begins with action (experiencing), moves through reflection (sharing, analyzing, and inferring), and ends with a call for action. When the action that is proposed is initiated, the cycle can begin again.

Exeter (2001) provides an interesting adaptation of the Kolb cycle (Figure 12.6). He stresses experiential activities followed by reviewing through reflection. Careful reflection and description of the experience will lead to conclusions and possible theories about the experience. This, in turn, will lead to planning in which the new learning will be applied to future activities.

USING EXPERIENTIAL LEARNING METHODS.   Tips for using experiential methods include the following:

1. Experiential methods can be combined with direct instruction. Set the stage by explaining terms and concepts and then assign an individual or group experiential setting.
2. Relinquish at least a portion of the control to students. At first, some teachers are reluctant to take the risk.
3. Vary the degree of teacher versus student control. Some experiential methods may be very structured (e.g., a game with set rules) and others completely unstructured (e.g., a role-playing improvisation).
4. Evaluation is not as cut and dried as recall or comprehension-level cognitive teacher-made tests. Initially, you may find it difficult to assess both process and product.

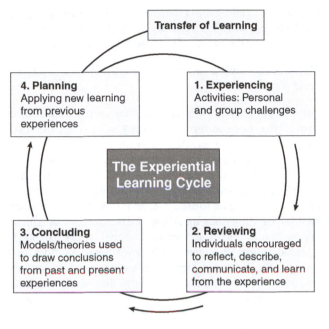

FIGURE 12.6 *Exeter Experiential Learning Cycle*
Source: Exeter, 2001.

5. Capitalize on the higher level of motivation that results from the use of experiential teaching methods.
6. Teach students interpersonal and group skills, which will reduce classroom management problems.
7. Use experiential learning methods to teach not only specific content but also the knowledge, values, skills, and abilities related to common essential learning (e.g., communication, critical and creative thinking, and personal and social values and skills).

An experiential approach enhances self-esteem, increases social and personal responsibility, and contributes to higher-level mental processes and creativity. Student involvement in the planning stage is critical. For example, if a class is visiting a legislature or parliament, discussion in the class could involve such questions as: "What do we need to know before our visit?" "What should we look out for during the visit?" "What questions should we ask when we are there?" "What special responsibilities need to be assigned?" Teachers can visit potential experiential learning sites. Many places—for example, museums—have excellent prepared materials and ideas for experiential learning tasks.

Games, Simulations, and Role Playing

Games can be defined as activities governed by rules that participants play to achieve game objectives by completing these activities successfully. *Simulations* use "real-life" situations, normally requiring participants to make decisions during and following an activity. Simulations may be game like or involve role playing. In *role playing,* participants play parts (assume roles) spontaneously in a situation or around a theme.

When students are actively engaged through games, simulations, and role playing, when they are responsible for their actions, when they reflect on their experiences, when they discuss their learning with peers, and when the experiences shape future experiences, motivation is increased and learning is enhanced and personalized. Learning is more complete because the cognitive aspects (information and thinking skills and processes) and affective aspects (values, attitudes, prejudices, and emotions) and often the physical aspects are critical. Games, simulations, and role playing as methods within the experiential strategy involve principles:

1. An activity for the game, simulation, or role play is done to achieve a purpose or one or more learning objectives.
2. Active involvement is needed if students are to learn the optimum amount from an activity.

3. The activity needs to be followed by debriefing that focuses on the decisions made, the effects of decisions (including feelings), and the effects of commitment for the future.
4. The process, to be most successful, should foster commitment by individuals.

Appendix 12.3 is a data collection instrument you can use to evaluate your skills in directing games, simulations, or role playing.

A PRACTICAL EXAMPLE.   Byerly (2001) presents a refreshing view of the importance of experiential learning for students. He sees experiential learning as having three primary components: *modeling*—the teacher demonstrating a skill; *collaborating*—the teacher or a guest working with students, or students working with peers; and *simulating* (enactment within a context that mirrors the real world) (p. 697). He believes that subject area classes can take on large-scale projects such as a model restaurant for home economics, a school representative election modeled on local, state, and national elections, or a model United Nations. "Experiential learning pops up across the curriculum as educators seek to give their students a sense of how learning works in the real world" (p. 698). Byerly recommends trying a large-scale project that may require considerable school and district support. Many teachers consider at least one large-scale experiential project, to give students a valuable learning opportunity. As an example, Byerly discusses a reenactment of a wagon train experience of the 1840s. The following are examples of significant stages of larger-scale experiential learning.

- Fund raising
- Building the context for the activity
- Doing extensive background teaching and research
- Having students help find answers to key questions (purpose of the wagon train, natural obstacles of the time, etc.)
- Instruction and practice sessions for particular roles
- Learning new skills (cooking on open fires or using Dutch ovens)
- Creating authenticity (costumes, props, etc.)
- Having the teacher and parents volunteer for specific roles
- Clear organization
- Promoting goodwill and hard work
- Documenting (photographs/videotape)
- Debriefing (what has been learned?) (pp. 697–699)

Use the data collection instrument in Appendix 12.2 to help you analyze the cases that follow. Your instructor may pose specific questions for your response.

CASE 12.4 Experiential Learning

All about Air

A grade 3/4 class is about to begin a unit on the topic "air." Their teacher, Mr. Chang, plans to introduce the topic by using an experiential approach. He has placed six science experiment stations around the room. Two of these demonstrate "Air occupies space," two demonstrate "Air has weight," and two show "Air exerts pressure."

He begins, "What if I told you, 'There's no such thing as air?' Do you think that's right? How many agree? How do we know there's such a thing as air?

Can we see it, feel it, hear it?" Mr. Chang asks for examples as proof.

After a short discussion, he continues, "Today we're going to find out some other things about air by doing experiments. I have listed names of experiment teams on this chart. Each team will work at the location specified. By following instructions at each station, you should be able to help answer the questions, 'How do we know air exists? What is it like?' Please follow your instructions carefully and carry out each experiment twice. Be sure to record, on the sheet provided, what happens. We'll have a chance to share the results afterward."

Mr. Chang has groups of four work at each experiment station. They follow the directions for their experiment and record the results on their data sheet. They discuss the activity animatedly as they work on the experiments.

After each group has done its experiment two or more times and recorded the results, Mr. Chang asks the groups to bring their data sheets to the large-group discussion area. Each group reports their results. The data sheets are gathered and, with the help of the students, the descriptions of what happened are recorded on large chart paper.

Mr. Chang says, "Let's look at the six descriptions. What patterns or similarities do we notice? Are there similarities in 1 and 2? In 3 and 4? In 5 and 6? Does something always happen? Is there anything that never happens?" The children enthusiastically discuss and compare their results.

Mr. Chang prompts, "Well, what did we learn about air? Do we have proof that air exists? Do we know more about what air is like?" Discussion continues until the following information is generated: air takes up space; air has weight; air pushes or has pressure. The children make new charts outlining and illustrating what they have learned. Data sheets are attached to the charts.

Mr. Chang closes with the following questions: "What are some examples of air taking up space? Exerting pressure? Weighing?" Students generate examples, including vehicle tires, balloons for decoration, bubble packing, filling tires, floats on airplanes, air-filled dinghies or rafts, and balloons moving when you let go of the end.

CASE 12.5 Experiential Learning

All about Water

Ms. Plaxton's grade 10 general science class is studying the topic of water. She likes to use an approach to instruction that is quite student centered. Students had read about water in the library and checked in the Science Center for illustrations of different sources of water. Ms. Plaxton required them to answer several questions about water supply sources, purity or impurity, purification methods, and effects on health and economics. She gave students a test on the topic of water.

Ms. Plaxton marked the test. When she analyzed the results, she was surprised that most students did not seem to know very much about the very common commodity of water. She wonders why. She has just heard about the experiential learning teaching strategy. Next year, she plans to use the complete experiential learning approach.

CASE 12.6 Discussion

Making Social Studies Interesting

Mr. Goldman, an avid student of history who believes strongly in its importance, would like to make his grade 11 social studies class interesting but spends much of his time lecturing. It is obvious that students are bored and are just putting up with him and the subject. He finds himself in a bind. The social studies department of his high school insists that he cover a certain amount and kind of information. His classroom is crowded, so group work is difficult. He has tried to hold class discussions on matters that he finds interesting but has been disappointed because of lack of participation by his students. Getting students to participate is like finding and pulling hens' teeth. Total class discussion, Mr. Goldman believes, can be very worthwhile. He is willing to give this approach one more try. He seeks your advice on how to use class discussion effectively.

LINKING PRACTICE TO THEORY

Experiential learning takes much planning and monitoring. Try the methods suggested in this chapter. Consider the benefits and the drawbacks. What skills and competencies do each approach require? Can they work for all school subjects? How would you meet the challenge of a field experience where this strategy was not encouraged? How can you use the experiences you give the students in your follow-up and debriefing? Experiential learning can involve much personal and emotional involvement by your students. What do you need to do to handle this well? Reflect on your experiences with this strategy and build your own approaches.

Summary

The direct, indirect, and individual study strategic approaches to instruction were presented in the last chapter. The interactive and experiential are two more. The interactive strategy makes use of discussion and sharing among individuals in the classroom and active student involvement. Group size ranges from the total class as a work group through pairs or triads to small work groups. Effective group operation depends on the use of communication and interpersonal skills. These and group skills should be taught. There are a huge variety of groups from which to choose. The teacher needs to monitor the operation of groups and intervene as necessary.

When the experiential instructional strategy is used, students are actively involved in the context to be studied. This strategy is often multisensory and inductive. True experiential instruction involves a cycle of experiencing, sharing, analyzing, inferring, and applying.

Activities

INQUIRY METHODS

1. Join a class discussion in which you and your peers report and discuss the inquiry approaches used by cooperating teachers that have been observed. Do not use teachers' names.
   (a) Describe the teacher behaviors.
   (b) List examples of why the approaches were effective.
   (c) List the basic inquiry processes used.
2. In a subject group, brainstorm topics that are often taught by the direct instructional strategy. Demonstrate how they could be more effectively taught using: (a) inductive and inquiry modes; (b) guided inquiry; and (c) unguided inquiry.

3. Join a subject group to design a lesson using guided inquiry. Using the same lesson topic, design a lesson using unguided inquiry. Have these presented, and ask for critique from the class. If this is not feasible, compare the two instructional approaches in your subject group.
4. Teach a microteaching or school lesson with an inquiry method target. A data collection instrument is provided in Appendix 12.1.
5. People often think that Sherlock Holmes "deduced" the solutions in his famous cases. To what extent can it be argued that he used an inductive approach? Discuss.

APPENDIX 12.1 *Inquiry Orientation Data Collection Instrument*

PROFESSIONAL TARGET—INDUCTIVE, INQUIRY ORIENTATION OBSERVATION GUIDE

Describe what was said and done and how students reacted.

1. Problem or objective understood

2. Adequacy, arrangement of facilities, materials, references

3. How, by whom, data was selected

4. How data was processed, what thinking skills were used

5. Teacher behavior: telling? asking?

6. Use of questions: open/closed, convergent/divergent, teacher/student initiated; use of probes and redirects

7. Teacher behavior: supportive? encouraging?

8. Who provided answers: teacher? student?

9. Manner in which ideas were tested, evaluated

10. Effect of introduction of new data or evidence

11. Application of concept, principle, or generalization to new situation

APPENDIX 12.2 *Experiential Learning Data Collection Instrument*

PROFESSIONAL TARGET—EXPERIENTIAL EDUCATION

Please describe what you hear and see and how students react.

Step	Teacher and Student Behaviors
Students "experience" an activity	
Sharing: students share observations and reactions or feelings about experiences	
Analyzing: students "talk through" the experience they shared, surface patterns, and interactions	
Inferring: students derive principles/ generalizations from their analysis that can be used in the future	
Applying: students tell how they will apply their learning and/or individuals report what they plan to do	

APPENDIX 12.3 *Games, Simulations, or Role-Playing Data Collection Instrument*

PROFESSIONAL TARGET—GAMES, SIMULATIONS, OR ROLE PLAYING

Please describe what you hear and see and how students react.

Step	Teacher and Student Behaviors
Intentions: What are students to know or be able to do as a result of the experience?	
Relevance: Are students relating the experience and learning to their personal lives? Are students involved emotionally and in decision making?	
Operation: Setting? Time? Role assignments? Number of participants? Resources or materials needed?	
Procedure: Rules? Sequence of events (warm-up, briefing, action conclusion)?	
Debriefing: Recalling the activity? Sharing learning and feelings? Pros and cons of potential decisions? Decision? Commitment? Plans for evaluation of carrying out commitment?	

13 The Collaborative Learning Strategy

Diversity among individuals is increasing and is everywhere. Teaching students the skills to interact effectively with diverse individuals is not a luxury, it is a necessity. (Johnson & Johnson, 1999)

Group Skills

The challenge for the teacher is to create a learning environment that promotes cooperative behavior, individual accountability and responsibility, and interdependence. (Centre for Staff Development, 2000)

The term collaborative learning is an umbrella term that includes various interactive approaches and methods for group work. Cooperative learning is an aspect of collaborative learning that takes a very specialist approach to group work. This involves positive interdependence rather than just sharing. A well-known example is the "jigsaw." These approaches are presented in this chapter.

Gross Davis notes, "students learn best when they are actively involved in the process. Researchers report that, regardless of subject matter, students working in small groups tend to learn more of what is taught, and retain it longer than when the same content is presented in other instructional formats. Students who work in collaborative groups also appear more satisfied with their classes" (1993, p. 147).

Collaborative learning, Gokhale (1995) observes, fosters development of critical thinking through discussion, clarification of ideas, and evaluation of others' ideas. If instruction is to enhance critical-thinking and problem-solving skills, collaborative learning is more effective than direct instruction. The

OBJECTIVES

You will be able to:

1. Define interactive teaching and describe patterns available to the classroom teacher.
2. Describe the special purposes of the classroom as a group.
3. Describe the developmental stages through which groups move and list interventions a teacher can use during these stages.
4. Describe stages of group development and teacher behaviors for creating a positive classroom group and list skills needed for effective group participation.
5. Discuss the nature of the class group as a social system and work group.
6. Describe how you can promote effective student interaction in a classroom.
7. List characteristics of effective class discussion.
8. Describe characteristics of different kinds of small groups.
9. Discuss how small groups can be used effectively and list benefits and limitations.
10. List the duties of group leaders and members.
11. Describe the essential components of cooperative learning.
12. Explain the advantages and disadvantages of cooperative learning and appropriate situations in which to use it.
13. Describe the phases for setting up cooperative learning models.
14. Explain how cooperative learning can reduce prejudice among students.
15. Include cooperative learning in a unit plan.

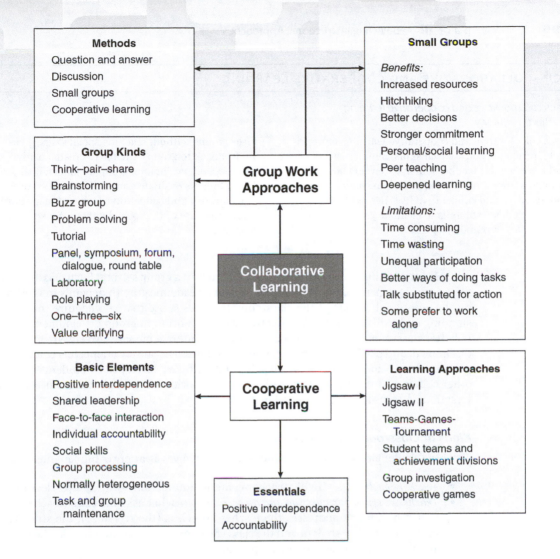

Methods

Question and answer
Discussion
Small groups
Cooperative learning

Group Kinds

Think–pair–share
Brainstorming
Buzz group
Problem solving
Tutorial
Panel, symposium, forum,
    dialogue, round table
Laboratory
Role playing
One–three–six
Value clarifying

Group Work Approaches

Collaborative Learning

Small Groups

Benefits:
Increased resources
Hitchhiking
Better decisions
Stronger commitment
Personal/social learning
Peer teaching
Deepened learning

Limitations:
Time consuming
Time wasting
Unequal participation
Better ways of doing tasks
Talk substituted for action
Some prefer to work
    alone

Basic Elements

Positive interdependence
Shared leadership
Face-to-face interaction
Individual accountability
Social skills
Group processing
Normally heterogeneous
Task and group
    maintenance

Cooperative Learning

Essentials

Positive interdependence
Accountability

Learning Approaches

Jigsaw I
Jigsaw II
Teams-Games-
    Tournament
Student teams and
    achievement divisions
Group investigation
Cooperative games

TCP—GROUP SKILLS

Develops group skills in the classroom

Builds rapport with whole class and establishes a cohesive class group; sets achievable, challenging goals for the class group or small groups; uses effective interpersonal and group skills (i.e., participation, consensus seeking, problem solving, conflict resolution, group accountability); models, teaches, and expects use of group skills.

Unaware of the class as a social group and appropriate pupil and teacher behaviors; does not model, teach, and expect use of group skills by pupils.

teacher, she says, needs to view teaching as a process of developing and enhancing students' ability to learn. The role is not to transmit information, but to facilitate learning. This, she says, involves creating and managing meaningful learning experiences and stimulating student thinking.

TCP—COLLABORATIVE AND COOPERATIVE LEARNING

*Uses collaborative and cooperative learning
methods regularly*

Uses collaborative and cooperative learning appropriately; teaches specific social skills; monitors group work and gives regular feedback; able to develop positive interdependence among group members; uses a variety of collaborative and cooperative (e.g. Jigsaw) learning methods; allows students to evaluate group effectiveness and accountability.

Uses groups without teaching social skills; gives no feedback to groups; unable to create positive interdependence among group members; does not have students evaluate group effectiveness; uses collaborative and cooperative learning inappropriately; unaware of the special nature of cooperative learning.

Most teaching and learning in schools occurs in a group setting. Each classroom develops a unique personality. A student's personal academic growth depends in large part on the emotional climate of the classroom. It makes sense that you acquire the understanding and skills that build an effective class. Attention to group development results in better classroom management because students interact more positively, are more self-disciplined, and participation in discussion is enhanced because students feel comfortable participating. And, the interpersonal skills and attitudes developed by students apply in other contexts. If the class is harmonious and task oriented, you can use a variety of interaction patterns to achieve education goals.

Kinds of Classroom Interactions

Teaching elementary, secondary, or adult students involves a variety of human interactions.

- *Teacher/whole class:* Highly teacher-centered interaction—for example, lectures.
- *Teacher/class during question and answer:* The teacher asks the class (teacher question); the student addresses the teacher and class (the response); the student responds to another student and the class (reaction); and the student asks the teacher and the rest of the class (student question).
- *Discussion with whole class:* (1) Teacher-guided discussion, in which the teacher steers the class or draws out certain points or principles; or (2) open discussion, a freewheeling discussion with no predetermined "answers."
- *Small-group discussions, projects, or assignments:* The class is divided into small groups. A large number of different small group formats can be used.
- *Cooperative learning:* Groups feature positive interdependence, promotive interaction aided by the reward structure, individual accountability, require communication, interpersonal, and group skills, and group processing to determine group effectiveness.
- *Student pair or triad:* Discussions, projects, assignments, or presentations.
- *Others:* Panels; case study; resource person; laboratory; committees; role playing or skits; simulations or games; forum; interviews; debates; symposia; or combinations.

The Class as a Group

Although some classroom work is one on one, teaching is differentiated from most other professions in that the teacher works with groups and most teaching and learning occurs in a group setting. The classroom is a complex social system in which many dynamic social forces operate: friendships, power and influence, communication patterns, member roles, and school, classroom, and peer-driven behavior norms.

When you ask questions or give an assignment, student responses are affected by your relationship with individuals, peer friendship patterns, and individual and subgroup attitudes. Students influence one another. A class either helps or hinders individual student or group learning. Group processes are always present. It makes sense to understand them.

The classroom as a whole is a work group. Effective teacher/student class groups work on making the environment pleasant and task oriented. They consciously focus on *task achievement* (academic goals and objectives), *group maintenance* (using interpersonal and group skills to build a strong group), and *group effectiveness* (reacting to changing tasks and to member and group needs).

1. *Task achievement:* to achieve academic goals by attaining curriculum goals. Task functions relate to a work orientation to fulfill subject-matter requirements of task achievement. *Social skills* include sharing information and ideas, asking questions, providing information, checking for understanding, summarizing, and keeping students on task.
2. *Group maintenance:* to build a strong class that works well together, in which members help and support each other. Group maintenance functions involve the feelings and interpersonal relationships of class members. The intent is to establish a cohesive and stable work group to efficiently achieve academic tasks. Examples of *group maintenance social skills* are checking for agreement, encouraging others, actively listening, paraphrasing, sharing feelings, responding to ideas, and checking for agreement.
3. *Group effectiveness:* learning how to react to changing tasks and the needs of individuals. Task achievement and group maintenance skills are needed for groups to work effectively.

An inventory, "My Behavior in Groups," which lists task achievement and group maintenance behaviors, is shown in Appendix 13.1.

"Membership" of students in an elementary school class is not voluntary, but as students move through high school, options become available. In a departmentalized high school, membership varies with the teacher and the students enrolled in different subjects. A class may have several teachers and so several social settings. Membership in adult education may or may not be optional. In some cases, employees are required to take courses.

NORMS.   Every group has *norms* (accepted rules for behavior). Rules established by the teacher may or may not be norms, depending on whether they are accepted and followed. Deviation from norms by a student leads to disapproval or rejection by group members, reprimand by the teacher, even expulsion. Examples of norms include the language used, the clothing worn, hairstyles, what one talks about, whom one talks to, and how much work one has to do. Rules a teacher or group leader tries to establish become norms only if the majority of the group accepts and follows them. Each subgroup in the classroom has norms that may or may not be entirely the same as classroom norms. Norms can either interfere with, or facilitate, achievement of curriculum objectives.

STRUCTURE.   Group structure also affects class effectiveness. *Group structure* is the pattern of relationships derived through the positions members of the group occupy. Three things affect structure:

1. *Roles:* indicates what people are supposed to do in the group. The two major roles (culturally defined but adapted by members of the class) are "teacher" and "student."
2. *Status:* the hierarchy of positions in the class. The behavior and ideas of some individuals have more influence (or power) than others, and some subgroups have more power than others. The teacher has the greatest formal status and usually is accepted as leader. How the teacher or other persons of high status behave toward an individual affects how that person is viewed by the class.
3. *Attraction:* the extent to which group members like each other and elect to work or play together. Attraction patterns affect the way individuals interact and communicate and thus their achievement. Deliberate effort is needed to build a constructive and cohesive class group.

GOALS.   Building an effective and cohesive group can help achieve curriculum objectives and the goals of the class. Goals can come from broader society, school officials, individual teachers, the student body, the specific class, or individuals in the group. One of the most difficult tasks of a teacher is harmonizing different goals. If the goals of these sources differ, the result can be conflict and trouble.

Fostering Group Development

Productive class groups do not happen by accident. As a teacher, try to foster self-concept development and group support for the growth of individuals by attending to three aspects of group functioning:

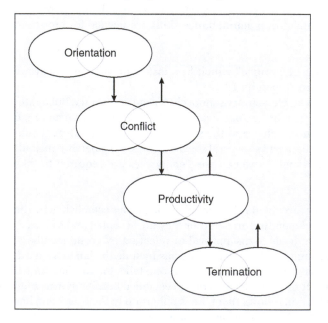

1. *Task achievement,* by initiating discussion, seeking and providing information, raising questions, providing meaningful group assignments, summarizing, and evaluating
2. *Group maintenance,* by encouraging participation, reducing anxiety, handling conflict, promoting cooperation, and clarifying feelings
3. *Group effectiveness,* by modeling, teaching, and requiring communication, interpersonal, and group skills

Class groups tend to move through relatively predictable stages from the first time they meet through to their last meeting. The stages are (1) beginning the group, (2) developing the group, (3) maintaining the group, and (4) phasing to the future (termination) (Figure 13.1).

1. *Orientation (beginning the group).* "What's expected of me?" "How do I fit?" "Will I make

FIGURE 13.1   *Group Development Stages*

a fool out of myself?" "Will the others like me?" "Will I succeed?" "Do I want to be here?" The *orientation stage* is a time of dependency on the teacher and uncertainty as class group members try to sort out their roles and the norms of the group. Relationships begin to be established, and initial participation may be tentative or superficial. Gaining approval of fellow class members is important, and individuals may fear disapproval or rejection. Leadership and influence may remain undecided.

The teacher can help by recognizing and respecting the needs of learners as individuals. Clear information should be given about the objectives, operational procedures, and evaluation for the class. Students can be helped to get to know each other through "ice-breaking" activities and having students engage in group activities that help members get to know and feel comfortable with one another. Norms, such as empathy, trust, openness, respect, acceptance, provisional try, risk taking, and commitment, can be expected. Characteristics of an effective group can be taught (e.g., the duties of group leaders and participants). Rules and routines can be taught and practiced.

2. *Conflict (developing the group).* The second stage is the *conflict stage.* Some anxiety, tension, and disagreement is normal and occurs as a result of increased participation and interaction as group members get to know each other better. A struggle for control may occur. Group members tend to test the leader and other members before the group settles in. As group identity builds, and if the group overcomes the problems of conflict, it can move into a period of group identity and cohesiveness development. Ways of working together emerge, and agreement is reached on behavior norms. It should be stressed that conflict is normal, and the teacher should emphasize that positive learning can result from reconciling differences and learning how to resolve conflicts. Learning how to use problem-solving, decision-making, conflict-resolution, and group-effectiveness monitoring strategies is beneficial.

3. *Productivity (maintaining the group).* Group cohesion is the primary characteristic of a well-functioning group. In the *productivity stage,* class members become good at attaining goals and become more flexible and adaptive in working together. Roles, status, attraction, and norms are established. Goals are accepted. Trust is high, the group is cohesive, and interpersonal conflicts are handled. Group members understand that it is normal to have "ups and downs."

4. *Termination of the group (phasing toward the future).* The teacher can prepare (early in the life of the group) for the phasing out (*termination stage*) by helping students see the ending of the group to be maturation leading to future growth and perhaps future groups. Friendships that have been established need not terminate with the group. The success of the class group can be reviewed, and attributes or skills still to be mastered can be positively identified.

Teacher Interventions for Building Effective Groups

Effective groups rarely occur by chance. Classes run in a mainly teacher-centered, lecture-dominated, write-papers-and-exams way rarely progress beyond the orientation (or conflict) stage. If this is so, the power of the group to help learning will not have been realized. Students learn best when they are actively involved. They need to hone relationship skills to achieve the affective objectives part of the curriculum and to acquire the skills needed to express acceptance, support, and to cooperate. They should support each other during interactions, reject nonsupportive, self-serving behaviors such as ridicule or blaming, and seek ways to improve cooperation. Suggestions for working with the group during the various development stages follow.

Beginning of the Group

1. Get-acquainted activities (introductions, name cards, and "ice-breaking" games)
2. Clearly laying out course (or unit or lesson) objectives, content, and evaluation
3. Teaching and having the class practice rules and routines
4. Activities to promote personal disclosure (as appropriate)
5. Instructor modeling of skills and behavior expected
6. Stating and expecting the principle of group support for individual growth
7. Using teaching methods that require interaction and use of positive norms
8. Teaching and providing activities for class members to learn interpersonal and group skills
9. Introducing and practicing group monitoring techniques

Developing and Maintaining the Group

1. Activities that foster further disclosure and openness
2. Activities that require use of positive, constructive norms
3. Activities that practice participation skills (e.g., listening, interacting, seeking information, sharing information, including and encouraging, clarifying, summarizing, and concluding)
4. Activities to extend interpersonal skills
5. Activities to practice leader, participant, group-effectiveness-monitoring roles
6. Activities that emphasize shared leadership, cooperation, and consensus seeking
7. Activities to practice brainstorming, buzzing, problem solving, and decision making
8. Activities to learn and practice negotiation skills such as listening, initiating, analyzing, diagnosing, interpreting, criticizing, and compromising and conflict resolution
9. Requiring group effectiveness monitoring and providing activities to practice systematic and nonjudgmental observation and reporting, soliciting and giving and receiving feedback, and interpreting data

Preparing for Group Termination

1. Activities that recall and review group experiences and achievements
2. Activities that identify the individual and group skills that have been learned
3. Activities to help the class see that termination leads to future growth
4. Activities to identify ways the current group, or individuals, might continue to provide support in the future

Communication, Interpersonal, and Group Skills

What makes a group effective is the consistent application of group skills: communication (interpersonal), trust, leadership, and conflict-resolution skills. These skills should be taught as purposefully as reading or math skills, using an experiential cycle. Make students aware of why a skill is needed and ensure that they understand what the skill is. Group events develop behaviors and skills.

Consensus Seeking and Decision Making

Whole-class and small-group discussions are often used to come to conclusions or make decisions. The teacher or group leader can make decisions autocratically, or decisions can be made by voting or by consensus. Consensus seeking is often treated as a part of decision making. Critical thinking skills and the process of decision making can be taught. (discussed in Chapter 14).

Setting consensus as a goal, though it may not be totally attained, encourages a group to consider the needs and wishes of all members. It requires listening skills, free exchange of information, acceptance of honestly held beliefs, checking for assumptions and biases, and carefully thinking through opinions. Minority opinions must be valued. Students should be able to stand firm on important issues if they have been carefully thought through, but blind stubbornness is not acceptable. Students should be willing to compromise when conflicts arise.

A useful model to seek consensus is the *One–Three–Six Method*. This involves: presenting the problem; asking individuals, privately, to record (preferably in positive terms) their top priorities; students form groups of three to combine lists and add any new ideas; groups of three form groups of six to combine lists and remove redundancy; a representative is chosen by each group of six to form a committee that combines all lists and arrives at a consensus; the committee reports to the class. This procedure can be repeated periodically.

CASE 13.1　The Class as a Group

Starting off Right

Mr. Festlinger is getting ready for his first class of the year. Sitting at his desk in the classroom, he looks at the empty desks in front of him. Tomorrow the seats will be full of new grade 7 students.

He believes he has done everything to be ready. He has carefully planned his courses and materials. All the resources he needs for the first few weeks are in place. He has his class list ready; in fact, he has everything he needs to actually teach.

What concerns him, however, is getting the class group off to a good start. He is thinking about how he can get the class to trust him and to cooperate with him and with one another. He thinks that perhaps he could begin with some group-building activities. One idea is a scavenger hunt game. The students will try to complete a sheet with such items as "someone wearing red"; "someone who has a pet cat"; and so on. It will be noisy, but the important thing is to establish group openness and support. Too many teachers, he thinks, get down to the academic work, whereas the important thing is group or community building.

He leaves his desk and walks about his room. He has arranged the desks in a way that should allow productive interaction and yet allow order and good management.

The arrangement is flexible enough for various types of groups to operate. Materials are in easy reach and arranged so students themselves can access and distribute them. The few basic rules he insists on and the most important procedures for the first few weeks are posted.

Mr. Festlinger is excited about meeting his new class. He is ready for opening day, but realizes that keeping his class as an effective group will need all his communication and interpersonal skills. He knows that the students will have their own concerns. They will want to gain the approval of their peers. There will be some anxiety and tension, even conflict. He must make sure he is a good model and set clear goals. There is much to do, but he is ready.

Collaborative Instruction and Learning

What Is the Collaborative Instruction Approach?

Collaborative learning is an approach to teaching and learning in which students interact to share ideas, explore a question, and complete a project. Collaborative (interactive) instruction methods range from class discussions through small-group methods or cooperative learning to using the Internet when working on an assignment (Figure 13.2).

FIGURE 13.2 *Collaborative (Interactive) Instruction Methods*

Source: Saskatchewan Learning (1991).

Human beings, to paraphrase Aristotle, are social animals. Significant learning occurs through interaction with others. The long-held notion that instruction should usually be teacher and print centered and occur in a classroom with desks in straight rows has been challenged. Collaborative (interactive) instructional strategies provide viable alternatives. In interactive situations, the behavior of individuals stimulate each other. It is a pattern of communication. Interactive strategies rely heavily on discussion and sharing among individuals. The term *collaborative* denotes an exchange of ideas and active participation.

Collaborative methods let students discover or state personal viewpoints instead of just repeating those presented. Interactive, discussion, and sharing or discourse methods let learners react to the teacher's or peers' ideas, experience, insights, and knowledge, and give rise to different ways of thinking and feeling. Students can learn from peer teachers, develop social skills, organize thoughts, and develop rational arguments. Compared to direct instruction strategies, teacher control is less, but this does not mean that you can relinquish responsibility. You control discussion time, the nature and topics of discussion, group composition and size, and reporting techniques. You need good observation, listening, interpersonal, and intervention skills.

Collaborative approaches are summarized in Table 13.1. If, for instance, you want active participation, increased motivation, and a high rate of retention, chose an interactive method that fosters these, such as problem-solving or decision-making groups. If recall of information and ability to perform step-by-step skills are desired, select a method that uses instructor or peer tutoring. If a high level of cognitive understanding, decision making, or interpersonal skills is the goal, pick an interactive method that calls for investigation and critical or creative thinking, for example, a debate. Cross-cultural understanding can be fostered through cooperative learning, role playing, or simulations. At times you will want a change of pace or to add flexibility to your repertoire by using games, role playing, skits, or simulations. Role playing and simulations incorporate the experiential learning strategy (see Chapter 12).

TABLE 13.1   *Selecting Collaborative/Interactive Instruction Methods*

Objective	Possible Method
Active participation, increased motivation, and a high rate of retention	Problem-solving and reporting groups
Recall, performance of step-by-step skills	Instructor or peer tutoring groups
High level of cognitive understanding, decision-making, or interpersonal skills	Investigative critical or creative thinking groups
Cross-cultural understanding	Cooperative learning, role playing, or simulations
Change of pace	Games, debates, simulations

You can choose from a range of grouping and interaction patterns including:

- Teacher (or student) presentations to the total class
- Teacher questions to the whole class and student responses
- Whole-class discussions
- Small-group discussions, projects, assignments, or presentations
- Student pair or triad discussions, projects, assignments, or presentations
- Small groups in front of the class (debates, panels, dialogues, forums, etc.)
- Teacher (or student) presentations, questioning, or discussions with split grade or ability groups
- Cooperative learning
- Combinations or variations of these

Groups and Collaborative Learning

THE CLASS AS A SOCIAL SYSTEM AND WORK GROUP.   The class is a *social system,* a community, affected by friendships, power and influence, communication patterns, member roles and school, peer-driven, and classroom norms. The class that has been helped to develop into a mature group does better, because positive interaction and participation improves self-concept. Threat is reduced, students are more comfortable with each other, feel free to take part actively, and can take risks because peer influence is positive. The classroom group is set up by society as an academic work group. The two major roles are "teacher" and "student." A hierarchy of status exists, and attraction patterns affect the way individuals interact and how well the class functions. You often work with the class as a whole, particularly when presenting information or step-by-step skills or conducting a class discussion.

There are times when a highly teacher-centered whole-class method is effective. However, it is often desirable for students to become more interactive and contribute to the development of the lesson. This can happen when question and answer and discussion are used skillfully. When this occurs, students feel their contributions are valuable and that they, individually, are responsible for the development of the lesson and the learning of classmates.

CREATING AN EFFECTIVE SOCIAL SYSTEM.   Cooperative and collaborative learning are significant educational trends that deserve considerable attention by educators. Tschannen-Moran and Hoy (2000) believe that "Collaborative learning strategies provide a powerful mechanism not only to address affective goals in education but also to enhance students' cognitive development" (p. 161). They say that collaborative learning increases student understanding of ideas and the ability to express them. Students are active constructors of knowledge, not passive recipients of information. These authors think that most teachers do not have the knowledge and skills to make the best use of collaborative learning strategies. They have created a five-part framework based on five "G's" (Figure 13.3):

- *Group characteristics:* Know the cognitive development, social and emotional maturity, and skills of the group.
- *Goal setting:* Be aware of the social skills and affective processes that are age appropriate for the group. Be aware of the cognitive development of individuals and the group as a whole. Set realistic goals.

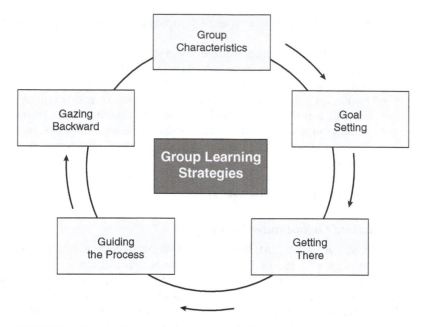

FIGURE 13.3   *Collaborative Learning Group Learning Strategies*
Source: Adapted from Tschannen-Moran & Hoy, 2000.

- *Getting there:* Design group tasks. Select learning strategies. Determine instructions, resources and rewards, and decide on assessment.
- *Guiding the process:* Move about the room and check for student understanding. Check for quality and quantity of interactions.
- *Gazing backward:* Reflect on what went well and where there were problems. Consider teacher directions, participation, time, and resources.

Small Groups

Effective small-group discussions do not happen by accident. Learn what is involved in conducting successful small-group discussions. Many authorities feel that much more use should be made of small groups. They are appropriate if you want to increase teacher–student and student–student verbal interaction and increase social skills so students adopt a responsible, independent mode of learning. Conditions in society make it imperative that people learn to relate well to others and that the school accepts its responsibility for teaching skills that will equip students to fill useful, responsible, and productive roles.

Some teachers have tried small-group methods and said, "I tried small-group discussions but students just sat there like bumps on logs" or "A waste of time, they just socialize!" Another said, "I have far too much important material to cover to use small groups." The problem in the first instance likely was that students were not adequately prepared for discussion and small groups; and the problem in the second case is that small-group methods lend themselves to certain kinds of content but not as well to other kinds.

Discover the readiness of the class to use small groups and, if necessary, intervene with activities that build these capabilities gradually. Training can take place with the class as a whole or within small groups as the need becomes evident. Stanford and Rourke

(1974) proposed the following classic arrangement of skills into categories, used in many current group approaches:

1. Getting acquainted and establishing trust
2. Taking responsibility (including taking the roles of initiator, contributor, clarifier, summarizer, evaluator, recorder, encourager, and harmonizer)
3. Encouraging others to contribute
4. Careful listening
5. Responding to other contributions
6. Setting clear goals
7. Learning to cooperate
8. Coming to consensus

Participants in a small group can be assigned roles. These provide a sense of purpose for each group member. Stanford and Rourke (1974) also summarize the roles students can be assigned and rotated through during small-group discussion, to help them learn "taking responsibility" skills.

- The *initiator* gets discussion underway, helps the group organize, and keeps it moving toward the goal.
- The *contributor* offers opinions, facts, anecdotes, or examples that could help the group solve the problem.
- The task of the *clarifier* is to make sure the terms, problem, and contributions by group members are understood by all. If needed, the clarifier suggests that added information be sought.
- The *summarizer* helps keep discussion relevant and to the point by bringing together and summarizing what has been discussed or learned to date. The summarizer also makes sure everybody in the group understands where the group stands on an issue.
- The job of the *evaluator* is to keep track of how well the group is progressing in its task and tactfully points out problems the group is having in working together.
- The main points of the discussion and the product of the group are noted by the *recorder*. On occasion, what was recorded is read back, to help the group recall what had been covered during discussion or to make sure it is accurate.
- The *encourager* facilitates participation by listening carefully, being friendly, complimenting members for their contributions, and inviting participation.
- The *harmonizer* acts as the peacekeeper by relieving tension (perhaps through humor), settling disputes, helping the group work out disagreements, and suggesting compromises. (p. 103)

A data collection instrument that can be used to evaluate group participation by role is provided in Appendix 13.2.

KINDS OF SMALL GROUPS.   There is an effective small-group method for almost any content. A surprisingly large array is available. Examples of small-group methods are provided below.

1. *Think–pair–share group.* A good way to encourage students to participate in small groups or in class while students extend their thinking and interaction is the

think–pair–share method, developed by Professor Frank Lyman of the University of Maryland Howard County Southern Teacher Education Center (Kagan, 1994). It begins with a short teacher presentation. So students consider more fully what was explained, you pose a question and ask students to spend a minute or two thinking alone about an issue or generalization. Then assign students to pairs to share their thinking. A good practice is to have one student make a statement to be paraphrased by the other until it is understood. This is followed by reversal of statement maker and paraphraser roles. Finally, each pair reports. Reporting can be to two or three other pairs or to the class as a whole. In reporting to the whole class, not all pairs need report. Reporting can be suspended when all major ideas have surfaced.

2. *The brainstorming group.* Brainstorming is a fun, useful, creative thinking technique that can be used to initiate problem solving. It can be included in any lesson. A group or individual may do it. When it is done in groups, it can be like a game. Four to nine people are given a particular problem, and in five to ten minutes, participants come up with as many ideas or suggestions as possible. Quantity of ideas is the main objective. Judgment about the value, implications, ideas, or suggestions is deferred. The basic rules are to

- Think of as many ideas as possible. Quantity is wanted (the greater the number, the more likely a winning idea).
- Withhold criticism; judgment is ruled out.
- Frill. Sometimes, the wilder the ideas the better—it is easier to tame down than to think up.
- Hitchhike. Seek combination and improvement. One idea can beget another idea, or a whole stream of other ideas.

Advantages of brainstorming include:

- The pressure to have an immediate "right" answer is removed.
- Creative potential can be released.
- Solutions to seemingly "unsolvable" problems can be initiated.
- It is fun—people like the freedom of expression.
- If several groups are involved, friendly and enjoyable competition occurs.
- When it is done by a group, people who would otherwise never speak up do so, because the climate is nonthreatening.
- It can be used any time a problem comes to light or at any time during a lesson as a refreshing change of pace.
- When it is used in a lesson, students are actively, not passively, involved in learning.

Limitations of brainstorming are that:

- Some people find it hard to get away from the "practical" or may feel that reasoned ideas are needed.
- Many ideas or suggestions are not worth anything.
- Pet ideas, or the ideas of some people, may have to be discarded.

3. *The buzz group.* "Buzzing" the solution to a problem involves considering the pros and cons of alternatives for solving a problem and making a decision. A starting point can be brainstorming. An individual or a group can buzz. As a teaching method, it involves every student in the discussion process. People are divided into groups of four to seven. For a limited time (five to ten minutes or so), people try to arrive at consensus about the

answer to a problem or question. A novel way to use buzzing is with statements such as, "Let's have a Buzz 36," or "We are going to do a Heinz 57." The first statement calls for groups of three to discuss a topic for six minutes; the second for groups of five to engage in a seven-minute discussion. There are many points in a lesson where buzz groups can be used. The basic rules of buzzing are that

- An issue or problem is presented.
- A leader and recorder for each group are picked by the teacher or elected; the leader sees that all group members participate and the recorder notes contributions.
- Consensus is sought.
- The leader reports areas of agreement (including the rationale) or alternative solutions if there is no agreement.

The limitations of buzzing are that:

- Some people may dominate.
- If all groups of the class deal with the same topic, contributions may be contradictory or hard to combine.
- Participants may need training in interpersonal and group skills.
- Monitoring may be needed to keep groups on task.

4. *Problem-solving group.* Group members, in a systematic way, seek the solution to a problem based on the "scientific method." The steps are: define the problem, brainstorm the likely causes of the problem, decide the most likely cause, brainstorm potential solutions, select the most likely solution (based on determination of pros and cons of alternatives), and decide when and how to implement the solution.

5. *Tutorial group.* Tutorial groups are set up to help students who need remediation or more practice or for students who can benefit from enrichment. The teacher or student leads a tutorial group. Greater attention to individual needs is possible, and students can participate more actively.

6. *Panel, symposium, forum, dialogue, and round table.* Rather than presenting information and ideas through lectures, assigned questions, or readings, you can have students do the job. This can be by setting up a *panel* (a group of students who discuss a topic before a class—chaired by either you or a student), a *committee* (a group of students is assigned by you or the class to learn about a topic and report), a *symposium* (several students become "expert" in a topic and give brief presentations to the class), a *forum* (a class discussion in which a problem is explored through question and answer and short statements under the guidance of a chairperson), a *dialogue* (two people discussing a topic in front of the class), or a *round table* (a group of students discussing an issue in front of a class). Students find these methods motivating. Conclude with a summation to ensure content is organized, correctly understood, and links to what is being studied.

7. *Laboratory group.* A laboratory group is formed to complete a project, an experiment, or practice something that has been presented. A common example is a chemistry laboratory group.

8. *Role-playing group.* In a role-playing group, each member is assigned a role to assume on a controversial topic. Students may or may not agree with the stance of the role they have been given. A role-playing group can bring out all sides of an issue or have students learn to understand the ideas or feelings of others. Role playing can be a good method for having students learn attitudes.

9. *One–three–six group.* The one–three–six group method can be used at almost any time during a lesson. Students are asked, as individuals, to record their opinion on an issue. Then individuals join two others and come to an agreement. Finally, two groups of three join and seek consensus. Each group of six reports to the class as a whole.

10. *Value-clarifying group.* Groups are presented with a value-laden topic. Each group is asked to seek alternative solutions, discuss the pros and cons of alternatives, and agree on a potential solution. The idea is for students to clarify their values and to learn to understand and tolerate the values of others. Value-clarifying groups should be used with care: this is a controversial method. Some educators believe it motivating and invaluable for developing critical thinking skills; others believe the approach to be a fad that is superficial and laden with inadequacies and problems.

USING SMALL-GROUP METHODS.   Some teachers believe that using small groups can lead to classroom management problems and off-task student behavior. However, attention to group development results in improved classroom management because students become more self-disciplined. Small-group methods should involve orderly grouping so students take part in informed cooperative interaction to share information, solve problems, make decisions, or help each other.

Classroom climate must be open, friendly, and nonthreatening. Group members need acceptance, trust, and security to contribute freely, speak their minds, and be safe from teacher and peer censure and pressure. You relinquish the dominant role in favor of being a learning coordinator, support and resource person, co-planner, and co-evaluator. Student responsibility for planning, executing, and evaluating is increased. Independence and cooperation should be encouraged and student contributions valued. This requires planning, and content relevant to student interests. Before discussion begins, students need content background for meaningful interchange. In short, discussions should not "pool ignorance."

Have a plan for students who are shy, lazy, or dominate discussion, and those who lead the group off task or are negative. Participation, goal setting, consensus seeking, problem solving, decision making, conflict resolution, and group-effectiveness monitoring skills can be taught and learned. This should not be left to chance.

As groups are at work, circulate and intervene as appropriate but avoid dominating. Contributions by all students should be promoted, and interpersonal and group skills stressed. Offer ideas, ask questions, cue, offer verbal and nonverbal reinforcement, and suggest group maintenance activities when needed. In the concluding stage, the results of interaction should be synthesized and summarized. Reporting must occur (oral or through a paper or project). Each group should evaluate its own effectiveness using specific rubrics.

Using Collaborative Learning Well

Mueller and Fleming (2001) agree that cooperative and collaborative learning are an important part of student learning. They suggest ways teachers can structure and guide group learning experiences. A key finding is that "children require periods of unstructured time to organize themselves and to learn how to work together toward a mutual goal" (p. 259). We tend to overstructure how tasks are to be achieved. However, if the task is clear, students often find their own way to achieve the goal.

Boxtel and Roelofs (2001) observe that collaborative learning can help students gain a deeper understanding of concepts, especially when students work together on tasks such as concept mapping. The concern is with how to construct knowledge. They argue that we tend to consider cognitive activities only, and that teachers must consider the "learning and thinking as social and situated processes" (p. 55). Students, they say, should be encouraged in "collaborative elaboration," trying to reach a shared understanding. The use of shared objects or tools can play a critical part in the discussion. Tools such as a text or other materials to experiment with give many students "exploration and manipulation possibilities" (p. 59). Simple Post-it notes on which students can write and arrange ideas help students to structure their shared discussions.

A teacher's planning guide for using small groups is given in Appendix 13.3 . A data collection instrument for use with microteaching or classroom lessons taught with the professional target of small-group teaching is provided in Appendix 13.4.

Benefits and Limitations of Group Methods

Although there are times when group work is very effective and times when another strategy or method should be used, most teachers agree that much more use should be made of small groups.

BENEFITS.   Impressive benefits can result through small-group methods:

1. Increased resources. "Two heads are better than one." A group has access to more information and has a broader background than does any individual. More insights are likely to occur. A group can create more ideas.
2. Members are often stimulated by the presence of others. Members may be motivated to help the group succeed for social approval reasons. "Ideas beget ideas." "Hitch-hiking" occurs.
3. Better decisions can result. Groups can produce better decisions than students working separately. Ideas can be clarified, refined, combined, and evaluated through the interaction of group members; therefore, decisions should be superior.
4. Group members may have a stronger commitment. If group members help hammer something out, they feel a stronger commitment to accept the result and follow through.
5. Students are more actively involved. Participation is likely to be active rather than passive. This increases motivation, learning, retention, and commitment.
6. Personal and social learning take place. Increased understanding of self, others, and group processes can result. Interpersonal and social skills can be improved and increased self-concept can result. Prejudices can be reduced. Students gain insights into the attitudes, reactions, and sensitivities of others and may examine and modify their behavior. Ability to contribute rationally and constructively can be improved.
7. Peer teaching is advantageous. Studies confirm that peer teaching is powerful. Some things are learned better and faster when taught by peers. Ideas are put in "student language" not "teacher language"; examples and explanations used by peers are often more relevant to students than teacher or text examples.
8. Learning may be deepened. Often, material is easily forgotten when it is memorized and not understood when direct teaching methods are used. When small groups are used, it is more likely that students will understand the thinking skills or processes involved. When this occurs, learning is more likely to be transferred to new situations.

LIMITATIONS.   You should be aware of the potential limitations of using small groups.

1. Group decision making takes time. More time is required for decision making or planning when it is done by a group than when it is done by an individual. The views of all must be heard, and disagreements may occur that take time to resolve.
2. Time may be seen to be wasted. Discussions, if not well conducted, not only take time, they waste it. Without able guidance or the use of group skills, discussion can wander, be misled, hindered, concerned with trivia, or lack conclusiveness.
3. Convictions may be suppressed. Some members may conform to avoid confrontation or risk censure. Less aggressive students may not be given a chance to present ideas.
4. Some tasks are better done by individuals, i.e., routine or simple tasks, or information acquisition. More material can be covered through methods such as lectures.
5. Talk may be substituted for action. "Visiting" may take precedence over productivity. In some instances, groups may be indecisive because no person is solely responsive for action. One or two individuals may do all the work.
6. Some students prefer to work alone. Unless small groups are used well and the benefits taught, some might rather work alone, thinking they can learn better. Some may be shy, lack social skills, or feel they will not be accepted.

It should be stressed that most disadvantages can be overcome. Doing so, of course, requires careful planning, instruction, and monitoring.

Group Structure and Member Duties

The productivity and health of groups depend on how they are structured. Effectiveness is also affected by how well students understand the duties of group leader and participants. This should be clearly presented or worked out at the beginning of the group.

You can control group size. Large groups (more than twelve members) require more structure and leadership than medium (seven to twelve members) or small (two to five members) groups. Seating should allow members to work together without violating personal space, and suitable materials should be available. Consensus and decision-making procedures should be taught and groups informed that consensus is not always possible or required. Task accomplishment activities should be stressed and a normal operational routine established. Each meeting should start with a statement of what is to done and end with an evaluation of group effectiveness. Groups should be told about meeting times and the completion date.

Group members should understand that each is accountable, that the group leader has specific duties and that others have specific duties.

Group members' duties are to:

- Be on time and attend all group sessions.
- Take an active part and contribute information and ideas.
- Contribute to group maintenance.
- Have a positive, rather than negatively critical, frame of reference.
- Listen when others speak, be empathetic, and hear others out.
- Respect and interact with other members.
- Respect individual differences.
- Avoid prejudices and keep biases out.
- Seek, and be open to, the ideas and suggestions of others.

- Encourage noncontributors to take part.
- Accept responsibility for the consequences of their behavior.
- Be sensitive to the feelings and concerns of others.
- Avoid self-serving, judgmental, blaming, grandstanding, or storytelling behavior.
- Be genuine and open.
- Support others and help them articulate their ideas.
- Help the group by summarizing, clarifying, mediating, praising, and encouraging.
- Use problem-solving, decision-making, and conflict-resolution frames of reference.
- Act as group leader, recorder, or group effectiveness monitor as appropriate.

The group leader's duties are to

- See that the "problem" is clarified.
- Get discussion started.
- Keep discussion moving.
- See that all phases of the problem are brought out.
- Keep discussion on topic.
- Encourage full participation and draw out nontalkers.
- Be objective.
- Rephrase and clarify statements, or have others do this.
- See that stage summaries and a conclusion are made.
- See that all members are treated with respect.
- Respect the confidence of the group.
- Report, or see that the thoughts of the group are fairly reported.

Discussion Approaches

Whole-class discussion requires teacher and students to interact verbally. It recognizes that knowledge is more than a string of correct answers and that much knowledge is gained through creative inquiry and active student participation. The purpose is to stimulate analysis and to interpret and shape attitudes. Discussion can be adapted to many classroom situations. For example, a "magic moment" in teaching and learning may occur if, during a presentation, you notice students are particularly interested in a topic and involve them in a discussion. This helps build a positive climate and leads to intrinsic student interest in the school subject.

Discussion can be guided carefully, step by step, through thought-provoking questions and, when appropriate, by interjecting information. This can be called *guided discussion*. On the other hand, discussion can be completely open and consist largely of student–student interchange. We call this *open discussion*. The former approach is effective for promoting understanding of important concepts; the latter is an exciting way for students to engage in high-level, creative thinking.

GUIDED DISCUSSION.   In guided discussion you, as teacher, are the discussion leader and authority source, and, when needed, information source. Guided discussion is used to guide students as they review what they have been studying, to promote understanding, or to develop ability to apply learning. In guided discussion you draw out the information needed and make frequent use of convergent (who, what, where, when) questions, prompts, and probes, and seek wide participation. Guided discussion is similar to guided discovery or inquiry.

OPEN DISCUSSION.   Open discussion is more difficult to conduct, but can be exciting and rewarding. It is freer flowing than guided discussion. You are a facilitator instead of an authority source or figure. You focus discussion, set boundaries, encourage participation (but unlike in guided discussion, not necessarily wide participation), and promote positive interaction. You listen and use paraphrasing, perception checking, open-ended questions and probes, but don't push the class toward predetermined conclusions. Avoid intervening too often (particularly with questions), because this may get in the way. Divergent ideas and originality are welcome, and high-level and critical and creative thinking are sought.

CONDUCTING DISCUSSION.   There is more to *discussion* (which is similar to a "businesslike" or on-topic conversation) than first meets the eye. Effective application of this teaching method requires a range of skills in planning, conducting, and concluding the discussion. Categories of skills include interpersonal exchanges, motivation, questioning, and reinforcement.

Effective discussions are based on material familiar to students. You set the stage, stress that opinions must be supported (based on evidence), and ensure that terms or concepts are understood. Good discussion is student centered. The rules of "common courtesy" prevail. Ideas can be challenged, but personalities must never be attacked.

Collaborative learning involves students in peer discussion. Chinn, O'Donnell, and Jinks (2000) say that teachers must consider carefully the structure of students' discourse so that students, who are encouraged to consider more detailed issues and questions, will produce more complex conclusions and learn more from one another. They suggest that (1) giving explanations, (2) elaborating on what they have learned, and (3) requesting clarification from their peers are beneficial. In other words, "It is not simply the activity of engaging in discourse that promotes peer learning but the quality of that discourse" (p. 78).

Good teachers establish a classroom ethos that is safe, fun, challenging, and at task. They demonstrate and encourage positive behaviors and avoid negative behaviors (Figure 13.4).

FIGURE 13.4   *Encouraging Positive and Discouraging Negative Behaviors*

Positive Behavior	Negative Behavior
• Encourage	• Blame
• Model listening skills	• Judge
• Are courteous	• Use put-downs
• Are genuine	• Use sarcasm
• Use empathy	• Use story telling
• Paraphrase	• Placate
• Seek information	• Rescue
• Check for feelings	• Theorize
• Ask for examples	• Distract
• Ask for opinions	• Clown
• Probe	• Show off
• Keep discussion on track	• Are rude
• Elicit stage/concluding summaries	
• Are businesslike	

ENCOURAGING PARTICIPATION.   You can do much to encourage positive and productive participation in class discussions and, for that matter, in small-group activities. Students should be taught to listen, take turns, encourage others to participate, and speak clearly to the point. Several techniques were presented in Chapter 8.

Effective discussion approaches were presented earlier. A data collection instrument you can use to get feedback on your use of the discussion target is provided in Appendix 13.5.

Peer Tutoring

Students often work alone. Schoolwork is typically based on competition rather than cooperation. When students teach students, a valuable dimension is added to teaching and learning. "Students should be put in situations where they have to reach to understand, but where support from other students or from the teacher is also available. Sometimes the best teacher is another student who has just figured out the problem" (Woolfolk, 2004, p. 52). You likely are familiar with the truism that if you really want to understand something, . . . teach it. Both the tutor and tutee can benefit. Cognitive and affective development is fostered through a student's conversations and interactions with others. Peers provide the information and support needed for intellectual growth. Successful peer tutoring seems to provide feelings of satisfaction and competence that improve self-concept.

Peer teaching can involve groups of three, four, or five, but most peer teaching occurs in pairs. When a teacher uses the peer tutoring method, students are placed in groups or two or more and provided with structured learning activities that include tutoring, practice, and feedback. Normally, students take turns teaching and being taught, answers are checked, and feedback is given.

Use the data collection instruments in this chapter to help you analyze the cases that follow. Your instructor may pose specific questions for your response. Suggest different arrangements and think about the advantages and disadvantages of each arrangement.

CASE 13.2 Collaborative Learning

Getting along with Each Other

Mr. Ramsingh, a student teacher, planned to have his grade 6 students do small-group discussion. The regular classroom teacher was skeptical about the idea; she said the students had never worked in groups before and doubted they could learn that way. But she was supportive to Mr. Ramsingh in his plan to try other approaches.

Mr. Ramsingh was confident the students would welcome the opportunity to become more involved in their learning. He began, "On the playground yesterday, there were many problems. Ms. O'Toole and I had complaints from several of you and from the supervisors. We are very concerned. It seems problems during the break are so great that no one is benefiting. I hope today we can work out ways that will make playground time more enjoyable for everyone. What I'd like you to do is to form groups of four." (The students began to look for friends to join.) "Each group will decide what the problems are and think of solutions." (Many students stopped listening and actively began to negotiate their group membership. Some began calling out to others, some left their desks for whispered discussions). "OK, you can get into your groups now. We'll finish in fifteen minutes and have all the groups report their solutions to the class before recess."

Most students rose and began to form groups. Four girls, by exchanging glances, decided to work together. They chose to work in the reading area. A

continued

fifth girl, who had been trying to get the attention of the four, was deliberately excluded. She returned to her desk, took out a library book, and began to read. Meanwhile, much loud discussion ensued. A pair chose each other and would not let anyone else join. Five boys decided to work together, though a sixth was vigorously protesting "That's not fair." The five moved to the reading area and tried to eject the group of girls in that area.

Mr. Ramsingh made suggestions, grouped children who lacked partners, and helped groups to find an area to work. Soon half the discussion time was gone. Mr. Ramsingh made a comment about the passing time, although many students did not hear him. As the children settled into their groups, their voices rose. Some began to complain about specific students on the playground; others wanted to defend those students. One group compared hockey card collections. Gustav

took charge of his group and began to list rules for the playground. Others in his group tried to enter the discussion, but he overruled their ideas and continued to develop his list. Mr. Ramsingh realized that each group should have had papers and pencils for recording; he quickly passed these out and spent time explaining the purpose of these materials to each group as he distributed them to. Two groups were still arguing about their work area. Just then the recess bell sounded.

The children looked up in amazement and frustration. "Hey, we're not finished." "We didn't get started!" "Marvin kept fooling around, Mr. Ramsingh." Some students seemed anxious at not having finished. Others argued loudly as they left the classroom, on the way to the playground. The classroom teacher looked stern and Mr. Ramsingh wondered how to salvage the lesson and whether he would be permitted the opportunity to try small groups again.

CASE 13.3   Collaborative Learning

Waning Enthusiasm

Ms. Treblioni, a grade 11 social studies teacher, really liked using small groups. She has the reputation of being one of the best teachers in the school system. With only a few exceptions, she has always had success with them. Most of her students this year really liked the group work that had been done to date. Recently, however, the students' enthusiasm for group work seemed to be waning. She suspected that the problem was mainly a handful of students. There was Trenton and Teresa, both very pleasant and sociable, who just seemed to let the others in whatever group they were in do all the work. Two other kinds of

problems had emerged. One involved Hazel, who just always had to have her way and dominated every group she was in. Nobody seemed to want to work with her anymore. Then there were Fred and Austin. Every time they were in the same group, they seemed to have to out-clown each other. The competition, though amusing, left the other group members disgruntled and Ms. Treblioni frustrated.

In the past, Ms. Treblioni had always solved problems by gently teasing erring students or privately encouraging them. This has not worked. What would you suggest?

CASE 13.4   Collaborative Learning

Bridging to Other Subjects

Mr. Shaw and his eighth-grade students begin each day with an open discussion. As the students come into the class, they pull their desks into a circle. Mr. Shaw joins the circle. The purpose of the discussion varies, but the topics usually come from the class. The students rotate the responsibility of chairing the discussion.

The chairperson's role is to help choose a topic, introduce the topic, keep the discussion on topic, encourage balanced participation, and bring the discussion to conclusion. Mr. Shaw had, earlier in the year, taught interpersonal and communication skills, so students carry out the responsibilities of the chair with confidence. Though it is not compulsory to take a turn, most students do. Mr. Shaw participates to clarify or summarize, but is careful to model effective group skills. Today, the students have just heard about the police shooting of a young man involved in a high-speed chase in a stolen vehicle. Their feelings about whether the shooting was inappropriate or not are strong. Heated discussion outside the school and in the corridors had occurred.

It's Megan's turn to chair. She begins, "Can everyone see and hear? Some people want to talk about the police shooting. Do you agree?" Most are in agreement, but Jason, who is an avid sports fan, suggests the topic be the nearly completed World Series. There are many moans, and several students support the shooting story. "Is anyone else interested in the World Series as a topic?" asks Megan. "I'd be interested another time," says Morgan, "But I think the shooting story is more important now." "I think so, too," added Jason. "It's the third shooting this year, and my dad says the police need better training." Megan looks around the group. "Do you all agree on this story?" The class indicates they agree. "OK, Jason?" "Yeah," responds Jason, "But let's not forget to have the Series. We could each pick the team we favor to win."

"OK," Megan begins, "Who knows the whole story of what happened with the shooting? We need to get the facts." One student gives an overview of what she heard on the news, and several others add details. Intense discussion occurs that requires monitoring by the chairperson to prevent interruptions and some students from dominating. There is support for the police action by some, who point out that stealing is wrong

and driving at high speeds is very dangerous. Others feel sympathy for the young man, whose crime seemed minor compared to the police action. Much of the discussion involves students stating views, sometimes in more than one way. There doesn't seem to be much listening to other positions or questions of other participants. Some students are becoming more emotional as they sense others may not be listening to their views.

Finally Mr. Shaw intervenes. "Let's see if we can figure out the issues here. I hear some people saying that because stealing is wrong, people who steal should be punished. I hear people saying that although stealing is wrong, police should not be able to shoot someone for that kind of crime. So there's an issue about stealing and there's an issue about whether the police action was appropriate. Are there any other issues?" "Another issue is that the boy who was shot was black," says Hamad. "My parents say police treat white people differently from minorities. All the shootings this year have been of black people." There is some agreement, although some students explain this by saying there is more crime committed by people from minority groups.

Megan seeks agreement on the issues and finds that everyone agrees stealing is wrong. The class does not agree on the appropriateness of the police action. As the discussion draws to a close, it becomes clear that agreement will not be possible. Megan asks for a summary of ideas or positions, and the discussion ends with a review of the positions.

Mr. Shaw is thinking of ways he can continue to build on the content of this discussion in other classes. He intends to extend this topic in both social studies and English.

Cooperative Learning

There is a pertinent film, based on a true story, called *October Sky,* which is set in the year 1957. A group of students in a small mining town in the United States is excited when the Soviets place the first satellite (*Sputnik*) into space. They decide to see if they can design, build, and launch model rockets. They realize that much scientific knowledge and skill are needed. Working together to solve many problems, they achieve success. They learn much math and physics in the process, and develop long-lasting skills and values. Experiences they share reveal that each person in the group was needed. They had engaged in cooperative learning.

To be called *cooperative,* learning needs to include certain elements: (1) *group interaction* (face-to-face interaction; the formation of groups to foster on-task behavior); (2) *social skills* (teaching and requiring interpersonal and group functioning skills); (3) *positive interdependence* (working together and mutual support; mutual goals; division of labor; dividing materials, resources or information among group members; and, giving joint rewards); (4) *individual accountability* for mastering the assigned material (responsibility as an individual and to the group); (5) *reflection* (students reflect and can share, and receive and give feedback). Furthermore, cooperative learning requires that students be taught, learn, and use interpersonal and group skills. Finally, students need to learn how to discover how well their learning groups function and the extent to which they use social skills to help members benefit from the working relationships in the group.

Modes of interaction are usually classified as individualistic, competitive, and cooperative. Most classrooms stress student interaction with the teacher and materials; cooperative learning also stresses interaction among students. Cooperative learning reaps the benefits of positive student interdependence as they work together in groups and support one another (Johnson & Johnson, 1980a). "Today, evolving constructivist perspectives on learning fuel interest in collaboration and cooperative learning" (Woolfolk, 2004, p. 492). Johnson and Johnson believe that many reasons for using competitive structures are more myth than reality and that individualizing instruction is not the only, or even the best, alternative to competition. Fears some teachers have about using cooperative goal structures are also myths. The authors say research shows that a cooperative goals structure should be the most frequent structure in the classroom but recognize the benefits of both competitive and individualistic structures (pp. 39–57). When a cooperative teaching strategy is used, emphasis is on cooperation, not competition.

Cooperative learning occurs in classrooms where students work in small groups on learning activities and receive recognition (or rewards) based on group performance. Groups are mixed in ability, and members are to help one another other. Believers claim that cooperative learning motivates students to do their best; they translate the language of the teacher and learn through this; they provide individual attention for one another. In cooperative learning, interaction to enhance learning and develop interpersonal and group skills is emphasized. It supplements the teacher's instruction by having students discuss information or practice skills originally presented by the teacher; sometimes cooperative methods require students to find or discover information.

Cooperative learning is *not:* (1) students sitting beside each other at the same table and talking as they do individual assignments, (2) students doing tasks individually, with those finishing first helping the others, or (3) giving a group assignment and one or two do most of the work to which others sign their names (Johnson & Johnson, in Brubacher, Payne, & Rickett, 1990, p. 77).

Essentials of Cooperative Learning

To improve student achievement substantially, two aspects must be present: (1) students work toward a group goal or recognition—for example a certificate; and (2) success is dependent on learning by each individual in the group (Slavin, 1987, p. 9).

Two things are essential to cooperative learning:

1. It entails *positive interdependence* among students in the task structure. Involvement of each group member is necessary for the group to complete the task. An interdependent task structure is created by having each responsible for a part of the task that cannot be completed by any other in the group—for example, the tutoring aspect. Positive interdependence can be fostered through a reward structure. Here, the final evaluation, if any, is dependent on the reward received by each student.

2. In designing cooperative learning tasks and reward structures, individual responsibility and accountability must be identified. Individuals must know exactly what their responsibilities are to the group, and they must be accountable to the group.

David and Roger Johnson's (1989) approach to cooperative learning has five basic elements:

1. *Positive interdependence.* Students need to believe they are responsible for their learning and that of members of their group.
2. *Face-to-face promotive interaction.* Students need to explain to each other what they are learning and help each other understand and do assignments.
3. *Individual accountability.* Each student needs to demonstrate mastery of the content studied.
4. *Social skills.* Effective communication, interpersonal, and group skills are needed.
5. *Group processing.* Periodically, groups must assess their effectiveness and figure out how it can be improved. (p. 80)

Cooperative Learning and Research

As part of a meta-analysis of research on a range of teaching strategies, research on cooperative learning was "overwhelmingly positive" and showed that cooperative modes are appropriate for all subjects (Joyce, Showers, & Rolheiser-Bennett, 1987, pp. 12–13). Cooperative learning involves group work that increases learning and adds other important dimensions. The positive outcomes are (1) academic gains, especially for minority and low-achieving students, (2) improved race relations among students in integrated classrooms, and (3) increased personal and social development among all students (Slavin, 1987). Slavin (1991) thinks that cooperative learning:

- Enhances student achievement; cooperative learning is most effective when groups are rewarded on the basis of the individual learning of group members.
- Consistently provides positive achievement effects when group goals and individual accountability are present.
- Produces effects on achievement that are about the same at all grade levels, all major subjects, rural or urban schools, and for high, average, and low achievers.
- Has consistent positive effects on self-esteem, intergroup relations, acceptance of academically handicapped students, attitudes toward school, and ability to work cooperatively. (p. 71)

It is not surprising that the research results are so strongly positive. People who talk about ideas with others "understand and remember" them better. Transfer from short- to long-term memory is enhanced. The support that comes from cooperation (in contrast to achievement-limiting competition) is "another plus."

Slavin (1991) reports that research on cooperative learning shows the following:

- For academic achievement, cooperative learning techniques are at least as good as traditional techniques, and usually significantly better.
- Contrary to what is sometimes claimed, it does not hold back high achievers. Cooperative learning methods are, usually, equally effective for all ability levels.
- Studies in senior high schools are about as positive as those in grades 3 to 9.

- Results are just as positive in rural, urban, and suburban settings.
- Cooperative learning methods have been equally effective with students of different ethnic groups.
- "People who cooperate learn to like one another." It has been consistently found that students' perceptions of each other are enhanced through cooperative learning.
- Cooperative learning methods promote positive intergroup relations; ethnicity barriers tend to break down, and more positive interactions and interethnic friendships occur.
- The barrier between physically and mentally handicapped children and their "normal" peers is reduced and the number of positive interactions and friendships increase.
- Cooperative methods increase students' self-esteem or self-concepts. (pp. 75–80)

Other positive outcomes include: greater liking of school, favorable attitudes toward doing well in school, a feeling of being in control of one's fate in school, greater cooperativeness and altruism, and increased time on task. One study found that cooperative learning resulted in students from lower economic backgrounds having better attendance, fewer brushes with the police, and higher behavior ratings. Another study shows that students taught cooperatively were rated higher on "measures of supportive, friendly, and pro social behavior; were better at resolving conflicts; and expressed more support for democratic values" (Slavin, 1991, pp. 80–81).

The success of cooperative approaches is not restricted to K–12 classrooms. Research shows that using cooperative modes with adults is beneficial and should lead to higher productivity (Johnson & Johnson, 1987b). The results are higher achievement, improved interpersonal relationships, greater social support, and enhanced self-esteem (p. 30). Figure 13.5 provides a summary of research on cooperative learning.

Cooperative versus Traditional Learning Groups

Effective traditional groups and cooperative learning groups require many of the same interpersonal and group skills, but they differ in significant ways. Table 13.2 shows the differences.

Cooperative Skills

Proponents of cooperative learning believe that there are no skills more important to humans than cooperative interaction (including interpersonal, group, and organizational

FIGURE 13.5   *Cooperative Learning Research*

1. Greater academic achievement	2. Positive social outcomes
"Lower"-order objectives	Better peer relationships
"Higher"-order objectives	Better social skills
High, average, and low achievers	More social support
Grade levels 2–12	Higher self-esteem
Rural, urban, suburban	Greater liking of subject, class, and school
All major subjects	Reduced prejudice
	Acceptance of academically handicapped
	Ability to work cooperatively

TABLE 13.2   *Cooperative versus Traditional Learning Groups*

Cooperative Groups	Traditional Groups
Interdependence and group accountability	Often not stressed
Normally heterogeneous	Often not homogeneous
Shared leadership	Appointed or elected
Responsibility for others' growth	Responsible for self-growth
Task and maintaining group emphasized	Emphasis on task
Social skills must be taught and used	Often ignored or assumed

skills). Particularly important are communication skills, building and maintaining trust, and controversy skills (Figure 13.6).

You can gradually introduce cooperative learning activities and games to help students acquire communication and helping skills and the basics of small-group organization and operation. These can create the necessary climate for carrying out cooperative learning strategies. Establishing the basic cooperative interaction skills helps groups to work together in completing their tasks. The goal is more than the specific subject matter as dictated by the teacher. It provides a way of acquiring or analyzing, or synthesizing information or skills.

Cooperative planning skills deserve special attention. They should be introduced gradually and practiced in various situations before starting a cooperative learning project; for example, discussions can be held with the whole class or small groups for ideas to carry out an activity such as planning a display or organizing a class trip.

When a cooperative learning method is being used, the teacher is always attending to two things: (1) achieving the learning task and (2) maintaining the group (including building interpersonal and group skills). It is important that cooperative norms of behavior be established. Students can practice interpersonal and group skills. This can be done independent of, or as part of, a group assignment. At times the group may have to put aside the academic learning to work on group maintenance. An example of this occurs when there is a conflict in a group that must be attended to if the group is to be productive.

Building and Maintaining a Trusting Climate

For cooperative learning to be effective, students need collaborative skills. It is particularly important to maintain a trusting climate. Relevant suggestions when using cooperative learning were provided some time ago by Johnson and Johnson (1975b):

- Encourage students to contribute information, ideas, thoughts, feelings, intuitions, hunches, and reactions openly to the group operation.
- Encourage students to share materials and resources.

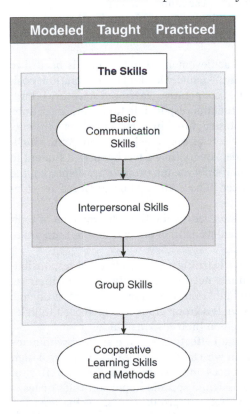

FIGURE 13.6   *Skills to Be Acquired for Effective Cooperative Learning*

- Encourage students to express cooperative intentions, acceptance, and support toward each other during their cooperative interactions.
- Ensure that students have the skills to express acceptance, support, and desire to cooperate.
- Point out rejecting and nonsupportive behaviors that shut off future cooperation, such as silence, ridicule, or superficial acknowledgment of an idea.
- Periodically have groups that are cooperative evaluate their behavior to ensure it is trusting and trustworthy and how cooperation could be improved. (pp. 105–106)

Principles of Cooperation

Cooperative learning principles involve positive task and reward structures and positive interdependence. A cooperative learning task structure exists when students tutor each other; a cooperative reward structure exists when a student's grade is the total of his or her grade and that of the tutor. Either task or reward structures can be used, or both can be used. A task is structured cooperatively when no one student can do the task alone—for example, requiring a group product. Another example is a "jigsaw," in which each group member is provided with a separate portion of the learning material but every group member is to learn all the material. Reward is structured cooperatively when grades of individuals are dependent on the scores of other team members (e.g., the group grade is based on the sum of the scores). Studies show that these kinds of rewards structures have a powerful influence in directing group efforts. The lowest achiever in a group (if that person's grade contributes heavily to the group grade) often is given much tutoring and support.

Positive interdependence occurs when the achievement of individuals is needed to help the group complete a task or receive a reward—usually leading to cooperation; positive facilitation will usually lead to cooperation. A cooperative classroom structure is built by creating student interdependence. Having students responsible for separate portions of the task fosters interdependence. If classes are structured in a traditional way, the success of one student results in the failure of another (e.g., only one person can get the highest grade and other students do not get that grade). Every time a teacher asks a student to respond to a question, others are not asked; and if only the top projects are displayed, the other students do not have their work recognized. These kinds of occurrences are common in competitive classrooms.

Individualistic task or reward structure is present when the achievements of individual students have no student impact on the achievement of other students; then, there is no incentive either to cooperate or to compete.

The key principles in effective cooperative learning are (1) individual responsibility, and (2) individual accountability. Individuals need to be keenly aware of their responsibilities to the group and must be accountable to it. Research shows that academic gains occur when groups are used only if the goal is a group grade to which each individual contributes, and if individuals follow through on their responsibilities.

Two kinds of individuals can obstruct group effectiveness: the student who reaps the benefits without contributing and the student who takes over the group. Group design should provide safeguards for individual differences and ensure respect for the effort of the less dominant. Each individual should be assigned specific important roles or tasks and be held accountable. Another technique is frequent group process evaluations and having groups conclude each meeting with a discussion of what to do to increase group effectiveness.

Students have different social motives. "Cooperative" students are (1) *altruistic*—they help others make gains; (2) *equality oriented*—they minimize personal achievement compared to the achievement of others; and (3) *group enhancement oriented*—they do their best to help the group achieve. Competitive students tend toward rivalry and being superior. Individualistic students tend to be self- rather than other centered; they are cooperative when there is a "payoff" and competitive when there is a chance of winning.

As students get older, they become individualistic and increasingly compare their achievements with those of others. Also, the need to cooperate or compete is influenced by students' cultural values. Minority, low-income, and rural students tend to have cooperative social motives, whereas white American students often have competitive social motives. Because traditional classrooms assume that motivation occurs through competition, educational outcomes are biased in the favor of majority students. Likely, the most effective classrooms provide meaningful rewards for all students, whether their social motives are individualistic, competitive, or cooperative.

Cooperative Learning Approaches

Cooperative team learning approaches described below are Aronson's Jigsaw, Slavin's Jigsaw II, Devries and Slavin's Teams-Games-Tournament (TGT), Slavin's Student Teams and Achievement Divisions (STAD), Sharan's Group Investigation, cooperative games, and using cooperation to reduce prejudice. These approaches share the feature of small teams, or social units, of students to promote interaction and cooperation.

JIGSAW. Jigsaw was developed to encourage peer cooperation and tutoring (Aronson, Blaney, Stephin, Sikes, & Snapp, 1978). Students are assigned to five heterogeneous, or "home," groups of five or six members. Academic material is broken into as many parts as there are groups. Students study their portion of the materials with the members of other "home" groups who have been assigned the same material. This is the "expert" group. "Experts" return to their "home" groups to teach their material to other group members. "Home" group members are dependent on the "experts" to be tutored to learn the material, therefore they are motivated to pay attention. Students are quizzed on all the academic material and receive individual grades (there is no team score). Group members are interdependent to the extent that they work together to accomplish the task but not interdependent regarding reward because they are graded as individuals. "Experts" have unique information that makes "home" group members value the contribution of each member. Jigsaw is used mainly in social studies and subjects for which it is important to learn from textual material. However, other creative approaches are possible.

JIGSAW II. Jigsaw II, described by Slavin (1978a), is a variation of Jigsaw. Students work in heterogeneous groups and each group is assigned a portion of the material. Students study the material assigned and then meet in "expert" groups. After this, students return to their "home" teams to teach their peers. Then, students take a quiz covering all the topics. Quiz scores, based on an individual improvement system, are used to form team scores. High-scoring teams are recognized in some way, such as in a bulletin or school newspaper. Interdependence is key to Jigsaw II: students depend on teammates to provide the information so they can do well on quizzes.

TEAMS-GAMES-TOURNAMENT. Slavin's (1978a, 1978b) Teams-Games-Tournament (TGT) format, based on motivation theory, involves competitive cooperation with individuals of similar ability competing against each other and with teams competing against one another. Students are assigned to four- or five-member teams. Teams are heterogeneous by ability (e.g., one low-ability student, two of average ability, and one of high ability), racial or ethnic background, and sex. The job of the teams is, through peer tutoring, to prepare each other for a tournament usually held once a week. Tournament tables are set up. Three students of similar academic achievement (determined by previous performance) are assigned to each table. The three highest performers are assigned Table #1, the next three highest sit at Table #2, and so on. When the game is over, contestants are scored. The highest performer of a trio earns 6 points, the mid-performer earns 4 points, and the low performer earns 2 points. Team scores are determined by adding the scores of the team members. The winning team is the one with the most points. It earns recognition through, for example, a newsletter. The composition of teams remains the same, and tournaments run for six to eight weeks. Tournament table group composition changes depending on scores earned by individuals. Performance in the first tournament decides table placement for the second tournament, performance in the second determines placement for the third, and so on. Reward interdependence is created in a team. The more members help one another, the better the team will do in tournaments.

STUDENT TEAMS AND ACHIEVEMENT DIVISIONS.   Like TGT, the Student Teams and Achievement Divisions (STAD) format involves competitive cooperation. Teams compete against each other; but, unlike TGT, games and tournaments are not used. Students, through peer assistance, review teacher-taught materials. The teacher distributes rewards to team members and uses an accounting system that avoids head-on student competition.

Students are assigned to heterogeneous teams of four or five members. Students, in teams, study for fifteen-minute weekly quizzes. Quiz scores are translated into team scores using "Achievement Divisions." The highest six scorers are placed in the same Achievement Division and their scores are compared to allocate points. (The top scorer gets 8 points, the second earns 6 points, etc. Students earning the next six highest scores form the second Achievement Division and points are allocated, etc.) The result is that students are compared only with those of similar ability, not the whole class. As in TGT, STAD involves competition among equals. Students do not interact with other members of their division; in teams, they help each other prepare for quizzes, and teams compete to win recognition for performance.

GROUP INVESTIGATION.   The Group Investigation (GI) model proposed by Sharan and Lazarowitz (1980) has students gather data, interpret the data through discussion, and synthesize individual contributions into a group product. The emphasis in GI is different from in TGT and STAD, which feature peer tutoring (rather than investigation and reporting). The teacher presents a general topic to the class, which is divided into groups to investigate and report on subtopics. After subtopics are chosen, groups break their subtopics into tasks for individuals and individuals and subgroups carry out their assignments to prepare group reports. The teacher is a facilitator and resource. The use of GI can be particularly effective for higher-order thinking skills and can be a very effective method in high school classes.

After a general topic is introduced by the teacher, the class is divided into two- to six-member heterogeneous task-oriented groups. Students often can pick the topic they would like to investigate, and this influences team membership. Individual groups meet with the teacher to clarify the goals of the investigation and plan how the investigation is to be conducted. Both in- and out-of-school resources can be investigated. Each group then carries out the plan and the teacher monitors progress and offers assistance as needed. Data are analyzed and evaluated and an interesting way of presenting or displaying what was learned to the rest of the class is determined. As coordinated by the teacher, groups then display or present their reports. Evaluation now takes place, with the teacher and students collaborating to decide the assessment methods. Evaluation should include assessment of higher-level learning. It can include individual or group assessment or both.

COMPARING TEAM LEARNING METHODS. Cooperative learning modes fall into two categories: those emphasizing peer tutoring (Jigsaw, TGT, and STAD), and those emphasizing group investigation. Sharan and Lazarowitz (1980) point out critical differences in the variety and source of information and the nature of the learning task, the nature of interpersonal relations and communications, evaluation of rewards for the academic product, and the organization of the classroom (Table 13.3).

In peer tutoring, the teacher presents information or identifies sources; in group investigation, information can be varied and broad and is gathered by students. Peer tutoring emphasizes acquiring information or skills; group investigation stresses analysis, interpretation, problem solving, and application. With respect to interpersonal relations and communications, peer tutoring teams stress peer instruction and drill within the team, whereas in group investigation, teams are part of mutual exchange that requires techniques such as idea or consensus seeking and decision making. Evaluation of, and rewards for, the academic product also differ. In peer tutoring, the academic product is independent, evaluation is mainly individual (test scores), and rewards tend to be extrinsic; in group investigation, the academic product is interdependent, evaluation is both individual and group, and the reward is mainly intrinsic (based on self-directed interest in the topic). In peer tutoring, the classroom is organized as several separate, uncoordinated, teams to achieve a uniform academic product; in group investigation the class is divided into teams to investigate portions of a broad topic that requires between-team coordination, reporting, and integration into a whole (Sharan & Lazarowitz, 1980, pp. 263–264).

Cooperation and interdependence in learning tasks are fostered by peer tutoring, that is, teaching classmates. Given practice and reinforcement, most children become rather good "teachers." Many learn better from peers than from adults, and benefit greatly

TABLE 13.3 *Comparing Peer Tutoring and Group Investigation Cooperative Learning*

Peer Tutoring	Group Investigation
Teacher provides the information	Students gather the information
Use: information/skill acquisition	Use: for problem solving, interpreting, applying
Peer tutoring (presenting/acquiring)	Information/idea exchange, planning, coordination
Evaluation: usually individual or done with group, done by teacher	Evaluation: individual and/or group; product is interdependent; done by teacher and/or students
Rewards: extrinsic; group recognition	Rewards: mainly intrinsic
Organization: aggregate of teams, same task	Organization: "group of groups," between-group coordination

from teaching other students. In their small groups, each team, rather than the class as a whole, becomes the social unit in which learning is pursued. Classroom instruction process changes from direct instructor control to allow for interaction among peers. Figure 13.7 compares peer tutoring and group investigation methods.

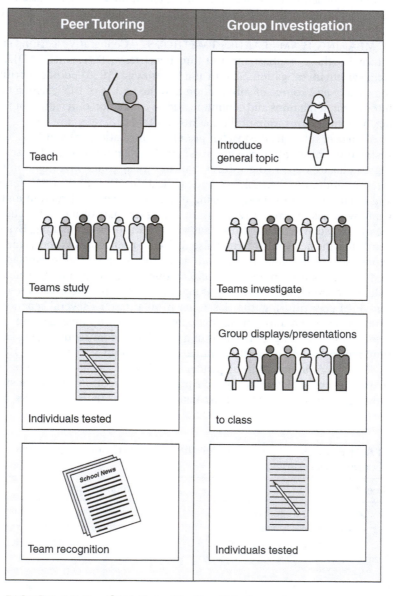

FIGURE 13.7   *Operation of the Peer Tutoring and Group Investigation Methods*

COOPERATIVE GAMES.   When one thinks of classroom games, one usually thinks of something offered as a reward, to provide a break in the academic schedule, or something the physical education teacher has students do. *Cooperative games* can be used to build academic learning. Play is a great medium for positive social learning. It is natural, active, and extremely motivating. While playing cooperatively, students can act, react, feel, and experience. Games can be used "to break the ice," practice interpersonal or group skills when a group maintenance activity is appropriate, or provide a change of pace and simultaneously develop students' social skills. They can be used to have students experience the process of cooperation and develop a positive mind set for it before a cooperative method is used. Many books on cooperative games are available. These describe hundreds of games, ranging from those that require no additional resources or materials to those that require relatively elaborate resources or materials.

Cooperative games are useful in achieving cognitive, psychomotor, or social curriculum objectives. They are "sharing" games: a big difference between cooperative games and most other games is that everybody "wins." The structure is cooperative, not competitive. People play "with" rather than "against" each other. Cooperative games allow maximum participation and opportunity for everybody to be involved. They are not graded or assessed and usually are self-paced and fun. In cooperative games, the more individuals help others, the more they and the group can achieve. So all can "win," the goals are mutual effort, fun, and helping others.

Cooperative games are powerful for positively shaping students' feelings about themselves and others. Competitive games can rob some of the opportunity to experience satisfaction and enjoyment and can lead to unfriendly and negative interactions. Cooperative games can reduce the students' feeling anxious, self-conscious, isolated, or unworthy. They enhance self-concept, creativity, and the ability to get along with others. Through well-designed cooperative games, students become more considerate and caring. Cooperative games can teach the values and behaviors we would like society to have.

Cooperative Learning and Reducing Prejudice

It seems clear, as Sharan and Lazarowitz (1980) state, that team learning "promotes positive interethnic contact under cooperative conditions" (p. 258). This is confirmed by Slavin (1983), who reviewed research on cooperative learning and intergroup relations. He agrees that there is "a strong positive effect of cooperative learning on intergroup relations" (p. 88). Cooperative groups increase interracial contact and lead to cross-racial friendships. Slavin hypothesizes that students learn it is acceptable to interact with members of other races, there is increased awareness of interracial similarities, and racial barriers to peer-group membership break down. Obviously, the more exceptions there are to a stereotype, the more a stereotype breaks down. This happens as a student interacts with (and becomes friends with) one person from another race who does not match the stereotype, then another, then still another, and so forth.

Studies show that the orientation of a classroom, competitive or cooperative, can have significant effects on the academic and social behavior of students, particularly for members of a minority group. Teachers in North America of Anglo or European ancestry often have cultural values characterized by emphasis on competition and winning. In contrast, cooperation was, and is, essential in rural, land-based societies and has become the basic cultural value in indigenous societies. The reward structure in most North American and European classrooms is based on competition. Teachers, then, may wonder why minority students generally do not do as well as majority students. One can say that these teachers, because of cultural background, make a prejudgment by using competitive modes. This prejudice is based on lack of knowledge of how minority students learn, while stressing the schooling expectations and values of a predominantly Anglo-European society. Perhaps if they had used cooperative learning teaching methods, the academic achievement of minority students would have been higher, majority-culture student achievement would have been at least as high, and intercultural social behavior could have been enhanced. Cooperative learning reduces prejudice.

Handling Problems

Some teachers do not want to risk using group work, believing that use of groups promotes off-task behavior and discipline problems. We argue that the opposite is true. Improved classroom management results when groups are established effectively. Teachers who use group approaches well find that misbehavior drops significantly. Because use of groups results in improved social skills, fewer problems arise and students who might be problems can be handled more easily. The thing to remember is that students must be taught how to use groups, and interacting skills must be taught and practiced.

Most students react well to cooperative learning modes; however, all teaching strategies, on occasion, encounter difficulties. Problems can arise with cooperative learning when assigning groups or with socially isolated, high-achieving, disruptive, or low-achieving students.

Care must be taken to assign students into compatible, yet heterogeneous, groups. Students may have limited experience in working with others, and some in-group divisiveness may occur. Careful monitoring of group operation is, of course, necessary. Stress the critical aspects of the operation of cooperative groups and have students engage in group-building exercises or games. This is usually enough, but in the rare cases where a personality conflict exists, you may need to intervene or even restructure a group.

You may have to help the *socially isolated student* become accepted and included by the cooperative group. Students can receive instruction in interpersonal skills before they are introduced to the class, giving the isolated student an opportunity to support the group; or you can assign a task (e.g., recorder) to the student at which he or she can be successful. As groups learn cooperative behavior, peer support (which promotes participation) does develop, and the isolated student should increasingly become included.

A *high-achieving student* may say, " I don't want to be in a group. I can do this better and faster myself." You may have to explain the benefits of cooperative group work, pointing out that when the high achiever explains something to another student, a deeper understanding is gained, and simultaneously, the student acquires important interpersonal and social skills. This student can be assigned a task (such as observer) that requires skill in tabulating, interpreting, and reporting data, giving the student a feeling of the importance of contributing to group achievement. Or you may wish to use bonus marks that can be earned by high-achieving students. These could be partially dependent on the quality of support lent to group development and achievement. On occasion, you may group high-achieving students together, to challenge them or encourage divergent thinking.

A *low-achieving student* may need to discover that he is worthy, has capabilities, and can help others. While low-achieving students may not be handicapped in the usual sense of this term, the techniques suggested by Johnson and Johnson (1980b) may work: assign clear, achievable roles to the student; train him in the interpersonal skills needed to participate; or, set criteria he can meet (perhaps varying what must be mastered for success).

As the group develops its ability to support individuals, the low achiever's self-esteem and performance will increase.

A *disruptive student* with poor interpersonal skills can benefit from cooperative learning. You may have to intervene to help the group deal with the problem. For instance, you may assign the disruptive student a task that keeps him or her constructively busy. The student, for example, may be asked to keep the data collection sheet on task achievement behaviors. Sometimes, however, the student has to be pulled out of the group, at least temporarily, until the problem has been solved.

Evaluating Cooperative Learning

When teachers use cooperative learning, they are concerned with both academic achievement and acquisition of cooperative behaviors. Kagan (1985) points out that: (1) groups should evaluate their process, (2) team members should evaluate each other, (3) individuals should evaluate themselves, and (4) presentations by groups should be evaluated by the teacher and class members (p. 153).

Sources of evaluation instruments, among others, are: Kagan's (1985) *Cooperative Learning: Resources for Teachers,* and Johnson and Johnson's (1985) *Learning Together and Alone: Cooperative, Competitive, and Individualistic Learning.* A source that provides an excellent summary of the process of evaluation with examples is Clark, Wideman, and Eadie (1990), *Together We Learn.* Assessing academic progress when cooperative models are used is, as usual, done through homework, assignments, projects, papers, or tests. Assessment of the behavior of students involves use of observation procedures that describe and record behavior. Usually, an observation sheet is used to record, descriptively and objectively, the nature and frequencies of student behaviors.

Behaviors appropriate for cooperative learning include:

I. *Leadership*
   A. Achieving the task
      1. Sharing information and opinions
      2. Seeking information
      3. Clarifying or elaborating
      4. Summarizing
      5. Checking progress toward the group goal
      6. Testing for, or facilitating, consensus
   B. Maintaining the group
      1. Including/encouraging/listening to others
      2. Expressing group feelings
      3. Relieving tension and harmonizing
      4. Setting or applying standards
      5. Compromising
      6. Helping solve problems
II. *Communication*
   A. Listening
   B. Describing behavior accurately
   C. Paraphrasing
   D. Perception checking
   E. Describing feelings
   F. Seeking feedback; providing it when solicited

III. *Displaying trust*
    A. Accepting others and their ideas
    B. Expressing support/intention to cooperate
    C. Following through on promises/responsibilities
IV. *Conflict resolution*
    A. Managing personal feelings/showing empathy
    B. Defining the problem
    C. Discovering sources of the problem
    D. Proposing potential solutions
    E. Selecting the best potential solution
    F. Trying the proposed solution
    G. Evaluating the attempted solution

Prepare a summative profile of each student's progress. You can include mastery of cognitive knowledge and skills, verbal and writing ability, cooperative ability, competitive ability, ability to work independently, and ability to solve problems. You can also record appreciation of a subject area, appreciation of learning, self-awareness of abilities, characteristics that help others, appreciation of cultural and individual differences, appreciation of being trustworthy, and valuing free and open inquiry into problems.

The Teacher's Role in Cooperative Learning Instruction

The teacher assigns the group goal, outlines operational procedures, establishes the evaluation system, and monitors group progress (Figure 13.8). As adapted from Johnson and Johnson (1978), your duties when using cooperative learning include the following.

1. Specify the instructional objectives.
2. Set the size of the group. Size depends on the age of students (two or three for young students), the resources available, the cooperative skills of group members, and the task.
3. Name the group members. Composition is usually heterogeneous by sex, ability, leadership qualities, and ethnic background. Sometimes students can be grouped by interests.
4. Structure the physical arrangement of the room. Consider movement patterns, separation of groups, and access to materials.
5. Make sure that suitable materials are available. Students may all need the same materials, or individuals may need different materials.
6. Explain the task, operational procedures, role expectations, and evaluation criteria. Make sure that expectations for the final product and student behavior are clear.
7. Observe students' cooperative behavior (interpersonal and group skills) progress toward the goal.
8. Be a consultant or intervene as needed to solve problems for achieving the task using cooperative behaviors. Remind students that they are accountable to their group. Group effectiveness forms can be completed by the groups themselves.
9. Evaluate the products of the groups using criteria that were set. Usually, each group member gets the grade assigned to the group. Consider how well students learned or accomplished the task and how well they helped each other.

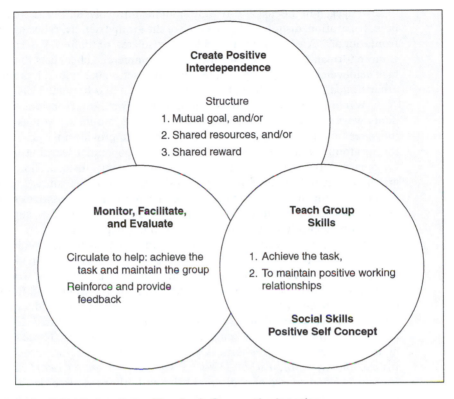

FIGURE 13.8   *Role of Teacher in Cooperative Learning*

Sonnier-York and Stanford (2002) stress "the need to target behavioral/social skills for each student" before students begin the project. The key, they say, is to "monitor," not "control" students, so they "learn on their own or from each other" (p. 42). The essence of cooperative learning is learning from each other, a process that plays a significant part in all authentic learning.

OBSERVATION AND INTERVENTION.   There are two key elements to the teacher's role: *observation* and *supportive intervention*. Though it may be difficult for the teacher to find time for observation during large-group instruction, cooperative learning allows teachers to observe, reflect, and intervene supportively. Keep on top of how groups are functioning, their interests and feelings, who is learning and who needs help. Observe to evaluate the learning occurring, to see if help is needed, to discover the nature of interaction, to decide if group maintenance intervention is needed, and to reflect about your use of the cooperative learning teaching method.

You can observe in two ways: globally or systematically. *Global observation* is informal and a good way to begin. It may lead to systematic observation to confirm or provide information upon which to base interventions. When you use global observation, record what you hear and see. Questions in your mind may include: "Are all students busily engaged in the task?" "Are any students uninvolved?" "Is there evidence of boredom, frustration, disquiet?" "Is the tone of the group friendly, relaxed, animated, or confrontational?" Are there any 'free riders' or 'isolates' or 'bullies'?" *Systematic observation* is more formal. It involves teacher-made or commercial checklists that specify essential task achievement and group-maintenance interaction behaviors. Examples of checklists are included in several cooperative learning texts and other materials.

When you intervene, do so in a supportive way. Interventions should lead to students working together more effectively. Students should see you as a helper, not as a judge ready to point a finger. It may be tempting to provide answers and solve problems for the group, but this defeats a major purpose of cooperative learning and denies students the opportunity to learn how to work through problems. Instead, show confidence in the group's ability to help itself. Intervention should consist of encouragement, patience, and opportunity for reflection. On occasion you can provide alternatives or sources for student consideration. To foster the groups' problem-solving abilities, suggest that they follow the problem-solving procedures described in Chapter 14.

When you use warm-up activities or intervene with task achievement or group maintenance activities, consider the Clark et al. reference mentioned above, Roger and David Johnson's (1990) cooperative learning warm-ups, grouping strategies, and group activities, and the 1988 manual by Johnson, Johnson, Bartlett, and Johnson, *Our Cooperative Classroom.* Another good reference, directed at early childhood students, is the Lorna Curran (in consultation with Kagan) 1990 book, *Cooperative Learning Lessons for Little Ones: Literature-Based Language Arts and Social Studies.* These references contain many good activity suggestions. A general reference that you should find valuable is Brubacher, Payne, and Rickett (1990), *Perspectives on Small Group Learning: Theory and Practice.* A good source of additional titles and other resources is the annual resource guide of *Cooperative Learning: The Magazine for Cooperation in Education.* The 1990 issue, edited by Nan and Ted Graves, *Cooperative Learning: A Resource Guide,* is Vol. 11, No. 1.

When a cooperative learning teaching method is used, the teacher should obtain feedback. A data collection instrument that can be used is provided in Appendix 13.6.

A data sheet on group participation is provided in Appendix 13.2. The authors suggest that students evaluate each other, and they provide a sample peer evaluation rubric (Appendix 13.7) that can be adapted to any age or grade.

Use the data collection instrument in Appendix 13.6 to help you analyze the cases that follow. Your instructor may pose specific questions for your response.

CASE 13.5 Cooperative Learning

Sharing Apples

In one group, five children sit facing each other. Jason is the "Writer" (recorder) and has a pencil and a sheet on which to record the group's answers. Samantha is the "Teller" (facilitator or chairperson), Arthur is the "Happy Talker" (encourager), Angie is the "Reader," and Jeannie is the "Checker."

The group is working through three problems they have been assigned. Jason finishes recording the group's answer. As he finishes, Samantha says, "We're ready for the next problem. What's next?"

Angie looks at the card in her hand and reads, "Nathan and Roger, three-year-old twins, woke up from their nap at Daycare. A staff member was preparing an apple for each of them. Roger said, 'Cut my apple in lots of pieces. I want to have more apple than Nathan.' The staff member cut Nathan's apple into six pieces and Roger's into twelve. Who had the most apple?"

"The same," Jason states. "They both get the same."

Arthur says, "But twelve is more than six. Everybody knows that."

"Wait a minute," interjects Samantha. "They each get one apple, right? So how could anybody get more? The pieces get smaller when you cut more of them."

"What do you think, Angie?" asks Jeannie.

"Samantha's right," Angie responds. "They only have one apple each. The pieces are different, that's all. Do you get that, Arthur? The twelve pieces are still one apple, the same as the six. The kids still have one apple each."

"OK. Right, I see how that works," says Arthur.

"Does everybody agree the twins both get the same?" asks Jeannie. The group members show agreement. Jason writes, "Both kids get the same."

"You got the answer pretty fast, Jason and Samantha," says Arthur. "And did a good job of explaining it, Angie."

CASE 13.6 Cooperative Learning

Comparing Economic Systems Cooperatively

Ms. Asuko has heard that cooperative learning, particularly the group investigation method, can be effective for teaching high school students. She is a bit doubtful but resolves to give it a try with a grade 12 unit on comparative economic systems.

She begins, "You have been doing group work in my class and know what is expected of participants and the group leader to work together well as a team. The group effectiveness sheets you used have helped you to work productively. You have discovered that learning through group work is significant and also fun. We are going to try a special form of group work. It is a cooperative learning method called 'group investigation.'" She explains that four heterogeneous groups of seven will be established and each group will be assigned a subtopic and workspace. She says, "Reference materials will be made available in the room, and others can be obtained from the school library or other sources. I will introduce the topic and provide a common topical outline that is to be followed by each group. Each group will research a subtopic and decide how they can present it in an interesting way to the rest of the class. I will debrief what has been presented and you will take a test based on questions submitted by each group. Grades will be a combination of group and individual scores. The topic you will be investigating is comparative economic systems." Ms. Asuko then assigns students to groups by topic (fascism, communism, socialism, and capitalism) and writes a work and reporting schedule on the chalkboard.

Most students appear interested, but Arden, a bright high achiever, asks, "Do I have to be part of a group? Can I do it all by myself?" Ms. Asuko replies, "No, I know you can do a very good job by yourself, but working effectively with others is an important consideration. Besides, effective group investigation often results in a deeper understanding than is possible when something is done independently. Give it a 'provisional try' to see if I am right." She then begins to introduce students to the elements of an economic system before she is to provide an outline that each group is to follow as it investigates its subtopic.

The following day, Ms. Asuko moves students into their groups to do two "ice-breaker" and "get-to-know-each-other-better" exercises. She then asks students to decide how they will approach their investigation.

CASE 13.7 Cooperative Learning

Significant First Nations Leaders

Mr. Sylvester is working through a unit on First Nations cultures. He wants to explore significant leaders in First Nations history. He has collected several key names, such as Chief Sitting Bull and Geronimo. He has put together a reading pack on five important First Nations leaders. It would take some time to teach each, so Mr. Sylvester has decided on a jigsaw approach. He has divided the class into five groups. These are the home groups. Each member of the home group has been given a different First Nations leader information pack. He asks his students to get together with the others who have the same material. These are his expert groups. He has given each expert group the same guiding questions: (1) In what period of time did the leader live? (2) In what region of North America? (3) Describe two significant events of the leader's life. (4) What was the leader's relationship with the white culture? (5) What main legacy did he leave?

The expert groups work away at their tasks. Some seem to have even broken into subgroups, with each working on one question. Mr. Sylvester then asks each expert to return to the home groups and complete a chart that outlines the names of the leaders and the answers to the questions. Mr. Sylvester is pleased with how hard the students have worked and he is looking forward to his discussion with the class. He is confident that each student will do well on the test he has prepared.

LINKING PRACTICE TO THEORY

What has been your experience with group work? What attitudes do you bring to the approach? How much preplanning seems to be involved? Many methods are suggested in this chapter. Try some of these and compare their strengths and weaknesses. Is more involved than you expected? What is the difference between collaborative and cooperative learning? Why is rapport with the whole class normally necessary before group work can be successful? What is the relationship between the theory in the text and the practice in your classroom? Were the guidelines helpful for giving meaning to your experiences?

Summary

Both collaborative and cooperative learning approaches stress teaching and learning from a "cooperative" rather than competitive or individualistic perspective. For either collaborative and cooperative learning to be effective, students must learn and use communication, interpersonal, and group skills.

Collaborative learning is an approach in which students interact or work together. Research shows that cooperative learning is effective, leading to greater academic achievement and positive social outcomes. Approaches to instruction in schools are often competitive, emphasizing individual achievement. This may not sit well with students from certain cultures. Students master knowledge by becoming experts in an area of knowledge and then by teaching this to other groups. Cooperative learning teaching methods can be particularly effective in bringing diverse students together. Students with different learning styles can make good contributions to the achievement of a group. The role of the teacher is critical.

Cooperative learning approaches teaching and learning from a cooperative rather than competitive or individualistic perspective. Research supports its effectiveness for academic and social gains and for reducing prejudice and discrimination. Students are divided into heterogeneous groups that are task and reward interdependent.

A data collection instrument you can use to evaluate group effectiveness is provided in Appendix 13.8.

Activities

WORKING IN GROUPS

1. You have been, and are, a member of several groups. What did these experiences teach you about yourself? About the way groups can operate? About how groups should be led?

2. Think about a situation in which conflict occurred in a group in which you were a member. How was the conflict handled? Could it have been handled better? How?

3. Should there be a difference in opening procedures between a long- and a short-term group?

4. Examine the room you are in now. How can it be best set up for a group meeting?

5. What are the most important things to consider near the final stage of the group? What do you think the group should be considering during the termination stage? What strategies would you suggest?

6. Form a group of from five to seven members. A classroom is also a group, albeit fairly large. What can teachers do at the beginning of the year to establish a cohesive, productive group? Brainstorm the kinds of conflict that might arise in a typical classroom. Provide suggestions for solving each kind of conflict.

7. Marks are sometimes allocated for the product of groups and for group operation. What problems does this pose, and how might these be overcome?

8. Engage in a formal debate on the following topic. "Resolved that use of group techniques by a teacher usually results in more management and discipline problems than for a teacher who does not use this instructional approach."

COLLABORATIVE LEARNING

1. In the last chapter you were asked to consider how much you gained when you performed some activity alone. Consider when you enjoyed being with others. How much did you learn? What skills did you develop? Share your findings with others in your group.

2. Join four or five others to play the "Cardinal Principles" game. Members cooperate to build a ten-card house. Each person is given two cards. Preplanning is not permitted. Proceeding clockwise, each student contributes one card at a time. Only four cards can be touching the table top, and no more than two cards can be laid flat. Eight

minutes are given. Debrief on your learning and feelings, and implications for effective group operation for achieving a task and having a harmonious, cohesive group.

3. Take part in a class discussion on the advantages and disadvantages of small-group learning. Follow this with a discussion on how to overcome the disadvantages.

4. Join a subject-interest group. Given five minutes, brainstorm as many topics in a subject area as you can think of that could lend themselves to using a small-group teaching method.

5. Join a subject group to examine the question, "What special classroom management and control considerations are present in the teaching of the subject, and how can these be best handled?" Assign one or two group effectiveness evaluators to collect data and report.

COOPERATIVE LEARNING

1. To help you understand cooperative learning, view the Johnson and Johnson video on *Circles of Learning,* which shows elementary and secondary classrooms where cooperative learning is used. Keep these questions in mind: (1) How are cooperative learning essentials manifested in these classrooms? (2) What problems arise and how can they be overcome?

2. Get into subject groups. Make a chart on the following interactive approaches to instruction: brainstorming, guided discussion, forums, panels, investigative groups, open discussions, debates, problem-solving groups, tutorial groups. The chart should have the following headings: name of interactive approach, example of approach, value (e.g., Investigative Group, examination of Darwin's impact on biology, very useful).

3. Consider a class you remember well in which you were a student. Describe briefly the class as a social group. Consider the friendships, communication patterns, roles, influences, and the like. Describe the class as a work group. Was it teacher or student centered? How successful was the class as a whole? What do you think is the relationship between the class as a social group and as a work group?

4. Select a subject topic that would benefit from discussion (e.g., We should still study Shakespeare in

school; Shakespeare should be dropped and more modern authors studied). Plan the class as both a guided discussion and as an open discussion. What are the merits of each?

5. Examine the following group roles: initiator, contributor, clarifier, evaluator, harmonizer, recorder, summarizer, and encourager. On cards, state: (a) the role that most suits you, and (b) the roles of two of your university classmates. Share and discuss your findings.

6. Cooperative learning does not just happen. The focus is on "we as a group" and not "I as an individual." Students need many skills to be successful in cooperative learning. Brainstorm what these skills are.

7. Schools are becoming more diverse in terms of ethnic background, economic background, and cognitive ability. How can such diversity be used to create effective learning situations?

8. Learn cooperative learning methods by using one of them, Jigsaw. Follow these steps:

Step 1: Introduction and overview of the activity.
Step 2: Formation of heterogeneous "home" groups, each with five or six members.

Step 3: Review of group functions; decision to practice specific functions and to monitor and evaluate them.

Step 4: Formation of "expert" groups; each home group is represented in each expert group. Expert groups will be formed for each cooperative learning model: (a) Jigsaw, (b) STAD, (c) TGT (d) group investigation, (e) cooperative games, (f) cooperative learning and prejudice.

Step 5: Expert groups receive training and use special materials explaining their topic.

Step 6: Expert groups prepare their procedure for tutoring home groups.

Step 7: Experts tutor (explain and drill) their home groups. Material is provided to aid in this activity.

Step 8: Progress of home groups is checked and groups prepare for testing.

Step 9: Each individual is part of an evaluation process that covers all the approaches.

Step 10: Results are posted for each group.

Step 11: Monitoring of both expert and home groups is provided for.

Step 12: The process is analyzed with the whole class.

APPENDIX 13.1   *Analysis of Personal Behavior in Groups*

MY BEHAVIOR IN GROUPS

Directions: Please circle the number that most nearly represents your normal behavior.
1 = much more often than most, 2 = more often than most, 3 = about average for the group,
4 = once in a while, and 5 = rarely or never.

Task Functions

1.	1	2	3	4	5	I offer facts, opinions, suggestions, ideas, and other relevant information.
2.	1	2	3	4	5	I ask for facts, opinions, suggestions, ideas, and feelings from others.
3.	1	2	3	4	5	I am a starter who proposes things to do to initiate action in the group.
4.	1	2	3	4	5	I help develop plans for how to proceed and keep the group on task.
5.	1	2	3	4	5	I summarize what has occurred to date and the major points made.
6.	1	2	3	4	5	I am a coordinator who pulls ideas together and harmonizes activities.
7.	1	2	3	4	5	I diagnose the difficulties the group has in working to achieve goals.
8.	1	2	3	4	5	I energize (stimulate) the group to achieve a higher quality of work.
9.	1	2	3	4	5	I apply the test of reality or practicality of ideas and alternatives.
10.	1	2	3	4	5	I evaluate, compare the standards and goals of the group with group decisions and what was accomplished.

Maintenance Functions

11.	1	2	3	4	5	I encourage others to participate, accept them, and am open to their ideas,
12.	1	2	3	4	5	I help solve conflicts and try to harmonize differences in opinion.
13.	1	2	3	4	5	I help cool tensions by joking, suggesting fun approaches or breaks.
14.	1	2	3	4	5	I use interpersonal skills and make sure that others understand each other.
15.	1	2	3	4	5	I check the climate by determining how members feel about the way the group is working and each other.
16.	1	2	3	4	5	I observe the process the group is using and help discover its effectiveness.
17.	1	2	3	4	5	I remind the group about its goals and standards and help keep it on task.
18.	1	2	3	4	5	I actively listen to others and am receptive to others' ideas.
19.	1	2	3	4	5	I support openness, encourage risk and individuality, and thus build trust.
20.	1	2	3	4	5	I encourage open discussion to solve conflicts and increase togetherness.

Based on the summary of task and maintenance functions provided by David and Richard Johnson
in Johnson, D., & Johnson, R. (2003). *Joining together: Group theory and group skills.* Boston:
Allyn & Bacon.

APPENDIX 13.2   *Group Participation Data Collection*

Assign each group member a number. When a contribution is made, under the appropriate heading, enter that number with a brief description of the behavior.

Behavior Description

Initiating (getting discussion going, helping the group organize, keeping the group moving toward the goal)

Contributing (offering opinions, facts, anecdotes, or examples that help the group solve problems or move on)

Clarifying (helping make sure that terms, the problem, and group member contributions are understood by all, suggesting that added information is needed)

Summarizing (keeping the group on track by providing stage or concluding summaries and making sure that everybody knows where everybody stands on a topic)

Evaluating (keeping track of how well the group is progressing and in a constructive way pointing out problems that are being encountered)

Recording (recording main points, reading the record back to help recall what was done and to check for accuracy)

Encouraging (listening carefully, being friendly and accepting, complimenting good contributions or effort)

Harmonizing (keeping peace, relieving tension [e.g., humor], settling disputes, working out compromises)

APPENDIX 13.3   *Small-Group Planning Guide*

Subject and Grade Level _____

Unit Name _____   Lesson Topic _____

Statement of the small-group tasks

Objectives to be achieved

Size of groups

How students are to be assigned to groups

Time allotment

Materials needed for each group

Meeting place for each group

Instructions given to groups regarding how they are to go about achieving their tasks

Interpersonal or group skills targets for groups

Evaluation criteria and method for task achievement

Evaluation criteria for interpersonal or group skills

APPENDIX 13.4   *Small-Group Discussion Data Collection Instrument*

PROFESSIONAL TARGET—SMALL GROUP DISCUSSION

Describe the actions, statements made, and student reactions.

Group Discussion Consideration	Descriptive Observations
1. Set, objectives, and tie-in to lesson	
2. How students are assigned to groups	
3. Group meeting place and time allocation assignments	
4. Instructions for group operation regarding academic task	
5. Instructions re interpersonal and group skills to be used	
6. Behavior of students during group operation	
7. Teacher interventions during group operation	
8. Reporting by groups and debriefing	
9. Assessment of groups' effectiveness	

APPENDIX 13.5   *Discussion Data Collection Instrument*

PROFESSIONAL TARGET—DISCUSSION

Record what was said and done and the reaction of pupils.

Discussion Skills	Observations

A. Focusing on topic
     Way topic was introduced
     Establishment of aims
     Restating of aims
     Irrelevancies redirected?
     Periodic summaries?
     Dealing with off-task behavior

B. Clarification of answers
     Paraphrasing
     Summarizing
     Probing
     Elaborating
     Analyzing

C. Promoting participation
     Use of students' ideas
     Use of silence
     Challenging
     Key questions
     Providing information

D. Varying interaction
     Setting of ground rules
     Use of eye contact
     Encouraging participation/interaction
     Seeking agreements

E. Closing discussion
     Summarizing
     Evaluation of discussion effectiveness
     Proposal(s) for follow-up

APPENDIX 13.6   *Cooperative Learning Target*

PROFESSIONAL TARGET—USING COOPERATIVE LEARNING GROUPS

Please describe what is said and done and how students react.

Aspects of the Teacher's Role	Descriptive Comments

1. *Arranging groups*
      Group size
      Heterogeneous assignments
      Time allotments
      Physical arrangements
      Providing materials

2. *Provision for positive interdependence*
      Providing the mutual goal
      Requiring sharing of resources
      Establishing the group and individual rewards

3. *Skill development*
      Explaining roles
      Identifying the interpersonal and group skills
      Practicing the skills

4. *Setting the task and goal structure*
      Stating the task and goal structures
      Checking for understanding

5. *Monitoring and providing feedback*
      Circulating and observing
      Helping with task achievement
      Helping with group maintenance
      Providing and using group-effectiveness instruments
      Providing for student self-evaluation

6. *Assessment*
      Providing quizzes or tests
      Assigning group and/or individual grades
      Using bonus marks
      Other kinds of recognition

APPENDIX 13.7   *Peer Evaluation Rubric*

Directions: Answer the following questions with (1) indicating the lowest and (4) indicating the highest amount of points. Who was your partner?

_____

Did this individual appropriately contribute to the group project?   1   2   3   4

Did this individual spend an appropriate amount of time developing materials?   1   2   3   4

Did this individual spend an appropriate amount of time typing?   1   2   3   4

Did this individual work collaboratively?   1   2   3   4

Was this individual motivated to help?   1   2   3   4

Did you have a positive experience collaborating with this individual?   1   2   3   4

Reflections: _____

_____

_____

_____

_____

_____

APPENDIX 13.8 *Group Effectiveness Data*

GROUP EFFECTIVENESS DATA COLLECTION SHEET

A chairperson and one or two group-effectiveness data collectors are appointed or elected. Observations are recorded objectively and findings are reported. Agreement about group effectiveness is reached and plans for making the group more effective are formulated.

Behavior	Description of Behavior

A. Chairperson

1. Seeing that problem is clarified

2. Discussion initiated and kept moving

3. All phases of problem brought out

4. Discussion kept on topic

5. Participation of all members encouraged

6. Stage and concluding summaries used

7. Statements rephrased if needed

8. Objectivity

9. Listening skills demonstrated

10. All persons treated with respect

11. Thoughts of group accurately reported

B. Participants

1. All members contribute reasonable amount

2. Ideas stated clearly and concisely

3. Prejudices kept out

4. Keeping on topic

5. Storytelling, digressions, showing off avoided

6. Helping others—phrasing ideas, clarifying, encouraging, listening

7. Respecting other's ideas/opinions

8. Not ridiculing, ignoring

9. Helping summarize, conclude

14 Teaching for Thinking and Problem-Based Learning

Thinking Skills and Processes

Problem solving is natural to young children because the world is new to them. They exhibit curiosity, intelligence, and flexibility as they face new situations. The challenge . . . is to build on children's innate problem-solving inclinations and to preserve and encourage a disposition that values problem solving. (Trafton & Midgett, 2001, p. 532)

As you teach, you want your students to think both critically and creatively about the subject matter. How can you ask questions to get them to think deeply? Can a thinking skill taught in one subject be used in another subject? Do your students think about their own thinking? Do you value their opinions and encourage them to take risks and try new ideas? The way teachers have been expected to teach has changed from transmission of knowledge (knowing content) to interpretation of knowledge (thinking about content), that is, that there should be much more emphasis on specifically teaching cognitive strategies. In other words, thinking skills and processes are highly important "content" too.

Recent focus on teacher effectiveness has been on acquisition of thinking skills (Peterson, Kromrey, Borg, & Lewis, 1990, p. 5). Research shows:

> Simply increasing teachers' awareness of the need to teach students how to think without providing training in the specific operations of teaching thinking has little chance of significantly changing classroom performance. . . . educators must systematically undertake specific training in higher order teaching in both preservice and inservice programs. (p. 10)

Eggen and Kauchak (2001) believe the best approach to teach for thinking occurs when it is taught explicitly *and* within the context of the regular curriculum (p. 343). Much earlier, Resnick (1987) said, "Higher order skills must suffuse the school program from kindergarten on and in every subject matter" (p. 48). An obstacle to the development of

OBJECTIVES

You will be able to:

1. Give reasons why thinking skills should be taught within the context of a subject.
2. Define and give examples of learning.
3. List examples of process and product learning.
4. Give examples of and use specific approaches to teaching thinking.
5. List and explain the advantages of higher-order thinking.
6. List and define thinking operations and core thinking skills.
7. Plan ways to encourage the development of dispositions needed for critical thinking.
8. Describe ways students can be taught critical and creative thinking skills.
9. Teach a cognitive skill and a cognitive process in a microteaching or classroom lesson.

Planning for Teaching a Thinking Skill

1. Specify skill label and definition
2. Determine the rules or steps in use of skill
3. Specify use of skill in the content studied
4. Decide how to model, explain, demo the skill
5. Decide how to provide guided/unguided practice
6. Decide how to evaluate
7. Decide how to transfer skill to other subjects
8. Decide how to transfer skill to life situations

Thinking Operations

Comparing
Classifying
Observing
Imagining
Hypothesizing
Criticizing
Collecting/organizing
Summarizing
Coding
Interpreting

Core Thinking Skills
(Marzano et al.)

Focusing
Information gathering
Remembering
Organizing
Analyzing
Generating
Integrating
Evaluating

Thinking Skills and Processes

Critical Thinking Procedures

Distinguish between facts and value claims
Discover reliability of sources
Check accuracy of statements
Distinguish between valid and invalid claims
Distinguish between what is irrelevant and irrelevant
Detect biases
Identify assumptions
Note the ambiguous/equivocal
Recognize inconsistencies
Determine argument strength

Thinking Creatively
(Rothstein)

Welcome class climate
Encourage exploration
Provide school time
Encourage broad interests
Foster the belief students can be more creative
Teach what's involved in being creative
Encourage acquisition and creative use of information

thinking skills is the growing demand for schools to teach more and more facts and information. "The idea that knowledge must be acquired first and that its application to reasoning and problem solving can be delayed is a persistent one in educational thinking" (p. 48). Arguably, the U.S. No Child Left Behind Act (NCLB), with its emphasis on standardized tests, tempts teachers to underemphasize teaching for thinking.

Beyer (1998) notes that teachers can provide a classroom learning environment that makes thinking possible and students willing to engage in it. You can make the invisible

The PBL Classroom

Teacher is facilitator/
  co-learner/mentor/guide

Faculty work in teams

Faculty structure is flexible

Students take responsibility/
  create partnerships

Structured problem is basis for
  course/motivation through
  real-life problems

Student initiative encouraged

Environment is collaborative
  and supportive

"One right answer" approach is
  is discouraged

Students evaluate themselves

**Creating a PBL Learning
Experience**

1. Identify a problem

2. Connect problem to
  students' world for authentic
  opportunities

3. Organize subject matter
  around the problem

3. Students define learning
  experience and plan how
  to solve problem

4. Encourage collaboration
  through learning teams

5. Students show results
  through a product or
  performance

**Problem-Based
Learning (PBL)**

PBL Characteristics

- Student centered
- Small groups
- Teacher as facilitator
- Problems as focus and stimulus
  for learning
- Problems vehicles for developing
  problem-solving skills
- Gain new information through
  self-directed learning

substance of thinking visible for students. This can provide students with an explicit guide and support for when they encounter difficult or complex thinking operations. Teachers should integrate instruction in thinking as they teach subject matter.

Importance of Thinking Skills and Processes

There is much controversy about the term *intelligence*. It is not easily quantified, and the debate about effects on intelligence of nature and of environment is ongoing. Intelligence is increasingly viewed as a set of *thinking skills and processes* that can be separately taught and learned. Of course, thinking skills are never "content" free; they are generic to, and can be applied to, all school subjects and used in daily life. While some believe "thinking"

TCP—THINKING SKILLS

*Uses specific instruction in the nature and use
of thinking skills and processes*

Specific instruction in the nature and use of thinking skills and processes; emphasis on problem-solving and critical thinking skills; objectives and evaluation reflect emphasis on thinking skill acquisition; asks many "why" and "what if" questions.

Sole focus on facts and information of an area of study; "right answer" emphasis; no opportunity for problem solving or critical thinking.

*Incorporates key thinking operations
and core thinking skills into teaching*

Key thinking operations such as comparing and classifying are a key part of teaching, as are the core thinking skills such as organizing and analyzing.

Teaching tends to focus on basic factual information that is accepted at face value without organizing material into new patterns through comparison, classification, and analysis.

Ensures that students use critical thinking procedures

Ensures students are familiar with the difference between facts and value claims, and that they check for bias, validity, and relevance in their research.

Students tend to accept all information at face value; little attempt by students to check material for bias, validity, and relevance; students unaware of critical thinking procedures.

is a matter of innate intelligence, many authorities acknowledge that "thinking" should be taught directly. They argue that there never is enough time to teach all the information that could usefully be taught and that we should reduce the time spent on teaching specific information and focus instead on teaching thinking skills. This is in harmony with the view of the teacher as a "learning facilitator" rather than an "information disseminator." The teacher, therefore, needs to facilitate transfer from one portion of a school subject to another, from one school subject to another, and from school to life. Perhaps the most important aspect of direct teaching of thinking as a skill is that it builds a youngster's self-image as a "thinker." Importantly, *problem-based learning* has been developed to help students acquire thinking skills and processes. In problem-based learning, students are presented with meaningful (authentic) situations to develop investigative, inquiry, and decision-making skills.

Also important is meta-cognition (thinking about one's thinking). Kuiper (2002), in a study of nursing practice and education, believes, "once learned, metacognition supports lifelong reflective thinking in divergent situations, enables one to handle ambiguity, assists with problem solving, promotes responsibility for actions, and fosters development of self-confidence for rapid decision making" (p. 78).

Organizing Knowledge and Learning

Learners can handle new information better if they understand how to organize it into patterns. Some approaches examined later in this chapter are coding and classification systems, comparing and contrasting, and sequencing.

Schooling must help students acquire strategies to organize information. Learners need ways to accomplish academic tasks. They need learning strategies (operating steps or patterns) to infer, predict, summarize, or hypothesize. Learning is *strategic*, in that there can be procedures or ways of executing a skill.

When students use certain learning strategies well, memory and comprehension are improved. Pressley and Harris (1990, p. 32) provide examples of effective strategies: summarization, imagery (creating an internal visual image of the content), activating prior knowledge (relating what is known to new content), self-questioning (composing questions that cut across different parts of the content), and question answering (teaching students to analyze questions as a part of attempting to answer them). When students can carry out a certain learning strategy well, they should be helped to learn when to use the strategy in new contexts across the curriculum—teaching for transfer.

The Importance of Thinking Well and Wisely

Sternberg (2003) suggests that the conventional approach to teaching creates "pseudo-experts"—students with expertise that does not mirror what is needed in real-world situations. He says we should teach for wisdom, "teaching them to think in the ways experts do" (p. 5). He suggests that teaching for *analytical thinking* means encouraging students to analyze, critique, judge, compare and contrast, evaluate, and assess; teaching for *creative thinking* means encouraging students to create, invent, discover, "imagine if," "suppose that," and predict; and teaching for *practical thinking* means encouraging students to apply, use, put into practice, implement, employ, and render practical what they know (p. 5).

In preparing students to think like experts, we "should teach children not only to think well, but also wisely" (p. 7). He claims, "those who have not learned to think wisely exhibit five characteristic fallacies in thinking" (p. 7):

1. The fallacy of unrealistic optimism (People think that they are so smart they do not think through what they do.)
2. The fallacy of egocentrism (People think the world centers around them. Wisdom requires one to know what one knows and does not know as well as what can be known and cannot be known.)
3. The fallacy of omniscience (People feel that they are not only experts in their fields, but also all-knowing about pretty much everything.)
4. The fallacy of omnipotence (The belief that if knowledge is power, then omniscience is total power. People who are in positions of power imagine themselves to be all-powerful.)
5. The fallacy of invulnerability (People's view that if they are all-knowing and all-powerful, they can do what they want.)

"Wisdom," Sternberg says, "is the use of successful intelligence and experience toward the attainment of a common good" (p. 7). This involves balancing three kinds of interests that should be informed by values: (1) intrapersonal (one's own); (2) interpersonal (other people's); (3) extrapersonal (more than personal—institutional).

Schools, then, should "consider the development of expertise in wisdom to be an important goal" (p. 7). This is because knowledge does not in itself create wisdom; wisdom provides a way to make important decisions and render important judgments, and wisdom represents an avenue to creating a better, more harmonious world (p. 7). Sternberg concludes that "an augmented conception of expertise takes into account wise and intelligent use of knowledge" (p. 8).

Classic Teaching Approaches

> Just as a traditional architect might borrow the fundamental elements and signature styling from a master architect, such as Frank Lloyd Wright, educators borrow from master craftspeople. They borrow from master cognitive psychologists and neurobiologists who have helped shape structures for the intellect. (Fogarty, 1999, p. 76)

Useful approaches are available to the novice teacher who wishes to teach thinking skills. The following names will be familiar. *John Dewey,* an American educator, was ahead of his time in suggesting that teachers must encourage the thinking and reflection of the child through the child's interaction with the world. Dewey wrote, "I believe that the only true education comes through the stimulation of the child's powers by the demands of the social situations in which he finds himself" (1933, p. 1). His writings make significant reading even today. *Jean Piaget,* a Swiss psychologist, recorded his observations of how children think. Many accept his model of child development and learning. To Piaget, the child cannot engage in certain intellectual tasks until he or she is psychologically ready. Children construct meaning—a concept further developed by Vygotsky and Bruner. Children are innately curious, love learning and asking questions. *Lev Vygotsky* (1978), a Russian psychologist, emphasized the social aspect of learning. He said, "Every function in the child's cultural development appears twice: first, on the social level, and later, on the individual level; first, between people (interpsychological) and then inside the child (intrapsychological). This applies equally to voluntary attention, to logical memory, and to the formation of concepts. All the higher functions originate as actual relationships between individuals" (p. 57). Vygotsky is known for the concept of the *zone of proximal development* (ZPD), the relationship between a student's actual and potential levels of development.

Other significant approaches to teaching thinking skills were developed by Bruner, Bloom, Wasserman, and Marzano.

Bruner: Content and Process

As early as 1967, Jerome Bruner introduced a theory of instruction that examined the relationship between *content* and *process.* Process is the cluster of diverse operations that surround the acquisition and use of knowledge. Through process, we use knowledge as a system for learning in contrast to only amassing information. Bruner said that curriculum should reflect not only the nature of knowledge, but also the process of acquiring it. Instruction should include the steps (stages, patterns, and behaviors) necessary to attain concepts or generalizations or to perform skills. Students need to learn the knowledge acquisition process to function well in a changing world.

Kearsley (2004) states that for Bruner, "learning is an active process in which learners construct new ideas or concepts based upon their current/past knowledge," and that "as far as instruction is concerned, the instructor should try and encourage students to discover principles by themselves. The instructor and student should engage in an active dialog (i.e., socratic learning). The task of the instructor is to translate information to be learned into a format appropriate to the learner's current state of understanding."

For Bruner, "a theory of instruction should address four major aspects: (1) predisposition towards learning, (2) the ways in which a body of knowledge can be structured so that it can be most readily grasped by the learner, (3) the most effective sequences in which to present material, and (4) the nature and pacing of rewards and punishments.

Good methods for structuring knowledge should result in simplifying, generating new propositions, and increasing the manipulation of information" (Kearsley, 2004).

Note again the emphasis on the thinking skills elements of discovery, active dialogue, building on what has been learned, and learner readiness.

Bloom's Taxonomy

Benjamin Bloom's cognitive taxonomy has been the most prevalent model for the teaching and learning of thinking skills. Many studies have used this taxonomy, hundreds of publications have referred to it, and many courses of study have been and are based on it. Many educators find the taxonomy useful as an instructional and evaluation tool. The taxonomy is described in Chapter 5.

Some authorities have concerns about Bloom's cognitive taxonomy and believe that teaching thinking skills should be done differently. Some instructional experts do not hold the notion that "knowledge" is low level and rote, but that knowledge often can be viewed in a more comprehensive way, it may be process or product, and declarative, procedural, or conditional. Few authorities now, including those who believe in Bloom's taxonomy, think the levels are strictly hierarchical or that learning must occur in a linear way.

Wasserman's Thinking Operations

Raths, Wasserman, Jonas, and Rothstein (1967) suggest that thinking skills or operations pertain to any school subject and level and that these can be taught. Their classification system is still widely used. By focusing attention on the teaching of thinking operations, they helped educators go beyond teaching for memorization of information. This is a good place for student teachers to start. By planning lessons that include a procedural (thinking skill or process) objective, you can modify your teaching to incorporate thinking skills. Raths, Wasserman, and Wasserman (1978, pp. 7–29) describe the following thinking operations.

1. *Comparing.* In the operation of comparing, students look for *similarities and differences*. We may choose two items for comparison that have a close relationship (e.g., two musical instruments); alternatively, we can select items that have more subtle relationships (e.g., a train and a caterpillar). Steps in comparing are (a) details are observed, (b) similarities are sought and sorted, (c) searching/sorting for differences, and (d) summarizing (in a list). Comparing activities lead students to additional insights and awareness. As a result of many experiences in making comparisons, students learn how to observe perceptively and compare before drawing conclusions.

2. *Observing.* When we are observing, we can make visual observations of data. Observing also can involve listening, touching, or smelling. The sense evidence used must be checked for accuracy. Students must be made aware of the possibility of distortion and thus false inference and misinterpretation. We want perceptiveness, acuity, and accuracy. Reporting is needed for the accuracy of observation to be checked. Observing should lead to more accurate data on which to base conclusions, and to greater understanding. Like any other skill, practice is required for proficiency.

3. *Classifying.* Classifying involves examining an assortment of items and sorting them into related groups. Each grouping is given a name. When they are classifying, students can process data mentally and organize them systematically. Ability to classify helps us bring order into our lives. Classifying requires three steps: (a) examining data, (b) creating categories, and (c) placing items in categories. The first two require advanced mental

activity and the third requires lower mental skills. We usually should avoid providing students with the categories so that students can exploit the full cognitive potential of this operation. Classification involves discovery of similarities and differences (as in comparing). Students should discover that, though a number of groupings are possible, each must have internal consistency. Normally, only one principle at a time is operative as groupings are established.

4. *Imagining.* For imagining, students are asked to let their minds travel to whatever vistas they can invent, to create freely and to exercise that part of the mind that often goes untapped. In imagining there is a release from rules and regulations and unbinding from data. Divergent thinking is promoted. Imagining leads to creations and inventions; it brings humor, joy, spontaneity, and beauty into our lives. A feeling of accomplishment and enhanced self-concept can result from this rich inner resource.

5. *Hypothesizing.* For the hypothesizing operation, students are to come up with a variety of possible explanations (hunches) for a question, problem, or situation. Hypothesizing involves identifying alternative possibilities and deciding which have the most credibility. High school students can be asked to go a step further to find ways of testing their hypotheses (which carries the operation to greater sophistication). Steps can be: (a) present the problem, (b) have students suggest ways to solve the problem, (c) have these ways considered and combined if appropriate, (d) ask students to anticipate what would happen if suggested solutions were tried, and (e) have students select a hypothesis. Hypothesizing helps free us from dogmatic assertions, from seeing life from only one perspective, and from "black or white" judgments. It lets students deal with problems in school learning and in their daily lives.

6. *Criticizing.* In the criticizing operation we ask students to "evaluate," "make judgments," and "offer opinions" to sharpen their sense of what is desirable or undesirable, high or low quality, and significant or trivial. Students should specify the *criteria* (standards) they use in making judgments. They should identify the evidence on which their judgments were made. Criticizing lets students use a higher level of cognition and sharpen the thinking skills that will improve the quality of their lives.

7. *Looking for assumptions.* Making an assumption means taking something for granted. In situations where a conclusion is drawn or a decision is being made, one or more assumptions enter. What we take for granted (or assume) may only be "probably true" or "probably false." Through this operation students can learn to identify assumptions (ones made themselves or those made by others). Learning to differentiate between what is assumed to be true and what is observable fact is at the heart of logical reasoning. Discrimination—scrutiny of assumptions—should occur. When students become skilled at identifying and examining assumptions, they will be less susceptible to propaganda, seductive advertising, and accepting experimental data as proof and conclusions as "right." They will be less likely to leap to conclusions that are based on limited data and less impulsive in their actions. Studying and practicing this skill is particularly important.

8. *Collecting and organizing data.* The ability to collect and organize information requires several skills: (a) locating information (deciding what are the proper references or appropriate sources, then locating those sources); (b) examining the data and selecting those that are relevant to the inquiry; (c) developing procedures that allow data to be assembled; and finally, (d) organizing data. That is, once sources are identified and tapped, the information culled and gathered, data should be organized. It can be organized into essays, reports, research proposals, menus, almanacs, and bibliographies, to name a few pos-

sibilities. Organizing data systematically, logically, and coherently is a complex task and sharpens our ability to locate and comprehend information.

9. *Summarizing.* Summarizing requires condensing and distilling the core message from a piece of work. Students must be able to state, briefly and coherently, the main ideas of something they have heard, seen, or read. Summarizing should be concise but not miss the big ideas. It involves differentiating between what is important and what may be left out. Summarizing skills increase students' abilities to understand. They develop the ability to discriminate and to discern the relevant from irrelevant, significant from insignificant, and consequential from trivial.

10. *Coding.* Codes communicate ideas in "shorthand." For example, an editor uses a shorthand code to communicate aspects of a manuscript to an author. As a thinking operation, coding is a shorthand system for pointing out thought patterns or expressions in the writings or speech of others. To illustrate, the code "X" can be used to identify extreme words and phrases such as "always," "never," "everybody" or "the best," "the worst," or "the only." "E-O" can be used to point out words and expressions of the "either–or" type. "Q" could be "qualifying expressions." "V" can be used to designate "value statements." As students use coding to examine utterances of others, they become more responsible for what they say.

11. *Interpreting.* Interpreting involves explaining the meaning that an experience (story, event, picture, film, poem, graph, chart, joke, body language, etc.) has for us. When we interpret, we put meaning into, and take meaning out of, a body of data. Our interpreting ability is dependent on how well we "read messages." We may misinterpret, which can get us into trouble. Sometimes we miss the meaning. Or we may generalize on insufficient evidence (going beyond the data to draw conclusions). Skillful interpretation increases meaning and understanding; continually misinterpreting severely handicaps the ability to understand and derive satisfaction from experiences.

Marzano's Core Thinking Skills Approach

A second approach to teaching basic thinking operations, that of Marzano, Brandt, Hughes, Jones, Presseisen, Rankin, and Suhor (1988), places core thinking skills into a schema or framework. It sets out eight major categories that are closely related to the steps one might follow in problem solving. Within the master schema, there are twenty-one subprocesses. With this framework, teachers can gradually understand how to use the skills.

Facts and information are the important raw materials for thinking. Knowing how, and having the skills to access and use these to "think," is at least as important! Marzano et al. suggest *core thinking skills* that occur in thinking processes. It should be noted the skills are not always sequenced exactly as in the pattern presented. These skills are outlined in the Hughes (Hughes & Jones, 1988) model (Figure 14.1).

- *Focusing.* Focusing occurs as we (1) define the problem (what is it, who has it, examples of it, when it must be solved, and what makes it a problem) and (2) set goals (short- and long-term outcomes).
- *Information gathering.* Information-gathering skills are brought to play as we (3) observe (pick relevant information) and (4) ask questions (clarify issues and meanings).
- *Remembering.* Remembering takes place when we (5) encode (repeat information, use associations or mnemonics; new information to make it accessible when needed) and when we (6) recall (bring to consciousness, surface when, where, or how information was originally learned).

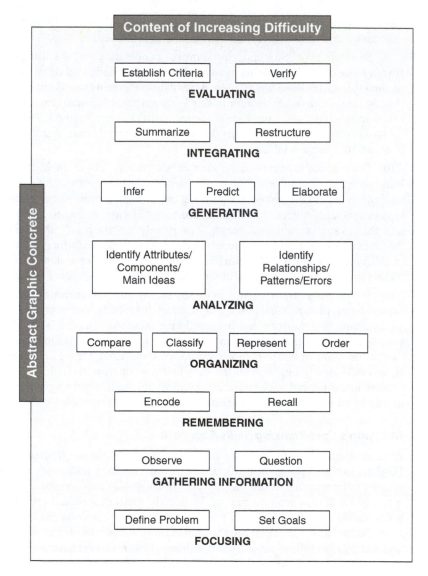

FIGURE 14.1 *Core Thinking Skills—The Hughes Model*

Source: Hughes & Jones, 1988; Marzano, Brandt, Hughes, Jones, Presseisen, Rankin, & Suhor, 1988.

- *Organizing.* Information is organized through (7) comparing (identifying similarities and differences), (8) classifying (grouping, categorizing, or sequencing items), (9) ordering, and (10) representing (showing how elements are related).
- *Analyzing.* This information is analyzed and checked for accuracy as (11) attributes and components are identified (recognizing, putting parts into a whole), (12) relationships and patterns are determined (identifying interrelationships), (13) main ideas and (14) errors are identified.

- *Generating.* We may generate new ideas by (15) inferring (identifying what reasonably may be true), (16) predicting (anticipating what will likely happen), and (17) elaborating (adding details, explanations, and giving examples).
- *Integrating.* We integrate what we have learned and come to a solution through (18) summarizing (condensing, selecting, and combining) and (19) restructuring (combining new knowledge with old into something new).
- *Evaluating.* So we can evaluate, (20) criteria are established and the solution is (21) verified. (pp. 68–114)

Carolyn Hughes (Hughes & Jones, 1988) adds a useful visual view (Figure 14.1) of the Marzano et al. skills. She thinks that content can be of increasing difficulty and that teachers should recognize that teaching/learning experiences (concrete, graphic, and abstract) should match learner readiness. Other approaches to core skills are Beyer's (1984) decision-making steps, and Baron and Sternberg's (1987) suggestions for selecting training skills programs.

Linking New Information to Prior Knowledge

Jones, Palincsar, Ogle, and Carr (1987) observe that researchers believe "information is stored in memory in [interrelated] knowledge structures called schemata" (p. 7). Learners draw on these memory banks as they reflect and make plans (p. 7). This is apparent when a person links previous experience to the solution of a problem or when he compares previous attempts to solve a problem (p. 8)—meta-cognition is involved. The ability to link new information with previous experiences is affected by several factors. One's perspective affects how new information is viewed (e.g., perspectives differ if a person views a proposed building site from an excavation-cost frame of reference rather than effect on environmental). Other variables relate to the characteristics of the learner. Lack of information or unorganized information can limit a person's ability to see patterns, chunk information, or derive analogies, and recognize similarities and differences between problems (p. 9).

Research shows that (1) success in learning situations often depends on the presence of specific previous knowledge, and (2) having prior knowledge is not enough if it cannot be accessed or if the learner cannot relate it to new information. It is important to build on what students know and the skills they have learned. Students may already know how to compare or paraphrase. For example, students must have learned, or must learn, skills such as encoding, organizing, and retrieving information (Jones et al., 1987, pp. 9–10).

Jones et al. (1987) contend that less able students may need explicit instruction in the use of thinking skills and that content and skills instruction should be adjunct to minimize interference. Instruction in strategic skills for the less able should have a strong content emphasis, and application to content areas should receive much attention. Instruction for other students should include thinking skills "within the context of content courses" (p. 17). Stress the transfer of strategic skills to alternative content areas.

Current Issues and Teaching Approaches

The Importance of Process

The *California Assessment Program* includes processes in measuring science and mathematics. Distinguishing between content and process learning is similar to distinguishing between subject-centered and child-centered education. It can be said that process learning is learning for the future, and content learning is learning about those things already discovered, formulated, restructured, and deemed important.

Teachers need to provide for the learning of process. A major decision in teaching is deciding when to extract procedural knowledge from the whole act. The dilemma of whether to teach a process directly or in the context of (embedded in) the curriculum is a concern. Both approaches are appropriate at times, and both are essential. If process is taught directly, provision must be made for transfer.

It is increasingly apparent that teaching for thinking must be a top educational priority if high school graduates are to take their place in our technically oriented society. Current school programs are not adequate. Much more school time must be devoted to thinking skills and integration of these across the K–12 curriculum. Too many students cannot respond effectively and critically to their environment.

An approach to the teaching of process you can use is shown in Figure 14.2. Be aware that teaching process is complicated and requires time and energy. In the long run, emphasis on processes can help achieve the more general goals of education. You will need to learn how to assess "process" learning. If you resort to "product" assessment only, the original purpose is defeated (see Baron & Sternberg, 1987, p. 224). Proper assessment requires the student to apply the process in a new context to see if transfer has occurred.

Processes normally include two or more thinking skills. All humans, by their very nature, are thinkers. As teachers, we want to help students think better, regardless of developmental stage. In addition to basic skills and facts, it is possible to identify higher-order skills and advance knowledge, that is, *content* and *process*. A danger is overemphasis on replication and application and underemphasis on *associative uses* or webs of associations students have and the *interpretive uses* or translation of ideas and giving meaning.

FIGURE 14.2   *Product- and Process-Oriented Classrooms*

The Product-Oriented Classroom	The Process-Oriented Classroom
− The teacher emphasizes, "What did you do?"	+ The teacher also emphasizes, "How did you do it?"
− Tasks revolve around items of content.	+ Tasks involve a "process" of learning.
− The answer is most important.	+ The means of finding an answer is as important as the answer.
− The teacher believes there is a body of content.	+ The teacher recognizes that content is only one component of the learning process to cover.
− The teacher evaluates the product.	+ The teacher also evaluates the process.
− The student "does."	+ The student "does" and thinks about what s/he did.
− The student often lacks an awareness of how s/he learns.	+ The student has a growing awareness of how s/he learns and can learn.
− Learning takes place through factual knowledge acquisition.	+ Learning occurs when students work through a process in which knowledge is manipulated and restructured to reach insight.
− Problem-solving skills develop automatically while learning the content.	+ Problem-solving skills develop while learning content and reflection on the process occurs while working with content.

Source: Contact, Canada Studies Foundation, Toronto.

Education must move beyond memory to educating minds. This is what schooling *should* be about. An approach to the teaching of process is illustrated in Figure 14.3.

There are three promising approaches to the teaching of thinking: *stand-alone, embedding,* and *immersion.* There is considerable material available to help you teach thinking skills through the stand-alone approach, for example, material by Wasserman (1978). Over the years, hundreds of workshops have treated teaching for thinking, critical thinking, and creative thinking in a generic way. The embedding approach builds thinking skills into the regular school subjects, as does the immersion approach. In the former, but not in the latter, thinking skills are made explicit. Embedding is the most commonly accepted. For most students, it is necessary to be explicit. In general, teachers must decide when practice on specific skills is necessary for automaticity. Better understanding occurs when skills are extracted and studied in isolation *as well as* in context. Apparently, "to be caught, it must be taught," and if transfer is to occur to other parts of a subject, to other subjects, and to life, this, too, must be "taught."

Not all basic knowledge should be taught before thinking skills. For instance, various forms of sequencing can be taught at an early age, and young learners can be taught and encouraged to develop their own sequencing system. The classroom should be interactive and activity oriented to foster learning and applying thinking processes and skills.

Teachers need to make decisions about the timing and activities for learning explicit cognitive skills and see that these skills are transferred to various contexts. This is especially true with young learners and those who have difficulty with the processes. Very often, those who complain about achievement in schooling are actually complaining about the lack of use of these skills in higher education and the workplace. Paul (1990) believes the issue is complex. The teacher must make decisions to assure growth in both procedural knowledge and system use and meaning, or the atomistic versus the holistic dilemma.

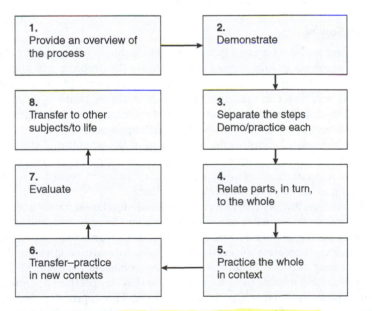

FIGURE 14.3   *An Approach to the Teaching of Process*

Dialectical Thinking

Another level of thinking to include in your teaching is the *dialectical.* "The first charac-teristic of dialectical thinking is that it places all the emphasis on change. . . . the second characteristic . . . is that it states that the way change takes place is through conflict and opposition" Rowan (2004). Using dialectical thinking is a bit like arguing with yourself. Barry and Rudinow (1994) believe that *dialectical thinking* is the ability to reflect criti-cally on personal thinking and to reason sympathetically using a frame of reference dis-tinct from or even opposed to that frame of reference. This could be called *reflective self-criticism.* Though Barry and Rudinow's suggestions are more appropriate for middle years and high school students, they can be adapted for elementary students.

The first step in the Barry and Rudinow plan is to pose a question for discussion, without presupposing a position. After preliminary discussion and clarification, students take positions they prepare to defend. They ask questions about the other positions and answer questions on their view. In teams with predetermined positions, various roles can be assigned and reassigned for practice. Then, each team prepares a defense to a position to which it was initially opposed. The exercise is recorded so students can review and cri-tique their performances. Variations of this strategy can be created.

Affective and Cognitive Strategies

An excellent web site, The Critical Thinking Community (www.criticalthinking.org) gives a strategy list of thirty-five dimensions of critical thought. It shows how the list can be used in remodeled lesson plans that add the critical thinking dimension. The full list is at www.criticalthinking.org/resources/TRK12-strategy-list.shtml.

Although Pettus and Blosser (2002) think it is important to teach thinking skills to students, they believe "students can creatively develop numerous strategies to aid their re-call of information and concepts. Frequently, they develop more up-to-date and relevant strategies and devices than their teachers" (p. 14).

Problem Solving

Students face problems every day, whether with schoolwork, peers, or at home. Students approach problems in four ways: (1) they ignore the problem and hope it will go away, (2) they ignore the problem and don't care if it goes away, (3) they attempt to solve the problem as best they can even though they do not have training in problem solving, or (4) they approach the problem in a sound and systematic way, having been taught how to do this. You can help students follow the fourth approach.

Problem solving requires the application of knowledge and skills to obtain a solu-tion or achieve a goal. Transfer of learning to a new situation must occur. Problem solv-ing has two aspects: recalling or acquiring the information needed to solve a problem, and following an effective problem-solving procedure.

At one time it was thought that problem solving should follow a sequence of problem definition, suggesting possible causes of the problem (hypotheses), and testing each hypoth-esis. The modern approach is based on what has been learned about how people process in-formation. Expert problem solvers do not begin by suggesting a large number of hypotheses and then testing each one. First they narrow the problem down by deciding the key features of the problem and relating these to information they have at their fingertips or can look up. Then they pick one or a few hypotheses for testing. This approach is time saving and works well because experts do not spend time investigating low-probability hypotheses. The approach requires rapid and accurate problem definition and pattern recognition. Students can be taught how to seek patterns, strategies, and thinking skills they can use to solve problems.

Sternberg (1990) emphasizes that students should discover problems for themselves. Life problems are not well structured, so application of rigid steps often does not work. School problems are usually decontextualized. Problem-solving steps may work for text problems but not "real" ones. Students who care about a problem, because it is theirs, are motivated to face it. Schools normally stop short of being practical; it is important to provide for transfer to life. Sternberg emphasizes that students must be taught how to plan to solve problems and the thinking skills to use.

Begin by having students learn problem-solving steps. When you do this, you help them discover how they like to represent problems—some can just think of the key features, others need to write these down, and others need a visual representation. While we should learn from experience, we often are prisoners of our experiences. Students can learn from experience, to break the chains of tradition and strive for novelty. Real-life problems rarely have a single solution, so students should guard against a "one-right-answer" expectation. At times a problem can be set aside for a while; after incubating, the answer may seem to "jump out." Rothstein (1990) suggests things you can do to help students improve their problem-solving ability.

- *Provide a climate that allows risk taking*. Encourage students to look at problems creatively and provide incubation time. Be accepting and sensitive to students' feelings.
- *Show students how to define the problem*. A problem that is well defined is "half-solved." Make sure students recognize the need to define the problem before they start to solve it. Help them learn to seek the essential features of the problem.
- *Teach students how to do problem analysis*. They should learn to differentiate between essential and nonessential information. Have them ask what materials they have to work with and how these can be used to solve the problem.
- *Have students learn to generate hypotheses*. They should not seek a hypothesis prematurely. Provide instruction and practice in the important skill of brainstorming.
- *Show students how to evaluate each hypothesis*. Students should learn not to jump to conclusions. Have them set criteria for evaluating hypotheses and record the implications or consequences of several hypotheses. Then have them select the best or combine hypotheses.
- *Teach students to recognize factors that affect problem solving*. Factors that influence problem-solving ability are acquiring the necessary information, defining the problem, and letting the problem incubate.
- *Show students how to use analogies*. Encourage students to seek cases that are similar to their problem and the solutions that were successful for these. This reduces the number of errors that will be made and the time needed to solve a new problem.
- *Have students practice solving problems and provide feedback*. They should be encouraged while they are practicing, and feedback should focus on the problem-solving process used rather than getting "the right answer" (pp. 268–270).

Problem-based learning is examined further later in this chapter.

Thinking and Decision Making

Decision making involves making a selection from among alternatives. It is a process (like problem solving, conceptualizing, and reflective thinking) that involves several thinking skills. *Decision making* usually involves (1) stating the desired goal or condition; (2) stating the obstacles; (3) identifying alternatives for overcoming each obstacle; (4) examining alternatives in terms of resources needed and constraints to their use; (5) ranking alternatives in terms of probable consequences; and (6) choosing the best alternative.

Using Questioning to Encourage Thinking

Questioning techniques were discussed in Chapter 8. Questions can be categorized into a hierarchy from low-level (facts and comprehension) through application to high-level (analysis, synthesis, and evaluation). Emphasis on higher-cognitive questions is more effective, particularly for students of average and high ability, while emphasis on fact questions is effective in mastery of basic skills (particularly for lower-ability students). Teachers often emphasize closed, single-right-answer, low-level questions, when emphasis on open-ended, higher-cognitive-level questions would be more effective. You learned how the use of probes and redirects can lead to higher-level thinking and that teacher acceptance of student ideas is positively correlated with student learning gains. Wait time of at least three seconds is critical, particularly for higher-level questions. Students should be encouraged to respond, and responses should be balanced among volunteers and nonvolunteers. Correct responses should be acknowledged, and praise should be used specifically and discriminately. The quality of teacher questioning, use of encouragement, and involvement and acceptance of students are important. The way you respond during question and answer affects whether thinking skills are being developed. Students should feel accepted, able to take risks; and using open-ended questions and sufficient wait time encourages thinking.

Examples of questions that encourage thinking are provided by King (1990). These questions and other ideas on encouraging thinking are available at the University of Texas at Austin's Division of Instructional Information and Assessment web site, www.utexas.edu/academic/diia/gsi/coursedesign/advanced.php.

- How would you use . . . to . . . ?
- What is a new example of . . . ?
- Explain why. . . .
- What do you think would happen if . . . ?
- What is the difference between . . . and . . . ?
- How are . . . and . . . similar . . . ?
- What is a possible solution to the problem of . . . ?
- What conclusions can you draw about . . . ?
- How does . . . affect . . . ?
- In your opinion, which is best . . . ? Why?
- What are the strengths and weaknesses of . . . ?
- Do you agree/disagree with this statement: . . . ?
- How is . . . related to . . . that we studied . . . ?

Symptoms present in classrooms with little encouragement for student thinking are:

- Extreme impulsiveness (emphasis is on doing, without much thinking behind it)
- Overdependency ("Tell me what to do, teacher")
- Dogmatic assertions ("Don't confuse me with data, my mind is made up")

- Inability to apply learned principles to new situations ("What am I s'pozed to do here?")
- Over-anti-intellectualism ("It's your job to tell us what to do")

Traditional expository teaching, characterized by teacher-dominated explaining, telling how, and showing, makes students passive rather than active. Learners need to be involved in acquiring knowledge. Provide acceptance, support, probes, and encouragement to think. Learning that emphasizes thinking is fragile, involving emotions, pressures, and the self-concept of students, dynamics of the class group, and the attitudes of the teacher.

Teaching for Thinking and Transfer

One of the most debated issues in the teaching of thinking is transfer. If you want transfer, teach for it. It should be emphasized in both the set and closure of a lesson and used gradually in more contexts until it is applied in contexts in which learners themselves seek transfer from previous learning.

Acquisition of thinking skills or processes includes *declarative* knowledge. Like a concept, the meaning of a process is always under construction. Thinking processes can even be taught to very young children through activity-oriented classrooms that have many opportunities for idea construction. Unfortunately, a recent study of first graders doing reading seatwork found that getting an activity done was more important than making sense of what they were doing. This suggests that teachers should emphasize the understanding and use of thinking skills.

Evaluation and Thinking

Not only should thinking skills be taught directly, they also should be part of evaluations. That is, if we want students to know and be able to transfer the use of specific thinking skills to new contexts, this must be part of the "reward system." Marks should be specifically allocated for how students use thinking skills in the subject they are studying (not just for recall of information or "getting the right answer"). If student progress using thinking processes and skills is not part of assessment, learning may degenerate to recall of content. The lowest level of evaluation is repeating a thinking skill in its simplest form and in a context already used. To extend evaluation, a skill must be evaluated as it is used in a slightly different context. Many approaches are necessary: written and oral, descriptions, recordings, broad and narrow, standardized, and self-monitoring.

Steps that you can follow when planning to teach a thinking skill are illustrated in Figure 14.4 on page 460.

Action Research

We believe that most teachers, at all ages and grade levels, are concerned about teaching for thinking. Pre- or inservice teachers can be helped to structure their work in this direction. Emphasize professional development and collaborative action research in which you begin with a structured position and, through an interactive and reflective approach, are led to a refinement of professional judgment. A research approach to development is pertinent for teaching thinking because of the political and moral aspects of thinking in various cultures. Related learning from research in early childhood, middle years, secondary, and adult education can provide a wealth of background. For instance, reading itself can be considered a higher-order thinking skill.

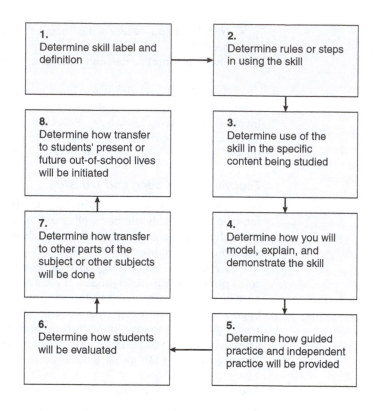

1. Determine skill label and definition

2. Determine rules or steps in using the skill

8. Determine how transfer to students' present or future out-of-school lives will be initiated

3. Determine use of the skill in the specific content being studied

7. Determine how transfer to other parts of the subject or other subjects will be done

4. Determine how you will model, explain, and demonstrate the skill

6. Determine how students will be evaluated

5. Determine how guided practice and independent practice will be provided

FIGURE 14.4 *Steps in Planning to Teach a Thinking Skill*

Critical and Creative Thinking

Critical Thinking

> Few educators . . . oppose the idea of getting students to think more critically . . . yet rhetoric outstrips practice. (Case & Wright, 1999, p. 179)

You want to help your students become good thinkers, people who think critically. Critical thinking, which many agree involves the use of skills, is a very cerebral thing. It should not be misconstrued that the skills are to be used in a mechanistic way. Having students acquire critical thinking capability needs to be a prime objective of all teachers, not something to be covered if and when the subject matter of the curriculum or textbook has been covered (Case & Wright, 1999, p. 179). To become critical thinkers, students need instruction on what is involved in doing critical thinking, interesting content, opportunity to practice it, and assessments of their attempts at critical thinking.

What Is Critical Thinking?

What is critical thinking? There is disagreement about what qualifies as critical thinking. Most authorities agree that critical thinking involves abilities, background concepts and information, and certain dispositions. Case and Wright (1999) ask, "Of what value in becoming a better thinker is there in asking students to assess the pro and con arguments on an issue if they are profoundly unaware of the standards they should use in critiquing competing pieces of evidence?" (p. 181). While most think dispositions (attitudes) and tools (skills) are involved, some, including McPeck (1990), believe there are no general abilities. It can be argued, however, that there are dispositions and tools that can be learned and transferred in a way that recognizes the uniqueness of disciplines, issues, or situations.

Scriven and Paul (1996) say that critical thinking is "the intellectually disciplined process of actively and skillfully conceptualizing, applying, analyzing, synthesizing, and/or evaluating information gathered from or generated by, observation, experience, reflection, reasoning, or communication, as a guide to belief and action." Earlier, Norris (1985) said, "Critical thinking is deciding rationally what to or what not to believe." Critical thinking can be summarized as "the ability to think about one's thinking so as to recognize its strengths and weaknesses and, as a result, redo and improve the thinking in improved form" (Scriven & Paul, 1996). In a nutshell, "Critical thinking . . . means making reasoned judgments" (Beyer, 1995, p. 8). Whatever the definition, the purpose is to, through questioning and inquiry while being sensitive to context, achieve understanding, evaluate points of view, and solve problems. The process of critical thinking is fundamental to education. For our purposes, we define *critical thinking* as fair-mindedly interpreting, analyzing, or evaluating information, arguments, or experiences with a set of reflective attitudes, skills, and abilities to guide our thoughts, beliefs, and actions. In short, critical thinking involves evaluating the credibility of information.

Critical Thinking Dispositions and Attitudes

Being able to think critically begins with an attitude of being disposed to consider, in a thoughtful and perceptive way, the problems and subjects of aspects of life. When we include critical thinking in schooling, we must emphasize, model, and encourage critical thinking dispositions. You can help your students develop critical thinking abilities by teaching them how to objectively and open mindedly seek answers to questions and problems, and teaching them how to investigate the causes of events. You can model and promote intellectual honesty, even though evidence challenges personally cherished beliefs. Students need to learn the importance of flexibility and have, but not be inhibited by, healthy skepticism until adequate evidence is surfaced. A patient, persistent, and systematic approach to arriving at conclusions and resolving differences needs to be valued, as does the attitude of respect for other points of view after listening carefully to those views.

Procedures and Skills

Authorities disagree about what is involved in critical thinking and when, where, and how it should be taught. We believe that critical thinking should be taught in both a generic and a subject-specific sense. It should not be taught in isolation, whether as a stand-alone topic or as part of a discipline, without providing for transfer—that's the important thing. If students practice critical thinking, content is *always* required—whether from a school subject or some other source. If, for example, it is taught as part of social studies, the teacher needs to help students bridge to, for example, science, English, and other subjects. Critical thinking in social studies is like critical thinking in science, is like critical thinking in solving a community issue, is like making a meaningful decision in a business, and is like making an appropriate choice about a personal quandary. Transfer may not occur unless you deliberately point out transfer possibilities and have students acquire the disposition to seek transfer to new situations.

Sternberg (1985) believes that teaching for critical thinking, "as it usually is done, inadequately prepares students for the kinds of problems they will face in everyday life"

(p. 277). He adds, "good thinking in one academic area does not guarantee good thinking in another." His solution is to have programs that sample a variety of content areas and thinking skills in a way that is "true to the way problems appear in our everyday lives" (p. 278). Critical thinking procedures and skills can be taught! Students need to practice this and, importantly, to practice discovering problems for themselves. Beyer's (1984) list of procedures may well have relevance today:

1. Distinguishing between verifiable facts and value claims
2. Determining the reliability of a claim or source
3. Determining the accuracy of a statement
4. Distinguishing between warranted or unwarranted claims
5. Distinguishing between relevant and irrelevant information, claims, or arguments
6. Detecting biases
7. Identifying stated and unstated assumptions
8. Identifying ambiguous or equivocal claims or arguments
9. Recognizing logical inconsistencies in a line of reasoning
10. Determining the strength of an argument (p. 557)

Paul and Elder (2001) describe intellectual traits that help critical thinking: intellectual humility, courage, empathy, autonomy, integrity, perseverance, confidence in reason, and fair-mindedness. Critical thinking, it can be argued, requires a set of dispositions (or attitudes) *and* specific processes and skills. These dispositions need to be taught (refer to Chapter 4).

The ability to think critically involves behavior that can be learned. One can examine the problem, identify the key issues, and ask the following questions: Are there any underlying assumptions? What generalizations can be safely made? What credible sources might shed light on the problem? What have we previously learned about the problem? What kinds of data are relevant? How adequate is the data? Is data presented in a biased or distorted way? How consistent and relevant is our argumentation? What can we do to ensure that personal bias does not affect what we do? What conclusions and possible solutions can be posed? What are the pros and cons of each potential solution. Which solution or what combination of solutions appears best? How can we test the solution or combination of solutions? If the test is not passed, what can be done to arrive at another possible solution to be tested?

Creative Thinking

TCP—CREATIVE THINKING

Ensures that students think creatively

Encourages creative potential of students; welcomes novel and imaginative responses; uses divergent approaches; models creativity and allows open-ended expression; experiential, inductive, and hands-on approaches.

Creativity not apparently welcomed; reliance on standard information; only "right" answers welcome; little attempt to encourage novel, imaginative, and creative ideas.

Creativity is not a single process. Though we recognize and value creative thinking, it defies precise description. *Creative thinking* can be viewed as forming new combinations of ideas to fulfill a need or as thinking in a way that produces original and appropriate results. Creativity has been linked to divergent thinking and originality of thought or execution. Although something can be creative (original) for an individual, it need not be original to mankind. Creativity is found in all areas of life and is not limited to the arts, to geniuses, or to the talented. Creative thinking should be structured into the curriculum and encouraged through open-ended challenges.

Teaching for Creativity

Every student has creative potential. Creativity can conflict with established rules, procedures, and patterns, and what is "correct." When you promote creativity, expect a mixture of novel, imaginative, and valuable answers, and also answers that may seem silly or bizarre. Let students think, solve problems, and use divergent ideas.

Teaching for creativity includes teaching thinking skills. Creativity has long been known to be the highest form of mental functioning. Some instructional strategies are more effective than others in producing creative responses in students. As never before, we need to help students develop creative thinking and feeling skills. Students who have had ample opportunity to use their creative talents will likely use them well throughout their lives. Barriers to creative thinking often are in students' minds; those who are intelligent but not very creative may be disinclined to be imaginative. The barriers may be due to social fears, fear of being wrong, lack of confidence, or the belief that they are not creative.

Model creativity and provide ample opportunity for creative expression by allowing students to express themselves in an open-ended manner and to seek different ways to do something or solve problems. Fear of failure or looking foolish limits creativity. Students must not feel their answers will lower their grades; trying new things should be praised, not suppressed. Small-group problem solving or decision making can promote creativity. Teach brainstorming and have students use it. Students also should be taught constructive disagreement, and that ideas and procedures can be challenged, but people and personalities must not be attacked.

Rothstein (1990) provides suggestions for teaching for creativity:

- *Encourage students to explore things in their environment.* Have them use all their senses and discover the messages sent through each and combinations of senses. Have them describe things they find interesting. Have them discover how to "look at things with fresh eyes."
- *Provide school time to encourage creativity.* Structure activities or exercises that require originality or problem solving. Have students suggest new uses for old things. Make frequent use of brainstorming and creative activities. Let them know that creativity is sought.
- *Encourage students to become interested in many things.* Vary activities, take students on field trips, bring in speakers, and use media to help students "stretch their minds."
- *Help students believe they can learn to become more creative.* Few inventors, scientists, or artists were very creative at first. Reward students who show evidence of creativity, and reward improvement.
- *Teach students what is involved in creativity.* Help them learn that creativity is influenced by the types, number, and originality of alternatives produced. Train students to use specific thinking skills and inquiry and problem-solving processes and how to transfer knowledge of these into new situations.
- *Encourage students to acquire information and use it to be creative.* Show students how knowledge can be used to create alternatives, analogies, or to make inferences (p. 274).

You can help students increase their creative talents by helping them develop *meta-cognitive talents*. For example, teach students how to generate questions about the material studied or ask them to propose activities. Participation helps them take control of learning. They can learn to explore things from a variety of perspectives and decide the consequences of the alternatives generated. Tell them that statements (or thoughts) such as "I can't" or "I don't know how" or "I'm too slow" are not permitted. Students can share ideas with peers and have these paraphrased. This teaches them to become better listeners, clarifies thinking, and fosters fresh ideas. Role playing and simulations can be used. Encourage students to become more hypothetical. Have them assume a stance or position with which they do not agree. Journals help students bring their thoughts together and translate them into constructive action. This can occur when students look back at what happened, how they reacted, decide how they could have reacted, and what they will do in the future.

Honig (2001) suggests ways to encourage creativity in young children:

1. Breaking up old ideas through encouraging new ideas and making children comfortable with ambiguity
2. Making new connections through the creative use of recycled materials such as paper rolls and pipe cleaners
3. Enlarging the limits of knowledge through taking apart old or broken objects such as hair dryers and battery-operated toys to see how they work
4. Allowing the onset of wonderful ideas through encouraging children to move about the classroom in their own creative ways (p. 37)

The way the teacher behaves and runs the classroom is at the core of teaching for both creative and critical thinking. The teacher needs to listen to, and value, students' ideas and opinions. The teacher should encourage students to value each others' thoughts and beliefs. Teachers must be flexible and not insist on conformity at all times. Open-minded discussion is important—students need to discuss their thinking, viewpoints, and attempts at analysis. They need to make decisions, examine alternatives, and act in accord with their decisions. Cooperative learning procedures can be used to advantage.

Teaching your students to think critically and creatively is demanding. Do you really need to know and understand the theory to be effective? Did the specific operations of classifying, organizing, and the like work? You may say, "I really want my students to think about what I teach." How do you achieve this? How does this ideal depend on planning and instructional skills? Do you see the teacher as a facilitator? How can the structures suggested in this text help you? Try the methods and reflect on your experience.

A data collection instrument is provided in Appendix 14.1 for your use when teaching for thinking as a target in microteaching or classroom lessons. You can use this instrument to help you analyze the cases that follow. Your instructor may pose specific questions for your response.

CASE 14.1 Thinking

All about a Farm

The grade 2 class had been involved in a farm unit for several days. They had learned about kinds of farms, farm animals, and farm machinery. Ms. Arnott wanted to build on the new learning and introduce

Different	*Comparing*	*Same*
Paul	*Jacques*	
brown hair	black hair	both are boys
taller	shorter	both are in grade 2
wearing runners	sock feet	both play soccer at recess
wearing a sweater	wearing a "Turtles" shirt	both are wearing jeans
blue eyes	brown eyes	both have short hair
		both are Montreal Canadians fans

the thinking skill of *comparing*. She planned, in consecutive lessons, to have the children: (1) compare two farm animals with which they were familiar to introduce comparing, (2) compare two live pet turtles (a snapping turtle and a box turtle), and (3) compare two stories. She thought the children would learn to transfer this skill if they used it in different situations.

In the first lesson, she began, "This afternoon, we're going to do something that's fun. It's called *comparing*. It's a special way of thinking about something and it's called a thinking skill. First, we will practice doing it together, then we'll do it with farm animals; tomorrow we'll try it with something else. Have you ever heard the word *compare*?" She writes the word on the board.

Some children had heard the word. They gave examples: "My mom compares prices when she shops." "I'm tall compared to my baby brother." "My sisters don't like to be compared."

"Those are good examples of how that word can be used. What do you think the word means?" Trish volunteered, "It means seeing if two things are the same."

Ms. Arnott recorded the word *same* on the board, under *Compare*. "Yes, if you look for things that are the same, it's called comparing. It means something else, too," said Ms. Arnott. "It means if you're as tall as your brother," Petra responded. Ms. Arnott asked, "If you are small and your brother is tall, are you the same?" "No, we're different." "So, comparing could be looking for ways things are different?" "Yes," answered Petra. Ms. Arnott wrote *different* under the *Compare* heading. "Now can you tell us what *compare* means?" Ivan answered, "*Compare* means looking for things that are the same and for things that are different." "That's right!" replied Ms. Arnott, "And that's what we're going to do."

"All right, let's see how this would work. I wonder if you can *compare* two boys in our class, just to see if you get the idea. How about Paul and Jacques? Paul and Jacques, stand at the front of the room. Let's make a place for information." Ms. Arnott clears a section of the board and writes the word *comparing* and the headings "Paul," "Jacques," "Different," and "Same" on the board (shown above). The children identify similarities and differences.

"That's great," said Ms. Arnott, "Now let's see if you can compare two farm animals we've been learning about. Which ones should we compare?" Many hands wave. After looking around, Ms. Arnott chooses Marcus. Marcus suggests goats and sheep.

Ms. Arnott gives directions for students to work in pairs, and then distributes papers to each pair. The papers are blank versions of the format used on the board. Ms. Arnott reviews information about goats and sheep with the class and asks them, in pairs, to begin discussing the information. "Decide which things are different, which are the same, and then record the information on your worksheets. When everyone is finished, we'll talk about them."

When the children have completed their task, using a general class discussion, Ms. Arnott asks students to share their responses. Following the discussion, in which she discovers students have the idea of similarities and differences, she concludes, "You all did a good job of comparing today. Tomorrow we'll do more comparing, but we'll look for things that are the same and different for two different kinds of turtles. I'm going to bring my pet box turtle and my pet snapping turtle. We'll look at them, touch them, and see what they eat and how they act in a new place. Then we'll decide what is the same and what is different."

CASE 14.2 Thinking

Assumptions about "Facts"

Mr. Goldstein wanted to teach more than information in his grade 10 science class. In a general way, he had been working on this for some time. He wanted his students to learn to process information rather than just receive and memorize it. It had become a habit to ask broad or open-ended questions and to make sure he waited three to five seconds before calling on a specific student. The number of probes and redirects he used had increased, and he encouraged students, at every opportunity, to become aware of their thinking processes. Though he knew it was a less certain way to conduct lessons, he encouraged divergent thinking, and student questions were obviously welcome.

Mr. Goldstein had decided that he was going to teach certain thinking processes and skills directly. To date, he had taught classifying, coding, and comparing and contrasting. To help his students develop critical thinking capability he decided to teach his students to be sensitive to the difference between statements of fact and assumptions.

Two containers of potato chips were displayed on Mr. Goldstein's desk. Students noticed these as they entered the room, wondering what he was up to today. One container was a large, puffed-up plastic bag and the other was a sealed cylinder one-quarter the size of the bag. "Which of these contains more?" he asked. Students found out that the large container

held 150 grams and the smaller container actually held 200 grams. They had assumed the large container held more.

"Some statements are clearly facts," he said. "For example, grass is generally green in the summer; and there are 5,280 feet in a mile. But, statements like 'It's not going to rain for another three weeks' or 'Sam is a good dancer because he was born in Jamaica' are *assumptions*. An assumption is a statement that is not supported, or not fully supported by evidence." He provided a few more examples that contrasted facts and assumptions. Next, he provided a handout that contained twelve statements. Students were asked to label those statements that were facts and those that were assumptions. Then, he divided the class into buzz groups of six to try to arrive at consensus on the issue of whether disposable containers should be used for food products. He said, "As you debate this issue, be very sensitive about your statements. If you think a statement is a fact, say so; if you are aware that it is an assumption, point this out. I will give you a signal when you have about ten minutes left. At this signal, discuss the implications of making decisions or recommendations based on assumptions." Students reported and he asked them to look for assumptions not only in science but also in other subjects, particularly, social studies, English, and consumer studies.

CASE 14.3 Critical Thinking

Arguing with Yourself

SARAH: Hello, Mark. You look like that statue . . . you know, Rodin—the thinker.

MARK: Well, that's "right on," because I am working out a lesson on the dialectic.

SARAH: The dial what?

MARK: Instead of the usual debates and discussions, it's a way of getting kids to look at both sides of an issue. It's good for critical thinking.

SARAH: How does it work?

MARK: You get a student, a group, or even the whole class to make a value claim on an issue. It could be something like smoking should be banned in all

public places. The students then say what is good, right, or worthwhile concerning the issue.

SARAH: So, they'd express a moral and ethical position.

MARK: Yes, it must be one on which there is an honest division of opinion. Then they'd give supporting arguments and reasons to support their position.

SARAH: That sounds reasonable.

MARK: Then, you get the individual or class to set out a value claim opposing that of the first value claim—in other words, an opposite moral and ethical position—and they must argue the position with supporting arguments.

SARAH: In other words, this dialectic is like a dialogue, like arguing with yourself?

MARK: Exactly. There are other things that should happen, but you have the main idea. Students would decide which value claim is the better, and the value claim has to pass certain intellectual tests.

SARAH: What kind of tests?

MARK: Can the claim apply to different cases? Can it pass a role-exchange test? And are the consequences of agreeing with these value claims acceptable morally and ethically?

SARAH: This sounds exciting. There are so many issues you could discuss. I'm going to try it with my next class.

Problem-Based Learning

TCP—PROBLEM-BASED LEARNING

Skilled and effective approach to problem-based learning

Skilled at setting up student-centered problem-based learning approaches; teacher is facilitator, ensuring that students explore problems themselves; carefully selects problems as focus of learning; students develop problem-solving skills as they direct their learning; meaningful information provided or suggested.

Little or no student-centered approaches; teacher controls and dominates the learning process; problems selected are unauthentic and not challenging; students learn few meaningful skills; information provided is uninteresting or inadequate.

> The interviewer handed the students a battery, a wire, and a light bulb and asked if they could make the bulb light. They could not. This might not be alarming if the students were fourth graders, but they were not. The students were clothed in caps and gowns as they prepared to graduate from Harvard and MIT. (Bracey, 1998)

This is the opening of *Minds of Our Own,* a three-part videotape series on our misconceptions about how the world works. The key idea "is that children bring to the classroom profoundly held ideas about how the world works, and these ideas are incredibly resistant to change," but "our pedagogy does not equip teachers to teach for understanding and then detect misunderstandings through assessment" (Bracey, 1998, p. 328). The reason the Harvard and MIT students could not solve the light bulb problem is similar to why many educators find it difficult to teach thinking, inquiry, and problem solving. We have preconceptions about how things should be. Bracey provides a revealing example of a "friend who doesn't like to boil water in a microwave oven because the water is never hot enough (for her, boiling water equals bubbles rising, not a set temperature)" (p. 329).

Church (2001) claims that "PBL, a well-documented instructional approach that originated in the field of medical education, has extended its application to many areas and taken many forms. . . . Clearly, collaboration, interacting with others, and thinking through situations to improve knowledge and solve problems are of interest to most professions" (p. 6).

Stressing the importance of problem-solving skills is not new. Students can be taught the procedures and processes of thinking and to recognize, define, and go about solving open-ended problems. They can learn to be fluent, flexible, and original in generating ideas—creativity can be learned by practicing it. Techniques of forecasting, too, can be learned. These involve defining and solving future-oriented problems. You can teach habits of mind and the tools students can use to cope with the present and the future.

What Is Problem-Based Learning (PBL)?

As you may have surmised, problem-based learning is any learning situation in which the problem drives the learning. Students discover they need the information or skills to solve a problem. To do this, they need to know how to access the information and how to use critical thinking and problem-solving skills. Problem-based learning is a student-centered method in which learners become increasingly independent of the teacher, who suggests educational materials and provides guidance (SIU, 2002). The teacher's function is to encourage, keep students on track, provide information or suggest sources of information, and be a fellow learner (Aspy, Aspy, & Quinby, 1993).

PBL, which values active learning, has the following characteristics:

- It is student centered.
- Learning occurs in small student groups.
- Teachers are facilitators or guides.
- Problems are the organizing focus and stimulus for learning.
- Problems are a vehicle for the development of problem-solving skills.
- New information is acquired through self-directed learning (SIU, 2002).

Why Use Problem-Based Learning?

The argument posed in the Southern Illinois University School of Medicine web site is that traditional schooling—kindergarten through medical school—leaves students disenchanted and bored with their education. Much of what was memorized is soon forgotten and what is remembered is hard to apply to tasks and problems. Many students can't reason effectively and are unable to take responsibility for their education. Many do not collaborate well with others. Education has been "an imposed set of rituals with little relevance to the 'real world.'"

Through PBL, traditional teacher and student roles change. Students assume more responsibility and so are better motivated with more feelings of accomplishment, "setting the pattern for them to become successful lifelong learners" they become "better practitioners of their profession" (MCLI, 2001). Learning becomes relevant and authentic, occurs in ways similar to how it will be used in the future, and higher-order thinking is promoted.

How Does Problem-Based Learning Work?

PBL is the kind of classroom organization that supports a constructionist approach (NCREL, 2002). Savoie and Hughes (1994) used a process to initiate a problem-based experience for students.

The process of PBL has students, in groups, confront a problem. They organize prior knowledge and try to discover the nature of the problem. Questions may be posed about what they do not understand. They then formulate a plan for solving the problem and decide the resources needed. Following this, they start to gather information with which to work to solve the problem. Potential solutions are generated. The pros and cons of each solution are considered, and a solution, or a combination of solutions, is selected to be tested. A data sheet you can use for problem-based learning is provided in Appendix 14.2.

CASE 14.4 Problem-Based Learning

Making Ancient Egypt Interesting

Two student teachers are in the staff room, discussing approaches to teaching. They have seen much lecture teaching in the school and want to try a more dynamic approach.

HASSIM: Do you think we could try a more challenging approach on the lesson on Ancient Egypt? How about that problem-based learning idea we learned about?

SARAH: We could try it with the section on the pyramids. First we have to give students a problem.

HASSIM: That's easy: "How were the pyramids built?"

SARAH: OK, then we have to use the knowledge they already have to get a clearer idea of the nature of the problem.

HASSIM: So, we'll ask them to brainstorm what they know, such as the size of the pyramids, when they were built, and the fact that most are made from huge blocks of stone.

SARAH: They'll need a plan to solve the problem of how the stones were moved and set in place.

HASSIM: They'll need to see what resources are available, like books, Internet ideas, and so on.

SARAH: And once they've enough resources, they can organize the information to solve the problem.

HASSIM: Sounds good. Let's give it a try.

CASE 14.5 Problem-Based Learning

Saving the Burrowing Owl

Mr. Duszik's grade 7 class was very excited. For their science class today their teacher had invited a special guest, Ellen Forsyth, from the government nature conservancy. She had brought with her a burrowing owl as part of her talk on ecosystems.

She asked the students if they had ever gone on nature hikes or camped with friends or family in the wilderness. All the students had, because Mr. Duszik worked hard to ensure that each grade experienced nature trips at least once a year. Ms. Forsyth asked the students what was the best part of these trips, and they all said it was when they saw rare birds or animals.

Not one of the students had ever seen a burrowing owl, and they were thrilled when Ellen finally took it out of its cage. They were surprised at how small it was—only about nine or ten inches tall. They loved how it looked at them, bobbing from side to side as if to get a better view.

When she was asked why it was called a burrowing owl, Ellen got the students themselves to think of possible reasons and, eventually, they thought it lived in the burrows abandoned by gophers or prairie dogs.

She explained that this creature and many others were in danger because there was so little natural grassland left. They needed whole areas of undisturbed prairie if they were to survive. She said she had a special problem she wanted the whole class to think about. How could creatures like the burrowing owl be saved from extinction?

First students defined the problem. How could large sections of undisturbed natural grassland be set aside for creatures like the burrowing owl? They decided they would need to know many things, such as what creatures were threatened, what possibilities for undisturbed environment existed, what agencies could help, what could they do to get people thinking about the issue, and what was being done already. They decided they should form teams and each should be in charge of a particular aspect of the problem.

They had lots to do and lots to learn. Ms. Forsyth smiled at their energy and enthusiasm. She told Mr. Duszik she had started in her career as a student in the class of a teacher who inspired them with real problems.

LINKING PRACTICE TO THEORY

Think about your school experience. Were you taught thinking skills? What subjects made you think about your learning? Do all subjects make you think? Try the approaches to teaching about thinking and problem solving suggested in this chapter. Are the ideas helpful?

This may be the last chapter before your field experience. For each chapter we have suggested you work with the theory and compare approaches in the text with your growing personal experience. There is a tendency sometimes to decry theory and believe the practicum will provide the "real experience" of teaching. The ideas that shape theory grow from the experiences of many teachers. Britzman (1991) describes a practice teacher who believed his internship would tell him what to do and how to teach. His "tendency to distance himself from his teaching strategies was evident. Most apparent, by the last stages of his student teaching semester, was he had no analytical framework from which to theorize about his experience. His experience appeared trapped in immediacy, subject to the pull of uncontrollable forces over which he had little control" (p. 159). Compare your lived experience of teaching with the theoretical framework in this text. This can have significance for your development.

Summary

Schools have typically neglected teaching for thinking, and transfer of thinking operations from one subject to another and to life. Emphasis has been on information acquisition and low-level content. Students need to do more than learn information. Thinking skills and processes need to be learned, as does the ability to use these in a variety of contexts. If teaching and learning are to be authentic, teachers need to teach for thinking. Some educators see stand-alone thinking skills or process learning as ineffective—believing that thinking skills are discipline specific and little transfer, if any, will occur. Others say a context is always required, but thinking skills are generic and teaching for transfer can occur.

If learning is orientated toward discovery of personal meaning and solving problems, each student, no matter his or her ability or background, tries to make sense of knowledge and experience, and uses his or her skills to do so. The student is constructing meaning. Your classroom can be a supportive community for learning and provide a caring environment that encourages constructive risk taking tempered by creative, critical thinking during individual and group work.

What should schooling accomplish? Philosophers and educational theorists have debated this for decades. Authentic, active, collaborative, problem-based learning is the direction proposed by many contemporary theorists.

Activities

1. You and your subject group choose a thinking skill, analyze it, and plan the steps to teach it.
2. In subject groups, examine lesson plans that you have previously used that could be considered essentially content based. Redesign your lesson plans to be: (a) process based rather than product based; and (b) using the core thinking skills (presented in this chapter).
3. Consider a lesson in school or college in which you were taught, or encouraged, to think. Compare your reflections with the creative and critical thinking charts in this text.
4. Plan a lesson in your subject area with the objective of teaching a thinking skill, which can be demonstrated to the class.
5. Choose a lesson plan you have previously prepared. Revise it to include the teaching of a thinking skill and to encourage the learning of a disposition or attitude.

6. Brainstorm examples of topics that could be discussed using the dialectic model.

7. Meet in subject groups. (a) Brainstorm lists of the most important creative and critical thinking skills that apply to your subject. (b) Indicate those skills that are essential to your subject.

8. Research constructionist teaching or review the section in this text. List the main similarities between constructionist teaching and problem-based learning.

9. Think of problems you have solved outside of school using the PBL model. Describe what you did. Take a "traditional" lesson you have taught. Redesign it using a PBL approach.

10. What would you consider the advantages and disadvantages of a PBL approach in your discipline?

APPENDIX 14.1 *Thinking Skills Professional Target*

PROFESSIONAL TARGET—TEACHING A THINKING SKILL

Please describe what you hear and see including how students reacted.

Teaching Aspect	Teacher and Student Behaviors
The skill label and definition provided	
Rules or steps for using skill provided	
Use of skill in the specific content under study	
Skill modeled (demonstrated and explained)	
Guided practice provided (and the context of practice)	
Independent practice provided	

APPENDIX 14.2 *Problem-Based Learning Professional Target*

PROFESSIONAL TARGET—PROBLEM-BASED LEARNING

Please describe what you hear and see including how students reacted.

Steps	Teacher and Student Behaviors
Problem identified	
Authentic problem connected to the life experiences of the students	
Students, in groups, confront the problem	
Students organize prior knowledge; identify the nature of problem	
Questions posed about what is not understood	
Students design a plan to solve the problem and identify resources needed	
Students gather information to solve the problem	
Solution(s) identified and evaluated	
Solution(s) tried	

Epilogue

The Field Experience

There has been much recent research regarding making the field experience viable. Maxie (2001) refers to a shift recognizing

> Teacher development and field-based experiences as complex processes . . . characterized by a focus on reflection and inquiry into teaching; an acknowledgement of the complexity of the work of teaching and life in schools; and an emphasis on the integration of the study and practice of teaching through collaborations between universities and schools. (p. 116)

This text was designed to support you as you proceed through your teacher preparation courses and practica. Through the models, strategies, methods, skills, and competencies described in the text and suggestions for professional development, you can develop a personal foundation for a meaningful and satisfying teaching career

The Field Experience as Experiential Learning

Your field experience is a form of experiential learning (described in Chapter 12). Specific and general goals must be set, the experience monitored, and reflections completed. Only with these key elements can your teaching experiences have focus and meaning. Examine the Kolb and Exeter models on experiential learning for the importance of the experiential–reflection cycle. Inquiry into and reflection about your teaching and life in schools are critical aspects of your field experiences.

The TCP as Goal and Assessment Guide

The Teaching Competence Profile (TCP) lists and describes many of the essential competencies of effective teaching. Each competence is based on sound practice and research. We suggest that you design an overall plan for practicing and developing your competencies during student teaching and internship. You can begin with basic, everyday competencies such as communication skills, giving directions, and basic classroom management, and move to more complex competencies such as inductive teaching, planning for experiential learning, or helping students learn critical and creative processes. Using the TCP as your guide, you can reflect on what you have learned about yourself, your colleagues, and students, and what abilities, attitudes, and values you have developed. Details on use of the TCP as a developmental plan were presented in Chapter 1.

Collaboration between Universities and Schools

We have suggested that you and your university teachers study and discuss the theory behind the TCP descriptors. Research, beyond what is presented in the text, can be explored, and readings in this text can be studied in more depth. Then, in microteaching, case studies, and initial school practice you can apply the competencies. For each lesson that you teach, we suggest that you have two goals: (1) planning and conducting lessons for the learning of your students, and (2) planning and successfully using a particular competence (target). Reflection about whether your intentions were achieved should be ongoing and provide the basis for further attempts with the use of targets. Let us repeat the essentials of the professional development process presented in Chapter 1. Using the descriptors for the competence, you design a data sheet so your partner or cooperating teacher can collect objective information on how you meet your target. You use the data as a basis for reflection and further inquiry. An example might be "How effective were you in asking higher-level questions?" "How did the students respond?" You can reflect about the information collected and, perhaps, go beyond simple questioning to thinking about how inductive and inquiry teaching might work.

Your cooperating teacher will become an important link between the theory you learn in university and the practice in the school. Your faculty advisor, who periodically observes your teaching, will likely be familiar with the competencies. In this way your university teachers and faculty advisor can be part of a coherent teacher education program. We suggest that the TCP provides focus for your ongoing teacher development and acts as a means for assessing your teaching competence. You, however, control the selection of competencies, so your professional development is personalized, specific, and developmental.

With this coherent process you can "move from thinking about educational matters in concrete, undifferentiated ways to thinking in ways that are more integrated, flexible and holistic" (Page, Rudney, & Marxen, 2004, p. 26). The experience, both the theory and the practice, will help you build your image as teacher.

Professional Development: Practice Teaching and Internship Competencies

Several competencies apply to your field experience. Most describe the general approach to the internship experience. The last four relate specifically to the professional development process described in Chapter 1. Reflect about the competencies described below as you gain personal experience in teaching.

TEACHER COMPETENCE PROFILE

Effective Performance	Ineffective Performance
Shows interest and commitment to teaching	
Active effort to improve teaching and extensive involvement in school programs and professional development opportunities: displays genuine concern for and enjoyment of children.	Lack of commitment to teaching; avoids getting involved in school, extracurricular, and professional development activities.
Demonstrates initiative	
Shows active interest and inner self-direction by volunteering constructive suggestions and assuming responsibility.	Shows apathy or reluctance to be involved; waits to be asked and/or directed.
Manner is dependable and mature	
Fulfills commitments responsibly; positive, but realistic, outlook; is concerned with self-betterment; acts independently but is sensitive to the needs and feelings of others; accepts and acts on constructive criticism; cooperative and pleasant without being compliant; addresses problems in a professional rather than personal way; shows excellent professional judgment; is tactful.	Unreliable, duties neglected or fulfilled in a haphazard or sloppy way; must be reminded or checked up on; defensive when constructive criticism is offered; moody and uncooperative; problems addressed personally rather than handled professionally; makes inappropriate professional judgments; is not tactful.

continued

*Deals effectively with interpersonal stress
and conflict*

Calm and composed under stress; maintains "professional cool," seeks and fosters satisfactory solutions to disagreements, conflicts, or misunderstandings; handles emergency solutions calmly and expeditiously; seeks assistance when appropriate; able to remain objective.

Easily flustered; displays unprofessional behavior such as sarcasm or blaming rather than seeking solutions; never admits that help may be needed; avoids addressing problems; acts in a defensive manner when challenged.

Demonstrates confidence and enthusiasm

Responds positively to new experiences and is willing to risk; is not threatened by unexpected events; is decisive and communicates a positive outlook, enjoyment, and high levels of interest to inspire others in a variety of situations; is dynamic.

Withdraws from challenge; makes inappropriate decisions based on emotion; avoids making decisions; is pessimistic, lacks expression of interest and enjoyment; is uninspiring.

Demonstrates creativity and flexibility

Actively incorporates new ideas and materials or uses traditional ideas and models in different integrative ways; models and encourages imagination; is able to change activities as the situation demands.

Follows commonly prescribed or suggested methods, in own presentations and in responding to others; focuses on specifics; limited imagination exhibited; cannot adapt teaching to changing demands.

Collaborates and cooperates with school staff

Typically listens to constructive criticisms and suggestions of others and is able to contribute criticisms and suggestions of his or her own with sensitivity to the norms of the school and needs of others; is tactful.

Typically submissive; follows directives from colleagues or makes inappropriate or indiscreet comments; antagonizes or irritates others.

Relates effectively to students' caregivers

Communicates effectively with students' caregivers; makes caregivers feel comfortable in the school; listens to concerns of caregivers without making premature judgments; encourages and achieves caregiver participation in the classroom.

Avoids students' caregivers and discounts their concerns.

Involved in student-related school activities

Actively contributes to the school co-curricular program; initiates new activities for students.

Avoids co-curricular activities; does not contribute in his or her areas of expertise.

Demonstrates interest in teaching

Active effort to improve teaching; extensive involvement in school programs and professional development opportunities; displays genuine concern for and enjoyment of children.

Lack of commitment to teaching; avoids getting involved in school, extracurricular, and professional development activities.

Observes a professional code of ethics

Observes principles of a professional code of ethics; commitment to students, school, profession, and community; resolves conflicts with sensitivity.

Violates precepts of a professional code of ethics; lacks commitment to students, school, profession, and community.

Practices the Professional Development Process:
(Professional target selection, pre/postconferences,
data collection methods, and analysis of data)

Consistently sets appropriate generic and subject-specific professional targets for each lesson and unit without being urged to do so; progresses creatively, as ready, from simple to sophisticated.	Seldom, if ever, sets targets; set only when urged; inappropriate to content of lesson; seldom varied.
In the preconference, based on preplanning, clearly presents and collaboratively plans for all essential lesson elements and a specific target; in the postconference participates actively and receptively in analysis of feedback and plans for future.	Uncooperative; avoids conferences; unprepared; does not solicit feedback; unreceptive to feedback.
Appropriately uses available instruments; often designs suitable instruments that result in specific, objective, and observable behavior.	Data collection instrument rarely provided; often inappropriate for target or lesson; onus on cooperating teacher.
Reviews data and initiates identification of key elements and patterns; forms, and takes ownership of appropriate generalizations or implications.	Usually doesn't analyze and interpret feedback; if attempted, fails to identify, or accept, data implications; relies on cooperating teacher's analysis and interpretation.

Implements change (plans for growth)
based on reflection on experiences

Incorporates feedback for improvement of: future lessons and professional growth through suitable targets; in an attempt to gain understanding about classroom practice and personal professional growth, often reflects on key events, records these and shares thoughts and questions with the cooperating teacher and faculty advisor; as a result, sets new directions and goals.	Rarely uses feedback to improve future lessons or select targets; does not reflect about, or ask questions about, personal professional growth or classroom practice through a journal or dialogue with the cooperating teacher or advisor.

Evaluates planning, instruction, and management

Periodically self-evaluated by reviewing documented process; sets long-term professional goals to direct future progress; monthly use of the Teacher Competence Profile.	Seldom takes time to evaluate progress; avoids effective use of the Teacher Competence Profile.

Participates in professional development opportunities

Regularly participates in staff development activities; seeks out information on professional development opportunities; attends professional meetings.	Avoids planned professional development opportunities; avoids professional meetings.

Self-Analysis during Your Teacher Education Program

As described in Chapter 1, you will likely want to assess your capability at different times during the course of your teacher preparations and note your progress with respect to the competencies in the TCP. A checklist you can use is given in Figure E.1.

FIGURE E.1   *Teacher Competence Checklist*

YOUR TEACHER COMPETENCE PROFILE (TCP) CHECKLIST

The TCP contains competencies needed by an effective teacher. They are included in and follow the sequence of chapters of the text. Descriptors for each competence that describe competencies as "Excellent" or "Not Evident" are included in Chapter 1.

Indicate your present capability with each competence on the checklist below, on the continuum from "Not Evident" to "Excellent."

This checklist can be used at the beginning and conclusion of each semester or year of your teacher education program if you are a novice teacher. If you are a practicing teacher, you could use it as a basis for planning personal professional development and assessing whether progress has been made.

	Not Evident										Excellent
Communication Skills											
Models appropriate voice and spoken and written language	0	1	2	3	4	5	6	7	8	9	10
Makes effective use of interpersonal skills	0	1	2	3	4	5	6	7	8	9	10
Diversity Issues											
Promotes the worth of all students	0	1	2	3	4	5	6	7	8	9	10
Responds to the needs of all	0	1	2	3	4	5	6	7	8	9	10
Attentive to learning styles	0	1	2	3	4	5	6	7	8	9	10
Attitudes and Values											
Helps students understand attitudes and values	0	1	2	3	4	5	6	7	8	9	10
Creates a positive classroom climate conducive to student-centered learning	0	1	2	3	4	5	6	7	8	9	10
Shows an interests in individual students	0	1	2	3	4	5	6	7	8	9	10
Encourages and supports students	0	1	2	3	4	5	6	7	8	9	10
Motivates students to participate	0	1	2	3	4	5	6	7	8	9	10
Assessment and Evaluation											
Identifies student academic, personal, and social strengths	0	1	2	3	4	5	6	7	8	9	10
Assesses change in student development	0	1	2	3	4	5	6	7	8	9	10
Involves students in assessment	0	1	2	3	4	5	6	7	8	9	10
Evaluates student progress	0	1	2	3	4	5	6	7	8	9	10
Keeps thorough, well-organized records	0	1	2	3	4	5	6	7	8	9	10
Provides diagnosis and remediation	0	1	2	3	4	5	6	7	8	9	10
Classroom Management											
Creates a positive classroom climate conducive to student-centered learning	0	1	2	3	4	5	6	7	8	9	10
Communicates and monitors expectations	0	1	2	3	4	5	6	7	8	9	10
Establishes and uses effective classroom routines and procedures	0	1	2	3	4	5	6	7	8	9	10
Handles minor disruptions in a positive way	0	1	2	3	4	5	6	7	8	9	10

FIGURE E.1 *Continued*

	Not Evident										Excellent
Uses a problem-solving approach to misbehavior	0 1 2 3 4 5 6 7 8 9 10										
Uses consultation when necessary	0 1 2 3 4 5 6 7 8 9 10										
Anticipates problems and plans for successful (preventative) management	0 1 2 3 4 5 6 7 8 9 10										
Uses management skills effectively	0 1 2 3 4 5 6 7 8 9 10										
Involves students in formulating classroom rules and consequences	0 1 2 3 4 5 6 7 8 9 10										
Exhibits understanding of student behavior	0 1 2 3 4 5 6 7 8 9 10										
Practices fairness and is consistent	0 1 2 3 4 5 6 7 8 9 10										

Lesson, Unit Planning and Delivery

Planning

	Not Evident	Excellent
Integrates skills and knowledge common to all subjects and adapts curriculum to individual needs	0 1 2 3 4 5 6 7 8 9 10	
Plans varied learner-centered activities	0 1 2 3 4 5 6 7 8 9 10	
Outlines long-range plans to guide student development	0 1 2 3 4 5 6 7 8 9 10	
Plans interdisciplinary thematic units	0 1 2 3 4 5 6 7 8 9 10	
Involves learners in the planning process	0 1 2 3 4 5 6 7 8 9 10	
Includes classroom management in plans	0 1 2 3 4 5 6 7 8 9 10	

Instruction

	Not Evident	Excellent
Demonstrates competence in basic instructional skills	0 1 2 3 4 5 6 7 8 9 10	
Teaches for holistic development (physical, social, emotional, cognitive)	0 1 2 3 4 5 6 7 8 9 10	
Varies teaching approaches and activities	0 1 2 3 4 5 6 7 8 9 10	
Ensures the participation and success of all students	0 1 2 3 4 5 6 7 8 9 10	
Engages students in instructional dialogue	0 1 2 3 4 5 6 7 8 9 10	
Provides motivating set and closure	0 1 2 3 4 5 6 7 8 9 10	
Orders and sequences content to meet learner needs	0 1 2 3 4 5 6 7 8 9 10	
Provides for transfer of learning	0 1 2 3 4 5 6 7 8 9 10	

Curriculum

	Not Evident	Excellent
Adapts curriculum to student needs	0 1 2 3 4 5 6 7 8 9 10	
Knows subject matter	0 1 2 3 4 5 6 7 8 9 10	
Exhibits knowledge of local and state curricula	0 1 2 3 4 5 6 7 8 9 10	

Questioning, Discussion, Seatwork, and Homework

	Not Evident	Excellent
Has effective questioning skills	0 1 2 3 4 5 6 7 8 9 10	
Conducts effective class discussion	0 1 2 3 4 5 6 7 8 9 10	
Sets meaningful seatwork and homework	0 1 2 3 4 5 6 7 8 9 10	

Teaching Concepts

	Not Evident	Excellent
Provides effective teaching of concepts and explanations	0 1 2 3 4 5 6 7 8 9 10	

Skills Teaching

	Not Evident	Excellent
Provides effective teaching of skills and demonstrations	0 1 2 3 4 5 6 7 8 9 10	

FIGURE E.1 *Continued*

	Not Evident		Excellent

Direct Instruction and Individual Study

Effective direct instruction/deductive/expository methods — 0 1 2 3 4 5 6 7 8 9 10

Effective use of the individual study strategy — 0 1 2 3 4 5 6 7 8 9 10

Employs resource-based teaching/learning with a wide variety of media and resources — 0 1 2 3 4 5 6 7 8 9 10

Uses instructional technology to enhance student learning — 0 1 2 3 4 5 6 7 8 9 10

Indirect Instruction and Experiential Learning

Effective use of inductive/inquiry methods — 0 1 2 3 4 5 6 7 8 9 10

Uses experiential learning regularly to encourage active learning — 0 1 2 3 4 5 6 7 8 9 10

Collaborative and Cooperative Learning

Develops group skills in the classroom — 0 1 2 3 4 5 6 7 8 9 10

Uses cooperative collaborative learning methods regularly to meet both academic and social goals — 0 1 2 3 4 5 6 7 8 9 10

Thinking Skills and Problem-Based Learning

Uses specific instruction in the nature and use of thinking skills and processes — 0 1 2 3 4 5 6 7 8 9 10

Incorporates key thinking operations and core thinking skills into teaching — 0 1 2 3 4 5 6 7 8 9 10

Ensures that students use critical thinking procedures — 0 1 2 3 4 5 6 7 8 9 10

Ensures that students think creatively — 0 1 2 3 4 5 6 7 8 9 10

Skilled and effective approach to problem-based learning — 0 1 2 3 4 5 6 7 8 9 10

Professional Development–Practicum Skills

General Internship Skills

Shows interest and commitment to teaching — 0 1 2 3 4 5 6 7 8 9 10

Demonstrates initiative — 0 1 2 3 4 5 6 7 8 9 10

Manner is dependable and mature — 0 1 2 3 4 5 6 7 8 9 10

Deals effectively with personal and interpersonal stress and conflict — 0 1 2 3 4 5 6 7 8 9 10

Demonstrates confidence and enthusiasm — 0 1 2 3 4 5 6 7 8 9 10

Demonstrates creativity and flexibility — 0 1 2 3 4 5 6 7 8 9 10

Collaborates and cooperates with school staff — 0 1 2 3 4 5 6 7 8 9 10

Relates effectively to students' caregivers — 0 1 2 3 4 5 6 7 8 9 10

Gets involved in student-related school activities — 0 1 2 3 4 5 6 7 8 9 10

Practices a professional code of ethics — 0 1 2 3 4 5 6 7 8 9 10

Professional Development Process

Practices the Professional Development Process (target selection, pre/postconferences, data collection, and analysis of data) — 0 1 2 3 4 5 6 7 8 9 10

Implements change (plans for growth) based on reflection on experiences — 0 1 2 3 4 5 6 7 8 9 10

Evaluates planning, instruction, and management — 0 1 2 3 4 5 6 7 8 9 10

Participates in planned professional development — 0 1 2 3 4 5 6 7 8 9 10

References

AAUW. (1992). *How schools shortchange girls: The AAUW report.* Washington, DC: AAUW Foundation, American Association of University Women.

Albert, L. (1989). *A teacher's guide to cooperative discipline: How to manage your classroom and promote self-esteem.* Circle Pines, MN: American Guidance Service.

Alberta Human Rights Commission. (1978). *Human rights: Respecting our differences, Students' manual.* Edmonton, AB: Department of Education.

Alderman, M. (1990). Motivation for at-risk students. *Educational Leadership, 48*(1), 27–30.

Allan, J., & Nairne, J. (1984). *Class discussions for teachers and counsellors in the elementary school.* Toronto: University of Toronto.

Allen, J. (1986). Students' perspectives, goals and strategies. *American Educational Research Journal, 23*(3), 437–459.

Alvino, J. (1990). A glossary of thinking-skills terms. *Learning, 18*(6), 50.

Amrein, A., & Berliner, D. (2003). The effects of high-stakes testing on student motivation and learning. *Educational Leadership, 60*(5), 32–38.

Amundson, K. (1993). *Speaking and writing skills for educators.* Arlington, VA: American Association of School Administrators.

Anderson, L., Krathwohl, D., Airasian, P., Cruikshank, K., Mayer, R., Pintrich, P., Raths, J., & Wittrock, M. (2001). *Taxonomy for learning, teaching, and assessing: A revision of Bloom's taxonomy of educational objectives.* (Abridged ed.). Boston: Allyn & Bacon.

Arends, R. (2004). *Learning to teach* (6th ed.). New York: McGraw-Hill.

Armstrong, T. (2001). *Multiple intelligences in the classroom.* Alexandria, VA: Association for Supervision and Curriculum Development.

Aronson, E., Blaney, N., Stephin, C., Sikes, J., & Snapp, M. (1978). *The jigsaw classroom.* Beverly Hills, CA: Sage.

Aronson, E., & Goode, E. (1980). Training teachers to implement jigsaw learning: A manual for teachers. In Sharan, S., Hare, P., Webb, C., & Hertz-Lazarowitz, R. (Eds.), *Cooperation in education* (pp. 47–81). Provo, UT: Brigham Young University Press.

Ashcraft, M. (2002). *Cognition* (3d ed.). Upper Saddle River, NJ: Prentice-Hall.

Aspy, D., Aspy, C., & Quinby, P. (1993). What doctors can teach teachers about problem-based learning. *Educational Leadership, 50*(7), 22–24.

Association for Supervision and Curriculum Development (ASCD). (2004, April). Update on NCLB: State backlashes, new flexibility, and private school choice. *EdPolicy Update, 3*(4). Available at www.ascd.org.

Ausubel, D. (1963). *The psychology of meaningful verbal learning: An introduction to school learning.* New York: Grune and Stratton.

Ausubel, D. (1968). *Educational psychology: A cognitive view.* New York: Holt, Rinehart and Winston.

Ausubel, D., Novak, J., & Hanesian, H. (1978). *Educational psychology: A cognitive view* (2nd ed.). New York: Holt, Rinehart and Winston. Reprinted, New York: Warbel & Peck, 1986.

Bailey, P. (1989). Elements in effective teaching: Direct instruction. Unpublished paper, University of Regina, Regina, SK.

Banks, J. (1999). *An introduction to multicultural education* (2d ed.). Boston: Allyn & Bacon.

Banks, J. (2003). *Teaching strategies for ethnic studies* (7th ed.). Boston: Allyn & Bacon.

Banks, J., & Banks, C. (2001). *Multicultural education: Issues and perspectives* (3rd ed.). Boston: Allyn & Bacon.

Barbe, W., & Swassing, R. (1979). *Teaching through modality strengths: Concepts and practices.* Columbus, OH: Zaner-Bloser.

Baron, J., & Sternberg, R. (Eds.). (1991). *Teaching thinking skills: Theory and practice.* New York: Freeman.

Barry, V., & Rudinow, J. (1994). *Invitation to critical thinking* (3d ed.). New York: Harcourt Brace Jovanovich.

BBC. (2002). *Digital change at the chalkface.* BBC News Online. Available at www.bbc.co.uk/news.

Beamon, G. (2001). *Teaching with adolescent learning in mind.* Thousand Oaks, CA: Corwin Press.

Beamon, G. (2002). Guiding the inquiry of young adolescent minds. *Middle School Journal, 33*(3), 19–27.

Beebe, S., Beebe, S., Redmond, M., Geerinck, T., & Milstone, C. (2000). *Interpersonal communication: Relating to others* (2d Canadian ed.). Boston: Allyn & Bacon.

Berliner, D. (1984). The half-full glass: A review of research on teaching. In Hosford, P. (Ed.), *Using what we know about teaching* (pp. 51–75). Alexandria, VA: Association for Supervision and Curriculum Development.

Berliner, D. (1987). Do they understand? In Richardson-Koehler, V. (Ed.), *Educators' handbook: A research perspective* (pp. 259–293). New York: Longman.

481

Berry, B. (2001, May). No shortcuts to preparing good teachers. *Educational Leadership, 58*(8), 32–36.

Beyer, B. (1984). Improving thinking skills: Practical approaches. *Phi Delta Kappan, 65*(8), 556–560.

Beyer, B. (1995). *Critical thinking*. Bloomington, IN: Phi Delta Kappa Educational Foundation.

Beyer, B. (1998). Improving student thinking. *The Clearing House, 71*(5), 262–267.

Blair, L. (2002). The right questions can improve student thinking and learning. *SEDL Letter, 14*(3). Available at www.sedl.org/pubs/sedl-letter/v14n03/6.html.

Bloom, B. (1968). Learning for mastery (UCLA-CSEIP). *Evaluation Comment, 1*(2), 1–12.

Bloom, B. (1982). The master teachers. *Phi Delta Kappan, 63*(10), 70–77.

Bloom, B. (1986). The hands and feet of genius: Automaticity. *Educational Leadership, 43*(5), 70–77.

Bloom, B., Englehart, M., Furst, E., Hill, W., & Krathwohl. (1956). *Taxonomy of educational objectives. Handbook I: The cognitive domain*. New York: David McKay.

Bonwell, C., & Eison, J. (1991, Sep.). *Active learning: Creating excitement in the classroom*. ASHE-ERIC Higher Education Report No.1. Washington, DC: George Washington University School of Education and Human Development.

Borich, G. (1998). *Effective teaching methods* (3d ed.). Columbus, OH: Merrill.

Borich, G., & Tombari, M. (1995). *Educational psychology: A contemporary approach*. New York: HarperCollins.

Bowd, A., McDougall, D., & Yewchuk, C. (1994). *Educational psychology for Canadian teachers*. Toronto: Harcourt Brace.

Bower, C. (2004, March 30). Discipline policies vary. *St. Louis Post Dispatch*. Available at www.stltoday.com/stltoday/news/stories.nsf/News/Education/C2BBB583711FAEC486256E640022A5F5?OpenDocument&Headline = Discipline + policies + vary.

Boyer, E. (1995). The educated person. In *Toward a coherent curriculum*. Alexandria, VA: ASCD Yearbook.

Bracey, G. (1998). Minds of our own. *Phi Delta Kappan, 80*(4), 328–329.

Brendtro, L., Brokenleg, M., & Van Bockern, S. (2002). *Reclaiming youth at risk: Our hope for the future*. Bloomington, IN: National Educational Service.

Brigman, G., & Campbell, C. (2003). Helping students improve academic achievement and school success behavior. *Professional School Counseling, 7*(2), 91–98.

Bristor, V., Kinzer, S., Lapp, S., & Ridener, B. (2002). The Teacher Education Alliance (TEA): A model teacher education program for the twenty-first century. *Education, 122*(4), 688–699.

Britzman, D. (1991). *Practice makes practice*. New York: State University of New York Press.

Brooks, J., & Brooks, M. (1993). *In search of understanding: The case for constructivist classrooms*. Alexandra, VA: Association for Supervision and Development of Curriculum.

Brown, B. L. (1998). *Task analysis strategies and practices*. Practice application brief. Available at www.cte.org/acve/docgen.asp?tbl = pab&ID = 70.

Brown, G., Bull, J., & Pendlebury, M. (1997). *Assessing student learning in higher education*. New York: Routledge.

Brown, S., & Kysilka, M. (2002) *Applying multicultural and global concepts in the classroom & beyond*. Boston: Allyn & Bacon.

Brualdi, A. (1998). Classroom questions. *Practical Assessment 6*(6). ERIC Document ED422407. Available at http://PARE online.net/getvn.asp?v = 6&n = 6.

Brubacher, M., Payne, R., & Richett, K. (1990). *Perspectives on small group learning: Theory and practice*. Oakville, ON: Rubicon.

Bruner, J. (1960). *The process of education*. Cambridge, MA: Harvard University Press.

Bruner, J. (1966). *Toward a theory of instruction*. Cambridge, MA: Harvard University Press.

Buchmann, M., & Schwille, J. (1982). Education: The overcoming of experience. Occasional Paper #63. East Lansing, MI: The Institute for Research on Teaching, Michigan State University.

Buchmann, M., & Schwille, J. (1993). Education, experience, and the paradox of finitude. In M. Buchmann & R. Floden (Eds.), *Detachment and concern*. London: Cassell and Co.

Bulgren, J., Deshler, D., Schumaker, J., & Lenz, B. (2000). The use and effectiveness on analogical instruction in diverse secondary classrooms. *Journal of Educational Psychology, 92,* 426–441.

Burden, P., & Byrd, D. (2003). *Methods for effective teaching* (3d ed.). Boston: Pearson Education.

Butler, D. (2002). Individualizing instruction in self-regulated learning. *Theory into Practice, 41*(2), 81–92.

Byerly, S. (2001). Linking classroom teaching to the real world through experiential instruction. *Phi Delta Kappan, 82*(9), 697.

Calderhead, J. (1988). The development of knowledge structures in learning to teach. In Calderhead, J. (Ed.), *Teacher's professional learning*. London: Falmer.

Campbell, B. (1990). The research results of a multiple intelligences classroom. *New Horizons for Learning 11*(1), 7. Avaliable at www.newhorizons.org/strategies/mi/campbell2.htm.

Campbell, C., Cordis, L., McBeath, A., & Young, E. (1987). Implementing responsive supervision. *The Canadian Administrator, 26*(6), 10–22.

Canadian Public Health Association. (1998). *Safe spaces: HIV prevention for gay, lesbian, and bisexual youth.* Ottawa, ON: Canadian Public Health Association.

Canadian Teachers' Federation. (1991). *Children schools and poverty.* Ottawa, ON: Canadian Teachers' Federation.

Canter, L. (1988a). Assertive discipline and the search for the perfect classroom. *Young Children, 43*(2), 24.

Canter, L. (1988b). Let the educator beware: A response to Curwin and Mendler. *Educational Leadership, 46*(2), 71–73.

Carbone, P. (1991). Perspectives on values education. *Clearing House, 64*(5), 290–292.

Case, R., & Wright, I. (1999). Taking seriously the teaching of critical thinking. In Case, R., & Clark, P. (Eds.), *The Canadian anthology of social studies.* Vancouver, BC: Pacific Educational Press.

Castle, K., & Rogers, K. (1994). Rule-creating in a constructivist community. *Childhood Education, 70*(2), 77–80.

CEED. (2000). *Social contracts: A proactive intervention for the classroom.* Tip Sheets: Proactive Ways of Intervening and Challenging Behavior. Early Childhood Behavior Project. Minneapolis, MN: University of Minnesota. Available at www.ici2.umn.edu/preschoolbehavior/tip_sheets/social.htm.

Center for Teaching and Learning. (1998). *Strategies for inclusive teaching.* Chapel Hill, NC: University of North Carolina. Available at www.unc.edu/depts/ctl/tfi2.html.

Center for Teaching and Learning. (2001). *Teaching for inclusion: Gender and your classroom.* Chapel Hill, NC: University of North Carolina. Available at www.unc.edu/depts/ctl/tfi3.html.

Centre for Staff Development. (2000). *Collaborative and cooperative learning.* University of Western Australia, Centre for Staff Development. Available at www.csd.uwa.edu.au/altmodes.

Charles, C. (2005). *Building classroom discipline: From models to practice.* Boston: Allyn & Bacon.

Checkly, K. (1997). The first seven . . . and the eighth: A conversation with Howard Gardner. *Educational Leadership, 55*(1), 8–13. Available at www.ascd.org/readingroom/edlead/9709/checkly.htm.

Chickering, A., & Ehrmann, S. (1996, Oct). Implementing the seven principles: Technology as lever. *AAHE Bulletin.* Available at www.tltgroup.org/programs/seven.html.

Childcare. (1983). *Presenter's guide for the audio-visual program, Childcare shapes the future: Anti-racist strategies.* New York: Council of Interracial Books for Children and the Multicultural Project for Communication and Education.

Chinn, C., O'Donnell, A., & Jinks, T. (2000). The structure of discourse in collaborative learning. *Journal of Experimental Education, 69*(1), 77–97.

Church, K. (2001). Review of the book *Problem-based learning: A research perspective on learning interactions. Educational Horizons, 80*(1), 6–7.

Cipani, E. (1998). *Classroom management for all teachers: 11 effective plans.* Upper Saddle River, NJ: Merrill.

Civikly, J. (1992). *Classroom communication: Principles and practices.* Dubuque, IA: Wm. C. Brown.

Clarke, J., Wideman, R., & Eadie, S. (1990). *Together we learn.* Scarborough, ON: Prentice-Hall.

Cohn, D. (2002, July 5). U.S. counts one in 12 children as disabled. Census reflects increase of handicapped youth. *The Washington Post,* p. B01.

Cooper, H. (1989). Synthesis of research on homework. *Educational Leadership, 47*(3), 85–91.

Cooper, H. (2001). Homework for all in moderation. *Educational Leadership, 58*(7), 34–38.

Cooper, H., Lindsday, J., Nye, B., & Greathouse, S. (1998). Relationships among attitudes about homework, amount of homework assigned and completed, and student achievement. *Journal of Educational Psychology, 90*(1), 70–83.

Coopersmith, S. (1967). *The antecedents of self-esteem.* San Francisco: Freeman.

Cotton, K. (1988). Close-Up # 5: Classroom questioning. *School Improvement Research Series.* Portland, OR: NW Regional Educational Laboratory. Available at www.nwrel.org/scpd/sirs/3/cu5.html.

Cotton, K. (1990). Close-Up # 9: Schoolwide and classroom discipline. *School Improvement Research Series.* Portland, OR: NW Regional Educational Laboratory. Available at www.wrel.org/scpd/5/cu9.html.

Cotton, K. (1991). Close-Up # 10: Computer assisted instruction. *School Improvement Research Series.* Portland, OR: NW Regional Laboratory. Available at www.nwrel.org/scpd/sirs/5/cu10.html.

Council on Interracial Books for Children. (1983). *Childcare shapes the future: Anti-sexist strategies.* K 305.8 C45. New York: Multicultural Project for Communication and Education Inc.

CPSER. (2004). *Homework policies.* Research Brief, Center for Policy Studies, Educational Research, and Community Development, Intermountain Center for Education Effectiveness, College of Education, Iowa State University. Available at http://icee.isu.edu/Policy/RBHomework.pdf.

CRESPAR. (2002). *Every child has the capacity to succeed in school and in life.* Center for Research on the Education of Students at Risk. Baltimore MD: Johns Hopkins University; and Washington, DC: Howard University. Available at www.csos.jhu.edu/crespar/index.htm and www.bridges4kids.org/articles/10-03/CRESPAR10-03.html.

Crick, N., Bigbee, M., & Howes, C. (1996). Gender differences in children's normative beliefs about aggression: How do I hurt thee? Let me count the ways. *Child Development, 67,* 1003–1014.

Cruickshank, D. (1985a). Applying research on teacher clarity. *Journal of Teacher Education, 36*(2), 44–48.

Cruickshank, D. (1985b). Uses and benefits of reflective teaching. *Phi Delta Kappan, 66*(10), 704–706.

Cruikshank, D., Bainer Jenkins, D., & Metcalf, K. (2003). *The act of teaching* (3rd ed.). Boston: McGraw-Hill.

CTE Home. (2003–2004). *Questioning strategies.* Center for Teaching Effectiveness, University of Delaware. Available at http://cte.udel.edu/TAbook/question.htm.

Curran, L. (1990). *Cooperative learning lessons for little ones: Literature-based language arts and social studies.* San Juan Capistrano, CA: Resources for Teachers.

Curwin, R., & Mendler, A. (1980). *The discipline book: A complete guide to school and classroom management.* Reston, VA: Reston Publishing.

Curwin, R., & Mendler, A. (1997). *As tough as necessary: Countering violence, aggression, and hostility in our schools.* Alexandria, VA: Association for Supervision and Curriculum Development.

Curwin, R., & Mendler, A. (1999). *Discipline with dignity.* Alexandria, VA: Association for Supervision and Curriculum Development.

Dale, E. (1969). *Audio-visual methods in teaching* (3rd ed.). New York: Holt, Rinehart & Winston.

Dalgarno, D. (2001). Interpretations of constructivism and consequences for computer assisted learning. *British Journal of Educational Technology, 32*(2), 183–194.

Daniels, V. (2000). *Classroom organization: How to deal with disruptive behavior in inclusive classrooms.* Teacher Vision in Cooperation with the Council for Exceptional Children. Available at www.teachervision.com/lesson-plans/lesson-2943.html.

Danielson, C. (1996). *Enhancing professional practice: A framework for teaching.* Alexandria VA: Association for Supervision and Curriculum Development.

Danielson, C., & McGreal, T. (2000). *Teacher evaluation: To enhance professional practice.* Alexandria VA: Association for Supervision and Curriculum Development.

Darling-Hammond, L. (1996). What matters most: A competent teacher for every child. *Phi Delta Kappan, 78*(3), 193–200.

Darling-Hammond, L., & Cobb, V. L. (1996). The changing context of education. In *The teacher educator's handbook* (pp. 14–62). San Francisco: Jossey-Bass.

Dave, R. (1975). In Armstrong, R. (Ed.), *Domains.* Tucson: Educational Innovators Press.

Davis, B. G. (1993). *Tools for teaching.* San Francisco: Jossey-Bass.

Davis, G. (1983). *Educational psychology: Theory and practice.* Reading, PA: Addison-Wesley.

Delpit, L. (1988). The silenced dialogue: Power and pedagogy in educating other people's children. *Harvard Education Review, 58*(3), 280–282.

Delpit, L. (1995). *Other people's children: Cultural conflict in the classroom.* New York: New Press.

Dembo, M. (1994). *Applying educational psychology* (5th ed.) (Annotated Instructor's Edition). White Plains, NY: Longman.

Dever, M., Hager, K., & Klein, K. (2003). Building the university/public school partnership: A workshop for mentor teachers. *The Teacher Educator, 38*(4), 245–255.

Devitt, J. (2004). Reducing fear of being stereotyped bolsters test performances, *NYU Today on the Web, 17*(7). Available at www.nyu.edu/nyutoday/archives/17/07/Stories/stereotype-aronson.html.

Dewey, J. (1897). My pedagogic creed. *The School Journal, 54*(3). Available at www.infed.org/archives/e-texts/e-dew-pc.htm

Dewey J. (1902). *The child and the curriculum.* Chicago: University of Chicago Press.

Dewey, J. (1933). *How we think* (rev. ed.). Boston: Heath.

Diaz, C., Massialas, B., & Xanthopolous, J. (1999). *Global perspectives for educators.* Boston: Allyn & Bacon.

Dick, W., & Carey, L. (2005). *The systematic design of instruction* (6th ed.). New York: Addison-Wesley.

Diem, K. (1998). *Enliven teaching and learning with a variety of instructional methods.* New Brunswick, NJ: Rutgers Cooperative Extension, N.J. Agricultural Experiment Station, State University of New Jersey. Available at www.rcre.rutgers.edu/pubs/publication.asp?pid = fs892.pdf.

Dietel, R., Herman, L., & Knuth, R. (1991). *What does the research say about assessment?* North Central Educational Laboratory (NCREL). Available at www.ncrel.org/sdrs/areas/stw_esys/4assess.htm.

Disney Working Partnership. (2004). *Teacher Center in Collaboration with Thirteen Ed On Line. Teaching to Academic Standards, Workshop 3.* Available at www.thirteen.org/edonline/concept2class/month3/index_sub7.html.

Dobbs, M. (2005, Jan. 7). Spellings promises fixes to No Child Left Behind law. *The Washington Post,* p. A5.

Dowler-Coltman, G. (1995). Homosexual youth in our schools. *The Canadian Executive, 14*(8), 12–16.

Doyle, W. (1977). The uses of nonverbal behaviors: Toward an ecological model of classrooms. *Merrill-Palmer Quarterly, 23,* 179–192.

Doyle, W., & Carter, K. (1987). Choosing the means of instruction. In Richardson-Koehler, V. (Ed.), *Educator's handbook.* New York: Longman.

Drayton, B., & Falk, J. (2001). Tell-tale signs of an inquiry-orientated classroom. *NASSP Bulletin, 85*(623), 24–34.

Drefs, I. (1989). Effective schools: The characteristics and outcomes. Unpublished paper, University of Regina, Regina, SK.

Dreikers, R. (1968). *Psychology in the classroom* (2d ed.). New York: Harper & Row.

Dreikers, R., Grunwald, B., & Pepper, F. (1982). Maintaining sanity in the classroom. New York: Harper & Row.

Driscoll, M. (2000). *Psychology of learning for instruction* (2d ed.). Boston: Allyn & Bacon.

DuBosq, J. (2002). Take it to the next level: Individualized instruction in technology education. *Tech Directions, 61*(7), 29–31.

Duncan, B. (1998). On teacher knowledge: A return to Schulmann. In *Philosophy of Education Society yearbook,* College of Education, University of Illinois. Available at www.ed.uiuc.edu/EPS/PES-Yearbook/1998/duncan.html.

Dunn, K., & Dunn, R. (1987). Dispelling outmoded beliefs about student learning. *Educational Leadership, 44*(6), 55–62.

Dunn, R., & Dunn, K. (1979). Learning styles/teaching styles: Should they . . . can they . . . be matched? *Educational Leadership, 36*(4), 238–244.

Dunn, R., Beaudry, J., & Klavas, A. (1989). Survey of research on learning styles. *Educational Leadership, 46*(6), 50–58.

Dunn, R., & Stevenson, T. (1995). Teaching diverse college students to study with a learning-styles prescription. *College Student Journal, 31*(3), 331–339.

Educational Research Group. (1995). *Active teaching and learning (ATaL).* College Station, TX: Educational Programs That Work, Educational Research Group, Texas A&M University.

Edwards, D. (1994). Learning and control in the classroom. *Journal of Instructional Psychology, 21*(4), 340–346.

Eggen, P., & Kauchak, D. (2001). *Educational psychology: Windows on classrooms* (5th ed.). Upper Saddle River, NJ: Merrill, Prentice-Hall.

Eggen, P., & Kauchak, D. (2003). *Educational psychology: Windows on classrooms* (6th ed.). Upper Saddle River, NJ: Merrill, Prentice-Hall.

Elksnin, L., & Elksnin, N. (2003). Fostering social-emotional learning in the classroom. *Education, 124*(1), 63–75.

Elliott, S., Kratochwill, T., Littlefield, J., & Travers, J. (1996). *Educational psychology: Effective teaching, effective learning.* Madison, WI: Brown & Benchmark.

Emmer, E., Evertson, C., & Worsham, M. (2003). *Classroom management for secondary teachers* (6th ed.). Boston: Allyn & Bacon.

Eric Digests. (1996). *Multiple intelligences: Gardner's theory.* Washington, DC: ERIC Clearinghouse on Assessment and Evaluation. Available at www.ed.gov/databases/ERIC_Digests/ed410226.html.

Erlandson, C. (2002). Creating a climate for learning. *Saskatchewan Bulletin, 69*(5), 12.

Erlandson, C. (2005). *Safe schools: Breaking the silence on sexual difference.* Saskatoon, SK: Saskatchewan Teachers' Federation.

Evertson, C., Emmer, E., & Worsham, M. (2006). *Classroom management for secondary teachers* (7th ed.). Boston: Allyn & Bacon.

Exeter, D. (2001). *Learning in the Outdoors.* London: Outward Bound.

Feldman, S. (2003). The right line of questioning. *Teaching Pre-K–8, 33*(4), 8.

Feldman, S. (2004). The Great Homework Debate. *Teacher to teacher: Issues affecting the classroom teacher.* Available at www.aft.org/teachers/t2t/0103.htm.

Finkel, E. (2003, Dec.). *Teacher evaluation.* Chicago: Catalyst, Community Renewal Society. Available at www.catalyst-chicago.org/12-03/1203danielson.htm.

Fogarty, R. (1999). Architects of the intellect. *Educational Leadership, 57*(3), 76–78.

Fordham University Graduate Schools. (2004). *Diversity among learners.* Available at www.fordham.edu/general/Graduate_Schools/index.html.

Fosnot, C. (2005). *Constructivism theory, perspectives, and practice* (2nd ed.). New York: Teachers College Press.

Four Worlds Development Project. (1982). *Sacred Tree teachers' guide.* Lethbridge ALTA Four Worlds Development Project, University of Lethbridge.

Freiberg, H. J. (1998) Measuring school climate: Let me count the ways. *Educational Leadership, 56*(1), 22–26.

Frieman, B., O'Hara, H., & Settel, H. (1996). What heterosexual teachers need to know about homosexuality. *Childhood Education, 73*(1), 40–42.

Friesen, D. (1991, Feb.). Action research as professional development: Collaborative inquiry into teaching. Presented to the Western Canadian Association for Student Teaching, Regina, SK.

Fritz, R. (1992). *A study of gender differences in cognitive style and volition.* ERIC Document ED354379.

Gaarder, J. (1994). *Sophie's world.* New York: Farrar, Straus, & Giroux.

Gage, N., & Berliner, D. (1998). *Educational psychology* (6th ed.). Boston: Houghton Mifflin.

Gagné, R. (1985). In Orlich, D., (Ed.), *Teaching strategies: A guide to better instruction.* Lexington, KY: Heath.

Gagné, R. M. (1985). *The conditions of learning and the theory of instruction* (4th ed.). New York: Holt, Rinehart, and Winston.

Gall, M. (1970). The use of questions in teaching. *Review of Educational Research, 40,* 707–721.

Gall, M. (1984). Synthesis of research on teaching. *Educational Leadership, 42*(3), 40–46.

Gall, M., Gall, J., Jacobsen, D., & Bullock, T. (1990). *Tools for learning: A guide to teaching study skills.* Alexandria, VA: Association for Supervision and Curriculum Development.

Gallagher, J. (1994). Teaching and learning: New models. *Annual Review of Psychology, 45,* 171–195.

Gardner, H. (1983). *Frames of mind.* New York: Basic Books.

Gardner, H. (1991). *The unschooled mind: How children think and how schools should teach.* New York: Basic Books.

Gardner, H. (1993). *Creating minds.* New York: Basic Books.

Garrity, C., Jens, K., Porter, W., Sager, N., & Short-Camilli, C. (1994). *Bully-proofing your school: A comprehensive approach for elementary schools.* Longmont, CO: Sopris West.

Gazda, G., Asbury, F., Balzer, F., Childers, W., Phelps, R., & Walters, R. (1999). *Human relations development: A manual for educators* (6th ed.). Boston: Allyn & Bacon.

Geddes, D. (1995). Keys to communication: *A handbook for school success.* In Herman, J. J., & Herman, J. I. (Eds.), The Practicing Administrator's Leadership Series, Thousand Oaks, CA: Corwin Press. ERIC Document ED377575. Available at www.vtaide.com/png/ERIC/Communication-Skills.htm.

Gibson, S. (1999). Integrating computer technology in social studies. In Case, R., & Clark, P. (Eds.), *The Canadian anthology of social studies: Issues and strategies for teachers* (pp. 227–234). Vancouver, BC: Pacific Educational Press.

Glasser, W. (1969). *Schools without failure.* New York: Harper & Row.

Glasser, W. (1985). *Control theory. A new explanation of how we control our lives.* New York: Harper & Row.

Glasser, W. (1989). *Control theory in the practice of reality theory.* New York: Harper & Row.

Glasser, W. (1993). *The quality school teacher.* New York: HarperCollins.

Glatthorn, A., & Baron, J. (1985). *The good thinker, teaching skillful thinking: A four-part video-based staff development program for educators.* Alexandria. VA: Association for Supervision and Curriculum Development.

Gokhale, A. (1995). Collaborative learning enhances critical thinking. *Journal of Technology Education, 7*(1). Available at http://scholar.lib.vt.edu/ejournals/JTE/jte-v7n1/gokhale.jte-v7n1.html.

Good, C., Aronson, J., & Inzlicht, M. (2003). Improving adolescents' standardized test performance: An intervention to reduce the effects of stereotype threat. *Journal of Applied Developmental Psychology, 24,* 645–662.

Good, T., & Brophy, J. (1995). *Contemporary educational psychology* (5th ed.). New York: Longman.

Good, T., & Brophy, J. (2003). *Looking in classrooms* (9th ed.). Boston: Pearson.

Goodlad, J. (1983). What some schools and classrooms teach. *Educational Leadership, 7*(40), 8–19.

Goodlad, J. (1984). *A place called school.* New York: McGraw-Hill.

Goodlad, J. (1990). *Teachers for our nation's schools.* San Francisco: Jossey-Bass.

Goodrich, H. (1997). Understanding rubrics. *Educational Leadership, 54*(4). Available at www.middleweb.com/rubricshg.html.

Goulet, L. (1987, February). The development of racial attitudes in children. Presentation to the Western Canadian Association for Student Teaching. Saskatoon, SK.

Grambs, J., & Carr, J. (1991). *Modern methods in secondary education* (4th ed.). Toronto: Holt, Rinehart & Winston.

Greenberg, K. (1996). *Zack's story: Growing up with same sex parents.* Minneapolis, MN: Lerner Publications.

Greene, M. (1991). Forward. In Britzman, D. (Ed.), *Practice makes practice.* Albany: University of New York Press.

Gregorc, A. (1979). Learning/teaching styles: Potent forces behind them. *Educational Leadership, 36*(4), 234–237.

Gregory, G., & Chapman, C. (2002). *Differentiated instructional strategies: One size doesn't fit all.* Thousand Oaks, CA: Corwin Press.

Gross Davis, B. (1993). *Tools for teaching.* San Francisco: Jossey-Bass.

Gudykunst, W., & Kim, Y. (1997). *Communicating with strangers: An approach to intercultural communication.* New York: McGraw-Hill.

Guignon, A. (1998). Multiple intelligences: A theory for everyone. *Education World.* Available at www.education-world.com/a_curr/curr054.shtml.

Guskey, T. (2002). Computerized grade-books and myth of objectivity. *Phi Delta Kappan, 83*(10), 775–780.

Hall, R., Hall, M., & Saling, C. (1999). The effects of graphical postorganization strategies on learning from knowledge maps. *Journal of Experimental Education, 67*(2), 101–112.

Hall, T. (2002) *Explicit instruction.* Wakefield, MA: National Center on Accessing the General Curriculum (CAST). Available at www.cast.org/ncac/index.cfm?i = 2875#pacing.

Halpern, D. (2000). *Sex differences in cognitive abilities* (3d ed.). Hillsdale, NJ: Erlbaum.

Hamel, A. (2004). Inclusion strategies that work. *Music Educators Journal, 90*(5), 33–37.

Hansen, J. M., & Childs, J. (1998). Creating a school where people like to be. *Educational Leadership, 56*(1), 14–17.

Hanser, L. (1995). *Traditional and cognitive job analysis as tools for understanding the skills gap.* Berkeley, CA: National Center for Research in Vocational Education, University of California. (ERIC Document ED 383842)

Hardman, M., Drew, C., & Egan, M. (2002). *Human exceptionality: Society, school and family* (7th ed.). Boston: Allyn & Bacon.

Hardman, M., Drew, C., & Egan, M. (2006). *Human exceptionality: Society, school and family* (8th ed.). Boston: Allyn & Bacon.

Harlow, J. (1972). *A taxonomy of the psychomotor domain: A guide for developing behavioral objectives.* New York: David McKay.

Hart, T. (2002, Winter). From mediocrity to mastery: Finding the patterns of knowledge. *Educational Horizons, 80*(2), 77–82.

Hatton, N., & Smith, D. (1995). Reflection in teacher education: Towards definition and implementation. *M. Teach, In House Resources,* University of Sydney, Faculty of Education and Social Work. Available at http://alex.edfac.usyd.edu.au/LocalResource/Study1/hattonart.html.

Heinmiller, B. (2000). Assessing student learning—and my teaching—through student journals. *ENC Focus, 7*(2). Available at www.enc.org/topics/assessment/altern/document.shtm?input = FOC1566-index.

Hellison, D. (1986, April). Cause of death—Physical education. *Journal of Physical Education, Recreation and Dance, 57*(4), 27–28.

Hellison, D. (1988, April). Cause of death—Physical education—A sequel. *Journal of Physical Education, Recreation and Dance, 59*(4), 18–21.

Hellison, D. (1990, Aug.). Making a difference—Reflections on teaching urban at-risk youth. *Journal of Physical Education, Recreation and Dance, 61*(6), 44–45.

Hellison, D. (1996). Teaching personal and social responsibility in physical education. In Silverman, S., & Ennis, C. (Eds.), *Student learning in physical education: Applying research to enhance instruction.* Champaign, IL: Human Kinetics.

Hellison, D. (2003). *Teaching responsibility through physical activity* (2nd ed.). Champaign, IL: Human Kinetics.

Hellison, D., & Templin, T. (1991). *A reflective approach to teaching physical education.* Champaign, IL: Human Kinetics.

Heroman, C. (2003). *Using technology for ongoing assessment.* Curriculum and Assessment, Teaching Strategies, Inc. Available at www.teachingstrategies.com/pages/page.cfm?pageid = 183.

Hicks, D. (1981). *Bafa Bafa in Minorities.* London: Heinemann Educational.

Higgins, N., & Sullivan, H. (1978). *Writing worthwhile objectives.* Tempe, AZ: Teaching for Competence.

Higgins, N., & Sullivan, H. (1981). *Assessing student learning.* Tempe, AZ: Teaching for Competence, College of Education, Arizona State University.

Honig, A. (2001). How to promote creative thinking. *Scholastic Early Childhood Today, 15*(5), 34–40.

Huba, M., & Freed, J. (2000). *Learner-centered assessment on college campuses: Shifting the focus from teaching to learning.* Boston: Allyn & Bacon.

Hughes, C., & Jones, B. (1988, March). Integrating thinking skills and processes into content instruction. Presented to the Third Annual Conference, Association for Supervision and Curriculum Development, Boston.

Hunter, M. (1971). *Theory into practice: Teach for transfer.* El Segundo, CA: TIP.

Hunter, M. (1984). Knowing, teaching, and supervising. In Hosford, P. (Ed.), *Using what we know about teaching.* Alexandria, VA: Association for Supervision and Curriculum Development.

Hunter, M. (1985). What's wrong with Madeline Hunter? *Educational Leadership, 42*(5), 57–60.

Hunter, R. (2004). *Madeline Hunter's mastery teaching increasing instructional effectiveness in elementary and secondary schools.* Thousand Oaks, CA: Corwin Press.

Iowa Testing Programs. (1999). *Using the tests: Testing students with special needs.* Iowa City, IA: University of Iowa. Available at www.uiowa.edu/ ~ itp/use-specialneeds.htm.

Jacobsen, D., Eggen, P., & Kauchak, D. (2002). *Methods for teaching: Promoting student learning.* Upper Saddle River, NJ: Merrill, Prentice-Hall.

Johnson, D., & Johnson, F. (1975a). *Joining together: Group theory and group skills.* Englewood Cliffs, NJ: Prentice-Hall.

Johnson D., & Johnson, F. (2003). *Joining together: Group theory and group skills.* Boston: Allyn & Bacon.

Johnson, D., & Johnson, R. (1975b). *Learning together and alone: Cooperation, competition and individualization.* Englewood Cliffs, NJ: Prentice-Hall.

Johnson, D., & Johnson, R. (1978). Cooperative, competitive, and individualistic learning. *Journal of Research and Development in Education, 1*(12), 3–15.

Johnson, D., & Johnson, R. (1980a). Cooperative learning: The power of positive goal interdependence. In Lyons, V. (Ed.), *Structuring cooperative learning: The 1980 Handbook.* Minneapolis: Cooperation Network.

Johnson, D., & Johnson, R. (1980b). The social integration of handicapped students into the mainstream. In Reynolds, M. (Ed.), *Social environment of schools.* Reston, VA: Council for Exceptional Children.

Johnson, D., & Johnson, R. (1990). *Cooperative learning: Warm-ups, grouping strategies, and group activities.* Edina, MN: Interaction Book Company.

Johnson, D., & Johnson, R. (1987a). *Learning together and alone: Cooperative, competitive, and individualistic learning.* Englewood Cliffs, NJ: Prentice-Hall.

Johnson, D., & Johnson, R. (1987b). Research shows the benefits of adult cooperation. *Educational Leadership, 45*(3), 27–30.

Johnson, D., & Johnson, R. (1989, April). Toward a cooperative effort: A response to Slavin. *Educational Leadership, 46*(7) 80–81.

Johnson, D., & Johnson, R. (1999). *Human relations: Valuing diversity.* Edina, MN: Interaction Book Company.

Johnson, D., Johnson, R., Bartlett, J., & Johnson, L. (1988). *Our cooperative classroom.* Edina, MN: Interaction Book Company.

Joint Field Experience Committee. (2004). Learning to teach: A shared responsibility. In *Internship Manual.* Regina, SK: Faculty of Education, University of Regina.

Jones, B., Palincsar, A., Ogle, D., & Carr, E. (1987). *Strategic teaching and learning: Cognitive instruction in the content areas.* Alexandria, VA: Association for Supervision and Curriculum Development.

Jones, J., & Pfeiffer, J. (Eds.). (1979). *Annual handbook for group facilitators.* San Diego, CA: University Associates.

Jorgenson, O., & Vanosdall, R. (2002). The death of science? What we risk in our rush toward standardized testing and the three R's. *Phi Delta Kappan, 83*(8), 601–605.

Joyce, B., Showers, B., & Rolheiser-Bennett, C. (1987). Staff development and student learning: A synthesis of research on models of teaching. *Educational Leadership, 45*(2), 11–23.

Joyce, B., Weil, M., & Calhoun, E. (2004). *Models of teaching* (8th ed.). Boston: Allyn & Bacon.

Kagan, S. (1985). *Cooperative learning resources for teachers.* Riverside, CA: Psychology Department, UCLA.

Kagan, S. (1994). *Cooperative learning.* San Juan Capistrano, CA: Kagan's Cooperative Learning.

Kameenui, E., & Carnine, D. (Eds.). (1998). *Effective teaching strategies that accommodate diverse learners.* Upper Saddle River, NJ: Prentice-Hall.

Kantrowitz, B., & Kalb, C. (1998, May 11). Boys. *Newsweek,* 55–60.

Kaplan, P. (1990). *Educational psychology for tomorrow's teacher.* St. Paul, MN: West.

Kauchak, D., & Eggen, P. (2003). *Learning and teaching: Research based methods* (4th ed.). Boston: Allyn & Bacon.

Kearsley, G. (2004). *Explorations in learning and instruction: Theory into practice.* TIP Data Base. Available at http://tip.psychology.org/index.html.

Keller, J. (1983). Motivational design of instruction. In Reigeluth, C. (Ed.), *Instructional-design theories and models: An overview of their status.* Hillsdale, CA: Erlbaum.

Kellerman, T. (1999). *Everything you wanted to know about FAS/FAE, but were afraid to ask!* Tucson, AZ: FAS Community Resource Center. Available at www.come-over.to/FASDAY.

Kennedy, M. (1991). Policy issues in teacher education. *Phi Delta Kappan, 72*(9), 658–665.

Kincheloe, J. (2004). The knowledges of teacher education: Developing a critical complex epistemology. *Teacher Education Quarterly, 31*(1), 49–66.

Kindlon, D., & Thompson, M. (2000). *Raising Cain: Protecting the emotional life of boys.* New York: Ballantine.

Kizlik, R. (2002). *Teaching and values.* ADPRIMA. Available at http://adprima.com/values.htm.

Kolb, D. (1976). *Learning style inventory.* Boston: McBer.

Kolb, D. (1984). *Experiential learning: Experience as the source of learning and development.* Englewood Cliffs, NJ: Prentice-Hall.

Kounin, J. (1970). *Discipline and group management in classrooms.* New York: Holt, Rinehart & Winston.

Kounin, J., & Doyle, P. (1975). Degree of continuity of a lesson's signal system and task involvement of children. *Journal of Educational Psychology, 67,* 159–164.

Kozioff, M., LaNunziata, L., Cowardin, J., & Bessellieu, F. (2001, Dec.) Direct instruction: Its contributions to high school achievement. *The High School Journal, 84*(2), 54–71.

Krathwohl, D., Bloom, B., & Masia, B. (1964). *Taxonomy of educational objectives. Handbook II: Affective domain.* New York: David McKay.

Kuiper, R. (2002). Enhancing metacognition through the reflective use of self-regulated learning strategies. *The Journal of Continuing Education in Nursing, 33*(2), 78–87.

Ladson-Billings, G. (1994). *The dreamkeepers: Successful teachers of African American children.* San Francisco: Jossey Bass.

Lang, H. (1990). Classroom management concerns of secondary teacher education preinterns. Presentation to the Western Canadian Association on Student Teaching, Brandon, Man.

Lasley, T. (1988). Defining the knowledge base: Prescriptions and principles. Unpublished paper, Department of Teacher Education, University of Dayton, Dayton, OH.

Latham, A. (1998). Rules and learning. *Educational Leadership, 56*(1), 104–105. Available at www.ascd.org/safeschools/e/9809/ssellatham.html.

Leinhardt, G. (2001). Situated knowledge and expertise in teaching. In Calderhead, J. (Ed.), *Teachers' professional learning* (pp. 146–168). London: Falmer.

Leinhardt, G., & Greeno, J. (1991). *The cognitive skill of teaching.* Norwood, NJ: Ablex Publishing Corporation.

Levin, T., with Long, R. (1981). *Effectiveness of instruction.* Washington, DC: American Association of Colleges of Teacher Education.

Lewis, R., & Doorlag, D. (2003). *Teaching special students: In general education classrooms* (6th ed.). Upper Saddle River, NJ: Merrill/Prentice Hall.

Loevinger, N. (1994). Teaching a diverse student body: Gender and your classroom. Charlottesville, VA: University of Virginia. In Center for Teaching and Learning. (1998). *Diversity in the college classroom: Teaching for inclusion.* Chapel Hill, NC: University of North Carolina. Available at www.unc.edu/depts/ctl/tfi3.html.

Macomber, H. (2003). *Listening top ten countdown.* Reforming Project Management. Available at http://weblog.halmacomber.com/2003_12_14_archive.html#107155525566587421.

Maehr, M. (1974). *Sociocultural origins of achievement.* Monterey, CA: Brooks/Cole.

Maker, C., Nielson, A., & Rogers, J. (1994). Giftedness, diversity, and problem-solving. *Teaching Exceptional Children, 27*(1), 4–19.

Marshall, C. (1991). Teachers' learning styles: How they affect student learning. *Clearing House, 64*(4), 225–227.

Martin, J. (1983). *Mastering instruction.* Boston: Allyn & Bacon.

Martorella, P. (1986). Teaching concepts. In Cooper, J. (Gen. Ed.), *Classroom teaching skills* (3d ed.). Lexington, MA: Heath.

Marzano, R. (2000). *Transforming classroom grading.* Alexandria, VA: Association for Supervision and Curriculum Development.

Marzano, R., Brandt, R., Hughes, C., Jones, B., Presseisen, B., Rankin, S., & Suhor, C. (1988). *Dimensions of thinking: A framework for curriculum and instruction.* Alexandria, VA: Association for Superivision and Curriculum Development.

Marzano, R., Marzano, J., & Pickering, D. (2003). *Classroom management that works: Research-based strategies for every teacher.* Alexandria, VA: Association for Supervision and Curriculum Development.

Maslow, A. (1962). *Toward a psychology of being.* Princeton, NJ: Van Nostrand.

Maxie, A. (2001). Developing early field experiences in a blended teacher education program; from policy to practice. *Teacher Education Quarterly, 28*(1), 115–131.

Mayer, J., & Salovey, P. (1997). What is emotional intelligence? In Salovey, P., & Sluyter, D. (Eds.), *Emotional development and emotional intelligence: Educational implications.* New York: Basic Books.

McBeath, A. (1989, March). *Reflections from an international perspective. On the education of teachers: Responses to the Academic Review Task Force.* Regina, SK: Faculty of Education, University of Regina.

McCarthy, B. (1986). *Hemispheric mode indicator (HMI).* Barrington, IL: Excel.

McCarthy, B. (1987). *The 4MAT system: Teaching to learning styles with right/left mode techniques.* Barrington, IL: Excel.

McCarthy, B., & Morris, S. (1994). *The 4MAT Course-Book. Volume 1.* Barrington, IL: Excel.

McDevitt, T., & Ormrod, J. (2002). *Child development and education.* Upper Saddle River, NJ: Merrill Prentice Hall.

McKinney, C., Gilmore, C., Peddicord, H., & McCallum, S. (1987). Effects of best example and critical attributes on prototype formation in the acquisition of a concept. *Theory and Research in Social Education, XV*(3), 189–202.

McLaughlin, J., Watts, C., & Beard, M. (2000). Just because it's happening doesn't mean it's working. *Phi Delta Kappan, 82*(4), 284–290.

McLeskey, J., & Waldron, N. (2004). Three conceptions of teacher learning: Exploring the relationship between knowledge and the practice of teaching. *Teacher Education and Special Education, 27*(1), 3–14.

MCLI. (2001). *Problem-based learning.* Maricopa Center for Learning and Instruction. Available at http://mcli.maricopa.edu/pbl/info.html.

McLuhan, M. (1994). *Understanding media: The extensions of man.* Cambridge, MA: MIT Press.

McMillan, J. (2001). Secondary teachers' classroom ssessment and grading practices. *Educational Measurement: Issues and Practice, 20*(1), 20–32.

McMillan, J. (2004). *Classroom assessment: Principles and practice for effective instruction* (3rd ed.). Boston: Allyn & Bacon.

McPeck, J. (1990). *Teaching critical thinking: Dialogue and dialectic.* New York: Routledge.

Medin, D., & Smith, E. (1984). Concepts and concept formation. *Annual Review of Psychology, 35,* 113–138.

Mitchell, R., Willis, M., Crawford M., & Chicago Teacher's Union Quest Center. (1977). *Learning in overdrive: Designing curriculum instruction, and assessment from the standards, A manual for teachers.* Golden, CO: North America Press; Washington, DC: The Education Trust.

Montague, E. (1987). *Fundamentals of secondary classroom instruction.* Columbus, OH: Merrill.

More, A. (1984, July). *Learning styles and Indian students: A review of research.* Paper presented at the Mokakit Indian Education Research Conference, London, Ontario. ERIC Document ED 249028.

Moore, J., Mintz, S., & Biermann, M. (1988). Reflectivity: The Edsel of education? In Waxman, H., Frieberg, H., Vaughen, J., & Weil, M. (Eds.), *Images of reflection in teacher education.* Reston, VA: Association of Teacher Educators.

Moore, K. (1989). *Classroom teaching skills: A primer.* New York: Random House.

Motamedi, V., & Sumrall, W. (2000, Spring). Mastery learning and contemporary issues in education. *Action in Teacher Education, 22*(1), 4–42.

Mueller, A., & Fleming, T. (2001). Cooperative learning: Listening to how children work at school. *The Journal of Educational Research, 94*(5), 259–265.

Mui, Y. Q. (2004, April 8). Md. plans to ease requirements of "No Child" law: Education officials may change how test results are interpreted. *The Washington Post,* p. AA10. Available at www.washingtonpost.com/ac2/wp-dyn?pagename = article&contentID = A58047–2004Apr7&notFound = true.

Muirhead, B. (2002, Feb.). Relevant assessment strategies for online colleges and universities. *USDLA Journal, 16*(1). Available at www.usdla.org/html/journal/FEB02_Issue/article04.html.

Murgio, M. (1969). *Communication graphics.* New York: Van Nostrand Reinhold.

National Association of Secondary School Principals. (1996). *Breaking ranks: Changing an American Institution.* Reston, VA: Author.

NCREL. (2002). *Learner-centered classrooms, problem-based learning, and the construction of understanding and meaning by students.* North Central Regional Educational Laboratory. Available at www.ncrel.org/sdrs/area/issues/content/cntareas/science/sc3learn.htm.

Newman, L. (2000). *Heather has two mommies.* Los Angeles, CA: Alyson Publications.

Newsweek. (1990). *Annual Editions: Child Growth and Development* (9th ed.).

Norris, J. (2003). Looking at classroom management through a social and emotional learning lens. *Theory into Practice, 42*(4), 313–318.

Norris, S. (1989). Can we test validly for critical thinking? *Educational Researcher, 18*(9), 21–26.

Novak, J. (1991). Clarify with concept maps: A tool for students and teachers alike. *The Science Teacher, 58*(7), 44–49.

Novak, J., & Gowin, D. (1984). *Learning how to learn.* New York: Cambridge University Press.

NWREL. (2000). *Motivating students to engage in class activities. Increasing student engagement and motivation: From time-on-task to homework.* Portland, OR: Northwest Regional Educational Laboratory. Available at www.nwrel.org/request/oct00/engage.html.

Office of Educational Research and Improvement (1993). *Performance assessment. Education consumer guide.* Office of Research, Office of Educational Research and Improvement, U.S. Department of Education. Available at www.ed.gov/pubs/OR/ConsumerGuides/perfasse/html.

Ogbu, J. (1999). The significance of minority status. Paper presented at the annual meeting of the American Educational Research Association, Montreal, PQ.

Orlich, D., Harder, R., Callahan, R., Kauchak, D., & Gibson, H. (1994). *Teaching strategies: A guide to better instruction* (4th ed.). Toronto: Heath.

Owens, R., Hester, J. L., & Teale W. (2002). Where do you want to go today? Inquiry-based learning and technology integration. *The Reading Teacher, 55*(7), 616–625.

OZ Teachers Net. (2004). *Teachers helping teachers.* Available at http://rite.ed.qut.edu.au/oz-teachernet/index.php?module = ContentExpress&func = print &ceid = 29.

Page, M., Rudney, G., & Marxen, C. (2004). Leading preservice teachers to water . . . and helping them drink: How candidate teachability affects the gatekeeper and advocacy roles of teacher educators. *Teacher Education Quarterly, 31*(2), 25–41.

Paik, S. (2003). Ten strategies that improve learning. *Educational Horizons, 81*(2), 83–85.

Parker, M., & Hellison, D. (2001). Teaching responsibility in physical education: Standards, outcomes, and beyond. *Journal of Physical Education, Recreation and Dance, 72*(9) 25–36.

Parsons, J. (1992). *What works: Ideas to teach by.* Edmonton, AL: Les Editions Duval.

Paul, R. (1990). *Critical thinking: What every person needs to survive in a rapidly changing world.* Rohnert Park, CA: Center for Critical Thinking and Moral Critique.

Paul, R. (2002). The art of generating and asking questions. *The Second International Conference, Preconference,* Sonoma State University. Available at www.criticalthinking.org.

Paul, R., & Elder, L. (2001). *Critical thinking: Tools for taking charge of your learning and your life.* Englewood Cliffs, NJ: Prentice-Hall.

Paulson, F., Paulson, P., & Meyer, C. (1991). What makes a portfolio a portfolio? *Educational Leadership, 48*(5), 60–63.

Performance Learning Systems. (2003). *Learning styles: Vitally important.* Performance Learning Systems. Available at www.plsweb.com/sec06.htm.

Perkins, D., & Salomon, G. (1989). Are cognitive skills context bound? *Educational Researcher, 18*(1), 16–25.

Perry, C., & Power, B. (2004). Finding the truths in teacher education field experiences. *Teacher Education Quarterly, 31*(2), 125–136.

Peterson, D., Kromrey, J., Borg, J., & Lewis, A. (1990). Defining and establishing relationships between essential and higher order teaching skills. *The Journal of Educational Research, 84*(1), 5–12.

Peterson, P., & Comeaux, M. (1987). Teachers' schemata for classroom events: The mental scaffolding of teachers' thinking during classroom instruction. *Teaching & Teacher Education, 3*(4), 319–331.

Pettus, A., & Blosser, M. (2002). Fun with learning and recall. *Science Activities, 38*(4), 10–14.

Pfeiffer, J., & Goodstein, L. (Eds.). (1982). *Annual handbook for group facilitators.* San Diego, CA: University Associates.

Piaget, J. (1929). *The child's conception of the world.* NY: Harcourt, Brace Jovanovich.

Piaget, J., & Inhelder, B. (1969). *The psychology of the child.* NY: Basic Books.

Pike, G., & Selby, D. (1999). *Bafa Bafa. In the Global Classroom 1.* Toronto, ON: Pippin Publishing Corporation, pp. 189–195.

Popham, J. (1999). *Classroom assessment: What teachers need to know.* Alexandria, VA: Association for Supervision and Curriculum Development.

Popham, J. (2003). *Test better, teach better: The instructional role of assessment.* Alexandria, VA: Association for Supervision and Curriculum Development.

Pressley, M., & Harris, K. (1990). What we really know about strategy instruction. *Educational Leadership, 48*(1), 31–34.

Provost, R. (1991). The value of ideas: The immersion approach to the development of thinking. *Educational Researcher, 20*(2), 3–10.

Purkey, W., & Novak, J. (1996). *Inviting school success: A self-concept approach to teaching, learning, and democratic practice* (3d ed). Belmont, CA: Wadsworth.

Raab, M. (2004). *How well are learning styles supported in the current design of online learning?* Available at www.netsoc.tcd.ie/ ~ martin/Portofol/Martin LiteratureReview.pdf.

Ramsey, P. (2004). *Teaching and learning in a diverse world: Multicultural education for young children* (3rd ed.). New York: Teachers' College, Columbia University.

Raths, L., Wasserman, S., Jonas, A., & Rothstein, A. (1967). *Teaching for thinking: Theory and application.* Columbus, OH: Merrill.

Raths, L., Wasserman, J., & Wasserman, S. (1978). *Pupil activity reference book: Thinking skills development program.* Westchester, IL: Benefic Press.

Redick, S., & Vail, A. (1991). *Motivating youth at risk.* Gainsville, VA: Home Economics Education Association.

Renner, P. (1983). *The instructor's survival kit* (2d ed.). Vancouver, BC: PER Training Associates.

Resnick, L. (1987). *Education and learning to think.* Washington, DC: National Academy Press.

Richetti, C., & Sheerin, J. (1999). Helping students ask the right questions. *Educational Leadership, 57*(3), 58–62.

Rink, J. (1996). Effective instruction in physical education. In Silverman, S., & Ennis, C. (Eds.), *Student learning in physical education: Applying research to enhance instruction.* Champaign, IL: Human Kinetics.

Riordan, C. (1997). *Equality and achievement: An introduction to the sociology of education.* Boston: Longman.

Robinson, M. (1995). Alternative assessment techniques for teachers. *Music Education Journal, 81*(5), 28–34.

Rogers, J. (1993, May). The inclusion revolution. *Research Bulletin 11, Phi Delta Kappa,* Center for Evaluation, Development, and Research, No. 1. Available at www.pdkintl.org/edres/resbul11.htm.

Rose, L., & Gallup, A. (1999). The 31st annual Phi Delta Kappa/Gallup Poll of the public's attitudes toward the public schools. *Phi Delta Kappan, 81*(1), 41–56.

Rose, L., & Gallup, A. (2003). The 35th annual Phi Delta Kappa/Gallup Poll of the public's attitudes toward the public schools. *Phi Delta Kappan, 84*(1), 41–56.

Rosenshine, B. (1979). Content, time, and direct instruction. In Peterson, P., & Walberg, H. (Eds.), *Research on teaching: Concepts, findings, and applications.* Berkeley, CA: McCutchan.

Rosenshine, B. (1987). Explicit teaching and teacher training. *Journal of Teacher Education, 38*(3), 34–36.

Rosenshine, B. (1988). Synthesis of research on explicit teaching. *Educational Leadership, 43*(7), 60–69.

Rosenshine, B., & Stevens, R. (1986). Teaching functions. In Wittrock, M. (Ed.), *Handbook of research on teaching* (3rd ed.) (pp. 376–391). New York: Macmillan.

Roth, W. (1999). Computers can individualize learning and raise group interaction skills. *The Education Digest, 65*(3), 27–31.

Rothstein, P. (1990). *Educational psychology.* New York: McGraw-Hill.

Rothstein, R. (1999). Blaming teachers. *The American Prospect 11*(2). Available at www.prospect.org/print/V11/2/rothstein-r.html.

Rowan, J. (2004). Dialectical thinking. The George Walford International Essay Prize. Available at www.gwiep.net/site/dialthnk.html.

Rowe, M. (1972). Wait-time and rewards as instructional variables, their influence in language, logic, and fate control. *Paper presented at the National Association for Research in Science Teaching,* Chicago, IL. ED 061 103.

Rowe, M. (1986). Wait time: Slowing down may be a way of speeding up. *Teacher Education, 37*(1), 43–50.

Royal Melbourne Institute of Technology (RMIT). (2004). *Teaching and Learning.* Melbourne, Australia. Available at www.rmit.edu.au.

Sadker, M., & Sadker, D. (2003). Questioning skills. In Cooper, J. (Ed.), *Classroom teaching skills* (7th ed.) (pp. 101–147). Boston: Houghton Mifflin.

Saskatchewan Learning. (1991a). *Instructional approaches: A framework for instructional practice.* Regina, SK: Saskatchewan Department of Education.

Saskatchewan Learning. (1991b). *Student evaluation: A teacher handbook.* Regina, SK: Saskatchewan Department of Education.

Saskatchewan Learning. (2004). *Global Issues: Unit 5, History 20.* Regina, SK: Saskatchewan Department of Education. Available at www.sasked.gov.sk.ca/docs/history20/unitv.html#over.

Savoie, J., & Hughes, A. (1994). Problem-based learning as classroom solution. *Educational Leadership, 52*(3), 54–57.

Scarborough Board of Education. (1997). *Policy on assessment and evaluation.* Scarborough, ON: Board of Education.

Schimmel, D. (1997). Traditional rule-making and the subversion of citizenship education. *Social Education, 61*(2), 70–74.

Schon, D. (1983). *The reflective practitioner.* New York: Basic Books.

Schon, D. (1990). *Educating the reflective practitioner.* San Francisco: Jossey-Bass.

Scott, E., & McCollum, H. (1993). Making it happen: Gender equitable classrooms. In Biklen, S., & Pollard, D. (Eds.), *Ninety-Second yearbook of the National Society for the Study of Education. Part 1, Gender and education* (pp. 174–190). Chicago: University of Chicago Press.

Scriven, M., & Paul, R. (1996). *Defining critical thinking.* Available at http://lok1.sonoma.edu/Cthink/University/univclass/Defining.nclk.

Shanker, A. (1985). Leading educators outline training needed by future teachers. *Phi Delta Kappan, 67*(4), 321.

Sharan, S., & Lazarowitz, R. (1980). In Sharan, S. (Ed.), Cooperative learning in small groups: Recent methods and effects on achievement attitudes and ethnic relations. *Review of Educational Research, 50*(2), 241–271.

Shenker, J., Goss, S., & Bernstein, D. (1996). *Instructor's resource manual for psychology.* Boston: Houghton Mifflin.

Shostak, R. (1977). Lesson presentation skills. In Cooper, J. (Ed.), *Classroom teaching skills* (1st ed.). Lexington, MA: Heath.

Shostak, R. (1982). Lesson presentation skills. In Cooper, J. (Ed.), *Classroom teaching skills* (2nd ed., pp. 111–145). Lexington, MA: Heath.

Shostak, R. (1986). Lesson presentation skills. In Cooper, J. (Gen. Ed.), *Classroom teaching skills* (3rd ed.), pp. 117–137. Lexington, MA: Heath.

Shulman, L. (1986). Those who understand: Knowledge growth in teaching. *Educational Researcher, 15*(2), 4–14.

Sigurthorsdottir, I. (2001). Philosophy for children in action: Iceland. *Thinking, 15*(4), 16–19.

Silverman, S., & Ennis, C. (1996). *Student learning in physical education: Applying research to enhance instruction.* Champaign, IL: Human Kinetics.

SIU. (2002). *Problem-based learning.* School of Medicine, Southern Illinois University. Available at http://pbli.org/pbl/htm.

Sizer, T. (1992). *Horace's compromise: The dilemma of the American high school* (3rd ed.). Boston: Houghton Mifflin.

Skinner, B. (1971). *Beyond freedom and dignity.* New York: Knopf.

Skinner, B. (1976). *Walden two.* New York: Macmillan.

Slack, J. (2002). *Questioning strategies to improve student thinking and comprehension.* Southeast Comprehensive Assistance Center, Southeast Educational Development Laboratory. Available at www.sedl.org/secac/ren/quest.pdf.

Slavin, R. (1978a). Student teams and comparison among equals: Effects on academic performance and student attitudes. *Journal of Educational Psychology, 70,* 532–538.

Slavin, R. (1978b). Student teams and achievement divisions. *Journal of Research and Development in Education, 12,* 39–49.

Slavin, R. (1983). *Cooperative learning.* Research on teaching monograph series. New York: Longman.

Slavin, R. (1987). Cooperative learning and the cooperative school. *Educational Leadership, 45*(3), 7–13.

Slavin, R. (1991). Synthesis of research on cooperative learning. *Educational Leadership, 48*(5), 71–82.

Sleeter, C., Torres, M., & Laughlin, P. (2004, Winter). Scaffolding conscientization through inquiry in teacher education. *Teacher Education Quarterly, 31*(1), 81–96.

Smerdon, B., Burkam, D., & Lee, V. (1999, Fall). Access to constructivist and didactic teaching: Who gets it? Where is it practiced? *Teachers College Record, 101*(1), 5–34.

Sonnier-York, C., & Stanford, P. (2002). Learning to cooperate: A teacher's perspective. *Teaching Exceptional Children, 34*(6), 40–55.

Sparks, D. (1999). Assessment without victims: An interview with Rick Stiggins. *Journal of Staff Development, 20*(2), 54–56.

SPDU/SIDRU. (1996). *Creating an inclusive classroom: Integrating students with special needs.* Regina, SK: Saskatchewan Professional Development Unit/ Saskatchewan Instructional Development Unit.

Stage, F., Miller, P., & Kinzie, J. (1998). Creating learner centered classrooms: What does learning theory have to say? *ASHE ERIC Higher Education Reports, 26*(4), 1–121.

Stahl, R. (1990). *Using "think time" behaviors to promote students' information processing, learning, and on-task participation, An instructional module.* Tempe, AZ: Arizona State University.

Stahl, R. (1994). Using "think-time" and "wait-time" skillfully in the classroom. ERIC Document ED370885. Available at http://atozteacherstuff.com/pages/1884.shtml.

Stanford, G., & Rourke, A. (1974). *Human interaction in education.* Boston: Allyn & Bacon.

Star, L. (1999, updated 2005). Is character education the answer? *Education World.* Available at www.gppgle.ca/search?q = character + education&hl = & start = 40&sa = N.

Stein, M., & Carnine, D. (1999). Designing and delivering effective mathematics instruction. In Steven, R. (Ed.), *Teaching in American schools* (pp. 245–270). Upper Saddle River, NJ: Merrill/Prentice-Hall.

Sternberg, R. (1985). Teaching critical thinking, Part 2: Possible solutions. *Phi Delta Kappan, 67*(4), 277–280.

Sternberg, R. (1990). Thinking styles: Keys to understanding student performance. *Phi Delta Kappan, 71*(5), 366–371.

Sternberg, R. (1990, Aug.). Problem solving: Teaching for thinking. Presentation to the Regina Board of Education Teachers. Regina, SK.

Sternberg, R. (2003). What is an "expert student?" *Educational Researcher, 32*(8), 5–9.

Sternberg, R., & Williams, W. (2002). *Educational psychology.* Boston: Allyn & Bacon.

Stevenson, J., & Dunn, R. (2001). Knowledge management and learning styles: Prescriptions for future teachers. *College Student Journal, 35*(4), 483–490.

Stewart, D. (1969). A learning-systems concept as applied to courses in educational training. In Witman, R., & Meierhenrey, W. (Eds.), *Education media: Theory into practice* (pp. 134–177). Columbus, OH: Charles Merrill.

Stiggins, R. (2002). Assessment crisis: The absence of assessment FOR learning. *Phi Delta Kappan, 83*(10), 758–765.

Stiggins, R. (2005). *Student-involved assessment for learning* (4th ed.). Upper Saddle River, NJ: Merrill/Prentice Hall.

Stiggins, R. J. (1993). Two disciplines of educational assessment. *Measurement and Evaluation in Counseling and Development, 26,* 93–104. Available at www.ericdigests.org/1998-2/career.htm.

Swanson, H. (2001, Oct.). Searching for the best model for instructing students with learning disabilities. *Focus on Exceptional Children, 34*(2), 1–15.

TeacherNet. (1995–2003). *Department for Education and Skills* (a resource to support the education profession. Available at www.teachernet.gov.uk/teaching andlearninglibrary/Behaviour_management.

Tennyson, R., & Park, O. (1980). The teaching of concepts: A review of instructional design research literature. *Review of Educational Research, 50*(1), 55–70.

Terry, M. (2001). Translating learning style theory into university teaching practices: An article based on Kolb's experiential learning model. *Journal of College Reading and Learning, 32*(1), 68–85.

Thompson, M. (1999). Keynote address at the Wellesley College Gender and Equity in Schools Conference: A Focus on Boys and Men.

Tiedt, P., & Tiedt, I. (2002). *Multicultural teaching: A handbook of activities, information, and resources* (6th ed.). Boston: Allyn & Bacon.

Tiedt, P., & Tiedt, I., (2006). *Multicultural education: A handbook of activities, information, and resources* (7th ed.). Boston: Allyn & Bacon.

Tomlinson, C. (1999). *The differentiated classroom: Responding to the needs of all learners.* Alexandria VA: Association for Supervision and Curriculum Development. Available at www.cedu.niu.edu/tedu/portfolio/diffclass.htm.

Trafton, P., & Midgett, C. (2001). Learning through problems: A powerful approach to teaching mathematics. *Teaching Children Mathematics, 7*(9), 532–536.

Tschanannen-Moran, M., & Hoy, A. (2000). Collaborative learning: A memorable model. *The Teacher Educator, 36*(2), 148–165.

Tubbs, S., & Moss, S. (2003). *Human communication: Principles and contexts* (9th ed.). Boston: McGraw-Hill.

Turnbull, R., Turnbull, A., Shank, M., Smith, S., & Leal, D. (2002). *Exceptional lives: Special education in today's schools.* Upper Saddle River, NJ: Merrill Prentice-Hall.

U.S. Department of Education. (1986). *What works: Research about teaching and learning.* Washington, DC: U.S. Department of Education.

Vaishnev, A., Globe Staff, & Deman, W. (2002, July 8). Special ed gender gap stirs worry. *The Boston Globe & Mail,* p. A1.

Van Boxtal, C., & Roelofs, E. (2002). Investigating the quality of student discourse: What constitutes a productive student discourse? *The Journal of Classroom Interaction, 36,* 55–62.

Van Manen, M. (1977). Linking ways of knowing with ways of being practical. *Curriculum Inquiry, 6,* 205–228.

Van Tassell, G. (1999). *Practical applications of current brain research: Classroom management.* Salt Lake City, UT: brains.org. Available at www.brains.org/classroom_management.htm.

Vigna, J. (1995). *My two uncles.* Morton Grove, IL: Albert Whitman & Company.

Vygotsky, L. (1962). *Thought and language.* Cambridge, MA: MIT Press.

Vygotsky, L. (1978). *Mind in society: The development of higher mental processes.* Cambridge, MA: Harvard University Press.

Walberg, H. (1990). Productive teaching and instruction: Assessing the knowledge base. *Phi Delta Kappan, 71*(6), 470–478.

Walls, R., Nardi, A., Von Minden, A., & Hoffman, N. (2002). The characteristics of effective and ineffective teachers. *Teacher Education Quarterly, 29*(1), 39–48.

Wang, M., Haertel, G., & Walberg, H. (1993). What helps students learn? *Educational Leadership, 51*(4), 74–79.

Wangsatorntanakhun, J. (1997, Sept.). *Designing performance assessments: Challenges for the three-story intellect.* Bankok, Thailand: Ruamru/dee International School. Available at www.geocites.com/Athens/Parthenon/8658.

Wasserman, S. (1978). *Put some thinking in your classroom.* San Diego, CA: Coronado.

Weber, W. (1990). Classroom management. In Cooper, J. (Ed.), *Classroom Teaching Skills*. Lexington, MA: D.C. Heath and Company.

Weber, W., Crawford, J., Roff, L., & Robinson, C. (1983). *Classroom management: Reviews of the teacher education research literature*. Princeton, NJ: Educational Testing Service.

Weinert, F., & Helmke, A. (1995). Learning from wise mother nature or big brother instructor: The wrong choice as seen from an educational perspective. *Educational Psychologist, 30*(3), 135–142.

Weinstein, C., & Mignano, A. (1993). *Elementary classroom management*. New York: McGraw-Hill.

Weiss, I., & Pasley, J. (2004). What is high-quality instruction? *Educational Leadership, 61*(5), 24–28.

Wiggins, G., & McTighe, J. (1998). *Understanding by design*. Alexandria, VA: Association for Superivison and Curriculum Development.

Wiggins, G., & McTighe, J., (2005). *Understanding by design*. Alexandra, VA: ASCD Publications.

Wilen, W., & Clegg, A. (1986). Effective questions and questioning: A research review. *Theory and Research in Social Education, 14*(2), 153–161.

Wilson, L., & Corpus, D. (2001). The effects of reward systems on academic performance. Westerville, OH: Middle School Journal, Research Articles, National Middle School Association. Available at www.nmsa.org/research/res_articles_sept2001.html.

Wiman, R., & Meierhenry, W. (1969). *Educational media: Theory into practice*. Columbus, OH: Charles Merrill.

Windschitl, M. (2000). Supporting the development of science inquiry skills with special classes of soft-ware. *Educational Technology Research and Development, 48*(2), 81–95.

Winzer, M. (1995). *Educational psychology*. (1995). Scarborough, ON: Allyn & Bacon Canada.

Wisconsin Department of Public Instruction. (2001). *Guidelines to facilitate participation of students with special needs in state assessments: Examples of test accommodations for students with disabilities*. Eau Claire, WI: State of Wisconsin Department of Public Instruction. Available at www.dpi.state.wi.us/dpi/oea/aspecneed.html.

Witkin, H., Moore, C., Goodenough, D., & Cox, P. (1977). Field-dependent and field-independent cognitive styles and their educational implications. *Review of Educational Research, 47*(1), 1–64.

Womack, J. (1966). *Discovering the structure of social studies*. New York: Benzinger.

Woolfolk, A. (2004). *Educational psychology* (9th ed.). Boston: Allyn & Bacon.

Wright, I., & Sears, A. (Eds.). (1997). *Trends and issues in Canadian social studies*. Vancouver, BC: Pacific Educational Press.

Zeichner, K. (1993). Educating teachers for cultural diversity (NCRTL Special Report). East Lansing, MI: National Center for Research on Teacher Learning.

Zeichner, K., Grant, C., Gay, G., Gillette, M., Valli, L., & Villegas, A. (1998). A research informed vision of good practice in multicultural teacher education: Design principles. *Theory into Practice, 37*(2), 163–171.

Zeichner, K., & Liston, D. (1987). Teaching student teachers to reflect. *Harvard Educational Review, 57*(1), 23–48.

Index

Abstract concepts, 280–281
Academic integrity, homework and, 270–271
Academic learning time, 181
Acceleration programs, 90
Action research, 5, 459
Active learning, in experiential learning, 384–387
Affective domain, 108–112
    activities, 126–127
    cognitive domain versus, 107
    importance of and teaching to achieve objectives, 109–110
    in skills teaching, 308
    teaching competencies in, 110–112
    thinking processes and, 456
Affective objectives, 207, 211–213
African Americans, lifestyles of, 72
Airasian, P., 213
Albert, L., 194
Alberta Human Rights Commission, 72–73, 74–75
Alderman, M., 116–119
Allan, J., 262–263
Allen, J., 166–167
Alternative assessment, 152–153
Altruism, in cooperative learning, 421
American Association of University Women (AAUW), 95, 97
American Indians, lifestyles of, 72
American Sign Language (ASL), 88
Amrein, A., 157
Amundson, K., 45–46
Anderson, L., 213
Anecdotal records, 138
Anticipation, by teachers, 184
Antiracist education, 75–76, 78–79
Arends, R., 204, 228, 257, 259–260
Armstrong, T., 67, 68, 89
Aronson, E., 421
Aronson, J., 81
Asbury, F., 41, 52
Ashcraft, M., 284
ASL (American Sign Language), 88
Aspy, C., 468
Aspy, D., 468
Assessment and evaluation, 132–162
    accommodating special needs learners, 154–155
    activities, 162

in Blended Elementary/Secondary Teacher Competence Profile, 13
    cases, 140, 160–161
    of cooperative learning, 427–428
    definitions in, 133–134
    grading and marking systems in, 149–152, 176
    importance of, 132
    issues and trends in, 155–160
    key concepts in, 132–135
    methods of organization in, 136–137
    methods of recording data in, 136, 137–139
    of ongoing student activities, 136, 140–142
    other forms of, 152–154
    quizzes and tests in, 136, 142–152
    Teacher Competence Profile (TCP) and, 30–31, 134
    techniques for, 135–145
    thinking processes and, 453–455, 459
Assessment stations, 136
Assigned questions, 346–347
Assimilation, integration versus, 80
At-risk learners, 116–121
    attribution theory and, 116–117, 118–119
    characteristics of, 92–94
    circle of courage and, 119–120
    helping, 117–119
    school environment for, 120–121
Attitudes and values, 107–131
    affective domain and, 108–112
    at-risk learners, 116–121
    attitudes, defined, 109
    in Blended Elementary/Secondary Teacher Competence Profile, 13
    cases, 123–126
    changing, 122
    critical thinking and, 461
    motivation and, 112–116
    taxonomies of educational objectives, 107, 211–213, 235–238, 252–253, 449
    in Teacher Competence Profile (TCP), 30, 110, 113
    teaching, 121–126
    and value-clarifying group, 408
Attribution theory, 114–119
    at-risk learners and, 116–117, 118–119
    in teaching concepts, 289

Auditory learning, 65–66
Ausubel, David, 221
Authentic assessment, 153–154
Authentic instruction, 1

Backward design approach, 160, 204–205
Bainer, D., 2, 63, 181, 257, 345
Balzer, F., 41, 52
Banks, C., 76
Banks, J., 76, 78, 101
Barbe, W., 65
Baron, J., 453, 454
Barry, V., 456
Bartlett, J., 430
Basic management skills, 176–179
Beamon, G., 371–372
Beard, M., 5
Beaudry, J., 62, 65, 70
Beebe, S., 47, 49–50
Beebe, S., 47, 49–50
Behavioral contracting, 190
Behavioral disabilities, 87
Behavior description, 50–51
Belief, respect for, 73
Berliner, D., 157, 227, 251, 258
Bernard, Sandy, 97
Bernstein, D., 245
Berry, B., 4
Besellieu, F., 341
Beyer, B., 444–445, 453, 461, 462
Bias
    in assessment and evaluation, 155–156
    in books and instructional materials, 80
    content, 155–156
    testing, 156
Bigbee, M., 96
"Big ideas," 342
Bilingual students, 88
Blair, L., 252
Blaney, N., 421
Blended Elementary/Secondary Teacher Competence
    Profile, 13–14
Bloom, Benjamin, 87, 107, 211–213, 252–253,
    359, 449
Bloom's Taxonomy, 107, 211–213, 235–238,
    252–253, 449
Blosser, M., 456
Bonwell, C., 384
Borg, J., 443
Borich, G., 47, 63, 114, 267
Bowd, A., 152
Bower, Carolyn, 188–189
Boyer, E., 201
Bracey, G., 467
Brainstorming group, 406

Brandt, R., 451–452
Brendtro, L., 119–120
Bristor, V., 25, 26
Britzman, D., xiii
Brokenleg, M., 119–120
Brooks, Jacqueline, 154
Brooks, Martin, 154
Brophy, J., 63, 87, 89, 95, 100, 114, 116, 118, 214,
    222, 254, 291
Brown, B. L., 317
Brown, G., 157
Brown, S., 71, 76–77
Brualdi, A., 247
Brubacher, M., 416, 430
Bruner, Jerome, 215, 287, 342, 448–449
Buchmann, M., 383
Bulgren, J., 287
Bull, J., 157
Bullied students, 90–91
Burden, P., 92–93, 205, 268, 313
Burkam, D., 341
Bush, George W., 157
Butler, D., 354
Buzz group, 406–407
Byerly, S., 388
Byrd, D., 92–93, 205, 268, 313

Calhoun, E., 101–102, 284, 288, 340
California Assessment Program, 453–455
Callahan, R., 63, 258
Campbell, Bruce, 68–69
Campbell, C., 17
Canadian Public Health Association, 98
Canadian Teachers Federation, 93–94
Canter, L., 194
Carbone, P., 121
Carey, L., 318–320
Carnine, D., 342
Carr, E., 453
Case, R., 460–461
Castle, K., 171
Causal attributions, 114–115
Center for Teaching and Learning, 102
Chapman, C., 234
Character education, 121
Charles, C., 176
Checking up, by teachers, 180, 184
Checkly, K., 67
Chicago Teacher's Union Quest Center, 206
Chickering, A., 384
Childers, W., 41, 52
Children of poverty, 92–94, 116–121
Childs, J., 120
Chinn, C., 412
Chunkers, 64

Church, K., 467
Cipani, E., 189–190
Circle of courage, 119–120
Civikly, J., 44
Clark, J., 427, 430
Classifying concepts, 287–298
Classroom climate
    classroom environment in, 174–175
    in cross-cultural teaching, 81–82
    effective, characteristics of, 173–174
    physical environment in, 174
    positive, establishing, 112
    school environment in, 175
    for small groups, 408
    to support classroom management, 173–175
Classroom management, 164–200
    activities, 196–197
    as affective teaching competency, 112
    background for, 164–168
    in Blended Elementary/Secondary Teacher
        Competence Profile, 13
    cases, 182, 184–186, 194–195
    common problems of, 167–168
    corrective approaches in, 186–191
    disruptive behavior and, 179–181, 187–188,
        189–191, 427
    effective, aspects of, 168
    guidelines for, 191–195
    preventive approaches in, 168–173
    student perspective on, 166–167, 176
    supportive approaches in, 173–186
    in Teacher Competence Profile (TCP), 31–32,
        169–170
Classroom teaching
    described, 26
    instruction in, 166, 174–175
    in practice of targets, 25–27
    professional journal and, 28
    steps for practicing targets in, 26–27
Clear communication, 47
Clegg, A., 254
Closure
    kinds of, 224
    lesson plan, 221, 224
Cobb, V. L., 42
Cognitive domain
    affective domain versus, 107
    Bloom's Taxonomy and, 107, 211–213, 235–238,
        252–253, 449
    moving beyond, 42–43
    in skills teaching, 307
    thinking processes and, 456
Cognitive objectives, 207, 211–213
Cohn, D'Vera, 104–106
Coladarci, T., 159–160

Collaborative learning, 401–415
    activities, 433
    benefits and limitations of, 409–410
    in Blended Elementary/Secondary Teacher
        Competence Profile, 13
    cases, 413–415
    discussion approaches in, 411–413
    effective use of, 408–409
    group skills in, 394–401, 403–408, 410–411, 433
    group structure in, 410–411
    member duties in, 410–411
    nature of, 401–403
    peer tutoring in, 413
    in Teacher Competence Profile (TCP), 37,
        395, 396
Combination task analysis, 320–321
Comeaux, M., 4
Communication skills, 41–57
    activities, 54–55
    in Blended Elementary/Secondary Teacher
        Competence Profile, 13
    case, 53–54
    communication disorders, 86–87
    components of effective communication, 41
    in groups, 400
    importance of, 41
    interpersonal, 47–53, 400
    moving beyond cognitive approach and, 42–43
    nonverbal, 45–46, 81
    oral, 45
    role of teacher in, 43–44
    self-knowledge and, 44
    in Teacher Competence Profile (TCP), 29, 42, 43
Community
    Critical Thinking Community, 456
    in cross-cultural teaching, 79–80
Competence, in circle of courage, 119–120
Computer-assisted instruction (CAI), 356–357
Computer-based education (CBE), 356
Computer-enriched instruction (CEI), 356
Computer-managed instruction (CMI), 356
Computers
    in assessment and evaluation, 159–160
    benefits and limitations of, 357–358
    in the classroom, 356–358
    individual study and, 355–358
Concept maps, 285–286
Concept teaching, 277–305
    activities, 303
    analysis of, 287–290, 300
    in Blended Elementary/Secondary Teacher
        Competence Profile, 13
    cases, 299–302
    concept maps and, 285–286
    cycle for, 297–298

Concept teaching, *continued*
  deductive and inductive approaches in, 296–297
  diversity and, 287
  kinds of, 280–283
  learner readiness and, 287
  learning, 283–284
  nature of, 277–287
  in Teacher Competence Profile (TCP), 35, 280
  teaching approaches and, 287–298
  textbooks and, 290–295
  understanding, 277–279
Concrete concepts, 280–281
Conferencing
  checklists for, 23
  in professional development, 18–19
Conflict resolution, 186, 399
Congruent communication, 47
Conjunctive concepts, 282
Consensus seeking, 400–401
Consequences of behavior, 186–187
Constructivist approach, 220–221, 340–343
Content objectives, 207
Continuing dialectical relationship, in teacher
    preparation, 6–7
Contracts, 136, 190
Cooper, H., 268–269
Cooperative games, 425
Cooperative learning, 415–432
  activities, 433–434
  approaches to, 421–425
  in Blended Elementary/Secondary Teacher
    Competence Profile, 13
  cases, 430–433
  cooperative skills in, 418–419
  elements of, 415–416
  essentials of, 416–417
  evaluating, 427–428
  group skills in, 394–401, 433
  handling problems in, 426–427
  prejudice reduction and, 425–426
  principles of cooperation for, 420–421
  research and, 417–418
  in Teacher Competence Profile (TCP), 37, 395, 396
  teachers and, 399–400, 428–430
  trusting climate for, 419–420
Coopersmith, S., 119–120
Coordinate concepts, 282
Cordis, L., 17
Core thinking skills (Marzano), 451–453
Corrective approaches, to classroom management,
    186–191
Cotton, Kathleen, 164, 246, 250, 253–254, 356–357
Council on Interracial Books for Children,
    78–79
Cowardin, J., 341

Crawford, J., 172–173
Crawford, M., 206
Creative thinking, 64, 462–467
  cases, 464–467
  and gifted, talented, and creative learners,
    89–90, 426
  nature of, 462–463
  teaching for creativity, 463–464
Crick, N., 96
Criterion-referenced evaluation, 135
Critical beliefs, in cross-cultural teaching, 76–77
Critical thinking, 460–462. *See also* Reflection
  dispositions and attitudes in, 461
  nature of, 460–461
  procedures and skills in, 461–462
  in teacher preparation, 6–7
Critical Thinking Community, 456
Cross-cultural teaching, 71–84
  accommodating cultural diversity in the
    classroom, 83
  antiracist education, 75–76, 78–79
  becoming a multicultural teacher, 78–79
  bias in books and curricular materials, 80
  cases, 84
  classroom climate and, 81–82
  classroom management in, 188–189
  critical beliefs and, 76–77
  effective teaching, 77–78
  empathy in, 77
  fairness in disciplining minority students, 188–189
  hidden curriculum and, 78
  integration versus assimilation in, 80
  intercultural communication in, 52–53
  knowledge and action in, 80
  learning about community in, 79–80
  learning style and, 69–70
  nature of culture, 71–72
  nonverbal behavior in, 81
  racial awareness in, 82–83
  respecting human rights and differences in, 2–75
  teaching methods and, 81–82
Cruickshank, D., 2, 63, 181, 183, 257, 345
Culture. *See also* Cross-cultural teaching
  learning style and, 69–70
  lifestyles of group and, 72
  nature of, 71–72
Culture of poverty, 72
Curran, Lorna, 430
Curriculum knowledge. *See also* Lesson and unit
    planning and delivery
  hidden curriculum, 78
  for special needs learners, 101–102
  in Teacher Competence Profile (TCP), 34–35,
    232–233
Curwin, R., 194

Dale, Edgar, 288
Daniels, V., 187
Danielson, C., vii, 9–12, 22–25, 28
Darling-Hammond, L., 25, 42
Dave, R., 107
Decision making
  assessing present teaching capability, 23–24
  as group skill, 400–401
  reflection and, 27
  in teacher preparation, 6
  thinking processes and, 457–458
Declarative content and objectives, 207
Deductive approach
  in skills teaching, 313–314
  in teaching concepts, 296–297
Delivery cycle, 14–17
  nature of, 16–17
  team planning and delivery, 17
Delpit, Lisa, 61
Deman, W., 95
Dembo, M., 114
Demonstrations, 327–330
  principles of, 329–330
  procedures for effective, 328–329
Deshler, D., 287
Deterring behaviors, of teachers, 179–180
Dever, M., 26
Devitt, J., 81
Dewey, John, 245, 341, 448
Dialectical thinking, 6–7, 456
Dialogue groups, 407
Diaz, C., 71
Dick, W., 318–320
Didactic questioning, 348
Diem, K., 214
Dietel, R., 153
Digital Change at the Chalk Face, 355–356
Direct instruction, 339–351
  activities, 362
  in Blended Elementary/Secondary Teacher
    Competence Profile, 13
  cases, 348–351
  constructivism and, 340–343
  nature of, 339–340
  in Teacher Competence Profile (TCP),
    36, 339
  teaching methods and, 343–348
Directions,
  by teacher, 182–186
  cases, 184–186
Disabilities, types of, 85–88. *See also* Special needs
    learners
Discipline. *See also* Classroom management
  defined, 166
  for minority students, 188–189

Discrimination, 73
Discussion, 257–264
  activities, 273
  in Blended Elementary/Secondary Teacher
    Competence Profile, 13
  cases, 263–264
  in collaborative learning, 411–413
  conducting, 257–258
  encouraging participation in, 259–260, 413
  guided, 258
  guidelines for effective, 258–259
  interaction patterns in, 261
  planning class, 261–263
  purposes of, 257
  talking circles in, 260–261
  in Teacher Competence Profile (TCP), 35
  unguided, 258
Disjunctive concepts, 282
Disney Working Partnership, 206
Disruptive behavior, 179–181, 187–188, 189–191, 427
Diversity issues, 58–106. *See also* Cross-cultural
    teaching
  activities, 103–104
  approaches to, 99–102
  in Blended Elementary/Secondary Teacher
    Competence Profile, 13
  children of poverty and, 92–94, 116–121
  classroom management and, 188–189
  fairness in disciplining minority students,
    188–189
  gender differences, 94–99
  importance of teaching about and for diversity,
    58–61
  intercultural communication, 52–53
  learning styles, 61–71
  sexual orientation, 97–98
  special needs learners, 84–92
  in Teacher Competence Profile (TCP), 29, 60
  in teaching concepts, 287
Dobbs, M., viii
Doorlag, D., 90, 100
Dowler-Coltman, G., 97
Doyle, P., 176
Doyle, W., 176
Drayton, B., 373
Dreamkeepers, The (Ladson-Billings), 83–84
Drefs, I., 120, 175
Dreikers, R., 194
Drew, C., 85, 93, 99–100, 187
Drill and practice, 347–348
Driscoll, M., 109
DuBosq, J., 355
Duncan, B., xiii, 8–9
Dunn, K., 62–63, 70
Dunn, R., 61, 62–63, 65, 70

Eadie, S., 427, 430
Educational Research Group, 181
Edwards, D., 193
Egan, M., 85, 93, 99–100, 187
Eggen, P., 41, 112–113, 151, 155, 159, 166, 254, 268, 283, 285, 443
Ehrmann, S., 384
Einstein, Albert, 201
Eison, J., 384
Elksnin, L., 43
Elksnin, N., 43
Elliott, S., 114
Embedding approach to thinking, 455
Emmer, E., 58, 164, 168, 171, 173, 176, 179, 194
Emotional disabilities, 87
Empathy, 48, 77
Engelhart, M., 211–213
English as a Second Language (ESL) students, 88
Enhancing Professional Practice (Danielson), 9, 11
Enhancing Student Achievement (Danielson), 11
Ennis, C., 313
Enrichment programs, 90
Erlandson, C., 98, 191
ESL (English as a Second Language) students, 88
Essay test items, 143–144, 145
Evaluation. *See* Assessment and evaluation
Evertson, C., 58, 164, 168, 171, 173, 176, 179, 194
Examples, in teaching concepts, 289–290, 291–295
Exceptionalities. *See* Special needs learners
Exemplars, 283–284
Exeter, D., 386, 387
Experiential instruction, 379–390
    activities, 390
    benefits and limitations of, 383
    in Blended Elementary/Secondary Teacher
        Competence Profile, 13
    cases, 388–389
    games in, 387–388, 425
    Kolb model of, 381–383
    nature of, 379–383
    purposes of, 381
    role playing in, 387–388
    simulations in, 387–388
    in Teacher Competence Profile (TCP),
        36–37, 379
    teachers and, 384–387
Explicit teaching, 342
External attributions, 114–115, 117
External locus of control, 115
Extrinsic motivation, 113

Falk, J., 373
Feedback. *See also* Assessment and evaluation
    characteristics of effective, 19–20
    disclosure and, 20
    giving, 20

receiving, 20
on seatwork, 270
in skills teaching, 309
Feelings description, 50, 51–52
Feldman, Sandra, 247, 265
Field dependence, 63–64
Field experience, Teacher Competence Profile (TCP)
        and, 22–23, 474–480
Field independence, 63–64
Finkel, E., 12
Fleming, T., 408
Focused imaging, 359
Focusing
    in classroom presentations, 215–216
    in group focus behaviors of teachers, 178–179
Fogarty, R., 448
Fordham University, 60–61
Formal concepts, 281–282
Formative evaluation, 134–135, 159
Forums, 407
Fosnot, C., 221
Four Worlds Development Project, 260–261
Freed, J., 139
Freiberg, H. J., 173
Frieman, B., 98
Fritz, R., 63
Functioning culture, 71–72
Furst, E., 211–213

Gage, N., 258
Gagné, Robert, 109, 218–219
Gagné Instructional Model, 218–219
Gallagher, J., 4
Gallup, A., 164
Games, 387–388, 425
Gardner, Howard, 63, 67–69, 89, 154
Garrity, C., 90–91
Gazda, G., 41, 52
Geddes, D., 46
Geerinck, T., 47, 49–50
Gender differences, 94–99
    cases, 98–99
    eliminating stereotyping, 96–97
    literature on effects of, 94–96
    sexual orientation and, 97–98
Genuineness, 48
Gibson, H., 63, 258
Gibson, S., 357–358
Gifted, creative, and talented learners, 89–90, 426
Gilmore, C., 284
Glasser, William, 192–193
Goals
    group skills and, 398
    proximate, for at-risk learners, 118
Gokhale, A., 394
Good, C., 81

Good, T., 63, 87, 89, 95, 100, 114, 116, 118, 214, 222, 254, 291
Good behavior game, 190
Goodlad, J., 25, 80, 82–83, 108, 343
Goodrich, H., 139
Goss, S., 245
Gowin, D., 285, 286
Grading and marking systems, 149–152, 176
Graves, Nan, 430
Graves, Ted, 430
Greathouse, S., 268
Greene, Maxine, xiii
Greeno, J., 4
Gregorc, A., 62, 63
Gregory, G., 234
Grigg, N., 87
Gross Davis, B., 394
Group assessments, 136
Group focus behaviors, of teachers, 178–179
Group Investigation (GI), 422–423
Group skills, 394–401
    activities, 433
    case, 401
    class as group, 396–398
    classroom interactions, kinds of, 396
    stages group development, 398–399
    teachers and, 399–400
Group work. See also Collaborative learning;
        Cooperative learning
    benefits and limitations of, 409–410
Grunwald, B., 194
Gudykunst, W., 53
Guidance, in skills teaching, 310
Guided discussion, 258, 411
Guided inductive inquiry, 370–373, 374
Guignon, A., 67–68
Gusky, T., 159–160

Hager, K., 26
Hall, M., 285
Hall, R., 285
Halpern, D., 95
Hamel, A., 89
Handouts, 345
Hansen, J. M., 120
Hanser, I., 317
Harder, R., 63, 258
Hardman, M., 85, 93, 99–100, 187
Harlow, J., 211–212
Harris, K., 447
Hart, T., 359
Hatton, N., 5, 6
Heinmiller, B., 141
Hellison, D., 312–313, 314–315
Helmke, A., 339
Hemispheric mode, 64–65

Herman, L., 153
Heroman, C., 159
Hertz-Lazarowitz, R., 422
Hester, J. L., 372
Hidden curriculum, 78
Hierarchical task analysis, 319–320
Higgins, N., 147
Hill, W., 211–213
Hispanic Americans, lifestyles of, 72
Holistic rating scales, 138
Homework
    activities, 273
    assessment and evaluation of, 141
    in Blended Elementary/Secondary Teacher
        Competence Profile, 13
    case, 271
    as instructional variable, 268–271
    in Teacher Competence Profile (TCP), 35
Honig, A., 464
Howes, C., 96
Hoy, A., 403–404
Huba, M., 139
Hughes, A., 468
Hughes, C., 451–453
Human rights, respecting, 72–75
Hunt, James B., Jr., viii
Hunter, Madeline, 11, 219–220, 311, 342, 343
Hunter Direct Instruction Lesson Approach, 219–220

Immersion approach to thinking, 455
Immersion programs, 88
Inclusion, 85, 99–101, 187–188
Indirect instruction, 368–379
    activities, 390
    in Blended Elementary/Secondary Teacher
        Competence Profile, 13
    cases, 378–379
    format for, 375–376
    guided inductive inquiry, 370–373, 374
    inductive approach to, 370–374, 376–379
    inquiry and, 369–379
    nature of, 368–369
    in Teacher Competence Profile (TCP), 36–37, 368
    teachers and, 375–377
    unguided inductive inquiry, 373–374
    using inquiry methods, 370–379
Individual assessments, 136
Individual disruptive incident barometer, 191
Individualization, in skills teaching, 311
Individualized instruction and technology, 355
Individual study, 352–361
    activities, 362
    advantages of, 354
    in Blended Elementary/Secondary Teacher
        Competence Profile, 13

Individual study, *continued*
cases, 360–361
computers and, 355–358
importance of, 352–353
methods for, 353–360
nature of, 352
in Teacher Competence Profile (TCP), 36, 352
Inductive approach
in indirect instruction, 370–374, 376–379
in skills teaching, 314
in teaching concepts, 296–297
Informal concepts, 281–282
Inhelder, B., 215
Inquiry methods. *See also* Experiential instruction;
Indirect instruction
nature of, 369–370
using, 374–375
Instability, 115, 117
Instruction. *See also* Classroom management;
Classroom teaching
classroom climate and, 174–175
defined, 166
Instructional materials
bias in, 80
concepts and, 290–295
Instructional planning. *See* Lesson and unit planning
and delivery
Instructional skills, 338–339
Instructional strategies. *See* Collaborative learning;
Cooperative learning; Direct instruction;
Experiential instruction; Indirect instruction;
Individual study; Teaching methods/strategies
Instructional variables, 213–218
activities, 272–273
in Blended Elementary/Secondary Teacher
Competence Profile, 13
cases, 255–256, 263–264, 267–268, 271
discussion and, 13, 35, 257–264, 273
homework, 13, 35, 141, 268–271, 273
questioning and, 13, 35, 245–256, 272–273,
346–348, 458–459
seatwork, 13, 35, 265–268, 273
in Teacher Competence Profile (TCP), 33–34, 35,
247, 257, 265
varying presentation, 214–218
Integration
of assessment in teaching process, 160
assimilation versus, 80
of thematic units, 231–232
Intellectual disabilities, 87
Interaction patterns, in classroom discussions,
261–263
Intercultural communication, 52–53
Interference, in skills teaching, 310

Internal attributions, 114–115, 117
Internal locus of control, 115
Intern Professional Profile (IPP), vii, 12–14
Interpersonal skills, 47–53
attributes of effective, 48
clear communication, 47
congruent communication, 47
in groups, 400
for helping others understand you, 50–52
intercultural, 52–53
listening, 47–48
in Teacher Competence Profile (TCP), 29, 43
for understanding others, 48–50
Interstate New Teacher Assessment and the Support
Consortium (INTASC), vii, 12
Intrinsic motivation, 113–114
Inzlicht, M., 81

Jens, K., 90–91
Jigsaw, 421
Jigsaw II, 421
Jinks, T., 412
Johari awareness model (Johari Window), 44
Johnson, David, 394, 416–420, 426–428, 430
Johnson, F., 435
Johnson, L., 430
Johnson, Roger, 394, 416–420, 426–428, 430
Joint Field Experience Committee, 12
Jonas, A., 449–451
Jones, B., 451–453
Jones, J., 384–386
Jorgenson, O., 372
Journals
assessment and evaluation of, 141
professional, 27–28
Joyce, B., 101–102, 284, 288, 340, 417

Kagan, S., 406, 427, 430
Kalb, C., 94–96
Kameenui, E., 342
Kantrowitz, B., 94–96
Kaplan, P., 265, 268, 269
Kauchak, D., 41, 63, 112–113, 151, 155, 159, 166,
254, 258, 268, 283, 285, 443
Kearsley, G., 448
Keller, J., 116
Kellerman, T., 93
Kim, Y., 53
Kincheloe, J., 41
Kindlon, D., 97
Kinesthetic learning, 65–66
Kinzer, S., 25, 26
Kizlik, R., 121
Klavas, A., 62, 65, 70

Klein, K., 26
Knuth, R., 153
Kolb, David, 63, 381–383
Kounin, Jacob, 173, 176–179
Kozioff, M., 341
Krathwohl, D., 107, 211–213
Kratochwill, T., 114
Kromrey, J., 443
Kuiper, R., 446
Kysilka, M., 71, 76–77

Laboratory, teaching. *See* Microteaching laboratory
Laboratory group, 407
Ladson-Billings, G., 83
Lang, H., 167, 180
LaNunziata, L., 341
Lapp, S., 25, 26
Latham, A., 171
Laughlin, P., 61
Leal, D., 85–87
Learning centers, 358
Learning disabilities, 87
Learning principles, 308–311
Learning styles, 61–71
    adapting to different, 70
    in cultural perspective, 69–70
    defining, 62–64
    hemispheric mode and, 64–65
    learning modality preferences, 65–66
    as personal, 61
    teaching style and, 70–71
    theory of multiple intelligences, 67–69
    types of, 63
Lectures, 343–346
Lee, V., 341
Left mode learners, 64
Leinhardt, G., 4, 339
Lenz, B., 287
Lesson and unit planning and delivery, 201–244
    activities, 234–238
    in Blended Elementary/Secondary Teacher
        Competence Profile, 13
    cases, 217–218, 224–225
    instructional variables in, 213–218
    lesson planning in, 218–225, 294–295
    phases of, 202–204
    planning approaches to, 201–207
    planning variables in, 207–213
    in skills teaching, 321–323, 324–325
    in Teacher Competence Profile (TCP), 33, 203,
        213–214, 232–233
    unit planning, 225–234
Letter grade system, 149–150
Lewis, A., 443

Lewis, R., 90, 100
Lifestyles of groups, 72
Lindsday, J., 268
Linear approaches, 204
Listening skills, 47–48
Littlefield, J., 114
Locus of control, 115
Loevinger, N., 95
Lyman, Frank, 406

Macomber, Hal, 47–48
Mainstreaming, 85, 99–101, 187–188
Maker, C., 154
Marking systems, 149–152, 176
Marshall, C., 70–71
Martin, J., 376–377
Martorella, P., 278, 282
Marxen, C., 12, 475
Marzano, J., 164–165, 176, 179
Marzano, R., 156, 164–165, 176, 179, 451–452
Masia, B., 107, 211–212
Massialas, B., 71
Mastery grading system, 150–151
Mastery learning, 358–359
Matching test items, 144, 148
Max, D. T., 249
Maxie, A., 5, 474
Mayer, J., 43
McBeath, A., 17, 167
McCallum, S., 284
McCarthy, B., 63–65
McCollum, H., 97
McDevitt, T., 93, 94
McDougall, D., 152
McGreal, T., 11–12
McKinney, C., 284
McLaughlin, J., 5
McLeskey, J., vii, 336, 344
McMillan, J., 132, 149, 153, 160
McPeck, J., 460–461
McTighe, J., 160, 204
Measurement, 134. *See also* Assessment and
    evaluation
Medin, D., 283
Meierhenry, W., 287
Mendler, A., 194
Metacognitive ability, 342–343
Metcalf, K., 2, 63, 181, 257, 345
Métis, lifestyles of, 72
Meyer, C., 137
Microteaching laboratory, 20–22
    described, 20–21
    professional journal and, 28
    steps for practicing targets in, 21–22

Midgett, C., 443
Mignano, A., 265
Milstone, C., 47, 49–50
Minds of Our Own (videotape series), 467
Minor disruptions, 179–181
Mitchell, R., 206
Montague, E., 265
Moore, K., 175
Morris, S., 64–65
Moss, S., 47, 52–53
Motamedi, V., 359
Motivation, 112–116
    activities, 127
    as affective teaching competency, 111
    attribution theory and, 114–116
    common sense factors in, 116
    defining, 113–114
    in Teacher Competence Profile (TCP), 113
Motor skills, in skills teaching, 312–313
Movement management behaviors, of teachers,
        177–178
Mueller, A., 408
Mui, Ylan Q., 157
Muirhead, B., 152
Multicultural teaching, 78–79. *See also* Cross-cultural
        teaching
Multiple-choice test items, 144–145, 148
Multiple intelligence theory, 67–69
    applying, 68–69
    list of intelligences, 67–68
Murgio, M., 214

Nairne, J., 262–263
Nardi, A., 2–4
Narrative grading system, 151
National Board for Professional Teaching Standards
        (NBPTS), vii, 12
National Council for the Social Studies (NCSS), 205
National Teacher Examination (NTE), 12
Nielson, A., 154
No Child Left Behind Act, viii, 109, 157–158, 444
Nonlinear approaches, 204
Nonverbal communication skills, 45–46, 81
Norm-referenced evaluation, 135
Norms, group skills and, 397
Norris, J., 42
Norris, S., 461
Note taking, 345–346
Novak, J., 120–121, 285, 286
Numerical grade system, 150
Nye, B., 268

Objectives
    activities versus, 209–210
    affective, 207, 211–213

    cognitive, 207, 211–213
    conditions of performance, 210–211
    describing student performance, 210
    importance of clear, 207–209
    lesson, 209
    planning, 207–213
    psychomotor, 207, 211–213
    teaching to achieve, 109–110
    writing, 209
Observation
    checklists for, 138
    cooperative learning and, 429–430
    professional journal and, 28
O'Donnell, A., 412
Office of Educational Research and Improvement, 152
Ogbu, J., 71
Ogle, D., 453
O'Hara, H., 98
One-three-six group, 408
Open discussion, 258, 412
Oral assessments, 143
Oral communication skills, 45
Orientation, in fostering group development,
        398–399
Orlich, D., 63, 258
Ormrod, J., 93, 94
Overgeneralization, 74
Overlapping behaviors, of teachers, 177
Owens, R., 372

Page, M., 12, 475
Paik, S., 339
Palincsar, A., 453
Panels, 407
Paraphrasing, 48, 49
Parsons, J., 233–234
Participation
    in discussions, 259–260, 413
    in skills teaching, 308
Pasley, J., 249
Pass-fail system, 150
Paul, R., 248–249, 455, 461
Paulson, F., 137
Paulson, P., 137
Payne, R., 416, 430
Peddicord, H., 284
Peer assessments, 136–137
Peer tutoring, 413
Penalties, in classroom management, 187
Pendlebury, M., 157
Pepper, F., 194
Perception checking, 48, 49–50
Performance assessment, 133, 141, 152. *See also*
        Assessment and evaluation
Performance skills, 312–313

Performance test items, 143
Perry, C., 4
Peterson, D., 443
Peterson, P., 4
Pettus, A., 456
Pfeiffer, J., 384–386
Phelps, R., 41, 52
Phrasing questions, 248–249
Physical disabilities, 85–86
Piaget, Jean, 215, 448
Pickering, D., 164–165, 176, 179
Planning variables, 207–213
    content, 207
    objectives, 207–213
Popham, J., 156, 158
Porter, W., 90–91
Portfolios, 137, 151
Positive interdependence, 416, 420
Poverty
    children at risk and, 92–94, 116–121
    culture of, 72
Power, in circle of courage, 119–120
Power, B., 4
Practice and drill, 347–348
Practice of skills, 323–324
Practice of targets, 20–27
    in classroom teaching, 25–27
    decision making in, 23–25
    designing data sheets, 24–25
    in field experience, 22–23
    in laboratory microteaching, 20–22
    planning targets, 24–25
Prejudice, 73, 425–426
Presseisen, B., 451–452
Presentations
    assessment and evaluation of, 140–141
    varying classroom, 214–218
Pressley, M., 447
Preventive approaches, to classroom
    management, 168–173
Prior knowledge, linking new information to, 453
Problem-based learning (PBL), 467–469
    in Blended Elementary/Secondary Teacher
        Competence Profile, 14
    cases, 469
    nature of, 468
    reasons for using, 468
    in Teacher Competence Profile (TCP), 37–38, 467
Problem solving
    in cooperative learning, 426–427
    problem-solving group for, 407
    thinking processes and, 456–458
Procedural content and objectives, 207
Procedural task analysis, 318–319
Procedures

in classroom management, 172
critical thinking and, 461–462
Professional Assessments for Beginning Teachers
    (PRAXIS), vii, 12
Professional development practica, 38–40
    general internship skills, 14
    professional development process, 14
Professional development process (PDP), 14,
    18–28. See also Teacher Competence
    Profile (TCP)
    competencies in, 475–477
    components of, 18–19
    conferencing in, 18–19, 23
    helping relationship framework in, 19–20
    practice of targets in, 20–27
    reflection in, 27–28
Professional journals, 27–28
    described, 27
    tips for keeping, 27–28
Prompted test items, 147–148
Prototypes, 283–284
Provost, R., 455
Proximate goals, for at-risk learners, 118
Psychomotor objectives, 207, 211–213
Purkey, W., 120–121

Questioning, 245–256
    activities, 272–273
    assigned questions, 346–347
    in Blended Elementary/Secondary Teacher
        Competence Profile, 13
    cases, 255–256
    didactic, 348
    distribution, 250–251
    to encourage thinking, 458–459
    levels of questions in, 252–254
    normal steps in, 247–248
    practices to avoid, 249–250
    procedures for, 247–250
    responses in, 254–255
    in Teacher Competence Profile (TCP), 35
    trends in, 245–247
    "wait time" in, 250–252
Quinby, P., 468
Quizzes and tests, 136, 142–152
    bias in, 156
    essay, 143–144, 145
    marking systems for, 149–152
    matching items, 144, 148
    multiple-choice, 144–145, 148
    oral, 143
    performance, 143
    preparing, 142–143, 146–149
    short-answer, 144
    true-false, 145, 148

Raab, M., 63
Racial awareness, in cross-cultural
    communication, 82–83
Racism
    antiracist education, 75–76
    approaches to change, 75–76
    causes of, 75
    defining problem of, 75
Ramsey, P., 97
Rankin, S., 451–452
Raths, L., 449–451
Rating scales, 138
Reacting, as affective teaching competency, 111
Readiness, 287
Reality therapy, 192–193
Redick, S., 92–93
Redirects, 254
Redmond, M., 47, 49–50
Reflection. *See also* Critical thinking
    defined, 112
    in dialectical thinking, 456
    professional journal and, 27–28
    in teacher preparation, 6–7
Reinforcement
    of desirable behavior, 180
    in skills teaching, 310
Relational concepts, 282
Relaxation training, 191
Reliability, 135
Removal time out, 190–191
Renner, P., 228
Renner Unit-Planning Sequence, 228
Resnick, L., 443–444
Respect, for human rights and differences, 72–75
Responses, in questioning, 254–255
Responsibility, in skills teaching, 314–315
Reston, Scotty, 141
Rewards, in classroom management, 187
Richetti, C., 252
Rickett, K., 416, 430
Ridener, B., 25, 26
Right mode learners, 64
RMIT Teaching and Learning Unit (Australia), 380
Robinson, C., 172–173
Robinson, M., 141
Roff, L., 172–173, 176, 178, 193
Rogers, J., 99, 154
Rogers, K., 171
Role playing, 387–388
Role-playing group, 407–408
Rolheiser-Bennett, C., 417
Rose, L., 164
Rosenshine, B., 265
Rothstein, A., 449–451

Rothstein, P., 114, 457, 463
Rothstein, Richard, 207
Round tables, 407
Rourke, A., 405
Routines, in classroom management, 172
Rowan, J., 456
Rowe, Mary Budd, 250, 252
Rubrics, 138–140
Rudinow, J., 456
Rudney, G., 12, 475
Rules
    in classroom management, 171
    dealing with misbehavior and violations
        of, 189–191

Sadker, D., 246, 250, 251
Sadker, M., 246, 250, 251
Sager, N., 90–91
Saling, C., 285
Salovey, P., 43
Saskatchewan Teachers' Federation, 98
Savoie, J., 468
Scapegoating, 74–75
Schimmel, D., 171
School environment
    for at-risk learners, 120–121
    classroom climate and, 175
School-university partnerships, 26
Schumaker, J., 287
Schwille, J., 383
Scott, E., 97
Scriven, M., 461
Seatwork
    activities, 273
    in Blended Elementary/Secondary Teacher
        Competence Profile, 13
    case, 267–268
    feedback on, 270
    as instructional variable, 265–268
    in Teacher Competence Profile (TCP), 35
Self-assessments, 136–137
Self-concept, and integration versus
    assimilation, 80
Self-evaluation, 151–152
Self-fulfilling prophecy, 74, 117
Self-knowledge, 44
Sensitivity to feelings, as affective teaching
    competency, 112
Sensory preferences, 65–66
Set, lesson plan, 221–222
Settel, H., 98
Seven Step Planning Model, 315–327
Severe and multiple disabilities, 87
Sex differences, 94. *See also* Gender differences

Sexual orientation, 97–98

Shank, M., 85–87

Sharan, S., 422, 423, 425

Sheerin, J., 252

Shenker, J., 245

Short-answer test items, 144

Short-Camilli, C., 90–91

Shostak, R., 214, 215, 217, 222–224

Showers, B., 417

Shulman, L., 3

Signal time out, 190

Significance, in circle of courage, 119–120

Sikes, J., 421

Silence

    in classroom presentations, 216

    "wait time" in questioning, 250–252

Silverman, S., 313

Simulations, 387–388

Skiba, Russ, 188

Skill domains, 306–308

Skills teaching, 306–334

    activities, 331

    in Blended Elementary/Secondary Teacher

      Competence Profile, 13

    cases, 325–327, 330

    demonstrations, 327–330

    nature of skills, 306–315

    Seven Step Planning Model for, 315–327

    in Teacher Competence Profile (TCP), 36, 307

Skinner, B., 194

Slack, Jill, 213, 252

Slavin, R., 416–418, 421–422, 425

Sleeter, C., 61

Small groups. *See also* Group work

    in collaborative learning, 404–408

    kinds of, 405–408

    methods for, 408

    roles in, 405

Smerdon, B., 341

Smith, D., 5, 6

Smith, E., 283

Smith, S., 85–87

Snapp, M., 421

Social attitude, respect for, 73

Social disabilities, 87

Soliciting, as affective teaching competency, 111

Sonnier-York, C., 429

Special needs learners, 84–92

    assessing and evaluating, 154–155

    at-risk students, 92–94, 116–121

    bullied students, 90–91

    cases, 91–92

    cooperative learning and, 426–427

    curriculum for, 101–102

    disabilities and learning problems, 85–88

    gifted, creative, or talented learners, 89–90, 426

    population trends, 104–106

    students with exceptionalities, 84–85

    working with, 88–89

Specific learning disabilities, 87

Splitters, 64

Stability, 115, 117

Stahl, R., 250–252, 254

Stand-alone approach to thinking, 455

Standardized tests, 135

Standards. *See also* Teacher Competence Profile

    (TCP)

    benefits of academic, 206

    critics of, 206–207

    in lesson and unit planning and delivery, 205–207

    in standards-based grading, 149

    for teacher preparation, 5, 12

Stanford, G., 405

Stanford, P., 429

Star, L., 121

Stephin, C., 421

Stereotyping, 73–74, 96–97

Sternberg, R., 94, 95, 114, 175, 284, 447, 453, 454,

    457, 461–462

Stevens, R., 265

Stevenson, J., 61

Stiggins, R. J., 132, 137, 149, 157, 158, 159

Structural immersion, 88

Structure, group skills and, 398

Students. *See also* Special needs learners

    at-risk, 92–94, 116–121

    beliefs about student learning, 62

    classroom management and, 166–167, 176

    computers and, 355–358

    conditions of performance of, 210–211

    in cross-cultural communication, 81–82

    describing performance of, 210

    learner expectations, 205

Students with special needs. *See* Special needs

    learners

Student Teams and Achievement Divisions

    (STAD), 422

Study skills, 360

Subordinate concepts, 282

Successful experiences, for at-risk learners,

    118–119

Suhor, C., 451–452

Sullivan, H., 147

Sumrall, W., 359

Summative evaluation, 135

Superordinate concepts, 282

Supportive approaches, to classroom

    management, 173–186

Supportive intervention, cooperative learning and, 429–430
Swanson, H., 341
Swassing, R., 65
Symposia, 407

Tactual learning, 65–66
Talking circles, 260–261
Task analysis, in skills teaching, 317–321
Teacher Competence Profile (TCP), vii, 6, 8, 9, 12–17, 22–25, 28–40
  assessment and evaluation in, 30–31, 134
  attitudes and values in, 30, 110, 113
  classroom management in, 31–32, 169–170
  collaborative learning in, 37, 395, 396
  communication skills in, 29, 42, 43
  cooperative learning in, 37, 395, 396
  curriculum knowledge in, 34–35, 232–233
  direct instruction in, 36, 339
Teacher Competence Profile (TCP), *(continued)*
  diversity issues in, 29, 60
  experiential instruction strategy in, 36–37, 379
  field experience and, 22–23, 474–480
  as goal and assessment guide, 474
  indirect instruction in, 36–37, 368
  individual study in, 36, 352
  instructional variables in, 33–34, 35, 247, 257, 265
  interpersonal skills in, 29, 43
  lesson and unit planning and delivery in, 33, 203, 213–214, 232–233
  motivation in, 113
  problem-based learning in, 37–38, 467
  for self-analysis, 477–480
  skills teaching in, 36, 307
  teaching concepts in, 35, 280
  thinking skills in, 37–38, 446
  using, xi–xii
TeacherNet, 180–181
Teacher preparation, 2–40. *See also* Teacher Competence Profile (TCP)
  applying research on, 2–9
  in Blended Elementary/Secondary Teacher Competence Profile, 13–14
  components of, 10, 13–14, 18–19, 28–40
  criteria for, 4
  for cross-cultural teaching, 4–5
  Danielson's model for, 9–17, 22–25
  delivery cycle and, 14–17
  growth areas in, 7
  hierarchy of capabilities in, 5–7
  model for, 9–17, 28–40
  personal attributes in, 4–5
  professional development and, 14, 18–28
  standards for, 5, 12

theory and practice in, 7–9
Teachers. *See also* Classroom climate; Classroom management; Classroom teaching; Cross-cultural teaching; Professional development process (PDP); Teacher preparation; Teaching concepts; Teaching methods/strategies
  affective teaching competencies of, 110–112
  characteristics of effective and ineffective, 2–4, 77–78
  communications role of, 43–44
  cooperative learning and, 399–400, 428–430
  expectations of, 205–206
  general principles for teaching diverse learners, 102
  gifted learners and, 89–90
  group skills and, 399–400
  hemispheric mode preference of, 64–65
  indirect instruction and, 375–379
  individual study and, 354, 355
  learning styles and, 62–63
  motivation of students and, 115–116
  multicultural, 78–79
  role in developing communication skills, 43–44
  teaching style of, 70–71
Teaching methods/strategies
  for at-risk learners, 118
  in cross-cultural communication, 81–82
  in direct instruction, 343–348
  in unit planning, 229–231
Teaching strategies, methods, and skills, 338
Teale, W., 372
Teams-Games-Tournament (TGT), 421–422
Technical capabilities, in teacher preparation, 6
Templin, T., 312–313
Terry, M., 382–383
Tests. *See* Quizzes and tests
Textbooks. *See* Instructional materials
Thinking operations (Wasserman), 449–451
Thinking skills and processes, 443–473
  action research and, 5, 459
  affective and cognitive strategies in, 456
  assessment and evaluation and, 453–455, 459
  in Blended Elementary/Secondary Teacher Competence Profile, 14
  cases, 464–467
  classic approaches to, 448–453
  creative thinking, 64, 89–90, 426, 462–467
  critical thinking, 6–7, 460–462
  decision making and, 457–458
  dialectical thinking in, 6–7, 456
  importance of, 445–446, 447
  importance of process in, 453–455
  in organizing knowledge and learning, 446–447
  problem-based learning, 467–469
  problem solving in, 456–457

questioning and, 458–459
in Teacher Competence Profile (TCP), 37–38, 446
Think-pair-share group, 405–406
Thompson, M., 97
Tiedt, I., 78, 81
Tiedt, P., 78, 81
Time out
removal, 190–191
signal, 190
Tombari, M., 47, 63, 114
Tomlinson, C., 101
Torres, M., 61
Total immersion, 88
Trafton, P., 443
Transfer, in skills teaching, 311
Travers, J., 114
True-false test items, 145, 148
Trust, in cooperative learning, 419–410
Tschanannen-Moran, M., 403–404
Tubbs, S., 47, 52–53
Turnbull, A., 85–87
Turnbull, R., 85–87
Tutorial group, 407

Unguided inductive inquiry, 373–374
Unit planning. *See* Lesson and unit planning and
delivery
University-school partnerships, 26

Vail, A., 92–93
Vaishnev, A., 95
Validity, 135
Value-clarifying group, 408
Values. *See* Attitudes and values
Van Bockern, S., 119–120
Van Manen, M., 5
Vanosdall, R., 372
Van Tassell, G., 194
Visual learning, 65–66
Von Minden, A., 2–4
Vygotsky, Lev, 257, 342, 448

"Wait time", in questioning, 250–252
Walberg, H., 5, 269
Waldron, N., vii, 336, 344
Walls, R., 2–4
Walters, R., 41, 52
Wasserman, J., 449–451
Wasserman, S., 449–451
Watts, C., 5
Weber, W., 172–173, 176, 178, 193
Weil, M., 101–102, 284, 288, 340
Weinert, F., 339
Weinstein, C., 265
Weiss, I., 249
Whole versus part learning, in skills teaching, 314
Wideman, R., 427, 430
Wiggins, G., 160, 204
Wilen, W., 254
Williams, W., 94, 95, 114, 175, 284
Willis, M., 206
Wiman, R., 287
Winzer, M., 87
Wisconsin Department of Public Instruction,
154–155
Withitness behaviors, of teachers, 176–177
Womack, J., 371
Woolfolk, A., 85, 87–89, 93–97, 165, 257, 258, 265,
283, 290, 413, 416
Worsham, M., 58, 164, 168, 171, 173, 176, 179, 194
Wright, I., 460–461
Written assignments, assessment and evaluation
of, 140

Xanthopoulous, J., 71

Yewechuk, C., 152
Young, E., 17

Zeichner, K., 83
Zone of proximal development (ZPD), 448